Mambo Montage

Mambo Montage

The Latinization of New York

Agustín Laó-Montes
Arlene Dávila

COLUMBIA UNIVERSITY PRESS
NEW YORK

Columbia University Press
New York, Chichester, West Sussex

Library of Congress Cataloging-in-Publication Data

Mambo montage : the Latinization of New York / edited by Agustín Laó-Montes and Arlene Dávila.
    p. cm.
  Includes bibliographical references and index.
   ISBN 978-0-231-11274-1 (alk. paper) — ISBN 978-0-231-11275-8 (pbk. : alk. paper)
    1. Hispanic Americans—New York (State)—New York—Ethnic identity. 2. Hispanic Americans—New York (State)—New York—Social conditions. 3. Hispanic Americans—New York (State)—New York—Social life and customs. 4. New York (N.Y.)—Ethnic relations. 5. New York (N.Y.)—Civilization. 6. Public spaces—Social aspects—New York (State)—New York. 7. Intercultural communication—New York (State)—New York. 8. United States—Civilization—Hispanic influences. I. Laó-Montes, Agustín. II. Dávila, Arlene M., 1965-
F128.9.S75 M36 2001
974.7′100468073—dc21   00-047548

CONTENTS

ACKNOWLEDGMENTS

As poetically spelled out by Ruben Blades in a salsa song, "There are eleven million histories in New York City." There are many stories and storytellers in this mambo, and it won't be possible to mention all of them. However, a few individuals need to be acknowledged for their special contribution for this project to become a reality. First, the editors want to acknowledge all the contributors for their valuable work and dedication. We also want to give special recognition to John Michel, our editor at Columbia University Press, for his confidence in the significance of this collection since its early stages and for his strong support throughout the whole process. The analytical substance and writing quality of *Mambo Montage* significantly gained from the critical comments of our two main readers, Román de la Campa and Steven Gregory. Thanks to them for their invaluable work. Also thanks to Máximo Colón, Lisa Maya Knauer, and Amilcar Tirado-Avilés for providing their photos to be included in this volume. Last but not least, we also want to acknowledge the meticulously efficient labor of the team at Impressions Book and Journal Services, who coordinated the actual production of the book. Finally, Agustín wants to dedicate this book to the five women he loves most: Grandma Mami Angela González; his mother, Jenny Montes; Diana Coryat; and his daughters, Aiyana and Emma Lao, who represent the future hopes of this labor of love.

CONTRIBUTORS

LUIS APONTE-PARÉS is an associate professor of community planning and Latino studies at the College of Public and Community Services of the University of Massachusetts, Boston. His research interests include the representation of Latinos in the urban milieu, the social formations and institutions of Latino gay men, and the history of Puerto Ricans in the United States. His most recent publications include articles on casitas as well as on the Puerto Rican struggles against displacement during the 1960s and 1970s in places such as El Barrio. Presently, Mr. Aponte-Parés is director of Latino Studies at the University of Massachusetts, Boston.

AMÍLCAR TIRADO AVILÉS is currently a professor affiliated with Carlos Albizu University (previously known as Caribbean Center for Advanced Studies), and the Interamerican University in Puerto Rico. He is a Ph.D. candidate in History at the Graduate Center of the City University of New York and previously was affiliated with the Center for Puerto Rican Studies at Hunter College, City University of New York. He has published essays on Puerto Rican women, nationalism, and labor movements and is preparing a book on the history of Puerto Ricans in El Barrio, East Harlem.

KAREN BACKSTEIN is an independent scholar who has written widely on Brazilian popular culture, dance, religion, and cinema. In addition to regularly teaching these topics in different academic institutions in the area, Ms. Backstein writes book and film reviews for *Cineaste, The Quarterly Review of Film,* and *The International Journal of Cultural Studies.* Her great love and major research area is Brazilian popular culture, and she enhances her appreciation of it by taking dance and percussion classes.

ADRIÁN BURGOS JR. is visiting assistant professor of American Social History at the James Madison College of Michigan State University. He has just completed his doctoral dissertation in History, entitled "Playing America's Game: Latinos and the Performance and Policing of Race in North American Professional Baseball, 1868–1959," at the University of Michigan. He is the author of several articles on Latinos in baseball and has appeared in *Greener Grass,* a documentary on Cubans in North American professional baseball.

MARY GARCIA CASTRO is a sociologist and associate researcher at the University Federal of Bahia (Center of Human Resources) and at the University of Campinas (Center of Studies on International Migration), Brazil. She is research scholar of the Conselho Nacional de Pesquisas (CNPq)– Brazilian National Commission on Research, coordinator of the International Migration Group at the National Commission of Population in Brazil and United Nations Educational, Scientific, and Cultural Organization (UNESCO, Brazilian representation) advisor on gender and culture. Her current publications and research are related to gender, race, class, politics of identities, culture, and power in comparative perspective.

ARLENE DÁVILA is assistant professor of Anthropology and American Studies at New York University. She is the author of *Sponsored Identities: Cultural Politics in Puerto Rico* and has just finished a book on the U.S. Hispanic advertising industry tentatively entitled *The Business of Culture: The Marketing of U.S. Latinos.* Her current work and research interests concern issues of identity, cultural politics, media, and urban studies.

CARLOS DORE-CABRAL is a sociologist affiliated with the Facultad Latino-americana de Ciencias Sociales (FLACSO) in the Dominican Republic. He is co-editor of *The Urban Caribbean* and *El Batey.* His research interests are public policy and migration.

JUAN FLORES is professor of Black and Puerto Rican Studies at Hunter College and in the Sociology Program at the City University of New York Graduate Center. His publications include *From Bomba to Hip-Hop: Puerto Rican Culture and Latino Identity, La venganza de cortijo y otros ensayos, Divided Borders: Essays on Puerto Rican Identity,* and other volumes and translations as well as multiple articles on Puerto Rican and Latino music, literature, and popular culture. He is also co-editor of two book series on Cultural Studies of the Americas and Puerto Rican Studies.

CHLOÉ S. GEORAS is a Ph.D. candidate in art history at Binghamton University. She is currently writing her dissertation on the postcolonial mutations of the Musée des Arts d'Afrique et d'Océanie in Paris. She is also a creative writer and has a forthcoming poetry book entitled *Rediviva: Lost in Trance.* Lations 1.

RAMÓN GROSFOGUEL is professor in the Sociology Department at Boston College. He is a research associate of the Fernand Braudel Center at State University of New York–Binghamton and of the Maison des Sciences de l'Homme in Paris. He has published many articles on Caribbean migration to Western Europe and the United States and on Latin American/Caribbean development.

José Itzigsohn is an assistant professor of Sociology at Brown University. He has published *Developing Poverty* as well as articles in journals such as *Ethnic and Racial Studies, Social Forces,* and *Sociological Forum.* He is interested in transnationalism, racial and ethnic identities, and also the political economy of development in Latin America.

Lisa Maya Knauer is a doctoral candidate in New York University's American Studies Program, where she is completing a dissertation on Afro-Cuban music and religion in and between New York and Cuba. Her publications include "La rumba y la santeria en New York y La Habana," in John Coatesworth and Rafael Hernandez, eds., *Huellas culturales entre Cuba y los EEUU* (La Habana) and "Rumba, comunidad e identidad en New York," in *Temas* 10, July-October 1997. She coproduced and directed "The Cuban Americans," a one-hour documentary broadcast nationally through the Public Broadcasting System (PBS) in Summer/Fall 2000.

Agustín Laó-Montes teaches Sociology at the University of Massachusetts at Amherst where he is also affiliated with the Centerfor Latin American, Latino, and Caribbean Studies, and with the program of African-American Studies. He is also a Research Associate of the Fernand Braudel Center at Binghamton University. He is currently completing a comparative study entitled "Postnationalist Decolonizations? Ireland, Puerto Rico, and the Coloniality of Power." His research fields include historical sociology, cultural studies, postcolonial theory, urban analysis, political economy, and political sociology. He has been an activist/organizer in Latin America/Caribbean, and in the United States for close to twenty-five years.

Nancy Raquel Mirabal is assistant professor of La Raza Studies at San Francisco State University. In addition to authoring several articles on the history of Cuban and Puerto Rican migration to the United States, she is currently working on a monograph on the early history of Afro-Cuban migration to New York and Florida. She is also directing a community oral history project on the gentrification of the Mission District in San Francisco and its impact on the longstanding Latino/a community.

Raquel Z. Rivera is a sociologist and independent scholar. She is currently working on a book entitled *New York Ricans from the Hip-Hop Zone* based on her dissertation. She is the author of various academic articles on hip-hop culture that focus on national identity and ethnoracial relations and has written numerous journalistic articles on rap music for publications such as *The San Juan Star, Stress,* and *In the House.*

Elsa B. Cardalda Sánchez is currently director of the Ph.D. Department of Clinical Psychology at Carlos Albizu University (previously known as Caribbean Center for Advanced Studies), where she teaches and conducts research on Puerto Rican children. She has also conducted research on the phenomena of community muralism both in New York City and Puerto Rico. Her works have been disseminated nationally and internationally, contributing in the areas of vulnerabilities and resilience in high-risk children.

VILMA SANTIAGO-IRIZARRY teaches Anthropology and Latino Studies at Cornell University, where she is also affiliated with the American Studies Program, the Institute for Public Affairs, and the Latin American Studies Program. She has published on the medicalization of ethnicity, constructions of ethnicity, and institutional culture and is currently developing a series of co-authored manuscripts on practical anthropology based on her extensive field research in urban areas.

LIZ ŠEVČENKO is a doctoral candidate in History at New York University and a grant writer for Charas/El Bohio Cultural and Community Center. Her dissertation, "The Real Great Society: Cultural Citizenship in the War on Poverty," explores how Youth Organizations United negotiated the boundaries of cultural citizenship and the place of Puerto Ricans in the national imaginary during the War on Poverty. At the Lower East Side Tenement Museum, Ševčenko is responsible for interpreting historic sites of the Lower East Side—including a sweatshop, a slave gallery, and a tenement building—as resources for contemporary activism.

JOCELYN SOLÍS is a doctoral candidate in the Developmental Psychology program of the Graduate Center of the City University of New York and has taught as an adjunct lecturer at the College of Staten Island and Brooklyn College. She is a Ford Foundation dissertation fellow and is completing her doctoral thesis on the formation of illegality as an identity, focusing on undocumented Mexican immigrants and their children.

WILSON VALENTÍN-ESCOBAR is a doctoral candidate in the Program in American Culture at the University of Michigan. He holds a master's degree in Sociology and is currently an Andrew W. Mellon fellow conducting dissertation research on the Latin Jazz scene(s) in New York City. His research interests include oral history, memory, performance studies, Latino/a popular cultures and musics, and cultural theory.

Mambo Montage

Mambo Montage

The Latinization of New York City

Agustín Laó-Montes*

> Carlos y Rebecca dance across the floor.
> They move in mambo cha-cha
> that causes the sweat of their bodies to swirl
> in a circle of tropical love.
>
> Rebecca y Carlos glide across the floor,
> and two become one in the land of salsa.
> The sweat of their bodies mingles with flute
> blowing high over splintered wooden floors,
> in notes that soar beyond the rooftops of El Barrio.
>
> —"Mambo Love Poem," Sandra Maria Estevez (1990:24)

> By what route is it possible to attain a heightened graphicness com-
> bined with a realization of the Marxist method? The first stop along
> this path will be to carry the montage principle over into history. That
> is, to build up the large constructions out of the smallest, precisely
> fashioned structural elements. Indeed to detect the crystal of the total
> event in the analysis of the small, individual moment.
>
> —Walter Benjamin, as quoted in Smith (1989:48)

> Si se quiere divertir, con encanto y con primor
> solo tiene que vivir un verano en Nueva York
>
> —Justi Barreto (for El Gran Combo)

New York is the capital of mambo and a global factory of latinidad. The
booming of mambo dance classes and the increasing popularity of Latin
music are visible signs of the latinization of the city. Lou Bega's "Mambo

*The author acknowledges the following individuals for their helpful comments in
previous versions of this introduction: Karen Backstein, Diana Coryat, Arlene
Dávila, Román de la Campa, Jorge Duany, Robert Farris Thompson, Juan Flores,
Ramón Grosfoguel, Winston James, Walter Mignolo, Nancy Raquel Mirabal, Tiffany
Patterson, Alberto Sandoval-Sánchez, Amilcar Tirado-Avilés, Immanuel Wallerstein,
and Kate Wilson.

#5," a hip-hop version of Pérez Prado's worldwide hit of the 1950s, after peaking at the top of the 1999 charts, is now a standard of U.S. pop entertainment. Dominican bands are now calling their new strand of merengue *mambo*. The word *mambo* itself is constantly used as a metaphor for New York's Latino cultures. This can be seen in titles such as that of John Leguizamo's performance piece "Mambo Mouth"; David Caballero's film *The Puerto Rican Mambo Is Not a Musical;* Pedro Pietri's play *Mambo Rhapsody;* and Sandra Maria Estevez's book of poems, *Bluestown Mockingbird Mambo.* A Web site named "Mambo Mall" displays the globalization of this mambomania as well as how the world is looking at New York as a symbolic center of Latino culture.

New York is a Latino metropolis and a mecca of the Black Atlantic.[1] This mambo you now hold in your hands is a montage of histories, cultures, economies, and politics of peoples now known as Latinos as well as a collection of essays on the latinization of New York City. *Mambo* is a creole word of multiple African ancestries.[2] It is the word for "priestess" in Haitian Vodu and for the songs of Cuban Congo (Palo Monte) religion. But it has also been used to connote the unintelligibility of African cultures to the West as illustrated in the colonial expression *mumbo jumbo*. *Mambo* is a versatile word used in Latin American and Caribbean vernacular speech to describe the pulse of the streets and the tone of the times. It names a musical movement that emerged in Cuba in the 1940s and was developed and disseminated to the world from New York and Mexico City in the 1950s. Since those times, the mambo has become a global style of music and dance.[3] In sum, mambo is a key cultural trope that connotes multiple meanings at the crossroads of African American, Caribbean, and Latin American cultures.[4]

New York is a montage of Latin American, Caribbean, and Afro-diasporic cultures. Montage is a quintessentially modern art form in which disparate images are collaged, overlapping or juxtaposed, in pictures or film. African American artist Romare Bearden used montage to represent the fragmented yet assembled sense of memory and community in Harlem.[5] Likewise, for German critical theorist Walter Benjamin, montage is a way of seeing and representing the metropolis in which historical and theoretical interpretations are grounded in the characters, architectures, images, snapshots, memories, narratives, and practices of everyday life. This Benjaminian method of montage encompasses both a detective investigation of the city as labyrinth and a semiotic reading of the city as an object of historical analysis (Benjamin 1973, 1983, 1985a, 1985b). The metropolis is viewed as a paradigmatic modern text, implying that the textures of urban life, as well as the ashes and traces of history in the city, are crucial to understanding the cultural and political contradictions of capitalist modernity (Buck-Morss 1990; Gilloch 1996; Steinberg 1996). This book, indeed, constitutes a kind of montage in the sense that it places various angles of reading, interpreting, and theorizing at center stage. *Mambo Montage* can be read as a set of writings on Latino politics and cultures in New York, the latinization of cityscapes, the historical production of latinidad, and the cultural and political meanings of the global phenomena of latinization.[6] If mambo can be described as a montage, because as a trope of tropes (Gates 1988)[7] it signifies the African diaspora in the Americas and the Latin American/Caribbean tropics of New York, this collection delivers a theoretical mambo that is a montage of multiple historical worlds and cultural genres. Here, the vernacular polyvalence and hybridity of mambo corresponds to the methodological heterogeneity of montage and to the collage of critical approaches presented by the authors.

Mambo montage, a concept embodied in the very form of this anthology, implies both a way of imagining latinidad and an angle of vision of the city and also encourages reading the "city-as-text" and writing the "text-as-city" (Gilloch 1996:15). *Mambo Montage* is a book representing several subject positions, intellectual locations, ideological viewpoints, and critical practices, just as a city does. It is an attempt to situate the historical production of Latino American identities, cultural expressions, and social movements in the context of New York City. It is also born out of an interest to evaluate the political meanings and implications of the current ubiquity and visibility of the language of latinidad in academic, state, commercial, and popular cultures.

More than trying to chronicle a people (Shorris 1992), conceptualize an emergent national formation (Fox 1996), describe a condition (Stavans 1995), or analyze the gap between ethnic labels and historical experience (Oboler 1995), *Mambo Montage* seeks to trace a genealogy of the production of discourses of latinidad as they have been (and continuously are) historically imagined and enacted in New York City. Each essay provides entry points into the actual processes through which Latino identities are constructed, performed, and contested in everyday life. This is done by exploring and analyzing the multiple sites in which latinidad is produced, enacted, and expressed within the particular context of New York City.

Mambo Montage represents an intervention in the ongoing discussions on the histories and cultures of U.S. Latinos/as as well as on the latinization of the United States. Being so, latinidad and latinization as unique discursive constructs must be defined. *Latinidad* is now a keyword in the emerging field of Latino Studies;[8] it is an analytical concept that signifies a category of identification, familiarity, and affinity. In this sense, *latinidad* is a noun that identifies a subject position (the state of being Latino/a) in a given discursive space. Latino/a identity refers to the specific positioning of peoples of Latin American and Caribbean descent living in the United States, a historical location with particular historical foundations, hemispheric linkages, and global projections. I contend that for latinidad to be "a useful category for historical analysis,"[9] it should be conceptualized as a domain of discursive formations.[10] Latinidad, however, does not denote a single discursive formation but rather a multiplicity of intersecting discourses enabling different types of subjects and identities and deploying specific kinds of knowledge and power relations. In these terms, it is not only possible to distinguish between governmental, corporate, and academic discourses of latinidad but also to analyze how latinidad is produced through the work of Latino community institutions and by means of aesthetic practices and social movements. This overall process of production of discourses of latinidad is what we call *latinization*. Here, a crucial distinction must be made between Anglo strategies of latinization and Latino tactics of self-definition and self-representation.

I propose that we employ two general complementary methods of inquiry, archaeology and genealogy, to develop an analytics of latinidad and latinization. *Archaeology* refers to the historical and social conditions of possibility and production of discourses of latinidad. In practice, it means investigating the historical foundations and social forces that made possible the emergence of those discourses. It also means exploring the analytical values of latinidad as an epistemological and political category. In turn, *genealogy* refers to the concrete practices and particular sites by which different discourses of latinidad are produced and performed. This implies researching the practical strategies by which, and the specific institutional sites in which, Latino/a comes into being as a subject position and as a way of codifying lived experiences. Such research requires studying the concrete modes of knowledge, narrative forms, cultural genres, and ideological formulations that shape discourses of latinidad in relationship to particular systems of power relations. In fact, *Mambo Montage* can be read as a set of genealogical studies on the latinization of the city of New York.[11]

We strategically adopt latinidad as a key analytical category, but *Latino/a* competes and overlaps with related labels that correspond to other fields of discourse. This results in what Alberto Sandoval-Sánchez calls a "mumbo jumbo of ethnic labels and categories (1999:11)." We can identify at least four different names that correspond to distinct sources and significations of identity: *Hispano/a, Latin, Latino/a,* and *Hispanic.* The nouns *latinidad* and *hispanidad* refer to ideologies of identification that often converge and are used interchangeably in everyday parlance but that indeed refer to different histories, ideologies, and meanings. For some time, it has been common to ascribe political meanings to *Hispanic* and *Latino,* using as the main criteria the contrast between the adoption of the former label in governmental and corporate rhetoric since the 1980s and the rise of the latter as a self-nomination since the Chicano and Nuyorican movements of the 1960s. However, a more careful genealogy should go much earlier in history and also identify the various usages and cultural/political meanings of different discourses of hispanidad and latinidad in time and space. For instance, it should recognize that when the idea of Latin America was coined in the nineteenth century by the French, *Hispano America* was already a signifier for the self-representation of the emerging Creole elites. Also, the denomination *hispano* in early-twentieth-century New York City was widely used as a sign of solidarity among working-class immigrants of Hispanic Caribbean and Spanish descent, as in the Liga Puertorriqueña e Hispana (Puerto Rican and Hispanic League). The term *Latin* had been used in the United States at least since the 1920s to refer to a stereotype of ethnic characters in Hollywood films (Latin lovers) and at least since the 1940s to refer to genres of Brazilian and Caribbean musics (Latin music).[12] An important point here is how imperial/colonial discourses of hispanismo and latinism[13] can be appropriated for their own uses and ideological agendas by working-classes and subaltern sectors, as exemplified in the popular adoption of the idea of Latin music. In any case, the main challenge is not to reify the signifiers and fix their meanings but to investigate their historicity and strategically employ their versatile value and multiplicity of meanings. Unfortunately, the persistent (and somehow agonizing) discussions on the comparative virtues and defects of *Latino* and *Hispanic* often pay more attention to the semantic values of the words (philology) than to their political and ideological entanglements (genealogy).

As a whole, the analytics of latinidad/latinization in *Mambo Montage* entails studies on the archaeologies of latinidad and genealogies of latinization. *Latinidad* (noun) signifies the historical archives and discursive categories, and *latinization*, derived from *latinize* (verb), signifies the multiple processes by which discourses of latinidad are coined and enacted in time and space. That is, archaeology studies the conditions and elements of discursive formations (latinidad), whereas genealogy investigates discursive practices or historically framed and situationally located processes of formation and transformation (latinization). The next two sections will explore the theoretical and methodological frameworks pertinent to developing archaeological and genealogical critical approaches to latinidad/latinization. After this, I will examine latinidad and latinization in the particular context of New York City.

LATINAMERICANITY AND THE MODERN/COLONIAL PRODUCTION OF PEOPLEHOOD

The historical underpinnings of latinidad go back to the invention of the Americas along with the rise of the West and the birth of capitalism as a modern/colonial world system circa 1492.[14] Latino identities are ultimately rooted in the histories of conquest, colonization, chattel slavery, labor exploitation, economic and political subordination, and political/cultural struggle that constituted Latin America as a world region and Latin Americans as a category of peoplehood. Underneath this historical trajectory is what we call the coloniality of power,[15] namely the systemic relationship between global hierarchies of power (capitalist, racial, patriarchal, cultural, interstatal) and modern/colonial definitions of identity (class, race, nationality, ethnicity, gender, and sexuality). These historically grounded world divisions of power and definitions of identity set the stage for the imagining of Latin America as a world region distinct from both Europe and the United States, especially in the conjunctures of the early-nineteenth-century Hispanic American wars for independence (and the Haitian Revolution) and the rise of the U.S. empire in the late nineteenth century.

The dialogical conception of Latin America in relationship to the United States as a "hemispheric dialectic of similarity and difference" (Belnap and Fernandez 1998:4) is clearly articulated in José Martí's essay "Nuestra America" (1963), originally written and published in New York City in 1891. Martí's distinction between "Our Mestizo America" (Latin America) and the "Other America" (the United States) indicates the hemispheric divide between Anglos and Latinos that ultimately informs any notion of latinidad.[16] The very idea of a Latin American identity was framed within the imperial "contact zone" (Pratt 1992:4) between the rising U.S. transoceanic empire and its southern neighbors, especially the so-called backyard of Central America and the Caribbean. This zone of unequal exchanges and uneven developments in the Americas configures a hemispheric field of domination, exploitation, resistance, and transculturation. In tandem with this, the transformation of populations and territories under former Spanish colonial possession into U.S. colonial subjects and colonized spaces (such as Louisiana in 1803, the conversion of more than half of Mexico into the U.S. Southwest after the Mexican-American War of 1848, and the rise of U.S. imperial domination in the Hispanic Caribbean after the 1898 Spanish-Cuban-American-Filipino War) inscribed the production of latinidad into the very definition of the U.S. territorial nation and national imaginary.[17]

There is a *longue durée* that constitutes a fundamental background to understanding the production of discourses of latinidad in the United States. This long-term historical duration begins with the European invention of the Americas as both the exotic lands of Tropicalia[18] and as the embodiment of the future of the West. This modern/colonial framework informs the emergence of latinamericanist discourses,[19] first in the context of the wars of independence against European imperial powers and later as expressions of the national and regional ideologies of self-definition developed by the Creole elites of the nascent Latin American nation-states partly against the Americanism of the U.S. empire. This historical outlook is crucial for two general reasons: first, memory is a constitutive element in any process of identification and a primary component in the struggle for hegemony, and second, History is not only about temporal change but also about persistent structures of domination and injustice. A world-historical perspective makes possible the conflation and connection of discourses of identity (nineteenth-century latinamericanism and twentieth-century latinidad) and hemispheric patterns of economic, cultural, and political inequality. Latinidad is historically rooted in the discourses of latinamericanism that established a historical sense of identity in the modern world (Latin American identities) as well as in the mass migrations, political exiles, conquest of peoples and territories, and processes of uneven development and unequal exchange that characterize the relations between Anglos and Latino/Americans both within and beyond the territorial boundaries of the United States. These historical groundings constitute the archives from whence to conduct our archaeological investigations of latinidad.

The largest and most important world city of the U.S. empire, New York has been an important site and reference point for Latin American and Caribbean political developments and cultural expressions since at least the last part of the nineteenth century. For instance, by the end of that century, New York City was a major base of operations in the organization of Hispanic Caribbean anticolonial political movements and an important space for the emergence of Cuban and Puerto Rican national and Latin American regional identities. Since then, New York has increasingly become an epicenter for the production of latinamericanist discourses whose subjects were first defined as Latin Americans (the hemispheric others of the United States and Canada) and later as Latinos, a category of identity and difference primarily within (but also beyond) the U.S. national space.

The historical universe of discourse from whence latinidad emerges as a category is signified by the notion of *peoplehood*,[20] which refers to the large collective identities (race, nationality, ethnicity) codified in the modern/colonial world system to name, classify, differentiate, homogenize, and regulate bodies and populations according to Western capitalist regimes of power and knowledge. Three interrelated processes define these categories of the modern self as colonial: first, the dominant geocultural division of the world in capitalist modernity between "the West and the rest" (Chinweizu 1975, Hall 1996); second, the hierarchical organization of political bodies (nation-states, world cities) as hegemonic (imperial, metropolitan) or subordinate (colonial, neocolonial); and third, the stratification (in terms of wealth, power, and culture) of human subjects and collectivities as races, ethnicities, nationalities, and civilizations. However, peoplehood is not simply the outcome of Western domination and capitalist exploitation, and neither colonial difference can be reduced to the global chain(s) of otherness (racial, ethnic, sexual, etc.) promoted by occidentalist discourses.[21] Modern peoplehood is also the product of countercolonial resistances and anticolonial movements as well as of collective self-fashioning and community-making, including the imagining of collective self and memory and existential practices of self-affirmation. In these terms, latinidad is both a category deployed within a variety of dominant spaces and institutions (state, corporate, academic) to label populations as well as a form of self-identification used by individuals, movements, and organizations to articulate a sense of community. In both cases, latinidad is enacted as a form of identification that denotes one or more of the three main referents of peoplehood: race, ethnicity, and nationality. In the next section, I will explore the manifold ways in which latinidad relates to each of these three categories of peoplehood.

LATINIDAD AT THE CROSSROADS OF RACE, NATION, AND ETHNICITY

Latinidad is mostly assumed to be an ethnic or panethnic category. It is also often understood (either through argument, by analogy, or through common sense) by using the language of nationhood or as a racial formation.[22] This mixture of categories, along with the great diversity of subject positions and historical locations (classes, genders, sexualities, races, nationalities, generations, and locales) among latinized people, leads some analyses to conclude that latinidad (and even more, hispanicity)[23] are mere fictions without much relevance to understanding social realities, power asymmetries, and cultural creation. *Latino* and *Hispanic* have been interpreted as labels imposed by the dominant powers to homogenize, regulate, and discriminate against Latin American populations in the United States, labels whose political effects undermine class politics and co-opt radical agendas (Gimenez 1988, 1992). Without denying the relative value of these allegations, I contend that latinidad could be used as a meaningful category of social analysis and political organization because being Latino/a is now a criterion for individual and collective identification that defines a domain of cultural production, influences the division and allocation of social wealth and power, and motivates the organization of social movements and institutions.

However, most scholarship on Latinos does not problematize the categorical status of latinidad. The most general assumption made is that Latino/a identity is an ethnic marker of a mosaic of nationalities with a common ancestry and history from south of the Río Grande and a shared condition and experience in the United States. In contrast, as the essays in *Mambo Montage* demonstrate, it is crucial to conceive latinidad not as a static and unified formation but as a flexible category that relates to a plurality of ideologies of identification, cultural expressions, and political and social agendas. In analyzing latinidad as peoplehood, my argument is twofold: first, that as historical constructs, race, nationality, and ethnicity each have their own particular discursive space at the same time that they are necessarily intertwined; second, that as a consequence, different discourses of latinidad and hispanidad are inscribed by these modern/colonial constructs in distinct but overlapping ways. I will now examine how discourses of latinidad relate to each of the categories of peoplehood (nationality, race, and ethnicity) as well as how they overlap.

Beneath most conceptions of latinidad lies a nationalist common sense. Latin American nationalisms always involved a relationship between region (Latin America as the Big Motherland) and nation (nationalities as small motherlands). Latino/a discourses build from that historic entanglement of region and nation by developing a sort of pan-Latino nationalism in which latinidad appears as an association of nationalities. In fact, given that nationhood appears to be natural and universal, most individuals and organizations tend to define their latinidad in relationship to their nationalities. The nationalist rationality in which peoplehood is defined in terms of an essentialist search for origins, fixed cultural traits, and a common destiny, a logic that promotes homogenization of difference and the exclusion of selected others (racial, sexual, etc.), can also shape discourses of Latino self-identification. This is the same kind of nationalist logic that anchored the nineteenth-century foundation of Latin American nation-states in occidentalist notions (such as Latin American civilization as part of the Hispanic race)[24] while predicating an ideology of racial democracy that was contradicted by the tacit exclusion of subaltern subjects (Indians, blacks, peasants, marginals) from membership in the national community.[25] In contrast, a revolutionary strand of nationalism guided the ideologies of Latino power against U.S. racial capitalism and imperialism articulated by the Chicano and Nuyorican movements in the 1960s.

Latinidad is shaped and defined by racial discourses, processes of racialization, and racisms. Latinized people(s) are subject/ed to (and engage in) several systems of racial classification and racist inequality.[26] Race is an open and chameleonic signifier. It refers to the modern/colonial classifications and global stratifications of peoples in terms of naturalized essences. The keystones of modern racial discourse are occidentalism (the alleged superiority of the West) and white supremacy, the idea of the so-called white race being superior to allegedly lesser races (civilizations, cultures, colors). Indeed, the civilizational distinction between Anglo-Saxons and Latin Americans both represents and establishes a geocultural racial divide. This civilizational mode of racial reasoning shows how race cannot be reduced to biological or somatic markers. Racial discourses always involve cultural criteria and are necessarily connected to nationhood. They are flexible, unstable, and ambiguous, and they acquire particular meanings according to spatio-temporal contingencies and structural articulations (DuBois 1940; Stoler 1997; Outlaw 1996; Lott 1999).

One of the main racial ideologies of latinidad defines Latinos as a third race, as it were, in between black and white—the bearers of an allegedly new mestizaje and hybridity, the so-called browning of America. The brown face refers to a register of racialization in which whiteness as a universal referent is contrasted to different categories of nonwhiteness such as red, yellow, mongrel, Creole, mulatto, which can also correspond to racialized nationalities (Chinese, Mexican, Puerto Rican). What this alleged hybridization of the racial and ethnic composition of U.S. society does is to highlight and enhance the nuances of a complex matrix of social and racial stratification.[27] The perception of Latinos as a mestizo race situated in the middle of the black and white binary is not only a hegemonic racialized notion of the other. It is also a guiding thread in several strands of latinismo. The notion of la raza latina articulates this racial discourse of latinidad through different means, from expressions of popular culture ("la salsa representando la raza latina")[28] to the self-characterization of Latino social movements for racial justice (Que Viva la Raza). In this last sense, *la raza* more than *race* signifies community and brings to light national and transnational constructions of latinidad.

In light of the historically specific, malleable, and contradictory nature of racist discourses, latinized populations and individuals have distinct experiences of racialization depending on differences such as class, color, gender, and nationality. Some of the most important distinctions are those drawn between conquered minorities (Chicanos and Puerto Ricans) and new immigrants (such as Colombians, Mexicans, and Ecuadoreans), between colonial/neocolonial migrants (Puerto Ricans and Dominicans) and immigrants from nation-states with more political autonomy and symbolic capital (such as Argentina and Brazil), and between Afro-Latinos/Indo-Latinos and Euro-Latinos.[29] In this context, it is relevant to ask, Are there any white Latinos, or are all Latinos people of color? These are complex questions to be examined. For instance, in the global chain of otherness, upper-class Euro-Latinos can be located within multiple hierarchies of whiteness[30] by which they can be considered white in their countries of origin, light mestizo in California, Creole in Louisiana, and Hispanic in New York City. If we use a more complex equation of race and class, we will notice that there are different layers of U.S. Latino subalternity according to factors as diverse as the timing and modes of incorporation of immigrants into U.S. society (Grasmuck and Grosfoguel 1997), the significance of Afro-Americans and Amerindians in the nationality (Dominicans and Mexicans versus Argentineans and Uruguayans), and placement within (or displacement from) labor and housing markets. Latino subaltern classes are doubly racialized in relationship to both the ways in which the racism of their places of origin is reenacted in the United States (Afro-Cubans and Guatemalan Mayans) and the manifold manners in which they are racialized in the United States by the racial state, institutions of civil society, and the racial common sense. In the United States, everyday racism is the most immediate source in the formation of a pan-Latino consciousness. The daily situations of discrimination, exclusion, stigmatization, humiliation, and violence, expressing various forms and levels of racism, encourage resistances and movements articulated by race, thus promoting definitions of latinidad as a racial formation.

In spite of all of these ways in which latinidad can be considered as a racial category, it is still mostly employed as an ethnic marker. In the United States, the rhetoric of ethnicity serves as a way to distinguish between an allegedly nonethnic, mainstream American core (implicitly white) and the internal others (ethnicized new immigrants and nonwhite second-class citizens). This ethnic paradigm plays the ideological role of obscuring and denying racism and colonialism as significant frames of identity/difference in the United States insofar as it reduced the histories of racialized peoples (such as African Americans and Puerto Ricans) to an immigrant analogy based on the experience of so-called European white ethnics (Irish, Italians, Jews, etc.).[31] However, ethnicity also indicates a form of classification and a process of subjectification and stratification (i.e., ethnicization). Hence, ethnicity as a construct is no less real than race and nationality because it signifies a strand of discourse with pertinent effects in processes of identification, affiliation, and stratification as well as in social divisions of wealth and power.

Given that ethnic classifications largely rest on cultural markers (such as language, religion, and nationality), there is a tendency to conflate ethnic discourses with peoplehood. However, if by marking ethnic boundaries, processes of ethnicization form a particular dimension in the constitution and allocation of social subjects, they also are necessarily entangled with racialization and nationalization. For instance, ethnicity can be used as a language for signifying different kinds of subcategories of race (such as West Indians, Afro-Cubans, and African Americans). Races are also founded on cultural criteria, which gives them an ethnic dimension as in the case of African Americans. Likewise, nationalities are based on a fictive ethnicity that enables the nation to be imagined as a community of shared culture and common past and destiny. In the United States, the dominant fictive ethnicity of the Anglo-Saxon ideal nation (Balibar 1990) has historically been the template against which immigrants (i.e., nationals) are simultaneously ethnicized and racialized. People(s) of Latin American and Hispanic Caribbean descent in the United States are triply ethnicized and racialized in relationship to their nationality (Colombians as an ethnoracial group), in terms of world regional identities (Latin American immigrants), and as a pannational/panethnic population (U.S. Latinos or Hispanics).

Latinidad has also been defined as a "pan-ethnicity . . . the development of bridging organizations and the generalization of solidarity among ethnic subgroups" (López and Espíritu 1990:198). To some extent Latino identity is, as in the panethnic argument, an outcome of coalition-building among different national/ethnic groups based on shared economic, political, and cultural subordination, an ensemble of different historical experiences, cultural expressions, and social locations—a montage of sorts. There is also a pannational/panethnic common sense based on common denominators such as language, an alleged common history, and appeals to Latin American backgrounds. Such an analysis (and commonsense understanding) does not sufficiently explore the articulations of ethnicization and racialization, and it limits the question of power to issues of organization and collective action. Interpretations of latinidad as panethnicity also tend to assume ethnonational identities as the unproblematized (virtually fixed) building blocks of a notion of ethnicity that is largely confined to ethnic relations in the United States.

Latinidad can also be conceptualized using Stuart Hall's notion of new ethnicity in terms of "how different subject positions are being transformed or produced in the course of the unfolding of the new dialectics of global culture" (1991:19). His main argument is that the "master concepts" (46) (nationality, class, race, and gender) that constitute "world historical identities" (20) in Western modernity have been decentered, fragmented, and eroded in the current phase of globalization of capital and culture. This process is accompanied by the rise of both global formations (World Bank, European Union) and local solidarities (new ethnicities), challenging the sovereignty of nation-states and the integrity of modern concepts of collective identity. Hall defines *ethnicity* as "the reach for groundings" (36) by the local margins excluded from dominant regimes of representation by means of retrieving lost histories and a cultural politics of difference. Hall's analysis of resistant forms of solidarity in the context of globalization, as well as his interpretation of processes of identification as multiple and contextually defined, is the closest to my own understanding of latinidad as a fluid postmodern category of identification capable of challenging modern definitions of peoplehood in terms of relatively fixed identities. However, given Hall's definition of new ethnicities as primarily local, his optimism toward the politics of the margins, and the predominance of the language of ethnicity; this framework will not suffice to grasp the complexities of latinidad.

BEYOND MASTER IDENTITIES: LATINIDAD AND TRANSLOCALITY

Latinidad should be analyzed as a transcultural, transnational, and translocal category. As discussed previously, U.S. Latino populations are the product of world historical hemispheric processes of economic colonialism, imperial political domination, and cultural imperialism that are constitutive of the U.S. territorial nation and empire and productive of mass migrations and political exiles to *el norte* as well as persistent inequalities within the imperial field. The historical framework within which Latino identities emerged and developed should be framed in the context of the imperial contact zone of colonial encounters between the United States and Latin

America/the Caribbean. This regional field of empire is also a zone of trans-culturation[32] in which a diversity of imperial and colonial locations (races, genders, nationalities, cultures, etc.) engage in unequal exchanges and power struggles. This logic transgresses simple dichotomies such as north and south, colonizer and colonized, and self and other. In this sense, latin-idad signifies complex processes of transculturation between different places and positionings within the contact zone. The geocultural and geo-political landscapes of latinidad are not confined to the U.S. national/local "zones of instability where the people dwell" (Fanon) but are also consti-tuted by the vast array of transnational flows and translocal linkages that compose latinidad as a borderland.

The caribbeanization of New York City has been described as a "trans-national socio-cultural system" between the city and the Caribbean (Sutton 1987:15). In the last two decades, there has certainly been a qualitative in-crease in the intensity and density of travel; communications; and circula-tion of peoples, commodities, representations, and political movements be-tween New York City, Latin America, and the Caribbean. We can now surely speak of a transnational field of exchanges or a space of flows be-tween the world city and a multiplicity of Latin American and Caribbean locales. Studies have shown the formation of transnational communities between towns in Mexico and transmigrants in New York (R. Smith 1996, 1997) as well as the transnational relocalization of kinship bonds. It is now also possible to talk about transnational social movements and trans-national political actors. It is even sound to theorize the existence of un-bounded diasporic national formations (Basch, Glick Schiller, and Szanton Blanc 1994) as in the cases of Puerto Rico and the Dominican Republic, where Nuyoricans and Dominicanyorks represent a substantial percentage of the national population and New York is a symbolically central territory in the national imaginaries. In such cases it is hard to make a distinction between nation and diaspora, but it is more adequate to talk about diasporic conditions. Indeed, diasporic perspectives move beyond the language of transnationalism to postulate the emergence of postnational identities, net-works, and formations (e.g., the Hemispheric Amerindian Movement, the Black Atlantic, latinidad).[33]

I propose that latinidad can best be analyzed in terms of translocation.[34] The notion of translocality refers at once to historical/structural locations, geographic scales, and subject positions. In contrast to the more common term *transnationality,* it is not centered in nation-states and nationalities but articulates geographic units of space (place, nation, region, world) with historical locations and subject positions (classes, genders, sexualities, races, ethnicities, nationalities, etc.). The concept of translocality as I am using it here is influenced by the politics of location that has been formu-lated by U.S. Third World feminism.[35] In these analyses, *location* refers to the multiplicity of subject positions (gender, sex, race, etc.) that inscribe the human body as a subject as well as the locales (geographic places and social spaces) from whence these subjects speak and assert their agency. What is at stake here is not a poststructuralist celebration of the play of differences but a theoretical and political understanding of how the multiple mediations (Mani 1989) that compose the self correspond to various axes of domination and a determination of the implications for framing struggles and developing coalitions. Identities are conceptualized as relational and complex processes that are differentially situated in diverse contexts of domination and resistance. Discussions of the politics of location tend to derive from diasporic and postcolonial perspectives trying to conceptualize the hybrid and translocal character of culture, power, and subjectivity in an era of continuous migrations, displacements, and deterritorialization/ reterritorialization of processes of cultural production and identification. This sort of analysis is key to understanding a fluid category such as latinidad that resists any simple categorization given its plurality of meanings and its multiple status as a marker of collective identity.

I contend that the politics of location should be more firmly grounded in a theory of translocation.[36] The concept of the coloniality of power, insofar as its links subject positions with structural locations in a global and historical perspective, is a powerful basis for the kind of translocal analysis that accounts for historical contingencies and local particularities without losing track of historical trends and structural patterns. By *location* I mean the multiple loci (class, gender, race, etc.) from which we enunciate as well as the various locales that we occupy in the social divisions of power and labor (at local, national, and global scales). In our case, the main questions are: what are the locations of latinidad, and how we are to define Latino locations? Historically, latinidad is located in the colonial horizons of modernity; that is, in the colonial and neocolonial migrations from Latin America to the United States, in the continuous relationship of imperial domination and colonial/neocolonial economic and political inequality in the Americas, in the persistence of hemispheric imperial/colonial difference between Anglos and Latin Americans (within and beyond national boundaries), and in the contact zones of colonial and neocolonial encounters in U.S. world cities (especially New York, Los Angeles, Chicago, and Miami). Latino locations are as diverse as any other cartography of differences in the global chain(s) of self and otherness. One of the distinctive features of latinidad is that because the Americas are historically at the intersection of world cultures, races, and civilizations, Latin Americans and Latinos (their offspring) are a rich melange of all the peoples that created the Americas.

The very conception and reproduction of latinidad as a historical location is grounded on a regional matrix of domination and exploitation involving a complex interplay of relationships of identity and difference. As Alicia Arrizon (1999:3) puts it, "latinidad mirrors the multiple identities that form the Latin American territory," and "the very complexities of latinidad may be the crucial distinguishing mark of Latino culture and identity in the Americas." This translocal character of Latino identities, in the double sense of being simultaneously enacted in various places and at different scales as well as being at the crossroads of various definitions of peoplehood and subject positions, is what make it a particularly ambiguous, unstable, and open category.[37] This is conceptualized with poetic wisdom in Gloria Anzaldúa's image of the borderland, a key metaphor that signifies the nature of latinidad as a space for negotiation of multiple positionings and perspectives.[38] From within Latino locations, it is from the critical edges, as in Sandoval-Sánchez's "queer margin" (1999:5) that we find the most enabling explorations of the transformative potential of a Latino/a politics of translocation. Sandoval-Sánchez himself frames an interpretation of latinidad in a translocal perspective when he states that he sees "the self as a site of consistent negotiation between discursive junctures and geo-political intersections" (1999:5). This is akin to Arrizon's contention of "the term latino/a as marking the in-between-ness embedded in the geo-political spaces where identity-formation occurs" (1999:4). In this schema, latinidad is conceived in a liminal space of oppositionality and is endowed with the potential of being a vector for transforming multiple forms of domination (sexual, gender, racial, etc.). Being at the crossroads of subalternity, latinidad could potentially serve as a framework to articulate postcolonial categories of peoplehood and could be a standpoint to formulate, to use Fernando Coronil's language, "post-imperial categories" to move "beyond occidentalism" (1995:51).

The versatility and elasticity of latinidad as a category also means that if it could be a building block for countercolonial movements, it could also be a stepping stone for a hegemonic corporate or governmental multiculturalism. The emergence of *Latino/a* as a hemispheric and even global form of identification is as much the product of genres of popular culture (such as mambo and salsa)[39] and social movements as it is of corporate marketing strategies (such as Univision and Hispanic advertising). For latinidad to have any significance as a category of intellectual and political discourse there needs to be evidence of its relevance in actual processes of subject formation and community-making. In spite of the transnational, transcultural, and translocal character of latinidad, the *differentia specifica*[40] that defines it as a form of identification lies in its historical production as a U.S.-based constellation of identities of peoples of Latin American and Caribbean descent living in the belly of the beast—hence, the need to investigate how latinidad is (or is not) produced in the context of particular power relations and trace its power effects (if any). Now our analysis must move from considering latinidad as category to considering latinization as process, from understanding Latino identity to mapping the makings of Latino identifications, and from the archaeologies of latinidad to the genealogies of latinization.

LATINIZATION: GENEALOGIES OF LATINIDAD AND TECHNOLOGIES OF LATINO SELVES

In *Megalopolis,* Celeste Olalquiaga (1992:76) defines latinization as a "process whereby the United States culture and daily practices become increasingly permeated by elements of Latin American culture imported by Spanish-speaking immigrants from Central and South America as well as from the Caribbean." She contends that this is symptomatic of a "postmodern condition" in which there is "an unprecedented degree of reciprocal appropriation and mutual transformation," involving changes such as "the latinization of urban culture in the United States, the formation of hybrid cultures such as the Chicano and Nuyorican, and the pop recycling of U.S. icons of both Latin American and U.S. culture" (82). She argues that "pop recycling" is the only one of these devices with a strong critical edge (in the form of "postmodern parody"), whereas latinization is virtually reduced to "the consumption of exotica" and "hybrid cultures" are characterized simply as a "nostalgia for the homeland" that "promote the isolation they should fight against" (80). In short, for Olalquiaga, latinization is a process by which "mainstream culture begins to be infiltrated by fragmented and scattered elements of language, music, film, iconography" and whose "most simple and elementary" form is "the commercial circulation of food and clothing appreciated mostly for their exotic quality" (80–81).

In *Tropicalizations,* Aparicio and Chavez-Silverman (1997) present a different analysis of latinization. They critically engage Olalquiaga's argument, given that for her "latinization is limited to reformulations of cultural icons by the dominant sector" that are virtually "synonymous with commodification" and that "she does not problematize the neo-colonial gestures of a mainstream society that appropriates and co-opts the subordinate cultural productions" (3). They take issue with her contrast between hybrid cultures ("nostalgic" Chicano and Nuyorican) and Latin American critical postmodern parodies, claiming that "Olalquiaga renders invisible the postmodern parodies of Chicanos/as and Niuyoricans" and that the "dismissal of nostalgia is the depoliticization of the neo-colonial status of U.S. Latinos" (4). In contrast, Aparicio and Chavez-Silverman understand latinization in relationship to a "post-colonial reading and writing of tropicalizations" in which the "notion of latinidad is contestatory and contested, fluid and relational" (15). They contend, contra other Latino scholars, that "latinidad cannot be contained" (15), either as a "type of organic understanding and appreciation of all things Latino"[41] or as simply "a critical shorthand valorizing seemingly authentic cultural practices that challenge both colonial and imperialist US. ideologies both in North and South America."[42] Instead, Aparicio and Chavez-Silverman introduce the concept of tropicalizations to signify both the "sets of images and attributes superimposed onto both Latin American and U.S. Latino subjects from the dominant sector" ("hegemonic tropicalizations") as well as "transculturation from below" or processes "by which subaltern Latino and Latina subjects and communities struggle to attain power and cultural authority" ("self-tropicalizations") (12). Self-tropicalizations are seen "as a tool that foregrounds the transformative cultural agency of the subaltern subject," whereas hegemonic tropicalizations are theorized as tropes of tropicalism or expressions of an imperial/colonial discourse analogous to Said's notion (1979) of orientalism.

In general, the criticisms by Aparicio and Chavez-Silverman of Olalquiaga are analytically and politically sound. Olalquiaga certainly reduces latinization to commodified culture, underestimates the aesthetic value and political efficacy of U.S. Latino cultures, and adopts a latinamericanist, intellectualist form of critique. But Aparicio and Chavez-Silverman do not give enough credit to Olalquiaga's critical edges, as in her analysis of parody and role inversion as "examples of how to resist colonial practices to the advantage of marginalized cultures" (82) and as a way of "reinverting roles in postcolonial culture" (86). Even more important for us is Olalquiaga's lucid analysis of certain forms of latinization as offsprings of the commodification of U.S. urban cultures in the context of the transnationalization and capitalization of cultural production and exchange. We also see latinization, as do Aparicio and Chavez-Silverman, as a fluid and relational process that arises from different sources and that has diverse ideological inspirations and political implications. Our own analysis of the latinization of New York will build partly on Olalquiaga's account of the commodification of ethnicity as well as on Aparicio's and Chavez-Silverman's postcolonial interpretation of latinidad as a hegemonic and counterhegemonic process of transculturation in the Western Hemispheric "contact zone" between the United States, Latino/America, and the Caribbean.[43]

In *Mambo Montage,* latinization is first and foremost a power process of social differentiation and cultural production. Latinization signifies the emergence of a space for discursive formations. Latinization is a process of both subjection and subjectivation.[44] It is a process of subject formation by hailing and labeling but also by means of self-affirmation and self-constitution. Here, latinization also signifies a mode of production and appropriation of urban space. Latinization is the production of latinidad by both the dominant powers and the subordinate social sectors. Thus, latinidad can be produced around different axes of identification: at one end, in relationship to markers of identity/difference such as language, race, culture, or immigration resulting in self-identification by Latinos and, at the other end, as a result of practices of othering (classification and homogenization) racialized and ethnicized populations by governmental, corporative, and intellectual discourses. In this sense, what I will call *latinization from above* refers to a process by which discourses of latinidad are produced as part of the organization of hegemony by dominant institutions. In contrast, *latinization from below* refers to the processes of Latino self-fashioning that arise from resistances against marginality and discrimination and as expressions of a desire for a definition of self and an affirmative search for collective memory and community. The main agencies for latinization from below are social movements and community institutions. The making of discourses of latinidad entails the production of forms of subjectivity (Latinos), modes of knowledge (intellectual, governmental, corporate, subaltern), and genres of cultural expression (oral, literary, performative, visual), which are framed by power imbalances at the same time that they have concrete power effects. These processes of latinization are derived from (and mediated by) different societal sources (the state, the market, the media, the academy, social and cultural movements) and are enacted in specific institutional sites (museums, churches, schools, social service agencies, restaurants, nightclubs).

As stated before, one of the main projects of *Mambo Montage* is to begin drawing the lines for a genealogy of latinization as it has been produced in New York City. Latinization is a process that is simultaneously local and global, and being a world city, New York is a key site for the globalization of latinidad. Before analyzing the latinization of New York and its implications for the global dissemination of latinidad, I will now present a general profile of the historical demographics and political economies of what we today call New York Latino/a.

NEW YORK LATINO/A: HISTORICAL DEMOGRAPHICS AND POLITICAL ECONOMIES

New York has been a center of imperial power, core capitalist activity, international labor migrations, and hemispheric transculturation since the late nineteenth century. As a main locus of economic, political, and cultural power in the modern world system, New York can be defined as a world city.[45] The legendary city of skyscrapers embodies in its built environment the cityscapes of empire. New York is paradigmatic of the urban landscapes of modernity and a herald of hegemonic political and cultural developments. As Walter Benjamin named Paris the capital of the nineteenth century, New York City has been called the capital of the twentieth century (Ward and Zunz 1992). There are many cities in and many facets to New York. As a world city, it can be seen from three angles: as a key node in the global networks and circuits of capitals, peoples, and representations; as a protagonic site of agency in the globalization of economy, politics, and culture; and as a place of dwelling with its own institutions, forms of domination and hegemony, social movements, cultural genres, and social struggles.

Late-nineteenth-century New York, an emerging world city for cultural, political, and economic activity, attracted artisans, proletarians, merchants, writers, and political activists from Latin America and the Caribbean. New York housed and hosted such founding figures of nineteenth-century Latin American politics and ideology as Ramón Emeterio Betances, Amelia Casanova de Villareal, Máximo Gomez, Juan Pablo Duarte, Eugenio María de Hostos, Antonio Maceo, José Martí, and Inocencia Martínez. Latin American and Hispanic Caribbean activists and leaders also contributed to the organization of the labor movement and to the rise of pan-African consciousness in the city, as exemplified by Afro–Puerto Rican Arturo Alfonso Schomburg, who became a member of Antillean anticolonial movements but also founded the first archives of African American history.[46]

The Spanish-Cuban-American-Filipino War of 1898 was a watershed in the hemispheric role of New York City as well as in the character and composition of its Latin American population.[47] As New York came to be the main U.S. imperial city of industry, trade, finance, and the emerging mass media, it also became a magnet for Latin American and Caribbean migrations. The aftermath of the 1898 war marked the emergence of the United States as an imperial power, consolidating the contact zone between Uncle Sam and the so-called Caribbean Backyard. The colonial appropriation of Puerto Rico after the 1898 Paris Treaty; the imperial regulation of Cuba with the 1901 Platt Amendment; the military occupations of Haiti and the Dominican Republic in 1914 and 1916, respectively; and the numerous military interventions in Central America during the same period set the stage for U.S. domination in the geopolitical and economic region. The increase of Latin American immigration in the twentieth century is a constitutive component of this imperial/colonial field of domination, resistance, and transculturation in the Americas. The restructuring of the Cuban and Puerto Rican economies and polities exacerbated unemployment and economic need at the same time that the newly established relationship with the United States opened the flow of travel and migration. Puerto Rican socialist and cigar maker Bernardo Vega writes in his memoirs about how at the beginning of the twentieth century, New York was an important node in the network of places (Puerto Rico; Cuba; and Tampa, Florida) where Hispanic Caribbean cigar manufacturers established their production shops and developed a dynamic working-class public sphere (Ramos 1991).

The 1920 U.S. Census registered 41,094 individuals of Hispanic descent in New York City,[48] of whom 21.2 percent were Cuban and West Indian, 17.9 percent were Puerto Rican, 18.9 percent were from Central and South America, and 35.7 percent were from Spain (Rosenwaike 1972; Haslip-Viera 1996). This shows close to 40 percent of the Hispanic population as being of Caribbean origin, a pattern that keeps growing over time and demonstrates the demographic diversity that has made New York a unique center of pan-Caribbean and Latin American encounters. It was in this period that Hispano organizations and Latin American neighborhoods *(colonias hispanas)* began to be created in the city (Sánchez-Korrol 1988). The 1930 U.S. Census recorded an increase of more than 100 percent (to 110,223) in what was then called the Hispano population of New York, with a substantial growth of Puerto Ricans to 44,908 (40.7 percent). From this time forward, because Puerto Ricans held U.S. citizenship with the Jones Act of 1917[49] and because of the island's particularly poor economy and its historical flows of exchange with the United States, they became the majority of Hispanos, Latinos, and Caribbeans (as they were variously termed) in New York until the 1980s. This facilitated Puerto Rican migrations and set the conditions (legal, political, and symbolic) for Puerto Ricans to become colonial citizens ("legal aliens," as put by salsa leader Willie Colón) in the heart of empire.

Puerto Rican migration to New York City increased substantially in the aftermath of World War II. Even though relative declines in the interwar period and particularly during the world economic crisis of the 1930s had temporarily slowed the trend, the Puerto Rican population of New York City grew from 61,463 in 1940 to 811, 843 in 1970. The industrialization process of the island in the late 1940s (Operation Bootstrap) and the political redefinition of the colonial relationship codified in the creation of the Commonwealth of Puerto Rico in 1952 marked the first mass migration by airplane in modern history. Imperial planning played an important role in this massive migratory process. (Grosfoguel 1997; Maldonado-Denis 1980). The patterning of Puerto Rico as a showcase for the post–World War II models of economic development and political modernization, which was intended to consolidate U.S. world hegemony, included encouraging large numbers of the island's residents to move to the U.S. mainland (Pantojas 1991; Grosfoguel 1997). This was overwhelmingly a labor migration (Bonilla and Campos 1986; History Task Force 1979) in which the large majority of Puerto Ricans became a "colonized labor force" (Santiago-Valles 1993:13) in the cities and in the countryside of the northeastern United States. In New York City, by far the first port of destination, Puerto Ricans arrived along with the second great influx of African Americans from the South. African American and Puerto Rican working classes came to share a niche in the labor market (mostly low-paid blue-collar and service) and a common condition of deprivation in housing, education, and health care as well as relative political powerlessness and racial discrimination (Torres 1995). In light of this, many of them shared workplaces and living spaces, this intimacy accounting for the birth of joint cultural creations (from doo-wop to hip-hop) (Flores 2000) and political sensibilities (e.g., the Young Lords and the Black Panthers) (Laó 1995) but also for the creation of a field of identity and difference in which Boricuas and Latinos were conceived in opposition to blacks, their immediate others (and often intimate enemies). The dramatic decline of manufacturing employment after the global economic crisis and restructuring that began in the early 1970s and the concomitant pattern of urban governance and development unscrupulously favoring the upper classes and eroding basic conditions of life (employment, housing, education, health, etc.) for the working classes once again grouped many African

Americans and Puerto Ricans (and eventually Dominicans) in a category of marginalized subalternity that has been stigmatized and vilified with discourse on the so-called underclass.[50]

The period from the end of World War II to the world economic slump of the mid-1970s (Mandel 1975; Amin et al. 1982) also featured two other major migrations from the Hispanic Caribbean to the city: the first after the Cuban Revolution of 1959 and the second with the Dominican political crisis dating from the fall of the Trujillo dictatorship in 1961 to the U.S. military invasion in 1965. Cubans have been in New York since the nineteenth century, but in the 1940s and 1950s, in the context of a deepening political and economic crisis in Cuba, labor migration of Cubans increased, which included musicians looking for better fortune in the city's booming culture industries (music, radio, film, etc.). In spite of their relatively small numbers, Cubans accumulated the symbolic capital to become representative of the Latin culture of New York. Cuban and Puerto Rican music, restaurants, and nightclubs became emblematic of the latinization of the city. Afro-Cubans had been visible in the cultural life of Harlem at least since the heyday of vaudeville theatre in the 1920s, and their religious traditions (such as Palo Monte and Regla de Ocha, or Santería) became highly influential in diasporic practices of the city's africanization since the 1950s.[51] After the 1959 Cuban revolution, the New York Cuban population grew from 42,694 in 1960 to a peak of 84,179 in 1970. The significantly white upper- and middle-class composition of the first post-1959 Cuban migration[52] and the substantial financial and political aids provided by the U.S. government to them as part of Cold War anticommunist policies (such as the Cuban Refugee Program of 1961 and the Cuban Adjustment Act of 1966) facilitated the ability of the new immigrants to obtain an unparalleled degree of economic success and cultural recognition (Grosfoguel 1994, 1997). The very possibilities for success led many Cubans to relocate (the censuses of 1980 and 1990 indicated a decrease of Cubans in New York from 63,189 to 56,041, respectively) to places where they could predominate (especially Miami and West New Jersey) and where they accumulated not only economic and symbolic capital but also demographic leadership and political power. It was not until the Mariel migration in the 1980s and the waves of *balseros* in the 1990s that we got a new group largely composed of working-class Cubans of color in New York City.

According to the U.S. Census of 1960, there were 13,293 Dominicans in New York City, but by 1970 the census indicated that number had grown to 66,914. Dominicans also have a long history in New York, a city that has historically been a frame of reference for a variety of movements and events related to and promoted by them, from nineteenth-century struggles for Dominican independence to the arrival during the 1960s and 1970s of political exiles from the authoritarian regimes of Trujillo and Balaguer (Torres-Saillant and Hernandez 1998; Rodríguez de León 1998). Particular restrictions on Dominican emigration were not abolished until the demise of the Trujillo dictatorship in 1961, and the boom of Dominican migration to New York began after 1965, when U.S. immigration reform allowed for a yearly ceiling of 120,000 from all countries and when 65,000 U.S. Marines invaded the Dominican Republic to crush a popular insurrection that demanded the reconstitution of a democratically elected government. Several factors promoted the mass immigration of Dominicans to New York City, including a concerted effort from the U.S. government to displace Dominican political dissidence out of the country (Mitchell 1992; Grosfoguel 1997), an exacerbation of unemployment in the post-1965 U.S.-oriented model of economic development, and the new opportunities for both legal and illegal immigration. The official count of the Dominican population of New York City more than doubled to 125,380 in 1980, and in 1990 it came up to 332,713, a total of 18.7 percent of the Latino community, making it the second-largest Latino ethnic group. At present, Dominicans and Puerto Ricans are the largest, most visible, and most influential Latino ethnonational groups in New York City, and they are the only ones that have elected officials from their own ranks to city and state government. However, their nationals are also overrepresented in the figures of unemployment and social marginality, and their neighborhoods (such as Washington Heights and East Harlem) are among the most vilified in hegemonic urban discourse. Consequently, the equation of solidarity and conflict that characterizes their relationships is crucial in defining latinidad and to the latinization of New York City.

Starting in the 1970s, significant changes began to take place in the composition and character of New York City's Latino population. The crisis in the world economy during that decade exacerbated economic malaise in Latin American and Caribbean countries, motivating unprecedented migrations to the United States. The corresponding economic restructuring involved a flight of most manufacturing activity away from New York City (and into other regions and countries), accompanied by massive movements of peoples toward metropolitan centers such as New York, a phenomenon that Saskia Sassen (1988) calls "exporting capital and importing labor." The census of 1980 counted 1,406,024 people of Latin American descent, and the one of 1990 elevated the total to 1, 783,511, or 23.7 percent of the city's population. These figures still showed that 72.1 percent of all New York Latinos were Hispanic Caribbeans, with Puerto Ricans representing 50.3 percent; Dominicans, 18.7 percent; and Cubans, 3.1 percent. These were followed by significant increases in the quantity of individuals self-identified as Colombian (from 6,782 in 1960 to 84,454 in 1990), Ecuadorean (from 4,077 in 1960 to 78,444 in 1990), and Mexican (from 8,260 in 1960 to 61,772 in 1990). Colombians are the third-largest group of Latinos in New York and one of the most culturally influential in the city's latinization in spite of their relative lack of formal political organization (Garcia Castro

1982a, 1982b; Urrea Giraldo 1982; Jones-Correa 1998). For instance, Colombians have a turf base (e.g., restaurants, community organizations, car services) in Jackson Heights, Queens, one of the most culturally diverse and well-known neighborhoods in the whole city, as well as a visible presence in the civic and cultural life of Latin New York. Evidently, these statistics' margin of error underscores the much-discussed tendency of the U.S. Census to undercount Latinos for a variety of reasons including socially and culturally biased methods of collection and the fact that many undocumented immigrants go unrecorded in these data, which may considerably change the numbers, especially if they come from places such as Mexico, Colombia, Ecuador, the Dominican Republic, and Central America, which still provide a large pool of the city's undocumented workers. This undocumented status is particularly important to assess the situation of Mexicans who arguably are the fastest-growing immigrant community in the city, occupy a particular niche in the metropolitan labor market, and protagonize a specific kind of latinization (i.e., mexicanization) of New York (R. Smith 1996, 1997; Solís in this volume).

Central Americans make up the next-largest group of New York Latinos in terms of geographic origin. The 1990 census counted 23,926 people from El Salvador, 22,707 from Panama, 22,167 from Honduras, and 15,873 from Guatemala residing in New York City. In the case of Salvadorans, Hondurans, and Guatemalans, the numbers are clearly related to the political turmoil and civil wars during the 1980s that provoked thousands of refugees to flee these countries (Mahler 1995). The contradiction between foreign policies that supported authoritarian regimes and armies in Central America and domestic policies that denied political asylum to refugees from this area[53] promoted the creation of another class of undocumented workers who came to fill jobs in the lower echelons of the service and garment industries. Panamanians had also been coming to New York in significant quantities since the political unrest and economic disturbances of the late 1960s and early 1970s, showing a demographic growth from 15,225 in the 1970 census to 22,707 in the 1990 census (Priestley 1998). Most Panamanians in New York are of Afro-Antillean descent and are therefore often labeled as West Indian or African American. These designations are not necessarily exclusive; people self-define simultaneously as Panamanian, Latino, West Indian, and African American and share spaces of living, work, creed, and leisure with members of all of these collective designations. Also, given that the symbolic center and largest concentration of Panamanians in New York City is in Brooklyn neighborhoods classified as West Indian (Crown Heights, Eastern Parkway), their political and cultural identities have tended to be codified more as Caribbean and African American than as Latino. These multiple racial and ethnic locations of Panamanians reveal the intersections but also the contradictions between caribbeanization and latinization and between Latino and Afro-American diasporas.

A large majority of Latin American immigrants and their offspring in New York City came as labor forces or turned into labor reserves. After the immigration reforms in the 1960s and the qualitative growth of world migratory movements since the 1970s (Cohen 1997), the majority of New Yorkers became either direct immigrants or of immediate immigrant ancestry. This implied the rise of new, multinational, and pluriracial working classes substantially composed of Latin American and Caribbean workers. The restructuring of the metropolitan economy away from traditional industrial production into one led by a highly stratified service sector expelled several contingents of racially subordinate workers (especially Puerto Ricans and African Americans)[54] from manufacturing employment and displaced many of them from the labor market. The cartography of new class actors also incorporated new immigrant workers predominantly from Latin America, the Caribbean, and Asia who came to work in the lower echelons of the service economy (as servitudes of the services) as well as a segment of immigrant labor (largely Dominican and Chinese) occupying blue-collar jobs in the remaining fragments of the manufacturing industry. Latin American and Caribbean immigrants, who have been arriving in quantity to New York since the 1970s, also organized neighborhood economies where ethnic entrepreneurs (Portes and Sensenbrenner 1993; Waldinger 1996; Bailey and Waldinger 1991) developed their own spheres of economic activity (sweatshops, car services) that constitute sources of profit for emerging petit bourgeois and small capitalist classes and employment (and exploitation) for local working classes. A middle stratum of Latino semiprofessionals (paralegals, finance specialists), as well as middle-range managers, grew in the new service economy. The charting of class divisions among Latinos should also register the difference between, on the one hand, a sector of civil service public workers and nonprofit service providers and, on the other, a sector of top-city bureaucracies and community service managers with higher incomes, better residential situations, access to political connections, and more cultural capital.

The 1990 census calculated that 1,737,927 individuals (a city in itself) from at least 19 countries of Latin America were then living in New York City, which represents more than double the 1960 figure of 757,231.[55] All the estimates for the year 2000 exceed two million, meaning that Latinos will comprise more than a quarter of New York City's inhabitants; close to 60 percent of the city's population will be made up of Latinos, African Americans, and Asians, making it a place where so-called minorities are now the majority. This also makes New York not only the most populated Latino city of the United States but also the most diverse and the largest one (along with Chicago and San Francisco) where no single national group (such as Mexicans in Los Angeles and Cubans in Miami) predominates— a uniquely pan-Latino metropolis.

MONTAGING THE MAMBO: LANDSCAPES OF LATINIDAD AND THE LATINIZATION OF CITYSCAPES

Mambo Montage is divided into four parts. The first part, "The Production of Latinidad: Histories, Social Movements and Cultural Struggles," opens with Nancy Raquel Mirabal's " 'No Country but the One We Must Fight For': The Emergence of an Antillean Nation and Community in New York City, 1860–1901," in which she shows how by the second half of the nineteenth century, New York City was a central headquarters in the organization of Hispanic Caribbean anticolonial movements as well as a key place and referent in the very constitution of Cuban and Puerto Rican national and Caribbean regional identities. She also demonstrates the diasporic element in the rise of Cuban and Puerto Rican nationalities in the context of New York City and considers the role of class, race and gender in the emergence of these national and regional (Antillean) definitions of identity. The second article, Adrian Burgos Jr.'s " 'The Latins from Manhattan': Confronting Race and Building Community in Jim Crow Baseball, 1906–1950" is a social and cultural history of the complex interplays among race, nationality, and ethnicity in the construction of Latino identities (particularly from the Spanish-speaking Caribbean) through baseball in the early twentieth century and how sport facilitated diasporic encounters between African Americans, Cubans, and Puerto Ricans that helped build translocal publics as well as an interethnic racial community in Harlem. This is followed by "Latino Caribbean Diasporas in New York," in which Ramón Grosfoguel and Chloé S. Georas analyze the relationship between global coloniality and the differential racialization of Caribbean immigrants in New York City as well as how U.S. imperial geopolitics and cultural politics account for inequalities of economic and symbolic capital between Puerto Ricans, Dominicans, and Cubans. The last two articles in this section (Laó-Montes's and Dávila's) historicize and problematize the making of Latino identities by means of political and cultural struggles and movements. In "Niuyol: Urban Regime, Latino Social Movements, and Ideologies of Latinidad," Laó-Montes discusses how Latino political identities emerge from within various struggles and movements such as those for immigrants' rights and racial justice and how they articulate distinctive projects of politics in relationship to the patternings of power in the urban scene and beyond. Like Grosfoguel and Georas, Laó-Montes analyzes the dynamics of power and the construction of identities in New York in terms of the interweaving of the local and global entanglements of the coloniality of power. The section closes with "Culture in the Battlefront: From Nationalist to Pan-Latino Projects," a piece in which Arlene Dávila traces the trajectory of cultural movements and the emergence of cultural institutions in East Harlem from the 1960s to the 1990s, emphasizing the visual arts. Dávila highlights the cultural politics of renaming institutional identities from

Puerto Rican to *Latino* and of redefining the arena of cultural contestation from community empowerment in the 1970s to minority representation in the 1990s.

In what remains of this introduction, I will present the rest of the book as part of the following discussion on landscapes of latinidad in New York City. The notion of landscape "connotes the entire panorama that we see: both the landscape of the powerful—cathedrals, factories, and sky-scrapers—and the subordinate, resistant, or expressive vernaculars of the powerless—village chapels, shantytowns, and tenements" (Zukin 1991:16). Landscapes are spaces of economic activity and cultural meaning, inscribing, organizing, and representing social power and social identities. Montage mapping of the city is a powerful representational device of modern (and postmodern) cityscapes. Christine M. Boyer contends that montage best represents "the very form of New York City as urban space" and characterizes the "landscape of contemporary city [as] composed of conflicting fragments, sliced or framed views, first cut out, extracted from the city fabric, and then set-up juxtaposed against each other" (1998:421). Along the same lines, James Donald observes that Eisenstein's cinematic "aesthetic of montage . . . self consciously used the experience of fragmentation that characterize the modernite of the city . . . to capture the complex syncopated rhythm of the metropolitan day (1999:76)."[56] New York cityscapes can be represented as a montage of a multiplicity of spaces, as a contested terrain of dominant, emerging, and residual landscapes, articulating different projects and styles of urbanism. New York's cityscapes are heterogeneous and contested, facilitating differentiated publics and representing opposing political and cultural projects. The latinization of New York refers to both the vernacular landscapes of latinidad and the growing visibility of signs of latinidad in the city's central landscapes of power.

The primary representations of New York's latinization are sensory images of the city: the sounds of salsa and bachata from the radios tuned to La Mega ("the authentic station of Latinos"); a visual montage of Dominican bodegas (grocery stores) with their open-air display of peppers and plantains, Puerto Rican flags waving from casitas[57] in community gardens, and Mexican street vendors offering colorful flowers in supermarket carts. But beyond the aesthetics of the barrios, the latinized sensorium of the city is also composed by other more central cityscapes, as exemplified in restaurants such as Patria ("the home of the Nuevo Latino") and Bolivar, where you can eat gourmet versions of a variety of Latin American dishes while enjoying the plush atmosphere and paying the high prices of Manhattan's exclusive East Side.[58] This contrast between the barrios' cultural economies and the exoticized consumption of latinidad is one of the most important tensions in the booming process of the city's latinization. To represent this tension, I distinguish two general yet intertwined domains of the latinization of the Big Apple: landscapes of latinidad and the latinization of central cityscapes.

The notion of landscapes of latinidad refers to the emergence of particularly Latino social spaces, expressive cultures, institutions, and organizations. The latinization of central cityscapes refers to the increasing presence of particular versions of latinidad in the dominant and most visible landscapes of power of the city. These two entangled domains constitute the contested terrain of the city's latinization. For instance, Sunday drumming jams in Central Park led by Afro-Cubans and Nuyoricans carve a multicultural space for the creation of community and in this way exemplify how Latino cultural expressions can become city traditions and means of transculturation by their appropriation of core urban spaces. Landscapes of latinidad are visible in the latinization of cityscapes in multiple ways and with variable meanings, ranging from Otabaleño Ecuadorean Amerindians playing Andean music in the 42nd St. subway station to the Quisqueya in the Hudson Festival (Duany 1994) celebrating Afro-Dominican traditions in the Cloisters Park.

Any demographic map of New York should represent the city as a vast cartography of latinized places and populations. The *New York City Latino Neighborhoods Databook* identified 54 Latino Neighborhood Areas (Hanson-Sánchez 1998). The large number, wide geographic dispersion, and great diversity that characterize and differentiate these places bear witness to the particular richness of New York's Latino neighborhoods.[59] For instance, in Jackson Heights or Corona, Queens, you can see a line of restaurants and nightclubs representing different parts of South America (Peru, Colombia, Ecuador, Uruguay, and Venezuela) along with Argentinean bakeries and Dominican beauty parlors. In Spanish Harlem, the historic Puerto Rican barrio, it is now customary for bodegas to sell Mexican chiles and tortillas, and the visual landscape now includes the traditional cuchifritos (Puerto Rican fried foods) near Mexican posts selling tortas and tacos. These Latin Quarters are the grassroots of New York's latinization and the main grounding for the practice of latinization from below. They are places for face-to-face Latino/American multinational encounters, national diasporic formations, panethnic identifications, and the emergence of a new ethnic and racial consciousness. These localized identities are ambiguous and complex and are forged within a dialectic of solidarity and conflict (between nationalities, classes, genders, etc.). Barrios also constitute the geographies where cultural and economic forms known as Latino (bodegas, hip-hop) emerge as part of the city's public culture and cultural economy. Hence, barrio popular cultures refer to the forms of cultural production and aesthetic expression emerging from the social locations and lived experiences of the city's Latin Quarters.

Mambo Montage showcases New York's Latino landscapes in two sections: "Latino/a Identities and the Politics of Space and Place" and "Expressive Cultures: Narrating, Imaging, and Performing Latinidad." The first of these sections opens with "Making Loisaida: Placing Puertorriqueñidad in Lower Manhattan," an article in which Liz Ševčenko analyses how the struggles since the 1960s for Puerto Rican self-affirmation and local empowerment in Manhattan's Lower East Side account for the latinization of the place, renamed Loisaida by its Latino residents. Elsa B. Cardalda Sánchez and Amílcar Tirado Avilés, in "Ambiguous Identities! The Affirmation of Puertorriqueñidad in the Community Murals of New York City," demonstrate the relationship between puertorriqueñization and latinization based on a historical, aesthetic, and social-psychological interpretation of community murals in East Harlem. Like Ševčenko, Cardalda Sánchez and Tirado Avilés's article explores the intricate relationship between nationality, panethnicity, and place in the articulation of urban struggles and in the production of urban space.

All of the articles in the section on expressive cultures investigate the relationship between Puerto Rican and Latino identities and cultural expressions. The aesthetic expressions of Latino/a New York are created over a broad range of genres (visual art, film, literature, music, performance, and photography)[60] and performed by individual authors and cultural movements. Each of these realms of cultural creation is now linked to cultural industries at the same time that they are terrains of cultural contestation. Literature is one of the main spheres through which Latino/a identities are created, narrated, and disseminated. In "Life Off the Hyphen: Latino Literature and Nuyorican Traditions," Juan Flores assesses the cultural politics of the canonization of the new Latino literature in contrast to the vernacular traditions of Nuyorican literature. New York has been a world mecca of Latin music at least since the mambo craze of the 1950s, and music is a pivotal medium of latinizing peoples and places. In "Nothing Connects Us All but Imagined Sounds," Wilson Valentín-Escobar, focusing on the performance of popular memory and the appropriation of public space at the funeral of salsa singer Héctor Lavoe, interprets the meanings of New York's salsa music in the configuration of a translocal Puerto Rican nation and a global Latino identity. Raquel Z. Rivera, in "Hip Hop, Puerto Ricans, and Ethnoracial Identities in New York," analyzes the racial and sexual politics entangled in hip-hop culture, drawing a complex picture of ethnoracial and gender identity and difference in the relationship between blackness, puertorriqueñidad, and latinidad. All of these pieces reveal something of the uniqueness of New York as a Latino metropolis in relationship to the historical importance of puertorriqueñidad as a main expression of what we now call latinidad as well as a key vector of latinization. They also show the tensions between puertorriqueñidad and latinidad as the relative centrality of Puerto Ricans in the city and among Latinos is being relativized. Another important historic relationship shown in the articles is that between Latinos from the Hispanic Caribbean (especially Afro-Latinos) and

African Americans (in the sense of U.S. blacks); both Burgos's and Rivera's articles show the tensions of race, ethnicity, and nationality in the negotiation of collective identifications and intergroup relationships.

The production of New York Latino space is place based at the same time that it is bound to larger networks and flows. The geographic contours of Latin New York range from the building and the block to global webs of style and music. For instance, the Bronx is known as the world's capital of salsa, and the National Puerto Rican Parade in New York now is the largest ethnic parade in the city as well as a translocal celebration of a diasporic nation and a carnival of latinidad. In this way, New York Latino landscapes are shaped by place at the same time that they are constitutive of more global spaces to articulate identity and community. New York Latino communities are both neighborhood settlements and translocal ethnoracial collectivities. Joselyn Solís, in "Immigration Status and Identity: Undocumented Mexicans in New York," studies the relationship between legal status, New York's Mexican identity, and the mexicanization of the city. Considering another transnational community, José Itzigsohn and Carlos Dore-Cabral analyze the intersections of race, nationality, and Latino panethnicity in the encoding and enactments of Dominican identities in New York, focusing on the Dominican enclave in Manhattan's Washington Heights. Looking at the question of space from the angle of landscapes of otherness and Latino locations, Luis Aponte-Parés, in "*Out*side/In: Crossing Queer and Latino Boundaries," discusses how Latino gay politics and queer landscapes can simultaneously transgress and challenge heterosexism and homophobia within landscapes of latinidad as well as racism and classism within mainstream queer cityscapes. The last article in "Latino/a Identities and the Politics of Space and Place" is Mary Garcia Castro's "Engendering and Coloring Labor Unions: Transcultural Readings of Latin American Women's Ways." Garcia-Castro does a feminist reading from her Brazilian location of how counterpointing histories, memories, and agendas of Brazilian and New York Puerto Rican women trade unionists can shed light in a project for a translocal hemispheric politics of working-class women of color.

The last part of the book, "Latinizing Cityscapes," discusses the carving of Latino spaces in New York's public sphere through genres of culture and politics and the production, inscription, and reconversion of latinidad in the city's central landscapes of power. The Latino media make up one of the main forces in the latinization of New York. The Spanish-language press has historically been a very important medium for the hispanization and latinization of the city.[61] Founded in 1911, *El Diario-La Prensa*, the Spanish newspaper with the largest circulation in the metropolitan area, describes itself as "the champion of the Hispanics" and plays an active role in chronicling and disseminating knowledge on New York Latino life; promoting a sense of pan-Latino unity; and advocating for Latino rights, cultural recognition, and political representation. The rise of New York's Spanish-language radio in the 1940s and of television in the 1960s facilitated and promoted the production of latinidad and the city's latinization even more. In 1998, La Mega was rated as first in audience share of all radio stations in New York. The growth of Spanish-language radio and television in New York, along with more globally oriented Latino cultural industries (music, record, performance, and magazines) enhanced the city's role as a key center in the translocal production of Latino/American popular and mass-mediated cultures.

New York is a world city of latinidad because of its Latino landscapes' vitality and because of its central spaces' relative latinization. In mainstream film and television, latinidad is largely invisible, and representations of New York Latino bodies and spaces are still dominated by tropes of urban ghetto life. Although some New York Latinos, such as Jennifer López and Marc Anthony, are becoming media celebrities and pop icons, they are still partly depicted as exotic bodies and exceptional brown faces. In the realm of corporate cultural industries, Latinos (or as they are more often called, Hispanics) are above all a large and growing market, and latinidad is thus a discourse produced with the purpose of enhancing marketability. In "The Latin Side of Madison Avenue: Marketing and the Language that Makes Us 'Hispanics,'" Arlene Dávila analyzes the transnational political economy and ethnoracial discourses of Hispanic marketing, one of the key cultural industries in the production of latinidad. She examines the cultural politics involved in the Hispanic corporate representations of Latino identity and culture and explores the tensions between Spanish-language versus English-language genres of Hispanic and Latino media.

In the local cultural economies of mainstream New York, latinization can also be a practice of cultural consumption of a commodified form of ethnicity. These commercial ethnoscapes of latinization are dispersed through scattered restaurants, nightclubs, performance spaces, dance and language classes, art galleries, and stores selling ethnic crafts and clothing, generally located in gentrified Manhattan neighborhoods such as Soho and Chelsea. New Yorkers enjoy a unique culture of leisure and an infrastructure of entertainment within which eating and dancing Latino is now an option not only in the Latin Quarters of Queens and the Bronx but also in the Anglocore of downtown and mid-Manhattan. Now, restaurants and clubs in Soho and the Village play Latin music (salsa, merengue, Brazilian, Cuban, plena) seven days a week, and traditional Latino Clubs such as the Copacabana and La Escuelita are now tourist attractions. An analysis of this mode of latinization of cityscapes by means of consumption, Lisa Maya Knauer's "Eating in Cuban" highlights the crucial importance of Cubans in the latinization of New York and analyzes the relevance of Cuban restaurants for various definitions of cubanidad.

The popularization of spaces for the consumption of ethnicity as a ritualized source of pleasure promotes a circumstantial and superficial engagement with the cultures of the perceived other and a deceptive sense of knowledge. For some, this means a latinization without Latinos except as entertainers or perhaps as casual sexual partners or behind-the-scenes workers. For others, consuming Latino/a otherness serves as a gateway to some sort of intercultural exchange, which can go as far as traveling, studying, becoming solidarity activists, marrying interracially, or going out to dance Latin. In "Taking 'Class' Into Account: Dance, the Studio, and Latino Culture," Karen Backstein analyzes dance as a space of transculturation and reflects on the meaning of Afro-diasporic (Brazilian and Cuban) dance classes for multicultural community-making and for the multiple definitions of Latino identity and New York's public cultures. Indeed, the increasing presence of Brazilians in the city often unsettles conventional views of both Latino and Brazilian identity and culture, and it presents one of the clearest challenges to close definitions of latinidad based on narrow criteria of language and history.

Strategies of latinization through the commodification of ethnicity leave intact the underlying structures of class, gender, sexual, and racial inequality that inform cultural and political power in New York City. In "Deceptive Solidity: Public Signs, Civic Inclusion, and Language Rights in New York City (and Beyond)," Vilma Santiago-Irizarry discusses how the scattered presence of Spanish and the marginalized inclusion of Latino cultures in central cityscapes reveal the political limits of legal struggles for language rights and the uneven character of New York's latinization. Even though language is a significant racial and ethnic marker and is one of the formative forces of discourses of latinidad as well as an inspiration to Latino social movements and claims of rights, the circumscribed impact of the politics of language reveals the limits of ethnic identity politics and of uncritical celebrations of latinization. In a way, the latinization of the city's central spaces is a facade or simulacrum foreign to the majority of working-class and economically marginalized Latinos who reside in its Latin Quarters. Paradoxically, the very same time when Latino cultural commodities are more in vogue is when Latino barrios and subaltern classes (especially Dominican and Puerto Rican) are increasingly vilified, criminalized, and labeled as dangerous and undesirable in the central landscapes of power of the city. Latinization is conceived in some conservative (and even liberal) discourses as a problem. In the most recalcitrant narratives, latinization is seen as a liability to the city, and the increasing numbers of Latinos are posited as a source for social ills such as unemployment and crime.

In the post–Civil Rights era, the dominant discourse is not one of bold exclusion but rather of the governmentalization and corporativization of multiculturalism, as in Mayor Dinkins's "Gorgeous Mosaic." We can also see the colonization of multiculturalism in Mayor Giuliani's paradoxical defense of immigrant rights as well as in the corporate promotion of cultural diversity as a market principle. These governmental and corporate discourses enable hegemonic strategies of latinization in which Latino culture is officially celebrated at the same time that Latino subaltern classes are excluded from centrally localized spaces. This mode of urbanism is characterized by a combination of privatization and policing of public space. The privatization of public culture as a strategy of neoliberal policy, a manifestation of a social space colonized by capital, is accompanied by the increasing militarization of New York's urban regime. Ironically, the appearance of diversification and democratization (latinization) in New York's commodified cultures is the sublime face of the fortress city. The rule of capital in the production of and access to a sanitized urban space is visible in the rise of standardized commodified spaces for entertainment and tourism (Sorkin 1992; Hannigan 1998). Perhaps the best example is the conversion of Times Square into a corporate theme park and the associated displacement of the sexual markets and abjected peoples (the homeless, sex workers, street dwellers) from the former red-light city.

The colonization of public space by means of neoliberal policies of privatization and policing is orchestrated by a partnership of corporate actors, the city government, and upper-/middle-class citizens, as exemplified in the increasing reliance on city-corporate ventures for managing parks and other public spaces (Zukin 1995). These governmental and corporate strategies of exclusion and marginalization are symptomatic of patterns of urban governance predicated on the combined effects of class and racial domination and of an urban economic growth model characterized by redevelopment through gentrification with a concomitant racialization of public space. Gentrification, or the redevelopment and repopulation of working-class neighborhoods (largely African American and Puerto Rican) with expensive housing and cultural economies of middle-class consumption, has the continuous and increasing effect of dismantling working-class publics, displacing tenants, and promoting homelessness (N. Smith 1996). The overall impact has been to exacerbate social ills (such as chronic poverty and unemployment) in the most directly affected communities and individual subjects of long-term coloniality, namely African Americans and Puerto Ricans. This overt racialization of the production and appropriation of urban space is contested by alternate local strategies of redevelopment, such as those creating Latino immigrant cultural economies (Dominican bodegas, car service networks) in the barrios. An important example of struggles over space is in ecological activists' fight to save community gardens and casitas against the impulses of savage capitalism, represented in Mayor Giuliani's attempt to sell the green spaces developed by largely Latino grassroots organizations.

The latinization of New York's landscapes of power also refers to the latinization of formal politics manifested in a Latino bureaucracy of city elected and appointed officials, in the constitution of Latinos as a political constituency and identity, and in explicitly Latino political organizations and social movements. However, the contested city is not simply about the political in the sense of the political system but also about politics in the sense of the deployment and contestation of power in all instances and at all levels of the urban social space. In this tenor, the cultural politics involved in struggles such as those over language rights, museum exhibitions, multicultural education, and the uses and meanings of public space are of crucial relevance. Latinization is also a contested terrain of politics manifested, from below, in struggles for needs and rights, as in the cases of working-class Latino students fighting for educational access and relevant course material (Puerto Rican, Dominican, and Latino Studies) at the City University and barrio residents advocating for the right to spaces (parks, gardens) for leisure and pleasure, community building, and cultural affirmation.

Given the intensity and density of transnational connections and global flows between New York and the rest of the world, the latinization of the world city is also key to making latinidad a translocal process of identification and cultural expression. The ongoing process of the caribbeanization and latinization of New York City gives rise to border zones for cultural production and political struggles such as the triangular borderland that now exists between the Dominican Republic, Puerto Rico, and New York. The rise of latinidad as a signifier of an emerging translocal political community within this triangular contact zone was exemplified at the November 1999 Latin American Women Movement Encounter at the Dominican Republic where Dominican and Puerto Rican women's activists from New York City jointly defined themselves as Latinas struggling for rights and justice in Santo Domingo, Puerto Rico, and New York (Weyland 2000).

As the oldest and most cosmopolitan world city of the Americas, New York is a borderland of global latinidad and a crossroads of Latino/American and Caribbean diasporas. Indeed, New York can be described as a microcosm of world cultures. This is partly motivated by metropolitan imperial desire (i.e., New York Centrism) but it also reveals the character of the city as a global crossroads, a City of Elegguá.[62] Eshú-Elegbá (in Cuba, Elegguá) is the orisha of communication and interpretation, the trickster and gatekeeper who presides over the crossroads. In this vein, a critical democratic vision of hybridity and fluidity of cultures is expressed in the aesthetic practices of what I call New York's Latina/o Postcolonial Montage.[63] For instance, in the performance arts of Carmelita Tropicana and Josefina Baez, the collages of Juan Sánchez, and the installations of Pepon Osorio and Anaida Hernandez, there is a juxtaposition of anti-imperial critique and re-americanization, social criticism and comedy, celebration and critical distance of Latino popular cultures, with the critical effect of both transgressing and reconstructing Latino identities. These aesthetic practices could be important forces in exploring the potential of latinidad to be an inclusive, open-ended, contestatory and emancipatory project of identification. In this sense, latinidad can be constructed as a montage and performed like a mambo. The principle of mambo in Congo cosmology as expressed in the Afro-Cuban and New York Afro-diasporic/Latino popular religion called Palo Monte implies a practice of community in terms of an interplay of identity and difference and the achievement of consensus based on individual freedom and fulfillment. In the final chant of a Palo ceremony, if there is no communal and individual self-expression and happiness, there is no mambo.[64]

This politics of latinization as a practice of freedom is also the thrust of what Chicana feminist historian Emma Pérez calls a "decolonial imaginary"; a vision for "desire, desire as revolution, desire as a medium for social change, desire as love and hope for a different kind of future—a postcolonial one" (1999:xix). Dancing the same kind of mambo, Nuyorican writer and performance artist Pedro Pietri, after drawing a landscape of despair and death, expressed a utopian vision of decolonization, Latino power, and desire at the end of his classic poem, "Puerto Rican Obituary" (1973):

> If only they . . .
> Juan
> Miguel
> Milagros
> Olga
> Manuel
> . . . make their latino souls
> the only religion of their race
> . . . Aquí the men and women admire desire
> and never get tired of each other
> Aquí Qué Pasa Power is what's happening
> Aquí to be called negrito
> means to be called LOVE.

NOTES

1. The notion of the Black Atlantic signifies the historical and geocultural threads that account for the linkages of African/Afro-diasporic cultures within the Atlantic System. To conceptualize the Black Atlantic as a historical formation does not mean positing an essentialized notion of African and/or of Afro-diasporic culture but rather to recognize how world capitalism and global racial hierarchies, on the one hand, and cultural practices of resistance and

self-affirmation, on the other hand, account for the emergence of African Afro-diasporic identities, consciousness, and cultural genres. For notions of the Black Atlantic, see Farris Thompson (1982), Linebaugh (1982), Gilroy (1993), Patterson and Kelley (2000).

2. In the words of Robert Farris Thompson, "*Mambo* is a creole word of ultimate Ki-Kongo ancestry . . . ultimately linked through Bantu cognation, to the Ki-Swahili term *jambo,* meaning 'what's up' 'how are things?' " Letter to the author, July 27, 1999.

3. The first Latin American genre of music and dance to be globalized by cultural industries was the Argentinean tango. This is partly related to the production of the imagery of Latin lovers by Hollywood since the 1920s. Thanks to Alberto Sandoval-Sánchez and Aníbal Quijano for bringing this to my attention. Concerning the globalization of so-called tropical music, the mambo was preceded by genres such as the rumba and the conga that were disseminated through the Hollywood musicals and other venues of the entertainment industries (like records and shows), but the mambo achieved far greater popularity and reached many more places as music and as a dance genre.

4. For an excellent general text on mambo written from a Cuban perspective, see Giro (1995). For an interpretation of the globalization of mambo music in the 1950s, see Pérez-Firmat (1994). For an analysis of the significance of mambo in the Black Atlantic, see Farris-Thompson (1982). For mambo as a cultural trope, see Laó-Montes (2000b).

5. Montage has been a principal aesthetic genre and philosophical-political principle in avant-garde art movements since surrealism and early-twentieth-century Russian cinema. Bearden's collages are a pillar of African American modernism.

6. As we shall see, processes of latinization are grounded in particular places (such as world cities) at the same time that they constitute global cultural economies and translocal identities. Derrida coined the notion of globalatinization referring to the globalization of references to the cultural heritages of Roman civilization (such as languages and religion) as well as their current signification through the performativity of new media and new structures of testimony and confession (Derrida and Vattimo 1996). The idea of latinidad and the corresponding politics of panlatinismo can be traced to nineteenth century French imperial discourses (as expressed by intellectuals like Renan) in competition with Anglo-Saxon powers. This in turn influenced the birth of Latinamericanist discourses in opposition to the U.S. in the same century. For the significance of Francophile Panlatinismo in the rise of Latinamericanism, see Phelan (1979).

7. A trope of tropes is a key figure of imagination and speech, namely one that enables a multiplicity of primary significations within a semantic and cultural field. I propose that Mambo is a key trope of latinidad and the African diaspora, similarly to Gates' argument of "The Signifying Monkey" as "trope of tropes" for African American vernacular aesthetics.

8. The notion of latinidad is increasingly becoming a common ground in Latino Studies. It is a already a keyword that facilitates intellectual and political dialogue (Williams 1985). For the notion of latinidad, see (among others)

Sandoval-Sánchez (1999), Noriega (1993), Arrizon (1999), Aparicio and Chavez-Silverman (1997), Flores (1997, 2000), de la Campa (1994, 2000).

9. I am suggesting that latinidad can be developed as a "useful category of historical analysis" analogously to the way that feminist historian Joan Scott (1988:29) argues for gender. The imperative need and the challenge to analyze the categorical status of *Latino* and *latinidad* is presented by Juan Flores in his "Pan-Latino/Trans-Latino: Puerto Ricans in the 'New Nueva York' " (2000:141–65). In general, Flores's work represents some of the most historically grounded and imaginative contributions to a genealogical analysis of Latino identity. Also see Flores (1997) and Flores and Yudice (1990).

10. I am using the concept of discursive formation in the tradition of Michel Foucault to signify not simply a narrative or a communicative act but also an enunciative ensemble that enables the production of a subject within a regime of power and knowledge and consequently has effects of power and is productive of particular forms of knowledge (see Foucault 1972, 1978a, 1978b, 1983). This line of analysis had partly enabled a field of studies of colonial discourse and postcolonial theory. See (among others) Said (1979), Bhabha (1994), Stoler (1995), Gandhi (1998), Spivak (1999), Pérez (1999).

11. Genealogy, more than bold historiography, is a way of analyzing how discourses are formed and transformed and how subjects emerge and act within regimes of power and knowledge. In light of this genealogy is also a strategy of critique that investigates how particular experiences, memories, and knowledges are marginalized, silenced, and made invisible while others are highlighted in the production of historical archives. Thus, genealogy could also be a way of "liberating the subjugated knowledges," promoting "countermemories," and enabling subaltern power against domination. In this sense, there is a correspondence between Foucauldian genealogy and Benjaminian montage because as a historiographic method montage is also a strategy of critique by means of investigating the hidden and repressed structures and practices of everyday life in the city and to re-present the totality from the perspective of the fragments. Both Foucaldian genealogy and Benjaminian montage involve writing histories as political interventions requiring a politics of memory and narration from the perspective of present struggles. See Benjamin (1973, 1999), Buck-Morss (1990), Dean (1994), Foucault (1977a, 1977b), Gilloch (1996), Smith (1989), Steinberg (1996).

12. The words Latin and Latino as used to signify civilizational categories have an older history in the Geocultural Cartographies of Identities in the Americas. This can be traced to the nineteenth century distinction (in Latin America, in the United States, and in Europe) between Anglos and Latins.

13. *Hispanismo* signifies a key imperial discourse of the Spanish Empire, *latinism* refers to the U.S.-produced imagery of the Latin other, and *latinismo* denotes an ideology of U.S. Latino power that emerged in the 1960s (Padilla 1985). However, critical traditions of hispanismo and latinism have been reconverted in popular and intellectual discourse. A discussion of the varieties of hispanismos and the different avatars of the rhetoric of latinism and latinismo is beyond the scope of this introduction. For an illuminative attempt to explore the diverse and contradictory meanings of all these signifiers, see Sandoval-Sánchez (1999).

14. The argument is that the European conquest and colonization after 1492 is a foundational moment in the production of modernity and coloniality as two sides of a coin marking the emergence of the modern/colonial world system with a new geography of world regions (the invention of the Americas but also of Europe and Africa), the rise of the West and occidentalism as the dominant historical imaginary, and the creation of the capitalist world economy. See, Quijano (1992, 1999), Dussel (1995), Wallerstein (1974, 1979), Mignolo (2000), Mudimbe (1988), Rabasa (1993), O'Gorman (1982), and Coronil (1995).

15. A central concept in this analysis is Aníbal Quijano's coloniality of power. Quijano argues that modern regimes of power are characterized by what he calls *coloniality,* which, as distinct from colonialism, is not simply defined by a relationship of formal domination between empire and colony but also by global and national/cultural hierarchies (gendered and sexualized) that are articulated differentially in time and space. He conceptualizes coloniality as an axis of domination and subjectification that is not the same as, but is necessarily articulated with, the axis of exploitation (i.e., capital and labor). See Quijano (1992, 1993, 1999a, 1999b). The notion of the coloniality of power had served as a key concept to facilitate dialogues and theoretical developments around questions of modernity, power regimes, subalternity, knowledge, and transformative ethics and politics. Among the scholars involved in those dialogues are Enrique Dussel, Walter Mignolo, Fernando Coronil, Kelvin Santiago-Valles, Gladys Jimenez, Ramón Grosfoguel, Chloé Georas, José David Saldivar, Norma Alarcón, Carol Boyce-Davis, Tiffany Patterson, Immanuel Wallerstein, and Sylvia Winter.

16. For this relational hemispheric perspective on power and identities in the Americas see, Saldivar, (1991), and Acosta-Belén and Santiago (1995).

17. The cases of Cuba and Puerto Rico in the context of the 1898 war clearly exemplify the different ways in which the so-called Caribbean backyard is constitutive of the U.S. imperial self. Louis Pérez Jr. (1998) demonstrates with detail how Cuba was discussed not only in state circles but also in U.S. public culture as an "American" matter. On the other hand, Puerto Rico represents the invisible because of repress face of empire insofar as it can show the hidden logics of U.S. imperialism. For a discussion of the importance of Puerto Rico for the rising transoceanic U.S. empire in the context of 1898, see Scarano (1998) and also Laó-Montes (forthcoming 2001b).

18. In my view, tropicalism, as the occidentalist imagining of the Caribbean tropics and the corresponding constructions of first the Amerindian and second the Afro-diasporic others, was the first modern expression of colonial discourse. See Hulme (1986). The meaning of tropicalism had been reconverted by movements such as the tropicalist movement in Brazil in the 1960s to denote a positive celebration of the so-called tropics. The relationship between the tropics and the act of uttering tropes of self-affirmation and subaltern resistance is productively explored in Aparicio and Chavez-Silverman (1997).

19. There are three ways in which I use the notion of latinamericanist discourses: first as European and U.S. imperial/colonial discourses on Latin America, in a fashion analogous to Said's orientalism; second, as Latin American Creole discourses on world regional and national cultures and identities that emerged

in the nineteenth century to distinguish the region and its countries from both Europe and the United States; and third, as an emerging strand of postcolonial critique from both U.S. Latinos and Latin American social movements and critical intellectuals who share a project of decolonization of power and knowledge. See Laó-Montes (forthcoming 2001a).

20. Wallerstein developed the concept of peoplehood to analyze the creation of a general field of collective identification in the modern world-system characterized by the production of narratives of a common past, culture, and ethnoracial stock; in relationship to current and future power conditions and political claims. He defines the three modern categories of peoplehood (race, nationality, and ethnicity) in terms of this ideological connection between past, present, and future, and by how they relate to regimes of labor exploitation and political/cultural domination in different locations of the modern world-system (Wallerstein 1991). Also see Dominguez (1989).

21. Coronil defines occidentalism the following way: "By 'Occidentalism' I mean not the reverse of Orientalism, but 'the ensemble of representational strategies engaged in the production of conceptions of the world that a) separates its components into bounded units b) disaggregates their relational histories c) turns difference into hierarchy d) naturalizes these representations; and, therefore e) intervenes, however unwittingly, in the reproduction of existing asymmetrical power relations (1997:15). The notion of "chain of otherization" is developed by Bolivian anthropologist Carmen Medeiros in her forthcoming doctoral dissertation.

22. See among others, Fox (1996), Almaguer (1994), and Omi and Winant (1986).

23. *Hispanicity* refers to a specific universe of discourse in which identity is signified by the label *Hispanic*. In contrast to hispanismo and hispanidad (and the label *Hispano*), which has a much older and complex genealogy, the immediate history of hispanicity as a discursive formation can be traced to the 1970s, when the tern *Hispanic* began to be used by the U.S. government and by corporate sectors (especially in advertising). An ironic landmark was the commercial labeling of the 1980s as the decade of the Hispanics in the middle of Reagan's conservative revolution and the new class war of capital against labor.

24. Today in New York City we still celebrate October 12 (known in the United States as Columbus Day) as El Día de la Raza with one of the largest Latino/ Hispanic parades in the city, El Desfile de la Hispanidad. There is a tradition of latinamericanist discourses that conceptualize Latin America (or as often called, Hispanoamerica) as a race in civilizational terms. In the late nineteenth century, perhaps the most celebrated ideologue was Uruguayan José Enrique Rodo, whose essay *Ariel* created school in the aftermath of 1898. In the 1920s the ideology of mestizaje gained special momentum with Mexican philosopher José Vasconcelos's notion of the cosmic race, and the educational and cultural policies that he promoted in Mexico were disseminated to other parts of Latin America as well as in Hispano communities in the United States. See Marentes (2001).

25. The continuity of colonial subalternity after independence within Latin American nation-states is an important historical grounding for what Aníbal Quijano calls the coloniality of power. See Quijano (1993).

26. In general, discourses of latinidad and hispanidad in New York City operate within five intertwined axes of racism that together form the global/regional hierarchies of race: the first is defined by the diversely constructed relationship (in time-space) between white and nonwhite; the second, by the equally contingent distinction between black and white; the third, by the civilizational divide between Anglo Americans and Latino/Americans; the fourth, by the circulation and transformation of Latin American and Hispanic Caribbean racist ideologies and practices in the circuits and travels back and forth between south and north; and the fifth, by the relationship between racial formation, urban space, and social power in the U.S. metropolis (and particularly in New York City).

27. Two studies that exemplify complex histories of racialization in subnational regions in the United States are Virginia Dominguez (1994) for Louisiana and Tomás Almaguer (1994) for California.

28. "La Salsa representando la Raza Latina" (in English "Salsa representing the Latin Race") is part of the lyrics of a song in Larry Harlow's record "La Raza Latina: A Salsa Suite" where latinidad is defined in relationship to a transnational cultural geography, the world of salsa. In the song (also called "La Raza Latina"), the Americas, the Antilles, Aruba, Cuba, Colombia Dominican Republic, Panama, Puerto Rico, Venezuela, and Africa are named as part of this cultural universe.

29. For "conquered minorities" see Blauner (1972), Flores and Yudice (1990) and Hernandez (1998). For colonial migrants, see Rodríguez (1989), Grosfoguel (1995a), and Flores (1997). For the concept of symbolic capital, see Bourdieu (1992).

30. Since their historical inception, Latinidad, Hispanidad, and Hispanicity had been signifiers of whiteness in some of their particular discursive incarnations (e.g., dominant state nationalisms, Latin American ruling classes) and of non-whiteness in others (e.g., Chicano Movement). Hence the racial ambiguity of these notions.

31. For critiques of the ethnic model in the United States, see Steinberg (1996) and Omi and Winant (1986)

32. The concept of transculturation was developed by Fernando Ortiz to conceptualize the unequal exchange (economic, political, and cultural) between different historical categories (such as colonizer-colonized, master-slave, black-mulatto-white, sugar-tobacco) that constitute and represent the politico-economic and cultural-symbolic national field of Cuba (or cubanidad). Mary Louise Pratt has extended the concept to what she defines as a contact zone of colonial encounters in the Americas. Also see Spitta (1995).

33. For diasporic perspectives, see Appadurai (1996), Gilroy (1993), Radhakrishnan (1996), Patterson and Kelley (2000), Laó-Montes (2000a). Juan Flores proposes several names to identify the transnational character of latinidad, including a *diasporic transnation*, a *world tribe*, and *pan-Latino/ trans-Latino*. See Flores (1997). For the transnational character of Latino/a identities and a transnational approach to their analysis in terms of a play of differences, see Mato (1997a, 1997b).

34. The concept of translocation has been used among others by Appadurai (1996), Santos-Febres (1991), Rafael (1995), Laó (1995).

35. For the notion of Third World feminism, see Mohanty (1991). For analyses of the politics of location from a postcolonial and Third World women's perspective, see Alarcón (1989), Mohanty (1987), Kaplan (1994), Frankenberg and Mani (1996), hooks (1989), Wallace (1989).

36. Brackette Williams presented a blueprint for a theory of location at the First Annual Zora Neale Hurston Lectures at Columbia University's Anthropology Department in the Fall of 1997.

37. For the ambiguity and instability of all categories of identity, see Butler (1993) and also Hall (1997).

38. The theoretical and political concepts of *border* and *borderland* are contributions from the Chicano movement and Chicano theory to contemporary critical theory and politics. For an excellent and paradigmatic statement of border theory, see Saldivar (1997).

39. In her article "Salsa as Translocation," Mayra Santos Febres argues that salsa is a "translocal phenomenon" that "cut[s] across national boundaries to create a community of urban locations linked by transportation, communication technologies, and the international market economy" (1997:180). Pérez-Firmat describes the mambo as "a bicultural creation with divided roots and multiple allegiances" and contends that it was "conceived in Cuba, nurtured in Mexico, and brought to maturity in the United States" (1994:80). I will add that the mambo in the sense of a genre of music and dance was conceived in the translocal webs of the Caribbean world cities with the United States in the 1940s and 1950s to eventually get plugged into the emerging global networks of music, performance, dance, and entertainment.

40. As suggested before (see endnote #6) the notion of latinidad is a foundation of nineteenth century latinamericanism. We can see it, for instance in Nicaraguan modernista poet Ruben Dario's idea of "Union Latina" (Dario 1898). Román de la Campa (2000b) writes about "latinidad norteamericana" to specifically locate discourses of latinidad produced in the United States. Here, I am contending that even though it is important to trace the historical legacies and the global/regional linkages (hence the need of a world-historical perspective) of contemporary discourses of latinidad produced in the U.S., it is also necessary to specify their particularity and current centrality.

41. Noriega (1993), as quoted in Aparicio and Chavez-Silverman (1997:15).

42. Roman and Sandoval-Sánchez (1995), as quoted in Aparicio and Chavez-Silverman (1997:15).

43. Alberto Sandoval-Sánchez proposes a notion of latinization as a "process of cultural appropriation" corresponding to discourses of "Latiness" or of the "Latin other" (1999:15). He also argues that " 'Latinization' differs from 'Latinidad' in that the latter results from Latino/a agency and intervention when U.S. Latinos/as articulate and construct cultural expressions and identity formations that come from a conscious political act of self-affirmation" (15). He also writes that for Aparicio and Chavez-Silverman, "Latinization is limited to reformulations of cultural icons by the dominant sector: it is, thus, synonymous with commodification" (15). It is interesting that this last argument is a (deliberate?) misreading of Aparicio and Chavez-Silverman (1997), who argue that to see latinization simply as commodification is a product of Olalquiaga's reductive view of latinization. I will argue

that Sandoval-Sánchez also has a limited view of latinization as well as an overly optimistic analysis of latinidad. It seems that he limits latinidad to the contestatory meanings and practices that derive from the traditions of the 1960s, and this obscures the existence of liberal and even conservative discourses of latinidad. Indeed, even commonsense usages of latinization signify a broader radio of meaning. For a broad-based analysis of latinization, see Davis (2000).

44. Balibar (1994) makes a useful distinction between being subjected (subjection) and developing subjectivity (subjectivation).

45. For the historical analysis of world cities, see Abu-Lughod (1999), Arrighi (1994), and Braudel (1984). The literature on world cities and global cities is now vast. Among the most important contributors are Friedman (1995), Knox and Taylor (1995), Grosfoguel (1995b), Sassen (1991), King (1990).

46. The historical relationship of peoples of Latin American and Hispanic Caribbean origin (that are here retrospectively called Latinos) with peoples from the other subregions of the Caribbean (such as West Indians and Haitians) and with African Americans is a very important aspect of New York Latino history that for reasons of space and particular focus I am not able to treat here as is warranted. For an excellent beginning to account for these histories, see James (1998).

47. The year 1898 was also when the five boroughs (Bronx, Brooklyn, Queens, Manhattan, and Staten Island) were consolidated into a single city, which is not an unrelated development as it marks when New York became a metropolitan core of the emerging U.S. empire. The 1898 war is to be placed in the context of the annexation of Hawai'i in the same period. Also, even though I am not including Puerto Rico in the name of the war given that there was not a war in Puerto Rico of the scale and significance as there was in Cuba and the Philippines, the Puerto Rican case is fundamental to understanding the territorial logics, economic purposes, racial discourses, and technologies of domination and representation of the rising U.S. empire. For this, see Santiago-Valles (1994), Scarano (1998), and Thompson (1995). For the relationship between 1898 and the question of media and empire, and particularly about the birth of cinema in the age of U.S. imperialism, see Shohat and Stam (1994).

48. Even though the category *Hispanic* in its current usage was adopted in the census of 1970, U.S. Census categories had been classifying people of "Spanish surname" or "Hispanic descent" and "ethnic stock" much earlier. In this short review, I won't be able to do a historical analysis of how these census categories reflect the changing and contradictory discourses on peoplehood and otherness in the United States. However, this is a very much needed task that I intend to pursue in a different project.

49. For the meaning of the Jones Act in terms of the racial and imperial aspects of U.S. citizenship, see Ringer (1983).

50. For critiques of the discourse on the so-called underclass, see Reed (1999), Gregory (1998), and Kelley (1997). For the shared economic and political space of African Americans and Puerto Ricans, see Torres (1995).

51. This is an area very much in need of research. My observations are primarily based on interviews with long-term Harlem resident, independent scholar, poet, babalawo, and tata nganga, Edward James.

52. This does not means that all Cubans who came to the United States after the 1959 Cuban revolution were white and upper class. This is testified in the growth of predominantly working-class Cuban communities such as West New York and the Cuban enclave in Union City, New Jersey. I am indebted to Jorge Duany for bringing this to my attention.

53. Indeed, the asylum policies were manifestly politically biased, giving asylum to Nicaraguans who opposed the Sandinista revolution and to Salvadorans and Guatemalans who opposed the guerrillas while denying it to thousands of individuals who suffered from the armed conflict but whose political status was unclear or against the U.S.-backed authoritarian regimes. This also contributed to the growth of the Central American population.

54. This pattern of inequality grounded in a systemic relationship of race, class, and coloniality also substantially affected other groups such as Dominicans. For Puerto Ricans, see Torres (1995) and Bonilla and Campos (1986). For Dominicans, see Hernandez, Rivera-Batiz, and Agodini (1998). For the relationship between economic marginalization and coloniality in New York City, see Grosfoguel and Georas in this volume.

55. The other two national categories that grew to a five-digit figure in the 1990 census were Peruvians, with 23,257, and Argentineans, with 13,934. In spite of the scanty research done on these two national groups in New York, it is evident that their growth was partly a result of the building of family and community networks given that they both had small communities in the city for more than 30 years (the 1960 census shows 2,297 Peruvians and 7,789 Argentineans). However, we hypothesize that in both cases the substantial growth of immigration since the 1970s was related to the rise of authoritarian regimes and to the Latin American regional economic crisis that hit formerly healthy economies such as those of Argentina, Venezuela, and Costa Rica (the 1990 census registered 4,752 Venezuelans and 6,920 Costa Ricans in New York City). In Peru, the civil war between the state military against Shining Path and Tupac Amaru guerrillas created a high number of disappeared and displaced persons, many of whom came to New York City.

56. Pérez Prado defined the mambo genre of music as a syncopated rhythm in the same manner that Eisenstein defined cinematic montage as an aesthetics representing the syncopated rhythm of the metropolitan day. This is yet another way in which the meanings of *mambo* and *montage* converge.

57. *Casitas* literally means "little houses," but in this context it means the wooden houses resembling Caribbean working-class architecture that are built in Puerto Rican barrios in New York City as a cultural practice for promoting memory, organizing community , and fostering identification.

58. The turning into names for commercial venues of two of the key signifiers of nineteenth-century latinamericanism (*Patria,* which means "fatherland," was the title of one of Martí's magazines in New York, and Bolivar is the last name of the most famous hero of the Latin American Wars for independence) dramatically exemplifies the currency of commercialized versions of latinidad. This goes along with the inscription of the icons and heroes of nineteenth-century latinamericanist discourses in the imperial cityscapes of Manhattan as exemplified in the monuments to Bolivar and Martí in Central Park.

59. Mike Davis, in his *Typology of Latino Urban Areas,* calls New York's Latino neighborhoods a "Multicultural Mosaic" and contends that "even on a fairly micro level, New York is far more pluricultural than any other major metropolitan core." (Davis 2000:41).

60. Unfortunately, we could not include articles on theatre, performance, and video/film in this volume. Hispano and Latino theatre in New York City dates back to the beginning of the twentieth century and has produced institutions such as the Puerto Rican Travelling Theatre and Intar as well as a thick volume of plays and equally thick crowds of playwrights. The Festival Latino in the Public Theatre was a highly visible and important event until it ended in 1993, and the Teatro Festival organized by the community theatre group Pregones placed New York at the forefront of U.S. Latino theatre. New York Latina/o performance art is also a very rich arena where latinidad is both celebrated and critiqued in productions ranging from large-scale performances such as Puerto Rican artist Pepon Osorio and choreographer Merian Soto's *Historias* to the postmodern parodies of Cuban Carmelita Tropicana, the satirical depictions of barrio popular cultures of Dominican Josefina Baez, and more recently the revival of poetry performance in several alternative spaces promoted by young poets such as Mariposa and Papyboy. The Latino Collaborative on Film and Video, created in the 1980s, exemplifies how the language of latinidad has been able to facilitate the creation of spaces for cultural organizing and aesthetic sharing.

61. As observed before, hispanization and latinization are necessarily related but are not the same. In this context, *hispanization* refers to the growing presence of the Spanish language in the city and *latinization* to the increasing significance of Latino culture. Latinization does not have to be based on the Spanish language, and indeed a great deal of the activity and developments that we call latinization involve English as the main language.

62. The idea of the City of Elegguá to allegorize the character of New York as a crossroads of cultures, races, genders, and sexualities from all over the world also lends itself as the title of Mexican performance artist Guadalupe Rodríguez's forthcoming doctoral dissertation in Performance Studies at New York University. Eshú-Elegbá is the orisha of signification and interpretation. Henry Louis Gates (1988) has drawn interesting parallels between Eshú-Elegbá and Hermes and suggests that Eshú-Elegbá should be claimed along with the Signifying Monkey as a foundation in a vernacular tradition of African American cultural criticism.

63. For reasons of space and focus, I could not engage the postcolonial debate in this introduction. To put it succinctly, I use the notion of the postcolonial to signify a critical outlook and practice that reveals and challenges the centrality of coloniality in modern regimes of power, modes of knowledge, and forms of subjectivity. This sort of critical theory implies a politics of decolonization as a key component of any project of justice and freedom. For two particularly illuminative interventions in the discussion on the postcolonial, see Shohat (1992) and Hall (1996). For an attempt of a postcolonial analysis of the late modern city, see Jacobs (1996).

64. I owe this interpretation to Cuban artist, art historian, and scholar of the African Diaspora, Bárbaro Martínez.

BIBLIOGRAPHY

Abu-Lughod, Janet. *New York, Chicago, Los Angeles: America's Global Cities.* Minneapolis: University of Minnesota Press, 1999.

Acosta-Belén, Edna and Carlos E. Santiago. "Merging Borders: The Remapping of America," *Latino Review of Books* (spring 1995): 2–12.

Alarcón, Norma. "Traddutora, Traditora: A Paradigmatic Figure of Chicana Feminism." *Cultural Critique* 13 (Fall 1989).

Almaguer, Tomás. *Racial Fault Lines: The Historical Origins of White Supremacy.* Berkeley and Los Angeles: University of California Press, 1994.

Amin, Samir, Giovanni Arrighi, Andre Gunder Frank, and Immanuel Wallerstein. *Dynamics of Global Crisis.* New York: Monthly Review Press, 1982.

Anderson, Benedict. *Imagined Communities: Reflections on the Origins and Spread of Nationalism.* New York: Verso, 1991.

Aparicio, Frances R. and Susana Chavez-Silverman, eds. *Tropicalizations: Transcultural Representations of Latinidad.* Hannover and London: Dartmouth University Press, 1997.

Appadurai, Arjun. *Modernity at Large: Cultural Dimensions of Globalization.* Minneapolis: University of Minnesota Press, 1996.

Arrighi, Giovanni. *The Long Twentieth Century: Money, Power, and the Origins of Our Times.* New York: Verso, 1994.

Arrizon, Alicia. *Latina Performance: Traversing the Stage.* Bloomington: Indiana University Press, 1999.

Bailey, Thomas and Roger Waldinger. "Primary, Secondary, and Enclave Labor Markets: A Training Systems Approach." *American Sociological Review* 56, no.4 (August 1991): 432–45.

Balibar, Etienne. "The Nation Form: History and Ideology." *Review* 13, no. 3 (1990): 329–61.

——— "Subjection and Subjectivation." In Joan Copjec, ed., *Supposing the Subject,* 1–15. New York: Verso, 1994.

Basch, Linda, Nina Glick Schiller, and Cristina Szanton Blanc. *Nations Unbound: Transnational Projects, Postcolonial Predicaments, and Deterritorialized Nation-States.* Langhoene, Pa.: Gordon and Breach, 1994.

Belnap, Jeffrey and Raul Fernandez, eds. *José Martí's "Our America": From National to Hemispheric Cultural Studies.* Durham, N.C.: Duke University Press, 1998.

Benjamin, Walter. *Illuminations.* New York: Schoken, 1973.

——— *Understanding Brecht.* New York: Verso, 1983.

——— "Central Park." *New German Critique* 34 (Winter 1985a): 28–58.

——— *One Way Street and Other Writings.* New York: Verso, 1985b.

——— *The Arcades Project.* Belknap, 1999.

Bhabha, Homi K. *The Location of Culture.* London: Routledge, 1994.

Blauner, Robert. *Racial Oppression in America.* New York: Harper & Row, 1972.

Bonilla, Frank and Ricardo Campos. *Industry and Idleness.* New York: Centro de Estudios Puertorriqueños, 1986.

Bonilla, Frank, Edwin Melendez, Rebecca Morales, and María de los Angeles Torres, eds. *Borderless Borders: U.S. Latinos, Latin Americans and the Paradox of Interdependence.* Philadelphia: Temple University Press, 1998.

Bourdieu, Pierre. *The Logic of Practice*. Palo Alto, Calif.: Stanford University Press, 1992.

Boyer, Christine M. *The City of Collective Memory: Its Historical Imagery and Architectural Entertainments*. Cambridge, Mass.: MIT Press, 1998.

Braudel, Fernand. *The Perspective of the World: Civilization and Capitalism 15th–18th Century*. Berkeley and Los Angeles: University of California Press, 1984.

Buck-Morss, Susan. *The Dialectics of Seeing: Walter Benjamin and the Arcades Project*. Cambridge, Mass.: MIT Press, 1990.

Butler, Judith. *Bodies That Matter*. New York: Routledge, 1993.

Chinweizu. *The West and the Rest of Us: White Predators, Black Slaves, and the African Elite*. New York: Random House, 1975.

Cohen, Robin. *Global Diasporas*. Seattle: University of Washington Press, 1997.

Coronil, Fernando. "Beyond Occidentalism: Toward Non-Imperial Geo-Historical Categories." *Cultural Anthropology* 11, no. 1 (1996): 51–87.

_____ *The Magical State: Nature, Money, and Modernity in Venezuela*. Chicago: University of Chicago Press, 1997.

Crahan, Margaret E. and Alberto Vourvoulias-Bush, eds. *The City and the World: New York's Global Future*. New York: Council on Foreign Relations, 1997.

Dario, Ruben. "El Triunfo de Caliban (1898)" *Revista Iberoamericana* Vol. LXIV, Nums. 184–185, Julio-Diciembre 1998 (edicion y notas Carlos Jauregui) (451–456).

Davis, Mike. *Magical Urbanism: Latinos Reinvent the U.S. Big City*. New York: Verso, 2000.

Dean, Mitchell. *Critical and Effective Histories: Foucault's Methods and Historical Sociology*. London: Routledge, 1994.

de la Campa, Román. "Latin Lessons: Do Latinos Share a World . . . or a Word?" *Transition* 63 (1994): 60–76.

_____ "Latinos and the Crossover Aesthetic." Foreword to *Magical Urbanism: Latinos Reinvent the U.S. Big City*, by Mike Davis. New York: Verso, 2000a.

_____ "Norteamerica y su Mundo Latino: Ontologias, Globalización, Diasporas." *Apuntes Posmodernos/Postmodern Notes* Fall 1999/Spring 2000: 2–17.

Derrida, Jacques and Vattimo Gianni, eds. *Religion: Cultural Memory in the Present*. Palo Alto, Calif.: Stanford University Press, 1996.

Dominguez, Virginia. *People as Subject, People as Object: Selfhood and Peoplehood in Contemporary Israel*. Madison: University of Wisconsin Press, 1989.

_____ *White by Definition: Social Classification in Creole Louisiana*. New Brunswick, N.J.: Rutgers University Press, 1994.

Donald, James. *Imagining the Modern City*. Minneapolis: University of Minnesota Press, 1999.

Duany, Jorge. *Quisqueya in the Hudson: The Transnational Identity of Dominicans in Washington-Heights*. New York: City University of New York, Dominican Studies Institute, 1994.

Du Bois, W.E.B. *Dusk of Dawn: An Essay Toward an Autobiography of a Race Concept*. New York: Harcourt Brace, 1940.

Dussel, Enrique. *The Invention of the Americas: Eclipse of "the Other" and the Myth of Modernity*. New York: Continuum, 1995.

Estevez, Sandra Maria. *Bluestown Mockingbird Mambo*. Houston: Arte Público Press, 1990.

Farris Thompson, Robert. *Flash of the Spirit: African and Afro-American Art and Philosophy*. New York: Random House, 1982.

Flores, Juan. "The Latino Imaginary." In Frances R. Aparicio and Susana Chavez-Silverman, eds., *Tropicalizations: Transcultural Representations of Latinidad*, 183–93. Hannover and London: Dartmouth University Press, 1997.

——— *From Bomba to Hip-Hop: Puerto Rican Culture and Latino Identity*. New York: Columbia University Press, 2000.

Flores, Juan, and George Yudice. "Living Borders/Buscando America: Languages of Latino Self-Formation." *Social Text* 8, no. 2 (1990): 57–84.

Foucault, Michel. *The Archaeology of Knowledge and the Discourse of Language*. New York: Travistock, 1972.

——— *Language, Counter-Memory, Practice: Selected Essays and Interviews*. Oxford: Blackwell, 1977a.

——— "Nietzsche, Genealogy, History." In Donald F. Bouchard, ed., *Language, Counter-Memory, Practice*. Ithaca, N.Y.: Cornell University Press, 1977b.

——— *The History of Sexuality Volume I: An Introduction*. New York: Pantheon, 1978a.

——— "Politics and the Study of Discourse." *Ideology and Consciousness* 3 (1978b): 5–21.

——— "The Subject and Power." Afterword to *Michel Foucault: Beyond Structuralism and Hermeneutics*, by Hubert L. Dreyfus and Paul Rabinow. 2d ed. Chicago: University of Chicago Press, 1983.

Fox, Geoffrey. *Hispanic Nation: Culture, Politics, and the Construction of Identity*. Secaucus, N.J.: Birch Lane, 1996.

Frankenberg, Ruth and Lata Mani. "Crosscurrents, Crosstalk: Race, 'Postcoloniality,' and the Politics of Location." In Lavie Smadar and Ted Swedenburg, eds., *Displacement, Diaspora, and Geographies of Identity*, 273–94. Durham, N.C.: Duke University Press, 1996.

Fraser, Nancy. *Justice Interruptus: Critical Reflections on the 'Postsocialist' Condition*. New York: Routledge, 1997.

Friedmann, John. "Where We Stand: A Decade of World City Research." In Paul L. Knox and Peter J. Taylor, eds., *World Cities in a World-System*, 21–47. Cambridge, England: Cambridge University Press, 1995.

Gandhi, Leela. *Postcolonial Theory: A Critical Introduction*. New York: Columbia University Press, 1998.

Garcia Castro, Mary. " 'Mary' and Eve's Social Reproduction in the 'Big Apple'—Colombian Voices." New York: Center for Latin American Studies, New York University, 1982a.

——— "Women in Migration: Colombian Voices in the Big Apple." *Migration Today* 10, nos. 3 and 4 (1982b): 23–32.

Gates, Henry Louis. *The Signifying Monkey: A Theory of African American Literary Criticism*. Oxford: Oxford University Press, 1988.

Gilloch, Graeme. *Myth and Metropolis: Walter Benjamin and the City*. Cambridge, England: Polity Press, 1996.

Gimenez, Martha E. "Minorities and the World-System: Theoretical and Political Implications of the Internationalization of Minorities." In Smith et al., eds., *Racism, Sexism, and the World-System*, 36–56. Greenwood, 1988.

_____ "U.S. Ethnic Politics: Implications for Latin Americans." *Latin American Perspectives* 19, no. 4 (April 1992): 7–17.

Gilroy, Paul. *The Black Atlantic: Modernity and Double Consciousness.* Cambridge, Mass.: Harvard University Press, 1993.

Giro, Radames. "Todo lo que quizo usted saber sobre el Mambo." In Radames Giro, ed., *Panorama de la Música Popular Cubana,* 231–44. La Havana: Editorial Letras Cubanas, 1995.

Grasmuck, Sherri and Ramón Grosfoguel. "Geopolitics, Economic Niches, and Gendered Social Capital among Recent Caribbean Immigrants in New York City." *Sociological Perspectives* 40, no. 2 (1997): 339–63.

Gregory Steven. *Black Corona: Race and the Politics of Place in an Urban Community.* Princeton, N.J.: Princeton University Press, 1998.

Grosfoguel, Ramón. "Caribbean Colonial Immigrants in the Metropoles: A Research Agenda." *CENTRO* 7, no. 1 (Winter 1995a): 82–95.

_____ "Global Logics in the Caribbean City System: The Case of Miami." In Paul L. Knox and Peter J. Taylor, eds., *World Cities in a World-System,* 156–70. Cambridge, England: Cambridge University Press, 1995b.

_____ "Migration and Geopolitics in the Greater Antilles: From the Cold War to the Post-Cold War." *Review* 20, no. 1 (Winter 1997): 115–45.

Hall, Stuart. "The Local and Global: Globalization and Ethnicity" and "Old and New Identities, Old and New Ethnicities." In Anthony D. King, ed., *Culture, Globalization and the World-System, 1900–1940,* 41–68. Binghamton: State University of New York Press, 1991.

_____ "When Was 'the Postcolonial'? Thinking at the Limit." In Ian Chambers and Lidia Curtis, eds., *The Postcolonial Question: Common Skies/Divided Horizons,* 242–60. London: Routledge, 1996a.

_____ "Who Needs Identity?" Introduction to Stuart Hall and Paul du Gay, eds., *Questions of Cultural Identity.* New York: Sage, 1996b.

Hannigan, John. *Fantasy City: Pleasure and Profit in the Postmodern Metropolis.* New York: Routledge, 1998.

Hanson-Sánchez, Christopher. *New York City Latino Neighborhoods Databook.* New York: Institute for Puerto Rican Policy, 1998.

Haslip-Viera, Gabriel. "The Evolution of the Latino Community in New York City: Early Nineteenth Century to the Present." In Gabriel Haslip-Viera and Sherrie L. Baver, eds., *Latinos in New York: Communities in Transition,* 3–29. Notre Dame, Ind.: Notre Dame University Press, 1996.

Hernandez, Ramona, Francisco Rivera-Batiz, and Roberto Agodini. *Dominican New Yorkers: A Socioeconomic Profile.* New York: City University of New York, Dominican Studies Institute, 1998.

History Task Force, Centro de Estudios Puertorriqueños. *Labor Migration under Capitalism: The Puerto Rican Experience.* New York: Monthly Review Press, 1979.

hooks, bell. "Choosing the Margin as a Space of Radical Openness." *Framework* 36 (1989).

Hulme, Peter. *Colonial Encounters: Europe and the Native Caribbean, 1492–1797.* London: Methuen, 1986.

James, Winston. *Holding Aloft the Banner of Ethiopia: Caribbean Radicalism in Early-Twentieth-Century America.* New York: Verso, 1998.

Jacobs, Jane M. *Edge of Empire: Postcolonialism and the City.* London: Routledge, 1996.

Jones-Correa, Michael. *Between Two Nations: The Political Predicament of Latinos in New York City.* Ithaca, N.Y.: Cornell University Press, 1998.

Kaplan, Caren. "The Politics of Location as Transnational Feminist Practice." In Inderpal Grewal and Caren Kaplan, eds., *Scattered Hegemonies,* 137–52. Minneapolis: University of Minnesota Press, 1994.

Kelley, Robin D.G. *Yo' Mama's Disfunctional: Fighting the Culture Wars in Urban America.* Beacon, 1997.

King, Anthony D. *Global Cities: Post-Imperialism and the Industrialisation of London.* London: Routledge, 1990.

Knox, Paul L. and Peter L. Taylor, eds. *World Cities in a World-System.* Cambridge, England: Cambridge University Press, 1995.

Laó, Agustín. "Resources of Hope: Imagining the Young Lords and the Politics of Memory," *CENTRO* 7, no. 1 (Winter 1995): 25–45.

——— "Islands at the Crossroads: Puertoricaness Traveling between the Translocal Nation and the Global City." In Frances Negron-Muntaner and Ramón Grosfoguel, eds., *Puerto Rican Jam: Rethinking Nationalism and Colonialism,* 169–88. Minneapolis: University of Minnesota Press, 1997.

——— "Unfinished Migrations: Commentary and Response." *African Studies Review* 43, no. 1 (April 2000): 54–60.

——— "Pan-Caribbean Circuits: Mambo and the Erotics of Translocality." Paper presented at the Brazilian Association of Comparative Literature Conference, Salvador, Bahia, Brazil, July 2000b.

——— "Latinamericanism: Crossing Genealogies/Transgressing Disciplines." In Immanuel Wallerstein, ed., *Structures of Knowledge in the Modern World-System* (forthcoming 2001a).

——— "The 1898 Spanish-Cuban-American-Philipino War: Clashing Hegemic Projects and Contending Occidentalisms." In Jo Labanyi and Sebastian Balfour, eds., *Reconfigurations of Empire: Cultural Perspectives on the 1898 War in the Caribbean and the Philippines.* London: Macmillan (forthcoming 2001b).

Linebaugh, Peter. "All the Atlantic Mountains Shook." *Labour/Le Travailleur.* 10, (1982): 87–121.

López, David and Yen Espíritu. "Panethnicity in the United States: A Theoretical Framework." *Ethnic and Racial Studies* 13, no. 2 (April 1990): 198–224.

Lott, Tommy L. *The Invention of Race: Black Culture and the Politics of Representation.* Cambridge, Mass.: Blackwell, 1999.

Lugones, María. "Playfulness, World-Traveling, and Loving Perception." In Gloria Anzaldúa, ed., *Haciendo Caras/Making Faces: Creative Critical Perspectives by Women of Color,* 390–402. San Francisco: an aunt lute foundation, 1990.

Mahler, Sarah J. *American Dreaming: Immigrants on the Margins.* Princeton, N.J.: Princeton University Press, 1995.

Maldonado-Denis, Manuel. *The Emigration Dialectic: Puerto Rico and the U.S.A.* New York: International Publishers, 1980.

Mani, Lata. "Multiple Mediations: Feminist Scholarship in the Age of Multinational Reception." *Inscriptions* 5 (1989): 1–23.

Mandel, Ernest. *Late Capitalism.* London: Verso, 1975.

Marentes, Luis A. *José Vasconcelos and the Writing of the Mexican Revolution* (New York: Twayne, 2001).

Martí, José. "Nuestra America." In *Obras Completas,* 15–23. La Havana: Editorial Nacional de Cuba, 1963.

Mato, Daniel. "Problems in the Making of Representations of All-Encompassing U.S. Latina/o–Latin American Transitional Identities." *Latino Review of Books* 3, nos. 1 and 2 (1997): 2–7.

____ "On Global and Local Agents and the Social Making of Transnational Identities and Related Agendas." *Identities: Global Studies in Culture and Power* 4, no. 2 (1997): 167–212.

Mignolo, Walter. *The Darker Side of the Renaissance: Literacy, Territoriality, and Colonization.* Ann Arbor: University of Michigan Press, 1995.

____ *Local Histories/Global Designs: Coloniality, Subaltern Knowledges and Border Thinking.* Princeton, N.J.: Princeton University Press, 2000.

Mitchell, Christopher. "U.S. Foreign Policy and Dominican Migration to the United States." In Christopher Mitchell, ed., *Western Hemisphere Immigration and United States Foreign Policy.* University Park: Pennsylvania State University, 1992.

Mohanty, Chandra Tapalde. "Feminist Encounters: Locating the Politics of Experience." *Copyright* 1 (Fall 1987): 30–44.

____ "Under Western Eyes: Feminist Scholarship and Colonial Discourses." In Chandra Mohanty, Ann Russo, and Lourdes Torres, eds., *Third World Women and the Politics of Feminism,* 51–80. Bloomington: Indiana University Press, 1991.

Mudimbe, V. I. *The Invention of Africa: Gnosis, Philosophy, and the Order of Knowledge.* Bloomington: Indiana University Press, 1988.

Noriega, Chon. "El Hilo Latino: Representation, Identity, and National Culture." *Jump Cut* 38 (1993): 45–50.

Oboler, Suzanne. *Ethnic Labels, Latino Lives: Identity and the Politics of (Re) Presentation in the United States.* Minneapolis: University of Minnesota Press, 1995.

O'Gorman, Edmundo. *The Invention of America: An Inquiry into the Historical Nature of the New World and the Meaning of Its History.* Bloomington: Indiana University Press, 1982.

Olalquiaga, Celeste. *Megalopolis: Contemporary Cultural Sensibilities.* Minneapolis: University of Minnesota Press, 1992.

Omi, Michael and Howard Winant. *Racial Formation in the United States: From the 1960s to the 1980s.* New York: Routledge, 1986.

Ortiz, Fernando. *Cuban Counterpoint: Tobacco and Sugar.* Durham, N.C.: Duke University Press, 1995.

Outlaw, Lucius T. *On Race and Philosophy.* New York: Routledge, 1996.

Padilla, Felix. *Latino Ethnic Consciousness: The Case of Mexican-Americans and Puerto Ricans in Chicago.* Notre Dame, Ind.: Notre Dame University Press, 1985.

Pantojas, Emilio. *Development as Ideology: Puerto Rico's Industrialization Process.* Río Piedras: University of Puerto Rico Press, 1991.

Patterson, Tiffany R. and Robin D.G. Kelley. "Unfinished Migrations: Reflections on the African Diaspora and the Making of the Modern World." *African Studies Review* 43, no. 1 (April 2000): 11–45.

Pérez, Emma. *The Decolonial Imaginary: Writing Chicanas into History.* Bloomington: Indiana University Press, 1999.

Pérez, Louis A., Jr. *The War of 1898: The United States and Cuba in History and Historiography.* Chapel Hill: University of North Carolina Press, 1998.

Pérez-Firmat, Gustavo. *Life in the Hyphen: The Cuban-American Way.* Austin: University of Texas Press, 1994.

Phelan, John L. *El origen de la idea de America* (Mexico: UNAM, 1979).

Pietri, Pedro. *Puerto Rican Obituary.* New York: Monthly Review Press, 1973.

Portes, Alejandro and Julia Sensenbrenner. "Embeddedness and Immigration: Notes on the Social Determination of Embeddedness." *American Journal of Sociology* 98, no. 6 (1993): 1320–51.

Pratt, Mary Louise. *Imperial Eyes: Travel Writing and Transculturation.* New York: Routledge, 1992.

Priestley, George. "Antillean Panamanians: Migration, Identity, and Politics." Unpublished manuscript, 1998.

Quijano, Aníbal. "Modernity, Identity, and Utopia in Latin America." *Boundary* 2 (1992): 140–55.

——— "Colonialidad y modernidad/racionalidad." *Peru Indígena* 13, no. 29 (1993): 11–21.

——— "The Coloniality of Power and Its Institutions." Paper presented at the Second Annual Conference of the Coloniality Working Group, State University of New York at Binghamton, April 1999.

Quijano, Aníbal, and Immanuel Wallerstein. "Americanity as a Concept, or the Americas in the Modern World-System." *International Journal of Social Sciences* no. 134 (1992).

Rabasa, José. *Inventing America: Spanish Historiography and the Formation of Eurocentrism.* University of Oklahoma Press, 1993.

Radhakrishnan, Rajagopalan. *Diasporic Mediations: Between Home and Location.* Minneapolis: University of Minnesota Press, 1996.

Rafael, Vicente L. *Discrepant Histories: Translocal Essays on Filipino Cultures.* Philadelphia: Temple University Press, 1995.

Ramos, Julio. Introduction to *Amor y anarquía: los escritos de Luisa Capetillo.* Río Piedras: Huracán, 1991.

Reed, Adolph Jr. *Stirrings in the Jug: Black Politics in the Post-Segregation Era.* Minneapolis: University of Minnesota Press, 1999.

Ringer, Benjamin B. *'We the People' and Others: Duality and America's Treatment of Its Racial Minorities.* New York: Tavistock, 1983.

Rodo, José Enrique. *Ariel.* Mexico, D.F.: Espasa Calpe Mexicana, 1948.

Rodríguez de León, Francisco. *El furioso merengue del norte: una historia de la comunidad dominicana en los Estados Unidos.* New York, 1998.

Rodríguez, Clara. *Puerto Ricans: Born in U.S.A.* Unwin Hyman, 1989.

Roman, David and Alberto Sandoval-Sánchez. "Caught in the Web: Latinidad, AIDS, and Allegory in *Kiss of the Spider Woman,* the Musical." *American Literature* 67, no. 3 (September 1995).

Rosenwaile, Ira. *Population History of New York City.* Syracuse, N.Y.: Syracuse University Press, 1972.

Said, Edward. *Orientalism.* Vintage, 1979.

Salvidar, José David. *The Dialetics of our America: genealogy, cultural critique, and literary history* (Durham: Duke University Press, 1991).

——— *Border Matters: Remapping American Cultural Studies.* Berkeley and Los Angeles: University of California Press, 1997.

Sánchez-Korrol, Virginia. "Latinismo among Early Puerto Rican Migrants in New York City: A Sociohistoric Interpretation." In Edna Acosta-Belen and Barbara R. Sjostrom, eds., *The Hispanic Experience in the United States*, 151–61. New York: Praeger, 1988.

Sandoval-Sánchez, Alberto. *José Can' You See?: Latinos On and Off Broadway.* Madison: University of Wisconsin Press, 1999.

Santiago Valles, Kelvin A. *"Subject People" and Colonial Discourses: Economic Transformation and Social Disorder in Puerto Rico 1898–1947.* Albany: State University of New York Press, 1994.

Santos Febres, Mayra. "The Translocal Papers: Puerto Rican Literature between Here and There." Ph.D. diss., Cornell University, 1991.

—— "Salsa as Translocation." In Celeste Fraser Delgado and José Esteban Muñoz, eds., *Everynight Life: Culture and Dance in Latino/America*, 175–88. Durham, N.C.: Duke University Press, 1997.

Sassen, Saskia. *The Mobility of Labor and Capital: A Study in International Investment and Labor Flow.* Cambridge, England: Cambridge University Press, 1988.

—— *The Global City: New York, London, Tokyo.* Princeton, N.J.: Princeton University Press, 1991.

Scarano, Francisco A. "Intervention or Possession? Puerto Rico, 1898, and the American Colonial Periphery." Paper presented at Conference on the Spanish-Cuban-American War at Lehman College of the City University of New York, October 1998.

Scott, Joan Wallach. *Gender and the Politics of History.* New York: Columbia University Press, 1988.

Shohat, Ella. "Notes on the Postcolonial." *Social Text* 31/32 (1992).

Shohat, Ella and Robert Stam. *Unthinking Eurocentrism: Multiculturalism and the Media.* New York: Routledge, 1994.

Shorris, Earl. *Latinos: Biography of a People.* New York: Norton, 1992.

Smith, Gary, ed. *Benjamin: Philosophy, Aesthetics, History.* Chicago: University of Chicago Press, 1989.

Smith, Neil. *The New Urban Frontier: Gentrification and the Revanchist City.* New York: Routledge, 1996.

Smith, Robert C. "Mexicans in New York: Memberships and Incorporation in a New Immigrant Community." In Gabriel Haslip-Viera and Sherrie L. Baver, eds., *Latinos in New York: Communities in Transition*, 57–103. Notre Dame, Ind.: Notre Dame University Press, 1996.

—— "Transnational Migration, Assimilation, and Political Community." In Margaret Crahan and Alberto Vourvoulias-Busch, eds., *The City and the World: New York's Global Future*, 110–32. New York: Council on Foreign Relations, 1997.

Sorkin, Michael, ed. *Variations on a Theme Park: The New American City and the End of Public Space.* New York: Noonday, 1992.

Spitta, Silvia. *Between Two Waters: Literary Transculturation in Latin America* (Texas: Rice University Press, 1995).

Spivak, Gayatri. *A Critique of Postcolonial Reason: Toward a History of the Vanishing Present.* Cambridge, Mass.: Harvard University Press, 1999.

Stavans, Ilan. *The Hispanic Condition: Reflections on Culture and Identity in America.* New York: HarperCollins, 1995.

Steinberg, Michael P., ed. *Walter Benjamin and the Demands of History.* Ithaca, N.Y.: Cornell University Press, 1996.

Stoler, Ann Laura. *Race and the Education of Desire: Foucault's History of Sexuality and the Colonial Order of Things.* Durham, N.C.: Duke University Press, 1995.

———. "Racial Histories and Their Regimes of Truth." In Diane E. Davis, ed., *Political Power and Social Theory.* Jai Press, Vol 11 (1997): 183–201.

Sutton, Constance R. "The Caribbeanization of New York City and the Emergence of a Transnational Socio-Cultural System." In Constance R. Sutton and Elsa M. Chaney, eds., *Caribbean Life in New York City: Sociocultural Dimensions,* 15–30. New York: Center for Migration Studies, 1987.

Thompson, Lanny. *Nuestra isla y su gente: la construcción del "otro" puertorriqueño en our islands and their people.* Río Piedras: Centro de Investigaciones Sociales y Departamento de Historia de la Universidad de Puerto Rico, 1995.

Torres, Andres. *Between Melting Pot and Mosaic: African Americans and Puerto Ricans in the New York Political Economy.* Philadelphia: Temple University Press, 1995.

Torres-Saillant, Silvio and Ramona Hernandez. *The Dominican Americans.* Greenwood, 1998.

Urrea Giraldo, Fernando. "Life Strategies and the Labor Market: Colombians in New York City in the 1970s." New York: Center for Latin American and Caribbean Studies, New York University, 1982.

Waldinger, Roger. *Still the Promised City? African Americans and New Immigrants in Postindustrial New York.* Cambridge, Mass.: Harvard University Press, 1996.

Wallace, Michelle. "The Politics of Location: Cinema/Theory/Literature/Ethnicity/Sexuality/Me." *Framework* 36 (1989).

Wallerstein, Immanuel. *The Modern World-System I: Capitalist Agriculture and the Origins of the European World-Economy in the Sixteenth Century.* San Diego: Academic Press, 1974.

———. *The Capitalist World-Economy.* Cambridge, England: Cambridge University Press, 1979.

———. "The Construction of Peoplehood: Racism, Nationalism, Ethnicity." In Etienne Balibar and Immanuel Wallerstein, *Race, Nation, Class: Ambiguous Identities,* 71–85. New York: Verso, 1991.

Ward, David and Olivier Zunz, eds. *The Landscape of Modernity: Essays on New York City 1900–1940.* New York: Russell Sage Foundation, 1992.

Weyland, Karin. "Dominican Women 'Con Un Pie Aquí y Otro Allá': Are National Narratives Threatened When Standing at the Crossroads of Local/Global Identities and Cultures?" Paper presented at Latin American Studies Association Conference, Miami, Florida, March 2000.

Williams, Raymond. *Keywords: A Vocabulary of Culture and Society.* Oxford: Oxford University Press, 1985.

Zukin, Sharon. *Landscapes of Power: From Detroit to Disney World.* Berkeley and Los Angeles: University of California Press, 1991.

———. *The Cultures of Cities.* Cambridge, Mass.: Blackwell, 1995.

FIGURE 1. Anti-Vietnam Demonstration on the West Side, 1970s. Photo by Maximo Colon

PART I

The Production of Latinidad

Histories, Social Movements,
Cultural Struggles

CHAPTER ONE

"No Country But the One We Must Fight For"

The Emergence of an Antillean Nation and Community in New York City, 1860–1901

Nancy Raquel Mirabal

> Cubans and Puerto Ricans! We suffer a common injustice. Let us be one in the revolution and in calling for the independence of Cuba and Puerto Rico. And tomorrow we shall be able to form a confederation of the Antilles!
>
> —*Comité Revolucionario de Puerto Rico, New York, 1867*[1]

> We have, Cubans, no country but the one we must fight for.
>
> —*José Martí*[2]

In 1868 anticolonial forces in Puerto Rico and Cuba revolted against the Spanish colonial government. For revolutionaries in Puerto Rico, the rebellion known as the Grito de Lares would be short-lived, lasting no longer than a month. For those in Cuba, on the other hand, the rebellion would turn into a ten-year struggle, becoming one of the longest revolutionary wars in Cuban history. The failure of Cubans to achieve independence during the Grito de Yara would spark further revolutionary efforts, including La Guerra Chiquita in 1879 and the Cuban War for Independence in 1895.[3]

Despite the differences in the length of each rebellion, both efforts at gaining independence greatly influenced how Puerto Rican and Cuban migrants in New York City would view themselves, their community, and their role in creating a distinct and independent nation.[4] This is not to say, however, that Puerto Rican and Cuban migrants agreed on a singular vision of what constituted nation, community, or a nationalist identity. On the contrary, the differences in opinion and in strategies employed would divide the migrant community and cause tensions among various factions. The annexationists and autonomists as well as the independentistas were locked in a political battle that often left the migrant community fragmented and tension filled.[5] At the center of much of the disagreement were questions related to class, race, and the involvement of the United States. In turn, these questions disrupted definitions of what constituted a shared political vision of nation. Once independent from Spain, how would the Puerto Rican and Cuban nation be defined? Whom would it include, and whom would it exclude? How would migrants reconcile their vision of what constituted a nation with the vision held by those on the island? The competing ideas about nation as well as national identity engulfed the migrant community in New York and forced a rethinking of politics, nation, community, and identity on a number of levels.

One of the tactics used by many in the Puerto Rican and Cuban migrant community during this period was to develop a mutual identity based on alliances and a common belief that their struggle was a shared one. The emergence of what revolutionaries would call an Antillean nation and national identity was a powerful reminder of how determined many were to avoid any form of political and economic control. Fundamentally distrustful of both Spain and the United States, Puerto Rican and Cuban independentistas geographically reconfigured the islands so that they would have no connection to any form of colonialism present or future. The use of the term *Antilles* signified an association with the Caribbean devoid of any outside influences. In other words, instead of looking to Spain and the United States, Puerto Rican and Cuban migrants would now look to Jamaica, the Dominican Republic, Haiti, and the West Indies to inform how they would define community and identity. As a result, the impact and importance of Africa, the African diaspora, and the history of the African slave trade in the Caribbean could no longer be avoided. Yet, as we will see later in the essay, negotiating and reconciling Africa within the exile and migrant nationalist movements would not be easy.

The creation of a shared Antillean nation and nationalist identity, one that was clearly imagined and shaped by nationalist rhetoric, reveals the ability of the migrant community to refashion itself to suit its political beliefs. As a result, Puerto Rican and Cuban migrants who subscribed to these notions ended up questioning the very idea of the nation-state as exclusive. For example, Cubans who believed in the concept of an Antillean nationalist identity would be at odds with Cubans who favored annexation to the United States even though they, too, viewed themselves as being Cuban. Because of the politics involved, being Cuban, as in this particular case, was not enough to sustain community. As a result, definitions of nation and national identity were continually in flux, causing the political migrant community to draw lines, make concessions, rethink the concept of nation, and forge alliances all in the name of making and solidifying a political community.

Nowhere was this more visible than in New York. With its long history of Puerto Rican and Cuban migration and settlement, along with it being the site where José Martí based his political operation and subsequently organized the Partido Revolucionario Cubano (PRC), New York was one of the few places where Puerto Ricans and Cubans lived and worked for a significant amount of time. By the 1830s Puerto Ricans and Cubans had fashioned an anticolonial movement. Political organizations, exile newspapers, cultural clubs, and revolutionary groups were already present in New York. As a thriving political community, the city was transformed into one of the most important and necessary sites for Puerto Ricans and Cubans to reimagine a distinct Antillean nation and identity while still remaining loyal to their own notions of what constituted an individual Puerto Rican and Cuban nation.

This distinction, the ability to create one concept of nation based on mutuality without relinquishing another concept based on cultural exclusivity, was one that was easily understood and, more importantly, invoked. This ability was manifested in the formation of a number of important political clubs in New York, including the influential Sociedad Republicana de Cuba y Puerto Rico, which was founded in 1865.[6] With time, Puerto Ricans and Cubans formed several other interacting and mutual revolutionary clubs that, as the records of Los Clubs Borinquen and Las Dos Antillas noted, were made up of "Puerto Ricans and Cubans who sympathized with the independence of Puerto Rico."[7] In the early 1890s the powerful PRC formed the Sección Puerto Rico to continue with the alliance-based politics initiated thirty years earlier by previous revolutionary clubs. For the PRC, this form of politics was especially useful in solidifying community and unifying what had been a fragmented migrant nationalist movement.[8] Yet by this time, much of the exile and migrant political activity had been dominated by the impending Cuban War for Independence and the ever-increasing possibility of U.S. intervention in Cuba. The speeches, newspapers, and journals often asked Puerto Rican activists and migrants to focus on the events in Cuba with the promise that once Cuban independence was secured, the movement would then direct its energies toward Puerto Rico.[9]

Along with the revolutionary and cultural clubs, exile newspapers played a large role in the production of a political community. Puerto Rican and Cuban migrants found and disseminated a series of publications that covered issues of concern for both Puerto Ricans and Cubans in the United States. Newspapers such as La Doctrina de Martí, La Verdad, El Yara, and El Porvenir were instrumental in encouraging and sustaining the separatist and nationalist movements. These publications, in conjunction with the numerous clubs, helped to redefine nation in terms of a mutual independence and liberation for both Puerto Rico and Cuba. The existence and, moreover, recognition of a mutual alliance between both communities was evident in the frequent use of the term las Antillas (the Antilles) in revolutionary literature and publications. At the same time, other forms of print media existed that expanded beyond nationalist and separatist rhetoric to serve other purposes needed in the building of a mutual political community.

One of the more influential publications, *La Revista Illustrada,* was founded in 1890 by the Puerto Rican revolutionary Sotero Figueroa. This publication was not only a voice for "la independencia de Cuba y Puerto Rico" but was also a forum for "artículos sobre asuntos de interés cultural y político para Hispanoamérica."[10] The many journals, *revistas,* and newspapers published by the Puerto Rican and Cuban communities informed and entertained but moreover helped to acclimate the increasing number of Puerto Ricans and Cubans migrating to New York during this period. In one article published by the separatist newspaper *La Gaceta del Pueblo* entitled "Nueva York por dentro: Una faz de su vida bohemia" (New York from the inside: A facet of its bohemian life), Francisco Gonzalo Marín, better known as Pachín Marín, offers newly arrived immigrants in New York some tips on how to "attain an intimate knowledge of this elephant of modern civilization."[11] Most of the advice Marín offers has to do with adjusting to the "incessant howling of the locomotives," to the "agitation of factories," and to the "vista of a million people hurrying past, trampling each other, yet going on their way as if nothing had happened." Marín's tone is both ironic and foreboding. He uses life in New York with its "eleven- or twelve-story building whose highest window seem to look down on you as if mocking your smallness"[12] as a way to get migrants to think about the differences between the United States and their home country. In spite of the technological advances and rapid industrialization, Marín reminds migrants coming to New York that life for a migrant who "does not speak English"[13] can be lonely and isolating. An underlying point in Marín's essay is the importance of creating community in New York while remaining conscious of U.S. political designs and maneuvers. The fear of the United States's overwhelming power and the possible consequences of buying into it were also on the minds of a number of Puerto Rican and Cuban revolutionaries who began to incorporate a distinctly anti-U.S. imperialist politics into their platform.

This tension between using the United States as a geographic site for building new nations from the outside while at the same time resisting the U.S. move toward empire was endemic to how many in the community viewed their position in the United States. This tension was most evident in the bitter rivalry between those migrants who advocated annexation to the United States and those who adamantly refused having any ties to it.

The existence of a parallel discourse among Puerto Rican and Cuban migrants was made more effective by their use of Spanish to articulate both publicly and privately their concerns, beliefs, and disagreements. In so doing, Puerto Rican and Cuban migrants reinforced the connection between what Benedict Anderson has written is the power of the printed media and consciousness, a connection that is part of the "embryo of the nationally imagined community."[14]

In this regard, Spanish was a tool by which Puerto Rican and Cuban migrants could create an exclusive and distinct political community that could exist and even thrive in a place where Spanish was not the official language. By using Spanish to discuss policy, tactics, and strategies, Puerto Rican and Cuban migrants were not only including those who spoke Spanish but also making a point to exclude those who did not. Furthermore, because the newspapers were written in Spanish, they could also be read by the population in Puerto Rico and Cuba. Often smuggled in by revolutionaries, the newspapers were read widely by political activists on the islands who desperately wanted and needed to know what was taking place outside of the island. Because the Spanish colonial government in Puerto Rico and Cuba censored newspapers or even made them unavailable to the public, the circulation of exile newspapers was both coveted and dangerous.

In addition to the use of Spanish, geographic location was also key to the development of a distinct Antillean community. Because New York was geographically located outside of both Puerto Rico and Cuba, not only could revolutionaries publish newspapers without fear of reprisal, but they could also remake the movement so that it would continually evolve. Ensuring that the movement would change and not become stagnant or irrelevant was key to its success. As long as Puerto Rican and Cuban revolutionaries remained outside of their respective homelands, they could imagine and articulate multiple definitions of nation and national identity at any given time to suit the current political climate in their homelands as well as in the United States.

The building of nation from the outside allowed Puerto Ricans and Cubans to move theoretical and ideological constructions beyond the purview of their respective homelands to reconstruct the parameters of nation. It also allowed them the space necessary to devise a language that spoke to this reconstruction. The development and ensuing use of a language that addressed the process of nation building from the outside is found in "With All and for the Good of All," one of the more famous speeches given by José Martí. In it Martí spoke of a patria, a homeland, "que *allí* se cae a pedazos" (that over *there* would fall to pieces) while "*aquí* se levanta"! (over *here* it rises).[15] In this passage, Martí makes clear the power of geographic location. As long as the Spanish colonial government remained in Cuba, it was doubtful that what Martí and other revolutionaries had in mind for Cuba would ever be realized.[16]

Locating nation outside of the islands also meant a reconfiguration of geography so that whatever was built in terms of politics, ideologies, institutions, and organizations in New York could in the end be transferred back to their respective homelands. The rhetoric of returns and returnings was pivotal to the overall success of the movement; after all, most migrants who advocated independence intended on moving back. In privileging returns and returnings as a viable option, New York City was delineated as a temporal site for building nations and a national identity. The creation of New York as a place of exile, migration, and temporary political refuge represented a different set of geographies that inspired Puerto Ricans and Cubans to cultivate alliances and continually reinvent themselves, a strategy that led to the formation of Las Dos Antillas.

LAS DOS ANTILLAS AND TOTAL INDEPENDENCE: DEFINING AN ANTILLEAN NATION AND NATIONALIST IDENTITY

During the late nineteenth and early twentieth centuries, the U.S. government was engaged in a policy of economic colonialism and geographical expansion. The unsteady political climate in Puerto Rico and Cuba seemed ripe with possibility to U.S. government officials, notably President William McKinley, who openly expressed his desire to economically and politically control much of the Caribbean. Many in the exile and migrant Puerto Rican and Cuban community who settled in New York City were aware of growing U.S. interest in the area and rightly suspected any attempts made by the U.S. government for assistance. At the same time, any discussion involving the possibility of annexation to the United States was quickly rejected by Puerto Rican and Cuban independentistas. It was the fear that Puerto Rico and Cuba could potentially fall into the hands of the United States that led the members of the all-women La Hijas de Cuba to denounce the actions of the members of the all-male Junta Revolucionaria de Cuba y Puerto Rico.[17]

On February 6, 1869, in the St. Julien Hotel located near Washington Square in New York City, fourteen Puerto Rican and Cuban women met to debate the recent political turns made by the Junta Revolucionaria de Cuba y Puerto Rico. At the head of the table sat Emilia Casanova de Villaverde, a staunch independentista who, as the acting president of Las Hijas de Cuba, wasted little time in accusing the members of the Junta of "annexationist maneuvers and betrayal of the independence movement."[18] The possibility that a revolutionary organization would include the United States as an ally was enough to usurp the power of men in a time when women had almost no institutional power in the movement. Denied formal membership to revolutionary and cultural clubs, women organized their own clubs where they would ironically wield a formidable amount of informal and collective power. It was from this power base that Casanova de Villaverde would be heard and later vindicated. Within a few months after the denouncement, the members of the Junta Revolucionaria de Cuba y Puerto Rico organized another group known as La Liga[19] whose objective was to "sway United States public opinion in their favor" by organizing "sympathizers in the United States." The problem with this, as the Puerto Rican labor organizer Bernardo Vega noted, was that this group, which had been founded by Juan

Manuel Macías, was made up of "North Americans motivated less by a desire for independence than by the hope that Cuba would be annexed to the United States."[20]

When the Puerto Rican revolutionary leader Eugenio María de Hostos was invited by La Liga in February 1870 to give a speech at one of its many functions, he spoke out against the formation of organizations such as La Liga as well as against what he viewed as a growing effort by its members to move closer toward annexationism.[21] A few years later the Puerto Rican revolutionary leader Ramón Emeterio Betances not only echoed María de Hostos's concern by protesting any possibility of annexation, but he furthered the reconfiguration of the parameters of nation when he called for a "new Antillean nation" to assert itself. The merging of nation, of a redefined political future that not only took both countries into account but also restructured its very geographic and theoretical location, was also on the mind of the Cuban leader José Martí when he wrote "it was a world that we are putting into balance: it is not simply two islands that we are going to liberate."[22]

By the time María de Hostos, Emeterio Betances, and Martí had given their speeches, a sizable and influential Puerto Rican and Cuban community was living and working in New York City. The community that had settled was dramatically different from the earlier migrants, who tended to be upper-class, landholding males interested in changing and reforming Spanish colonial policies. By the mid- to late nineteenth century, people from those islands arriving at New York were on the whole working-class male and female migrants[23] in search of employment in the garment factories and in the city's growing cigar industry. With the end of slavery in Puerto Rico in 1873 and in Cuba in 1886, the number of black Puerto Rican and Cuban migrants also increased significantly.

By the late nineteenth century, Puerto Rican and Cuban revolutionaries in New York could no longer avoid the role of race and class in the movement or the impact of the African diaspora. This is not to say, however, that Puerto Rican and Cuban migrants in New York were able to negotiate race and class within the movement in the same way they were able to incorporate it into its revolutionary platform. For the exile and migrant nationalist movement to remain unified, the leaders of the movement needed to articulate what role race and class would play in the building of a future Puerto Rican and Cuban nation, respectively, something that past revolutionary movements had failed to do. Intense political divisions and tensions needed to be addressed and resolved. For women, the exile nationalist movement had changed little from the separatist organizations of the 1860s to the powerful PRC of the 1890s: their coalitions and alliances were still viewed as auxiliaries to the larger, male-dominated organizations. Although women organized separate clubs and worked tirelessly for the revolution, the masculinist rhetoric and nature of the movement provided them with little room to maneuver themselves within it. They remained, despite their efforts and relative power, outside of the decision-making body of what was quickly becoming the main exile nationalist organization, the PRC.

The rise of the cigar industry in New York City during the mid- to late nineteenth century led to an increase in the number of working-class migrants traveling to the United States in search of employment. The cigar factories would also attract a large number of black Puerto Ricans and Cubans who were finding it difficult to secure jobs back home. The inability of both islands to absorb the mass incorporation of the new wage labor caused many to leave their home for the United States. Once in New York, however, black Puerto Ricans and Cubans had to negotiate an identity that had less to do with being Puerto Rican and Cuban than with being black. Although many became an integral part of the exile and migrant nationalist movement, their existence infused the movement with a different set of meanings that many in it were not ready to handle. In short, the rhetoric being espoused by the nationalist movement during the late nineteenth century was one that equated racial equality with independence.

On January 22, 1890, La Liga Sociedad de Instruccíon y Recreo was founded in New York as a space where black Puerto Ricans and Cubans could both organize and discuss methods used by the independence movement to address racial tensions among the migrant community. Established by, among others, Martí, the Afro-Cuban Rafael Serra, and the black Puerto Rican Sotero Figueroa, La Liga was an all-black organization that was set up as a "training school for the revolution."[24] In addition to being a place where members could meet freely to strategize and discuss political issues, La Liga offered its members formal classes where they could learn about the revolutionary wars and their role in securing independence. According to the historian Philip Foner, José Martí, for instance, taught night classes where he instilled "in his students pride in being Cuban" and emphasized "the important place that the masses of Negroes and whites had to occupy in the liberation movement and in the future of the republic." So instrumental was La Liga that Foner considered it "an important development in the revolutionary movement."[25] What Foner does not explain, however, is why La Liga was organized in the first place and furthermore why women were not asked to become members or to participate.

The problem with continuing to position La Liga as a solution to the racial tensions among Puerto Ricans and Cubans is that we lose sight of the reasons why it was necessary to form an all-black organization in the first place and the reasons that compelled leaders and members of the integrated nationalist movement to form such an organization. Outside of racial conditions in New York that did have an impact on the community, did any factors within the community contribute to the decision to organize La Liga? The historical records that speak to the founding of La Liga do not discuss or mention if racial tensions within the community led to its being organized in the first place. We know little of the impact that La Liga, as an all-black club formed by leaders of the PRC, had on the nationalist movement. What is clear is that the formation of La Liga was a key element in the organization of black Cubans and Puerto Ricans. A few years after La Liga was founded in New York, a second chapter was established by Afro-Cubans in Tampa. La Liga de Instrucción de Tampa was one of the few all-black exile nationalist organizations in Florida. The creation of a similar club reveals that a dialogue concerning race and nationalism was indeed taking place among black Cubans and Puerto Ricans.

At the same time that race was forcing a re-analysis of nation, independence, and revolution within the community, it was also part of the everyday life of Cuban and Puerto Rican migrants of all backgrounds. The racial conditions in New York during this period often made it difficult for many Puerto Ricans and Cubans to take care of the basic needs of revolutionary work such as leasing buildings and finding places to meet or have functions. In fact, this proved to be a major problem. In his memoirs, the Puerto Rican activist, socialist, and cigar worker Bernardo Vega recounts how members of one of the oldest and most respected female revolutionary clubs in New York, La Liga Antillana, were left with little choice but to negotiate racial exclusion and discrimination in New York. Formed in the 1860s, it was "completely interracial with all of its activities shared by white, black, and mulatto women."[26] Because the club encouraged a mixed membership, the members of La Liga Antillana were faced with difficulties in organizing, setting up events, and even finding places to meet. As Bernardo Vega noted, the members found that most of the meeting halls "shut their doors to them." As a result, the women met in private homes and held events in places provided by the "Socialist Party and the Cigarworker's Union."[27]

Vega's recollections provide a rare glimpse into how Puerto Rican and Cuban migrants negotiated racial conditions in New York. Yet he, like many of his contemporaries, also fails to discuss the working of race among the community itself. What is certain, however, is that the existence of all-black clubs; Martí's persistent calls for racial harmony and his insistence on working closely with Afro-Cuban activists such as Paulina Pedroso, Rafael Serra, and the Afro–Puerto Rican Sotero Figueroa; and the historical silences complicate how we examine the workings of race among Puerto Rican and Cuban migrants.

The increased migration of cigar workers during the late nineteenth century also forced the PRC to reconsider its role as a purely political organization. The popularity of labor unions and the frequent labor strikes forced the party to begin to address labor concerns and to incorporate labor (hesitantly at first) into its revolutionary platform. For the first time, its members were merging U.S. economic realities with Puerto Rican and Cuban nation building. The PRC had little choice but to support the labor strikes called by the Puerto Rican and Cuban cigar workers and to form alliances with the unions that by the late nineteenth century had become as strong as many of the revolutionary clubs. Although formal nationalist organizations found themselves having to shift their political platforms to adapt to the needs of the community, cigar workers were always clear concerning the connections between revolution and labor and their role in bringing about change; they were known to pay dues to local revolutionary clubs as well as to the PRC. The *lectores* (readers) who sat above the workers on a scaffold read radical presses and always kept the workers informed on daily political developments.

In April 1898 the United States intervened in the Cuban War for Independence, better known as the Spanish-American War. The United States entered the conflict during its last stages and within a few months was victorious against Spain. The ensuing military and political occupation of both Puerto Rico and Cuba drastically changed and altered definitions of exile, immigration, and nationalism for the migrant community in New York. The U.S. actions in Cuba signaled an end to the exile nationalist movement, causing revolutionary clubs and the PRC to disband only months later. For the Puerto Rican and Cuban community in New York, the end of the war and subsequent beginning of U.S. attempts at building empire put an end to the political alliances and revolutionary work. Bernardo Vega noted the drastic change when he wrote that "once the thunder of revolutionary struggle against Spain had subsided in the Antilles, the Cuban and Puerto Rican emigrant community in New York fell silent."[28]

The silence was further marked when representatives from the United States and Spain signed the Treaty of Paris, which transferred Cuba, Puerto Rico, the Philippines, and Guam to the United States on December 10, 1898.[29] This action would lead to U.S. policies in Puerto Rico and Cuba designed to limit those countries' political power and expand U.S. political and economic influence on both islands. In 1900 the United States implemented the Foraker Act in Puerto Rico, which ended the military government on the island and provided a civil structure modeled after that of the United States, with three separate branches of government. It also granted the U.S. government the power to select Puerto Rico's governor and cabinet members. A year later the U.S. government demanded that Cuban legislators either add the Platt Amendment to the Cuban Constitution or continue to be militarily occupied by the U.S. military. With only a few votes, the Cuban government decided to accept the Platt Amendment, which provided the United States with the right to intervene in Cuba's affairs any time the U.S. government deemed it necessary.[30]

One of the most damaging aspects of the U.S. occupation and action was the use of a colonialist language that soon became part of the public dialogue. This was particularly evident in a speech given by Brigadier-General William Ludlow on November 16, 1899, at a meeting for the Cuban

Orphan Society in New York City. The then acting military governor of Havana was invited by the members of the society to discuss the "situation in Havana."[31] In General Ludlow's opinion, Cuba, along with Puerto Rico, the Philippines, and Guam, were territories that had recently been "orphaned" and were in need of protection and governance. As a result, they were unable to "govern their own affairs."[32] During most of the speech, General Ludlow went on to argue that it was in the best interest of all involved for the United States to govern islands and populations that have "no discipline, no management," and "no comprehension of government."[33] Although Ludlow made a case for U.S. intervention in Puerto Rico and Cuba, he failed to mention past revolutionary wars or the efforts of the migrant community to gain their independence from Spain and to ward off possible annexation by the United States. There was no discussion concerning the interests of Puerto Rican or Cuban people.

The silencing of the Puerto Rican and Cuban independentistas in both their respective homelands and in New York City led to a rethinking of nation and community. It also caused Puerto Rican and Cuban migrants to reevaluate the role of nationalists leaders such as the delegado of the PRC, Tómas Estrada Palma, in helping to engineer the U.S. intervention. The combined silences as well as the great disappointment felt by the nationalist movement had a dramatic affect on the migrant community. To begin with, the end of the war effectively changed the parameters of a defined political community by doing away with the conceptions and uses of exile. Puerto Ricans and Cubans who had been exiled by their respective countries were now free to return. However, for many this meant returning to a nation not of their own making. For those who had not been formally exiled but who nonetheless considered themselves part of a larger Antillean community, their countries' new status signaled a change in how they would reconfigure a shared political identity and community.

Although the end of the war forced a rethinking of politics as it pertained to nation building, it did not end the political relationships developed between both communities during the mid- to late nineteenth century. Instead, many of those relationships were now transferred to labor. Puerto Rican and Cuban migrants who remained in New York created political communities devoted to labor organizing in the many cigar factories in New York and Florida. As a result, the cigar industry was transformed into a terrain for asserting identity and, in turn, resisting demands made by cigar manufacturers to change how the Antillean community viewed themselves as workers and migrants. The tension manifested itself in the refusal of the majority of Puerto Rican and Cuban cigar workers to belong to North American labor unions. Instead, they opted to form their own labor unions such as La Resistencia, which had ties to labor unions in Cuba.

In addition to rejecting U.S.-based labor unions, active Puerto Rican and Cuban cigar workers continually went on strike as a means to assert control over the means of production, which were in constant danger of being changed. The familiar work spaces where Spanish was spoken and lectores would read Spanish newspapers and novels were slowly disappearing as a result of rapid mechanization. By the 1920s, when the majority of cigar factories attempted to modernize, Puerto Rican migrants in New York would be given U.S. citizenship, further compromising the status of Puerto Rico as nation.[34] For the majority of Cubans living in New York, the rise of the repressive administration of Gerardo Machado in Cuba prompted a refashioning of migrant politics targeted at ending the machadato as well as the Platt Amendment.[35]

The political and economic changes in Puerto Rico and Cuba effectively altered how the migrant Antillean community would organize. As a result of their status as citizens, Puerto Ricans migrated en masse to New York, creating distinct Puerto Rican colonias as well as a powerful Puerto Rican nationalist movement.[36] Cubans, on the other hand, found themselves separated into distinct communities located in not only New York but also in Tampa, Key West, and to a lesser extent New Orleans. Because Cubans were not U.S. citizens, their movements back and forth were more restricted and subjected to U.S. immigration policies. Nonetheless, Puerto Ricans and Cubans continued to build mutual and shared communities. This time, however, the communities would reflect a myriad of mutual interests including labor, music, literature, sports, and a shared migrant history in New York.

The Cuban Revolution of 1959 and the ensuing exile changed the politics surrounding community building among Puerto Rican and Cuban migrants. Definitions of what constitutes a shared nationalist identity, even if imagined, have taken on altogether different meanings. Questions concerning the meaning of nation in a period of intense globalization, of crafting a mutual migrant identity in the face of generational change, and of building political alliances in a time of political uncertainties have left Puerto Rican and Cuban migrants with little choice but to once again reinvent themselves. This time, however, the reinvention will have to be one that takes into account migrants from other Antillean nations such as the Dominican Republic, Haiti, and Jamaica as well as one that is equipped to respond to globalization, the dynamic of overlapping diasporas, racialization, and transnationalism. Infused with a different set of meanings, the recasting of an Antillean migrant identity and community that challenges past configurations of geography might be what is needed to finally, as Martí once wrote, put the world "into balance."

NOTES

1. According to Josefina Toledo, this quote first appeared in a publication entitled "Patria, Justicia, Libertad, Habitantes de Puerto Rico." It was published in New York on September 1, 1867. See Josefina Toledo, "Ramón Emeterio Betances en la génesis de los clubes Borinquen y Mercedes Varona" (unpublished paper in possession of the author). I thank Agustín Laó-Montes

for bringing this article to my attention. This quote also appears in Bernardo Vega, *Memoirs of Bernardo Vega: A Contribution to the History of the Puerto Rican Community in New York,* ed. César Andreu Iglesias (New York Monthly Review Press, 1984), 48.

2. José Martí, *Obras Completas* (Havana: Instituto Cubano del Libro, 1963–1973), 3:54–62.

3. Unfortunately, the nature of this essay does not lend itself to an expanded discussion of the revolutionary wars in Puerto Rico and Cuba. For a more in-depth examination of the history of the Puerto Rican and Cuban revolutionary wars, please refer to Olga Jiménez de Wagenheim, *El Grito de Lares: sus causes y sus hombres* (Rio Piedras: Ediciones Huracán, 1986); and Fernando Picó, *Historia general de Puerto Rico* (Rio Piedras: Ediciones Huracán, 1988). For more on the Cuban revolutionary movement in particular, see Louis A. Pérez Jr., *Cuba Between Reform and Revolution* (Oxford University Press, 1988); and *Cuba Between Empires, 1878–1902.* (Pittsburgh: University of Pittsburgh Press, 1987).

4. It is important to note that migrants from the Dominican Republic lived and worked in New York during this period and as a result were involved in the movements, albeit on a smaller scale. Club records do reveal the existence of members who were from the Dominican Republic. Yet these members were involved in clubs that focused on Puerto Rican and Cuban independence. The revolutionary wars in Cuba (and to a lesser extent, Puerto Rico) dominated the political activism of the migrant community to the point that by the late nineteenth century almost all migrant political activity was directed toward Cuban independence from Spain. See Sherri Grasmuck and Patricia Pessar, *Between Two Islands: Dominican International Migration* (Berkeley: University of California, 1991). By the early years of the twentieth century, Dominican migrants began to organize political organizations and clubs in New York City. Records of clubs, such as El Club Cubano Interamericano, reveal how Puerto Ricans, Cubans, Dominicans, and even African Americans organized clubs during the 1930s and 1940s. See Nancy Raquel Mirabal, "De Aquí, De Allá: Race, Empire, and Nation in the Making of Cuban Exile and Immigrant Communities in New York and Tampa, 1823–1924," Ph.D. diss., University of Michigan, 2000.

5. The political lines were not always so neatly drawn among the migrant community. For instance, it was common for some migrants to want independence from Spain and still cultivate an economic and political relationship with the United States. Yet in short the three main factions consisted of the annexationists, who advocated the annexation of Cuba to the United States; the autonomists, who questioned the idea of completely disconnecting from Spain; and the independentistas, who wanted nothing short of total independence.

6. The club was founded by Juan Manuel Macías and the exiled Puerto Rican José Francisco Basora. After war broke out in Cuba in 1868, the club was renamed the Junta Revolucionaria de Cuba y Puerto Rico. Please see Vega, *Memoirs,* 48. Also see Gerald E. Poyo, *With All and for the Good of All: The Emergence of Popular Nationalism in the Cuban Communities of the United States, 1848–1898* (Durham, N.C.: Duke University Press, 1989), 10–11.

7. "Oficio No 1, Esquila al General Rius Rivera," New York, March 18, 1896. The clubs met in a hall located on 101 Street and Third Avenue. Arthur Schomburg papers, roll 7:0881, Schomburg Center for Research in Black Culture, New York Public Library.

8. The exile nationalist and separatist movements that organized in response to the Ten Years War in Cuba were factionalized and tension filled. The Cuban exile and migrant community could not agree on a single overriding policy or strategy, causing the exile movement to fail. The inability of the exile movement to remain unified had a great impact on the success of the war in Cuba. In 1878, after ten years of fighting, Cuban rebels lost the war. It was believed that the indecisiveness and infighting present in the exile nationalist movement contributed to the failure. With this in mind, nationalist leaders, most notably José Martí, were determined to unify the movement at all costs.

9. The records of the PRC do not make clear how the exile nationalist movement based in New York intended to address the political situation in Puerto Rico. Although members continually responded to the situation in Puerto Rico, they do not reveal what specific actions they expected to take once Puerto Rico was liberated from the Spanish and moreover what role the migrant community would play in Puerto Rico's independence. This makes it difficult to fully understand the role of the Sección de Puerto Rico and why at this point, after so many years of working together as full partners, Puerto Rican issues were relegated to a section of the PRC.

10. In English the phrase reads "articles concerning the cultural and political interests in Latin America." See Josefina Toledo, *Sotero Figueroa, editor de Patria* (Havana: Editorial Letras Cubanas, 1985), 38.

11. Francisco Gonzalo Marín, "Nueva York por dentro: Una faz de su vida bohemia," in *The Latino Reader: From 1543 to the Present,* ed. Harold Augenbraum and Margarite Fernández Olmos (New York: Houghton Mifflin, 1997), 108.

12. Ibid., 108–9.

13. Ibid., 108.

14. Benedict Anderson, *Imagined Communities: Reflections on the Origin and Spread of Nationalism,* rev. ed. (New York: Verso, 1993), 44.

15. José Martí, "Con todo y por el bien de Todos," in *Política de Nuestra América* (México, D.F.: Siglo Veintiuno, 1977), 216.

16. Martí's revolutionary ideas and actions were not lost on Spanish authorities, who exiled Martí to the United States in 1880.

17. The Junta Revolucionaria de Cuba y Puerto Rico was formed in 1866 in New York. Please see Toledo, "Ramón Emeterio Betances"; and *Sotero Figueroa, editor de Patria.*

18. Vega, *Memoirs,* 51.

19. This particular club called La Liga should not be confused with the club of the same name that was formed in 1891 by black Puerto Ricans and Cubans. Despite having the same name, these two clubs had little in common.

20. Vega, *Memoirs,* 53.

21. Ibid.

22. See Toledo, "Ramón Emeterio Betances," 5–6.

23. Puerto Rican and Cuban women who migrated during the early part of the nineteenth century were usually upper class and migrated to New York mainly to accompany their husbands or to work in the separatist and nationalist movements. It was not until the 1880s that the number of Puerto Rican and Cuban women migrating to New York increased significantly. Please see Virginia E. Sánchez-Korrol, *From Colonia to Community: The History of Puerto Ricans in New York City* (Berkeley: University of California, 1983).

24. Philip Foner, ed., *Our America: Writings on Latin America and the Struggle for Cuban Independence* (London: Monthly Review Press, 1977), 12.

25. Ibid.

26. Vega, *Memoirs*, 66.

27. Ibid.

28. Ibid., 83.

29. "A Treaty of Peace Between the United States and Spain," Articles, I, II, III, IV, and V, 55th Congress, third session, Senate doc. no. 62, Part 1 (Washington, D.C.: U.S. Government Printing Office, 1899), 5–11.

30. A number of secondary sources do a good job of discussing both the Foraker Act and the Platt Amendment at length. See Louis A. Pérez Jr., *Cuba Under the Platt Amendment, 1902–1934* (Pittsburgh: University of Pittsburg Press, 1986); *Cuba Between Empires*; and *The War of 1898: The United States and Cuba in History and Historiography* (Chapel Hill: University of North Carolina Press, 1998). Also refer to Sánchez-Korrol, *From Colonia to Community*; and Adalberto López and James Petras, eds., *Puerto Rico and Puerto Ricans: Studies in History and Society* (Cambridge, Mass.: Schenkman, 1974).

31. Brigadier-General William Ludlow, Governor of Havana, "Reception Tendered by the Cuban Orphan Society" (speech given on November 16, 1899, and published by the Cuban Orphan Society; New York Public Library, 1901, microfilm p74082), 2.

32. Ibid., 2–3.

33. Ibid., 4.

34. In 1917 the Jones Organic Act was passed, extending U.S. citizenship to all Puerto Ricans. The act further compromised the status of Puerto Rico as a nation because it restructured the country's government body and also decreed English to be its official language.

35. In 1924 Gerardo Machado was elected president of Cuba. Supported by the United States, he attempted to set up a reformist government in Cuba. Determined to economically diversify the island, Machado looked to the United States to strengthen his support and to acquire even more foreign investments. This did not sit well with the labor unions such as the Confederación Nacional Obrera de Cuba and the newly formed Cuban Communist Party, which were founded in 1925 and viewed Machado's efforts as detrimental to Cuban workers. His repression of labor unions and organizations critical of his administration would come to a head in the general strike of 1933. The strike, as well as the violence, imprisonment, and

executions that followed it, prompted a migration of Cubans who were against the machadato to New York.

36. I am referring to organizations such as the Partido Socialista Puertorriqueño, which was founded in 1915 as the political arm of the labor movement. According to the historian Blanca Silvestrini, the basic platform of the party "centered on labor-related social and economic reforms." See Silvestrini, "Contemporary Puerto Rico: A Society of Contrasts," in *Puerto Rico and Puerto Ricans,* ed. Adalberto Lopez and James Petras, 153.

CHAPTER TWO

"The Latins from Manhattan"

Confronting Race and Building Community in Jim Crow Baseball, 1906–1950

Adrián Burgos Jr.

THE CUBANS TAKE THE FIELD

A chilly wind swirled about Dyckman Oval as the New York Cubans readied themselves. Although New York City seemed cultural worlds away for the club's new Latino players, the opening-day scene at Dyckman was familiar for most; some of the players had appeared in the black baseball circuits as early as 1916. Unlike the other Negro League teams that called New York City home, the Cubans played the majority of their home games in Harlem and Manhattan. Fans and local reporters took note, adopting the Cubans as "Harlem's own" and referring to them as the "Latins from Manhattan."[1]

Under the ownership of Alejandro Pompez, a Latino of Cuban descent, the New York Cubans baseball club introduced the majority of Latino talent to the Negro Leagues and New York City's baseball fans between 1935 and 1950.[2] Composed of Latino and African American players, the team featured a high level of talent, including, among others, future Major Leaguers Orestes "Minnie" Miñoso, José "Pantalones" Santiago, and Edmundo "Sandy" Amoros. More significantly, the team provided a cultural link that mediated the distance between home and diaspora for the city's Latino population.

Despite perceptions of segregation as a Southern phenomenon, New York City staged a significant part of the U.S. segregation drama throughout the twentieth-century era of Jim Crow baseball, 1906–1950.[3] More Major League and Negro League organizations called New York City home than any other North American city. Latinos appeared on each of the city's Major League teams before the breaking of baseball's color line in 1947: the New York Yankees, the New York Giants, and the Brooklyn Dodgers. Their appearance on these teams started with Cuban-born Angel Aragon's brief stint with the Yankees in 1914; players such as Adolfo Luque, Miguel Angel González, and José Rodríguez followed during the 1910s. Latinos' first regular participation in black baseball circuits occurred in 1906 with the appearance of the Cuban Stars.[4] Over the next four decades, Latinos appeared on several Negro League clubs that called New York City home: the Brooklyn Royal Giants, the Lincoln Giants, the Cuban Stars, the New York Black Yankees, and the Brooklyn Eagles—which moved to Newark after the 1935 season. Home of these different big league clubs, New York City served as a primary point of entry for Latinos into North American professional baseball.[5] Upon examination, the history of the New York Cubans and the social interactions of Latinos in Harlem unveil the manner in which the "Latins from Manhattan" were exposed to the social and economic realities of race and segregation in a northern city.

Latino participation in the building of Black Harlem underscored the Spanish-speaking Caribbean's place within the African diaspora. Latino settlement in New York City resulted in the formation of communities in Harlem, Brooklyn, and the Bronx. The community formation process in Harlem exposed the intricacies of race and place among Latinos within a transnational context, particularly as it challenged their racial location within their own national communities. Conflicts over competing notions of blackness and over racial politics revealed how Harlem served as a nodal point of intersecting diasporas. Therefore, interactions in Black Harlem elicited a more nuanced understanding of the manner in which Black and Latino identities have been articulated through cultural practices, social interactions, and collective political struggle in the everyday realm.[6]

In spite of Major League baseball's racial segregation, Latino players felt most at home on the baseball diamond because most of them were already familiar with the sport that reigned as the national pastime in Cuba, Puerto Rico, and the Dominican Republic. The transition these players faced in the United States paralleled that encountered by other Latino immigrants and echoed issues with which U.S.-born Latinos had to deal. Their arrival in the North American leagues in the 1910s and 1920s coincided with the pioneering settlement of Latinos in several New York City neighborhoods. On New York City's streets, in its factories, or on its baseball diamonds, Latinos from throughout the Spanish-speaking Americas interacted with U.S.-born whites and blacks. Their articulation of new identities acknowledged the intricacies of race and place in a society that was undeniably race conscious. For many, their interactions aided the process whereby they became more than Cubans, Puerto Ricans, or Dominicans; it facilitated their becoming Latino.

Composed of English- and Spanish-speaking fans, the stadium crowds at Dyckman Oval and later the Polo Grounds offer a microcosm of the city's people-of-color community; its diversity allows this analysis to extend beyond the playing field and into community life. When we go back in time to revisit Harlem during its renaissance, we find a community much more culturally and ethnically diverse than what most people today envision when they hear "Black Harlem." Harlem was home to not just African Americans but also Antiguans, Trinidadians, Puerto Ricans, Dominicans, and Cubans. Harlemites shared more than the geographical area that constituted Harlem; together, they forged an "intra-racial ethnic community" that served as a creative center for black culture.[7] In writing Harlem's poetry or stories, as did Countee Cullen or James Baldwin; acting and singing on its stages, as did Paul Robeson or Harry Belafonte; collecting black cultural artifacts, as did bibliophile Arturo "Arthur" Schomburg; or playing professional baseball, as did Rodolfo "Rudy" Fernández, Harlemites blurred the binary notion of home and diaspora. After all, migrants and immigrants did not leave one society and replace it with another; rather, they lived in both, sometimes uncomfortably and certainly confusingly, but never with the resolute distinctions we often read into the past.

In rapid order, new languages and accents and the introduction of foods that brought new smells wafting through its neighborhoods, coupled with different musical sounds, marked a heterogeneity that professions of racial sameness in Harlem both hid and revealed. In Harlem, Spanish commingled with English, cricket players met baseball players, and fathers and mothers passed judgment over their children's associates either because they hailed from the rural South or the Caribbean. Yet when Harlemites rallied behind a political figure such as Marcus Garvey or Vito Marcantonio, picketed local merchants, or rooted for the New York Cubans, they engaged in a process of community building through which a Latino community emerged alongside an African American community, with both contributing to Harlem's unique cultural vitality.[8] Settlement in New York City not only influenced community formation but also kindled a shared sense of blackness based on consciousness of race and diaspora.

The strategies that Latinos formed to combat racial assignment and segregation reflected their expanding racial knowledge.[9] A number of Latinos opted to settle in black communities throughout the city. Many developed a renewed appreciation of their African cultural heritage and lineage from the African diaspora. Their interactions with African American and West Indian neighbors capture participation in what historian Earl Lewis has labeled "overlapping diasporas"—the movement of African-descended people to new locations within the Americas that followed initial forced removal from the African continent in the age of slavery.[10]

The makeup of the New York Cubans' following provides a prime setting to examine baseball's role in the emergence of a Latino identity that developed pan-Latino and transnational dimensions.[11] On city streets, rag-tag teams of boy and girls played stickball imagining their ascendance into *las grandes ligas,* while in city parks, their fathers, elder siblings, relatives, and neighbors played on teams such as the Borinquen All Stars, Ciudad Trujillo, or the Black Puerto Rican Stars. Participation in organized leagues and informal games reconnected Latinos across generations, national boundaries, and physical geography. Among Latino men, on-field success contributed to off-field solidarity. More significantly, success validated their masculinity in a sport where most Latinos endured a subordinated status and in a society where they could only exercise a circumscribed citizenship. Consequently, whether as fans or as players, participation in baseball cultivated a sense of pride and commonalty and helped assuage the toll of physical relocation, economic exploitation, and racialization in U.S. society.

NINETEENTH-CENTURY LATINO PIONEERS

The twentieth-century ethnoracial context in which Latinos participated in what many sportswriters have referred to as "America's game" had its nineteenth-century antecedents in direct participation by Latinos and indirect references to them in black baseball. Latino participation in the big leagues dates back to the early 1870s with Cuban-born Esteban "Steve" Bellán's appearance in the National Association. The first U.S.-born Latino, California native Vincent "Sandy" Nava, broke into the National League in the mid-1880s. Their careers reflected baseball's growth beyond the northeastern United States and its emergence as a national game. More importantly, their presence expanded the lexicon of race in the national game.

Bellán left Cuba in the midst of political turmoil that precipitated the Ten Year's War against Spain (1868–1878). New York City was among the preferred destinations for Cuban immigrants. Bellán's arrival came as part of the anticolonial struggle of the Cuban elite, who sought to safeguard their children by having them educated in the United States. He picked up America's game while attending St. Johns College (present-day Fordham University), playing on the varsity baseball team, the Rose Hill Club, before leaving to pursue a career as a professional ballplayer.[12] Like Bellán, a generation of Cubans picked up the game while attending secondary school, military academy, or college in the states; they would become primary carriers of the game to Cuba.[13]

The baseball career of Vicente Nava reveals a different historical path than that of most Latinos who entered the North American playing fields before integration. When Nava arrived in the National League in 1882, his physical appearance—noticeable foreignness and racial difference—drew notice. Intrigue about Nava's identity prompted the press, fans, and fellow players to refer to him as "the Spaniard." The mark he carried was never more clearly revealed as when the *Detroit Free Press* published "Nava Pinafored" during Nava's rookie year (1882). Reprinted by other newspapers in the National League circuit, the parody hailed Nava as "the Spanish catcher on the Providence club," an act that marked his ethnoracial difference from the rest of the league's players.[14]

Transmitters of racial knowledge, the North American press performed an important role in constructing the Latino players' difference. By the 1900s, the sporting press carried regular accounts of North American teams that toured Cuba. Their coverage relayed baseball's popularity in Cuba by providing game recaps, excerpts from players' correspondence, and seasonal summaries. The *New York Clipper* provided perhaps the most extensive coverage of Latino baseball from the 1870s to the 1890s.[15] Collectively, these papers' coverage contributed to the construction of a Spanish type in North American professional baseball, familiarizing fans with the ethnoracial difference of players from the Spanish-speaking Americas. This latter point held particularly true for New York City fans exposed to black baseball's first elite team, the Cuban Giants.

Formed in 1885 and comprised solely of African American players, the Cuban Giants represent an important link between the history of black professional baseball and Latino baseball. The extent to which the Cuban Giants manipulated racial types to masquerade as Cuban has been widely debated. At the center of this debate is a 1938 *Esquire* article in which black baseball's first historian, Sol White, recounted the genesis of the Cuban Giants. In that interview given more than fifty years after the team's formation, White discussed the extent of the Cuban Giants' racial masquerade, claiming that players on the team spoke "gibberish to each other which, they hoped, sounded like Spanish."[16]

The act of consciously identifying the team as Cuban reveals that before the twentieth century, African Americans had acquired the racial knowledge of a Cuban type they could imitate. Much as in any masquerade, convincing others of one's authenticity as Cuban was not the most important element of the performance. Rather, the coy manipulation of the possibility of being Cuban made the masquerade successful and posed the most significant challenge to U.S. racial categories by inserting consideration of nationality and ethnicity. Thus, the team's manipulation of Cuban identity reflected an awareness of the limitations their race placed on their professional aspirations. Aware of the Cuban Giants' on-field success, other black teams at the professional, semiprofessional, and local level followed suit and also played on the racial ambiguity invoked by the Cuban name. Finally, their masquerade signaled North American baseball's internationalization, in which African American and Latinos participated.[17]

Formation of the Cuban Giants occurred in the initial stage of black baseball's formal organization, a movement necessitated by the implementation of Major League baseball's color line (1889). Into this segregated world entered the Cuban Stars team during its initial visit in 1906, followed ten years later by Alejandro Pompez's Cuban Stars. On the field, these Latino clubs faced intense competition, playing elite black teams and white professional and semiprofessional clubs. The off-field dynamics of their participation in Jim Crow baseball provide a compelling snapshot of the manner in which segregation structured economic and social opportunity.

In the twentieth century, Latinos discovered the power of segregation and subsequently wandered to "their" side of baseball's racial divide: Major League baseball for those who could pass as white and the Negro Leagues for all others. Their participation on both sides of baseball's racial fault line reveals how the story of racial exclusion is much more textured than a mere black-white dichotomy would allow. This aspect of U.S. race relations found no more compelling stage than the professional diamonds where the lived experience of African Americans and Latinos contradicted the popular discourse of an egalitarian society.

ALEJANDRO POMPEZ AND THE NEW YORK CUBANS PLAY BALL

The life story of Alejandro Pompez, a participant in the internationalization of Negro League baseball, reveals two significant aspects of Latino history: migration and the Americas as an interconnected cultural sphere. Pompez's career embodied geographical movement within the Americas and underscored the translocal aspect of baseball as American culture. As a baseball entrepreneur, Pompez recognized that a market existed for Latino baseball in the states, linking him and his teams to the larger story about baseball in Latino communities. In addition, Pompez's involvement in black baseball management illuminates how segregation operated on multiple levels. Not only was on-field interracial competition heavily circumscribed in the Major Leagues, but segregation also affected those involved in the operations of professional leagues.

Born in 1890, Pompez lived his early childhood in Florida before his family joined the flock of return émigrés to Cuba following the end of Spanish colonial rule (1898). Living in Cuba during his teenage years made an indelible impression on him, for it was there that Pompez "was infected with baseball's atmosphere that was ingrained in the Republic."[18] At twenty years of age, Pompez moved to New York, where he developed a close relationship with Nat C. Strong, an influential figure in New York City baseball who controlled booking events at Major League stadiums and other local parks. The two enjoyed a mutually beneficial relationship; working with Pompez enabled Strong to strengthen ties with Latino baseball, and Strong's tutelage prepared Pompez for his career as a baseball team owner and sports promoter.[19]

Pompez's direct involvement in professional baseball began in 1916, when he organized his Cuban Stars club and toured the Caribbean. Upon returning to the states, the club participated several years in the eastern black baseball circuit before joining the Eastern Colored League in 1923, where it played until the league's collapse in 1929. These experiences gave Pompez the necessary background to build the New York Cubans organization, exposing him to African American, Cuban, Puerto Rican, and Dominican talent. With the foundation that Pompez built, the New York Cubans recovered from a fitful start in their inaugural season (1935) to claim the regular-season National League title, thereby qualifying to face the Pittsburgh Crawfords in the Negro League World Series. The Cubans eventually lost an exciting seven-game series to the talent-laden Crawfords, which featured future Hall of Fame inductees James "Cool Papa" Bell, Oscar Charleston, Satchel Paige, and Josh Gibson.

The Cubans-Crawfords matchup revealed the inherent conflict between fan loyalty, racial identification, and geographic location. The Cubans' roster featured a mixture of Caribbean-born Latinos and U.S.-born African Americans, whereas the Crawfords' roster included only African Americans. New York's African American fans faced a choice: they could privilege racial and national identification with fellow African Americans or maintain their developed loyalty to Pompez's predominately foreign-born contingent. In Harlem everyday life such issues emerged often, but decisions whether to choose race versus national identification were not so predictable. Sharing the cultural world and the geographical space popularly referred to as Black Harlem, many of Harlem's African American, Afro-Caribbean, and Latino residents developed a familiarity with the economic and racial barriers that each faced. Consequently, in midst of economic turmoil and tense race relations, Latinos and blacks banded together on different occasions, participating in organized protests, economic boycotts, and in the race riots of 1935 and 1938.[20] Similarly, they joined forces to protest baseball's continued racial segregation and to celebrate the triumphs of their Negro League teams.

The business activities of Pompez captured the limitations U.S. racial ideology and segregation placed on those not in the Anglo mainstream in the 1930s. Like others of his day, Pompez's connection to the city's black and Latino communities did not begin or end with baseball. Much like Gus Greenlee, longtime owner of the Pittsburgh Crawfords, Pompez funneled earnings from numbers running and other business activities to finance his professional team.[21] Well connected with the city's underworld bosses, Pompez eventually joined forces with Dutch Schultz's operation when the latter muscled his way into Harlem's gambling scene. In 1936, Pompez was indicted for his role in the city's policy racket. His indictment, which arose from District Attorney Thomas Dewey's campaign to root out vice and crack down on the policy racket, produced front-page headlines in the city's black newspapers. Instead of opting to stay and fight the charges filed, Pompez fled. His hasty departure disrupted the Cubans' 1936 campaign and caused the club to cease operations the following season.[22]

Captured in Mexico after a year in flight, Pompez negotiated a deal with Dewey to turn state's evidence. In exchange for testifying against Jimmy Hines, a Tammany Hall Democratic official who protected Schultz's operations, Pompez received a two-year probation. Pompez's testimony proved to be a critical cog in Dewey's case against Hines, who was eventually convicted in his 1938 trial.[23] Although implicated for his role in the numbers racket, Harlemites were quite forgiving of Pompez, especially compared with their animosity toward the city officials who protected Schultz's criminal operations.

Pompez's participation in Harlem's sporting world and underground economy challenged the perception that numbers runners were no more than hoodlums who took advantage of their predominately working-class constituency. Through his baseball teams, numbers operation, and other business ventures, Pompez employed hundreds of Harlemites and circulated tens of thousands of dollars within the black economy. Knowledge of this perhaps influenced *New York Age* sportswriter William E. Clark's opinion of Pompez's role in the policy racket scandal:

> We have known him for over a period of more than 15 years and
> have always found him a square-shooter in his dealings with his
> players and the public. He has sacrificed time and money to
> build up Negro baseball in New York. . . . To our way of thinking
> his crimes are no worse than those of bookmakers who accept
> bets on horses.[24]

Clark was not alone in framing Pompez's activities in a positive light; numerous others felt a debt of gratitude toward Pompez for his role in facilitating their own entry into Black Harlem's community life.

Pompez's business dealings reflected the interconnected and overlapping character of Harlem's black and Latino communities. The housing arrangements that Pompez made for his players demonstrates how these worlds overlapped. When pitcher Rodolfo Fernández departed Cuba for the first time in 1932, he benefited from Pompez locating him conveniently close to *el barrio latino* and the team's home field, a pattern repeated for many of his teammates. Fernández believed that Pompez's help enabled him to endure the hardship that Harlem's black and Latino population faced during the Depression.[25] As a whole, these arrangements reveal that Pompez established a multiethnic network that included African American, Jamaican, and Latino households. This network enabled Pompez to strategically place players in homes that fostered connections with Harlem's black community, exposed them to English, and provided access to familiar cuisine. It made life *en el norte* bearable; professional baseball made it possible.

JUGANDO EN NUEVA YORK: RACE, MEMORY, AND DIASPORA

Baseball's significance as a cultural institution and a mediating influence on the settlement process of Latino and West Indian immigrants is engrained in the collective memory of these overlapping communities. Memories of attending or participating in games unveiled the multiple purposes they served. Regardless of level, baseball provided them space to create community and, as historian Earl Lewis labels the process, to form congregation—that is, to join together a collectivity in the formation of informal networks or formal institutions that supports their ability to withstand segregation's dehumanizing effect.[26] Baseball games provided a place for them to remember their past, forge new identities, and find common cause with others who called Harlem home.

Baseball thrived as part of Latino culture in New York City, leaving an impression on countless Latinos who settled or were raised in the city, among them the Puerto Rican poet Piri Thomas. Born to a Cuban father and a Puerto Rican mother at Harlem Hospital in 1938, Thomas learned baseball from his father, who played in the city's semiprofessional leagues. Thomas's reflections moved him back through time and space:

> My father was a fine athlete. I remember when as a child, man, we were living in *unos barrios*, 113, 112 and 114, and 115 [street]. . . . Anyway, *papi* loved playing baseball. He used to take us to what I used to call the country, Central Park.
>
> I used to go watch my father when he played ball. Since we were kids I used to be massaging my father with my sister. . . . We learned how to give them . . . to get *papi* ready. We used to cheer him when he played in the field; then he made me batboy. He talked to the team to make me batboy. In those days, my father played for whatever teams he could get onto, whatever teams *papi* was able to play on: the Black League, Black Stars, on the Puerto Rican Stars, and he played on the Cuban Stars.[27]

Games at Central Park were more than Sunday outings for Thomas; they signified the reappropriation of public space, a place to re-create a place to call home; to meet with fellow Latinos, blacks, and Puerto Ricans; and, of course, to play ball. These were all aspects that permeated Thomas's recollections.

> But most, most were the World Series in Central Park because
> teams thought that this was ours. They [the Major Leagues]
> didn't allow us to go in theirs, but we made our World Series.
> And the teams, they all played seriously and there were some
> heavy betting going on, and the whole energy. And just like any
> World Series, there were selling going on, but it was *cuchifrito*
> not very much hot dogs.[28]

Similar memories were shared by other Harlemites such as Everard Marius,
a West Indian also born in Harlem. For those like Marius, whose family
hailed from the British Caribbean, baseball replaced cricket as their sport
of choice. Marius remembers how playing baseball represented an
important part of his identity formation, his Americanization if you will.[29]
Sports, then, combined with food, music, and other leisure-time pursuits to
allow average folks to recuperate from the demands of their wage-earning
jobs and to recreate themselves in communion with others.

Oral narratives and newspaper accounts detail another important and
interrelated story, the participation of Latinos in overlapping diasporas. As
migratory professionals who played throughout the Americas, Negro
League players formed friendships and relationships with other Americans
of African descent, exposing them to different possibilities. Caribbean
leagues provided African Americans the chance to play on and manage
integrated clubs. Similarly, Latino participation in North American leagues
enabled them to join the assault on baseball's myth of white supremacy
decades before Jackie Robinson became the twentieth century's first African American to play in the majors. In addition to professional opportunities, African Americans and Latinos acquired new language skills and
adapted their cultural practices through these relationships. More significantly, their experience in the Negro Leagues and the Caribbean leagues
enabled them to envision a common shared past, thereby extending and
deepening an appreciation of the African diaspora.[30]

Of course, differences as much as similarities characterized the African
diaspora and relationships between Latino and African American players.
Sometimes these differences intruded into the clubhouse and onto the playing field. At the very least it was a feeling shared by certain followers of
the New York Cubans who feared that the team's diversity would hamper
its ultimate success. One *New York Age* sportswriter, Lewis Dial, made note
of rumors that attributed the team's rocky 1935 start to internal divisions
among players: "The New York Cubans look like a real classy outfit, man
for man, but for some reason or other, they fail to jell. It is rumored among
fans that the Cubans and the Americans don't seem to pull together."[31]

The writer proposed a solution: splitting the players into two distinct
clubs, one entirely Latino and the other disproportionately African American. Guided perhaps by his own sense of the complexities of race or how

players had worked together in the Caribbean, Pompez did not follow this plan. Instead, he waited. After a slow start, the Cubans built a winning streak that propelled them within a game of the Negro League title.[32]

The place of Spanish-speaking Caribbean people of African descent in an English-speaking place in the diaspora exposed the complexities of language and region as few other examples could. Language, when attached to history and social perception, had a dexterous quality that transformed meaning and understanding. However, this was an uneven and often a painstakingly slow process, as became increasingly apparent to Latinos. Early in the twentieth century, the North American sporting press developed the practice of labeling all Latino players, regardless of national origins, Cuban. Luis Rodríguez Olmo, the second Puerto Rican Major Leaguer, encountered this practice in the early 1940s while rising through the minor leagues in the states. When the *Sporting News* wrote a brief article on the up-and-coming Puerto Rican, the Olmo family took notice of its reference to "Roberto Olmo, 21-year-old Cuban outfielder." Olmo's brother wrote the national sporting sheet to express his dismay:

> His correct name is Luis Rodríguez Olmo, but he is known as Luis Olmo, and he is a Puerto Rican, a proud American citizen.
> So far his name has been given out correctly only once, when you published the reserve lists. Later he was called Lewis Elmo and now as Roberto Olmo. Some confusion with Spanish names.[33]

The national press was not alone in applying the homogenizing Cuban label. Despite Harlem's Spanish-speaking population being predominately Puerto Rican and the New York Cubans club including Dominicans, Puerto Ricans, and Panamanians, the *New York Age* also proved susceptible to this misperception. Generally applied, the label negated aspects of the city's diverse Latino population; it also diminished ongoing struggles that Puerto Ricans and other Latinos experienced in New York City, among them labor exploitation, discrimination, cultural adaptation, and colonialism.[34]

Popular use of the Cuban label in the twentieth century may be attributable to Cubans reaching the Major Leagues decades before other Latino groups entered. The Cincinnati Reds' 1911 signing of two Cubans, Rafael Almeida and Armando Marsans, captured the ability of some players from the Spanish-speaking Americas to maneuver the racial divide. Although they could pass, their racialization by fellow players and the press marked their place at the periphery of whiteness; they were nominally white.[35]

The experience of Latinos who played in the Major Leagues during segregation differed significantly from Latino players incapable of transgressing the color line. Latinos in the Negro Leagues endured the dual impact of their perceived race and ethnicity. They were not just too dark skinned but were also foreign, spoke a different primary language, and partook in cultural practices unfamiliar to North Americans. These work conditions contributed to a sense of alienation and made the option of playing in a Spanish-speaking country attractive to Latinos. Thus, in the 1940s they and African Americans took advantage of the option to play in an integrated league in Mexico; the Mexican League paid well compared to the Negro Leagues. The loss of talent to the Mexican League did not represent the greatest threat to the Negro Leagues, however; in hindsight, it was Major League integration.

LATINOS ENTER THE GRAND BALLGAME: RACE, IDENTITY, AND MASQUERADE

During the 1930s and 1940s, civil rights and political organizations included baseball integration as part of their social equality campaigns that followed the hardening rather than softening of segregation after World War I. Vigilant of those who entered the Major Leagues, integrationists contended that because the majors already admitted ethnic groups that were not necessarily perceived as white when they first arrived, the time had arrived to grant African Americans entry. What was it, they wondered, that encouraged a nation to ignore the fine physical and mental capabilities of black players? A direct answer was not forthcoming, but the quiescence fueled the drive for change.

The preference for race produced one of North American professional baseball's greatest social ironies. Members of the Caribbean world who would have otherwise been considered nonwhite, if not black, gained certified admissions to compete in the Major Leagues by using the power of cultural and racial markers to reconfigure social rules. Upon first glance, players from the Spanish-speaking Americas were viewed as racially ambiguous. Concerned with mollifying segregationists, organizations that signed these players facilitated the performance of racial masquerade. This process typically involved an organization conducting a background check into a player's family. If it was found to be suitable, organizations defended their signings by attaching ethnic labels such as Castilian or Latin, thereby projecting a nonthreatening whiteness while negating African ancestry. This defense set the stage for a performance in which these players, who otherwise would have been excluded from the majors, were all too willing to participate. For players like Almeida and Marsans, performing as white Latins or Castilians did not mean losing their foreignness. This identity only imposed a nominal whiteness and allowed them to continue speaking Spanish and other cultural practices. Continuing these cultural practices, however, ensured they would not secure the same status as white Americans.

Racial masquerade worked in multiple ways, both in terms of performers and audience. In the late nineteenth century, it enabled European immigrants, mostly German and Irish, to validate their claims to whiteness through participation in or consumption of blackface minstrelsy. Opportunities for racial masquerade in U.S. culture were abundant in the 1920s and 1930s as new forms of mass entertainment emerged, perhaps none as prominent as Al Jolson's popularly received blackface performance in the 1927 talking movie *The Jazz Singer*.[36] Thus, in the early twentieth century, Italian and Jewish immigrants also acted out their Americanness through their participation in new cultural practices (i.e., attending movies) that called upon a process of racialization that emphasized their difference from the nation's black population.

Latino participation in racial masquerade in North American baseball is more complex and varied than the shorthand word *passing* would denote. The historical role of the Caribbean in the African diaspora and the race intermixture that occurred in slave and postemancipation societies of the Spanish-speaking Americas complicate the racial past of Latinos. Nationalist and anticolonial struggles in Cuba, Puerto Rico, and the Dominican Republic during the late nineteenth and early twentieth centuries all relate the vexing role of race in the imagining of nation.[37] Their processes of national identity formation illuminate how historical actors are multipositional subjects—that is, individuals consist of a dense grid of subject positions in which different aspects of the self become evident in different situations. For example, the native-born Cuban elite encountered a choice between identifying with Spain or Cuba during the various wars for independence; their decision involved privileging one identity (Cuban) over another (Spanish). Thus, when one examines individual lives, it is conceivable that at certain moments someone might claim a piece of herself that others would observe as inauthentic. At this moment it might be said that she is trying to pass for what she is not. But looking from the individual outward, *passing* is a peculiarly flat descriptor. It fails to capture the ways in which many actors remained what they had always been while simply altering the vectors of understanding and power.

Everyday residents of Harlem and sporting figures who came from throughout the African diaspora learned to manipulate, if not master, the poetics of racial masquerade. Albertus "Cleffie" Fennar, an African American player, recalled how he joined Pompez's Havana Cuban Stars in 1934. "I was approached by the Cubans to play with the Havana Cuban Stars; the manager of that team was a former big leaguer named José Rodríguez." In an interview with the author, Fennar explained that Rodríguez gave him a pseudonym under which he would play for the Cuban Stars.

AB: You are Roger Dario Fennar?

CF: That was the name that I played under when I played with the Havana Cuban Stars. They changed my name to Dario.

AB: How did you pick those names?

CF: I didn't pick them, they gave them to me.

AB: Oh, they gave them to you?

CF: Jose Rodríguez, told me, let's see, he said I am going to put your name as Dario, he was a good second baseman in Cuba.[38]

To carry out the masquerade, Fennar learned how to speak a little Spanish, expanding his cultural repertoire while meeting the expectation that others would have of Dario the Cuban.

Fans who grew up rooting for New York's big league teams recognized the ironic truths of race. Throughout the twentieth century, older European immigrant groups, grudgingly at first, made room for the inclusion of newer immigrants into the fraternity of whiteness. This was a process that blacks and Latinos observed and from which they learned. Around them Slavs, Italians, and Jews from eastern and southern Europe essentially became whiter and whiter as the century advanced. Attempting to subvert the popular beliefs of whites that they could tell black from white, many blacks twisted the narrative line by inserting language. Everard Marius was never as honest as when he made this comment:

> As a matter of fact, in those days in order for a black ballplayer to get in what was more or less the white Major League, all he had to do was become a Cuban. You know that racism was there. In fact, language would (not as much as today) but language at one time could get you across as not being an ordinary Negro. Some of my relatives used to take advantage of that, speaking creole and all of that business.[39]

As Marius explained, linguistic abilities had the power to transform an ordinary Negro into an "extra-ordinary Negro." This positioned them to possibly extract social benefits denied to those who only spoke the U.S. version of standard English. Racial masquerade, then, involved the manipulation of several cues or markers that signify one's cultural and racial identity: the phenotype associated with being black in the U.S. context(s), language practices such as bilingual skills, and name changes to mask one's presumed ethnic or racial identities. For Fennar, masquerading as Cuban protected his athletic eligibility to play college football, because Dario was the professional and not Fennar, whereas for Marius's relatives, it helped to distance themselves from being considered ordinary Negroes. In the case of Latino pioneers, racial masquerade ensured their entry into the Major Leagues.

CONCLUSION: WARMING UP FOR INTEGRATION

Through the early 1940s, attempts at evading Major League baseball's color line had not produced positive results for African Americans. Sportswriters who championed the integration cause formed a series of counterarguments to the prevailing ideas that supported segregation. Some pointed to the Italians and the few Jewish players, each heretofore questionably white, who joined the whitened ranks of the Major Leagues once dominated by Irish and Germans in the 1920s and 1930s.[40] Others took note how a range of Latinos, from the light-skinned Luis Rodríguez Olmo to the darker-skinned "mulatto" Roberto Estalella, had entered from 1935 onward. For individuals familiar with the history of Cuba and Puerto Rico, the growing Latino presence gave hope for the game's integration.

When the Cincinnati Reds signed their first two Cuban players in 1911, black newspapers speculated about integration's inevitability. *New York Age* columnist Lester Walton wrote forthrightly about the signing's implications on race in America's game:

> With the admissions of Cubans of a darker hue in the two big leagues it would then be easy for colored players who are citizens of this country to get into fast company. The Negro in this country has more varied hues than even the Cubans, and the only way to distinguish him would be to hear him talk. Until the public got accustomed to seeing native Negroes on [sic] big leagues, the colored players could keep their mouths shut and pass for Cubans.[41]

In spite of the popular belief shared by Walton that African Americans could pass as Cuban, no African American successfully accomplished this feat. However, a contingent of North Americans shared their suspicions that several Latinos with African ancestry did break into the Major Leagues.

Guardians of Major League baseball's racial status quo came under continual attack starting in the mid-1930s. Various New York City sportswriters pressed the city's Major League teams to sign Negro League stars, hoping that such a move would revive the Brooklyn Dodgers and the New York Giants franchises.[42] Resistance to change was firm despite public statements by Major League owners and executives that race did not matter. National League President Ford Frick insisted that "beyond the fundamental requirements that a major league player must have is unique ability, good character and habits, I do not recall one instance where baseball has allowed race, creed or color to enter the selection of its players."[43] In a similar mode of denial, Yankees President Lee MacPhail offered two reasons why baseball's color line did not exist owing to the Major Leagues' malevolence. First, the Negro Leagues were a large source of revenue for the

Major Leagues. Second, the Major Leagues did not want to steal contracted players from the Negro Leagues, which most organizations did anyway once integration began in 1947.[44] Veiled in a discourse that validated the Negro Leagues while disputing the existence of a color line, Major League owners continued to bar blacks and the majority of Latinos.

The growing ethnic diversity of the Major League players also spurred the protest of integrationists. *New York Age* reporter Lewis Dial could not stand the hypocrisy of those who claimed race did not play a role in baseball. Reflecting on one failed career in the Major Leagues, Dial wrote in 1936, "John McGraw was caught sneaking one [African American] into the league under the guise of a Cuban-American." Dial, knowing the answer before posing his question, continued: "If the president of the league is right, then why did the late McGraw have to sneak this player into the league as a Cuban-American?"[45] Racial masquerade as Cuban or Indian performed by black players did not guarantee entry into the majors, as Dial's question noted. Nevertheless, a number of Major League officials made use of their knowledge of the in-between space that individuals from the Spanish-speaking Americas occupied in the U.S. racial system. Although some of these organizations took the risk of signing these players, their entry did not translate into acceptance. In 1939 Buster Miller, another *New York Age* columnist, noted the manner in which race continued to matter despite the increasing diversity:

> It is true that the doors of organized baseball are open to Indians,
> Cubans, Porto Ricans [sic], Hawaiians, etc. but only if their skin,
> hair and features will pass muster as evidence of membership in
> the white race. This writer defies any member of the above
> mentioned national groups to obtain entrance into the major
> leagues with a black skin. Or even mahogany colored, lest he be
> hailed as a "nigger" as was Adolfo Luque, swarthy Cuban
> pitcher of the New York Giants, by the "sportsmen" when he
> made his first appearance on the mound in St. Louis.[46]

Miller's reference to Luque and other Latino players revealed how Latinos could serve as a case study in the incompleteness of the masquerade as an enduring strategy. It also disputed the notion that African Americans could pass unscathed as Cubans.

Latinos who entered the segregated Major Leagues gained admission without any promise of acceptance. Their lighter skin color offered only momentary relief in a nation that closely scrutinized ancestry for any tell-tale sign of falsified claim. This meant that although light-hued Latinos may not have been discernibly black, it was dubious that many viewed them as white. They, therefore, lived in that liminal state between racial poles, and few escaped the harsh reality of life in the in-between spaces of a race-conscious land. In such a context, skin color drew attention and distinction, requiring each individual to use his racial knowledge to define and redefine the contours of his world.

In the same fashion that the Latins from Manhattan could bring together a multiethnic contingent to the ballpark, the everyday reality of race and place in New York City and the United States facilitated the building of a Black Harlem that was an "intraracial ethnic community." Despite living in a northern city, these people were eminently aware of the impact of racial segregation; it shaped everything from where they could shop and work to the professional baseball teams on which they could play. Racial masquerade presented just one survival strategy that members of Black Harlem carried out. In the end, their awareness of racial politics in the United States enabled them at different moments to forsake individual agendas and mobilize against the institutional forms of racial segregation that affected their lives, a strategy that eventually brought greater political power to Harlem.

NOTES

This project's research was funded in part by a Spring/Summer Research Grant from the University of Michigan's Office of the Vice President for Research. The project also benefited from a residency at the Center for Puerto Rican Studies through its Graduate Student Summer Research Fellow program as well as the intellectual guidance of Juan Flores, Amilcar Tirado, and Roberto Rodríguez-Morazzani. Special thanks go to Professor Earl Lewis, for his mentorship; Wilson Valentín, for partaking in discussions on Latino popular culture; all who shared their oral narratives; and my family, who hosted my New York stay. Finally, thanks to Dolly Túa-Burgos, the strongest supporter of this project, who also assisted in researching the New York Age during her "free time" in the summer of 1996.

1. Lewis E. Dial, "The Sports Dial," New York Age, August 10, 1935, p. 8; "Attraction at the Polo Grounds, Sun.," June 21, 1945, p. 11; and "Cubans and Stars Meet in Exhibition This Sunday at P.G.," April 17, 1948, p. 7.

2. Referential labels for individuals from the Spanish-speaking Americas have long been an issue among scholars and the various constituent national/ethnic groups. A particular concern they have expressed is how the use of panethnic labels tends to erase profound differences along lines of ethnicity or national origin. For the purposes of this essay, Latino is employed as an ethnoracial category for those individuals from the Spanish-speaking Americas, whether U.S. or foreign born, who entered into the ranks of North American professional baseball. This usage is adopted for two primary reasons. First, it is employed in recognition of the manner in which Major League baseball and North Americans in general tended to treat individuals from the Spanish-speaking Americas as an undifferentiated mass during baseball's Jim Crow era—this conveyed most effectively through coverage from the U.S. mainstream and sporting press. Second, the experience that these individuals

gained while in the North American playing field developed a sense of shared history among these players, facilitating the articulation of a common identity as individuals from the Spanish-speaking Americas that transcended national boundaries. Thus, *Latino* refers to Cubans and Cuban Americans, Mexicans and Mexican Americans, Puerto Ricans, and Venezuelans, among other represented groups. Dominicans, who numbered less than five in the Negro Leagues (1920–1950), did not enter into the Major Leagues until September 1956, when Ozzie Virgil appeared with the New York Giants. Thus, Dominicans did not emerge as significant contributors to Latino baseball in the United States until almost a full decade after racial integration was initiated (April 1947).

3. The dates I use (1906 and 1950) mark Latino participation in Jim Crow baseball in the twentieth century, starting with the development of a black baseball circuit that included Molina's Cuban Stars and ending with the demise of the Negro Leagues as a major league. This date recognizes how integration merely began with Jackie Robinson's 1947 appearance with the Brooklyn Dodgers and that segregationist practices continued to affect the lives of racial minorities after his arrival into the majors.

4. Two different Cuban Stars teams participated in the Negro League circuits: the Pompez-owned squad that played predominately in the east, and the other, operated by Agustín "Tinti" Molina and based out of Chicago. Consequently, baseball historians refer to Molina's team as Cuban Stars West and Pompez's club as Cuban Stars East. Todd Bolton, "Beisbol Behind the Veil: Latin Americans in the Negro Leagues," *Ragtyme Sports,* December 1994, 23; and James A. Riley, *The Biographical Encyclopedia of the Negro Baseball Leagues* (New York: Carroll & Graf, 1994), 203.

5. I use *big leagues* to refer to the highest level of professional baseball among racial lines, the Major Leagues for whites and the Negro Leagues for nonwhites. On the experience of Latinos in the Negro Leagues, see Adrian Burgos Jr., *"Jugando en el Norte:* Caribbean Players in the Negro Leagues, 1910–1950," *CENTRO: Journal del Centro de Estudios Puertorriqueños* 8, nos. 1 and 2 (Spring 1996): 128–49; and Lisa Brock and Bijan Bayne, "Not Just Black: African-Americans, Cubans, and Baseball," in *Between Race and Empire: African-Americans and Cubans Before the Cuban Revolution* (Philadelphia: Temple University Press, 1998), 168–204.

6. In this chapter, I use *Black* to refer to the multiethnic community and cultural identity forged at diasporic sites in the Americas. Contrarily, *black* refers more to skin color. This is done because the lack of suitable terminology to describe the ability of people of African descent in the Americas to share a sense of commonalty without erasing profound differences has challenged social commentators for some time. Blackness, after all, is an incomplete social identifier. Merely labeling the population "Black" does not necessarily address the heterogeneity and internal tensions that existed among Harlem's residents. Yet this study unveils some of the ways in which various people of the African diaspora built community around notions of race and an awareness of a common origin that connected them.

7. From 1910 to 1940, Harlem underwent an extreme transformation, changing from a middle- and upper-working-class neighborhood composed primarily of

white Euroamericans to a predominantly black working-class neighborhood. Harlem's blacks came from all over the Atlantic world: the U.S. South, the West Indies, and the Spanish-speaking Caribbean. Uneasy around these new immigrants, many whites fled Harlem. Irma Watkins-Owens offers the concept of "intraracial ethnic community" to explain Black Harlem's heterogeneity; see *Blood Relations: Caribbean Immigrants and the Harlem Community, 1900–1930* (Bloomington: Indiana University Press, 1996).

8. Marcantonio, an Italian American, served as a U.S. congressman representing the East Harlem district from 1934–1936 and 1938–1950. On his relationship with Harlem's Puerto Rican community, see Felix Ojeda Reyes, "Vito Marcantonio and Puerto Rican Independence," *CENTRO* 4, no. 2 (Spring 1992): 58–64; and Gerald Meyer, "Marcantonio and El Barrio," *CENTRO* 4, no. 2 (Spring 1992): 66–87.

9. *Racial knowledge* refers to the manner by which individuals maintain (and always add to) a personal storehouse of knowledge based on their everyday interactions where specific practices, acts, styles, images, etc., develop racial significance. This reservoir of knowledge is then used in their daily interactions, i.e., to survey their physical surroundings or to interpret history or current events. As a concept, racial knowledge seeks to build on African American historian Evelyn Brooks Higginbotham's notion of a metalanguage of race by focusing on the manner in which individuals maintain and expand this racial vocabulary. Higginbotham, "The Metalanguage of Race," *Signs: Journal of Women in Culture and Society* 17 (1992): 251–74. For an examination that employs racial knowledge in examining the role of race in twentieth-century Cuba, see Frank Guridy, "Race-Making and Racial Politics in Cuba," *Rethinking Race in Cuba Seminar,* Institute of Latin American Studies, University of London, December 9, 1999 (paper in author's possession).

10. The concept of overlapping diasporas helps illuminate the ways these groups saw their lives and their historical pasts as fundamentally interconnected as well as how their diasporic consciousness facilitated community formation once in Harlem. See Earl Lewis and Adrian Burgos Jr., "Race, Baseball, and the Making of Urban Identities," in *Skin Color: The Multiple Meanings of Race in Twentieth Century* (forthcoming). For a discussion on how overlapping diasporas aid analyzing the history of African American community formation, see Lewis, "To Turn As on a Pivot: Writing African Americans into a History of Overlapping Diasporas," *American Historical Review* 100 (June 1995): 765–87.

11. On the articulation of pan-Latino identity in New York City in the late twentieth century, see Juan Flores, "Pan-Latino/Trans-Latino: Puerto Ricans in 'New Nueva York,' " *CENTRO* 8, nos. 1 and 2 (Spring 1996): 170–86.

12. Bellán contributed to the establishment of Cuba's professional league by serving as an advisor, player, and team manager. He was not alone in the Fordham connection. Doctor Carlos Zaldo, the founder of one of Cuba's most storied franchises, Almendares Club, also picked up the game while at Fordham. Ildefonso Ortega, "Historia del Club Almendares," Negro League Folder, "Magazine 'Fotos' from Puerto Rico," Ashland Collection, National Baseball Library and Archive, Cooperstown, N.Y. (hereafter NBLA).

13. Baseball arrived to Cuba in the midst of economic turmoil and political disaffection with its colonial ruler, Spain. Its arrival at this moment enabled nationalists to frame culture (including baseball) as a site for political contestation, one that facilitated the articulation of Cuban national identity as historian Louis Pérez has ably demonstrated. See Pérez, "Between Baseball and Bullfighting: The Quest for Nationality in Cuba, 1868–1898," *Journal of American History* 81 (September 1994): 493–517. On baseball's role in Cuban nationalist movements, also see Roberto González Echévarria, "The Game in Matanzas: On the Origins of Cuban Baseball," *Yale Review* 83 (July 1995): 62–94.

14. Nava played with Providence (National League) from 1882 to 1884 and with Baltimore (American Association) in 1885 and 1886. There were several markers of Nava's difference. Difficulty pronouncing his Spanish first name, Vicente, among English speakers quite possibly contributed to his acquiring the nickname "Sandy," according to baseball historian Joel Franks, a researcher of baseball in California (personal communication, October 1998). On the labeling of Nava as Spanish or a Spaniard, see "Eighteen-Inning Game and Only One Run Made," August 1882; and "The Opening Game of the Base Ball Season in Providence," April 8, 1883, Nava Player File, NBLA. Lyrics dedicated to Nava appeared in *Chicago Tribune,* June 25, 1882. Thanks to nineteenth-century baseball historian Jerry Malloy for sharing this document; a slightly different version appears in Lee Allen, *The Cincinnati Reds* (New York: G. P. Putnam's Sons, 1948), 96–97.

15. The *New York Clipper* baseball columnist regularly made references to Bellán's New York City connection when providing box scores of Cuban professional league games, alluding to Bellán's days as a player with the New York Mutuals and the Rose Hill club.

16. Most historians have accepted White's claim, although it has come under some scrutiny. Jerry Malloy, for one, raises the concern that no other primary documentary evidence validates White's 1938 account. Moreover, White did not make such a claim about the Cuban Giants speaking gibberish in his 1907 publication *Sol White's Official Base Ball Guide* (Philadelphia: Schlicter, 1907), reprinted by the University of Nebraska Press in 1995 with an introduction by Malloy. A historian of nineteenth-century baseball, Malloy does offer an alternative version of the team's genesis based on an October 1887 *New York Age* article. White is quoted in Alvin Harlow, "Unrecognized Stars," *Esquire,* September 1938, 75, 119–20. On the Cuban Giants formation and Sol White, see Malloy, "The Birth of the Cuban Giants: The Origins of Black Professional Baseball," *Nine* 2, no. 2 (Spring 1994): 236; and Malloy, "The Strange Career of Sol White, Black Baseball's First Historian," *Nine* 4, no. 2 (Spring 1996): 217–36.

17. The initial appearance in Cuba by an African American team occurred possibly as early as 1882. An 1886 *Trenton Times* article uncovered by baseball historian Jerry Malloy alludes to several Cuban trips led by S. K. Govern, who later managed the Cuban Giants in 1886. Although further verification of these trips has yet to be located, it is conceivable that the trip's impact was reflected in the team's name because members of the Govern-led contingent formed the

nucleus of the Cuban Giants team. Malloy, "Sol White and the Origins of African American Baseball," *Sol White's History of Colored Base Ball,* lx.

18. José Alvarez de la Vega, "Pompez Affectionately Remembers His Trip to Puerto Rico," *Puerto Rican Deportivo,* July-August 1947, 15 (translation mine). Some confusion exists about Pompez's birthplace, listed in secondary sources as Havana, Tampa, and Key West, Florida. In the 1947 interview, Pompez stated that he was born in Key West and grew up partly in Tampa and partly in Havana.

19. Strong booked games for the Cuban Stars in the early 1910s while they were in the East. Strong had a strained relationship with black baseball, however, owing to his role as a booking agent and owner of several independent clubs: the Bushwicks (white) and the Brooklyn Royal Giants (black).

20. Historians have discussed the 1935 race riot in a number of ways. Most agree that rumors that a young boy, Angelino Rivero, had been beaten while in police custody served as a spark. However, most studies elide the significance of the boy's ethnicity, Puerto Rican, and how a multi-ethnic group—African American, West Indian, and Puerto Rican—rallied in protest of alleged violence against one of their children. On Harlem's economic conditions and political mobilization, see Cheryl Greenberg, *"Or Does It Explode?": Black Harlem in the Great Depression* (New York: Oxford University Press, 1991).

21. Prior to Dutch Schultz's arrival, Pompez had helped introduce the numbers game in Harlem. An outlawed game of chance, the numbers game operated similar to a lottery, where participants select three numbers from 000 to 999. Players placed anywhere from a penny to many dollars in bets. The winning numbers were often pulled from published sources, such as the stock market or a ballplayer's batting average, and paid off at a 600:1 ratio. The numbers operators, contributing to its illegality, however, could manipulate the winning number. "Dewey Says Hines Influenced Police," *New York Times* August 18, 1938, p. 1. For a discussion of numbers running in urban contexts, see Victoria Wolcott, "The Culture of the Informal Economy: Numbers Runners in Inter-War Black Detroit," *Radical History Review* 69 (1997): 46–75. Pompez joined Schultz's outfit under duress; on Schultz's forceful takeover, see Watkins-Owens, *Blood Relations,* ch. 9, "The Underground Entrepreneur,"136–48. For more on Pompez's legal ordeal, see Appendix A in James Overmyer, *Queen of the Negro Leagues: Effa Manley and the Negro Leagues* (Lanham, Md.: Scarecrow Press, 1998), 272–79. On Gus Greenlee's involvement in Negro League Baseball and the policy racket, see Rob Ruck, *Sandlot Seasons: Sport in Black Pittsburgh* (Urbana: University of Illinois Press, 1993), especially ch. 5, "Gus Greenlee, Black Pittsburgh's 'Mr. Big.' "

22. A *New York Age* article declared: "Alexander Pompez of 409 Edgecombe avenue, owner of the New York Cubans basebal[l] team and lessee of Dyckman Oval, was reported indicted Monday on the testimony of alleged 'numbers' collectors as a 'banker' in the policy racket." "Alexander Pompez Beats Arrest in Mexico City," May 21, 1937, p. 1.

23. On Pompez's indictment, flight, and the Hines trial, see *Pittsburgh Courier,* "Harlem Numbers Banker Caught in 'Gun-Battle,' " April 3, 1937, pp. 1, 4, and "Pompez May Talk," November 6, 1937, pp. 1, 4. Also see *New York Times,* "Policy Racketeer Caught in Mexico," March 29, 1937, p. 1; "Extradition Fight

by Dewey Fugitive," and "Prisoner Says He Will Fight," March 30, 1937, p. 2; and "Dewey Says Hines Influenced Police," August 18, 1938, pp. 1, 12–13; "Pompez's Story at Trial," August 20, 1938, pp. 1, 7. Thanks to James Overmyer, Negro League historian, for sharing these important documents.

24. *New York Age,* April 2, 1938, p. 8.

25. Fernández remembered the period's dire conditions: "At that time, we lived in family-houses. One family would rent out two rooms, and another family would rent one room out because that was a really difficult time period. We paid three dollars a week rent. But the ballplayers were not the only ones who were earning very little money, those with the jobs here, many of them were only making seven or eight dollars a week." Fernández, interview by the author, New York, February 1995.

26. See Earl Lewis, *In Their Own Interest: Race, Class, and Power in Twentieth-Century Norfolk, VA* (Berkeley: University of California Press, 1994), 90–96.

27. Interview by the author with Piri Thomas, tape recording, New York, June 5, 1996. The author of numerous works, Thomas is best known for his provocative autobiography *Down These Mean Streets* (New York: Knopf, 1967).

28. Thomas, interview.

29. Everard Marius, interview by the author, tape recording, Harlem, N.Y., July 16, 1996.

30. Several African Americans who played in the Negro Leagues discussed friendships with Latino teammates in their autobiographies. See Monte Irvin with James A. Riley, *Nice Guys Finish First: The Autobiography of Monte Irvin* (New York: Carroll & Graf, 1996); and Hank Aaron with Lonnie Wheeler, *I Had a Hammer: The Hank Aaron Story* (New York: HarperCollins, 1991).

31. *New York Age,* June 22, 1935, p. 8.

32. *New York Age,* July 25, 1935, p. 8. Despite success during the Cuban Stars' initial season, another *Age* reporter, William E. Clark, expressed similar reservations two years later, contending that the team's failure to win a championship was rooted in the team's national composition. *New York Age,* August 7, 1937, p. 8.

33. Newspaper clipping, "Olmo a Puerto Rican," *The Sporting News* April 18, 1940, Luis Rodríguez Olmo Biographical File, NBLA. Olmo played four seasons with the Brooklyn Dodgers (1943–1945, 1949) and briefly with the Boston Braves after spending the 1946–1948 seasons in the Mexican League.

34. For autobiographical narratives about Puerto Rican migrations to New York City, see Cesar Andreau Iglesias, ed., *Memoirs of Bernardo Vega: A Contribution to the History of the Puerto Rican Community in New York* (New York: Monthly Review Press, 1984); and Jesus Colón (foreword by Juan Flores), *A Puerto Rican in New York and Other Sketches* (New York: International, 1982).

35. For analysis of Latino experience, see Daniel C. Frio and Marc Onigman, " 'Good Field, No Hit': The Image of Latin American Baseball Players in the American Press, 1876–1946," *Review/Review Interamericana* 9, no. 2 (September 1979): 199–208; and Samuel J. Regalado, *Viva Baseball!: Latin Major Leaguers and Their Special Hunger* (Urbana: University of Illinois Press, 1998).

36. On the role of racial masquerade in U.S. popular culture in the early twentieth century, see Michael Rogin, "Making America Home: Racial Masquerade and Ethnic Assimilation in the Transition to Talking Photos," *Journal of American History* 79 (December 1992): 1050–77.

37. The literature on the role of race in the structuring of national identity has grown significantly over the last decade and is too expansive to list here. I include several works here that reflect the tenor of these conversations. On Puerto Ricans, see Winston James, "Afro-Puerto Rican Radicalism in the United States: Reflections on the Political Trajectories of Arturo Schomburg and Jesus Colon," *CENTRO* 8, nos. 1 and 2 (Spring 1996): 92–127; Miriam Jimenez Róman, "*Un hombre (negro) del pueblo:* Jose Celso Barbosa and the Puerto Rican 'Race' Towards Whiteness," 8–29; and Roberto Rodríguez-Morazzani, "Beyond the Rainbow: Mapping the Discourse on Puerto Ricans and 'Race,' " 149–69. On Cubans, see Alejandro de la Fuente, "Race, National Discourse, and Politics in Cuba," *Latin American Perspectives* 25, no. 3 (May 1998): 43–69; Aline Helg, *Our Rightful Share: The Afro-Cuban Struggle for Equality, 1886–1912* (Chapel Hill: University of North Carolina Press, 1995); Nancy R. Mirabal, "Telling Silences and Making Community," in *Between Race and Empire,* 49–69; and Rebecca J. Scott, " 'The Lower Class of Whites' and the 'Negro Element': Race, Social Identity and Politics in Central Cuba, 1899–1909," in *La Nación Soñada: Cuba, Puerto Rico y Filipinas ante el 98* (Madrid: Doce Calles, 1996), 179–91. On Dominicans, see Jorge Duany, "Reconstructing Racial Identity: Ethnicity, Color, and Class Among Dominicans in the United States and Puerto Rico," *Latin American Perspectives* 25, no. 3 (May 1998): 147–72; and Lauren Derby, "Gringo Chicken with Worms: Food and Nationalism in the Dominican Republic," in *Close Encounters of Empire: Writing the Cultural History of U.S.-Latin American Relations* (Durham, N.C.: Duke University Press, 1998), 451–93.

38. Albertus "Cleffie" Fennar, interview by the author, tape recording, Daytona Beach, Fla., March 17, 1996.

39. Marius, interview.

40. *New York Age,* April 27, 1935, p. 5.

41. *New York Age,* October 16, 1937, p. 8.

42. *New York Age,* July 29, 1939, p. 8.

43. Dial quoted Frick from Powers's *Daily News* column. *New York Age,* August 1, 1936, p. 8.

44. "President of the Yankees Baseball Club Tells Mayor Has No Intentions of Signing Negro Players," *New York Age,* September 22, 1945, p. 1. As it would turn out, despite public pressure, the Yankees were be the last of the city's Major League teams to have a black ballplayer don its uniform.

45. *New York Age,* August 1, 1936, p. 8.

46. *New York Age,* February 25, 1939, p. 8.

CHAPTER THREE

Latino Caribbean Diasporas in New York

Ramón Grosfoguel and Chloé S. Georas

The 'Latino' category collapses the differences between and among colonial/ racial subjects, colonial immigrants, and immigrants in the U.S. empire. These distinctions have important implications for understanding the positive or negative reactions of dominant Euroamerican groups toward a particular Latino ethnicity. Colonial subjects have historically been the target of racist representations in the Euroamerican imaginary as a particular expression of the worldwide history of colonialism. For instance, Puerto Ricans constitute a colonial group of the U.S. empire that has been the target of many racist stereotypes. Because they also constitute the largest Latino population by ethnicity in New York City, their stereotypes have established a precedent with which new Latino immigrants must negotiate to the extent that they are frequently confused with Puerto Ricans in the hegemonic imaginary. This produces a contradictory relationship among different Latino groups. Many Colombians, Mexicans, Dominicans, Cubans, or Ecuadoreans in New York City make an effort to avoid being conflated under the rubric of Puerto Ricans for multiple and complex reasons. This is not merely a romantic attempt to mark out a distinct cultural identity. After all, to be taken for Puerto Ricans could be useful for illegal immigrants who want to take provisional cover under the former's guarantee of U.S. citizenship. This ethnic strategy of disentanglement has more to do with an effort to circumvent the racialized and stereotypical construction of Puerto Ricans. To be identified as Puerto Rican in the ethnic/racial hierarchy of New York City is a racist marker for a new Latino immigrant. The association of Puerto Rican identity in the Euroamerican imaginary with traits such as laziness, criminality, stupidity, and a tendency toward uncivilized behavior has important implications in the labor market, seriously affecting the new immigrants' opportunities.[1]

The main argument of this article is that the contemporary location of Latino migrants in New York City's racial/ethnic hierarchy needs to be understood in relation to the historical-structural dynamics of racialized colonial subjects of the U.S. empire.[2] New immigrants negotiate the labyrinth of racial otherness always in relation to the histories of racialization of the empire's colonial subjects. Some immigrants' identities fall under the umbrella of the colonial/racial subjects in the U.S. empire (colonial immigrants), whereas others are able to disentangle themselves from those histories, experiencing a more successful incorporation to the host society (immigrants). Those immigrant groups that cannot disassociate themselves from being identified or associated with the colonial/racial subjects of the empire become colonial immigrants despite never having been directly colonized by the United States. The notion of "coloniality of power" developed by Aníbal Quijano (1992) for the Latin American context can be very useful in understanding these contemporary racial dynamics in the United States. Coloniality of power addresses how social power relations today continue to be organized, constituted, and conditioned by the European/non-European axis built globally during centuries of Western colonial expansion. By using this concept, this article attempts to reconceptualize three social processes: 1) the construction of Puerto Ricans as a colonial racialized minority in the Euroamerican imaginary; 2) the transformation of Dominicans into colonial immigrants in the New York metropolitan area,[3] that is, how Dominicans became "Puerto Ricanized"; and 3) why the pre-1980s Cuban migrants were able to disassociate themselves from the "Puerto Ricanization" experienced by the Dominicans.

Puerto Ricans have migrated to New York since the turn of the century, but the largest migration occurred in the 1950s (Centro de Estudios Puertorriqueños 1979:186–87). The mass migration of Dominicans started more recently, after the U.S. invasion of the Dominican Republic in the mid-1960s (Grasmuck and Pessar 1991:20–21). Although Cubans have also migrated to the United States since the turn of the century, they came in larger numbers between 1960 and 1980 as anticommunist refugees (Boswell and Curtis 1984:40–42).

The class origin of the post-1950 Puerto Rican migration is similar to the pre-1960 African American migration to New York City. It has been predominantly from unskilled/rural labor extraction with low income and low educational levels (Friedlander 1965; Gray 1966; Osofsky 1966; Ottley and Weatherby 1967; Levine 1987; Grosfoguel 1995).[4] By contrast, the Dominicans who arrived between 1965 and 1985 were mainly from urban middle sectors of the working classes with higher skill levels than their native country's average workers (Bray 1984; Grasmuck and Pessar 1991).[5] However, despite these differences, both the Puerto Ricans and the Dominicans in New York City are at the bottom of the labor market, experiencing the worst economic conditions. Puerto Ricans and Dominicans have the highest unemployment rates (13.5 percent and 16.5 percent, respectively), the lowest labor force participation rates (58.6 percent and 63.6 percent), and the highest poverty rates (38.3 percent and 32.4 percent) in the New York metropolitan area (Grasmuck and Grosfoguel 1997). The Cubans who arrived in the New York metropolitan area between 1960 and 1980 also came from skilled urban middle sectors (Cronin 1981; Boswell and Curtis 1984:49), but unlike the Dominicans, they were able to improve their socioeconomic situation. The relevant questions are: Given the higher socioeconomic background of the Dominicans relative to the Puerto Ricans, why did the former end up in a similar structural position to the latter in New York's labor market? Given the similar class origins of the Dominicans and the pre-1980s Cuban migrants in New York, why did the situation of the former deteriorate and that of the latter improve? This article discusses the diverse experiences of Latino Caribbean migrants in New York City to understand their present location in the racial/ethnic hierarchy of the city. Issues of coloniality, language, and identity are crucial to understanding these multiple forms of incorporation.

SYMBOLIC CAPITAL AND GLOBAL COLONIALITY

In the symbolic field of New York City's racial/ethnic hierarchy, ethnicities are invested with different social value. Symbolic capital (Bourdieu 1977), that is, a capital of prestige and honor, varies for each group contingent upon its historical positioning in the racial/ethnic hierarchy of the city. Groups at the top of this hierarchy enjoy a high or positive symbolic capital, that is, social prestige. Prestige is frequently translated into greater economic opportunities and access to economic capital. Groups at the bottom of the racial/ethnic hierarchy have a low or negative symbolic capital, that is, no prestige, and their identities are usually tied to a negative public image. These groups suffer discrimination in the labor market and thus encounter barriers to economic opportunities.

Here identities will be treated as relational, that is, as relations of differences with other groups' identities, and embedded in multiple structural levels (global, state, local). Group identities are shaped through social relations with other groups in a symbolic field of dominant and subordinate groups. Social identities are relationally constructed and reproduced in a complex and entangled political, economic, and symbolic hierarchy that produces an unequal accumulation of symbolic, political, and economic capital for different economic classes, races/ethnicities, genders, and other socially classified groups. The dominant groups of the symbolic, economic, and political fields are the ones with the power to hegemonize the social classifications of a society. This power of classification is in turn related to the colonial history of the United States.

W.E.B. Du Bois was one of the first intellectuals in the United States to conceptualize the subordination of racialized subjects within the core of the capitalist world economy as part of colonial relations. As he said in 1945:

> We must conceive of colonies in the nineteenth and twentieth centuries as not something far away from the centers of civilization; not as comprehending problems which are not our problems—the local problems of London, Paris and New York. They are not something which we can consider at our leisure but rather a part of our own present local economic organization. Moreover, while the center of the colonial system (and its form and pattern) is set in the localities which are called definitely colonies and are owned politically and industrially by imperial countries, we must remember also that in the organized and dominant states there are groups of people who occupy a quasi-colonial status: laborers who are settled in slums of large cities; groups like Negroes in the United States who are segregated physically and discriminated against spiritually in law and custom; groups like the South American Indians who are the laboring peons, without rights or privileges, of large countries; and whole laboring classes in Asia and the South Seas who are legally part of imperial countries and, as a matter of fact, have their labor treated as a commodity at the lowest wage, and the land monopolized. All these people occupy what is really a colonial status and make the kernel and substance of the problem of minorities. (1970:183–84)

For Du Bois, racialization and colonization are entangled processes. Racial discrimination interrelates with colonial processes of using the labor force of domestic groups such as blacks in the United States as a "commodity at the lowest wage." Du Bois's conceptualization of the colonial status that minorities occupy in the centers of empire relates to the late-1960s concept of internal colonialism. Robert Blauner's (1972) approach to this concept provided a framework for understanding the different forms of incorporation of diverse ethnic/racial groups within the United States. Blauner makes an important analytical distinction between immigrants and internal colonial groups. Those groups that were incorporated into the United States as part of an experience of immigration had a more privileged form of incorporation than those that were incorporated through violence as part of an imperial/colonial expansion. European groups of different ethnicities formed part of the immigrant experience, whereas people of color experienced colonization.

Blauner uses this analytical distinction to deconstruct the so-called immigrant analogy. The foundational myth of the nation, the American Dream, portrayed the United States as the land of opportunities to which immigrant groups of all social and racial origins had equal access. In this myth, all immigrant groups experienced difficulties in the first generation, but after a few generations they were able to become socially mobile. According to Blauner, this myth cannot explain the colonial experience of racialized groups in the United States. An important distinction has to be made between immigrant labor and colonial labor, above all as regards the forms of labor. Immigrant labor was incorporated as wage labor, whereas colonized groups suffered coerced forms of labor.

Although this conceptualization is historically accurate, it is not useful for understanding the post-1965 period. Once the old colonial forms of coerced labor disappeared and the 1964 Civil Rights Amendment was passed, it was conceptually difficult to sustain an internal colonialism approach when examining the experience of the new, post-1965 immigrants and domestic minorities. One of the limitations of internal colonialism as a concept lies in its reduction of colonial relations to the presence of a colonial administration or colonial methods of labor control. Colonialism is understood as consisting of extra-economic mechanisms or institutions, such as a colonial administration or colonial methods of labor coercion. Therefore, many scholars (including Blauner himself) abandoned the internal colonialism approach altogether for the so-called postcolonial period. However, to think of the post-1965 period as a complete, discontinuous break with the past is inaccurate. Although the racial/ethnic hierarchy has changed with the ascension of some groups, previously classified at the bottom, to intermediary positions (Koreans, Jamaicans, or Cubans), there are still important continuities with the colonial past given that Euroamericans remain at the top of the hierarchy and people of color remain at the bottom. How can we think about the continuities of the colonial past while acknowledging the discontinuities? How can we reconceptualize the notion of internal colonialism in a way that accounts for the post-1965 transformations/complexities of the race/ethnic hierarchy of the United States?

One limitation of recent approaches to racial dynamics is that racial categories are dehistorized or disconnected from the colonial histories of the United States. For example, the racial formation approach developed by Omi and Winant (1986), although important for understanding the shifting meanings of race across time and crucial for a nonreductivist approach to race, still underestimates the historical continuities between colonial and postcolonial times. Their conceptualization is useful for understanding the discontinuities but limited when addressing the historical continuities.

We can conceptualize colonial continuities in the present by transcending the limitations of the internal colonialism approach and moving toward an approach that accounts for a noneconomistic analysis and noncoerced forms of reproduction of a disenfranchised colonial labor force. The recent postcolonial literature has tried to address this issue in the field of literary criticism and cultural studies. However, the *post* in the term *"postcolonial"* itself implies a temporality that undermines the initial intention of conceptualizing colonial continuities in the present (McClintock 1992; Shohat 1992). There is no *post* in colonial/racial hierarchies in the world today. There are cultural and political processes that reproduce a colonial situation without the presence of a colonial administration or colonial laws to visibly enforce a colonial subordination. Peruvian sociologist Aníbal Quijano (1991, 1992) develops a new conceptualization to understand the historical continuities of the racial/ethnic hierarchies in Latin American from the colonial past to the present. Quijano conceptualizes the emergence of an international division of labor at a global scale simultaneously with the emergence of a global racial/ethnic hierarchy as a result of the European colonial expansion in the sixteenth century. There is no *pre* or *post* to the formation of both hierarchies in the capitalist world system. Racist culture is not instrumental to capitalist accumulation but is rather an integral and inherent feature of historical capitalism (Wallerstein 1983).

According to Quijano's concept of the coloniality of power, after independence, when the formal juridical/military control of the state passed from the imperial centers to the newly independent countries, white elites still controlled the social and political structures of Latin American societies, marking a continuity of colonial domination over indigenous and black populations now within the newly emergent nation-states. Coloniality of power names the continuities in the so-called postcolonial era of the social hierarchical relationships of exploitation and domination between Europeans and non-Europeans built during centuries of European colonial expansion and based on cultural and social power relations. Thus, *coloniality,* as opposed to *colonialism,* names the contemporary processes of colonial/racial domination of a racialized/ethnic group by a dominant group without the existence of colonial administrations.

The importance of the concept of coloniality of power for the study of race is that it provides a framework to understand why the present racial/ethnic hierarchy of the capitalist world system is still "constituted on [cultural] criteria originated in colonial relations" (Quijano 1992:167). The coloniality of power historicizes and explains why today certain groups are at the bottom of the hierarchy while others remain at the top. To focus only on color alone is limited, and those who do risk falling into the trap of color reification. Although diverse colonized groups may be phenotypically indistinguishable from dominant groups, they can nevertheless be racialized as inferior others in a colonial situation. The Irish in the British empire are a good example of how racialization is not directly linked to skin color but to a location within a colonial relation. As will be discussed later, the same process occurs with "white" Puerto Ricans in the United States. This is why we prefer to use the category 'colonial/racial subjects of empire' rather than simply 'racial subjects'. Racial categories are built in relation to colonial histories of empire. They must be looked at together. Thus, the shifting meanings and structures that Omi and Winant (1986) conceptualize as a "racial formation" we prefer to call a "colonial/racial formation." Shifting meanings about race have a historical continuity that can only be understood in relation to the colonial legacies of empire.

If the concept of coloniality of power is stretched beyond the nation-state to a global scale, we can speak of a global coloniality (Georas 1997). Despite the eradication of the juridical-political institutions of colonialism, global coloniality names the continuities of colonial practices and imaginations across time and space at a global level in a so-called postcolonial period. This can explain why an immigrant group from a sending society that was not a colony of the metropole to which they migrated can enter the labyrinth of colonial constructions of identity. For example, Turkish immigrants in Germany suffer the oppression of a German racist/colonial culture that originates in the European colonial expansion without Turkey ever having been a German colony. Thus, Turks in Germany are, in our conceptualization, colonial immigrants.

The global coloniality of power from colonial to postcolonial times helps us understand the ongoing power of the white male elites to classify populations and exclude people of color from the categories of citizenship and in the imagined community called the nation. The civil, political, and social rights that citizenship provided to members of the nation were selectively expanded over time to white working classes and white middle-class women. However, internal colonial groups remained second-class citizens, never having full access to the rights of citizens and to the imaginary community called the nation (Gilroy 1987). The coloniality of power is constitutive of the metropolitan nation-states' narratives of the nation. Who belongs and does not belong to the nation is informed by historical power relations between Europeans and non-Europeans. The persistence of a colonial culture informs and constitutes social power today.

The central aspect of the concept of coloniality of power is that it allows us to understand the interface between racist/colonial cultures and social power relations with a long colonial history in the capitalist world system. It shows how social power today is still informed by cultural criteria built over a long colonial history. Yet it is important to highlight that coloniality is not a homogeneous but rather a heterogeneous process. There are multiple forms of colonialities according to the different colonial legacies and the diverse histories of colonial empires. Although colonial subjects of an empire have a longer history of racialization than some recent immigrants, this does not mean that the latter are immune to the racial categorization applied to the former. There are immigrant experiences that can only be understood in relation to the coloniality of power of the host society (colonial immigrants), whereas other immigrants were able to escape certain forms of coloniality (immigrants) owing to their skin color, class origins, and/or the state's policies.

In the United States, the social classification of peoples has been hegemonized by male elites of European descent (so-called whites) throughout a long historical process of colonial/racial domination over Native Americans, Africans, and other non-European subjects. This reflects how the categories of modernity such as citizenship, democracy, and national identity have been historically constructed through three axial divisions: 1) between labor and capital; 2) between Europeans and non-Europeans (Quijano 1991); and, we add, 3) between male and female. White male elites hegemonized these axial divisions. In the United States, this coloniality of power is constitutive of the symbolic racial/ethnic hierarchies. Euroamerican elites have historically deployed their symbolic capital, that is, the power of social prestige, to classify, racialize, and subordinate colonial subjects.

Global cities are today the new contact zones of colonial encounters. According to Mary L. Pratt, contact zone refers to "the space of colonial encounters, the space in which peoples geographically and historically separated come into contact with each other and establish ongoing relations, usually involving conditions of coercion, radical inequality, and intractable conflict" (1992:6).

Although Pratt uses the notion of contact zones to talk about the space of colonial encounters during the European colonial expansion, it can be a useful concept to use in contemporary global cities today. What is common to Puerto Ricans and African Americans is their respective long historical relationships as colonial/racial subjects within the U.S. empire and their subordinated location in the reproduction of those hierarchies today. Global cities today are "microcosms of empire" (Georas 1997:33) that reproduce within their spaces the racial/ethnic hierarchies of the old colonial empires. The symbolic capital (negative or positive) attached to the identity of different groups in the racial/ethnic hierarchy of a global city is related to the ongoing coloniality of power despite the formal elimination of colonialism as a political system in the late twentieth century.

AFRICAN AMERICANS AND PUERTO RICANS AS COLONIAL/RACIAL SUBJECTS

In the United States, the word *ethnic* has historically referred to cultural differences among white European groups (e.g., Italian, Irish, German), whereas racial categories have been used to refer to people of color (e.g., black, Asian, Hispanic), thus erasing ethnic differences within these racially classified groups. Categories such as Latino or Hispanic, although politically useful for certain struggles, mix together diverse ethnic groups with heterogeneous experiences that cannot be subsumed under a single label. However, since the 1960s, *ethnic* in the United States has become a code word for "race." *Ethnic* refers to those racialized groups excluded from the imagined community of white America. This shift in the dominant discourses on race occurred as a response to the 1960s Civil Rights movement. Rather than characterizing groups along racial lines, *ethnic* was coined as the new term. This emerging dominant discourse was elaborated by Nathan Glazer and Daniel P. Moynihan (1963) in their now classic *Beyond the Melting Pot: The Negroes, Puerto Ricans, Jews, Italians, and Irish of New York City.* In it, the experience of people of color in the United States is equated to that of the white immigrants from Europe at the beginning of the twentieth century. By transmuting racial discrimination into ethnic discrimination, Puerto Ricans and African Americans can go through the same experiences as any other ethnic group and eventually be economically, socially, and politically incorporated as were the white European migrants before. Consequently, poverty and marginalization are due to a cultural problem within the ethnic community rather than a structural problem of discrimination by Euroamerican dominant groups. This approach obliterates the history of racial/colonial oppression experienced by African Americans and Puerto Ricans: the former's long colonial history of slavery and political/racial barriers to upward mobility and the latter's colonial regime that expropriated the land and incorporated the people as cheap labor in sugar plantations first and later in manufacturing in Puerto Rico and the United States. Puerto Ricans and African Americans are not simply migrants or ethnic groups but rather colonial/racialized subjects in the United States. Both are formally citizens but without being able to exercise their full rights owing to the history of racial/colonial oppression. Even if the formal colonial barriers to social mobility have disappeared, African Americans and Puerto Ricans still encounter the old racial/colonial stereotypes as barriers to equality and social mobility in a contact zone of colonial encounter such as New York City.

Although there have been Puerto Ricans and African Americans in New York City since the nineteenth century, their mass migration did not occur until the early 1900s, when European migration was restricted and labor shortages increased due to World War I (Ottley and Weatherby 1967). As part of the war efforts, African Americans and Puerto Ricans were recruited in manufacturing industries and low-wage services in New York City (Ottley and Weatherby 1967; Centro de Estudios Puertorriqueños 1979; Sánchez-Korrol 1983). Labor agents, aided by the U.S. Labor Department, directly recruited blacks from the South and Puerto Ricans from the island. New York City became one of their main destinations.

The 1924 Immigration Act that restricted European migration to the United States further accelerated the massive migration of these internal colonial subjects to New York City. As the white workers became upwardly mobile with their increased skills and job opportunities in higher-wage industries, the low-wage manufacturing jobs in the garment and apparel industries became an undesirable economic sector identified with racialized minorities. During the 1920s and 1930s, African Americans became the main source of cheap labor in New York City's manufacturing sector and low-wage services. Puerto Ricans were the second largest group, with approximately 30,000 newcomers in the 1920s. The racialization of these colonial subjects was reflected in the low pay they received in the garment industry sweatshops relative to whites of different ethnicities. As early as 1929, Puerto Ricans and African Americans earned $8 to $13 per week, whereas Jews and Italians earned $26 to $44 per week (Laurentz 1980:90, 104). As Du Bois would say, the colonial status of these groups is related to having "their labor treated as a commodity at the lowest wage."

The racialization of the Puerto Ricans as inferior others in New York City was entangled with the racialization of the African Americans. Puerto Ricans settled initially close to African American communities such as Harlem (Sánchez-Korrol 1983). Given the large numbers of mulattos, blacks, and mestizos among the Puerto Rican migrants, many were initially confused in the white social imaginary with African Americans. The social construction of racial categories in the United States, where one drop of black blood is enough to be classified as black, was a fertile ground for the initial classification of Puerto Ricans as African Americans. The following account is typical of many pre-1950 Puerto Rican migrants in New York:

> When I came to New York everything was rationed, sugar, rice, everything. So my *mamá* sent me to get a ration card. My cousin Gino, the one who had written suggesting I come here, went with me. He spoke the language much better than I, so he did all the talking. I noticed the girl there was writing down everything in a questionnaire. She asked my nationality and my cousin answered "Puerto Rican," but she wrote down "Negro." My cousin protested, "No, no, no, not Negro, Puerto Rican." She gave him a look but she erased "Negro" and wrote down "Puerto Rican." It was my first experience of that kind up here.
> (narrated by Soledad, as quoted by Lewis 1966:227)

The history of Puerto Ricans in New York City is in many ways intertwined with that of the African American community. Puerto Ricans were African Americanized in New York City, the new contact zone of colonial encounter. But the social construction of Puerto Ricans as inferior others in the Euroamerican social imaginary is something that goes back to the colonial incorporation of the island as a result of the 1898 U.S. invasion. There was an autonomous construction of Puerto Ricans as inferior subjects dating from the beginning of the twentieth century that was later mobilized against Puerto Rican migrants in the metropole (Thompson 1995). However, as will be discussed later, it was after 1950 that the distinct racialization of the Puerto Ricans in New York City acquired a more pronounced form.

The African American mass migration to New York City diminished after 1950. However, this was not the case for the Puerto Ricans. After World War II, Puerto Rican migrants were incorporated in larger numbers to New York's labor market. Why were Puerto Ricans massively recruited in the 1950s rather than Chicanos, African Americans, Dominicans, Cubans, or Jamaicans? Capitalist accumulation can explain the labor demand of the metropole but not which ethnic group would be massively recruited. To answer this question, we must understand the ideological/symbolic global strategies of the United States during the Cold War.

As part of a long negotiation process between the Truman administration and Muñoz's colonial government during the late 1940s, the international training ground for the Point Four Program was located in San Juan (Grosfoguel 1992). The idea was to make Puerto Rico a symbolic showcase of the U.S. capitalist model of development for the Third World. Puerto Rico became part of the core state's strategy to gain symbolic capital vis-à-vis the Soviet Union. Between 1950 and 1970 more than 30,000 members of the Third World elites visited the island and stayed from six months to two years as part of the Point Four Program. The purpose of this program was to sell the Puerto Rican model of development to the Third World elites who would, in turn, sell it to their fellow citizens. The condition of possibility for the success of showcasing Puerto Rico was to encourage the migration of the poorest sectors of the island, many of them mulattos, to the urban centers of the United States.

After World War II there was a great demand for cheap labor in manufacturing industries in urban centers such as New York, Chicago, and Philadelphia. However, to understand why Puerto Ricans rather than Jamaicans or Chicanos were recruited, we must understand the global ideological/symbolic strategies of the United States and Puerto Rico's concomitant role. The elimination of the lower strata of the island made possible the upward mobility of those who remained, making possible the formation of a symbolic showcase. The Truman administration provided one of the most important institutional mechanisms promoting the flight of young men and women "who wish to go to the mainland": a reduction of the airfares between the island and the mainland. This policy paved the way for the first mass airway migration in world history. Approximately 600,000 Puerto Ricans, mostly rural unskilled workers, migrated to the mainland in twenty years. Because the Puerto Rican showcase was the island rather than the migrants, the United States channeled its resources to the island. Those who migrated ended up in the urban ghettos of a metropole with one of the highest poverty rates.

Unable to place Puerto Ricans in a fixed racial category (white or black) owing to the mixed racial composition of the community, Euroamericans increasingly perceived them as a racialized other. Puerto Ricans became a new racialized subject, different from whites and blacks, sharing with the latter a subordinate position to the former. The film *West Side Story* probably marked a turning point where Puerto Ricans truly became a distinct racialized minority, no longer to be confused with blacks or Chicanos in the Euroamerican social imaginary (Pérez 1997; Sandoval-Sánchez 1997). As was discussed earlier, this racialization was the result of a long historical process of colonial/racial subordination in the island and the mainland (Thompson 1995; Vázquez 1991). The racism experienced by Afro–Puerto Ricans in many instances can be stronger than that experienced by lighter-skinned Puerto Ricans. However, no matter how blonde or blue-eyed people may be or whether they can otherwise pass as white, the moment they identify themselves as Puerto Rican, they enter the labyrinth of racial otherness. Puerto Ricans of all colors have become a racialized group in the social imaginary of Euroamericans, a group whose racist stereotypes include such traits as laziness, violence, criminal behavior, stupidity, and dirtiness. Although Puerto Ricans form a phenotypically variable group, they have become a new race in the United States. This highlights the social rather than biological character of racial classifications. The deprecative classification of Puerto Ricans as "spics" in the symbolic field of New York designates the negative symbolic capital attached to this identity.

In New York's racial/ethnic division of labor, Puerto Ricans occupied the economic niche of low-wage manufacturing jobs. By 1960, more than 50 percent of Puerto Ricans in New York were incorporated as low-wage labor in this sector (Grasmuck and Grosfoguel 1997). During the 1960s, Puerto Ricans' successful struggles for labor rights made them too expensive for the increasingly informalized manufacturing sector. Simultaneously, the deindustrialization of New York led to the loss of thousands of manufacturing jobs. Most of the manufacturing industries moved to peripheral regions around the world, while those that stayed in New York informalized their activities. The manufacturing industry, in constant need of cheap labor, relied heavily on new Latino immigrants, legal or illegal, who had even fewer rights than internal colonial subjects such as Puerto Ricans. The expulsion of Puerto Ricans from manufacturing jobs and the racialized, segregated educational system that excluded Puerto Ricans from the best public schools produced a redundant labor force that could not reenter the formal labor market. This led to the formation of what some have called the Puerto Rican underclass, which we prefer to call a colonial/racialized labor force. Unable to find jobs, many Puerto Ricans developed strategies, legal or illegal, to survive the crisis. Currently, only 14 percent of Puerto Ricans are in manufacturing, and more than 50 percent are either unemployed or out of the labor force (Grasmuck and Grosfoguel 1997).

THE "PUERTO RICANIZATION" OF DOMINICANS IN NEW YORK

There was hardly any Dominican migration to the United States during the Trujillo dictatorship. Only after the 1961 U.S.-backed military coup against Trujillo did emigration take off. The migration process was politically induced by the political elites of the United States and the Dominican Republic as a safety valve against social unrest and political instability. Several studies on Dominican migration have mentioned this geopolitical strategy designed to perpetuate a stable pro-U.S. government (Báez-Everszt and D'Oleo Ramírez 1986:19; Mitchell 1992:89–123; Grasmuck and Pessar 1992:31–33). U.S. foreign policy toward the Caribbean concentrated on avoiding another Castro-style regime. U.S. military forces invaded the Dominican Republic to defeat the constitutionalists' forces in 1965 as part of this containment strategy. The amount of migration increased after this military intervention. From 1961 to 1965, 35,372 Dominicans were legally admitted to the United States. During the 1966–1970 postinvasion period, the amount of legally admitted Dominicans increased to 58,744 (Grasmuck and Pessar 1992:20). Most of the migrants came from urban middle sectors, and some of them were politically active against the regime.

The admittance to the United States of people who could represent a political threat was a mechanism to guarantee political stability in the Dominican Republic. This coincided with the Immigration Act of 1965, which facilitated skilled-labor immigration to the United States. Compared with other countries in the Western Hemisphere, the Dominican Republic (with a total population of less than five million people) has one of the highest rates of legal immigration to the United States. There was no deliberate legislation but rather a policy of active permissiveness and encouragement of Dominican entry to the United States. Other than this policy of actively fostering Dominican migration to guarantee political stability, no policies addressed the incorporation of Dominican immigrants to the United States. The geopolitical interest of fostering migration to achieve security in the Dominican Republic did not translate into a policy of active incorporation. Instead, Dominican immigrants were left to fend for themselves.

Dominicans in the New York metropolitan area initially settled in Puerto Rican communities located in the Lower East Side, the South Bronx, and Brooklyn (Hendricks 1974; Guarnizo 1992; Grasmuck and Pessar 1991). They relied on Puerto Rican social networks to find jobs, to acquire information about services in the city, and to avoid *la migra* by assuming a Puerto Rican identity (Hendricks 1974; Guarnizo 1992). Like Puerto Ricans,

Dominicans were racially mixed, but probably more of them were of African descent. Moreover, most of the Dominicans could not speak English. Their accents when speaking English were not significantly different from that of Puerto Ricans speaking English. The often-quoted phrase "they all look alike" had a lot to do with the fact that they all sounded alike. Thus, Dominicans remained indistinguishable from Puerto Ricans in the Euroamerican social imaginary. Even Dominicans who made an effort to distinguish themselves from Puerto Ricans to avoid being associated with their negative symbolic capital were unsuccessful. As José X, a Dominican informant, said: "In New York City if you are not White nor Black then you belong to a third racial category called 'Puerto Rican.' I am constantly telling White Americans that I am Dominican not Puerto Rican but they seem not to get it" (X 1997). In many instances, whites could not distinguish them from the supposed Puerto Rican race. Dominicans were subsumed under the categories of the coloniality of power directed at Puerto Ricans. Thus, even though Dominicans came predominantly from an urban middle-sector class/educational background, that is, a higher class background than the majority of Puerto Ricans, it was not an accident that Dominicans came to occupy the same economic niche as the Puerto Ricans in the racial/ethnic division of labor of New York City. They became colonial immigrants because their process of incorporation was closer to the experience of the colonial/racial subjects of the empire that preceded their arrival.

As racialized noncitizens, Dominicans were an even cheaper source of labor than Puerto Ricans. Dominicans replaced the so-called expensive Puerto Rican labor force in the manufacturing sector (Grasmuck and Grosfoguel 1997). Many Dominicans worked in New York City's sweatshops, not even earning the federal minimum wage. Moreover, the illegal status of many Dominicans provided a disenfranchised labor force for the U.S. low-wage manufacturing industry. Illegality has provided a new mechanism to produce a colonial status among immigrant populations. The coloniality of power of the city, where social power is still in the hands of whites, facilitated the transformation of Dominican labor into a new colonial/racial group within New York City. They became colonial immigrants.

By 1980, Dominicans had formed their own ethnic community in Washington Heights. They started to be identified by many Euroamericans as a racialized other distinct from Puerto Ricans. However, the Puerto Ricanization of the Dominican migrants in New York City's racial/ethnic division of labor was an accomplished fact by then. The social construction of Dominican identity in the Euroamerican social imaginary was associated with similar stereotypical traits toward those colonial/racial subjects within the city such as laziness and criminality. By 1980, around 50 percent of the Dominican labor force in New York City worked as cheap labor in manufacturing.

During the 1980s, Dominicans experienced the largest migration flow to New York City. However, the deindustrialization of New York accelerated during these years. Many Dominicans either lost their jobs or were replaced by even cheaper sources of labor such as Ecuadorean, Mexican, and Chinese immigrants. This displacement, plus the large numbers of new Dominican immigrants entering the labor force and unable to find jobs in their traditional economic niche, formed a massive, racialized, redundant labor force. The labor market marginality of the Dominican community reached similar proportions to those of Puerto Ricans. The Dominican community has experienced the same processes that the Puerto Rican community has experienced but in a compressed length of time (Grasmuck and Grosfoguel 1997). As colonial immigrants they lived a similar experience to the colonial/racial subjects of the U.S. empire.

CUBAN MIGRATION

Most of the Cuban migrants in the New York metropolitan area arrived between 1960 and 1980 and settled in Union City, New Jersey. Many Cubans came to New York by way of the Havana-Miami "freedom flights" between 1965 and 1973. These Cubans were part of an urban skilled labor migration (Prieto 1984:7). Similar to the Dominican experience in New York City, Cubans were also confused with Puerto Ricans. Given the similar class/educational/Latino origin of Cuban and Dominican migration, how did Cubans avoid ending up at the bottom of the labor market with the Puerto Ricans? First, most of the Cuban refugees before 1980 were considered white (Pedraza-Bailey 1985a:23). However, being phenotypically white does not necessarily preclude racialization in the Euroamerican social imaginary. As the Dominican example illustrates, association with Puerto Ricans is a racializing factor irrespective of a person's color. Ethnic social practices and a Puerto Rican accent can also color a person. The pre-1980s Cuban migrants managed to escape the negative symbolic capital of Puerto Rican racialization through the billion-plus dollars they received from the U.S. government's Cuban Refugee Program.[6] Every city where Cubans settled received millions of dollars in government assistance to cover expenses in education, welfare, hospitals, and other public services for the refugees. This made them radically different from Puerto Ricans. Every local government perceived Cuban settlement as a financial gain for a city rather than a burden, whitening the perception of their difference in the imaginary of white America. As a Puerto Rican informant from East Harlem said, "The federal government dipped the Cuban refugees in Clorox." They became whitened in the Euroamerican imaginary. Therefore, Cubans escaped the symbolic subordination of the coloniality of power experienced by the colonial/racial subjects of the empire. The media as well as the government represented Cubans as a model minority that had managed to lift themselves by their bootstraps (Pedraza-Bailey 1985b).

The development of a positive symbolic capital for the Cubans was part of a global strategy of the United States during the Cold War. The United States made Cuban refugees a symbol of the superiority of capitalism over socialism in its efforts to influence the population in Cuba. The Cuban success story in the United States was a symbolic tour de force for the U.S. government vis-à-vis the Soviet model of Cuba (Grosfoguel 1994). Thus, the federal services that Cubans received were superior to those available for citizens or residents of the United States and, for that matter, other immigrants at the time (Dominguez 1992:31). Cubans were the only ethnic group in the United States that received European-style welfare. Welfare in Europe includes a national system of free health care, education, job training, job placement, etc.; Cubans received free bilingual training, educational assistance, health care, legal recognition of their professional degrees from Cuba, job training, assistance to seek jobs, unemployment benefits, and many other services through the Cuban Refugee Program. This massive assistance increased after 1965 when President Johnson created a task force that included the Departments of State, Labor, Agriculture, Commerce, Housing and Urban Development; the Office of Economic Opportunity; and the Small Business Administration (SBA) to coordinate federal assistance to avoid burdening local communities where these refugees were or resettled (see Johnson 1966). In addition to their role as a showcase of capitalism, Cubans were used as a model minority against the Civil Rights movement of the internal colonial/racial minorities during the 1960s. In Miami as well as in Union City, New Jersey, and New York City, cities with a large concentration of Cubans, the SBA practiced institutional racist policies against Puerto Ricans and African Americans while disproportionately favoring the Cubans in the provision of loan programs. For example, in Miami the SBA gave Cubans 66 percent of its total loans between 1968 and 1979, compared with only 8 percent given to African Americans (Grosfoguel 1994:358–59). Similarly, successful entrepreneurship among the Cubans in Union City can be correlated to assistance from the SBA. A survey done with over 120 Cuban-owned firms in Union City found that 73 percent had acquired their initial capital through the SBA's direct or guaranteed bank loans (Cronin 1981). Approximately 80 percent of the total initial capitalization of the 120 Cuban-owned firms consisted of SBA direct and guaranteed bank loans. This study found that the SBA in New Jersey and New York City favored Cubans over Puerto Ricans in their loan programs even though around 70 percent of the Cuban entrepreneurs had completed only eight years or less of formal education and came from class origins similar to those of Puerto Ricans. The study raises the following question: If current Union City Cuban small-business owners share a similar educational and economic profile to Puerto Ricans in the metropolitan area, why have

Puerto Ricans not experienced the same entrepreneurial success? This study found that when Puerto Ricans called the SBA offices in New Jersey and New York City, 75 percent and 80 percent of the callers, respectively, were given the wrong information or the runaround. When Cubans called the same SBA offices, 84 percent of the callers in New Jersey and 70 percent in New York received the correct information. The study concluded that there was a broad institutional discriminatory policy favoring Cuban refugees and excluding Puerto Ricans. Cubans (approximately 700,000 people by 1975) received approximately $1.3 billion in federal assistance between 1961 and 1974 (only fifteen years), close to half of the total foreign aid of the United States to Brazil (a country of more than 100 million people) between 1945 and 1983 (thirty-eight years) (Grosfoguel 1994:359). This privileged treatment of Cubans was due to the geopolitical symbolic strategies of the Cold War. As Pedraza-Bailey states:

> While the Cuban state utilized the exodus to externalize dissent, on our shores the question remains: Why should the United States so eagerly receive the exiles? Because in America during the Cold War years, all the political migrations—the Hungarians, Koreans, Berliners, and Cubans—served a symbolic function. When West and East contested the superiority of their political and economic system, the political exiles who succeeded in the flight to freedom became touching symbols around which to weave the legitimacy needed for foreign policy. (1985b:154)

This global symbolic strategy translated into economic resources for the Cuban refugees, increasing their ethnic symbolic capital. The most dramatic representation of how Cuban identity was associated with positive symbolic capital was the humorous 1969 movie *Popi,* in which a Puerto Rican from a New York City ghetto with three jobs decided that the only way he could give his sons a better life was to turn them into Cuban refugees arriving in Miami. He trained his sons to be Cuban and put them off the coast of South Florida to pass them off as refugees. After their "rescue" by the Coast Guard, they received all the benefits for Cuban refugees. This sadly hilarious film documents the positive symbolic capital associated with Cuban identity and its relation to state resources.

During the 1980s, thousands of Cuban refugees from the Mariel migration went to New York City from Miami. These migrants were from a more popular class background than the pre-1980s Cuban migrants. Moreover, a large number of the marielitos were Afro-Cubans. Given the phaseout of the Cuban Refugee Program in the late 1970s, these migrants did not have access to state assistance and in turn were not cushioned against racial discrimination. As a result, the marielitos were Puerto Ricanized in New York City and "African Americanized" in Miami. They suffered a marginalization in the labor market similar to that of Puerto Ricans and Dominicans in New York City. They became part of the colonial immigrants living a social process similar to the colonial/racial subjects of the U.S. empire.

CONCLUSION

The coloniality of power, global state ideological and symbolic strategies. and the racial/ethnic symbolic field of New York City are all crucial determinants to understanding the differences among Latino Caribbean migrants. An important distinction for Latino Caribbean migrants is whether they are colonial/racial subjects, colonial immigrants, or immigrants. Immigrants do not enter a neutral space when they migrate. In the U.S. case, a racial/ethnic hierarchy with a long colonial history precedes the immigrants' arrival. Colonial migrants have a longer history of racialization in the white imaginary of the metropolitan populations owing to their colonial history within the U.S. empire. Some immigrants enter the labyrinth of the colonial/racial subjects (colonial immigrants), whereas others escape this subordination, having a more successful sociopolitical and labor market incorporation (immigrants). The coloniality of power experienced by the Puerto Ricans affected the incorporation of migrants from Caribbean nation-states that were perceived by the dominant Euroamerican populations as culturally similar to these colonial/racial subjects. This was the case for Dominicans who were adversely affected through their association with a Puerto Rican racial/ethnic identity in the Euroamerican imaginary. Dominicans entered the Puerto Rican social networks, sharing their same destiny in the New York racial/ethnic hierarchy. They became incorporated as colonial immigrants living a similar experience to the racial/colonial subjects of the empire. As was discussed earlier, language was a crucial factor constraining the Dominicans' possibilities for building an identity separate from that of the Puerto Ricans. They ended up sharing a negative symbolic capital with the Puerto Ricans.

However, there are also factors at the global level that determine how new arrivals are received in the metropolitan society and affect their incorporation as immigrants, colonial immigrants, or colonial/racial subjects. The United States developed symbolic and military/security strategies in the Caribbean during the Cold War that differentially affected migration processes. Mass migration of the Dominican urban middle sectors was fostered by the United States as part of a strategy to gain political stability and to avoid the emergence of another Cuba. Puerto Rico and Cuba waged the symbolic Cold War battle between the United States and the Soviet Union. In the Puerto Rican case, the showcase was the island, not the migrants. The migration of rural, unskilled labor was the condition of possibility for the success of Puerto Rico as a U.S. showcase. Thus, U.S. state resources were channeled to the islanders rather than the migrants. In the pre-1980 Cuban experience, the showcase was the migrants, not the island. Thus, U.S. state resources were channeled to the migrants while the islanders suffered a trade embargo. Pre-1980 Cubans in the United States were not perceived as a burden by the local communities in which they settled, thanks to millions of dollars of assistance from the federal government. Thus, Cubans developed a positive symbolic capital in the Euroamerican imaginary, becoming incorporated as immigrants closer to the white populations in the racial/ethnic hierarchy, a process that neither Dominicans nor Puerto Ricans enjoyed. This helps one understand why, unlike the Dominicans, pre-1980 Cuban refugees were able to escape the networks of, and the racialization attached to, the Puerto Rican community in New York City.

NOTES

1. A similar process occurs with new immigrants of African descent in relation to colonial subjects of the U.S. empire such as the African Americans. Many immigrant groups of African descent whose identity is perceived as indistinct from African American in the Euroamerican social imaginary have been ascribed the same racist stereotypes as the latter. Some black groups emphasize ethnic identity over racial identity to avoid the stereotypes against African Americans in the United States. Still, there are groups of African descent whose identity is perceived as distinct but still suffer racist discrimination owing to the pernicious prevalence of color in the Euroamerican imaginary.

2. This article will emphasize the racial categories as constructed in the Euroamerican social imaginary, which are the dominant racial categories used in the United States. For reasons of space, it will not deal with how racial categories are constructed within each racial/ethnic community. Racist perceptions of subordinated groups are not exclusively white phenomena, even though it is important to acknowledge that Euroamerican racist perceptions represent the society's dominant views.

3. The unit used in this article is the New York metropolitan area, which is larger than New York City. We sometimes used *New York* or *New York City* interchangeably to refer to the New York metropolitan area.

4. Most of the unskilled rural migrants from Puerto Rico came between 1950 and 1970. After 1970, since Puerto Rico had changed from a rural to an urban society, most of the migrants kept coming from unskilled labor backgrounds but from urban areas rather than rural zones. During the 1980s, skilled labor and middle classes migrated from Puerto Rico to Florida and Texas. However, most of the Puerto Rican migrants to New York City kept coming from unskilled labor backgrounds (Grasmuck and Grosfoguel 1997).

5. As time passed, the Dominican migration has included large numbers of people from poor sectors of the Dominican Republic. This was especially so during the 1980s (see Grasmuck and Grosfoguel 1997).

6. This section refers only to the pre-1980 Cuban refugees. It does not refer to the 1980s Cuban migration, collectively better known as the marielitos, which largely comprised Afro-Cubans. By the time the marielitos came to the United States, most of the federal assistance programs for Cuban refugees were finished. Thus, the marielitos were unable to escape being racialized as did the Cuban refugees before 1980.

BIBLIOGRAPHY

Báez-Everszt, Franc and Frank D'Oleo Ramírez. *La emigración de dominicanos a estados unidos: determinantes socio-económicos y consecuencias.* República Dominicana: Fundación Frederich Ebert, 1986.

Blauner, Robert. *Racial Oppression in America.* New York: Harper & Row, 1972.

Boswell, Thomas and James R. Curtis. *The Cuban-American Experience: Culture, Images, and Perspectives.* New Jersey: Rowman & Allanheld, 1984.

Bourdieu, Pierre. *Outline of a Theory of Practice.* Cambridge, England: Cambridge University Press, 1977.

Bray, David. "Economic Development: The Middle Class and International Migration in the Dominican Republic." *International Migration Review* 18 (1984): 217–36.

Centro de Estudios Puertorriqueños. *Labor Migration under Capitalism: The Puerto Rican Experience.* New York and London: Monthly Review Press, 1979.

Cronin, Denise Margaret. "Ethnicity, Opportunity and Occupational Mobility in the United States." Ph.D. diss., State University of New York, Stony Brook, 1981.

Dominguez, Jorge I. "Cooperating with the Enemy?: U.S. Immigration Policies toward Cuba." In Christopher Mitchell, ed., *Western Hemisphere Immigration and United States Foreign Policy,* 31–88. University Park, Pa.: The Pennsylvania State University Press, 1992.

DuBois, W.E.B. "Human Rights for All Minorities." In Philip S. Foner, ed., *W.E.B. DuBois Speaks: Speeches and Addresses 1920–1963,* 174–91. New York: Pathfinder, 1970.

Friedlander, Stanley. *Labor Migration and Economic Growth: A Case Study of Puerto Rico.* Cambridge, Mass.: MIT Press, 1965.

Georas, Chloé. "From Colonial Empire to Culture Empire: Re-Reading Mitterand's Paris." Master's thesis, Binghamton University, 1997.

Gilroy, Paul. *"There Ain't No Black in the Union Jack": The Cultural Politics of Race and Nation.* Chicago: University of Chicago Press, 1987.

Glazer, Nathan and Daniel P. Moynihan. *Beyond the Melting Pot: The Negroes, Puerto Ricans, Jews, Italians, and Irish of New York City.* Cambridge, Mass.: MIT Press, 1963.

Grasmuck, Sherri and Ramón Grosfoguel. "Geopolitics, Economic Niches and Gender Social Capital: Caribbean Migrants in New York City." *Sociological Perspectives* 40, no. 3 (1997): 339–63.

Grasmuck, Sherri, and Patricia Pessar. *Between Two Islands: Dominican International Migration.* Berkeley: University of California Press, 1991.

Gray, Lois Spier. "Economic Incentives to Labor Mobility: The Puerto Rican Case." Ph.D. diss., Columbia University, 1966.

Grosfoguel, Ramón. "Puerto Rico's Exceptionalism: Industrialization, Migration and Housing Development, 1950–1970." Ph.D. diss., Temple University, 1992.

—— "World Cities in the Caribbean: The Rise of Miami and San Juan." *Review* 17 (1994): 351–81.

—— "Depeasantization and Agrarian Decline in the Caribbean." In Philip McMichael, ed., *Food and Agrarian Orders in the World-Economy,* 233–53. Westport, Conn.: Praeger, 1995.

Guarnizo, Luis. "One Country in Two: Dominican-Owned Firms in New York and the Dominican Republic." Ph.D. diss., Johns Hopkins University, 1992.

Hendricks, Glenn T. *The Dominican Diaspora: From the Dominican Republic to New York City. Villagers in Transition.* New York: Teachers College Press, 1974.

Johnson, Lyndon B. "Letter Establishing a Task Force on the Impact of the Cuban Refugee Program, November 18, 1965." In *Public Papers of the Presidents of the United States: Lyndon B. Johnson,* 1119–20. Washington, D.C.: U.S. Government Printing Office, 1966.

Laurentz, Robert. "Racial/Ethnic Conflict in the New York City Garment Industry, 1933–1980." Ph.D. Dissertation, State University of New York, Binghamton, 1980.

Levine, Barry B. "The Puerto Rican Exodus: Development of the Puerto Rican Circuit." In Barry B. Levine, ed., *The Caribbean Exodus,* 93–105. New York: Praeger, 1987.

Lewis, Oscar. *La Vida: A Puerto Rican Family in the Culture of Poverty—San Juan and New York.* New York: Random House, 1966.

McClintock, Anne. "The Angel of Progress: Pitfalls of the Term 'Post-Colonialism'." *Social Text* 31 and 32 (Spring 1992): 1–15.

Mitchell, Christopher. "U.S. Foreign Policy and Dominican Migration to the United States." In Christopher Mitchell, ed., *Western Hemisphere Immigration and United States Foreign Policy,* 89–123. University Park, Pa.: The Pennsylvania State University Press, 1992.

Omi, Michael, and Howard Winant. *Racial Formation in the United States: From the 1960s to the 1980s.* New York: Routledge, 1986.

Osofsky, Gilbert. *Harlem: The Making of a Ghetto.* New York and Evanston: Harper Torchbooks, 1966.

Ottley, Roi and William Weatherby. *The Negro in New York: An Informal Social History, 1626–1940.* New York: Praeger, 1967.

Pratt, Mary Louise. *Imperial Eyes: Travel Writing and Transculturation.* London and New York: Routledge, 1992.

Pedraza-Bailey, Silvia. "Cuba's Exiles: Portrait of a Refugee Migration." *International Migration Review* 29 (1985a): 4–34.

—— *Political and Economic Migrants in America: Cubans and Mexicans.* Austin: University of Texas Press, 1985b.

Pérez, Richie. "From Assimilation to Annihilation: Puerto Rican Images in U.S. Films." In Clara Rodríguez, ed., *Latin Looks,* 142–63. Boulder, Colo.: Westview, 1997.

Prieto, Yolanda. "Cuban Migration of the '60s in Perspective." Occasional paper no. 46. Center for Latin American and Caribbean Studies, New York University, 1984.

Quijano, Aníbal. "Colonialidad y modernidad/racionalidad." *Perú Indígena* 29 (1992): 11–21.

Sánchez-Korrol, Virginia E. *From Colonia to Community: The History of Puerto Ricans in New York City, 1917–1948.* Westport, Conn.: Greenwood Press, 1983.

Sandoval-Sánchez, Alberto. "West Side Story: A Puerto Rican Reading of 'America.' " In Clara Rodríguez, ed., *Latin Looks,* 164–79. Boulder, Colo.: Westview, 1997.

Shohat, Ella. "Notes on the Post-Colonial." *Social Text* 31 and 32 (Spring 1992): 99–113.

Thompson, Lanny. "Nuestra isla y su gente: la construcción del otro." In *Our Islands and Their People.* Río Piedras, Puerto Rico: Centro de Investigaciones Sociales y Departamento de Historia de la Universidad de Puerto Rico, 1995.

Vázquez, Blanca. "Puerto Ricans and the Media: A Personal Statement." *CENTRO* 3 (1991): 5–15.

Wallerstein, Immanuel. *Historical Capitalism.* New York: Monthly Review Press, 1983.

Wieviorka, Michel. *La France Raciste.* Paris: Editions Du Sueil, 1992.

X, José. Interview by author. Paris, France, Summer 1997.

———— Interview by author. New York, Spring 1995.

CHAPTER FOUR

Niuyol

Urban Regime, Latino Social Movements, Ideologies of Latinidad

Agustín Laó-Montes*

> Identity . . . is a process, a project, it's a historical movement. . . . And in this sense, it isn't possible to define an identity because no utopia of identity has any future if the utopia of liberation is detached from it. I think that . . . this specific crossroads between the utopia of identity and the utopia of liberation . . . is truly the legacy of all societies that have been constituted . . . in relation to colonial domination.
>
> —*Aníbal Quijano, quoted in Velarde (1991:49)*

> If movements are the social domain which most readily escape the confines of the inherited . . . collective action can become the terrain of the exploration of the possible.
>
> —*Alberto Melucci, (1996:13)*

> We can think of cities as a new frontier . . . charged with the possibility of fundamental transformation in the West. The global city is, perhaps, the premier arena for these battles—it is the new territory where the contemporary version of the colonial wars of independence are being fought. But today's battles lack clear boundaries and fields: there are many sites, many fronts, many politics.
>
> —*Saskia Sassen (1996:197)*

"Hoy por Juan Rodríguez, mañana por nosotros," "¿Por qué lo mataron? Porque era Latino,"[1] chanted Estella Vasquez (Dominican), along with Howard Jordan (Puerto Rican) in the front line of a march against police brutality in the summer of 1988. What began with a crowd of around 1,000 activists of a booming movement for racial justice and in opposition to police brutality in New York City swelled at the end to include almost 5,000

*Thanks to Roberto Alejandro, Stanley Aronowitz, Roman de la Campa, Diana Coryat, James Cohen, Arlene Dávila, Steven Gregory, Ramon Grosfoguel, Sintia Molina, Felipe Pimentel, Kelvin Santiago-Valles, Arturo Escobar and Kate Wilson for their helpful comments on prior versions of this chapter.

marchers, most of whom joined the demonstration in a route that crossed two largely Latino working-class Brooklyn neighborhoods (from Bushwick to the Williamsburg Bridge). As an activist with the Latino Coalition for Racial Justice and a participant in the march, I witnessed[2] how the appeals to a common sense of rage against the violence of state racism ("Why did they kill him? Because he was a Latino") and the call for a community of destiny ("tomorrow for ourselves") moved the residents of the neighborhoods to join the cry of protest. It was, as Richie Pérez said in our evaluation meeting, a sort of *despojo* (collective healing), a prime moment of collective action when being Latino meant belonging to a racialized population, in spite of all differences within it. The following day, the front page of *New York Newsday*[3] showed a panoramic view of the march, led by people carrying the Puerto Rican and Dominican flags.

This article will analyze the emergence of Latino identities in New York City through collective action and political organization.[4] It will emphasize the constitution of latinidad as a collective identification by means of social movements. However, more than attempting to give a unified picture of the struggles for the empowerment of an allegedly homogeneous Latino community, this paper explores how the play of differences (class, race, nationality, gender, sexuality, place, ideology, organization) account for diverse strands of Latino politics (cultural, racial, social, sexual) as well as contending ideologies of latinidad. To do this, after mapping some general historical landscapes of Latino politics in New York City, I will introduce a typology of five distinct yet often overlapping political ideologies of latinidad: ethnic Keynesianism, Latino grassroots populism, Hispanic neoliberalism and neoconservatism, latinamericanist vanguardist radicalism, and Latino radical democratism. Throughout the article, I also will also try to deconstruct and evaluate the multiple meanings and political values of a number of keywords (empowerment, community, citizenship, social justice) in Latino politics. I will end with some reflections on the implications of the politics of Latino identity/difference in the prospects for radical democracy and social justice in New York and in the global scene.

THEORETICAL PRELUDE: GLOBAL COLONIALITY, URBAN REGIME, AND THE RIGHT TO THE CITY

Before sketching the historical horizons in which Latino political identities are enacted through collective action, it is important to frame the discussion in the particular arena of politics in which these struggles take place, namely, New York City's urban regime. New York is a particular place of politics and a specific domain of the political,[5] but it is also a node within larger (global, regional, and national) frameworks of power. A world city, New York is geopolitically located in between the U.S. nation-state and the modern world system.[6] New York City is legally and fiscally subordinate to the U.S. federal and the New York state government at the same time that it is culturally and economically linked to global landscapes reaching beyond the limits of the nation-state. Its local government has the fiscal scale, relative autonomy, and influence to form a political entity with a degree of sovereignty analogous to a city-state. Hence, New York should be analyzed as both a local field of power[7] and an important unit in a global web of power relations and political bodies. I conceptualize the patterning of these constellations of power (local-national-global) by integrating the notion of urban regime to Aníbal Quijano's theory of the coloniality of power.[8]

Quijano represents the coloniality of power as an intersection between two historical axes framing modern regimes of power: one characterized by the relationship between capital and labor (the axis of exploitation, class, and capital accumulation), the other depicting the relationship between the West and "its Others" (the axis of domination, culture and intersubjectivity). In this way, he historicizes the primary forms of identification that frame modern subjectivities (race, nation, ethnicity, gender, sexuality) as colonial categories, constituted through world historical processes of capitalist exploitation and Western domination. This colonial power dynamic, which is at the heart of capitalist modernity, and its ongoing historical process of globalization encompass such diverse phenomena in time and space as the conquest/invention of the Americas, chattel slavery and the rise of the Atlantic System, twentieth-century U.S. imperialism, and the post–World War II ghettoization of African Americans and Latinos as neocolonial subjects in U.S. cities.

Even though these entangled processes of exploitation and domination (economic, racial, sexual, cultural), and the struggles they entail, are historical products of the global structuring of inequality, they acquire particular shapes and meanings in specific contexts (rural, urban, national). A key process explained by the notion of the coloniality of power is the organization, in modern capitalism, of a system of nation-states characterized by a structure of domination (political-economic and ideological-cultural) between metropoles and colonies that continued even after the demise of formal political colonialism.[9] This came along with the emergence of a modern urban system that integrates metropolitan and peripheral cities in the same schema of uneven development (King 1990). Accordingly, world cities, like their states (local and national), were configured as part of this modern/colonial patterning of power relations. After the post–World War II decline of formal colonialism and with the increase of neocolonial migrations to the metropoles, world cities became central scenarios for neocolonial domination and strategic terrains in the current globalization of coloniality.[10] Hence, colonial difference and modern/colonial hierarchies (class, race, gender, sexual) of wealth, power, and culture are constitutive forces of world cities' urban regimes (see Mignolo 2000).

Here, *urban regime*[11] refers to the dominant political sphere of a world city, the multilayered process by which domination and hegemony (racial, class, patriarchal, cultural) are organized and contested across the institutions and throughout the social fabrics of urban space. New York's urban regime is shaped by global processes and structural constraints (capitalist economic logics and ruling classes, transnational racial and sexual hierarchies, geopolitics), by institutional demands to facilitate economic growth and political stability (law and order), and by the urban dynamics of social power. The hegemonic strategies and the practices of coercion (legal, discursive, physical, financial) that together define the core of urban governance are partly successful in integrating political energies to the institutions (political parties, urban state) and political cultures of the regime. On the other hand, New York has always been, and persists as, a protagonic scenario for many struggles and experiments of social power by a variety of social movements.

Social movements are, perhaps, the most active vehicles for contesting domination and developing counterhegemonic strategies in urban regimes. In this fashion, they are also a main arena of struggles for the decolonization of power. In general, there are two intertwined ways in which we understand social movements: as fields/waves of activism and as collective actors. In the first sense, they are analyzed as "social movement webs" (Alvarez 1997:87), or "action systems . . . plural, ambivalent, often contradictory . . . hidden networks of groups, meeting points, and circuits of solidarity which differ profoundly from the image of the politically organized actors" (Melucci 1996:115). In this register, it is possible to talk about a Latino social movement in New York City just as we refer to a women's, gay, labor, or ecological movement. In the second sense, social movements can be described as collectivities whose claims and actions are able to challenge (and even transform) power relations while they constitute themselves as socialities and political actors.[12] Here, social movements appear as purposeful collective actions to claim material and symbolic resources at the same time that they are spaces for identity building and community making. In this manner, we write about particular Latino social movements (racial justice, immigrant's rights, language rights), and social movement organizations (Latino Coalition for Racial Justice, Latinos United for Political Action) as venues for the making of Latino identities and Latino publics in New York. These webs of collective action enact collective identities[13] in the course of a diversity of struggles (over space, meaning, memory, resources, etc.); take place and have effects at different levels (neighborhood, workplace, city, transnational); use disparate tactics; vary in organizational form; and have different ideological profiles, political targets (state, corporation, landlord), and strategic goals. In general, movements are relatively fluid and autonomous and are among the most dynamic elements in politics; by introducing new claims of rights, entitlements, participation, representation, membership, and identity they open and diversify the political terrain and even the very terms of politics. They are, then, key agencies in the continuous process of signification, contestation, and performance of citizenship.[14]

A barometer of the quality and degree of integration and participation in a given social and political space, citizenship is an uneven process and a contested terrain. World cities such as New York are central scenarios in contemporary contests about membership, rights, participation, recognition, and representation in a political community—the very stuff of modern citizenship. New York is a political laboratory where the speed and intensity of social struggles, the density and diversity of social movements, and the continuous flow of migration push for a constant renovation of claims of right and definitions of membership. In New York, where difference (ethnic, sexual, etc.) is an explicit principle in the organization of social identities and political life and where patriotic loyalties and affiliations of peoplehood are multiple and often overlap, citizenship is a particularly fluid process, a framework in which urban subjects (racial, neocolonial, diasporic) fight in many ways for their right to be citizens of the world city. In short, New York is a fertile ground for the continuous rise of social movements and contending discourses of citizenship. It is an epicenter for transnational (Amerindian) and diasporic (Africans in the Americas, Puerto Rican) social movements at the same time that it is a place of dwelling with numerous and vibrant urban social movements. Consequently, New York is an important playground and a strategic battleground for both dominant and subaltern modernities.[15]

In light of its extraordinary concentration of wealth, power, prestige, culture, and activity, New York is a magnet to both capital and labor, a global terrain of class formations and struggles. This also makes New York an imperial contact zone (Pratt 1992) for neocolonial encounters and the associated struggles for racial justice, ethnic recognition, diasporic citizenships, and so on. As the economies of the city have been transformed in the current phase of crisis and restructuring in the capitalist world economy, there is a growing latinization of New York's working classes as well as a systematic marginalization of latinized labor forces from both employment and consumption. The latter social sector represents a substantial percentage of the city's Latino population, and it has been stigmatized and vilified with a widespread discourse on the so-called underclass that pervades the dominant representations of Latino cultural and social space (e.g., criminalization of barrios) and is deployed by the ruling classes and the corporate media. The overrepresentation of those more crucially and directly affected by long-term colonialism (Dominicans and Puerto Ricans) in this marginalized subaltern sector (which has also been termed a "colonized labor force" and a "racial/colonial labor formation")[16] reveals the relation between coloniality and subalternity in New York's urban regime.

In spite of all the substantive differences among peoples hailed as Latinos, latinidad remains as a marker of otherness both in the core discourses of U.S. identity and citizenship and in the ethnoracial hierarchies of New York's urban regime, governmental and corporate multiculturalism notwithstanding. In New York's urban discourses and equations of power, Latinos constitute a politically subordinate social category. In a way, the very affirmation of latinidad as a relevant criteria for political identity contains an element of transgression to dominant definitions of Americanness, a practical challenge to the monologic ideal of "America" as the heart of whiteness and the heir of the West. In this sort of imperial gaze, the city itself appears as a space of otherness, an unruly place in light of its concentration not only of foreigners but of more intimate aliens, the racialized minorities (African Americans, Latinos) who now are the new urban majority.

These very conditions of urban coloniality (discrimination, powerlessness, marginality, criminalization) differentially experienced by particular Latino social sectors, along with the manifest (and unconscious) desires for belonging, memory, recognition, and self-worth, encourage the rise of Latino social movements and motivate the organization of Latino spaces. But as latinidad is a historical discourse and Latino political identities are products of struggles, I will lay out a historical map of the emergence of Latino politics in New York City.

MAPPING THE LATINIZATION OF THE POLITICAL AND THE POLITICS OF LATIN NEW YORK

As the main world city in the U.S.-Caribbean regional nexus, New York has been an important place for Latin American and Caribbean politics since the latter part of the nineteenth century. The Cuban Revolutionary Party was founded in New York in the latter years of that century by Cubans and Puerto Ricans advocating a program of anticolonial nationalism from the perspective of exile. A different genealogy of politics is derived from Puerto Rican socialist labor organizers, who created a Latin American presence in the U.S. labor movement since the beginning of the twentieth century, as testified in the *Memories of Bernardo Vega* (1984). Both of these are examples of political activity that was located in, but not primarily focused on, the urban scene, the former from the standpoint of the exiles for whom New York was primarily a convenient site to fight Spanish colonialism and the latter in the name of working-class internationalism (see Mirabal, this volume, p. 57).

By the 1930s, there was a scale of population,[17] level of organization, and institutional network to produce self-identifications such as *colonia puertorriqueña* and *comunidad hispana* (Sánchez-Korrol 1994). At this juncture, the self-denomination as Hispanos expressed the centrality of language as a marker of difference and as a terrain of political contestation, indicating an experience of exclusion and the associated struggles for rights and redress. This was the period in which the Hispano politics of the city began to be led by Puerto Rican Pioneros, namely, those who pioneered struggles and opened spaces (jobs, unions, Spanish-language and neighborhood institutions, etc.) for peoples of Latin American and Hispanic Caribbean descent living in New York. In this tenor, organizations such as the Liga Puertorriqueña e Hispana took the lead in developing claims for resources and representation at the same time that it combated discrimination against puertorriqueños and Hispanos. Important examples of two distinct forms of collective action in that period are the 1935 riot, which erupted after an incident of racial violence against a Puerto Rican in East Harlem,[18] and the campaign (also in Spanish Harlem) that led Oscar Garcia to be the first Puerto Rican (and Hispano) elected to state office in 1938. During the great Puerto Rican migration to New York (late 1940s to early 1960s), there was a wave of neighborhood organizing and ethnic-based political action demanding fair services and public goods (education, health care, housing) as well as formal representation in the urban regime (political parties and local government) (Jennings and Rivera 1984). These energies and resources mobilized by this sort of community activism were to some extent transformed into quasi-governmental social service agencies, integrated into the city's (Lindsay's urban reform) and federal government's (Johnson's War on Poverty) soft gestures to build a welfare state. In contrast to this strand of politics, there was a cadre of labor and community organizers, many of them affiliated to the American Labor Party and the Communist Party (Myers, Ojeda), who were key in the organization of Puerto Rican and Hispano community institutions (Puerto Rican Day Parade)[19] as well as a relatively small but militant nationalist movement for Puerto Rican independence. By the second half of the 1950s, after the Red scares of McCarthyism and the relative decline of labor activism epitomized by the formation of the AFL-CIO, there was a rise of community liberal ethnic politics to the detriment of class-oriented radical politics (Aronowitz 1996; Katznelson 1981). Consequently, the political movements and social struggles of the next period (the 1960s) partly emerged as a reaction against the governmentalization of Puerto Rican and Hispano politics, thus representing a challenge to the status quo.

The world historical conjuncture that we call the 1960s (Katsiaficas 1987) was characterized by the rise of antisystemic movements (Arrighi, Hopkins, and Wallerstein 1989) that partly reshaped the scope, form, and dynamics of politics, thus redefining the very nature of the political. The new social movements of the 1960s challenged conventional politics by questioning the ability of the institutions of liberal democracy (the capitalist state, political parties) to keep their promise of freedom and equality, by politicizing aspects of individual and social life that had been considered private (gender, sexuality) and/or non- or prepolitical (ecology), introducing new and renewed political subjects as main agents of change (youth,

African Americans, Latinos, Asian Americans, gays and lesbians, women, students, colonial subjects), and redefining the principles of democracy by means of a radical practice of participatory decision making at all levels of society.

One of the key pillars of the 1960s was the Black Power Movement. An analogous movement was organized among Latinos (led by youth) from coast to coast. The Chicano and U.S. Puerto Rican revolutionary nationalist movements that were born in the late 1960s were very much inspired by the Black Power Movement. This gave birth to a political generation (Rodríguez-Morazzani 1992) whose political culture was largely characterized by an oppositional racial and class consciousness against the inequalities and exclusions promoted by what they defined as a system of U.S. capitalism, racism, and colonialism, both domestic and abroad (Acuña 1988; Barrera 1979; Muñoz 1989). It is in this juncture (late 1960s/early 1970s), with the emergence of a radical politics of identity against colonial negations of self (and for self-affirmation of popular culture and memory), that the term *Latino* gained momentum as a common denominator for U.S. peoples of Latin American descent. In this context, the substantive Latino signified an anticolonial politics that unified Latin American peoples beyond national borders (thus the Chicano slogan "we are a people without borders") against U.S. imperial power. As we have seen, until the 1960s, the political organization of Latinos in New York was primarily Puerto Rican, indicating a relationship between nationalism and panethnic politics. Also, as mentioned earlier, before the 1960s the most common descriptor for people of Latin American/Hispanic Caribbean descent in the city was not *Latino* but *Hispano.* The appeal of the label *Hispano* demonstrates the significance of language in the making of U.S. Latino/Hispanic identities at the same time that it shows the historically changing character of the political meanings and cultural values of ethnoracial designations. Thus, in the 1960s it became shared knowledge that although the self-designation as Latino implied valorizing our African and Amerindian roots, the word *Hispanic* had a eurocentric and racist edge. This shift was symptomatic of a period of a very dynamic politics of renaming (Chicano, Black) as explicit strategies of decolonization.

The Nuyorican/Latino urban movements for "people's power" in the 1960s also formulated an ideology of community control. Here, community empowerment referred to local power to address interests and satisfy needs by means of grassroots organizations and neighborhood institutions at the same time that it involved a politics of ethnoracial representation. In New York, struggles such as the one for school decentralization and the establishment of school boards (Katznelson 1981) mobilized residents of African American and Latino barrios. The language of "empowering" the "Latino community" became common sense through struggles for collective consumption (in domains such as education, health care, and housing), in the fights to develop policies and institutions for cultural democracy (such as El Museo del Barrio and Taller Boricua), and in promoting political representation and community self-management.[20] The idea of community blurred distinctions among a variety of agencies (social movements, neighborhood organizations, political groupings) of different sorts. For instance, revolutionary nationalist movements such as the Young Lords Organization that were born reacting against ethnic bureaucracies (Puerto Rican social service bureaucracies), and that initially made moves and demands for local institutions of radical democracy (People's Church) eventually became identified with efforts to integrate Puerto Rican leaders into the power structures or to organize service-oriented community organizations led by professional social workers (Laó 1995). In other words, quite distinct ideologies of political community, and opposing democratic projects, got conflated under the rubrics of ethnic power and community control. In spite of these ambiguities and differences, the rhetoric of community proved crucial for any politics of Latino power in New York City.[21]

Since the world systemic crisis of the 1970s, there has been a tremendous increase and diversification of the population of Latin American and Caribbean descent in the city. This eventually resulted in the growth of new immigrant organizations (mutual-aid societies, social clubs, cultural institutions) divided by countries of origin but also in a new wave of neighborhood organizing and political activity that was largely shaped by nationality but that also began to be defined as Latino. For example, the strength and significance of the movement for educational rights in the primarily Dominican Washington Heights neighborhood motivated naming a citywide coalition advocating for bilingual education and parents rights as the Puerto Rican/Latino Educational Roundtable. The name itself revealed a relative shift from Puerto Rican to Latino politics.

In the 1980s New York City became a herald of a new urbanism characterized by neoliberal economic policies (privatization, fiscal austerity, gentrification, rule of capital), intense racialization of politics, deep socioeconomic polarization, and a dominant common sense of fear and policing. In this new urban regime, the dominant landscapes of power (the capital of capital and the cunning of civilization) clashed with its landscapes of otherness (the racial city of ethnics and immigrants, the marginal city of colonized labor forces). In this context, the rise of social struggles, neighborhood organizations, citywide coalitions, and political groupings under the name *Latino* indicated the making of political identities that corresponded to emerging ethnic and racial discourses. In this context, a nascent constellation of struggles (cultural, political, economic), organizations, institutions, and informal practices of resistance and self-affirmation together constituted (intentionally or not) what we now call a Latino social movement by virtue of the pertinent effects of its different strands of activism in the political sphere and in the cultures of the city.

Latino social movements and organizations developed particular demands, articulating claims for Latino rights (Latino Rights Project). In general, what emerged as Latino issues (immigration, labor, language, racism) corresponded to the principal ways in which the urban regime promoted inequality and discriminated against latinized subjects. Newly formed organizations such as Latinos United for Political Action (LUPA) played an important role in promoting movements for immigrant rights, political representation, and racial justice, in which leading Latino activists from different nationalities collaborated.[22] Other groupings based on nationality (such as the National Congress for Puerto Rican Rights) embraced not only ethnonationally defined struggles but also general issues taken as being of concern to Latinos in general, such as bilingual education and racial violence.

New York's Latino movements arise and act in particular places and are uttered from specific subject locations. The transformation of barrios into multinational Latino enclaves frames a dialectic of solidarity and conflict between different kinds of Latinos. A common experience of place and work, as well as a common location in metropolitan ethnoracial hierarchies, serves as raw material for the emergence of common expressive cultures, collective actions, and panethnic families. But the intimacy and familiarity of living and working together (and of being classified as same by the dominant culture) also highlight differences (nationality, class) and facilitate conflicts. This dynamic of cooperation and competition characterizes the rise of movements and the formation of organizations and coalitions that came to be defined as Latino. For instance, in Washington Heights, a Coalition for Latino Empowerment was organized in the 1980s, with cochairs representing Dominicans, Puerto Ricans, and Cubans, at the same time that there was a great deal of electoral competition (especially between Puerto Ricans and Dominicans). In the same neighborhood, movements and organizations named after nationalities (Asociación Comunal de Dominicanos Progresistas) integrated members from different national origins and built coalitions with explicitly panethnic organizations (Nuevos Horizontes Latinoamericanos) to struggle for collective consumption (education, housing), Latino rights (immigration), and local power. Community became the keyword for gluing these fluid and complex processes of identity formation by means of collective action. A common sense of community began to be built in light of shared living spaces, workplaces, and ethnoracial locations and in spite of vast differences and not insignificant conflicts.

New York Latino movements are attached to and identified with specific neighborhoods. Some of these struggles are strictly neighborhood based, whereas others have larger vocations and implications. For instance, Los Sures (Williamsburg, Brooklyn) became a central site in the citywide movement for Latino empowerment by means of action groups such as the Southside Political Action Committee, which in the 1990s organized struggles and ran campaigns against housing discrimination and environmental racism as well as for political representation (including citywide redistricting) and cultural recognition. In the same barrio, El Puente (now also the Academy for Peace and Justice) had been a central site since the 1980s for struggles concerning issues such as multicultural education and language rights, Latino youth empowerment, Latino youth cultural affirmation (hiphop culture), community environmental justice (Toxic Avengers), and against imperialist intervention (Young Latinos for Peace during the Gulf War). In Washington Heights, Dominican activists mobilized immigrants (documented and undocumented)[23] in the early 1980s to exercise their right to vote in school board and area policy board elections in order to elect Dominican, Puerto Rican, Cuban, and African American representatives and presided over the organization of the first community-based Latino coalition for immigrant rights in the city, the Northern Manhattan Coalition for Immigrants' Rights.

These struggles for immigrant and refugee rights have had a long-lasting impact in the city. A citywide broad-based campaign in the 1980s (led by LUPA) calling for a mayoral executive order of nondiscrimination against immigrants resulted first in Mayor Koch sending a memorandum and then Mayor Dinkins issuing the order for all immigrants to enjoy city services free of the fear to be reported to the U.S. Immigration and Naturalization Service. Even Mayor Giuliani, a conservative Republican, declared himself as a champion of immigrants' rights despite the alleged national consensus at the federal level that "we" have an "immigration problem" that needs to be attacked with exclusionary legislation and punitive measures. In a city where one of every three residents is foreign born and that can boast a rich tradition of movements for immigrant rights, it is a political imperative to recognize some kind of rights and entitlements (de facto citizenship) for immigrants. However, the issue of immigrant rights is controversial among Latinos. It has been embraced by some sectors as a Latino struggle for rights and against discrimination. But it is rejected by other Latinos (born and naturalized citizens and even legal residents) as an issue that belongs to other nationalities (it's a Dominican issue according to some Puerto Rican politicos) and/or to new immigrants who can allegedly decrease the voting capacity and overall status of the imagined community.

Perhaps the most vibrant movement-issue mobilizing latinidad as a political identity in New York is the struggle against police brutality and for racial justice that has been in crescendo for the last three mayoral administrations. New York has a serious problem of racial violence, and one of its most heinous expressions is in the pervasive practices of police brutality against people of color. In the last twenty years there has been a substantial increase in police brutality against Latinos in New York City. In spite of a great deal of organization and mobilization that has taken the issue to the center stage of politics and media attention and even after the achievement of a movement's demand for a creation of a civilian review board to watch police activity, police abuse (especially against African Americans and Latinos) continues to grow.[24] This is clearly an expression of the structural racism that partly shapes the institutions, policies, representations, and power divisions in the urban regime. In light of this, daily struggles against racialized police harassment have promoted a common sense of exclusion among racial others (Latinos). In this vein, movements against police brutality make a call for racial justice while they mobilize (and constitute) latinidad as a political identity.

In 1987, a core group of activists (mostly Dominicans and Puerto Ricans) organized the Latino Coalition for Racial Justice as part of a movement to protest against both a wave of racial violence (by police and civilians) against nonwhites and the neoliberal, racially biased administration of Mayor Koch (Mollenkopf 1992). This type of racial politics was a key factor in the election of David Dinkins as the first African American mayor in New York in 1989, but the problem continued during his term, fostering the continuous organization of Latinos around the problem of racial violence and against police brutality as its most patent expression. A particularly climatic moment was the so-called Washington Heights riot in 1991, when the neighborhood erupted after Kiko Garcia (Dominican) was murdered in cold blood by an Irish American policeman. After the election in 1993 of former U.S. attorney Rudolph Giuliani as mayor of New York City, policing became the defining rationality of an urban regime explicitly looking to restore "civility" and to ensure "security" by rescuing (militarizing and privatizing) public spaces from the "antisocial deviance" of the dangerous classes (the homeless, African American/Latino youth, "ghetto underclass"). This overtly racialized mode of governmentality (Foucault 1979), with its emphasis on policing social behavior, executing law enforcement, and elevating the police body to a quasi-heroic role, fueled police brutality. A number of incidences of police assassination of Latinos (Anthony Baez, Manuel Mayi) motivated the organization of a Latino Parent Coalition against Police Brutality, including the Mothers of Police Plaza, a group of mothers of Latino victims of police brutality who organized weekly rallies at the city's police headquarters.

In short, the experience of racial violence (symbolic and physical) in everyday life (schools, stores, subways, jobs, prisons), as well as the pervasiveness of racism in the urban regime and particularly the increase of police brutality against racial others, promoted the emergence of latinidad as a political identity by means of movements for racial justice. The rallying together behind the two national flags (Puerto Rican and Dominican) and the chanting of antiracist slogans of justice for Latinos in the 1988 Justice for Juan Rodriguez march mentioned at the beginning of this article demonstrate a racial common sense by which latinidad is primarily framed as a form of racial consciousness. As the urban racial state homogenizes targeted groups—merging Dominicans, Puerto Ricans, etc., into one category— it catalyzes and facilitates the formation of oppositional identities through collective action. A popular critique of racism, grounded on lived experiences of exclusion, discrimination, and violence, along with the practices of collective action organized by the Latino Coalition, revealed the strengths of the movement insofar as race became a premise for community making, a resource of sameness in oppression that sparked the subaltern group's ability to fight back.

Latino social movements in (and of) New York City vary in their struggles, agendas, organizational forms, outlooks, and tactics. Thus, they range from neighborhood grassroots organizations (Washington Heights Tenant Union), citywide coalitions (Latinos for Jesse Jackson), transnational networks (Latin American Women of Color Organization, Latina feminism), and placed-based movements[25] with a global projection (Centro Salvadoreño New York, Latino Immigrant Organizing Project) to urban movements colored by ethnoracial struggles and meanings (racial justice, police brutality, spatial appropriation). They can also be classified as political movements when looking to carve spaces in the formal domain of politics (Southside Political Action Committee, Latinos United for Political Action) and as cultural movements when cultural politics is the main arena of mobilization (Latino Media Collaborative, Rincón Criollo–Casita Community Garden) and can be informal (graffiti art, hip-hop culture) or formal (Almighty Latin Kings and Latin Queens) expressions of urban youth culture and "street" struggles. Latino movements can be defined in many ways depending on their identities, interests, goals, and targets, including the following: housing (Committee to Save East Harlem, Inner City Press/Squatters), labor (Center for Immigrant Workers), education (United Bronx Parents), national (National Congress for Puerto Rican Rights), racial (Latino Coalition for Racial Justice), panethnic (Ciudadanos Concientes de Queens), youth (Dominican Youth Union), gay and lesbian (Somos Hermanas), ecological (Toxic Avengers), women (Atabex-Axe Women Center), students (Fuerza Latina), legal (Latino Rights Project), and immigration (Immigrant Workers Organizing Project). Finally, they can be components of larger movements of various concerns such as AIDS advocacy (ACT UP Latino Caucus), solidarity (Latinos for a Free South Africa), peace (Young Latinos for Peace), and language (Committee for a Multilingual New York).

In short, New York's Latino social movements are the main vehicles through which daily resistances (struggles and self-affirmations) are translated into collective action, social and cultural struggles are politicized, and political identities are produced. Latino movements serve as media for contesting oppression, claiming rights, and affirming identity and dignity in a variety of social settings (home, work, school, university, street, park, prison, mall, and media) and in this sense they could be important means for the decolonization of Latino lifeworlds as well as key agents in the constitution of alternate Latino spaces (relational, geographical, cultural, and political). These spaces vary from Sunday soccer leagues, social clubs (Garifuna Town Associations), art and performance centers (Ollantay Gallery, Pregones Community Theatre), grassroots feminist institutions (Dominican Women Development Center), AIDS education cultural centers (Música Against Drugs), and underground radio stations (East Harlem Radio Latino) to community gardens and casitas. They configurate alternate publics insofar as they are by their very nature (ethnic, racialized) outside of the dominant "economies of signs and space" (Lash and Urry 1994) of the urban regime. These ethnoracial public spaces (or "subaltern counterpublics")[26] are not homogeneous; rather, they are contested terrains on their own where contending interests, needs, and projects debate each other according to the class, racial, sexual, ideological, or generational identity of the agents involved.

As Latino social movements are inscribed by a double dialectic between internal and external differences (class, race, nationality, ethnicity, gender, sexuality), they are arenas where collective identities emerge in a fluid process of exchange, involving negotiations of difference and the building of solidarity through the articulation of shared interests, meanings, and concerns in opposition to common others. Discourses of latinidad are produced and performed through processes of exchange, competition, alliance, and negotiation in which solidarities are built through collective action. In this sense, narratives of Latino unity and empowerment arise in the intersection between the practices of subalternization and homogenization (racialization and ethnicization) of people of Latin American descent by the dominant U.S. society (urban regime and imperial nation) and the practices of resistance and self-constitution of social movements. Latino movements are grounded on shared locations (social, cultural, racial) and emerging structures of feeling (barrio popular cultures, street sensibilities), at the same time that they are venues for the tailoring and rehearsal of expressive cultures and political identities. Likewise, Latino movements help to carve alternative publics, which in turn frame the practices of resistance and self-affirmation where Latino identities are coined and enacted.

In sum, the heterogeneous, multifaceted, and even incoherent struggles enacted under the rubric of *Latino* in New York can be seen as a Latino social movement.[27] This is pertinent because of the overall effects of these struggles in building latinidad as a political identity and, therefore, as a standpoint for claiming rights and resources and advocating for better conditions of participation and membership. In this sense, the movements, organizations, and individuals whose activity shape this ensemble of political and cultural effects that we call a Latino Social Movement are the most active agents in the latinization of city politics. However, there are substantive differences (class, generation, nationality, immigration status, colonial condition, etc.) among latinized subjects as well as contending po-

litical projects and ideologies of latinidad. In light of this, I will now turn
to examine the overall terrain of New York Latino politics by analyzing its
different political logics.

LATINO POLITICS AND IDEOLOGIES OF POWER

In explaining how the term *Latino* emerges and is enacted as a form of identification in various arenas of power, it is important to highlight the differences and contradictions among political ideologies of latinidad.[28] Now I
will chart five different ideologies of Latino power and briefly analyze their
politics. These political logics do not perfectly fit the theories and practices
of actual social movements and political organizations. They are instead entangled in the contradictory political discourses embedded in the actual performance of politics. Hence, the following categories are not necessarily exclusive but serve to distinguish among broad strands of politics and political
cultures. A more fleshed-out and nuanced nomenclature of ideologies of latinidad should include an account of how these political cultures articulate
with different ethnic discourses, racial projects, social and economic programs, and cultural politics. However, this typology is useful as a framework to enter into the labyrinth of New York Latino politics and start distinguishing between political projects and agendas for identity, citizenship,
democracy, and social justice between Latino collective actors.

Ethnic Keynesianism[29]

This hegemonic ideology of Latino empowerment guides most Latino urban
politics. Indeed, it functions as a set of principles shared by the rest (excluding the neoliberal/neoconservative), and in this sense, it is the most
widespread form of Latino politics. Here, Latinos are usually represented
as the fastest-growing minority, the largest new bloc of potential voters with
a booming market power. The key principles that orient this outlook are
the ability and responsibility of the state to solve social problems through
the supply of public goods and the elevation of ethnicity[30] as the main
category of social, cultural, and political identity. This implies an organic
notion of ethnic community that seeks to override differences (class, racial,
gender, sexual) within the collectivity and to overlook structural and institutional patterns of inequality.

As a political imaginary is associated with a pluralistic notion of the
political domain as basically a plain field where Latino interest groups organize to advocate for a fair share of the pie, their success depends on the
resources that they are able to mobilize. This entails an understanding of
social power as a process of equal competition and the urban state as a
mediator and provider of resources. Hence, this political rationality (ethnic

liberalism) obscures questions of domination and subalternity at the same time that its scope of framing politics tends to be local/urban and contemporary. Latino ethnic Keynesianism articulates a notion of citizenship as comprising social service entitlements and electoral participation based on legal membership in a formal political community. Therefore, its claims are for Latino rights for political representation and cultural recognition as full partners in a liberal democratic polity where individual freedoms are complemented by group rights (affirmative action). Likewise, social justice is understood as redistribution of wealth through ethnic social mobility and government transfer payments. Hence, the politics of Latino identity is the principal mechanism to correct social and political asymmetries and the main foundation for the achievement of social justice. This tends toward a politics of ethnic (national and/or panethnic) competition leading toward a parceling of political subjectivities and a weak orientation for coalition building.

The practical strategies of this ideological outlook and political repertoire range from direct action to lobbying, but the overall logic of practice is informed by a search for resources, representation, and recognition from the dominant institutions of society and particularly the state. In general, this is the ideology guiding the politics of most political organizations that advocate for Latino electoral representation, of social service agencies, and of movements that mobilize to advocate for solutions to social ills through state policies (like coalitions for socially conscious distribution of the state budget). As a hegemonic ideology it integrates various social sectors, but the main leadership is from the professional-managerial and political-bureaucratic classes, which largely base their power on a relationship of brokerage between the ethnic community and the urban regime.

Latino Grassroots Populism[31]

This primarily refers to the dominant version of the politics of neighborhood organizing and Latino urban social movements. But it is also an ideological underpinning of the overall movement for Latino power in New York City. It is common sense in the widespread principle of Latino empowerment at the community level. In this schema, the main movers of change and bearers of collective power are the grassroots, and the key subjects of popular sovereignty are the Latino people, who are a community by virtue of ethnic (overlapping with national and/or racial) affiliation and place of residence. Urban populism is for the most part the political logic of Latino neighborhood activism for collective consumption (housing, education, health care) and local power (share of representation, services, and resources), the terrain of urban social movements.

In this political tradition, social justice is primarily understood as the achievement of a fairer system of ethnic opportunity and a more equal share of social resources for ethnic populations. Conventionally, in Latino liberal urban populism, there is no systematic analysis of the sources and mechanisms of social power. This implies an understanding of the status quo of social and political inequality in terms of elite control, corruption, and bad leadership. It also involves an instrumentalist view of the state and a fuzzy notion of domination in which subalternity is seen as a temporary moment of subjection to be surely solved by ethnic self-organization and a proper representation in the political system. There is also a loose appeal to class and racial sensibilities, but the key principle of political identification is still a notion of ethnic solidarity that tends to marginalize the political significance of internal differences (such as gender and sexuality). In New York, Latino populist movements push liberal frameworks of urban citizenship to their limits insofar as their struggles entail an extension of the franchise (immigrant's social rights), a redefinition of membership in the political community (a multicultural city), and a relative decentralization of political decision making (local means of Latino power). However, given the fragmented character of social struggles in New York (and the United States) and liberal urban populism's inability to articulate a coherent vision of change, Latino grassroots organizing and activism mostly focus on local/ short-term problems (a tenants' strike, an incinerator). To a large extent, the organizing energies and activism of such movements result in grassroots organizations (Asociación Comunal de Dominicanos Progresistas, Ciudadanos Concientes de Queens) becoming service agencies or integrating within the urban regime as a politically functional opposition.

There are basic political convergences between Latino grassroots populism and ethnic Keynesianism. They are both confident about the virtues of liberal democratic politics, and they both pursue a representational politics of Latino identity. However, the former is primarily anchored on community-level coalition building, whereas the latter is more focused on the regime's political organizations (parties, interest groups) and state institutions.

Hispanic Neoliberalism and Neoconservatism

This strand of Latino politics is largely produced and disseminated by the Hispanic[32] bourgeois and professional-managerial classes. Its most visible expression is the growing presence of Hispanics in the Republican Party, as championed by official ideologues of a conservative latinidad such as Linda Chavez.[33] Theoretically, in this outlook latinidad is not a political identity but a cultural identity that should be confined to the private sphere. This is consistent with a notion of the public as a sphere of individual free competition mediated by a market that facilitates participation in a system of legal equality. Hence, in this political logic, to mobilize Latino identity for political purposes is against the rules of democratic politics (individual competition) because it allegedly entails privileging a so-called special interest. In the same vein, social policies devised to address economic injustices and social inequalities (the welfare state, economic policies) are rejected as hostile to the holy principles of the natural efficiency and freedom of the market.

There has always been a thin strand of Latino conservatism, but today it is a developing movement[34] that paradoxically is mostly led by individuals who benefited from the same programs (such as affirmative action) that they are now opposing. Hispanic neoconservatives are part of a larger movement for immigration control, monolingualism (English), and so-called traditional American values. They also promote neoliberal and neoconservative policies predicating a free market and minimal government intervention in the economy (privatization, decentralization) while increasing government intervention in controlling what they define as deviant behavior and ensuring civility and security. Thus, Latino conservatism is complicitous of the new wave of imperial patriotism and reactive nationalism suturing a bipartisan national consensus against the "dangerous classes" (African American/Latino inner-city youth, urban aliens, racialized immigrants) and favoring a strong police state with hard-handed policies of crime control at home and a "war against drugs" both at home and abroad.

Conservative discourses are mostly produced and led by ruling sectors because they articulate the boldest narratives of domination (class, patriarchal, racial), but there is an increasing conservative appeal to members of subordinate sectors (white working classes, African American and Latino middle classes) whose sense of disempowerment, hopes, and fears are addressed by a rising political culture of "authoritarian populism" (Hall 1988) that is able to displace their political energies and codify their desires with concerns such as security against the perceived other (immigrants, African American/Latino marginal subaltern sectors). The conservative appeal to New York Hispanics is more successful in calling for neoliberal policies of free-market capitalism (community business, self-help, privatization) and a regime of surveillance (policing, security) than in promoting anti-immigrant sentiments. This is symptomatic of a New York urban regime characterized by escalating racial and class polarization, spatial fragmentation, political alienation, and social violence.

In New York City, Latino political shifts toward neoconservatism are dramatically exemplified with the political history of Herman Badillo, who began as a neighborhood activist in the 1950s, became a leading reform Democrat in the 1960s (making it as far as the U.S. Congress), and after a series of defeats as a mayoral candidate, joined the Republican Party and became Mayor Giuliani's main Latino advisor, championing policies against open admissions and bilingual education at the City University of New York. This trend of leadership is also seen in the emergence of progentrification, antigrassroots Democrats such as former councilman Antonio Pagan. Hispanic conservatism is also manifest in grassroots organizations that follow neoliberal ideologies of self-help in defense of Hispanic business (a sort of Hispanic capitalism) and in cultural conservatives organizing with religious militancy against gay and lesbian and abortion rights (Rev. Ruben Diaz from the Bronx). Ironically, in spite of the assimilationist politics of overriding differences in favor of an allegedly mainstream U.S. culture, neoconservative Latino leaders get their political capital because of their ascribed latinidad.

Latinamericanist Vanguardist Radicalism

This strand of Latino politics has two main branches: the Latin American left in the United States and U.S. Latino radicalism. In this political tradition, latinamericanity is a signifier of a world region (Latin America) in a neocolonial relationship with U.S. imperialism at the same time that *Latino* denotes a subject position of ethnoracial and ethnonational subordination in the U.S. systems of stratification. The growth and diversification of Latin American and Caribbean migrations to New York City since the 1960s (especially since the 1980s) nurtured the rise of Latin American left-wing organizations with anti-imperialist politics of exile and in solidarity with liberation struggles. Most of the political work of this activist cadre was directed to raise financial and political support for the struggle in the home countries. But they also built a significant left-wing political community and a cultural public sphere in New York.[35] The main U.S. world city became a microcosm for the enactment of the Bolivarian ideal of Latin American unity in the coalitions, demonstrations, and social and cultural life of the latinamericanist solidarity movement.

In this political tradition, domination and exploitation are structural conditions imposed by transnational capitalism and U.S. imperialism, and the urban state tends to be seen as the local representative of the rule of capital, class, and empire, a mere instrument of power. In this schema, oppression is synonymous with class and colonial (national, racial) domination, and liberation is a goal to be pursued by revolutionary nationalist organizations and class-based groups. Thus, urban trenches were, at first, of secondary importance to solidarity with national liberation and international class struggles. An initial rejection of electoral politics as hopeless and the ascription to a maximalist program of no less than radical reforms or wholesale revolution caused this movement to lack a practical politics of the possible. Paradoxically, the instrumentalist view of the urban state led left-wing organizations to target state power and resources in the 1980s, at the peak of the crisis of socialism and Third Worldism and when hopes for immediate reforms were aroused by the rise of national and urban social democratic coalitions (the Rainbow Coalition).

In this manner, many activists and organizations of the Latin American left got involved in community struggles and became active players in urban politics. Issues of social justice that appeal to left-wing sensibilities such as racial justice, bilingual education, immigrant and refugee rights, and labor democracy attracted latinamericanist radicals as both professional organizers and rank-and-file activists. This sector of the Latino activist community, along with Latino/American intellectuals, also played an important role in raising issues of democratization of U.S. foreign policy toward Latin America and the Caribbean. In this context, latinamericanist radicals converged with U.S. Latino revolutionaries and community activists in movements such as those for opposition to U.S. intervention, for racial justice, and even to elect "progressive" Latino candidates for political office. A peculiar example in the electoral arena was a very brief effort in the 1980s to build a New York Latino progressive political party, El Partido de la Nueva Alternativa. The Latinamericanist left had historically been indifferent or opposed to legal citizenship in the United States not only because of reluctance to engage in electoral politics but also because of their reduction of anti-imperial politics to nationalism. However, in participating in citywide campaigns (immigrant/refugee rights, racial justice) and in local power struggles, they also engaged in the kind of activism that contributes to enlarging the franchise and redefining the terms of urban citizenship.

Nonetheless, to some extent activists and organizations of the Latinamericanist left have also been integrated into the organizations and institutions of the social democratic opposition and the liberal democratic establishment of the urban regime. In this way, this strand of politics also converges with ethnic Keynesianism and Latino populism. This is testimony to how the instrumentalism and vanguardism of the traditional left[36] allowed for their subordinate integration into the urban regime. That is to say, their view of urban power simply as state power (a tool of capitalism and imperialism) and their understanding of leadership as a special quality of a vanguard who possess a correct line and a right analysis converged with a politics of locating the left in key positions of power. This also relates to the lack of significance of the question of democracy in this tradition and particularly to the implications of the principles of political freedom for leadership and decision making.

Latinamericanist vanguardist activism as a strand of politics and as a political community is now minimal. However, the organizational network, activist cadre, and the demands of Latin American solidarity are now constitutive elements of the political landscapes of the city. Latin American solidarity claims are now framed as secondary issues in city politics (as witnessed by a city council resolution against the U.S. Navy's operations in Vieques). Latinamericanist claims also persist as the main focus of New York branches of Latin American traditional left-wing and social democratic political organizations.

Latino Radical Democratism

Radical democracy, generally speaking at the present moment, is not an explicit ideological or political orientation of Latino social movements and political organizations. This political paradigm now mostly operates as a tendency embedded in the principles and practices of various expressions of collective action. Indeed, grassroots organs of popular power (subaltern, working class) in what we now retrospectively call New York's Latino community go back at least as far as the immigrant mutual-aid and labor organizations of the early 1900s. The principles of community control and people's power that have been central to Latino urban social movements in New York since the 1960s are important components of the radical democratic political culture that we inherited from that era of crisis and change. But to a large extent this historical effort to radically democratize liberal democracy ended up being integrated into the hegemonic power structures. However, this should not make us overlook the importance of this radical populist ideology's elements of continuity, particularly in several practices (often heterogeneous, fragmentary, and localized) of popular organization and subaltern resistance. Elements of radical democracy persist in popular political cultures, in grassroots struggles for local power, and in social movements (relatives of Latino Victims of Police Brutality, the City University of New York student movement) that by their character and actions continue to challenge or seek to transform the urban regime.

If radical democracy is a political horizon that implies a continuous effort to achieve freedom and justice at all levels of social life, then a multiplicity of resistances and movements that at least partly occur under the rubric *Latino* exercise in daily practice (at home, in the streets, in universities, at workplaces) a radical democratic rationality. As these struggles cover the whole territory of power in the city, movements range from gay and lesbian efforts to democratize AIDS activism (ACT UP Latino Caucus) and Latina feminist organizations against domestic violence (East Harlem Victims Intervention Program) to grassroots labor organizing (Center for Immigrant Workers) and squatters' challenges to gentrification (Inner-City Press).

In this arena of politics, as it will be in any radical democratic political discourse, latinidad is a link in a chain of differences, a form of identification that does not play a privileged role in the definition of political identity. As political identities are multiple and contingent, communities (ethnic and otherwise) are also divided and conflicted by differences (class, gender, sexuality). This view of the play between identity and difference is consistent with an analysis of power as a multilayered web of relationships of inequality and resistance spread throughout society. In this sense, an important distinction between the liberal politics of Latino grassroots populism and the radical populism of radical democratic discourses is that although for the former the state is the main target, ultimate arbiter, and major provider in its search for resources, recognition, and representation, for the latter the state is an important link in a more complex network of power, and maintaining autonomy from it is a basic principle in a more general search for freedom and social justice.

Given that in this outlook, politics is characterized by a plurality of power struggles and political identities, social movements are considered key agents for social transformation. Also, the various terrains, targets, and demands of social movements correspond to a diversification of their claims of rights, entitlements, and participation. In fact, this politicization of different aspects of social life (public, private, and even intimate) by social movements represents a redefinition of the content of citizenship. In this vein, Latino movements in New York can articulate a language of civil rights (Latino Rights Project) or a rhetoric of human rights (AIDS education and treatment as a right to life) and/or develop new definitions of rights and needs (language, immigration). The proliferation of spaces of contestation and organization associated in one way or another with the politics of latinidad holds a promise of the possibility of these expressions of resistance to become a powerful web of social movements and for these in turn to become a transformative force in the city with all the global implications this has. However, as stated earlier, a Latino radical democratic politics is more of a project than an actual program. In the next section, after a general assessment of Latino Politics in New York City, I will close with a discussion on some of the challenges for such a project.

DECOLONIZING/DEMOCRATIZING POWER: NEW YORK LATINO MOVEMENTS AND GLOBAL CHANGE

The emergence of Latino political identities and the rise of an arena of Latino politics in New York City has effected changes in the urban regime. Today, there is an ongoing process of latinization of New York's political sphere. Latinos are now considered a primary constituency; Latino leaders are integrated into the dominant institutions of power, and Latino organizations are recognized players and significant vehicles for representation in city politics. This representational politics is the dominant strand of political culture in Latino activism as well as the putative horizon of Latino politics. Accordingly, the overall effect of Latino activism in New York City has been in the realm of representation in the double sense of a political demand for Latino concerns to be priorities of city policy and for Latino leaders to be in government as well as a cultural demand for positive recognition of Latino histories and cultural expressions.[37] Undoubtedly, the activism of this predominantly liberal politics of ethnic representation has borne fruits. There is now a milieu of elected and appointed officers (city, state, and federal) who configure a New York Latino political class. Likewise, there is an infrastructure of social service and educational institutions explicitly organized to address the needs of Latino communities. In general, educational advocacy and affirmative action have promoted a Latino professional-managerial class with some influence in the social, political, and cultural life of the city.

Nonetheless, the overall impact of the liberal politics of ethnic representation has proven to be much less than expected. The American Dream of social mobility has become reality only for a few, and the majority of Latinos are still either in the lower echelons of the working class or marginalized from formal employment. In spite of the relative opening of political space, Latinos remain politically subaltern in the urban regime, as demonstrated by the limited political influence and condition of disenfranchisement of Latinos as a community. Also, despite celebrations of the gorgeous mosaic of diversity in the liberal (and even neoconservative) discourses of multiculturalism, in the many trenches of the cultural politics of Latino self-affirmation there is a daily struggle against the dominant practices of devalorization and disrespect. In short, the limits of the liberal agenda for Latino empowerment are also the limits of reforming the urban regime while leaving its structures of domination intact.

From a different angle of politics, Latino social movements can act as transformative agents, rehearsing new ways of doing politics, performing innovative practices of citizenship, and creating alternate (and even oppositional) publics. Latino movements are the political agencies with more potential to advance Latino politics beyond the confines of liberal democratic representation. Although the Latino regime's[38] organizations (political groups, community institutions) tend to perform a strict politics of ethnic representation, Latino social movements engage in a plurality of struggles addressing a diversity of axes of injustice. This has two significant implications: first, that Latino social movements can be means not only for the production of Latino identities but also for latinidad to become an arena for the negotiation of difference (class, race, gender), and second, that Latino movements can be vectors for larger agendas of democratization and social justice. Against the grain of their political potential, Latino social movements in New York tend to be of limited scope and short sighted. They mostly articulate particularistic claims and pragmatic remedies and, generally speaking, lack a transformative vision to change the very frameworks of power that re-produce inequalities. As we have seen, Latino movements are ideologically inclined toward liberal populist political discourses and tend to become integrated as junior partners in the urban regime. When this happens, their political energies are usually converted into "venues of containment" of a transformative politics (Dávila, this volume, p. 161).

Given this scenario, we need to develop critical theories of Latino politics. Arguably, the main task for such a theoretical practice should be to devise, from within the movements and/or in collaboration with them, an analysis of the achievements, virtues, potentials, and limits of Latino politics while producing (in theory and practice) Latino radical political discourses. In the case of New York Latino social movement(s), the most general question is how to move forward "from protest to proposal" (Fals-Borda 1992:305), or from a politics of resistance and representation[39] to a politics of transformation and liberation. I contend that this entails advancing the political horizon beyond liberal ethnic representation toward a radical democratic political imaginary (Smith 1999). The definition and concrete meaning of radical democracy is a matter of much debate. I stress that the adjective *radical* implies a will to change the very conditions of domination and exploitation at all levels and that the noun *democracy* signifies a form of polity of participatory popular rule and a society of substantial equality. Thus, in a radical democratic society, there should be "equal access to the material resources necessary for self-development and for meaningful participation in social, cultural, political, and economic decision-making," all of which imply the need for "a radical democratization of existing state structures and social formation, a profound redistribution of power, and a dismantling of the structures that institutionalize inequality: exploitation, sexism, homophobia, racism" (Smith 1999:31). This is not fully enacted anywhere, but as we have seen, the principles of redistributive justice, social egalitarianism, participatory democracy, cultural self-development, and collective empowerment of subaltern categories (genders, sexualities, races, classes, nationalities) are partially embedded in the practices of Latino social movements.

I will close by briefly discussing four key challenges for developing a Latino radical democratic politics in New York City. The first challenge is for Latino politics to become a transformative force of both relations of domination and exploitation in the urban regime. This entails assessing the efficacy of Latino activism in terms of its effects in several specific yet intertwined spheres of injustice (economic, political, sexual, racial, and cultural).[40] These domains of inequality can be considered both internal and external to the Latino imagined community. Therefore, a Latino radical democratic politics will require a politics of justice in all of these spheres of injustice, both within Latino movements and institutions and at the same time in the whole urban regime. In absence of this double process of democratization, Latino movements will tend to integrate as subordinates into the institutions of the urban regime.

This relates to our second challenge, which is the promotion of critical political identities and a broad-based politics of alliance. Here, the biggest challenge is to promote Latino solidarity while promoting the affirmation of differences as a premise to fight inequality (class, racial, gender, and sexual). This implies a Latina/o politics of location, meaning that because everybody's subjectivity is defined by a multiplicity of subject positions (class, race, gender, etc.), political agency involves multiple axes of solidarity around a plurality of struggles. The broader political task is to build a new hegemonic bloc grounded in a diversity of claims for freedom and justice. Here, the main question is how the "chains of otherness" (class, race, gender, etc.) that correspond to modern/colonial domination at all levels (urban regime, nation, empire, and world system) are to be translated into political "chains of equivalences" (Laclau and Mouffe 1985) among the movements to create radical democratic popular hegemonic blocs. The promotion of radical hegemony entails a remaking of political identities by means of a process of political exchange between particular struggles and movements that should encourage a practical understanding of the entanglement of different forms and levels of oppression. As put by feminist political theorist Wendy Brown, this involves both "a radical transformation of political subjectivity and a radical democratization of power" (Brown 1995:5).

The third challenge to a Latino radical democratism is to develop a politics for the decolonization of power. As I have argued throughout this article, coloniality is central to modern power relations and specifically to New York's urban regime. If what we call the coloniality of power signifies the colonial content of modern power regimes, then decolonization should be seen as a process that involves concerted efforts for stripping power relations from all the forms and practices of political, economic, and cultural domination of modern capitalism and Western hegemony. This means a multilayered politics of decolonization across all the historical locations, social spaces, and geographic scales colonized by capitalism and occidentalism. In this sense, democratization and decolonization are two sides of the same coin. A radical democratization of social relations implies a decolonization of social power, and a substantial decolonization of power entails a radical democratization of polity, culture, and economy. A Latino radical democratic politics ought to address the two main axes of the coloniality of power: exploitation (class and economic inequality) and domination (race, sex, gender, culture, and knowledge) to develop a politics of equality and justice, that is to say, a politics of freedom and liberation.

In this vein, as Latino subalternity is a localized articulation (in the urban regime) of global hierarchies of class and peoplehood (race, nation, ethnic), Latino movements can become anticolonial and could have countercolonial effects. New York Latino struggles for democratization, by means of movements for racial justice, language rights, immigrant rights, representation and participation at different levels of the city's decision making, and the like, can also become struggles for the decolonization of the urban regime. Accordingly, insofar as struggles for Latino citizenship challenge anglocentric definitions of U.S. citizenship and identity, they could also facilitate the decolonization of citizenship.[41]

In short, at the heart of a Latino radical democratic politics there should be a strategy of decolonization based on an understanding of the colonial underpinnings of power at the global, national, and urban levels. This means identifying the workings of Western cultural hegemony, imperial domination, and colonial exploitation in the urban scene.[42] These modes of coloniality are visible throughout the textures of city life in phenomena ranging from the eurocentric cultural policies of mainstream museums to the economic marginalization, vilification, and police violence to which colonial/neocolonial citizens such as Puerto Ricans and Dominicans are subject. Finally, a New York Latino politics of decolonization should be informed by an alternative vision of emancipation, what Chicana feminist historian Emma Perez (1999) calls a "decolonial imaginary."

As New York's urban regime is a strategic link in the global configurations of the coloniality of power, the project of a New York Latino radical democratic politics should also be framed in larger landscapes of power.

The relationship between coloniality and globality refers to the temporal scope and spatial scale of New York Latino politics. The fourth and last task for a Latino radical democratic politics should be to develop a language and devise strategies grounded in a global and historical understanding of the configuration and unfolding of power. Most of urban politics is conceived in terms of the city and the short term. But the temporalities and spatialities of the world city are linked to larger landscapes of economic, political, and cultural power. Given New York's protagonic role within the U.S. empire as well as within the modern/colonial world system, its urban regime constitutes a worldly field of domination, and the struggles of the city have the ability to connect globally and project historically. The key location of the city within the new geography of centrality and marginality (Sassen 1996) places it as a world center for capitalist accumulation and Western domination but also for world migrations, global diasporas, and transnational social movements—hence the need to analyze both the historical foundations and structural limits of the urban regime as well as the transnational projections and historical possibilities of oppositional (and transformative) movements.

New York City is a prime space not only for the production of world hegemony and cultures of rule but also for subaltern counterpublics and countercolonial movements. New York Latino social movements are linked to webs of collective action in national and transnational scenarios. This is exemplified by transnational movements for Afro-diasporic unity across the Americas and in hemispheric struggles of Amerindians for retrieval of memory and redefinitions of the historical borders and names of this world region.[43] As the joint forces of imperial planning and capitalist accumulation promote globalization and regionalization, the emergence of hemispheric labor forces within the imperial contact zone set the conditions of possibility for the regional organization of labor movements. In this context, transnational networks of movements and nongovernmental organizations in movements such as grassroots feminism and new labor organizing (UNITE, maquiladora workers) are also becoming transnational political actors, thus helping to redefine the territories of politics. This recasting of political agency corresponds to definitions of membership and participation at various scales of politics and in various polities, which often implies redefinitions of citizenship and political community along translocal frames of membership. Here, there is a relationship between the globalization of the political[44] and the deterritorialization and relocalization of Latino political identities. However, Latino social movements yet have to articulate a language and an outlook expressive of the multiple levels and linkages relevant to developing a transformative politics of decolonization/democratization.

New York City increasingly looks, sounds, smells, tastes, and feels like a transnational enclave geographically located and juridically integrated in the United States but characterized by translocal linkages and multiple spaces-of-flows that reach far beyond the limits of the nation-state. As the main world city of an empire that defines its territorial nation as a land of immigrants, New York is becoming a federation of diasporas. Its cosmopolitanism is not only one of global dominant classes (Robbins 1998) but also of subaltern translocal solidarities. New York is one of the key epicenters from which the notion of latinidad emerges as a worldly translocal form of identification (latinos del mundo), preserving and enlarging its role as a principal headquarter of Latin American and Caribbean radicalism. As world-city dwellers, latinized subalterns engage in multiple struggles for the right to the city and its pleasures. Thus, the right to the city means the right to freedom, to explore and invent new and more fluid ways of life and self-definition, and to create new and re-create older forms of political community out not only of need but also from desire.[45] This "utopistics" of the world city (germinating a "radical municipalism" and serving as a midwife for a decolonized cosmopolis),[46] is founded on the immense diversity of its publics; the incredible vitality of its own time-space; and the extraordinary concentration of wealth, power, and prestige incarnated on its body. The politicized bodies of the world city are surely major battlefields in the new configurations of global power and resistance. From their world-city trenches, fighting for democracy at work, in the streets, at universities, and in many more fronts; by combating the everyday ubiquity of violence, surviving the imminence of early death in the inner city, and affirming peoplehood against denial of memory and self; and in transforming the very definition of identity and citizenship in the city and in the empire-nation, New York Latino struggles and movements keep constructing new modes of political agency and performing their potential of being significant collective actors in the rapidly globalizing battles for justice and freedom.

NOTES

1. An English translation would be "Today for Juan Rodríguez, tomorrow for ourselves"; "Why did they kill him? Because he was a Latino."

2. This article can be described as an analytical report of more than twenty years of the author's being an activist, organizer, and public intellectual in New York City. To a large extent my political and intellectual activity has been performed in relationship to objectives of social justice and Latino empowerment. As a sociologist, a particularly important experience was as a field researcher with the CAMEO (Community, Autobiography, Memory, Ethnography, Organizing) project of the Center for Cultural Studies of the City University of New York, Graduate Center, between 1992 and 1994. This gave me the opportunity to return, as it were, to Latino communities to do participatory action research and collaborative research, thus developing a methodology of producing analytical knowledge by participating in critical community affairs and establishing a productive dialogue between university scholars, community intellectuals, artists, activists, and community folk.

3. *New York Newsday,* July 7, 1988.

4. In this context, by *Latino identities* I mean expressions of self-identification that, although mediated by many other subject positions (class, gender, sexuality, etc.) and constituting partial, perhaps circumstantial, and sometimes simply performative aspects of identification, play an important role in the definitions of such subjects as actors in power struggles. As we shall see, *Latino* as an important self-designation of social movements is a post-1960s phenomenon, and therefore, when we classify earlier movements as Latino, we are imposing present categories on our understandings of the past. It is impossible to make sharp distinctions between political, social, and cultural identities, but I find useful Laclau's definition of political identities as "the politicization of social identities" because it helps us to conceptualize how political subjectivities are not given and political struggles are not necessary, but instead arise in processes in which power relations become explicit matters of political contention and subjects become political actors. In turn, cultural identities can be built through the same process of politicization of subjectivities, which is an important aspect of the rise of Latino identities (Laclau 1994).

5. In this discussion, *politics* refers to all fields of power relations at all levels of social life, and *the political* refers to a specific sphere by which politics is submitted to public scrutiny and mediated by social institutions. Among others, see Ranciere (1995) and Mouffe (1992b).

6. The notion of a modern world system as a basic and necessary unit of analysis for sociohistorical interpretations of capitalist modernity was theoretically formalized by Wallerstein (1974). There are different theories of historical world systems as well as different conceptualizations of capitalist modernity as a particular world system. Hence, more than a world-systems theory, there are world systems and world historical perspectives, which is where I situate my particular methodological orientation. For the central importance of world cities in world systems (or in global dynamics) see Abu-Lughod (1999), Arrighi (1994), Braudel (1992), King (1990), Sassen (1991), and Knox and Taylor (1995).

7. The notion of urban field of power as I am developing it here denotes a spatial configuration of politics with localized strategies of domination and hegemony; specific patterns of social classification and stratification; and

particular political cultures, organizational forms, social struggles, social movements, and claims of citizenship and democracy. For the theoretical notion of field of power, see Bourdieu (1999).

8. The concept of the coloniality of power is an analytical tool that serves as a common ground for various efforts to rethink modernity and to articulate a postcolonial perspective from the standpoint of U.S. Latino/Latin American historical locations. Two important examples of such a project are the Coloniality Working Group that is now housed at the Fernand Braudel Center at Binghamton University and Walter Mignolo's latest book (2000).

9. Quijano (1992) makes a crucial distinction between coloniality and colonialism. *Coloniality* refers to the colonial undersides of modern regimes of power and processes of subjectification and identification. *Colonialism* refers to a specific form of coloniality that is defined by a political and military relationship of domination by metropolitan nations and dominant classes over colonized territories and populations. Coloniality persists after the end of formal political colonialism as demonstrated by the persistence of colonial hierarchies of race, class, and gender after independence in Latin America. Indeed, Quijano originally developed the notion of coloniality to explain the persistence of racial and ethnic inequalities after independence in the newly emerging Latin American nations as well as the economic, political, and cultural subordination of Latin America as a region in the capitalist world economy. On the colonial character of modern political bodies, see Balibar (1991), Chatterjee (1993), Cooper and Stoler (1997), Shapiro (1997), and Quijano (1992, 2000).

10. The coloniality of power is by definition a world historical phenomena, a basic feature of the modern world system, which in that sense had always been global. However, the notion of global coloniality is useful to conceptualize the global dispersion and dissemination of colonial situations and colonial difference in late modernity/late capitalism when the main forms of colonial domination are not necessarily associated with formal political colonialism between nation-states. See Mignolo (2000); Grosfoguel and Georas, this volume; and Laó-Montes (unpublished manuscript).

11. As it should be clear in the rest of the article, I am not adopting the conventional usage of the notion of urban regime in U.S. political science, where it is generally used as a synonym for the urban polity or as a more specific analytical term to name the political coalitions (partnerships of corporate, professional-managerial, political, and working/poor classes) that allegedly preside over urban governance. I am developing my own concept of urban regime, partly building from the attempts in England and the United States to create a theory of urban governance (and urban governmentality) on the basis of a critical dialogue between urban regime theory and the regulation school but also as an attempt to conceptualize the urban patterning of the coloniality of power as a spatial unit of the structuration of global power relations. See Judge, Stoker, and Wolman (1995) and Lauria (1997).

12. In this manner, social movements have been defined as "forms of collective action with a high degree of popular participation, which use non-institutional channels, and which formulate their demands while simultaneously finding

forms of action to express them, thus establishing themselves as collective subjects, that is, as a group or social category" (Jelin 1986:18).

13. The assumption here is that there is a dialectic between the ascribed cultural identities of the social actors (national, ethnoracial, gender, etc.) and the identifications that emerge from the process of collective action (latinidad).

14. The concept of citizenship that I am using here is not a mere juridico-political one. It also signifies the struggles that give content to practices of belonging, enfranchisement, and participation in a political community. Groups and individuals follow different paths and uneven developments in their forms and levels of citizenship because they claim different kinds of rights (civic, political, social, and cultural) that correspond to a variety of needs and interests and also arrive at different degrees of integration and entitlement. For the question of the city and citizenship see Halston and Appadurai (1996), Jenson (1996), and Isin (1996). For a good summary of the discussions on citizenship, see Schafir (1998). Also see Alejandro (1993, 1998).

15. The notion of subaltern modernities was developed by Fernando Coronil (1997) to conceptualize modernity not simply as the cultural productions and political discourses of the centers of capitalist and occidentalist power but also in terms of the coproduction of modern history from subordinated regions and countries and by subaltern peoples.

16. Santiago-Valles (1993:13) uses the term *colonized labor forces* to signify the conditions of overexploitation; displacement from work; underconsumption; and subaltern racialization, sexualization, and gendering of colonial subjects. Grosfoguel and Georas (this volume) developed the notion of racial/colonial labor formations to conceptualize the systematic exclusion from substantial citizenship, economic marginalization, and cultural subalternization of colonial immigrants and racial/colonial citizens in the metropoles.

17. By the 1930s there were 110, 223 individuals of Hispanic descent in New York City, and 40.7 percent of them were Puerto Rican. For more on this, see the introduction to this volume.

18. See Sánchez-Korrol (1994:131–66). Also see James (1998:232–57). I am grateful to Winston James for providing references from the archives of Jesus Colon regarding the severity of the problem of racial violence against Puerto Ricans, as well as of the related movements against racism, in the New York City of the 1930s. This should be a matter for further research.

19. See Valentin (1991). Gerena Valentin was an activist in the American Labor Party in the 1940s and a main organizer of the Puerto Rican Day Parade in the 1950s. In the 1960s he was elected to the New York City Council.

20. This shows how the primarily Puerto Rican social movement of the 1960s and 1970s in New York City fulfilled the three requisites that urban sociologist Manuel Castells (1983) suggests need to be present for urban struggles to become urban social movements, properly speaking. These are collective consumption, political empowerment, and cultural identity. For the U.S. (particularly in New York City) Puerto Rican movement of the 1960s, see Torres and Velazquez (1995).

21. There are various sources of ambiguity in the language of community. On the one hand, insofar as it provides a discursive framework for any expression of solidarity, it is a crucial component of any project of liberation. On the other

hand, to the extent that the ideal of community justifies overriding differences in the name of an organic unity, it becomes a limit to democracy and freedom. For a feminist radical democratic critique of the ideal of community, see Young (1990). For an eloquent discussion of the virtues of the language of community in the emergence of oppositional racial politics in England, see Gilroy (1987). In any case, the "we" that is implied in the making of community should not be assumed but is the product of social domination, social struggles, and processes of identification and group formation.

22. Interview by the author with Howard Jordan, founding member of Latinos United for Political Action (LUPA) and also of the Latino Rights Project, August 1998. LUPA is perhaps the first organized expression of the new politics of Latino identity. It was organized by Puerto Rican and Dominican activists in 1982 to advocate for a Latino Agenda by means of political action around issues such as immigrant rights and language rights and through the running of electoral campaigns to elect progressive Latino elected officials. Also see Totti (1987).

23. The relatively big turnout of voters in these polls included a high percentage of undocumented people and legal residents without U.S. citizenship (i.e., formal federal recognition). This gave a concrete sense of local citizenship that was expressive of an increasing disjuncture between formal and substantive citizenship. For instance, Puerto Ricans and African Americans have had formal citizenship for decades but are for the most part disenfranchised, which prevents them from enjoying substantial membership in the U.S. polity. In this context, the struggles for citizenship gain sense not only at the level of legal membership in the nation-state but also at other levels including the urban regime and more global political arenas.

24. The movement against police brutality in New York City acquired broad-based mass dimensions after Abner Louima (a Haitian immigrant) was sexually abused while in police custody in 1997 and after Amadou Diallo (an African immigrant) was shot over forty times by a special unit of the New York City Police Department that mistook him as being a rapist. Both incidents called not only citywide but also national and international attention to the question of police brutality in New York City as a matter of human rights abuse. The strength of this movement triggered one of the most serious political crises faced by Giuliani's administration and by the urban regime itself.

25. Arturo Escobar (2000) formulates a useful distinction between *place-based* and *place-bound* movements to indicate the persistent importance of locally based movements in relationship to processes and discourses of globalization. Presentation at the University of Massachusetts at Amherst, Fall 1999.

26. Nancy Fraser uses the phrase "subaltern counterpublics" to designate "alternative publics . . . parallel discursive arenas where members of subordinated social groups invent and circulate counterdiscourses, which in turn permit them to formulate oppositional interpretations of their identities, interests, and needs" (1997:81). A more limited (only class-oriented) but excellent attempt to critique the univocal vision of the public sphere is Negt and Kluge (1993). For racial publics see Black Public Sphere Collective (1995). For an illuminating discussion on theories of the public sphere and how they relate to citizenship, see Alejandro (1993).

27. Flores and Yúdice also formulate a "new social movement approach to Latino identity" (1990:58).

28. In this article, I used the notions of ideology and discourse interchangeably, meaning both ideationally informed forms of practice and symbolic systems that constitute subjectivities and project action. In this section, I am using ideology primarily as a political program in the sense that it corresponds to conventions of practice at the same time that is predicated on given premises and understandings of politics and society. A useful methodology for the analysis of political ideologies is Chatterjee's (1993) version of the distinction between the thematic (the philosophical and ethical principles) and the problematic (the practical dispositions and strategies).

29. The appellation *Keynesianism* is used to denote a politics of social reform by means of state policies of promoting economic growth that will allegedly enlarge the proverbial pie and, consequently, provide more pieces and a better distribution of wealth for all. This political common sense is named after British economist John Maynard Keynes and corresponds to a liberal theory and practice of ethnic politics predicated on the centrality of ethnic interest groups to mobilize resources and advocate for representation in the political system.

30. For a critique of the ethnic model as a pillar in U.S. hegemonic discourses of "race relations" and ethnic relations in light of the fact that establishing the European immigrant path as the paradigm establishes the assumption of a fictive mainstream U.S. culture and a corresponding denial of colonial (race and class) inequality, see Blauner (1972) and San Juan (1992). For a similar critique that entirely rejects the colonial question, see Omi and Winant (1986).

31. The concept of populism is perhaps one of the most debated in political theory. I am using it following Ernesto Laclau's understanding of populism as based on the specific relationship between the state and the people. Thus, populist movements seek to advocate for popular aspirations and to represent the will of the people. Because of this, populisms by themselves are amorphous and can support ideologies as diverse as fascism and social democracy. Latino grassroots populism is a version of U.S. urban populism in the tradition of Saul Alinsky. For the theoretical contradictions of the notion of populism, see Laclau (1977:143–99).

32. As noted by many others before, the term *Hispanic* as used after the 1980s is associated with governmental and corporate discourses and is therefore allied with conservative thinking.

33. Linda Chavez is a national cadre and organic intellectual of the Republican Party, a visible leader in the campaigns for English-only monolingualism and against immigrant rights, and an important ideologue in blaming African American and Latino women for the problems of poverty in racialized communities.

34. An important question here is whether we can call this conservative politics a movement. I contend that it is a movement-like politics because of its often radical tactics, popular appeal, and grassroots organizational forms as well as its aggressive rhetoric and contradictory will to revolutionize in order to conserve and go back to order. In this sense it is a movement with the effect of being an antimovement. A clear example is the Cuban-American

Foundation, an anticommunist grassroots membership organization whose deceased member Jorge Mas Canosa was, arguably, one of the most politically influential Latinos in the United States.

35. A whole set of institutions such as Taller Latinoamericano and Casa de las Américas as well as cafe-teatros such as El Caney and Rincón Taino composed this Latin American left-wing cultural sphere.

36. Aronowitz (1996) makes useful distinctions between the traditional left and the new left and between social radicalism and cultural radicalism.

37. Gayatri Spivak conceptualizes masterfully these two senses of representation in her seminal essay "Can the Subaltern Speak?" For a recapitulation of the argument, see Spivak (1999).

38. Here I am using the notion of Latino regime inspired by Adolph Reed's concept of a black regime (1995, 1999) to signify the dominant political establishment in terms of leadership, organization, and ideology.

39. I am not arguing against representation per se. I am pointing to the need to move beyond a strictly representational politics, which involves an understanding of the limits of representation in general as well as a critique of the liberal democratic notions and means of representation. Likewise, it is not a condemnation of electoral politics but a call to analyze the limits of electoralism and the implications this has for exploring other forms of political action and more participatory forms of democracy.

40. This differentiated discussion of justice relates to Michael Walzer's notion of "spheres of justice" (1983) but also to the discussion in feminist theory (Benhabib 1996; Fraser 1997; Philips 1993; Young 1990) on the relationship between principles of justice based on redistribution and principles of justice based on recognition.

41. Linda Alcoff (1999) and Eduardo Mendieta (1999), two self-defined Latino philosophers, have developed the notion of Latino or Hispanic citizenship to conceptualize how latinidad can be a frame for claiming rights and developing a collective memory and self with the effect of redefining the U.S. political community along more heterogeneous democratic lines.

42. For the question of the persistence of legacies of empire in the social relations and built environment of the postcolonial late capitalist city, see Jacobs (1996). For global cities as places that exemplify "the ongoing weight of colonialism and postcolonial forms of empire on major processes of globalization today," see Sassen (1996: 190).

43. An important example is the Amerindian move to rename the Americas with the Kuna expression *Abia Yala,* which means "the land of all of us."

44. What Connolly calls the "dispersion of the political" (1993:xx) and Grewal and Kaplan describe as "scattered hegemonies" (and also call a "neocolonial transnational regime of governmentality") (1994:xx) indicates a global process of reconfiguration of power relations where nation-states do not play the same central role not only in regulating economy but also in organizing domination and hegemony. This is what we call global coloniality or the dissemination of Western economic, racial, and sexual hierarchies across different levels of life without need of state regulation or even mediation. Hence, there is the emergence of new institutions of governance (European Union, World Bank) that are not primarily grounded to nation-states and that are not necessarily

made accountable to subaltern constituencies. There is also the emergence of new actors (nongovernmental organizations, transnational social movements) as well as forms of citizenship and political community. This last point is exemplified in the rise of multiple loyalties (dual national citizenships) and the growing importance of world cities as arenas of citizenship as well as in discourses of citizenship projected into more global scenarios (e.g., languages of human rights and global citizenship). However, in the absence of clearly defined structures of world governance as well as of political languages capable of apprehending the new constellations of power while advancing strategies for radical change, the challenge for everyone is to adjust politics to these significant changes. See Held (1995), Archibugi, Held, and Köhler (1998), and Teivanen (2000).

45. Donald (1999:96) contends that today "the city as a place of politics—axiomatically the polis—has returned to haunt and reanimate political theory and philosophy," triggering "a renewed interest in thinking about questions of citizenship, republicanism and the possibilities of a radical democratic political culture based on difference and passion rather than on consensus and technical standards."

46. For the concept of utopistics as a practical utopia grounded on the concrete potential for radical change, see Wallerstein (1998). Warren Magnusson (1999) has developed the notion of radical municipalism to conceptualize the potential of global cities to become places to open political space for contestation and for experimentation of new forms of social life and political community. This, he argues, is because of the vitality and global projection of its social movements and because of the possibility of decentering the state in the urban polity in favor of multiple definitions of political loyalty and more participatory processes of democratic life. Alvarez (1997) uses the notion of radical urban regime to analyze attempts of local radical democratic power in Brazilian cities.

BIBLIOGRAPHY

Abu-Lughod, Janet. *New York, Chicago, Los Angeles: America's Global Cities.* Minneapolis: University of Minnesota Press, 1999.

Alcoff, Linda Martin. "Latina/o Identity Politics." In David Batstone and Eduardo Mendieta, eds., *The Good Citizen*, 93–112. New York: Routledge, 1999.

Alejandro, Roberto. *Hermeneutics, Citizenship, and the Public Sphere.* Albany: State University of New York Press, 1993.

—— "Impossible Citizenship." In Karen Slawner and Mark E. Denham, eds., *Citizenship After Liberalism*, 9–32. Peter Lang, 1998.

Alvarez, Sonia. " 'Deepening Democracy': Popular Movement Networks, Constitutional Reform, and Radical Urban Regimes in Contemporary Brazil." In Robert Fisher, ed., *Mobilizing the Community: Local Politics in the Era of the Global City.* New York: Sage, 1993.

—— "Reweaving the Fabric of Collective Action: Social Movements and Challenges to 'Actually Existing Democracy' in Brazil." In Richard G. Fox and Orin Starn, eds., *Between Resistance and Revolution: Cultural Politics and Social Protest*, 83–117. New Brunswick, N.J.: Rutgers University Press, 1997.

Archibugi, Danielle, David Held, and Martin Köhler. *Re-imagining Political Community: Studies in Cosmopolitan Democracy*. Palo Alto: Standford University Press, 1998.

Arrighi, Giovanni. *The Long Twentieth Century: Money, Power, and the Origins of Our Times*. New York: Verso, 1994.

Arrighi, Giovanni, Terence Hopkins, and Immanuel Wallerstein. *Antisystemic Movements*. New York: Verso, 1989.

Aronowitz, Stanley. *The Death and Rebirth of American Radicalism*. New York: Routledge, 1996.

Balibar, Etienne. "The Nation Form: History and Ideology." In Etienne Balibar and Immanuel Wallerstein, eds., *Race, Nation, Class: Ambiguous Identities*, 86–106. New York: Verso, 1991.

Benhabib, Seyla, ed. *Democracy and Difference: Contesting the Boundaries of the Political*. Princeton, N.J.: Princeton University Press, 1996.

Black Public Sphere Collective. Special issue. Public Culture. 1995.

Blauner, Robert. *Racial Oppression in America*. New York: Harper & Row, 1972.

Bourdieu, Pierre. "Rethinking the State: Genesis and Structure of the Bureaucratic Field." In George Steinmetz, ed., *State/Culture: State-Formation after the Cultural Turn*, 53–75. Ithaca, N.Y.: Cornell University Press, 1999.

Braudel, Fernand. *The Perspective of the World: Civilization and Capitalism 15–18th Century*. Vol. 3. Berkeley: University of California Press, 1992.

Brown, Wendy. *States of Injury: Power and Freedom in Late Modernity*. Princeton, N.J.: Princeton University Press, 1995.

Castells, Manuel. *The City and the Grassroots: A Cross-Cultural Theory of Urban Social Movements*. Berkeley: University of California Press, 1983.

Chatterjee, Partha. *The Nation and Its Fragments*. Princeton, N.J.: Princeton University Press, 1993.

Connolly, William E. *Identity/Difference: Democratic Negotiations of a Political Paradox*. Ithaca, N.Y.: Cornell University Press, 1991.

—— *The Ethos of Pluralization*. Minneapolis: University of Minnesota Press, 1995.

Cooper, Frederick and Ann L. Stoler, eds. Introduction to *Tensions of Empire*. Berkeley: University of California Press, 1997.

Coronil, Fernando. *The Magical State: Nature, Money, and Modernity in Venezuela*. Chicago: University of Chicago Press, 1997.

Donald, James. *Imagining the Modern City*. Minneapolis: University of Minnesota Press, 1999.

Escobar, Arturo. "Culture, Economics, and Politics in Latin American Social Movements Theory and Research." In Arturo Escobar and Sonia E. Alvarez, eds., *The Making of Social Movements in Latin America: Identity, Strategy, and Democracy*, 62–85. Boulder, Colo.: Westview, 1992.

—— "Culture Sits in Places: Anthropological Reflections on Globalism and Subaltern Strategies of Localization." Paper presented at Five College Faculty Symposium on Globalization, Postdevelopment, and Environmentalism, Hampshire College, June 2000.

Fals-Borda, Orlando. "Social Movements and Political Power in Latin America." In Arturo Escobar and Sonia E. Alvarez, eds., *The Making of Social Movements in Latin America*, 303–17. Boulder, Colo.: Westview, 1992.

Flores, Juan and George Yudice. "Living Borders/Buscando America: Languages of Latino Self-Formation." *Social Text* 8, no. 2 (1990): 85–116.

Foucault, Michel. "Governmentality." *Ideology and Consciousness* 6 (1979): 5–21.

Fraser, Nancy. *Justice Interruptus: Critical Reflections on the "Postsocialist" Condition.* New York: Routledge, 1997.

Gilroy, Paul. *"There Ain't No Black in the Union Jack": The Cultural Politics of Race and Nation.* Oxford University Press, 1987.

Grewal, Iderpal and Caren Kaplan, eds. *Scattered Hegemonies: Postmodernity and Transnational Feminist Practices.* Minneapolis: University of Minnesota Press, 1994.

Hall, Stuart. *The hard road to renewal: Thatcherism and the crisis of the left.* London: Verso, 1988.

Halston, James and Arjun Appadurai. "Cities and Citizenship." *Public Culture* 8, no. 2 (Winter 1996): 187–204.

Held, David. *Democracy and the Global Order: From the Modern State to Cosmopolitan Governance.* Stanford, Calif.: Stanford University, 1995.

Isin, Engin F. "Global City-Regions and Citizenship." In Roger Keil, Gerda Wekerle, and David V. J. Bell, eds., *Local Places in the Age of the Global City,* 21–37. Toronto: Black Rose Books, 1996.

James, Winston. *Holding Aloft the Banner of Ethiopia: Caribbean Radicalism in Early Twentieth-Century America.* New York: Verso, 1998.

Jelin, Elizabeth. "Otros silencios, otras voces: el tiempo de la democratización en Argentina." In Fernando Calderón, ed., *Los movimientos sociales ante la crisis.* Universidad de las Naciones Unidas, 1986.

Jennings, James and Monte Rivera, eds. *Puerto Rican Politics in America.* Greenwood, 1984.

Jenson, Jane. "Post-Fordist Citizenship: Struggling to be Born." In Roger Keil, Gerda Wekerle, and David V. J. Bell, eds., *Local Places in the Age of the Global City,* 13–20. Toronto: Black Rose Books, 1996.

Judge, David, Gerry Stoker, and Harold Wolman, eds. *Theories of Urban Politics.* New York: Sage, 1995.

Katsiaficas, George. *The Imagination of the New Left: A Global Analysis of 1968.* Boston: South End Press, 1987.

Katznelson, Ira. *City Trenches: Urban Politics and the Patterning of Class in the United States.* Chicago: University of Chicago Press, 1981.

King, Anthony. *Urbanism, Colonialism, and the World-Economy: Culture and Spatial Foundations of the World Urban System.* London: Routledge, 1990.

Knox, Paul and Peter J. Taylor, eds. *World Cities in a World-System.* Cambridge, England: Cambridge University Press, 1995.

Laclau, Ernesto. *Politics and Ideology in Marxist Theory: Capitalism, Fascism, Populism.* London: Verso, 1977.

—— *The Making of Political Identities.* London: Verso, 1994.

Laclau, Ernesto and Chantal Mouffe. *Hegemony and Socialist Strategy: Toward a Radical Democratic Politics.* London: Verso, 1985.

Laó, Agustín. "Resources of Hope: Imagining the Young Lords and Politics of Memory." *CENTRO* (Winter 1995): 325–45.

Laó-Montes, Agustín. "Global Coloniality and Urban Regime: Conceptualizing Latino Politics in the World City." Unpublished manuscript.

Lash, Scott and John Urry. *Economies of Signs and Space.* New York: Sage, 1994.

Lauria, Mickey, ed. *Reconstructing Urban Regime Theory: Regulating Urban Politics in a Global Economy.* London: Sage, 1997.

Magnusson, Warren. *The Search for Political Space: Globalization, Social Movements, and the Urban Political Experience.* Toronto: University of Toronto Press, 1996.

—— "Unicity, Megacity, Global City." *Working Papers in Urban Governance and Democracy* 99, no. 1 (1999): 108–16.

Melucci, Alberto. *Challenging Codes: Collective Action in the Information Age.* Cambridge, England: Cambridge University Press, 1996.

Mendieta, Eduardo. "Becoming Citizens/Becoming Hispanics." In David Batstone and Eduardo Mendieta, eds., *The Good Citizen,* 113–32. New York: Routledge, 1999.

Mignolo, Walter D. *Local Histories/Global Designs: Coloniality, Subaltern Knowledges,* Border Thinking. Princeton, N.J.: Princeton University Press, 2000.

Mollenkopf, John Hull. *A Phoenix in the Ashes: The Rise and Fall of the Koch Coalition in New York City Politics.* Princeton, N.J.: Princeton University Press, 1992.

Mouffe, Chantal. Democratic Citizenship and the Political Community." In Chantal Mouffe, ed. *Dimensions of Radical Democracy,* 225–39. London: Verso, 1992a.

—— *The Return of the Political.* London: Verso, 1992b.

Myers, Gerald. *Vito Marcantonio: Radical Politician 1902–1954.* Albany: State University of New York Press, 1989.

Negt, Oskar and Alexander Kluge. *Public Sphere and Experience: Toward an Analysis of the Bourgeois and Proletarian Public Sphere.* Minneapolis: University of Minnesota Press, 1993.

Ojeda, Felix. *Vito Mercantonio y Puerto Rico: Por los Trabajadores y Para la Nacion.* Rio Piedras: Ediciones Huracan, 1978.

Omi, Michael and Howard Winant. *Racial Formation in the United States: From the 1960s to the 1980s.* New York: Routledge, 1986.

Pérez, Emma. *The Decolonial Imaginary: Writing Chicanas Into History.* Bloomington: Indiana University Press, 1999.

Phillips, Anne. *Democracy and Difference.* University Park: Pennsylvania State University Press, 1993.

Pratt, Mary Louise. *Imperial Eyes: Travel Writing and Transculturation.* New York: Routledge, 1992.

Quijano, Aníbal. "Colonialidad y modernidad/racionalidad." *Peru Indígena* 13, no. 29 (1992): 11–21.

—— "¡Qué tal raza!" Pamphlet published by Centro Comomtario de Salud Mental de Villa El Salvador. Lima, Peru, 2000.

—— "Coloniality of Power and Social Classification." *Festschriften,* forthcoming.

Ranciere, Jacques. *On the Shores of Politics.* London: Verso, 1995.

Reed, Adolph, Jr. "Demobilization in the New Black Political Regime: Ideological Capitulation and the Radical Failure in the Postsegregation Era." In Michael Peter Smith and Joe R. Feagin, eds., *The Bubbling Cauldron: Race, Ethnicity, and the Urban Crisis,* 182–208. Minneapolis: University of Minnesota Press, 1995.

_____ "The Black Urban Regime: Structural Origins and Constraints," in *Stirrings in the Jug: Black Politics in the Post-Segregation Era*, 79–116. Minneapolis: University of Minnesota, 1999.

Robbins, Bruce. "Comparative Cosmopolitanisms." In Pheng Cheah and Bruce Robbins, eds. *Cosmopolitics: Thinking and Feeling Beyond the Nation*, 246–64. Minneapolis: University of Minnesota Press, 1998.

Rodríguez-Morazzani, Roberto. "Puerto Rican Political Generations in New York: Pioneros, Young Turks, and Radicals." *CENTRO* 4, no. 1 (1992): 96–116.

Sánchez-Korrol, Virginia. *From Colonia to Community: The History of Puerto Ricans in New York City*. Berkeley: University of California Press, 1994.

San Juan, E., Jr. *Racial Formations/Critical Transformations: Articulations of Power in Ethnic and Racial Studies in the United States*. Atlantic Highlands, N.J.: Humanities Press, 1992.

Santiago-Valles, Kelvin. "Looking at One's Self Through the Eyes of Others: Coloniality and the Utopia of Identity." Paper presented at the "Fixed Identities in a Moving World" conference, Graduate Center, City University of New York, April 1993.

Sassen, Saskia. *The Global City: New York, London, Tokyo*. Princeton, N.J.: Princeton University Press, 1991.

_____ "Analytic Borderlands: Race, Gender, and Representation in the New City." In Anthony King, ed., *Re-presenting the City: Ethnicity, Capital, and Culture in the 21st-Century Metropolis*. New York: New York University Press, 1996.

_____ *Globalization and Its Discontents: Essays on the New Mobility of People and Money*. New York: New Press, 1998.

Schafir, Gershon, ed. *The Citizenship Debates: A Reader*. Minneapolis: University of Minnesota Press, 1998.

Shapiro, Michael J. *Violent Cartographies: Mapping Cultures of War*. Minneapolis: University of Minnesota Press, 1997.

Smith, Ann Marie. *Laclau and Mouffe: The Radical Democratic Imaginary*. New York: Routledge, 1999.

Smith, Robert C. "Transnational Migration, Assimilation, and Political Community." In Margaret E. Crahan and Alberto Vourvoulias-Busch, eds., *The City and the World: New York's Global Future*, 110–32. New York: Council on Foreign Relations, 1997.

Spivak, Gayatri. *A Critique of Postcolonial Reason: Toward a History of Vanishing Present*. Harvard University Press, 1999.

Teivanen, Teivo. "Overcoming Economism." Paper presented at The Political Economy of World Systems Conference, Boston College, March 2000.

Torres, Andres and José E. Velazquez, eds. *The Puerto Rican Movement: Voices from the Diaspora*. Philadelphia: Temple University Press, 1995.

Totti, Xavier. "The Making of a Latino Ethnic Identity." *Dissent* (Fall 1987): 537–42.

Valentin, Gilberto Gerena. Interview by Stanley Aronowitz, Agustín Laó-Montes, and Pedro Angel Rivera as part of the CAMEO Project of the City University of New York–Graduate School Center for Cultural Studies, Lares, Puerto Rico, January 1991.

Vega, Bernardo. *Memoirs of Bernardo Vega: A Contribution to the History of the Puerto Rican Community in New York*. New York: Monthly Review Press, 1984.

Velarde, Nora. "Aníbal Quijano: la modernidad, el capital, y América Latina nacen el mismo día." *Sociedad y Política* 10 (enero 1991): 49; translation by Kelvin Santiago-Valles.

Wallerstein, Immanuel. *The Modern World System I: Capitalist Agriculture and the Origins of the European World Economy in the Sixteenth Century.* Academic Press, 1974.

—— *Utopistics: Or, Historical Choices of the Twenty-First Century.* New York: New Press, 1998.

Walzer, Michael. *Spheres of Justice: A Defense of Pluralism and Equality.* New York: Basic Books, 1983.

Young, Iris Marion. *Justice and the Politics of Difference.* Princeton, N.J.: Princeton University Press, 1990

CHAPTER FIVE

Culture in the Battlefront[1]

From Nationalist to Pan-Latino Projects

Arlene Dávila

> We are experiencing a cultural renaissance, a period of assertion and affirmation. . . . It is part of a revolution, a revolution which must be fought on every front. And the passion of our art must take its rightful place in this battleground because it is an instrument that condemns, enlightens and creates understanding.
>
> —*Felipe Dante (c. 1970s)*[2]

> I know, I already know, I am convinced already, all my life, that I have a Spanish cultural element, but I have never known about an Indian element, or African, in my culture. And I am now in a stage where I am going into that question. And then, if you, like others, interpret my attitude as anti-Spanish, "chevere," but I know that I want to know about what is Indian and Black and to hell with the Spanish question.
>
> —*Jorge Soto (1974)*

Although art, identity, and politics are increasingly at the forefront of contemporary analysis, such issues have long been closely intertwined in U.S. Latino cultural politics. Behind the leading Latino cultural and artistic institutions today lie the struggles for self-empowerment in the 1960s by both Chicanos and Puerto Ricans, who made cultural initiatives central to their quest for political enfranchisement.[3] To date, however, although more research is due in this area, we are considerably more familiar with the politicization of culture within the Chicano nationalist movement than with how similar processes reverberated in New York City, even though they are precursors to some of the foremost Latino cultural and artistic institutions in this country.[4] These include El Museo del Barrio, the Association of Hispanic Arts, the Caribbean Cultural Center, and other initiatives that were born out of the struggles of Puerto Rican artists, educators, and cultural workers for greater representation in the late 1960s and have since been pivotal for the public projection and definition of images of latinidad. An analysis of these earlier cultural initiatives is crucial if we are to analyze their scope and ensuing repercussions in a context in which these are increasingly the subject of scrutiny and reappraisal. Today, the relative popularity attained by Latin American art, as evinced in its internationalized commercialization and exhibitions in mainstream museums since the 1980s, suggests that much was gained from these earlier struggles, yet there is nevertheless great pessimism and skepticism among the city's Latino artistic and cultural community about whether anything of substance was indeed gained from these efforts.[5]

What follows engages these issues through an examination of the cultural struggles led by Puerto Rican artists and activists in New York City during the late 1960s and early 1970s as well as of the projects they engendered, the opportunities they opened, and the issues that have since affected the artistic and cultural initiatives on behalf of not only Puerto Ricans but also other Latino populations in the city. My goal is to contribute to the growing literature on the relationship between art, museums, and identity by providing a historical view of some of the issues impacting the growth and development of some important Latino cultural institutions since the 1960s.[6] Of course, by taking the late 1960s as my point of departure, I am not suggesting that cultural initiatives had been absent from the political and social endeavors of Puerto Ricans and other Latino groups in earlier decades. In the mid-1920s there were already at least forty-three self-identified Hispanic organizations in New York City, many of which included cultural work or civically oriented activities, whereas the Puerto Rican hometown clubs, which gathered Puerto Rican immigrants around their respective hometowns, celebrated a range of cultural and artistic programs (Sánchez-Korroll 1994). From the 1960s onwards, however, cultural and artistic work was not solely a complement to wider social projects but rather the center point of a variety of groups intent on fostering pride and increasing the representation and empowerment of the Puerto Rican population through the discovery, preservation, and promotion of culture.[7] My analysis probes the politicization of culture by Puerto Rican artists and activists at this time and examines the processes through which their artistic and cultural projects were transformed into institutions that are still relevant and highly contested in the contemporary context.

My examination will focus on the creation and ensuing development of El Taller Boricua, a workshop of Puerto Rican artists, and El Museo del Barrio, a Latino and Latin American museum, two institutions founded in the late 1960s that have since served as catalysts for the general recognition of Latino art and artists in New York City and beyond. Members and founders of El Taller Boricua have been central to the development of the new Julia de Burgos Latino Cultural Center in East Harlem, whereas El Museo Del Barrio, a formerly all–Puerto Rican museum, has recently shifted its mission to represent all Latin American cultures, primarily focusing on those present in the United States. Both of these centers have historically operated from El Barrio, the East Harlem New York City community that is considered the quintessence of a Puerto Rican and, increasingly, of a Latino neighborhood in the city's ethnically inscribed geographic landscape, rendering them into public strongholds of Latinness within New York City and beyond, and thus into good entry points for our discussion.

I will start by examining some of the original goals of these projects from the standpoint of a number of their original founders and then move to consider some of the issues that have since affected their scope and programs.[8] In particular, I look at the factors leading to their transformation from grassroots efforts to institutionalized structures and affecting their shift in focus from a primarily Puerto Rican to a pan-Latino orientation. Ultimately, I will argue that these initiatives provided for an important social movement to the extent that they constituted "purposive collective actions whose outcome, in victory as in defeat" (Castells 1997:3), contributed to the ensuing, though partial, representation of latinidad. Similar to Chatterjee's (1986) discussion of cultural nationalism in colonial situations, it was at the level of revoking specific forms of ethnic dominance that the cultural battles waged their most frontal attack through their reassessment of Puerto Rican and, later, of Latin culture. What these initiatives were unable to subvert, however, was their marked and subordinate status in relation to the city's artistic and cultural landscape. This situation will be traced to both the politics of multiculturalism into which these projects were ultimately incorporated and to the very field of art production in which these projects were framed from the outset. Specifically, within the context of cultural pluralism and later multiculturalism in which these cultural movements emerged into projects, they simultaneously served as vehicles of empowerment and of containment of difference within the structures of the art world and the larger context of contemporary U.S. society. As such, I will argue that their ability to be a conduit of Latino "cultural citizenship" was constrained from their onset to the extent that we consider cultural citizenship not solely a means to expand claims to entitlements (Flores and Benmayor 1997) but also a means to reformulate the frameworks of recognition and debate. Following Rosaldo and Flores, a number of authors have argued that Latinos, as well as other subordinated groups in United States, may "claim space in society and eventually claim rights" by attaining cultural citizenship through cultural assertions that may serve as a means of expanding claims for future political entitlements (1997:15). As we will see later, however, affirmations of cultural citizenship are incapable of addressing the pervasiveness of dominant constructs of citizenship, nation, and race. Specifically, expanding claims for entitlement may leave untouched the structures of subordination, thereby simultaneously rendering the attained rights into venues of containment and subordination, as will be noted in this essay.

ART AND THE POLITICS OF RECOGNITION AND CONTAINMENT

Movements are seldom unified but rather are made up of a conglomerate of events, interconnected projects, and influences well beyond those that may eventually lead to concrete projects or permanent institutions. Such was the case with what a variety of Puerto Rican artists and cultural activists described to me as a "cultural revolution" involving an emphasis on the assertion of Puerto Rican identity through art and cultural initiatives in the late 1960s and early 1970s. As we shall see later, this cultural revolution was not a contained or isolated project but was directly involved in the context of the times. By the 1960s, cultural pluralism had become the dominant political discourse, and the state-led programs of distribution, such as the War on Poverty, had helped fuel ethnicity as a medium for politics and thus led to a concern over the promotion and preservation of a distinct cultural identity (Herbstein 1978). This revolution was similarly influenced by, and part and parcel of, the greater struggles for civil rights, a concern over decentralization of art and services, and also by a diversity of political actors from the Young Lords to the Movement for the Independence of Puerto Rico, leading activist groups in the late 1960s and 1970s to become involved in revolutionary populism, social service, and work toward the independence of Puerto Rico (Torres 1998). This is evident in the development of El Taller Boricua and El Museo del Barrio.

Implicated in all of these developments, El Taller Boricua originated from the rejection of and opposition to the prevailing high art, social club, and Hispanic orientations dominating Puerto Rican and Hispanic art and cultural institutions of the time by a number of Puerto Rican artists. For the founders of El Taller, this stance was most directly embodied by Friends of Puerto Rico, Inc., one of the first institutionalized organizations devoted to the promotion of Puerto Rican art in the city, in which the idea of establishing a populist art workshop was first born. Friends of Puerto Rico had been founded in the mid-1950s with private funds by Amalia Guerrero, a Puerto Rican art patron married to a Cuban entrepreneur, with the goals of promoting "pride among Puerto Ricans in their Puerto Rican and Hispanic roots" as well as of combating the growing prejudice against Puerto Ricans by "[offering] to the North American people a show of the culture and cultural history of Puerto Rico" and a place where people "could know, and admire our singers, actors, painters, sculptures, poets, writers" (Gil de la Madrid 1969:19, quoting Amalia Guerrero). Its activities revolved around art exhibits, theater and dance classes, and the celebration of upscale events awarding prizes for renowned intellectuals and personalities. As such, it was geared to and attracted a mostly middle-class and professional Puerto Rican constituency intent on emphasizing Puerto Rico's Hispanic roots as a means of proving Puerto Rico's artistic contribution within conventional standards of art and culture.

Notwithstanding the institution's exclusivity, Friends of Puerto Rico would be a great influence to El Taller's development insofar as it functioned as a key meeting ground for older and younger Puerto Rican artists in the city. Indeed, the founders of El Taller consisted of artists who had been invited to its artists-in-residence program or who had obtained working space in exchange for performing maintenance work around the premises. They included an all-male group of younger U.S.-born or-based Puerto Rican artists such as Adrian Garcia and Armando Soto, who had attended the School of Visual Arts under the G.I. Bill, as well as established artists from the island such as Carlos Osorio and later Rafael Tufiño, who had been actively involved in the commonwealth's nationalist cultural efforts in its popular education and graphic arts division.[9]

Although diverse in their backgrounds—Carlos Osorio and Rafael Tufiño, for instance, had attained national recognition on the island as opposed to their younger New York–based counterparts—El Taller artists shared important commonalities. Primary among them was their commitment to Puerto Rico's independence, following the pattern of most activists of the times, which linked the fate of the Puerto Rican communities in the states with the struggle on the island (Torres 1998). El Taller members also shared a rejection of the Friends of Puerto Rico's fine arts and Hispanic orientation, which was contrary to the cultural nationalism that accompanied larger struggles for civil empowerment and was seen by Puerto Rican artists both as a denial of a Puerto Rican identity and a rejection of the African and indigenous elements of Puerto Rican culture. They were also similarly critical of the institution's high-art outlook, which they regarded as being divorced from the needs of the larger Puerto Rican community and at odds with what would become a prevalent view of the times: that art needed to be not in galleries but directly connected with the everyday reality of the people. Indeed, differences in focus and emphasis between Friends of Puerto Rico and what would become El Taller would become evident in subsequent years. By the mid-1970s, Friends of Puerto Rico had developed into Cayman Gallery as a Latin American gallery in Soho, far from the Puerto Rican enclaves in the city. El Taller Boricua, for its part, after leaving the premises of Friends of Puerto Rico, relocated to East Harlem's El Barrio directly across the street from the Young Lords headquarters, where its art was immediately connected to the social struggles of the times.[10]

This stress on the social functions of art is evident in El Taller's rejection of formal organization: it was not organized as an institution but as a loose collective of artists with no formal membership other than their commitment to work, and it was the streets of El Barrio, rather than a slick gallery, that became their permanent exhibition space through outdoor and travelling exhibits. This stance was again informed by the context of the times. Up to the 1960s, Puerto Rican politics had undergone a process of professionalization leading to a number of social and nonprofit institutions intent on integrating Puerto Ricans into mainstream society. These efforts, along with the availability of antipoverty funds and programs, had undergone a process of bureaucratization that had further diverted them from their immediate community (Rodriguez-Fraticelli, Sanabria, and Tirado 1991; Herbstein 1978). By turning to grassroots politics, cultural workers were therefore rejecting the then-current formalization of politics to embrace instead a revolutionary grassroots struggle orientation, although we shall see that their initiatives could not resist similar bureaucratic transformations. This lack of concern for institutional boundaries is also evident in the close relationship between El Taller and El Museo del Barrio, both having been founded in 1969 within a few months of each other's inception. During the early stages of both organizations, artists in El Taller provided many of the cultural workshops in El Museo and worked closely in its development. All were part and parcel of the common and larger historical goal of the times: the expansion of the available sites and venues to showcase and assert Puerto Rican culture.

Marcos Dimas, an early founder of El Taller and still one of its current administrators as of 1999, recalled that they saw themselves as a solidarity movement. As he stated, "What we wanted to do was about educating the community, we saw ourselves as an art movement, a political movement, a solidarity movement to other struggles, such as the students' movements and all others who looked to us and would tell us 'vamos a tener una protesta' and there we were, making posters, and participating" (1997). Their goals were directed to their immediate community, not limited to the geographical space of El Barrio but rather to the greater Puerto Rican diaspora—hence their full name of El Taller Alma Boricua, embodying their wish to serve as the "cultural soul of the community" in solidarity with the larger context of the times.

Yet El Taller's concern with the decentralization and democratization of art did not develop in a vacuum. Decentralization was a key demand of a variety of civil rights initiatives seeking greater community control over schools and services by individual communities as well as a key preoccupation of the artistic community. In particular, decentralization was a key concern of the Art Workers Coalition, an antiwar and activist group that militated for multiracial representation in museums and other measures to increase representativity in the city's museums in which they themselves participated (Lippard 1990). Among other issues, this group lobbied for the involvement of artists in museum boards as well as for the decentralization of museums' collections and for the opening of branches in minority communities where art could be brought into people's everyday lives. Such demands, along with the rise of state and federal arts funding, would lead to the development of neighborhood museums and community art spaces by mainstream institutions intent on serving minority communities as well as to minority-generated institutions such as The Studio Museum of Harlem and El Museo del Barrio that were intent on self-representation, as I will discuss later.

However, true to the double political orientation of Puerto Rican political initiatives of the times (informed by and directed at both the U.S.- and island-based Puerto Rican communities), the goal of decentralization was simultaneously fed by island-specific artistic developments. Through the involvement of artists Rafael Tufino and Carlos Osorio, the populist cultural policies initiated by the government of Puerto Rico in the 1940s and 1950s reverberated in New York City. Just as these policies had made grassroots education a priority and graphics and posters a medium of communication for the promotion of social change, printmaking and graphic art work became central components to El Taller's political and social goals in New York City. El Taller was hence transformed not solely into a cultural soul but also into an artistic satellite for the production of educational materials to accompany artistic tours and workshops for schools and colleges, which were simultaneously developing Puerto Rican Studies departments and programs, as well as for mainstream museums that were now seeking workshops and lectures to meet the growing demands for ethnic representation.

El Museo del Barrio, for its part, was similarly involved in larger social struggles of civil empowerment in the late 1960s. In particular, this was the result of the growing demands for educational equity and for the representation of Puerto Rican history and culture in public schools, issues that provoked demonstrations and boycotts throughout the 1960s. The idea to develop a nonschool educational program that would provide Puerto Rican children with a positive self-image came out of a group of parents and educators from community school district 4.[11] It aimed to counter the effects of racism and prejudice that they felt were impairing their children's education. Its funding came entirely from the New York State Board of Education, and it was housed in one of the district's four schools until 1971. At that time, it was incorporated as a nonprofit entity called Amigos del Museo del Barrio, Inc., and moved to El Barrio (first briefly to 116 East Street and later to Third Avenue between 107 and 108th Streets) to achieve greater independence from the board of education and to diversify its funding sources, both of which were intended to strengthen its role as a Puerto Rican cultural institution.

Like El Taller, El Museo did not arise or conceptualize itself along traditional lines or as a formal museum, although we will see that this identity would ultimately impact its future development. Rather, El Museo was conceived by its founders as a community museum that, following the emergent model of such institutions, sought to place people rather than collections at the center of its mission. Its staff were mostly educators and artists rather than museum professionals, and its goals were those of social empowerment rather than artistic display. As its first director, artist Rafael Ortiz, recalled, the museum was an attempt to "come to terms with our cultural disenfranchisement," just as groups such as the Young Lords were dealing with Puerto Ricans' political and economic disenfranchisement, pointing to the organic relationships within other cultural movements and projects of the time (Glueck 1970:J-4). Accordingly, it had to be more than a stuffy museum; it had to bridge distinctions between folk and fine culture and thus serve to validate people's material culture in the present. The vision of its first director was to even do without walls and to develop instead a traveling museum that would visit different communities and revolve around multimedia exhibitions rather than around objects,[12] although this idea never materialized as it clashed with the needs of parents and educators for more concrete and permanent manifestations of their efforts.

In terms of programming, El Museo was geared toward asserting Puerto Ricanness in the city, both by promoting the island's roots and historical past among New York–born or –based Puerto Ricans as a means of attesting to the existence of a rich and "proud-worthy" past and present and, most importantly, by reevaluating the history and legacy of Puerto Ricans in the city. In particular, it served, as did other cultural initiatives of the time, as a medium through which to negotiate and bridge differential evaluations of island- and U.S.-generated cultural expressions, whereby island-based examples of Puerto Ricanness were considered the most authentic manifestation of Puerto Rican culture.[13] Of course, the differential evaluation of geographically bound over diasporic culture is not unique to the case at hand but is a documented trend of the process of cultural representation— dominant views of cultures as concrete and identifiable entities tied to a distinct past and territory have long fostered the devaluation of diasporic cultural expressions in relation to those connected to a geographically bounded territory (Rosaldo 1993; Segal and Handler 1995). The central place of Puerto Rico as symbolic resource to combat the subordinate and minority position of Puerto Ricans in the states, however, made the need to negotiate these distinctions an utmost priority. As recalled by Fernando Salicrup, a present administrator at El Taller, engaging in cultural work confronted them with the colonized mentality that contributed to the unequal validation of artists from the island and from the city, with the view that "to have a Puerto Rican art show we had to have people from Puerto Rico" (1997).

Indeed, in searching for materials to embody Puerto Ricanness, New York–based cultural workers often turned to the same traditions that had already been objectified on the island as embodiments of Puerto Rican culture. Directors of El Museo del Barrio even traveled to the island to meet with representatives of its cultural institutions, such as Ricardo Alegria, founder of the island's Institute of Puerto Rican Culture, to "bring culture back," as an artist-administrator stated, further attesting to the unequal evaluation of diasporic over island culture. Responding to a different context, however, their initiatives were also distinct. For one, grounded in U.S.

racial politics, they drew mostly on the subverted African and Indian legacies rather than on the rural and whitened past that was and is still emphasized by the island's cultural policies and institutions. El Museo and El Taller adopted iconography of the Taino (the island's pre-Columbian population) in their logos: El Taller artists seized a Taino symbol as a means of self-identification, and both institutions organized workshops and activities to promote knowledge of the Taino among youth. Similarly, traveling exhibitions and educational kits were assembled on history and culture, highlighting Puerto Rican history from the pre-Columbian period to the present, as a means of empowerment through the dissemination of Puerto Rican cultural knowledge.[14] These institutions were also unique in their interest in validating the New York Puerto Rican experience and its particular sense of aesthetics. Marta Moreno-Vega, former director of El Museo (1971–1974), recalls that the aim was to promote the elements that make Puerto Ricans Puerto Ricans wherever they are, which involved adopting a diasporic consciousness in which the nation is conceived not as a bounded territory but as a people. It was in this spirit that El Museo organized exhibitions on the history of El Barrio and that replicated the environment of Puerto Rican living spaces in the city. As she explained: "The idea was to showcase art that people could relate to, the similarities in the colors of the flora and fauna of Puerto Rico in the living rooms, things that identified us that were not supposed to be in cases, we tried to reflect what we are, we aimed to distill the pride, the historical memory, and that what happens in our home is part of our art and culture" (1997).

From our discussion so far, it is evident that a variety of interconnected events led to this cultural revolution and that the projects it engendered were initially quite informal and directly involved in the self-empowerment of Puerto Ricans in the city. Almost from the outset, however, larger structural factors ranging from government funding requirements to the larger field of art production would have a direct impact on the scope and ensuing institutionalization of these initiatives. As early as a year after their founding, these institutions were receiving small grants from the New York State Council on the Arts (NYSCA) and from city agencies that imposed new constraints on these institutions, particularly as they sought to come to terms with these new cultural centers not on their own terms but in terms of an already validated cultural establishment. In 1972, for instance, three years after its founding, El Museo del Barrio received over $110,000 from, among others, the National Endowment for the Arts (NEA), the New York Urban Coalition, NYSCA, and The Rockefeller Brothers Funds (Amigos del Museo del Barrio, Inc. 1973).

State funding for the arts in New York City had its origins in 1960, when the New York Arts Council was founded at the initiative of Governor Nelson Rockefeller. This made New York a pioneer and model for government arts funding, which was not adopted at the federal level until 1965 with the creation of the NEA. Behind these policies was the view that the city should nurture its role as an international artistic and cultural center, a view that reverberates today: New York city's artistic and cultural sector is not solely a key center of the global symbolic economy (Zukin 1996) but also a recognized export industry highly regarded for its economic impact and its role in strengthening the state's overall attractiveness.[15] Initially, NYSCA's funding was directed entirely at the Metropolitan Museum of Art and other mainstream institutions, but by the late 1960s, pressure from grassroots groups and the growing context of pluralism had contributed to the growth of special programs for ethnically based cultural institutions. (Pankratz 1993). In 1967 and 1968 the Ghetto Arts Program, later renamed the Special Arts Program, was created in NYSCA, and later NEA's Expansion Arts was created at the national level. The Ghetto's Arts Program's goals aimed to "provide artists in ghetto communities with the opportunity to develop their talents and present their work, and . . . to encourage activities that relate art to the everyday life of the ghetto. It aims at involving in its work professional minority artists who recognize a stake in the community in which they themselves developed and in which they continue to live" (New York State Council on the Arts 1969:85).

Needless to say, this mission was full of contradictions that are not foreign to current debates on the politics of multiculturalism. For one, instead of incorporating and legitimating the demands and populist definitions of art advanced by these institutions, it framed the work and scope of so-called ghetto institutions solely as a matter of representing their talents and works to the ghetto community. As Gino Rodríguez, founder and director of The Alternative Museum in New York City and a critic of these initiatives, countered, "This was a matter of giving us the money so we would stay in el barrio, you are happy here and we are happy there. They are not saying come to our home and feast in our table." Related to this is the whole concept of neighborhood museum. It would be impossible to determine the exact chronology of this concept, but it should be noted that rather than being the exclusive outcome of grassroots efforts, these museums were the result of compromises and accommodations between, on the one hand, the demands of minority communities for greater and equal representation and, on the other, the mainstream museums' refusal to meet these demands on their own terms, which would have required the transformation of the very definition of mainstream art and institutions.

These issues became evident during the Seminar on Neighborhood Museums held in 1969 at the Brooklyn Children's Museum with the support of NYSCA and other art agencies to delineate the concept of a neighborhood museum or a "museum for the people" and to debate its feasibility in terms of programming, administration, and community participation.[16] The meeting, though originally planned for New York State museum directors, attracted hundreds of participants nationwide, including museum directors and local arts council representatives, along with representatives of some of the newly founded neighborhood museums, such as The Studio Museum and El Museo del Barrio. It also evolved into a heated discussion that triggered criticisms from African Americans and Latinos in the audience about the top-down nature of many neighborhood initiatives, the lack of minority representation at the meeting, and the extent to which it would serve as a "hip cop out" for the mainstream museum establishment. In particular, the concept was seen as a substitute for the demands that minority artists receive an equal footing at institutions such as the Metropolitan Museum and that such establishments share their collections with the newly founded institutions, instead of their having to always rely on multimedia and educational programs.

Other criticisms were voiced at this meeting. What I would point out here is that neither government funding nor support for special programs at this time was an absolute accomplishment. Rather, these gains were always involved in the politics of encompassing and accommodating, if not neutralizing, demands for full representation. In particular, such strategies helped reinforce distinctions between the supposedly universal mainstream art institutions and ethnic ghetto museums, whose inability to meet universal standards of art and culture was reaffirmed through these distinctions. Government funding also constrained the nationalist and political outlook of these institutions. As succinctly expressed by artist Nitza Tufiño, who was originally involved in both El Taller and El Museo, "We were getting money from the establishment, so we knew that there were certain things of which you could not talk about in workshops and activities. The thing was how to deal with that, and get the money, and still do the job" (1997). Similarly, Taller administrators recalled the difficulty of applying to state funding sources while conducting programs that could have been seen as contradictory to the U.S. system, such as workshops that promoted the figure of Puerto Rican nationalist leader Pedro Albizu Campos. They were well aware that such initiatives could be perceived as militant and subversive rather than as purely educational as intended by the funding sources, particularly at a time when African American and Latino organizations such as the Young Lords were subject to government persecution and surveillance. El Taller's premises were raided a number of times, and although these events were never explained, Taller members not surprisingly saw them as connected to their nationalistic programming. Tapping government funds was therefore always a matter of strategizing, or as Dimas (1997) explained, a matter of veiling their work by writing very general and generic proposals for "the promotion of Puerto Rican history and its cultural and artistic expression" while adopting a more politicized outlook in practice.

Funding also raised issues of professionalization. Recall that it was not cultural and political revolutionaries but professionals, even though ghetto ones, that these grants had in mind when they were first developed. The issue was simple, as Marta Moreno-Vega stated when recalling the pressure she felt during the mid 1970s: "Now you had to continue creating the 'aura' to get the monies" (1997). This in turn meant that artists could not be administrators and that the latter could not pass as artists, and this eventually led to a distancing from the original roots of these institutions and their connection to grassroots activism. Government funding also required that these ethnic and grassroots institutions resemble the traditional model of nonprofit art institutions with a board, trained and paid staff, and "quality" programs (Pankratz 1993). Indeed, while government funding in New York has embraced accessibility of services and the representation of a variety of constituencies as criteria since the mid-1970s, quality and professionalism have always remained paramount to its mission of maintaining New York as a "national cultural center."[17]

Thus, within a couple years of their establishment, these entities were on their way to becoming incorporated into the city's cultural and artistic landscape as well as into its funding and the larger evaluative structures of the arts establishment. Evidence of their ability to strategize through such structures, however, would be shortly forthcoming: the same actors involved in their development would go on to lead a variety of Latino-oriented institutions in the city that, though still marginal to the mainstream art structures, would be far from the fluid entities they once were: Marta Moreno-Vega, a former director of El Museo, went on to develop the Association of Hispanic Arts and later the Caribbean Cultural Center; writer Jack Agueros, another director of El Museo (1977–1985), was pivotal in the shift from Friends of Puerto Rico into the Cayman Gallery as a Latin American art gallery; and artist Nitza Tufiño, who worked at both El Museo and El Taller, became involved in the development of the short-lived yet highly influential Museum of Contemporary Hispanic Art (mid 1980s–1992).

LATINIZING CULTURE: FROM NATIONALIST TO PANNATIONALIST PROJECTS

Up to now I have argued that both El Museo and El Taller were outcomes of processes of struggle and of the active compromises with the larger evaluative structures of the art world. As we saw, these negotiations would lead to their transformation from grassroots organizations to institutionally based projects as the political and social climate changed from one of community empowerment to one of minority representation. Yet also common to many of the institutions developed at this time was their eventual transformation from Puerto Rican to Latino/Hispanic entities. We must ask whether this change represented the consolidation of a pan-Latino identity among these and other Latino cultural and artistic institutions or whether this transformation was also part of the negotiations involved in the institutionalization of these earlier projects. Through a discussion of the recent shift in El Museo del Barrio's changing mission toward representing all Latino and Latin American cultures primarily in the United States, I suggest that both processes are at play.

The first thing that should be noted is that since the mid-1970s this transformation has been conceived of as a need resulting from either changing demographics, the larger context of Latin American art, or the preference of funding sources, suggesting that these changes may have little connection with people's acceptance or rejection of Latinness as an encompassing identity or a representational category. Elsewhere, I discuss how the latinization of this formerly Puerto Rican institution is more closely connected to larger dynamics of contemporary U.S. identity politics than to particular demographic developments in the neighborhood itself (Dávila 1999). Specifically, while New York City's population has indeed undergone a process of latinization, with a greater and more diversified Latino population from Mexico, Central America, and the Dominican Republic, the East Harlem neighborhood of El Barrio, which El Museo del Barrio has historically claimed to represent, has remained a primarily Puerto Rican enclave. Indeed, while the Puerto Rican population in the city has dwindled from 80 percent of the Latino population in the 1960s to only 43 percent in the 1990s, Puerto Ricans are still 79.2 percent of El Barrio's Latino's population, which overall stands at 57.3 percent (Hanson-Sánchez 1996). Larger issues beyond immediate demographic changes are thus clearly behind El Museo's transformation. It is not my intention to discuss all the different factors behind this development, yet for the purposes of this work I would like to draw attention to the continued association made by previous directors of El Museo between the professionalization of this institution and the broadening of its scope to represent Latin American populations (Wilson 1984; Moreno 1997). This was already evident in the late 1970s, when the administration of Jack Agüeros conceived of broadening El Museo's mission to include other Latin American cultures as part of a larger goal of professionalizing the museum to establish for it a respectful place within the realm of international art. As discussed by María-José Moreno, these new goals were evidenced in its change of logo—the culturally loaded Taino hieroglyphic was replaced by a much vaguer logo of arched windows—and in unfulfilled plans to change El Museo's name to disconnect it from its barrio orientations (1997:114).

Evident in these concerns is the abiding permanence of dominant evaluations of art as universal and valuable in and of itself, devoid of ethnic identity or utilitarian purpose.[18] The actors involved in these initiatives had struggled to rename one of the Metropolitan Museum of Modern Art's wings after Puerto Rican nationalist leader Pedro Albizu Campos along with the Art Workers Coalition's decentralization committee, and they had lobbied for greater inclusion of Latino artists in mainstream shows and institutions (Wilson 1984). Similarly, issues regarding the recognition of different aesthetics—that Latino art is not only folklore or ethnic art; that it is diverse in styles, themes, and aesthetics; and that it should not be solely judged according to Western artistic standards—were central to greater claims for representation. Their demands were therefore those of inclusion in their own terms, as in the epigraph at the beginning of this essay, a call to "tear down the racist barriers which insist on denying our place as rightful contributors" (see endnote 1).

However, although similar concerns would reverberate up to the present, the most daring quest—these artists' attempts to reframe the very definition of art by gaining acceptance on their own terms rather than on those of mainstream institutions—would quickly come to an end. Seeking to come to terms with the dominant structures of art production and evaluation, these institutions found themselves implicated in discourses of high culture that were directly at odds with their grassroots origins if they were to avoid the risk of continued marginalization. And in seeking to validate projects in terms of larger structures and frameworks, the extension to the representation of Latin American art became paramount. For it is Latin American art, not Puerto Rican or U.S. Latino art, that has attained an international reputation as well as a position in the market and in the overall art establishment (Goldman 1994; Fusco 1995). This has been particularly the case after the 1980s, when the so-called Latin art boom, marked by the internationalized commercialization of Latin American art and its relatively greater exposure in mainstream museums, has further consolidated Latin American art as an academic, curatorial, and marketing category for any type of Latin art or artist, whether Mexican or Chicano, U.S.-born Puerto Rican or Chilean. In this context, to not transform themselves into Latin American institutions and to not frame their programs and exhibitions in terms of this larger category would be construed as obstacles to achieving greater scope and significance, and most significantly, funding.

Needless to say, the positioning of projects against the larger category of Latin American art and the hiring professional staff, among other measures, have not rid El Museo and other Latino institutions of their subordinate status vis-à-vis mainstream institutions. Central to the dynamics of subordination is the pervasiveness of such marked status, which remains the point of reference for evaluative estimations, limiting future efforts at self-representation by ethnically marked institutions.[19] Thus, although El Museo del Barrio has achieved a higher standing within the city's artistic landscape since its transformation into a Latin American institution, its staff still complain that "it is still up to us to be up with the mainstream museums," that these latter "will not come to our institutions, or notice our artists."

However, their marginal position should not divert us from the important role played by Latino-oriented or -directed institutions in relation to the larger cultural landscape in the city and beyond. Particularly relevant here is their location in New York City, an international center for the validation of trends, artists, and cultural products, which transforms any self-identified Latino/Latin American initiative into a likely contested terrain for the variety of interests involved in the promotion of Latin American art. Specifically, these institutions are of interest to curators interested in learning, discovering, or showcasing Latin artists as well as to a greater and more diversified number of Latin American artists, who see them as entry points to the competitive New York market, and even to corporations, which find them ideal venues to address Latinos either as a homogeneous population or as groups of distinct nationalities. Indeed, the latinization of the programming has been accompanied by a more diversified source of funding support. El Museo's change in mission, for instance, has attracted new funders from ministries of culture of different Latin American countries to private corporations, allowing the institution to decrease its traditional dependency on public funds.[20]

In this way, the latinization of New York's cultural landscape cannot be analyzed apart from the greater context affecting the funding and evaluation of Latin American art, and it is these processes that are most likely to continue to affect the consolidation of this category. This is particularly the case given that, at the local level, the current emphasis on Latino exhibitions and the latinization of programs and institutions often emerges as a contested and sometimes problematic development. For one, this trend has not benefited all similarly defined Latin artists in an equal manner. Although the category of Latin American art has evolved into the dominant classification supposedly encompassing U.S.- and Latin American–based artists irrespective of class, race, ethnicity, or length of stay in the United States, among other variables, U.S.-based Latinos have not benefited from the interest in Latin American art as much as their Latin American counterparts. Specifically, deterritorialized Latino artists are more likely to be devalued as minority rather than as national artists, and their art is more likely to be disregarded as narrow, more local than universal, or too political and inferior in relation to the eurocentric tendencies reproduced in Latin American art and scholarship, which largely prioritize European aesthetic standards and techniques.[21]

In this context, the latinization of cultural institutions and programs in the city has often served to veil distinctions and inequalities among the so-called Latin American artists. These are the processes behind recent debates over the transformation of El Museo's mission among Puerto Rican artists and among some of the original actors involved in its development. As I have noted elsewhere, some artists see this change as surrendering a space for asserting Puerto Ricans' identity, as part of a strategy of gentrification "to move Puerto Ricans away from their roots," or as the eradication of past struggles in a context in which the popularization of Latin art and culture is simultaneously bringing to light existing inequalities among Latin American artists (Dávila 1999:194–95).

Of course, these views are not antithetical to the simultaneous embrace of the discourse of latinidad by Puerto Rican artists, pointing toward the existence and development of contending discourses and ideologies of Latin Americanism and latinidad. This is particularly so given that since the 1980s, Latin-oriented shows have evolved into the primary exhibition venue for Puerto Rican and other Latin artists in the United States, furthering the extension and blurring of Latino/Latin American appellations among artists and curators alike. After all, the popularization of Latin American art has not been accompanied by the inclusion of Latin artists within mainstream museums or in thematic or conceptual shows, processes that remind us of the partial containment and recognition of ethnic differences that are intrinsic to the politics of multiculturalism and representation. Thus, although critical of the politics of multiculturalism and of the panethnic categories that are currently used to encompass them, most artists with whom I spoke are nevertheless compelled to advocate the need for more Latino-oriented shows and museums.

For Puerto Rican artists, however, who are rendered as colonial U.S. citizens as a result of the island's ambiguous political relationship as a free associated state of the United States, their Latin American identity is even more doubtful. For these artists, claiming a Latin American identity often involves having to educate people about Puerto Rico's Latin American background. This was one of the primary reasons behind the change of El Museo's mission, as explained by Susana Torruella-Leval, the institution's director (1993–present), to inform Latin American art scholars that "Puerto Rico is part of Latin America" (1997). Reminiscent of the institution's earlier attempts at expanding territorially bounded definitions of identity to legitimate the Nuyorican experience, El Museo is thus similarly confronted today with the need to legitimize the diasporic, nongeographic character of Puerto Ricans' Latin roots.

However, the latinization of cultural projects and institutions is not solely guided by artistic considerations. Appealing to Latino panethnicity also affords contemporary cultural workers with a powerful medium in which to contest monolithic cultural politics. This discourse is not deemed subversive as the discourse of Puerto Rican nationalism once was, and today in El Barrio it is highly utilitarian. This issue came to light when discussing the establishment of the Julia de Burgos Latino Cultural Center in East Harlem, an umbrella institution that would gather a number of Latin artistic, theatrical, and musical groups in one location, as well as El Museo's Latino mission with artist and community activist Fernando Salicrup. As he plainly put it, these initiatives "help stop gentrification" (1997). For him, what was most important not only about the Julia de Burgos Latino Cultural

Center, which he, along with El Taller and The East Harlem Community Planning Board, is spearheading, but also about El Museo del Barrio's recent spotlight is the possibility that these projects could be a way to safeguard East Harlem as a Latino stronghold through their simultaneous symbolic and physical claim to the area. Considering the proximity of these institutions to the prime real estate area of New York's Upper East Side, it is easy to understand his concern. This closeness makes El Barrio a prime candidate for development and gentrification, processes that this area is rapidly undergoing. And although it is difficult to assess their ability to stop gentrification, it is also evident that in this context, these initiatives take on added importance in marking identity in and through space, thereby serving as "inscriptions of resistance" (Koptiuch 1997:241, after Franco 1985) by reinforcing the area's Latino cultural identity. In this way, as he went on to describe the Julia de Burgos Latino Cultural Center, it was evident that appealing to a pan-Latino identity was a powerful move within the context of local identity politics in El Barrio. In this context, Latino/a identity is being deployed to save the area's Puerto Rican history from gentrification while appealing to an increasingly diversified Latino population not only in El Barrio but also within the realm of the city's planning agencies and thus to place culture at the center of empowerment in the city.

I started this discussion by suggesting that the cultural initiatives of the late 1960s and 1970s provided important social movements that contributed to the recognition of latinidad but not to the transformation of the frameworks of recognition and debate that affected their evaluation. These processes should be evident already: not only were these once-fluid ventures transformed into institutionalized projects, but they have also been pitted against dominant evaluative hierarchies, forcing them to endlessly try to reverse the subordination status stemming from the politics of multiculturalism and from the field of art production in which these struggles were initially framed. Part and parcel of the processes of multiculturalism are processes of exclusion from the structures of representation, with the result that these institutions did manage to bring about representation to Puerto Ricans and continue to engage in similar processes on behalf of a larger Latino/Latin American population but always in terms of an already validated cultural establishment. Multiculturalism and identity politics notwithstanding, it is "universal," not ethnic, art and types of institutions that have the most legitimacy, and it is their standards that have since shaped the development and ultimately the fate or evaluation of Latino projects. Nevertheless, although always the result of compromises, the institutionalization of these early Puerto Rican cultural initiatives would indeed help set an important precedent to the city's artistic landscape. Issues of artistic and cultural participation as well as of funding and representation have since been implicated in matters of rights and entitlement. What we are reminded of is that the expansion of claims for political enfranchisement through representation may do little to affect the processes of subordination that may simultaneously render rights, representation, and entitlements into venues of containment. Faced with this realization, the frustrations of cultural workers today take on added meaning as signs of a general awareness of the compromises ensuing from earlier struggles or perhaps as guides toward alternative fusions of culture and politics.

NOTES

1. This article first appeared in *Museum Anthropology* 23(3).
2. Undated leaflet (c. 1970s), a "call to artists to tear down the racist barriers which insist on denying our place as rightful contributors," circulated by Felipe Dante, New York–based photographer and writer. Leaflet found in artist Marcos Dimas's scrapbook on El Taller Boricua, El Taller Boricua, New York, during interview by the author (July 1997).
3. See the report by the National Association of Latino Arts and Culture (1995) for a brief historical account of the context behind the foundation of Latino cultural institutions in this country.
4. Although more work can be done in this area, the Chicano cultural nationalist movement of the 1960s and the particular context of the West Coast have been explored by a variety of scholars such as Goldman (1994), Ybarra-Frausto (1991), and Cockcroft (1977). New York's cultural movements led by Puerto Ricans in the 1960s, however, have not received comparable scholarly attention.
5. Some traveling exhibitions linked to this Latin art boom in the late 1980s include "Hispanic Arts in the United States: Thirty Contemporary Painters and Sculptors," organized by the Museum of Fine Arts in Houston; "The Latin American Spirit: Art and Artists in the United States, 1920–1970," by the Bronx Museum of the Arts; and "Art of the Fantastic: Latin America 1920–1970," by the Indianapolis Museum of Art. For a discussion of artists' skepticism about Latin art's current situation, readers may consult Moreno-Vega and Greene (1993) and Villa (1995).
6. Studies in this area range widely and include examinations of the role of museums in shaping particular cultural identities and on the different processes and interests impacting the growth, operations, and development of museums and cultural institutions (see, among others, Bright and Bakewell 1995; Handler and Gable 1997; Kaplan 1994; Karp, Mullen Kreamer, and Lavine 1992; and MacClancy 1997).
7. For discussions of how 1960s cultural and grassroots initiatives departed from those of previous decades and a discussion of their relation to the logics of the 1960s struggles for civil empowerment, readers may consult Rodríguez-Fraticelli, Sanabria, and Tirado (1991) regarding the nonprofit sector up to the 1960s and the memories of activist and educator Antonia Pantoja (1988) as well as the testimonies of Dimas and Salicrup in the catalogue for El Taller Boricua's twentieth anniversary (El Museo del Barrio 1990).
8. This paper is based on interviews and conversations with the founders and major actors behind the development of these institutions, most of whom are

still active in the Puerto Rican and Latin art milieu in New York City. Those interviewed include the artists Nitza Tufiño, Marcos Dimas, Andres Garcia, Rafael Ortíz, Fernando Salicrup, Pepon Osorio, and Juan Sánchez and the administrators Susana Torruella-Leval, current director of El Museo del Barrio; Marta Vega, director of the Caribbean Cultural Center; Jane Delgado, from the Bronx Museum of the Arts; and Gino Rodríguez, from the Alternative Museum. All interviews were conducted in the spring and summer of 1997. I have also selected these institutions because of my familiarity with these centers since the late 1980s, through having worked at them or attended their activities or through discussions of their work and operations.

9. Specifically, these artists were active in the Commonwealth of Puerto Rico's Division of Community Education (DIVEDCO), which centered around mobile educational and literacy workshops presented mostly in rural communities. DIVEDCO worked mostly through visual materials. Millions of booklets and posters were produced and distributed in rural communities along with hundreds of short films that served as the basis for staff-led community meetings and discussions. The topics covered a vast array of issues, but mostly aimed to direct people on how to deal with modernization and adapt to changes in family structure, diet, and other areas of social life. See Dávila (1997).

10. The relationship between El Taller and the Young Lords merits more attention than I can provide in this paper. I should note, however, that not only did El Taller work closely with the Young Lords but they also shared common members, such as the noted Nuyorican artist Jorge Soto.

11. See Quintero (1964a, b, c) for news articles about the educational demands of Puerto Rican communities and their struggles against the educational system leading to resolutions such as the development of culturally specific initiatives such as that of El Museo del Barrio. See Aquino Bermudes (1972) for an assessment of the effects of racism on the educational gains of Puerto Rican children and for a discussion of El Museo's role in developing bilingual-bicultural initiatives.

12. Interview with Rafael Ortíz by Jasmín Rivera, summer 1996.

13. For a discussion of these issues, see the historical Workshop on Culture sponsored by Hunter College's Puerto Rican Studies Department in 1974 with the goal of, among other issues, assessing and developing a critical perspective on Puerto Rican culture and analyzing both the relationship and the disjunctive experiences between island- and U.S.-based Puerto Ricans and their cultural expressions (Center for Puerto Rican Studies 1974). See also Lassalle and Pérez (1997) for a discussion of how dominant coordinates of identity, race, and nationality impinge upon the representation of Puerto Rican culture in the U.S. context.

14. Readers interested in learning more about El Museo's program in its early origins may consult its bilingual educational publication, *Quimbamba,* which was published throughout the 1970s.

15. A recent report by the Alliance for the Arts estimated that in 1997 the arts would contribute $16 billion dollars to New York State's economy. The

cultural nonprofit sector in particular is the largest employer among all sectors of the industry (Alliance for the Arts 1997).

16. See Harvey and Friedberg (1971).

17. These views are represented in many annual reports by NYSCA. See, for instance the New York State Council on the Arts (1975:8).

18. For discussions of the Western-based construction of art having intrinsic value in opposition to the cultural and social context in which it develops, see Marcus and Myers (1995), and see Bright and Blackwell (1995) and Lippard (1990) for a discussion of how these constructions affect the evaluation of Latin art.

19. For these issues, see Dominguez (1994); for the particular construction of Puerto Ricans as marked racial minorities, see Urciuoli (1996).

20. A larger discussion of El Museo del Barrio's development and its sources of funding is found in Moreno (1997).

21. See Gomez Peña (1996) and Fusco (1995) for a larger discussion of these issues.

REFERENCES

Alliance for the Arts. 1997. *The Economic Impact of the Arts on New York City and New York State (Executive Summary)*. A Report to Governor George E. Pataki and Mayor Rudolph W. Giuliani. New York: New York State Council on the Arts.

Amigos del Museo del Barrio, Inc. 1973. "Annual Report." *Quimbamba* (New York: El Museo del Barrio).

Aquino Bermudes, Federico. 1972. "Education and Puerto Rican Identity." *Quimbamba* (New York: El Museo del Barrio): 5–6.

Bright, Brenda and Liza Bakewell. 1995. *Looking High and Low: Art and Cultural Identity*. Tucson: University of Arizona Press.

Castells, Manuel. 1997. *The Power of Identity*. Oxford: Blackwell Publishers.

Center for Puerto Rican Studies, Taller de Cultura. 1974. *Los puertorriqueños y la cultura: crítica y debate/Culture and the Puerto Ricans: Critique and Debate*. New York: Center for Puerto Rican Studies.

Chatterjee, Partha. 1986. *Nationalist Thought and the Colonial World*. London: Zed Books.

Cockcroft, Eva. 1977. *Toward a People's Art: The Contemporary Mural Movement*. New York: Dutton.

Dávila, Arlene. 1997. *Sponsored Identities: Cultural Politics in Puerto Rico*. Philadelphia: Temple University Press.

—— 1999. "Latinizing Culture: Art, Museums and the Politics of Multicultural Encompassment." *Cultural Anthropology* 14(2): 180–202.

Dominguez, Virginia. 1994. "A Taste for 'the Other': Intellectual Complicity in Racializing Practices." *Current Anthropology* 35(4): 333–42.

El Museo del Barrio. 1990. *Taller Alma Boricua, 1969–1989, Reflecting on Twenty Years of The Puerto Rican Workshop*. New York: El Museo del Barrio.

Flores, William and Rina Benmayor. 1997. *Latino Cultural Citizenship: Claiming Identity, Space and Rights*. Boston: Beacon Press.

Franco, Jean. 1985. "New York Is a Third World City." *Tabloid* 9: 12–19.

Fusco, Coco. 1995. *English is Broken Here: Notes on Cultural Fusion in the Americas.* New York City: New Press.

Gil de la Madrid, Antonio. 1969. "Realización de un hermoso sueño: el centro puertorriqueño para las relaciones culturales." *El Diario/La Prensa,* 27 de abril, p. 19.

Glueck, Grace. 1970. "Barrio Museum: Hope Sí, Home No." *The New York Times,* July 30, p. J-4.

Goldman, Shrifra. 1994. *Dimensions of the Americas: Art and Social Change in Latin America and the United States.* Chicago: University of Chicago Press.

Gomez Peña, Guillermo. 1996. "The Multicultural Paradigm: An Open Letter to the National Arts Community." In Gerardo Mosqueros, ed., *Beyond the Fantastic: Contemporary Art Criticism from Latin America.* Cambridge, Mass.: MIT Press.

Handler, Richard and Eric Gable. 1997. *The New History in an Old Museum.* Durham, N.C., and London: Duke University Press.

Hanson-Sánchez, Christopher. 1996. *New York City Latino Neighborhoods Databook.* New York: Institute of Puerto Rican Policy.

Harvey, Emily Dennis and Bernard Friedberg. 1971. *A Museum for the People. A Report of Proceedings at the Seminar on Neighborhood Museums.* New York: Arno Press.

Herbstein, Judith. 1978. "Ritual and Politics of the Puerto Rican Community in New York City." Ph.D. diss., City University of New York.

Kaplan, Flora. 1994. *Museums and the Making of Ourselves.* London: Leicester.

Karp, Ivan, Christine Mullen Kreamer, and Steven Lavine. 1992. *Museums and Communities.* Washington, D.C.: Smithsonian Press.

Koptiuch, Kristin. 1997. "Third-Worlding at Home." In Akhil Gupta and James Ferguson, eds., *Culture, Power, Place: Explorations in Critical Anthropology.* Durham, N.C.: Duke University Press.

Lassalle, Yvonne and Marvette Pérez. 1997. " 'Virtually' Puerto Rican: Dis-Locating Puerto Rican-ness and Its Privileged Sites of Production." *Radical History Review* 68: 54–78.

Lippard, Lucy. 1990. "Socio-Political Implications." In *Taller Alma Boricua 1969–1989, Reflecting on Twenty Years of the Puerto Rican Workshop.* New York: El Museo del Barrio.

MacClancy, Jeremy. 1997. *Contesting Art: Art, Politics and Identity in the Modern World.* London: Berg.

Marcus, George and Fred Myers. 1995. *The Traffic in Culture: Refiguring Art and Anthropology.* Berkeley: University of California Press.

Moreno, María-José. 1997. "Identity Formation and Organizational Change in Nonprofit Institutions: A Comparative Study of Two Hispanic Museums." Ph.D. diss., Columbia University.

Moreno-Vega, Marta and Cherryl Greene. 1993. *Voices from the Battlefront: Achieving Cultural Equity.* New Jersey: Africa World Press.

National Association of Latino Arts and Culture. 1995. *Historical Survey and Current Assessment of Latino Arts and Cultural Organizations in the United States,* ed. Pedro A. Rodríguez. National Association of Latino Arts and

Culture in collaboration with Hispanic Research Center at the University of Texas at San Antonio.

New York State Council on the Arts. 1975 "Executive Director's Statement." In *NYSCA Annual Report (1975–1976)*. New York: New York State Council on the Arts.

——— 1969. "Ghetto Arts Program." In *NYSCA Annual Report (1969–1979)*. New York: New York State Council on the Arts.

Pankratz, David. 1993. *Multiculturalism and Public Arts Policy.* London: Bergin and Garvey.

Pantoja, Antonia. 1988. "Puerto Ricans in New York: A Historical and Community Development Perspective." *CENTRO* 7(5): 21–31.

Quintero, Luis. 1964a. "Borincanos hablarán por si mismos en la cuestión escolar." *El Diario/La Prensa*, 2 de febrero.

——— 1964b. "Grupos de derechos civiles no creen en promesas; afirman iran al boicot." *El Diario/La Prensa*, 31 de enero.

——— 1964c. "Rebelión puertorriqueña contra el sistema escolar de Nueva York." *El Diario/La Prensa*, 30 de enero, p. 1.

Rodríguez-Fraticelli, Carlos, Carlos Sanabria, and Amilcar Tirado. 1991. "Notes Toward a History of Puerto Rican Non-Profit Organizations in New York City." In Herman A. Gallegos and Michael O'Neill, eds., *Hispanics and the Non-Profit Sector.* New York: Foundation Center.

Rosaldo, Renato. 1993. *Culture and Truth.* Boston: Beacon Press.

Sánchez-Korrol, Virginia. 1994. *From Colonia to Community: The History of Puerto Ricans in New York City.* Berkeley: University of California Press.

Segal, Daniel and Richard Handler. 1995. "U.S. Multiculturalism and the Concept of Culture." *Identities: Global Studies of Culture and Power* 1(4): 391–408.

Soto, Jorge. 1974. Participant's comment. *Los puertorriqueños y la cultura: crítica y debate/Culture and the Puerto Ricans: Critique and Debate.* New York: Center for Puerto Rican Studies. Taller de Cultura.

Torres, Andrés. 1998. "Political Radicalism in the Diaspora: The Puerto Rican Experience." In Andrés Torres and José Velázquez, eds., *The Puerto Rican Movement.* Philadelphia: Temple University Press.

Urciuoli, Bonnie. 1996. *Exposing Prejudice, Puerto Rican Experiences of Language, Race and Class.* Boulder, Colo.: Westview.

Villa, Carlos. 1995. *Worlds in Collision: Dialogues on Multicultural Art Issues.* San Francisco: San Francisco Art Institute

Ybarra-Frausto, Tomas. 1991. "The Chicano Movement/The Movement of Chicano Art." In Ivan Karp and Steven Lavine, eds., *Exhibiting Cultures: The Poetics and Politics of Museum Display.* Washington, D.C.: Smithsonian Press.

Wilson, Patricia. 1984. "Puerto Rican Art in New York: The Aesthetic Analysis of Eleven Painters and their Work." Ph.D. diss., School of Education, New York University.

FIGURE 2. Pro-Central American Demonstration in the mid 1980s. Photo by Maximo Colon

FIGURE 3. Roberto Borrelli and his Kubata Folkloric Group at a Caribbean Festival in Lincoln Center. Photo by Maximo Colon, 1984

PART II

Expressive Cultures

Narrating, Imaging, and Performing Latinidad

CHAPTER SIX

Life Off the Hyphen

Latino Literature and Nuyorican Traditions

Juan Flores

In 1990 literary history was made when for the first time a book by a Hispanic writer won the Pulitzer Prize for fiction, generally considered the most prestigious honor in American literature. *The Mambo Kings Play Songs of Love,* the second novel by Cuban-American author Oscar Hijuelos, tells the story of two musician brothers, Cesar and Nestor Castillo, who arrive from Cuba in 1949 to try their luck on the New York music scene. Though not an untroubled immigrant success story, the Castillo brothers do get their piece of the American Dream when in 1955 they appear in a scene of the *I Love Lucy* show. The book's success, however, was boundless, having been helped along by what has been called "the most highly promoted Hispanic book in history by a major press."[1] Before culminating in the Pulitzer, recognition gathered in approving reviews, extensive exposure, advance sales of foreign rights, and a movie deal. By 1990 the time was right for a Hispanic Pulitzer, and when *Mambo Kings* rose to the top the door was thrown open for the entry of "Latino literature" onto the landscape of mainstream American letters.

The accolades were not at all unanimous, however, even among Latinos, many of whom believe that the book (and its insidious movie version) only repeat and reinforce some of the most nagging stereotypes of Latinos. Besides, the touted Pulitzer has never been regarded as a sure stamp of literary quality, many past awards having gone to books that were quickly forgotten and subject to more qualified reviews once they were read more closely. The Pulitzer board and juries, responsible for finalizing decisions since the first fiction award in 1948, have been composed almost entirely of white males, predominately professional journalists, with the first woman, non-white, nonjournalist board member admitted as late as 1980. Their perspective on literature is reflected in the principles which have guided the novel prize since its inception in 1917, where it is stated that the honor will go to the works that best present "the whole atmosphere of American life and the highest standard of American manners and manhood."[2] When the president of Columbia University Nicholas Butler Murray assumed his lengthy and influential role in the history of the prizes, the word "whole" was changed to "wholesome." The primacy of patriotic and moralistic criteria have led some to the view that "the Pulitzer Prize novels make a significant if negative contribution to the history of American fiction,"[3] while as early as 1935 Malcolm Cowley already was voicing his objection to the conventionalism and amateurishness of some of the prizewinners, and to the conservative biases of the prize itself. For Cowley, the prize implies "a guarantee to the American public that chosen books have nothing in them to shatter conventions or shake the state, nothing to drive the stock market down or interrupt the sleep of virgins."[4]

In the case of *The Mambo Kings Play Songs of Love,* the board and the jury (composed that year of the president of the Guggenheim Foundation, writer and critic Diane Johnson, and an English professor from Bowling Green State University) were divided, some preferring the other finalist, E. L. Doctorow's *Billy Bathgate,* others not liking either book. Once the prize had been announced and the movie hit the theaters, the songs of praise for Hijuelos's work became more muted, and the response of Latino readers ambivalent at best. While major Latino literature publisher and promoter Nicolás Kanellos, for example, refers to it as "the best Hispanic book ever published by a large commercial press," his judgment is qualified when he notes that "the novel drags in the middle and towards the end, without the benefit of a hard-driving plot. Its insistence on detailing the culture and spirit of the times and its repetitive reminiscence are somewhat tiring."[5] The Latino commentator for the *Village Voice,* Cuban-American Enrique Fernández, finds many objections to the claim that the book is "well-researched" in its historical references, pointing out some of the many anachronisms and other inaccuracies with regard to Latin music history. He concludes that "something tastes flat," and mentions that "the night Hijuelos's Pulitzer was announced, [some critical Latino] friends threatened to start a ruckus outside his house."[6] Perhaps the sharpest critical note is sounded by the young New York Puerto Rican writer Abraham Rodríguez, who points to the rampant sexism of the book as one of its most glaring retrogressions: "It took Hispanic women like thirty years to get over that macho bullshit," he says, "and he brings it all back, and they reward him with the Pulitzer. I think he's full of shit."[7]

Though hardly a breakthrough in literary terms, *The Mambo Kings* will likely retain its landmark status if only for its timelessness, the big prize establishing it as the book that inaugurated "Latino literature" as an accepted, English-language component of the multicultural canon, and as an attractive marketing rubric, in the 1990s. Several commentators speak in terms of "before and after" the event, noting the sudden plethora of works by Latinos published by major presses, the new space for Latino listings in catalogues and bookstores, and the promotionals featuring Latino writers— all in the decade since the award.[8] Beyond the expected celebrations, Hijuelos has become the author of choice to write prefaces to the many anthologies of Latino literature, where the inclusion of selections from his own work is all but obligatory.[9] After all, while some of the scenes in his laureled novel may well "interrupt the sleep of virgins," the overall effect is to bolster that "wholesome atmosphere of American life"; like Desi Arnaz, who has a preponderant symbolic role in the novel, it signals a modus vivendi between "Latino" culture and the coziness of the American living room, all the more welcome by our times when the Latino population has grown so alarmingly immense in size and diversity. As "full of shit" as he may be, Hijuelos helped provide the needed handle by winning the Pulitzer, the proof that a Latino book could make it into the long-elusive American mainstream, and the foundational fiction, as it were, of a legitimate, subcanonical concept of "Latino literature."

Not that a literature by U.S. Latinos is new, of course, its history extending back to the beginnings of American letters and encompassing a succession of discernible stages and periods.[10] The decades preceding the first "Premio Pulitzer" saw the publication of many works of Latino fiction and poetry, some of greater significance than *The Mambo Kings,* and even the idea of an embracing, pan-Latino heritage had been promoted by many critics and publishers, notably the Arte Público Press at the University of Houston. What is new about the post-Pulitzer period, in fact, is not so much the writing itself, which has tended to carry forward with the thematic and stylistic concerns of the previous years, but the prevalent notion of a Pulitzer-eligible Latino literature—that is, a literature by U.S. Latinos that is compatible with the prescribed "wholesomeness" of American life, a literature that, with all its play on cultural differences, matches up convincingly to the "standards of American manners and manhood." The coronation of *The Mambo Kings* heralded the ascendancy of a Latino literature which, however nostalgic for the old culture and resentful of the new, is markedly assimilationist toward American society and its culture, thus departing from the contestatory and oppositional stance characteristic of much writing by Latino authors in the past. Two prominent Latino critics, speaking specifically of Hijuelos, have referred to it as a Latino literature, and life, "on the hyphen," where the hyphen is embraced as an equal sign.[11]

Gustavo Pérez Firmat, the Cuban-American writer and professor of Latin American literature, entitles his intriguing book *Life on the Hyphen: The Cuban-American Way* (1994). His goal is very specific: to characterize the idiosyncrasy of Cuban culture in the U.S. setting, and to mark off what he refers to as the "one-and-a-half generation," that is, the generation of Cubans like himself, whose formative experience lies midway between those who grew up in Cuba before migrating ("too Cuban to be American") and the second generation, like the author's children, who grew up here and are "too American to be Cuban," Pérez Firmat traces this sequence of adaptations and negotiations between the Cuban and the American as links in what he calls the "Desi chain," refractions of Desi Arnaz's TV character Ricky Ricardo, "the single most visible Hispanic presence in the United States over the last forty years."[12] With Desi as the paradigm, and the elaborate discussion of the *I Love Lucy* show comprising the strongest section of the book, *Life on the Hyphen* ranges widely through Cuban-American literature and popular culture, with ample reference to Gloria Estefan and the Miami Sound Machine and to the historical placement of the mambo craze of the 1940s and 1950s. But it is Oscar Hijuelos and *The Mambo Kings,* where the "Desi chain" has the same fictional role as it has for Pérez Firmat's cultural discourse, that is clearly the most direct catalyst and exemplum for the enactment of the distinctively Cuban-American "life on the hyphen." While making due note of the criticisms of the book, and himself noting its many errors and dogged "anglocentrism," Pérez Firmat speaks of the "beguiling richness of the novel" and is obviously taken by this emblematic evidence of his theories of immigrant adaptation over the generations. He even ventures explanations for the book's blatant phallocentrism, and for the multitude of historical and linguistic errors, chalking them up to the task of cultural "translation." In the process, he offers the most extended and insightful interpretation of *The Mambo Kings* to date.[13]

With his subtitle and repeated insistence throughout the book, Pérez Firmat aims to limit himself to the "Cuban-American" way, the particularity of that hyphen, and that instance of Latino immigration adaptation. But as his reference to Desi as "the single most visible *Hispanic* presence" belies, the agenda of *Life on the Hyphen* is more ambitious than that: his lens may be "one-and-a-half generation" Cuban-American, but the cultural landscape is that of the contemporary United States as a whole. Inspired by a *People* magazine cover story devoted to Gloria Estefan, the book opens by taking this sign of celebrity as "a fair indication of the prominent role that Cuban Americans [no hyphen here] are playing in the increasing and inexorable—latinization of the United States; by now, few Americans will deny that, sooner or later, for better or for worse, the rhythm is going to get them."[14] Interest is not focused here on the hyphen in "Cuban-American," or the establishment of the neologism "cubanglo" as the most precise designation of Cuban one-and-a-halfers. As an extension of this group-specific discourse, Pérez Firmat is talking about "hyphenation" itself as a bicultural process, a pattern of cultural hybridization. At one point, his musings on Cubano-Americanism issue directly into a broad, three-stage theory of immigrant group experience; though Cuban-American examples prevail, his whole point is to explicate the paradigmatic passage of immigrant cultures and communities from the stages of "substitution" to "destitution" to "institution" in adjusting to the new "home country" and settling in. And among the immigrants, Cuban-Americans of course share their hyphenation with other Latinos, of whose generalized experience it is taken to be a "prominent" example.

It is important to bear these broader fields of validation in mind when addressing what Pérez Firmat regards as the distinctive quality of Cuban-American cultural placement in the U.S. setting. "I realize," he writes, "that mine is not a fashionable view of relations between 'majority' and 'minority' cultures. Contemporary models of culture contact tend to be oppositional: one culture, say white American, vanquishes another, say Native American. But the oppositional model, accurate as it may be in other situations, does not do justice to the balance of power in Cuban America" (6). To "oppositional" he prefers "appositional," for the "balance of power" in this case is defined by "contiguity" rather than "conflict," by "collusion" rather than "collision." This particular case, he contends, puts the lie to other, more "fashionable" views of ethnic relations and culture contact in that the hyphen, the ultimate mark of hybridity, signals equilibrium and not tension. Unlike other "minority" cultures, and at odds with the experience of many other Latino groups, "over the last several decades, in the United States, Cuba and America have been on a collusion course, . . . display[ing] an intricate equilibrium between the claims of each culture" (6). At no point venturing a historical or sociological explanation of this unique and exceptional circumstance, the author nevertheless upholds the representative stature of his case in point. Like his cherished hyphen, Pérez Firmat's analysis "is a seesaw, . . . tilt[ing] first one way, then the other" (6) between exceptionalism and generalization, between the "Cuban-American way" and the "Hispanic condition."

While Pérez Firmat's *Life on the Hyphen* retains a Cuban-American focus despite its forays into broader cultural and theoretical terrains, Ilan Stavans in *The Hispanic Condition* (1995) will do with no such narrow boundaries; he subtitles his book expansively *Reflections on Culture and Identity in America*. Here the hyphen—he calls his introductory chapter "Life in the Hyphen"—marks not just the "cubanglo" dilemma, but takes on hemispheric proportions, "the encounter between George Washington and Simón Bolívar,"[15] or even, at a civilizational level, between Shakespeare and Cervantes. Stavans, who arrived in the United States from his native Mexico as late as 1985, has been quick to insert himself into the culture wars, bringing with him an essayistic style comprised of warmed-over Octavio

Paz and a postmodernist metaphysics of the border. Despite the constant appeal to the relational aspects and indeterminacy of cultural identities, the "Hispanic condition" as portrayed here rests on decidedly essentialist, and existentialist, assumptions. The sense of "displacement" experienced by Cuban-American exiles, for example, "as a struggle, as a way of life, as a condition, . . . is, and will remain, a Latino signature. . . . To be expelled from home, to wander through geographic and linguistic diasporas, is essential to our nature" (59).

With all his cosmic claims, though, Stavans is mainly interested in the new "Latino literature." In *The Hispanic Condition* and other books, numerous anthologies and countless articles, he has become the most frequent commentator on the subject, and the critic who has been most intent on configuring a Latino literary canon in the 1990s. Though perhaps most familiar with the Mexican American tradition, he nevertheless has ample reference to Cuban-American, Puerto Rican, Dominican, and other Latino writers, and his professional training in Spanish and Latin American literatures allows him to range widely—though often diffusely—over the "Hispanic" literary landscape in the widest sense. Unfortunately, what is gained with this potentially welcome framework of cultural kinship and solidarity is lost in the need for specificity and more rigorous differentiation among the varied group perspectives.

For Stavans, *The Mambo Kings Play Songs of Love* is a "dazzling novel," a "moving account of brotherly love in the New York of the 1950s, which traced the impact and influence of Latin rhythms north of the border" (14, 56). References to the book and the Pulitzer abound in *The Hispanic Condition* (though they are unaccompanied by any extended critical analysis), and along with Sandra Cisneros and Julia Alveraz, Hijuelos clearly takes on canonical status here and in Stavan's other writings.[16] Thinking of Hijuelos he asks the question that centrally concerns him: "What does he as a Cuban-American share with Chicana Sandra Cisneros and Dominican-American novelist Julia Alvarez, author of *How the García Girls Lost Their Accents,* other than an amorphous and evasive ethnic background?"[17] At no point do the intervening issues of class position accessibility to the newly forming literary market figure in his calculations, which despite his many historical digressions continually revert to an internally cultural unit of discourse. Indeed, though he is groping for inclusive, pan-Latino affinities and associations, Stavans is notably selective in his conception of the Latino canon and the conditions of its formation. He favors, among other variables, the "literary" works, those most reminiscent of and compatible with Latin American literary models, especially those of the "boom."

As for group perspective, though his knowledge of Chicano literature is strongest, he is inclined toward that of the Cuban-American; the present-day "Hispanic condition" is most closely tracked as another link in the "Desi chain." "Arnaz's ordeal," he comments, "as Hijuelos knows . . . , is every Latino's dream of making it big in America. Among Latinos, Cuban-Americans symbolize success and progress, assimilation but self-awareness" (58). What would here seem to be a marking off of Cubans among the other groups—the sense of success and progress, assimilation and upward mobility—is repeatedly treated as the "new" element in all of Latino life; "something essential is changing in the texture of the Latino community," he claims, for "behind the much-publicized images of poverty, drugs and violence, upward mobility is indeed taking place" (189). Like Pérez Firmat, Stavans maintains that what is new, "a different approach to the Latino metabolism," is the demise of the idea of Latino culture as resistance, the replacement, in his words, of "the concept of negative assimilation" (14–15). Though he shies away from a sense of the Latino hyphen as signaling "collusion," his notion of "collision" is far from the politically grounded resistance historically associated with Latino cultural expression. In league with Latin American magical realism (which he calls "eminently marketable"), Latinos are here presented as "soldiers in the battle to change America from within, to reinvent its inner core" (14–15).

What is "new" about the recent Latino writing, and goes to inform it as a marketing category, is that it seeks to be apolitical, and here that foundational Cuban-American is again joined by Julia Alvarez as the trendsetter: "Hijuelos signals a trend by the new generation of Cuban-Americans and shies away from politics, as does Julia Alvarez in her fictional study of well-off Dominican girls in the United States" (56). With all his disclaimers and fanciful notions of "implosion," Stavans is talking about crossing over, making it into the mainstream, assimilation. The "explosion of Latino arts" which is "overwhelming the country," and which involves a strange gallery of examples, from William Carlos Williams and Joan Baez to Anthony Quinn and Oscar Lewis (!), means above all a move into the heart of American mass culture. Toward the end of *The Hispanic Condition,* Stavans pauses to wonder what it is all about, whether there is any substantive change involved in all the novelty and hype. "Is the pilgrimage from the periphery to mainstream culture," he asks, "one in which the entire Latino community is embarked? Aren't many being left behind?" (187). It is interesting that Stavans allows himself such second thoughts amidst his flurry of enthusiasm. Unfortunately, these questions find no substantive answers within the conceptual framework in which he conducts his "reflections on culture and identity in America."

LATINO LITERATURE AND CULTURAL CAPITAL

There are few Puerto Ricans in *The Mambo Kings,* and when they do appear it is usually as underworld mobsters, typically garbed in "tan suits." Toward the end of the book, as a kind of afterthought in the endless love life of the protagonist Cesar Castillo, there is Lydia, a working-class Puerto Rican woman whose caring relation to the aging but ever libidinous musician is marred by an undertone of personal opportunism. Otherwise, though, the Latin New York of the first Hispanic Pulitzer is entirely Cuban, even though it is set at a time when Puerto Ricans far outnumbered other Latino groups and was written when the Cuban population in New York had declined to relative insignificance. Even the Latin music scene in New York, which in the 1950s was already largely populated by Puerto Rican musicians, is basically a Cuban affair in Hijuelos's novel, renowned Puerto Ricans like Rafael Hernández, Noro Morales, Tito Puente, and Tito Rodríguez getting frequent mention and an occasional cameo appearance but no formative role in either the music or the narrative. It is worth recalling in this regard that Machito's "Afro-Cubans," the supreme orchestral achievement of the whole "mambo kings" era, were almost all New York Puerto Ricans.

The invisibility of New York Puerto Ricans in their own social habitat, while presumably not the intention of the author, is not casual either, for the cultural world of The Mambo Kings is "Latino" in a certain selective sense. Aside from its obvious masculinist and heterosexual emphasis, it is the white, middle-class Latino whose experience and perspectives prevail throughout the book. Though they run into some harder times in New York, the Castillo brothers are from a landowning family in Oriente, not of the status of the Arnaz's of the Santiago elite, but they had their means and prospects, and their domestic help; they can even pass as Ricky Ricardo's cousins. They speak proudly of their Spanish background, their father having migrated from Galicia and stubbornly upheld the noble bloodline. They are cubanos, yes, but above all "gallegos"; they are from the mountains, but fashion themselves more as caballeros than "guajiros." They are "mambo kings," masters of Afro-Cuban music, yet the protagonists' deepest love is not the mambo but "songs of love," the bolero.[18] Unable to ignore the reality of racism that plagued the Latin bands, the white "mambo kings" recall it as indignities suffered by the "black musicians," as though they were a rare and marginal presence on the scene.[19] In general, "blackness," pressing poverty, and other markers of social oppression are "othered" in this evocation of New York Latino life, with the African American, even more thoroughly than the Puerto Rican, being a total nonpresence in the book.

Fully in line with the theoretical orientations of Pérez Firmat and Stavans, the concept of "Latino" in The Mambo Kings involves the privileging of privilege. Claiming to represent cultural traits shared by all Latinos, they typically have recourse to language, religion, and a Spanish-inflected mestizaje (mixing) while evading differential relations of power among the groups involved. The result is an idea of Latino life based on what might be termed the "highest common denominator," one that highlights motives of success and opportunity and underplays issues of poverty and inequality as extraneous to the dynamics of Latino culture. The "condition" and concerns of middle-class exiles, bearing with them and reproducing the cultural capital inherent in their family lines, become the paradigm of the Latino experience. The communities forged of working-class migrations from colonized countries and regions recede into the background of this "Latino" landscape, and often find representation as fearful, hostile, inner-city jungles. The hyphenated Latino—the hyphen standing for equilibrium, "collusion," or even Stavans's wishful "implosion"— is fully compatible with white social identity in the U.S. racial formation, while blackness, especially as embodied by the African American, is typically distanced from the terrain of representative Latino experience.

Latino literature, as that category has emerged in contemporary canon-formation, is circumscribed from this perspective. To begin with, most of the prominent writers, those who appear in the anthologies, publish with major houses, and win literary prizes, are from this background of class and racial privilege. Beyond that, even those whose origins are more humble and disadvantaged, such as Puerto Rican authors Esmeralda Santiago and Judith Ortíz Cofer, tend to thematize their own upward mobility and distance themselves from the crasser aspects of inner-city barrio life, as is evident from their aloof treatment of African Americans. But writers like Dominican American Julia Alvarez, Cuban American Cristina Garcia, and Colombian American Jaime Manrique are more representative in this sense; writing in English though fluent in Spanish, broaching controversial themes of gender and sexuality, they offer up glimpses of middle-class Latino life in the metropolis, with all the travails and fits of nostalgia, but consistently from the vantage point of those who need not worry about being taken for Blacks or ghetto-dwellers.

But the bifurcation of Latino writing and canon-making goes beyond the more explicit matter of the social provenance of the favored authors, or even the thematic and stylistic features of the works themselves. The difference, I would suggest, which goes to explain such privileges and critical predilections, lies in the differential positioning of the varied Latino groups in the prevailing structures of power and domination within the United States and internationally. Those whose collective identities in the United States were constituted by a long-standing history of conquest and colonization generate a literary expression which contrasts with that of comparatively recent arrivals from countries with less direct ties to U.S. imperial power. In particular, Chicano and Nuyorican writing stands out among the emerging "Latino" literary configuration, sharing many of the bicultural themes with other works in that category but usually presenting a markedly divergent angle on society. As in the case of other aspects of social experience, the variations within the literature now classified as "Latino" need to be dissected critically with these structural contrasts clearly in view. Interestingly, the different placement of Puerto Ricans as compared with other Hispanic groups in New York was recognized early on in the community's history; already in 1928 an editorial in the weekly *Gráfico* spoke of Puerto Ricans as "the most vulnerable group of those which comprise the large family of Ibero-Americans. Truly it seems a paradox," the article continues, "that being American citizens these should be the most defenseless. The reality is sad, but true. People of Puerto Rican background find themselves completely unprotected [desamparados] in this American metropolis. While the citizens of other countries have their consulates and diplomats to represent them, the children of Borinquen have no one."[20]

In terms of literature and culture, this sociologically grounded variation within the pan-Latino concept refers to a differential relation to cultural capital, that is, to differing institutional infrastructures of production and consumption.[21] The newly arrived "Latino" writers, immigrating from countries relatively free of direct colonial subordination, find some degree of accommodation within the support structures provided by their nation-states of origin. Unlike their Nuyorican and Chicano counterparts, they are viewed, however opportunistically as "overseas" representatives of their countries, and are thus eligible to turn to their varied embassies and cultural attachés for support, recognition and exposure. Many of the readings and gatherings, book publication parties, and other commemorative events for New York writers of Dominican, Colombian, Mexican, and Honduran extraction are routinely convened under the auspices of their respective consulates or government-formed literary societies, which in cooperation with publishing houses also facilitate publication and promotion of their diasporic writers and artists.[22] Of course, many of these writers write in Spanish and have literary training, and are thus easily considered integral to their national literatures. But even English-language authors like the Dominicans Julia Alvarez and Junot Díaz, in addition to their access to major U.S. publishing opportunities, gained rapid recognition in the Dominican Republic and among Dominican writers, which included the translation and publication of their work.[23] It is this cultural capital as an institutional infrastructure that has meant for the making of a "Latino" literary community in New York and, nationally, an umbrella of legitimation for the diverse but structurally akin writers of Latin American and Spanish background. For obvious political reasons, the situation is of course different for Cuban American writers, who have not had the same kind of governmental support by way of the mission and interest sections. But in the Cuban case too the cultural and literary projection of the diaspora has remained an intense diplomatic issue, and the privileges accorded the exile community have meant for an influential infrastructure to the benefit of the artistic and literary community in the United States.[24]

Cultural capital of this kind has been virtually absent for the Puerto Rican writers, especially those also lacking in educational and linguistic advantages. Selectively, some of them find a place among their fellow "Latinos" in the anthologies and literary assemblies, but as a group, movement, or tradition, Nuyorican writing and authors run askew of the prevailing model. Dismissed or ignored by the Puerto Rican government and literary establishment, what they have had by way of an infrastructure was built from the ground up, with no auspice or recognition coming from any official entities. Cultural institutions on the Island, such as the Instituto de Cultura Puertorriqueña and the Ateneo Puertorriqueño, have virtually never found occasion to include Nuyorican writers in their ambitious literary programs and publications. Indeed, it is this lack of mediation which is in part responsible for the seemingly unbridgeable divide between the two settings of Puerto Rican culture, a gulf that has led Nicholasa Mohr among other New York writers to speak of a "separation beyond language."[25] On the New York side, the Puerto Rican government's Office of the Migration has indeed served the interests of the migrant population in its nearly fifty years of activity since the late 1940s; but that entity was always considered part of the Department of Labor and devoted its energy entirely to issues of employment and social services. The closest it came to cultural policies was its facilitation with basic literacy and English-language skills, and the simplistic promotion of Puerto Rican cultural traditions. Its function became particularly anachronistic with the emergence of a new generation of New York Puerto Rican politics and culture in the 1960s, when community-based and nongovernmental organizations were formed to fill the representational void.[26]

This lack of a diplomatic sphere and cultural politics oriented toward the needs and concerns of the diaspora is directly attributable to the ongoing colonial status of the Puerto Rican government. Along with the overwhelmingly working-class composition of the postwar migration, with its attendant low level of cultural literacy, it is this absence of a public infrastructure of literary institutions that accounts for the sharp differentiation in the social position and prospects characteristic of today's Latino writing. New York Puerto Rican cultural workers have been made painfully aware of this vacuum and have responded by establishing makeshift, neighborhood spaces like the Nuyorican Poet's Café and the New Rican Village to accommodate the rising generation of bilingual and English-language writers. As a way to dramatize the quasi-diplomatic aspirations of such grassroots efforts at official institution-building, the example set by the New Rican Village has in recent years been directed toward the founding of the "Puerto Rican Embassy"; with his usual ironic irreverence, Nuyorican poet Pedro Pietri has teamed up with photographer Adal Maldonado in the issuing of Puerto Rican passports, complete with photos and to the accompaniment of Puerto Rican music and literary recitals. More explicitly, Lourdes Vázquez, a poet and fiction writer who has lived stretches of time in both Puerto Rico and New York, has written about the agonies of the colonial writer in the absence of a diplomatic apparatus to address the nation's literary life. Speaking with envious admiration of the successful consular promotion of writers from Colombia, the Dominican Republic, Nicaragua, and the English Caribbean, she comments repeatedly, "No es el caso nuestro" ("such is not our situation").[27] She recognizes that in the field of popular music New York's Puerto Rican culture has been able to transcend geographic and political divides ("Salsa has been our most complete ambassador"), but concludes by referring again to the frustrations of writers and other artists with no established structures to turn to, or contend with. We are "trying to understand," as she puts it, "how to lay claim to a citizenship in a non-independent country. Here we are asking, where is the structure of government that nourishes us? Here we are wondering, where is the governmental agency to which we can pass the bill for such unrecognized individual effort, so many hours of creativity, discussion, and study."[28]

As the dramatis personae of *The Mambo Kings* illustrate, it is the Puerto Ricans who are "left behind" in the prevalent category of Latino literature. Not that they are totally or systematically excluded from the emerging canon, or that their literature is without parallels and commonalities with other writing under that heading. It is the particular social situation of that literary community when contrasted with that of other Latino nationalities, their differential access to literary and cultural capital as a result of direct colonial relations, that eludes their conceptualization of Latino writing as set forth by critics like Pérez Firmat and Stavans. For if the Latino hyphen as a sign of equilibrium stands for this interplay of cultural politics at an international level, Puerto Ricans in the United States live a life "off the hyphen." As is frequently noted, of all the ethnic groups it is the Puerto Ricans who pointedly refuse the hyphenation of their identity despite generations of life here and a rich history of interaction with U.S. culture at all levels. The term "Puerto Rican American" is rarely used by Puerto Ricans themselves, and when it is, as in the prestigious anthology of recent Latino literature *Iguana Dreams,* it stands as an immediate sign of unfamiliarity.[29] Rather than embracing the hyphen, or playing with it lovingly in the manner of Julia Alvarez, Puerto Ricans typically challenge that marker of collusion or compatibility and erase it as inappropriate to their social position and identity. In the case of colonial Latinos, another kind of punctuation and nomenclature is in order.

"LOWERCASE PEOPLE"

"Puerto Rican American," scowls Miguel, the protagonist of Abraham Rodriguez's novel *Spidertown.* "What a loada shit."[30] "It's not shit, Miguel," responds his girlfriend Cristalena. "It's people trying to find their own identities." But Miguel sticks to his point, distrusting any term that will make it appear either that he is American or that he comes from Puerto Rico. "I know my identity," he says. "I'm a spick. I like spick, okay? It tells me right away what I am. It don't confuse me into thinkin' I'm American. I'm a spick, okay? Thass how whites see you anyway" (267). *Spidertown* is set in the South Bronx of our own time, a return in the 1990s to the "mean streets" of inner-city Puerto Rican life first fictionalized by Piri Thomas in his 1967 autobiographical novel *Down These Mean Streets*. It is the story of young people, teenagers caught up in the engulfing, seemingly inescapable world of crack-dealing, gang warfare, and everyday violence; not once does the scene shift from the run-down streets and abandoned buildings, from the desperate, hopeless life of the ghetto. Time and time again we are reminded that it is a world modeled after the American Dream, that it follows the rules of capitalist society. But at the same time, it is a bitter abortion of that dream, a "business" lacking in any real social power or recognition. And the people who inhabit it, the impoverished, uneducated children of the Puerto Rican migration, are condemned to an outcast status, invisible and finding no representation of any kind in the alien culture that surrounds them. "Born to rule the streets and make alliances and break them," it is said toward the end of the book. "Just like world powers and big corporations and successful businesses, It was bigger than all of them. Miguel and Spider and all those shadows, they were tiny pins on a map, they hardly registered at all. Their kind came and went. They didn't write about them or direct plays or paint murals about their lives. They were all walking shit. Whether they lived in the South Bronx or Bed-Stuy or Harlem or Los Sures. It didn't matter. They didn't exist. They were all lowercase people" (288)

Standing at opposing extremes, *Spidertown* and *The Mambo Kings* illustrate the range of what is labeled as "Latino literature." Though written in the same years, in English, and by second-generation male authors, they portray diametrically contrasting realities and exemplify incompatible views of literature and its relation to society. While Hijuelos's prizewinner is built of nostalgia and the abiding power of cultural representation, *Spidertown* has no *I Love Lucy* show to harken back to, much less the dreamy reminiscences of a long-lost Cuban countryside. Abraham Rodriguez is mercilessly, programmatically antinostalgic, the unabating presentness of the action contributing directly to the sense of entrapment and alienation of the social experience. In spite of the historical backdrop suggested by Hijuelos, though, both in *The Mambo Kings* and in his first novel *Our House in the Last World* (1985), it is the nonretrospective young Bronx author who seeks to offer a sense of social context and an explanation for the Latino lives captured in his book. The class and racial gulf between the two books could not be more obvious, Hijuelos maintaining a middle-class and "white" perspective and Rodriguez never leaving the world of the Latino bordering on destitution and intricately associated with blackness and the African American experience.

As for gender, the difference is equally striking. While both books center on male experience, *The Mambo Kings* leaves the relation of subordination unquestioned and intact, wallowing in a naturalized phallocentrism and relegating the many women characters to passive, dramatically ineffectual roles. In *Spidertown,* on the other hand, while examples of misogyny and homophobia abound, it is the young women who serve as catalysts of challenge and change and stand up to that stubbornly sexist environment by word and example. Miguel's girlfriend Cristalena, "a girl with a name like a poem," would seem a direct parallel to the "beautiful Maria of my soul" immortalized for her idealized purity in the Castillo brothers' hit ballad; but thankfully Christalena is no goody-two-shoes, and wages a battle for independence of her own. Loving her, rather than reinforcing the Latin lover stereotype and leaving him his only domain of emotional power, leads Miguel to a bold and decisive rejection of that value system. In a lovemaking scene toward the end of *Spidertown* this serious life-change is made explicit: "In the world Miguel'd grown up in you start with backyards and rubble lots and then you conquer girls. You get your way with them and you learn that's the way, in life you are supposed to get your way. The woman is supposed to know where she's at, where she BELONGS. It was all in his blood. To be THE MAN. The woman just did what the man said. That was respect. Tradition. Yet Miguel was throwing it all away, the ghosts of a hundred million Latin machistas all hanging their heads and cursing him" (308).

As mentioned, it is its conservative, traditionalist treatment of women that Rodriguez finds most directly objectionable about the first Hispanic Pulitzer, and why he considers its author "full of shit." "It took Hispanic women like thirty years to get over that macho bullshit, and he brings it all back," he says of Hijuelos and his prizewinning book. His point is not that machismo is a thing of the past in Latino culture, but that it has been challenged by women, including women writers. Despite his iconoclasm and the sharply antihistoricist, here-and-now quality of his fictional settings, Rodriguez voices a sense of tradition here, an awareness that others have come before him in his literary project. Though he uses the term sparingly, he knows that he is a "Nuyorican" writer, recognizing that he is on a social turf staked out by Piri Thomas and relying in the lyrical sequences of his prose on a style reminiscent of the familiar cadences of poets like Pedro Pietri and Victor Hernández Cruz. He is also aware that since that outburst of literary expression by U.S. Puerto Ricans in the late 1960s, several women writers have emerged to present a different picture of the experience, such that the world of the Puerto Rican barrios can no longer be conceived of in literary terms without taking into account the contributions of Nicholasa Mohr, Judith Ortíz Cofer, Esmeralda Santiago, and others. This sense of a heritage, of belonging to a trajectory of literary representations of a historically forged community, differentiates the writing of long-resident Latino groups from that of more recent arrivals.

Even the Cuban experience in the United States, which does extend back to the past century and has given rise to a protracted literary representation, is different from the "Nuyorican" in this regard. For though Cuban American literature, with that of Mexican Americans and Puerto Ricans, counts as one of the three oldest among the Hispanic traditions, the tradition in this case is decidedly different from those two others because of the radical break occurring after the Cuban Revolution of 1959. For with the sharply altered social composition and ideological orientation of the exile population, Cuban Americans did not partake of the major political and cultural movements of the 1960s and 1970s which have been so formative of both Chicano and Nuyorican literary history. As a result, whereas a young contemporary writer like Abraham Rodriguez can harken back to the work of Piri Thomas and the Nuyorican poets, and even Island writers like Pedro Juan Soto, Julia de Burgos, and José Luis González, Cuban Americans like Hijuelos and Cristina Garcia have little by way of precedence in the literature produced by Cubans in the U.S. setting, the great, pathbreaking José Martí notwithstanding. The new "Latino" literature as it has been constructed in the 1990s, with all its assimilationist proclivities, now takes this relative newcomer experience, that of the "foreigner," as its prevalent model, while the longer-standing, resident Latino presence and literary background is more liable to be what is "left behind."

For it is not just differences in thematic concerns and stylistic features that distinguish these two variants of Latino literary expression. There is also, perhaps underlying the contrasts, the hyphen, that is, the differential sociological placement and grounding of the writing and social identity of its subjects. In *Spidertown* the main character Miguel is supposed to be writing a book about his mentor in the drug business, Spider; in fact, at several points his boss even commissions him to document his "amazin' life." But from early on Miguel dismisses the idea of becoming a writer as a "dead dream." "Miguel shouldn't have even blurted it out, because it was dumb. There weren't any Puerto Rican writers. Puerto Ricans didn't write books. Miguel had never even seen one" (62). But Spider doesn't relent, posing his question "how's the book coming?" throughout the heated action of the novel. By the end, Miguel does hand over his tapes of interviews with Spider, and perhaps the reader is to understand *Spidertown* itself as the fruit of Miguel's literary labors. Nevertheless, the incompatibility of literature as a profession and the social setting of the novel remain a constant, and echo something the author himself witnessed during his schooldays in the South Bronx. Rodriguez recalls frequently that when he mentioned he wanted to be a writer, his teacher told him it was impossible because there was no such thing; Puerto Ricans don't know how to write. Forever the rebel, Rodriguez would not be dissuaded by these admonitions and went on to disprove them with a prolific career. But he has continued to recognize the improbability of literature coming from neighborhoods like his own, and from a people bereft of literary infrastructures and cultural capital like the Puerto Rican community in the United States.

The literature of "lowercase people" is a "lowercase" literature, a literature deriving from sources other than those identified with formal education and cultural literacy. Asked if he chose to write because he liked reading, Rodriguez answered, "No, it wasn't about books. It was about writing. My father, it's all his fault, really. He used to write poems, these beautiful, long, longing, yearning poems about Puerto Rico. . . .My first memory is hearing the typewriter. He used to rent these really big typewriters and type on them, and I remember that *clack, clack, clack.* When I was little, I used to sit on his lap and bang on it. Really, the whole writing thing is about typewriters; it's got nothing to do with literature at all."[31] Rather than philosophical ideas or artistic creativity, writing in this sense is a preeminently tactile, physical, oral experience; the sound of the typewriter, the touch of the keys, the perception of letters, words, sounds, images—such is the basis of the writer's craft among the formally uneducated. What the budding author inherited from his father was obviously not the flowery versifying in the Latin American modernist tradition ("he was into Neruda") but the artisan practice. The typewriter was for him what drums or a guitar might be for the aspiring musician: the physical tool of the trade, the object required to express himself. As a "lowercase literature," Nuyorican writing is illustrative of oral tradition and not an institutionalized, canon-forming literature conceived of as a profession.

Not that Abraham Rodriguez, the "lowercase," "amazin' spick" writer, didn't read books, of course; on the contrary. He has clearly become well-versed in the writings of other U.S. Puerto Rican authors, as well as those from the Island and by other Latinos. He has also read widely among other U.S. writers, especially African American literature. Black literature, in fact, and Black culture and opposition politics, hold a special place for him, standing in his view as a model and inspiration for Puerto Rican aspirations; at the end of *Spidertown,* it is his reading of Richard Wright's *Native Son* that helps push Miguel to his final resolve to quit the crack business and move on with his life. Sanchez, the almost unbelievably enlightened Puerto Rican cop who gave him a copy of *Native Son,* is clearly the raisonneur when he says to Miguel, "Sometimes I feel more Puerto Ricans should read it. We could learn so much from the black man" (322). But Rodriguez's literary education goes beyond these more directly accessible sources and extends to the canon of European fiction. Through *Spidertown* the philosophical problematics of Sartre are brought into play by Miguel's friend Amelia, a college student and crack addict, and there is continual reference to Miguel's own reading matter, notably Dickens and Tolstoy. Dostoevsky is an even more obvious influence on Rodriguez's portrayal of the eerie ghetto underground and the psychological desperation of his adolescent characters.

But his all-time favorite, beyond even Gorki and Kafka, is Balzac, and Rodriguez has been called "the Balzac of the Bronx."[32] He refers to Balzac as the "cool guy" when talking to school children on his local speaking engagements, and calls him "my most favoritist writer in the whole planet."[33] Surely it is the sheer ambition of the "Comédie Humaine" that captures Rodriguez's fantasy, who aims for a similarly totalistic portrait of contemporary inner-city life; as he sees it, his first book, *The Boy Without a Flag: Tales of the South Bronx* (1992), is but the first installment in a long-term project of "Scenes from Ghetto Life" meant to emulate Balzac's "Scenes from Provincial Life." What most impresses the young Puerto Rican writer, however, is not so much the details of nineteenth-century French society as such, but the rigorous realist method of which Balzac is the undisputed master. For what Rodriguez means by a "non-literary" kind of writing is one, like that of Balzac and the great realists, which confronts social reality directly, as everyday lived experience and institutions, rather than as a mediation of what is conveyed in books and other means of representation. *The Mambo Kings,* for instance, while not particularly bookish, relies for its social framing and narrative coherence on the refraction of Cuban-American life and Latin music by means of television and Desi Arnaz; without that representational device, any sustained interest in the book's character and plot would all but vanish. Nuyorican literature, on the other hand, and the writing of "lowercase people" in general, stands face-to-face with social experience, however harsh and however saturated with mass culture, with its characters, voices, and story lines all recognizable denizens of the "mean" but real streets.

Though he is part of a Nuyorican tradition in writing, and knows himself to be, Rodriguez's relation to that tradition is anything but smooth, and his disposition anything but happy. Indeed, the appeal of Balzac and his own appeal to classical realist fiction may be in part directed at what he sees as the evasiveness of the previous generation of Nuyorican writers and their irrelevance to contemporary Puerto Rican conditions. He delights in "pissing on" his out-of-touch elders, ranting that they are "stuck in another era": "You'd think that I'm coming from a different place than those people. And while I respect literature, I don't see any use in stories about the blessed Diaspora forty years ago or of the first time I saw a snowflake. I think we should go beyond that now."[34] Piri Thomas, Pedro Pietri, Miguel Piñero, Nicholasa Mohr, Ed Vega, Judith Ortíz Cofer—the "older writers" had been formative for him, helping him belie the words of his teachers that there were no Puerto Rican writers. But when putting these writings to the test of present-day realities, and in view of the formidable political dilemma that underlies them, Rodriguez voices a dissatisfaction that he believes he shares with many of his contemporaries. "We've got young 14-year-old kids blasting each other to hell with automatic weapons, and the island has the same problem. I think these are bigger things, and we've got to find a way. . . . This is not all about politics. These are the dynamics of writing, but of course politics has to do something to it" (140–41).

With all his bouts of youthful fury, which lashes out in many directions and not only toward his fellow "spick writers," Rodriguez is announcing his sense of belonging to a new literary generation. The 1980s and 1990s are new times, marked off socially from the previous, properly "Nuyorican" years by the ebbing of the political and cultural movement of the 1960s and 1970s and the conclusive dashing of all hopes for Puerto Rican equality and independence. The intervening period saw the transition from "el barrio" to "Spidertown," the definitive placement of the U.S. Puerto Rican population at the bottom of the socioeconomic and political hierarchy as a result of regional and transnational restructurings. The "mean streets" had gotten even meaner with the infusion of crack, and had found a distinctive mode of cultural expression in hip-hop. And of course Puerto Rico, the idyllic homeland and cultural womb for most of the earlier Nuyorican writers, appears now at a still greater remove; though the consequences of its colonial politics still bear down on today's U.S. Puerto Ricans, the evocation of the Island no longer carries the same symbolic weight or literary interest. Speaking about books that wallow in the past, Rodriguez says that "as a young person I was never interested in this kind of book. They had nothing to offer me because I didn't see anything I could really relate to inside of them. In terms of the voice, in terms of the language, in terms of the subject matter, nothing. It's like writing about the island. It's a myth to me. The island is a myth. I like reading about it, but it's a myth" (141).

The demographic outcomes of these same social changes indicate that even the term *Nuyorican* has become an anachronism. In the early 1970s, when New York Puerto Rican writing was coming into its own, most U.S. Puerto Ricans lived in New York City, and the city's Latino population was over 80 percent Puerto Rican.[35] Both proportions have changed dramatically since, such that by 1990 more than 50 percent of Puerto Ricans lived in U.S. settings other than New York City, and the Puerto Rican proportion of the city's Latino population, while still the largest, had declined to lower than 50 percent. Poet Tato Laviera was one of the first to acknowledge the inappropriateness of the usage because of diasporic dispersion around the country, and proposed, leaving room for poetic license, the alternative *AmeRícan*, "with an accent on the i."[36] In any case, even "post-Nuyorican" won't do because of its lingering geographic specificity, though the overused prefix "post-" may well be pertinent to the generational relation in this case.

Abraham Rodriguez is not alone in his generation, though he claimed until recently that he does not "know any young Puerto Ricans who write." In a way, of course, it is the women prose writers who initiated the generational shift, moving away from the male-centered version of the migration and growing up experience. But in Rodriguez's own chronological generation, there is Willie Perdomo, who takes up themes of race and identity in his poems like "Nigger-Rican Blues" and has published a book with Norton, *When a Nickel Costs a Dime.* Other young voices are also beginning to be heard, often in the context of hip-hop or performance art, and some of them are young women. María Fernández, for example, whose nickname is "Mariposa," is from the Bronx, a graduate of NYU, who has been reciting her poetry at cultural and political gatherings in and around New York City for several years. She agrees with Rodriguez about the need for something new in the writing, a feel more in tune with the times. One of her poems, in fact, proposes still another possible designation for the present literary generation. In "Ode to the DiaspoRican," Mariposa presents the intense bicultural dilemma, familiar from the poems of Sandra María Esteves, in a setting that is New York but could readily be in any other enclave of the scattered "diaspoRico." The poem reads in part: "Some people say that I'm not the real thing / Boricua, that is / cuz I wasn't born on the enchanted island / cuz I was born on the mainland / . . .what does it mean to live in between / What does it take to realize / that being boricua / is a state of mind / a state of heart / a state of soul. . . / *No nací en Puerto Rico / Puerto Rico nació en mi. . .* [I wasn't born in Puerto Rico / Puerto Rico was born in me]."[37]

The other demographic shift marking off "diaspoRican" writing from its Nuyorican antecedent is the latinization of New York City, which brings us back to "Latino literature." The dramatic growth and diversification of "Latin New York" over the past decades, corresponding to developments throughout the country, has meant that Dominican, Colombian, Mexican, and many other Latino voices have joined those of the Puerto Ricans in presenting the migratory and diasporic experience. New and different versions of the story proliferate, many of them at extreme variance with those more characteristic of the Puerto Rican case in its contours and details. Predictably, the logic of social categorization generates a literary rubric to correspond to the demographic label, and "Latino literature" emerges as the new construct conditioning all literary production by Latinos of all national backgrounds. Suddenly the Puerto Rican writers have an umbrella, a point of access to mainstream multicultural literature that had so long eluded them. But along with the opportunities, for both recognition and potential creative sharing, there is for the Puerto Rican especially the pitfall of renewed marginalization and, on the other end, dilution of the collective experience.

And in 1990, as though to punctuate this precarious transition, *The Mambo Kings* wins the Pulitzer. As expected, the "older" Puerto Rican writers were disgruntled, and as expected, Abraham Rodriguez did not share their dejection. "They seem to be stuck in another era," he says of them. "The last time I was with those people, we were all sitting at this table, and they were all criticizing Oscar Hijuelos because he had just gotten a Pulitzer. It's just a waste of time. I don't see why writers do that. They should go home and write something. If they didn't sit around a table drinking, talking about other writers so much, arguing about Faulkner all day, maybe they'd get some work done."[38] If their work is indeed about "life off the hyphen," the need is strong in the present generation to dispel the anxieties over canons, prizes, and other marketing conveniences, and to concentrate more on bringing the "lowercase people" to literary life.

NOTES

1. Nicolás Kanellos, *"The Mambo Kings Play Songs of Love"* (review), *Americas Review* 18.1 (1990): 113.
2. Cited in W. J. Stuckey, *The Pulitzer Prize Novels: A Critical Backward Look* (Norman: University of Oklahoma Press, 1966), 7. See also John Hohenberg, *The Pulitzer Prizes: A History of Awards in Books . . .* (New York: Columbia University Press, 1974), and J. Douglas Bates, *The Pulitzer Prize: The Inside Story of America's Most Prestigious Award* (Secaucus, N.J.: Carol, 1991)
3. Stuckey, *The Pulitzer Prize Novels,* 262.
4. Citied in ibid., 250.
5. Kanellos, *"The Mambo Kings"* (review), 113.
6. Enrique Fernández, "Exilados on Main Street," *Village Voice,* May 1, 1990, 85.
7. Quoted in Alexandra Kuczynski, "Spider Man: Novelist Abraham Rodríguez Clocks the Bronx," *Paper* (May 1993): 20.1.
8. Examples of this assertion as to the historical importance of *The Mambo Kings* and its Pulitzer may be found in Harold Augenbraum, ed., *Latinos in English: A Selected Bibliography of Latino Fiction Writers of the United States* (New York: Mercantile Library, 1992), 12, and from a very different perspective, Marc Zimmerman, *U.S. Latino Literature: An Essay and Annotated Bibliography* (Chicago: March/Abrazo Press, 1992), 38.
9. See, for example, Lori M. Carlson, ed., *Cool Salsa: Bilingual Poems on Growing Up Latino in the United States* (New York: Fawcett Juniper, 1994), and Delia Poey and Virgil Suarez, eds., *Iguana Dreams: New Latino Fiction* (New York: HarperCollins, 1992).
10. Historical overviews of the "Hispanic literary heritage" may be found in Ramón Gutiérrez and Genaro Padilla, eds., *Recovering the U.S. Hispanic Literary Heritage* (Houston: Arte Público, 1993), as well as in Harold Augenbraum and Ilan Stavans, eds., *Growing Up Latino: Memoirs and Stories—Reflections on Life in the United States* (Boston: Houghton-Mifflin, 1993), and Zimmerman, *U.S. Latino Literature.* See also William Luis, *Dance Between Two Cultures: Latino Caribbean Literature Written in the United States* (Nashville: Vanderbilt University Press, 1997).
11. See Gustavo Pérez Firmat, *Life on the Hyphen: The Cuban-American Way* (Austin: University of Texas Press, 1994), and Ilan Stavans, *The Hispanic Condition: Reflections on Culture and Identity in America* (New York: HarperCollins, 1995), whose first chapter is entitled "Life in the Hyphen," 7–30.
12. Pérez Firmat, *Life on the Hyphen,* 1.
13. Ibid., 136–53. Another lengthy discussion of *The Mambo Kings* may be found in Luis, *Dance Between Two Cultures,* 188–214.

14. Pérez Firmat, *Life on the Hyphen*, 1. Subsequent page numbers are cited in the text.

15. Stavans, *The Hispanic Condition*, 19. Subsequent page numbers are cited in the text.

16. See, for example, Augenbraum and Stavans, eds., *Growing Up Latino*, xi–xxix.

17. Stavans, *The Hispanic Condition*, 19. Subsequent page numbers are cited in the text.

18. For a discussion of the mambo-bolero contrast in *The Mambo Kings*, see Pérez Firmat, *Life on the Hyphen*, 149–53.

19. See Oscar Hijuelos, *The Mambo Kings Play Songs of Love* (New York: Farrar, Straus, Gioux, 1989), 165–66.

20. *Gráfico*, March 27, 1928, 2; as quoted (in part) in Virginia E. Sánchez-Korrol, *From Colonia to Community: This History of Puerto Ricans in New York City* (Berkeley: University of California Press, 1994), 73.

21. For an extended discussion of the concept of "cultural capital" and its bearing on literary canon-formation, see John Guillory, *Cultural Capital: The Problem of Literary Canon Formation* (Chicago: University of Chicago Press, 1993). See also, for the theoretical foundations of this analysis, Pierre Bourdieu, *The Field of Cultural Production* (New York: Columbia University Press, 1993), especially the essay "The Market of Symbolic Goods," 112–41.

22. See, for example, Eduardo Márceles Daconte, ed., *Narradores Columbianos en U.S.A.* (Bogotá: Instituto Colombiano de Cultura, 1993), and Daisy Cocco de Fillippis and Franklin Gutiérrez, eds., *Stories from Washington Heights and Other Corners of the World: Short Stories Written by Dominicans in the United States* (New York: Latino Press, 1994).

23. On this point I am grateful for insights from Daisy Cocco de Filippis, Pedro López Adorno, and David Unger among others involved in the current "Latino literature" scene in New York. For a related discussion, see Arlene Dávila, "Art and the Politics of Multicultural Encompassment: 'Latinizing' Culture in El Barrio," *Cultural Anthropology* 14.2 (1999): 180–202.

24. For a more critical approach to Cuban American cultural experience and differentiation from that of resident Latino minorities, see the essays by Cuban American critic Román de la Campa, "The Latino Diaspora in the United States: Sojourns from a Cuban Past," *Public Culture* 6.2 (Winter 1994): 294–317, and "Miami, Los Angeles, and Other Latino Capitals," *Postdata* (Puerto Rico) 9 (1994): 65–74.

25. See Nicholasa Mohr, "Puerto Rican Writers in the United States, Puerto Rican Writers in Puerto Rico: A Separation Beyond Language," in Denis Lynn Daly Heyck, ed., *Barrios and Borderlands* (New York: Routledge, 1994), 264–69.

26. See Michael Lapp, "Managing Migration: The Migration Division of Puerto Rico and Puerto Ricans in New York City, 1948–68" (Ph.D. diss., Johns Hopkins University, 1990) 303ff.

27. See Lourdes Vázquez, "Nuestra Identidad y sus espejos," *El Nuevo Día* (San Juan), February 9, 1997, 8.

28. Ibid., 9.

29. See Poey and Suarez, eds., *Iguana Dreams*, xviii.

30. Abraham Rodriguez, *Spidertown* (New York: Penguin, 1993), 267. Subsequent page numbers are cited in the text.

31. See Rodriguez interview in Carmen Dolores Hernández, ed., *Puerto Rican Voices in English* (Westport, Conn.: Praeger, 1997), 137–55 (quote from 152).

32. See Jonathan Mandell, "A Posse of One: The Balzac of the Bronx," *New York Newsday*, July 19, 1993, 39, 42–43.

33. See Steve Garbarino, "Urgent Fury: Abraham Rodriguez Jr.," *New York Newsday*, August 9, 1992.

34. Rodriguez, in Hernández, ed., *Puerto Rican Voices in English*, 140. Subsequent page numbers are cited in the text.

35. For further details and analysis, see "Pan-Latino/Trans-Latino: Puerto Ricans in the 'New Nueva York,' " ch. 7 of the present volume.

36. See Tato Laviera, *AmeRícan* (Houston: Arte Público, 1985).

37. María Fernández, "Ode to the DiaspoRican," in *AHA! Hispanic Arts News* (February–March 1998): 14.

38. Rodriguez, in Hernández, ed. *Puerto Rican Voices in English*, 140.

CHAPTER SEVEN

"Nothing Connects Us All But Imagined Sounds"

Performing Trans-Boricua Memories, Identities, and Nationalisms Through the Death of Héctor Lavoe

Wilson Valentín-Escobar

Se te olvidó decir que yo soy el hombre que respira debajo del agua.

Si yo me muero mañana / mañana por la mañana / no quiero que nadie llore / no quiero que digan nada.

—*Héctor "Lavoe" Pérez*

Pulling you this way and that, mimesis plays this trick of dancing between the very same and the very different. An impossible but necessary, indeed an everyday affair, mimesis registers both sameness and difference, of being like, and of being Other. Creating stability from this instability is no small task, yet all identity formation is engaged in this habitually bracing activity in which the issue is not so much staying the same, but maintaining sameness through alterity.

—*Michael Taussig (1993:129)*

On Tuesday afternoon, June 29, 1993, one of Salsa music's greatest *soneros* (improvisational singers), Héctor Juan Pérez, commonly known as Héctor Lavoe, passed away at St. Claire's hospital in New York City. Lavoe died of a heart attack, bringing to an end his struggle with HIV. Héctor Lavoe's passing marked a turning point in the world of Salsa music as well as in the transnational Puerto Rican and Latina/o communities in the United States, Puerto Rico, and Latin America.[1] Thousands of Lavoe's admirers in Puerto Rico, la República Dominicana, Venezuela, Colombia, Perú, Panama, New York City, Chicago, and other urban and national hubs conducted vigils in his name. Throughout New York City, the songs and sounds of Héctor Lavoe's music emanated from people's homes, car stereos, and boom boxes, blurring the boundaries between public and private cultures.[2] The popular La Mega FM radio station in New York City played Lavoe's music all week long, motivating his followers and admirers to sing and dance, almost in unison, in the streets of *la Gran Manzana* (the Big Apple).

Nancy Rodríguez, disc jockey for Pacifica radio station WBAI in New York City, also aired a three-hour musical tribute to Héctor Lavoe soon after his death, remembering him in interviews with various Salsa music artists who discussed his musical career and personal life as well as his impact, contributions, and historical significance in Salsa music. Shortly after his death, T-shirts with imprints of Héctor Lavoe's face wrapped up in a Puerto Rican flag were produced and sold, and they soon became one of the hottest-selling items that summer. Musicians and Salsa singers, as they performed live in concert halls, street fairs, and Salsa clubs, paid homage to Héctor Lavoe by declaring that "el cantante de los cantantes todavía vive con nosotros" (the singer of singers continues to live with us).

Seven years after his death, Héctor Lavoe continues to be a cultural hero who has been memorialized through various cultural forms including urban street murals; theatrical productions; poetry recitals; clothing bearing his image; commemorative Salsa concerts throughout Latin America, the Caribbean, and the United States; and re-releases of his musical recordings. In addition, he is mimetically embodied in some of Salsa's contemporary singers, such as Marc Anthony, Van Lester, and Domingo Quiñonez. These simulations of "restored behaviors" may represent a symbolic form and link to the past of musical lineage and history that entails respect for elders, predecessors, and ancestors and are grounded in a spiritual, historical, and musical repertoire or tradition that transcends temporal and spatial conditions (Roach 1996:3). This active process of memorializing Lavoe through various styles, forms, and practices is the catalyst that guides my analysis. I argue that the circuitous mimetic and altered practices of Héctor Lavoe signify trans-Boricua communal imaginations. In the process, Lavoe's Salsa music and performances help to construct national and diasporic imaginations.[3] In memorializing Héctor Lavoe, Puerto Ricans in the diaspora— in this case, "Diaspo-Ricans" (Pagan 1997)—articulate and affirm their identities and nation-ness in a social and geographical location that Homi Bhabha describes as the "ambivalent margin(s) of the nation-space" (1990:4). In this in-betweenness of negotiated and transnational identities and cultural productions, Héctor Lavoe's music creates a feeling of national belonging that transgresses geographical boundaries.

The style and forms that these performances embody—be they oral history, song, dance, mural art, or ritual ceremonies—articulate the complexity of enacting translocal narratives of identity and memory. Analyzing Héctor Lavoe's burial ceremony as both a text and performance allows us to witness the encoded memories and nationalisms that embodied this collective ritual. Lavoe's death and the ensuing struggle that followed over his corpse and burial illuminate the ways in which identity is still very much contingent on place. Yet Lavoe still becomes a floating trans-Boricua who traverses disparate geographical locales while also engaging multiple discourses regarding Puerto Rican nationalisms, identities, and historical agency. In the process, Lavoe has become a "performed effigy" of Diaspo-Rican alterity, trans-Boricua memories and cultural histories, and a meto-nymic symbol of latinidad (Roach 1996:36). A performed effigy, as described by Joseph Roach, is the organized activity that provides "communities with a method of perpetuating themselves through specifically nominated me-diums or surrogates" channeled via a "set of actions that hold open a place in memory into which many different people may step according to circum-stances and occasions" (36). Surrogation is a rite of passage that sacrificial effigies come to represent. For Puerto Ricans living within and outside of Puerto Rico, Lavoe's corpse becomes a trans-Boricua effigy that embodies and interpolates overlapping nationalist and diasporic narratives, enacting a surrogate process constituted by diasporicity, transnationalism, and col-lective memory.

Deceased cultural heroes such as Lavoe are reincorporated into over-lapping and competing narratives of the nation. Much like cultural artifacts, constructions of memory are ever-changing (Canclini 1992, 1993). Different contexts create various meanings for cultural texts; similarly, popular and manufactured memories and commemorative practices or ceremonies con-struct local meanings of deceased cultural heroes such as Lavoe. Oral his-tories and media institutions generate both collective memory and manu-factured memory, which travel across multiple social locations and contribute to the formation of a larger public memory. In the case of Lavoe, these histories and meanings are in constant flux, articulated distinctly by members of various generations and across numerous geographical spaces. The Janus-faced fluid meanings encoded in commemorative practices can then be described as *memoria resemanticada* (resemanticized memory), a reformulation of diverse meanings produced and attached to particular in-dividuals and events across temporal and spatial boundaries and social con-ditions. Whether Lavoe is imagined as an "unchanging, incorruptible," au-thentic Puerto Rican *jíbaro,* or as a Diaspo-Rican sonero claiming New York City as his new home, these positions exemplify how local communities exercise their historical agency and come to comprise a trans-Boricua/trans-migratory imaginary.[4] These shared memories not only transcend the dual and Manichaean polarities between the geographical sites of Puerto Rico and New York but also emphasize the diasporicity that embodies cultural practices between both translocales and how each shapes the perceived other (Flores 1996; Basch, Schiller, and Blanc 1994). Transmigrant imagi-nations incorporate diasporic narratives into the traditional inscriptions of the nation, entangling and deterritorializing bounded historiographies that encompass the various embodied forms, practices, and "collective mentali-ties" that migrate across national and diaspora communities produced through Lavoe and that also reconstitute him before and after his death.[5] The collective mentalities that re-enact and re-present Lavoe are more than simple reappearances; they are mimetic reinventions rooted in translocal community rituals and performances (Roach 1996; Taussig 1993). Although resemanticized constructions of Lavoe inscribe varying memories, identities, and narratives surrounding his life and death, they also demonstrate the vibrancy of translocal Puerto Rican communities. In the act of resemanticization, Lavoe is then crowned a surrogate successor of tradition and difference, evoking diasporic alterity and national sameness.

EL HOMBRE QUE RESPIRA DEBAJO DEL AGUA/THE MAN WHO BREATHES UNDER WATER

Héctor Lavoe was born Héctor Juan Pérez in Ponce, Puerto Rico, on September 30, 1946, to Panchita and Luís Pérez. He grew up listening to and studying the music of Puerto Rico's most famous folklore and popular musicians and singers, such as Ramito, Chuito el de Bayamon, Odilio González, and Daniel Santos. Salsa singers whom he also admired, and who would later influence his singing style, were Cheo Feliciano and Ismael Rivera. In 1960, Lavoe dropped out of school and began singing for local bands in Ponce. Against his father's wishes, Héctor Pérez left for New York City in 1963, when he was only seventeen years old. Upon arriving, he quickly started singing with several bands, such as the New Yorkers, Kako and His All-Stars, and the Tito Puente Orchestra. Soon thereafter, the promoter Franquis christened Héctor with the nickname Lavoe, which meant *La Voz* (The Voice).[6] Shortly thereafter, Héctor met the South Bronx–born Willie Colón, a young and emerging musician who began his Salsa career with the support of the late Al Santiago, the former owner, founder, and producer of Alegre Records. Santiago, who helped Colón and Lavoe record their first album, also owned and operated one of the first labels to record New York–based Salsa music.

In 1967, Lavoe joined Willie Colón's band, and together they recorded their first album, entitled *El Malo*. This record, argued critics and musicians, lacked the "superior" musicianship and arrangement complexity found in the music performed by more established musicians such as Tito Puente, Tito Rodríguez, and Charlie and Eddie Palmieri (Rondón 1980). Regardless of this criticism, the album was a great success for a number of reasons. The music performed by Willie Colón and Héctor Lavoe consisted of Salsa and Boogaloo songs, which spoke to a younger generation of Puerto Ricans born and raised in New York City, and also signified the Nuyorican culture and identity at the time.[7] Their music was distinguished by its brash, urban, or "street" barrio sound and philosophy that departed from Cuban-influenced musical arrangements performed in ballroom settings.

The New York Salsa sound—shaped by racial, gender, social, cultural, economic, migratory, and political ideologies and processes, with its distinct instrumentation, phrasing, and arrangements—highlights local agency in reconstructing innovative techniques within and across musical traditions

(Alvarez 1992; Aparicio 1998; Berríos-Miranda 1997, 1998; Canclini 1992, 1993; Leymarie 1994; Negus 1999; Quintero-Rivera 1989, 1998; Quintero-Rivera and Alvarez 1990; Rondón 1980). For example, the New York trombone and "trompanga" (trombones played with violins in charanga) sound performed by Ray Baretto, Willie Colón, Manny Oquendo and Libre (formerly Conjunto Libre), Eddie and Charlie Palmieri, and Efrain "Mon" Rivera heavily emphasized trombone instrumentation and arrangements. The so-called singing trombone assumed a leading role, while other brass, wind, string, and percussive instruments became supportive instruments. The new leading role of the trombone changed in relation to how other instruments were arranged and performed within other music scenes. Another characteristic of this New York Salsa sound was the philosophical attitude that musicians brought to its construction. The attitude to experiment with tradition often created eagerness to modify musical paradigms. In this process, the new tradition that emerged—in varying degrees—was a reformulation and resemanticization of musical texts and boundaries. New York–based musicians were less ethnocentric than their Cuban counterparts in their willingness to mix other folkloric and musical traditions into the creation of Salsa. Many Salsa arrangements incorporated the heterogeneous urban spatial economy of the city, reflecting and articulating the transnational consciousness of many musicians and consumers. Although bands from Havana or New York may share similar orchestrations, the particular instruments emphasized and the phrasing employed during a recorded or live performance register the aural distinctions that develop within a musical scene and tradition.[8]

In addition to reformulated instrumentation and experimentation, faster Son (3-2) and Rumba (2-3) clave patterns were also developed, reflecting the pace of the city.[9] This free mixing of African American jazz, rhythm and blues, Cuban music, and Puerto Rican folkloric styles such as Bomba, Plena, and Seis is testament to the artistic renaissance and philosophical approach of the time, collectively contributing to the artistic distinctions found in the musical styles (including Latin Jazz) created in New York.[10] Yet despite the innovation involved, the New York brash sound was often considered to be a product of unskilled musicianship.

Described as untrained musicians (outside of the classical musical conservatory), Cesar Miguel Rondón portrays Colón, Lavoe, and many of their contemporaries as musicians who functioned "por el oído y no por el conservatorio" (by ear and not by their conservatory training) (Rondón 1980:50). They further flaunted this unpolished image of themselves through the bad-boy barrio construction represented in the title track song of Colón and Lavoe's first album, "El Malo" (The Bad One). In this song, Willie Colón and Héctor Lavoe express their social marginality and "Macho Ca-ma-chismo" through the strident trombone arrangements and the following lyrical commentary:

Quien se llama el malo	[Who is called the bad one
no hay discusión	there is no discussion
El malo de aquí soy yo	the bad one here is me
porque tengo corazón	because I have heart]

The trombone arrangements punctuated Lavoe's jíbaro twang as well as the young salseros' barrio philosophy.

Lavoe and Colón, along with Eddie and Charlie Palmieri, Ray Barretto, Joe Cuba, Johnny Colón, Ricardo Ray and Bobby Cruz, and others, were recognized as helping to create the distinctive Nuyorican sound of Salsa in their 1960s and 1970s Fania label recordings (Rondón 1980). In addition to the *El Malo* album (1967), Colón and Lavoe's other popular recordings were *The Hustler* (1968); *Guisando/Doing a Job* (1969); *La Gran Fuga/The Big Break* (1971); *Crime Pays* (1972); *Cosa Nuestra* (1972); *Asalto Navideño,* volumes 1 (1971) and 2 (1973); *El Juicio* (1972); *Lo Mato* (1973); and *The Good, The Bad, The Ugly* (1975), among others. They released some of Salsa's most popular songs on these albums, including "Soñando Despierto," "Piraña," "Aguanile," "La Murga," "Esta Navidad," "No Me Llores Mas," "Hacha y Machete," "Todo Tiene Su Final," "Guisando," "No Me Den Candela," "Che Che Cole," "El Malo," "Juana Peña," and "Te Conozco." With the success of each album, Lavoe and Colón became a tag team known as "Los Malotes de la Salsa"—the bad boys of Salsa.

Interestingly, this bad-boy masculine image that Colón and Lavoe portrayed in their albums and performances may have contributed to the similar images adopted by many rappers from the late seventies to the current period. More important to this essay, Colón's and Lavoe's album covers were in intertextual dialogue with cinematic representations of New York City organized crime. Prime examples include the album covers for *Guisando/Doing a Job* (1969); *Crime Pays* (1972); *The Good, The Bad, The Ugly* (1975); and *Cosa Nuestra* (1972). In the latter, Colón reverses the syntactical order of *Nuestra Cosa* to *Cosa Nuestra,* mnemonically similar to the underground Italian American organization often referred to as the Cosa Nostra (i.e., the Mafia). The album cover amusingly mimics the urban myth that organized crime kills its enemies near the Fulton Fish Market on the south side of the Manhattan Island waterfront (hence the phrase "swimming with the fishes"). Additionally, Colón may be suggesting that Salsa, as "Our [Latin] Thing," refers to both the Fania-sponsored documentary on the history of Salsa in New York City and a musical genre distinct from the Cuban Son. In the foreground of the album cover, Willie Colón is wearing a black suit and blue shirt. He holds a black fedora hat with his right hand while it rests on his chest as if in a farewell gesture; his other arm props up what appears to be a black leather trombone carrying case doubling as a rifle case (the trombone is his weapon). With a cigar dangling from his lips, which incidentally repeats the phallic image of the rifle case, he gazes upon a corpse wrapped in a brown blanket. In the background his figure straddles the Brooklyn Bridge on the right and the Manhattan Bridge on the left.[11]

The bad-boy album covers cannot simply be dismissed as examples of youthful indiscretions; rather, they are heavily laden with class and gender symbolism. The album covers signify other masculine-driven representations of national mythologies and identities such as the Wild West (*Guisando/ Doing a Job* and *The Good, The Bad, The Ugly*), urban street gangs (*Asalto Navideño*, volumes 1 and 2; *La Gran Fuga*), organized crime (*Crime Pays*), and ethnic rivalry (*Cosa Nuestra*). In the course of these self-representations, Lavoe and Colón draw on these mythical constructions to recast the personal and collective. Album covers become more than textual self-representations but are also self-reflexive metaperformances of diasporic identities and musical style. Lavoe and Colón actively refashion what it means "to be a Puerto Rican," complicating the culture of poverty and criminal depictions of Puerto Rican culture (while carefully playing with and exaggerating them) and consequently subverting traditional discourses surrounding urban life in the diaspora.[12] Contrary to adopting a stereotypical rags-to-riches (im)migrant narrative, Lavoe performs a variety of urban and ethnic roles and begins to refashion his own identity. The association with Colón further confers a Diaspo-Rican identity on Lavoe, who undergoes a transformation of doubly signifying island and diaspora translocality, rural jíbaro and urban Nuyorican. The triangulation is further completed by virtue of Lavoe's birthplace, upbringing, and jíbaro aesthetics, which confer authenticity to the New York–born Colón. Together, Willie Colón and Héctor Lavoe represent the translocal spaces of the Puerto Rican transnation while also signifying modern and postmodern moments of identity formation. Overall, it may seem that binary oppositions of identity are at work in these albums, but they are entangled, nonlinear, and postmodern (re)presentations of trans-Boricua imaginations.

In 1974, Willie Colón left the band to pursue other paths within Salsa music. In spite of his departure, Colón continued to produce many of the albums that Héctor Lavoe recorded with Fania records. With the original band members now in Lavoe's band, they continued to produce successful albums such as *La Voz* (1975); *The Good, The Bad, The Ugly* (1975); *De Ti Depende* (1976); *Comedia* (1978); *Héctor's Gold* (1980); *Revento* (1985): *¡Que Sentimiento!* (1981); *El Sabio* (1980); *Strikes Back* (1987); *Recordando a Felipe Pirela* (1979) and *The Master and The Protégé* (1993).[13] In 1988, Lavoe was nominated for a Grammy award for his album *Strikes Back,* a nomination many feel belatedly recognized the talent of one of Salsa's best singers. Some of the popular songs that emerged from these albums were "Hacha y Machete," "El Periódico de Ayer," "Mi Gente," "Comedia," "El Todopoderoso," "Songorocosongo," "De Ti Depende," and "Rompe Saragüey." Many followers often note that Héctor's improvisational skills were the best in the Salsa music scene. In some cases, during a live performance he would improvise a theme with audience participation for an estimated time of fifteen minutes. Although success continued after Willie Colón's departure, Lavoe juggled many personal tragedies that overwhelmed and affected his personal and professional life.

Transnational imaginations operate in Lavoe's declaration that "I am the man who breathes under water" (Yo soy el hombre que respira debajo del agua). This declaration is more than light banter exchanged between Johnny Pacheco and Lavoe during a 1975 performance published in the *Live at Yankee Stadium* album.[14] Rather, it serves as a prophetic commentary and takes on metaphoric dimensions for Lavoe's life and death. These transatlantic connections fuel a transmigratory imagination between Puerto Rico, Latin America, its diaspora, and other U.S.–based Latina/o communities.

The transatlantic movement of both Puerto Rican Plena and Salsa music is an example of musical texts and practices resemanticized within and across a spatial economy. In their distinctive and differentiated ceremony, the diaspora is distinguished from the national community by the style invoked in social and cultural celebrations and practices. As Benedict Anderson has argued, communities are imagined and "are to be distinguished not by their falseness/genuineness, but by the style in which they are imagined" (1991:6). Moreover, Plena music participants signify a class position as well as their social location through their musical practice. Anderson's theory offers a backdrop to understand how resemanticized Plena music performances are both mimetically linked and altered in New York City (Taussig 1993).

The resemanticization of Plena in the diaspora operates in both the level of meaning and musical style. Jorge Pérez's (1991) research on Plena delineates the distinct variegated music styles performed in New York City and Puerto Rico. He describes the role of distinctive instrumentation, technology, and social commentary as central differences in how Plena music is performed across both localities. The work of the Puerto Rican historian Angel Quintero-Rivera provides a basis to further enrich the discussion. Salsa music, he notes, is a cultural form that promotes confrontation between opposing social classes. Salsa music and its lyrics became the medium to critique Puerto Rican second-class citizenship. Quintero-Rivera more importantly argues that Salsa in New York assumed the role and social function that the musical forms of Bomba, Plena, and Seis have in Puerto Rico. Although these musical forms were media for communal expression, Quintero-Rivera argues that they, along with Salsa in New York, are musics of "class interaction" (1989:30). Because of their social position and cultural traditions, Nuyoricans creatively readapted Salsa into music that critiqued their social realities and affirmed their cultural identity. This dialectical is linked to how identities are produced through practices, making distinctions within an overlapping system of meanings. The works of Pérez and Quintero-Rivera help to document and further contextualize the resemanticized cultural performances of Plena music and the funeral as distinctive diasporic practices.[15]

Many of Lavoe's friends, fellow musicians, Salsa music promoters, and music journalists have described his life as plagued with adversity. In 1988 Lavoe attempted suicide by jumping out of a ninth-floor room at the Regency Hotel in San Juan, Puerto Rico, breaking both his legs, one hip, and several ribs, causing massive internal bleeding. This attempted suicide was a response to the distress that overcame his personal life. For example, his seventeen-year-old son was accidentally shot and killed. Shortly thereafter, Héctor's mother-in-law was brutally murdered in Puerto Rico, and a mysterious fire destroyed his home in Queens, leaving four relatives dead. Also, Lavoe frequently battled his drug addiction, which adversely affected his professional life. His addiction often made him late to many performances and regularly aroused the anger of promoters and club owners. His tardy appearances were so common that Lavoe deflected his lateness on to audience members and fans, jokingly communicating through song and statements that they had arrived too early for the performance. Yet if his tardiness created any animosity, it surely dissipated at the news of his death on June 29, 1993. Lavoe's fans remember the urban jíbaro salsero as a cultural hero, although at times they forget that he died of an AIDS-related complication. This selective omission and repression of Lavoe's distress is shaped and constituted by a national and diasporic narrative and mythology regarding Puerto Rican and Latino masculinity and sexuality, Salsa as a masculine and heterosexual practice and scene, and finally Latino culture and its selected cultural heroes. More important, with AIDS considered to be a gay disease, the logical inference would attribute a gay identity to Lavoe as well. As a cultural hero, this association would now inflict the Puerto Rican nation and its diaspora with the virus. Despite this historical amnesia regarding Lavoe's health and passing, he is both a tragic figure of urban mythology and a crowned martyr of the trans-Boricua and Latino communities. As a cultural hero, Lavoe may conjure up not just national and diasporic inscriptions but also a reworking of subaltern historiography where competing discourses and narratives are subverting and entangling official accounts of the past.[16] Lavoe's request to be buried next to his son in St. Raymond's cemetery in the Bronx was honored, and he was interred on July 2, 1993.

• • •

For two days, thousands of people from New York's Latino communities, particularly Puerto Ricans, paid homage to Héctor Lavoe by offering their condolences at the Frank E. Campbell Funeral Home, located on 81st Street and Madison Avenue. Throngs of people lined up to see Lavoe's body, and the crowds circled an entire New York City block up to and around 5th Avenue and 82nd Street. Annually, Puerto Ricans congregate in this area of Manhattan to celebrate the Puerto Rican Day Parade in early June. On this occasion, however, citizens whose public cultural expressions are often relegated to working-class, ethnic neighborhoods appropriated this heavily policed Upper East Side space by singing and dancing to Lavoe's music. With Lavoe's voice and Colón's strident trombone blaring from boom boxes and car stereos, subaltern bodies and cultural practices disrupted the sanctioned schedule that allowed them to occupy this space for only one day in June. The occasion of Lavoe's death allowed Puerto Ricans and other Latinos to rupture the spatial and temporal dichotomies that govern their annual parade festivity as well as the everyday expression of public culture.[17]

The appropriation of this affluent New York City neighborhood takes on a particular significance given the ambivalent social and political location of Diaspo-Ricans in between two nation spaces. In both the island and in the United States, the social location of the diaspora lies within a colonial dilemma of ambiguity in which institutional recognition is not sanctioned or superficially recognized. This social liminality may help to explain the public cultural expressions of Puerto Ricans during the burial and funeral procession. The lacuna between social cultural practices and public culture can provide insight to an understanding of public culture as described by Arjun Appadurai and Carol A. Breckenridge. Public culture is distinct from sanctioned national culture. It encompasses a "zone of cultural debate" serving as "an arena where *other* types, forms and domains of culture are encountering, interrogating and contesting each other in new and unexpected ways" (1988:6, emphasis added). In between "national culture"—which is a contested mode—defined by the nation-state, and commercial culture, public culture is "directed to audiences without regard to the limits of . . . locality or social category" (1988:6). In the public gathering and public performances of Salsa music and dance around the Frank E. Campbell funeral home, admirers of Héctor Lavoe and his music mediated this space and decentered the practices of a homogenized and purified geography and soundscape, putting forth a new site for Latino culture. Despite police surveillance, the power to occupy this geographical space with subaltern diasporic bodies with the once-outlawed West African clave rhythms piercing the Upper East Side soundscape informs us of the nexus of space, culture, and power. Moreover, it addresses the importance of occupying and redefining restricted territories marked by elite and privileged communities. This shift and occupancy of the aural and physical contact zones (Pratt 1991) continued at Héctor Lavoe's funeral procession and burial.

The funeral mass was held at St. Cecilia's Catholic Church on 105th Street in El Barrio. As Héctor Lavoe's body was being taken out of the church and into the hearse, hundreds of his followers outside began shouting, "¡Que Viva Héctor Lavoe! ¡Héctor Lavoe Vive! ¡Tú eres eterno! ¡Se fue pero se queda!" (Héctor Lavoe lives! You are eternal! He left but remains with us!). Other's clapped and sang the Plena song "Que Bonita Bandera,

Que Bonita Bandera, La Bandera Puertorriqueña!" (What a beautiful flag, What a beautiful flag, the flag of Puerto Rico!), referring not only to Lavoe's Puerto Rican nationality but also claiming him as a cultural hero of Puerto Rico. Fans continued to perform Plena music and interwove Salsa music throughout the funeral procession. The public performance around the hearse and throughout the procession between the church and the cemetery demonstrate the resemanticized practices of Plena and Salsa enacted during the funeral as well as the liminal social position of the Diaspo-Rican community. For example, various sectors of the crowd performed and sang Plena music with Spanglish lyrics, while other groups performed Salsa music. At times, the soundscape became indistinguishable because both musical styles were being performed simultaneously. Marching, dancing, walking, and singing through the noisy urban streets between El Barrio in Manhattan and St. Raymond's cemetery in the Bronx, pleneros and salseros used microphones and speakers to help carry their voices within this urban metropolis. As stated previously, Salsa in the diaspora serves a similar social function to the Plena in Puerto Rico. Plena and Salsa were performed interchangeably during the ceremony, illuminating the fluid movement between both musical styles in memorializing Lavoe.

The funeral procession to St. Raymond's cemetery lasted six hours. And during this time the crowd and those following the *caminata* (procession) played, sang, and danced to Héctor Lavoe's music. At the cemetery, many climbed on top of mausoleums and continued to sing Plena music in tribute to him during the final benediction and hours after the lowering of the coffin into the grave. One Plena song, sung by those present at the cemetery, canonized Héctor as a plenero and national hero by placing him among a community of Puerto Rican pleneros:

Túmbalc a Cortijo
Túmbale a Ismael
Túmbale a Lavoe
como le gustaba a él.

[Pay homage to Rafael Cortijo,
Pay homage to Ismael Rivera,
Pay homage to Héctor Lavoe
the way Héctor would have wanted]
(This refrain is also a praise of great valor.)

and
Fuego al cañon, fuego al cañon,
Así se respeta a Héctor Lavoe.
[Fire to the canon, fire to the canon,
this is how we must respect Héctor Lavoe.]

This acclamation and reclamation can be viewed and interpreted in a number of different ways. It not only recognizes the historical significance that Lavoe has on Puerto Rican music but also elevates him into the male pantheon of pleneros: Mon Rivera, Rafael Cortijo, and Ismael Rivera.[18] Canonizing Héctor Lavoe in this pantheon upholds and reproduces a masculine hegemony in Plena music while also accenting the gendered construction of public culture and the way in which masculinity shapes collective memory and national celebrations. This action also constructs Plena music as the national music of Puerto Rico. Lavoe's class position is racialized into this black Puerto Rican musical tradition as he is canonized and remembered in the process.

This public reclamation of Héctor Lavoe as plenero can be read as an attempt to reclaim and remember him as an authentic and true Puerto Rican and *ponceño*. Working on the premise that Plena is the authentic music of Ponce and Puerto Rico, in this performance it may serve as a means of authenticating Héctor Lavoe through this musical tradition, creating a reversion back to homeland references. Lavoe was not a plenero but a salsero popularly recognized by many as "el cantante de la Salsa" (the singer of Salsa music) and "el cantante de los cantantes" (the singer of singers) (Rondón 1980:125, 126). In the process of being memorialized, Lavoe, unlike Ismael Rivera, who was a performer of Plena music, crosses genres from Salsa into Plena. This crossing highlights the agency exercised by diasporized accounts of memory and commemoration and the role that collective memory has in reconstructing meaning, historical events, and figures. Besides historical reconstruction, this crossing may also be attributed to the arrangements that constitute Salsa music in New York City. Because Salsa is not a rhythm but a "way of making music," encompassing various genre elements including Plena, the reconstruction of Lavoe as plenero may also be rooted in the way he incorporated Plena music and lyrics into his live Salsa performances.[19] Overall, the fluidity of historical meanings demonstrates how collective memory functions to mitigate racial and class boundaries while also claiming them.

This process directs us to examine the agency exercised in the social imaginary articulated through performance. Memory and performance coalesce to become an "organized field of social practices" on the one hand and a "form of [negotiated] sites of agency and [transnational] fields of possibility on the other" (Appadurai 1993:274). Agency is exerted in the commemorative musical performance of Lavoe while also negotiating the floating transnational significance he draws from overlapping and connected communities across disparate locations on one hand and negotiating the difference between everyday life and structural processes on the other. Embedded in this crossing of genres is a crossing of racial and class positions, fronting a unified community while also erasing and diluting racially coded distinctions.

In Puerto Rico it is customary for deceased Salsa and Plena musicians to receive very large funeral processions and celebrations at the Plaza de Salsa, also referred to as La Plaza de los Salseros (the plaza of Salsa musicians). In Héctor Lavoe's funeral celebration, El Barrio in New York City and St. Raymond's Cemetery in the Bronx become the surrogate embodiments mimetically representing La Plaza de los Salseros. Close resemblance of the Lavoe funeral to those celebrated at the plaza informs us of the flexibility of a cultural repertoire to create an impression of reversion linked to a lineage of homeland practices. There is no doubt that this may be a factor, particularly in the ancestral connection to history and spiritual reverence to the deceased. Joseph Roach reminds us that the voices of the dead continue to be heard in the bodies and practices of the living (1996:xiii). However, as already argued, the public performance style of the funeral and burial in New York City was not simply an attempt of reversion but a celebration that articulated qualities of diversion.[20]

In addition, what also can be decoded from this performance and ceremony is the continued acknowledgment of the transnational identity of Lavoe—as both Nuyorican and ponceño—and the continued hybridity of Plena musical history and its contributors beginning with, for example, Joselino "Bumbún" Oppenheimer (Flores 1993). This acclamation of Héctor Lavoe as a plenero recognizes the impact that a Diaspo-Rican singer can have on a national Puerto Rican musical tradition, symbolizing the impact of transmigrancy upon island cultural expressions.

Immediately after Lavoe's death, a number of articles were published on his life and impact on Salsa music and Nuyorican history. One letter published in the Puerto Rican newspaper El Nuevo Día continued to enforce the authenticity argument. The letter petitions the government of Puerto Rico to excavate the bodies of Héctor Lavoe and his son, Héctor Jr., from their Bronx burial ground at St. Raymond's cemetery and have them sent and buried in Puerto Rico. The logic, as articulated in the letter, is that "it is obvious that el coquí cannot rest in a land outside Borinquen [Puerto Rico]" (Valle and Méndez 1993:125).[21] Yet a month earlier, Héctor's daughter, Priscilla, who lives in Puerto Rico, made a public acknowledgment in the same newspaper responding to the island community's demand to have Héctor buried there. She notes: "Comprendemos que el pueblo de Puerto Rico desearía que sepultaramos a Héctor en Ponce, pero la voluntad de él fue otra. En Noviembre pasado (1992) yo lo visité y me dijo que en cualquier momento esperaba fallecer y que quería que lo enterraran con [el hijo in el Bronx]" [We understand that the Puerto Rican community desires to have Héctor buried in Puerto Rico, but his wish was different. In November 1992, I visited him and he told me that should he ever die, he wanted to be buried with his son in the Bronx] (Torres 1993:25).

Implicit in the writers' nationalism are the linkages between land, identity, and memory. From the writer's perspective, geographical borders and "biological bonds of solidarity" supersede the deterritorialized transnational community of the Puerto Rican diaspora (Basch, Schiller and Blanc 1994:269). In this case, the land where diasporas reside is perceived as less authentic. The irony here is that nationalism is rooted within a geographical "body" and location, where the "bodies" of deceased heroes buried in soil within a specific location "baptize" the land, helping to contribute to the mythology of the nation. Bodies of land and biologically rooted bodies yield a solidarity within the traditional and obfuscating discourse of nationalism. The discourse of bodies penetrating land/bodies further contributes to gendered notions of land and nation, where the land is maternal, waiting to be penetrated, while the nation is masculine, ready and needing to return home (McClintock 1996). Lastly, Valle and Méndez failed to recognize how some of Puerto Rico's national heroes and intellectuals, such as Eugenio María de Hostos and José Luis González (to name a few), are transnationals buried outside the geographical borders of Puerto Rico. Héctor's buried body in the Bronx can also be perceived not simply as a body outside its home but also as an extended transnational character of the Puerto Rican community. Here, the ruptured nation exists translocally, in multiple pieces. I think the Puerto Rican sociologist Agustín Laó captures this imagery best in his description of the translocal sites of the Puerto Rican nation: "La Isla del encanto" to "La Isla en-cantos" [the island of enchantment to the island in pieces] (1997:173). Being buried in the Bronx, outside the borders of Puerto Rico, sustains the national myth of a tragic hero dying in the belly of the beast. The insistence to return his body accents how space, geography, and land are integral to traditional constructions of nationalism but also expands traditional discussions of the nation via the Diaspora.

As a performer Héctor sang, like Mon and Ismael Rivera and Rafael Cortijo in Puerto Rico, to the marginal lumpen who struggle daily to *sobre-vivir* (survive) across various transnational communities, including the United States, Puerto Rico, Venezuela, Colombia, and Panama among others. He was considered by many to be una voz del pueblo (a voice of the people) and poeta de la calle (street poet), articulating the experiences of those who were and continue to be marginalized from the economy (Colón 1993:30). Cesar Miguel Rondón notes that "la presencia del barrio en [Héctor] era fuerte . . . Siempre [acentuando] el toque marginal, de cantante del barrio, callejero, que nunca jamás podría admitir la sofisticación en su expresión" [The presence of the barrio in Héctor was strongly obvious . . . He frequently accents a touch of marginality in his expression] (1980:123). One respondent interviewed for this project perceived Héctor Lavoe and his music as the "voice of the street in *both* places," referring, obviously, to Puerto Rico and New York. The respondent explains: "Héctor Lavoe, like Ismael Rivera [before him], talked to people who had been down and out and who had seen bad things and triumphed. That's why people identified with them. Héctor and Ismael had lasted; they survived; ellos sobrevivieron" (Pérez 1996). This analysis does not divide the nation but roots the memory of Héctor Lavoe with the experiences of those within the diaspora and the island. Like nationalism, memory is linked and expressed with sites and places. This respondent's transmigratory imagination describes the transnational character of the Puerto Rican community by referring to "both places" or what is commonly termed "acá y allá" (here and there) (Flores 1996). Yet the respondent further highlights how Héctor's music addressed the lumpenproletariat across a transnational community. In other words, rather than just essentializing the nation as a monolithic community confined within a particular geography, the respondent provides a more complex perspective by addressing the class distinctions within the nation, including those sectors to which Héctor and Ismael sang. Moreover, he articulates a transmigrant imagination, superimposing and blurring the collective memories and places of those in both locations.

The respondent also notes how both men were admired because of the similar lives they lived vis-à-vis their transnational listening audience. In other words, the lives and experiences of Ismael Rivera and Héctor Lavoe were similar to those of their listening audience. It is for these reasons that "people identified with them" (Pérez 1996). In addition, at the time of Ismael Rivera's death in 1987, Héctor Lavoe became the diasporic and transnational successor of "el sonero mayor" (the master singer). However, unlike Ismael Rivera, who represented and signified a specific historical moment and style of Salsa music, Héctor Lavoe became a transmigratory effigy constituted by competing and overlapping significations of diasporic alterity and national restoration.

One of Héctor's most popular songs, "Mi Gente" [My People], written by band leader, flutist, and coproducer of Fania Records, Johnny Pacheco, is considered by some of the respondents interviewed for this project to be the Nuyorican national anthem. The transformation of this Salsa song into an anthem allows listeners to remember the death of Héctor Lavoe and his music as well as to memorialize him as a transnational representative of the nation. "Mi Gente" addresses the listeners as belonging to Héctor Lavoe and him to them. Lavoe is positioned as the spokesperson and signifier of the translocal nation. Again, as in the male pantheon of Plena music, a jíbaro ponceño becomes the chosen transnational representative. Lavoe is *diasporized* by his listening audience in New York City and *nationalized* by the community of listeners in Puerto Rico. This practice acknowledges how the song articulates and represents both the diasporic and national identity(-ies) and experiences of Puerto Ricans and other Latinos/as.

There is a collective emotional affinity that emerges when listening to the song "Mi Gente" that is, as some respondents note, the connectedness they feel to the larger community of Salsa listeners and other Puerto Ricans (Fontañez 1996; Pérez 1996; Ruiz 1996). This is similar to Alessandro Portelli's critique of the relationship between memory, orality, industrial folk music, and labor among the working class in Italy; this song "lives in the memory of an emotion" (1991:187). The collective and historical experiences shared by many listeners simultaneously reinforce a shared emotion of solidarity (1991:174). In this case, the collective experiences of the diaspora serve as the source for its writing and presentation and for how it is remembered and encoded in the song and memory of its listeners. This shared agency of resignifying "Mi Gente" to an anthem demonstrates the discursivity and malleability of popular culture and music, where time, memory, and locality change the meaning of the song. Although the lyrics have remained the same since its inception, the meanings attached to them by a collective body of listeners have changed during the course of Lavoe's musical career and, more dramatically, after his death across different spaces. This Diaspo-Rican national anthem extends the anthems of Puerto Rico as well as provides a distinctive and fluid lineage to the nation. Interestingly, how the anthem gets resignified to represent both the diaspora and the island nation is further testament to Lavoe's reconstruction as a floating signifier of national sameness and diasporic agency.

This perspective on music, emotion, and nation is linked to the sentiment of nationalism. Although shaped by essentialist categories of "the people," this emotion transcends national boundaries and communities, dialogically sharing experiences rooted in solidarity of sound and collective memory. It comes as no surprise then that live concerts performed by the Fania All-Stars in Puerto Rico, Venezuela, Colombia, and other Latin American countries and within various locations in the United States include a performance of Lavoe's song "Mi Gente." However, the song is now inverted to "Que Canten Su Gente" (Let His People Sing), referring here to Héctor's people/community (Fania All-Stars 1994 and 1997). The audience, identified as Héctor's community, sings in unison to the emotionally charged lyrics, creating a shared memory and emotion of the late sonero. What is more important, "Mi Gente" and its derivative, "Su Gente," interpellate (Althusser 1971) the imaginary relationships of individuals, which constitute them to imagined transnational communities. The song helps to construct and position these imaginary relationships to a transnational community, synthesizing collective memories, transnationalisms, and identities across multiple spaces.

Héctor is also remembered by some not just as a Nuyorican but also as a jíbaro from the city of Ponce whose singing style embodied both Puerto Rico and New York simultaneously. His voice is described as having both a Nuyorican "brashness" as well as a Puerto Rican jíbaro (country) sound (Pérez 1996; Ruiz 1996). Interestingly, the musician, musical arranger, bandleader, and Lavoe's close friend Willie Colón articulates this simultaneity. In an interview with Pacifica Radio's Nancy Rodríguez, Colón describes Lavoe's diasporality in this way: "Although Héctor was born in Ponce, he became a symbol of the New York Salsa sound during the 1960s and 70s"

(Colón 1996). Ray Barretto, band leader, conguero, and fellow member of the Fania All-Stars with Héctor Lavoe and Willie Colón, describes the doubleness of Lavoe in this way: "What made Lavoe a little different from the little guys was that he was closer to the jíbaro thing from Puerto Rico and that's what made him different. That's what people loved about him. He [also] projected that Barrio quality and that was his strength" (Barretto 1996). I think Rubén Blades articulates it best when reflecting upon the significance, singing style, and doubleness of Héctor Lavoe: "[Héctor's singing style], delivery, and the things that he said were more street than what my tastes at the time could understand. It was a very New York slang style, a more N[u]yorican approach. Héctor's strength was his power in terms of inventing things. He would invent things that reflected upon life in New York and also a dose of jíbarito [country], of Puerto Rican in him. Héctor's gift was his New York brash, in your face style with that pristine crystal clear voice that he had. *Héctor's style was more a mixture of emigrant Boricua and N[u]yorican*" (Blades 1993:17, my emphasis).

Embodying both Puerto Rican and New York identities and musical styles simultaneously alludes to the complexities that constitute the diasporality of his musical performances and identities. Héctor's orality and singing style became transmigratory with his movement to New York City. Rather than just seeing his Nuyorican brashness as an additive layer disconnected from his jíbaroness, I argue that both identities equally shaped and constituted who he was and what and how he sang and performed. Rather than just seeing a Puerto Rican jíbaro singing *in* New York, Héctor became a Nuyorican who transformed his identity from Héctor Pérez to Héctor Lavoe in New York City. This transformation and doubleness that embodied and shaped his music and identity speak to the process of diasporality that shape, reshape, and recategorize genres and identities (Bhabha 1996). The mobility of music and identities in diasporas fragments the ways in which the past and present are narrated and imagined (Hall 1990). Because music, according to Mark Slobin, resides at the margins of "the person and the people . . . it presents a crucial point of articulation in viewing diasporic life" (1994:244). The doubleness of jíbaro and Nuyorican, the singing of and being shaped by multiple social and cultural factors within New York and Puerto Rico, presents Lavoe as an intercessor of diasporic processes that are constantly converging, "producing and reproducing . . . through transformation and difference" (Hall 1990:235). In the case of Lavoe, his voice and singing style not only embody his doubleness but also represent and mirror the social experiences that Héctor shared with other Diaspo-Ricans.

The emphasis on his linguistic sound is coupled with Héctor Lavoe's ability to improvise and "think on his feet," telling stories and ideas to the clave meter of Salsa music. The ability to "improvisar" (improvise) in "el espíritu de la clave" [in the clave spirit] within Salsa music is what distinguishes a good from a bad Salsa singer (Alvarez, 1992:35).[22] Of the interviews I conducted for this paper and the oral and literary sources to which I referred, many if not all mention Héctor's talent to improvise. This concentration on his voice and sound speaks to the importance that orality plays in codifying diasporic and homeland linguistic traditions and identities. In addition, the movement from the page to the performance emphasizes the importance Héctor had in mediating and resemanticizing the written word/musical lyric. In other words, the move from the literate/written text to the oral performance becomes a mediated act of transcription (Edwards and Sienkewics 1990:37). Lavoe's ability to free himself from scripts and prewritten codes allowed him to become a vortex of multiple significations simultaneously. Regardless of the songwriter's location, he was able to embody and project the linguistic styles of both island and New York communities.

CONCLUSION

To speak about the intersecting authentic and transnational identities and musical style of Héctor Lavoe is to acknowledge how much Diaspo-Rican cultures have equally become a part of Puerto Rico. This transmigratory perspective shifts the colonialist binary model of Puerto Rico being the center of culture and the diaspora as the natural imitators of that authentic culture. This shift emphasizes the fluid and scattered processes that shape diasporic transmigratory cultures. Diasporality rather than ethnicity reshifts our attention to how the larger social constructions and processes of power—imperialism, coloniality, circular migration, and race, to name just a few—are intricately intertwined with identity formation and musical construction. Moreover, diasporality denaturalizes authentic perceptions of cultural origins and the one-way process that obliterates historical and cultural processes.

When Puerto Ricans and other Latinos gathered to pay homage to Héctor Lavoe across the various barrios of the diaspora, Puerto Rico, and Latin America, they articulated shared memories, feelings, and identities. These multiple sites converged through the transnational imaginations embodied in surrogate media of performance and collective memory. The burial of Héctor Lavoe's body at St. Raymond's cemetery and the ensuing controversy over his return to Puerto Rico still exemplify the importance of locality for nationalist and diasporic discourses. In the transnational circuit of resemanticized memories, Lavoe's corpse is not confined to its Bronx location but becomes an effigy that performs and surrogates overlapping and competing discourses of trans-Boricua memories, cultural histories, and Diaspo-Rican alterity. The polysemy of meanings and memories that encode community agency create Lavoe as a sacrificial effigy for a historical rite of passage. However, this rite of passage is not limited to him; other popular singers, artists, and cultural heroes, such as Frankie Ruíz, Guadalupe Victoria Yoli (La Lupe), and Tito Puente may come to shed light on other dimensions of diasporicity and transnationalism. In doing so, they inform us that there is no single rite of passage and that these historical constructions and formations are flexible and expansive. Thus, a closer examination of other historical figures may continue to show how resemanticized meanings and memories continue to develop across distinct social and geographical spaces. In June 29, 1993, Lavoe's last breath of life brought together distinct and translocal communities bonded by their collective memory and transnational imaginations of his life and music. The songs "Mi Gente," "El Cantante," and "Periódico de Ayer" were heard across various geographic locations, but the common bond that connected these communities was these imagined sounds.

NOTES

The title of this essay is from Benedict Anderson's *Imagined Communities,* 2d ed. (London: Verso, 1991), 145.

In the span of conducting this research and writing (and rewriting!) this essay, many friends, colleagues, professors, and relatives offered their assistance. First, I thank Professors Frances R. Aparicio, Susan Douglas, Travis Jackson, Richard Cándida Smith, Betty L. Bell, and June Howard for reading earlier drafts of this essay. Friends and colleagues at the University of Michigan who reviewed earlier drafts include Adrián Burgos Jr., Alexandra M. Stern, María Elena Cepeda, Mérida Rúa, and the members of La Colectiva Research Group. Many thanks to my brother Eddie Valentín and my cousin Luis Vázquez for sharing their musical knowledge and record collections. I want to especially thank Graciela Hernández for her insightful readings and patient editing. Friends and colleagues who agreed to be interviewed and/or assisted me with the interview process include Ramón Rodríguez, Luis Bauzó (both from the Harbor Center for the Performing Arts in New York City), Richie Pérez, Larry Harlow ("El Judio Maravilloso"), Madélena Fontáñez, and Mario Ruíz. Big kudos to the library and research staff at El Centro de Estudios Puertorriqueños, Hunter College, City University of New York, for welcoming me as a graduate student researcher during the summer of 1996 and for sharing their time, resources, and knowledge, particularly Roberto Rodríguez, Juan Flores, Blanca Vázquez, and Pedro Rivera. A special acknowledgement to the filmmaker Leon Gast for allowing me to review his video footage on Héctor Lavoe. Finally, the Office of Academic and Multicultural Initiatives, the Office of the Vice President for Research, Rackham School of Graduate Studies, and the Program in American Culture, all at the University of Michigan, Ann Arbor, provided financial resources that made this project possible. Dedico este ensayo a mi familia, especialmente a mi mamá Felicita Escobar Valentín (1938–1999). Like all intellectual projects, this work is collectively influenced but individually written. That notwithstanding, any errors and shortcomings are obviously my own.

1. The use of the term *Salsa* here is a *deliberate* marker to distinguish it from Son, which is a Cuban musical form. Rather than placing quotation marks

around the word *Salsa*—which is often done by some academic scholars to describe it as a euphemism for Cuban music—I purposefully capitalize the first letter to define it as a cultural arts expression that emerged in New York City during the 1960s and 1970s. Salsa, in other words, is not simply "refashioned Cuban musical rhythms" but rather, "a way of making music." For an insightful discussion on the distinction between Salsa and the Cuban Son, see Alvarez (1992); Aparicio (1998); Berríos-Miranda (1997, 1998); Quintero-Rivera (1998); Quintero-Rivera andAlvarez (1990); Negus (1990); Rondón (1980).

For a "culture of poverty" perspective on Salsa and the Puerto Rican community(-ies), Manuel (1994).

2. For a discussion on public culture, see Appadurai and Breckenridge (1988).

3. Diaspora is a "concept that illuminates the transnational workings of identity formation and challenges fixed and essentialist conceptions. Diasporas are the result of the scattering of peoples, whether as the result of war, oppression, poverty, enslavement or the search for better economic and social opportunities, with the inevitable opening of their culture to new influences and pressures. Diaspora as a concept offers new possibilities for understanding identity, not as something inevitably determined by place or nationality, and for visualizing a future where new bases for social solidarity are offered and joined, perhaps via the new technologies." See Gilroy (1997:304). Smadar Lavie and Ted Swedenburg (1996:1–25) also offer a definition and a comparative analysis of diaspora with other concepts and identities. For a critical and comprehensive analysis surrounding the diaspora discourse, see Clifford (1994) and Young (1995). In my opinion, Stuart Hall provides the most insightful use of this concept. Refer to Hall (1990, 1995, 1996a, 1996b).

4. *Jíbaro* means different things to different people and can be employed to describe various sectors of the Puerto Rican population. Important in this essay is the constant flux that the term signifies. The term often refers to an agricultural peasant living and working in Puerto Rico as well as to behavior and cultural practices that are often aligned with them. The term is often used in a derogatory manner, meaning "hick" or "backward," although it also refers to native purity. *Jíbaro* usually connotes a racially white, male, pure, static, and native idea of Puerto Rican authenticity. Crucial to this essay is how jíbaro constructions are now enacted by Diaspo-Ricans through popular culture. As a consequence, many island-based Puerto Ricans view U.S.-based Puerto Rican cultural expressions as "hick" because they often embody static and nostalgic depictions of the island. In other words, the hick is not simply residing in Puerto Rico but is now part of the diaspora and its social and cultural practices. To complicate this further, intra-Diaspo-Rican authenticity discourses parallel the jíbaro discourse between the island and the United States. This discourse arises between and among the translocal Puerto Rican communities residing in Massachusetts, California, Hawaii, Illinois, Connecticut, Florida, New York, Pennsylvania, and other U.S. states. Because of the mass migration of Puerto Ricans to New York during the first half of the twentieth century, Nuyoricans often construct themselves—and are

constructed—as the authentic Diaspo-Ricans, whereas Puerto Ricans residing in other U.S. cities are perceived as inauthentic. Often times, Puerto Ricans in the United States may also consider their New York counterparts as backward hicks unable to realize the (im)migrant narrative. For a discussion on the authenticity debate among Puerto Ricans in the diaspora, see Rúa (2000). For a detailed and insightful historical analysis of the jíbaro as a discursive and historical figure, see Scarano (1996) and Guerra (1998).

5. According to Hutton, "collective mentalities" is a concept developed by the French Historian Philippe Ariès. Collective mentalities can be defined as "old ways of thinking [that] do not completely disappear but continue to coexist with new ones. . . . Within tradition, the past remains the ground of the past present. The time of tradition cannot be plotted as a succession of discrete states of mind in which new habits displace old ones. To plot changes in mentality the historian must take into account the on-going, dynamic relationship between habit and improvisation. A habit of mind is modified within a larger structure of collective attitudes. Improvisation, therefore, alters the structure of memory in the process of being integrated into it. Within that structure, every modification of a habit represents a tension between old and the new. Old and new ways of thinking are coordinates that coexist in roughly inverse proportion, if the structure of collective memory is considered over a long period of time. . . . [A] history of mentalities appropriated the technique of the ancient art of memory: it assigned the meaning of the past to images rather than events, and it located these within larger mental structures. Historical change was [then] revealed through the way in which the structures were modified" (1993:101–2).

6. I'm unsure of the correct spelling of Lavoe's promoter Franquis. According to Al Santiago and Johnny Pacheco, Franquis gave Héctor the nickname Lavoe because of his excellent voice and singing style. This information is included in the live radio broadcast produced by Nancy Rodríguez and aired by WBAI FM in New York City (1996).

7. For a discussion on Boogaloo music, see the interview with Johnny Colón in Boggs (1992). Also see Flores (2000).

8. For an excellent discussion regarding music scenes and local sounds, see Finnegan (1989), Kruse (1993), Shank (1994), Feld (1994), and Cohen (1994).

9. For a discussion on clave, please refer to Gerard and Sheller (1989).

10. For a great overview regarding New York and Puerto Rican Salsa, see Vázquez (1999).

11. This masculine image of Salsa continues today but with kinder terms and pretty-boy images. Contemporary examples include "el caballero de la Salsa" [the gentleman of Salsa], which is used in reference to the Puerto Rican singer Gilberto Santa Rosa, and "el gallo de la Salsa" [the rooster of Salsa], which is used to refer to Tito Rojas. Other examples of current gendered terms are *Salsa dura* and *Salsa monga*. The former is used to describe a Salsa sound that is commonly attributed to the music performed during the 1960s and 1970s in New York City, whereas the latter derisively describes Salsa arrangements that contain little or no brass and percussive sounds and/or improvisational swing. Salsa dura and Salsa monga may draw on masculine/sexual discourses that connote binary interpretations of gender: femininity versus masculinity,

"active" versus "passive." These remarks are speculative and deserve further attention. To date, the most complete analysis concerning gender, Puerto Rican identity(-ies), and Salsa is Aparicio (1998).

12. Lewis (1965) and Chavez (1991) best illustrate the culture of poverty perspectives that shaped both public policy and public discourses regarding Puerto Ricans.

13. For a complete discography, refer to the two-CD collection, *Héctor Lavoe: The Fania Legends Collection, Volume 1*, Fania JM 700.

14. Fania All-Stars *Live at Yankee Stadium Volume 1*. Fania XSLP 00476. According to César Miguel Rondón (1980:101), the actual recording occurred during a live performance in the Clemente Coliseum in San Juan, Puerto Rico.

15. Scholars and journalists have discussed the symbolic form that performers' funerals have on constructing collective identities and memories. See Roach (1996); Rodríguez Juliá (1991); and Ruíz (1995).

16. For a review of historical and collective memory, myth, and power, see Portelli (1991), Samuel and Thompson (1990), Bodnar (1989), Halbwachs (1992), and Tonkin (1992).

17. The Frank E. Campbell Funeral Home is located one avenue east of the Metropolitan Museum of Art, an institution that regulates and legitimizes public knowledge of national and marginal culture(s).

18. Interestingly, Lavoe is thus far the only white Puertorriqueño in this pantheon of pleneros.

19. For a discussion on Salsa "as a way of making music," see Quintero-Rivera (1998).

20. For a discussion of reversion and diversion within diaspora communities, see Glissant (1989). Glissant's theory of reversion/diversion highlights the difference between "the transplanting of a people who continue to survive elsewhere and the transfer of a population to another place where they change into something different, into a new set of possibilities." Those who become transplanted maintain ties and cultural values in their new localities by practicing reversion. Reversion is an "obsession with a single origin: one must not alter the absolute state of being. To revert is to consecrate permanence, to negate contact" and believe in fixed beings (14). On the other hand, a population that changes into something different welcomes and practices diversion, which is a "return not to origins but to entanglement or continued Creolization" (26).

21. A coquí is an amphibious organism native only to the ecosystem of Puerto Rico and is unable to survive outside of the island; it is thus considered to be truly Puerto Rican. It is common to hear people compare their Puerto Rican identity to a coquí, linking their identity to it. This helps to explain the discourse and the underlying logic employed in the editorial.

22. Many contemporary critics note the difference between a sonero per se and a singer in Salsa music. The former follows in the tradition of a singer's ability to improvise and "rhyme a story" spontaneously during a live performance. The latter suggests that a Salsa singer may have a "pleasant" voice and adequate singing skills but does not have the ability to improvise while performing before a live audience. At the time of this writing, examples of popular soneros would be Ismael Rivera, Gilberto Santa Rosa, José "Cheo" Feliciano, Domingo Quiñones, Victor Manuel, and Cano Estremera; on the

other hand, Salsa singers who are not regarded as soneros would be Marc Anthony, Brenda K. Starr, and India (Linda Caballero). It is obvious that most Salsa singers are male and are inheritors (and maintain their domination as transmitters and guardians) of an oral tradition. Interestingly, this suggests how masculinity and gender constitute the underlying criterion for soneros and Salsa singing styles.

BIBLIOGRAPHY

Althusser, Louis. 1971. *Lenin and Philosophy and Other Essays.* Translated by Ben Brewster. New York: Monthly Review Press.

Alvarez, Luis Manuel. 1990. "La libre combinación de las formas musicales en la salsa." *David y Goliath* (Buenos Aires, CLASCO) 57 (October): 45–51.

—— 1992. "La presencia negra en la música puertorriqueña." In *La tercera raíz: presencia africana en Puerto Rico,* edited by Lydia Milagros González, 29–41. San Juan: Centro de Estudios de la Realidad Puertorriqueña-Instituto de Cultura Puertorriqueña.

Anderson, Benedict. 1991. *Imagined Communities: Reflections on the Origin and Spread of Nationalism.* 2d ed. New York: Verso.

Aparicio. Frances R. 1998. *Listening to Salsa: Gender, Latin Popular Music and Puerto Rican Cultures.* Hanover: Wesleyan University Press.

Appadurai, Arjun. 1993. "Disjuncture and Difference in the Global Cultural Economy." In *Phantom Public Sphere,* edited by Bruce Robbins, 269–95. Minneapolis: University of Minnesota Press.

Appadurai, Arjun, and Carol Breckenridge. 1988. "Why Public Culture?" *Public Culture Bulletin* 1, no. 1 (Fall): 5–9.

Barretto, Ray. 1996. Interview by Nancy Rodríguez. *Ritmo y Aché Radio Program.* Pacifica Radio, 8 September.

Basch, Linda, Nina Glick Schiller, and Cristina Szanton Blanc, eds. 1994. *Nations Unbound: Transnational Projects, Postcolonial Predicaments, and Deterritorialized Nation-States.* Langhorne, Pa.: Gordon and Breach.

Berríos-Miranda, Marisol. 1997. "Con sabor a Puerto Rico: The Reception and Influence of Puerto Rican Salsa in Venezuela." Paper presented at "The Rhythms of Culture: Dancing to Las Américas," An International Research Conference on Popular Musics in Latin[o] America, the University of Michigan, Ann Arbor, March 21–22.

—— 1998. "Salsa: Whose Music Is It?" Paper presented at the American Studies Association Annual Conference, "American Studies and the Question of Empire: Histories, Cultures, and Practices." Seattle, Washington, 19–22 November.

Bhabha, Homi K. 1990. "Introduction: Narrating the Nation." In *Nation and Narration,* edited by Homi K. Bhabha, 1–7. New York: Routledge.

—— 1996. "Culture's In-Between." In *Questions of Identity,* edited by Stuart Hall and Paul Du Gay, 53–60. Thousand Oaks, Calif.: Sage.

Blades, Rubén. 1993. Interview by Alfredo Alvarado. *New York Latino: Music, the Arts, and More* 6 (Fall): 17, 24.

Bodnar, John. 1989. "Power and Memory in Oral History: Workers and Managers at Studebaker." *The Journal of American History* 75(4): 1201–21.

Canclini, Néstor García. 1992. "Cultural Reconversion." In *On Edge: The Crisis of Contemporary Latin American Culture,* edited by George Yudice, Jean Franco, and Juan Flores, 29–43. Minneapolis: University of Minnesota Press.

———. 1993a. *Transforming Modernity: Popular Culture in Mexico.* Austin: University of Texas Press.

———. 1993b. "The Hybrid: A Conversation with Margarita Zires, Raymundo Mier, and Mabel Piccini." *Boundary 2* 20, no. 3 (Fall): 77–92.

———. 1995. *Hybrid Cultures: Strategies for Entering and Leaving Modernity.* Minneapolis: University of Minnesota Press.

Chavez, Linda. 1991. *Out of El Barrio: Toward a New Politics of Hispanic Assimilation.* New York: Basic Books.

Cohen, Sara. 1994. "Identity, Place and the 'Liverpool Sound.' " In *Ethnicity, Identity and Music: The Musical Construction of Place,* edited by Martin Stokes, 117–34. New York: Berg.

Colón, Willie. 1967. *El Malo.* Fania SLPCD 337. Compact disc.

———. 1968. *The Hustler.* Fania SLPCD 347. Compact disc.

———. 1969. *Guisando/Doing a Job.* Fania SCPCD 370. Compact disc.

———. 1971. *Asalto Navideño.* Fania SLPF399. Compact disc.

———. 1972. *Cosa Nuestra.* Fania SLP 384. Compact disc.

———. 1972. *Crime Pays.* Fania SLP 00406. Compact disc.

———. 1972. *El Juicio.* Fania LPCD 00424. Compact disc.

———. 1973. *Asalto Navideño, Volume 2.* Fania SLP 449. Compact disc.

———. 1975. *The Good, The Bad, The Ugly.* Fania SLP 484. Compact disc.

———. 1976. *La Gran Fuga.* Fania SLP 394. Compact disc.

———. 1993. "Héctor Lavoe." *Claridad,* 9 to 15 July, p. 30.

———. 1996. Interview by Nancy Rodríguez. *Ritmo y Aché Radio Program.* Pacifica Radio, 8 September.

Edwards, Viv and Thomas J. Sienkewics. 1990. *Oral Cultures Past and Present: Rappin' and Homer.* Oxford: Basil Blackwell.

Fania All-Stars. 1975. *Live at Yankee Stadium Volume 1.* Fania XSLP 00476. Compact disc.

———. 1994. *Live.* Fania-684. Compact disc.

———. 1997. *Viva Colombia.* Latina 225. Compact disc.

Finnegan, Ruth. 1989. *Hidden Musicians: Music-Making in an English Town.* New York: Cambridge University Press.

Flores, Juan. 1993. *Divided Borders: Essays on Puerto Rican Identity.* Houston: Arte Público Press.

———. 1996. "Broken English Memories." *Modern Language Quarterly* 57(2): 381–95.

———. 2000. *From Bomba to Hip-Hop: Puerto Rican Culture and Latino Identity.* New York: Columbia University Press.

Fontañez, Madélena. 1996. Interview by the author. Tape recording. New York, 2 July.

Frith, Simon. 1992. "The Cultural Study of Popular Music." In *Cultural Studies,* edited by Lawrence Grossberg, Cary Nelson, and Paula Treichler, 174–86. New York: Routledge.

Guerra, Lillian. 1998. *Popular Expression and National Identity in Puerto Rico: The Struggle for Self, Community, and Nation.* Gainesville: University Press of Florida.

Halbwachs, Maurice. 1992. *On Collective Memory.* Edited and translated by Lewis A. Coser. Chicago: University of Chicago Press.

Hall, Stuart. 1990. "Cultural Identity and Diaspora." In *Identity: Community, Culture, Difference,* edited by Jonathon Rutherford, 222–37. London: Lawrence and Wishart.

—— 1995. "Negotiating Caribbean Identities." *New Left Review* 209: 3–14.

—— 1996. "New Ethnicities." In *Black Cultural Studies: A Reader,* edited by Houston A. Baker Jr., Manthia Diawara, and Ruth H. Lindenborg. Chicago: University of Chicago Press.

Hall, Stuart, and Kuan-Hsing Chen. 1996. "The Formation of a Diasporic Intellectual." In *Stuart Hall: Critical Dialogues in Cultural Studies,* edited by David Morley and Kuan-Hsing Chen. New York: Routledge.

Hutton, Patrick H. 1993. *History as an Art of Memory.* Hanover, N.H.: University Press of New England.

Kruse, Holly. 1993. "Subcultural Identity in Alternative Music and Culture." *Popular Music* 12: 33–41.

Laó, Agustín. 1997. "Islands at the Crossroads: Puerto Ricaness Traveling Between the Translocal Nation and the Global City." In *Puerto Rican Jam: Essays on Culture and Politics,* edited by Frances Negrón-Muntaner and Ramón Grosfoguel, 169–88. Minneapolis: University of Minnesota Press.

Lavie, Smadar and Ted Swedenburg. 1996. "Introduction, Displacement, Diaspora, and Geographies of Identity." In *Displacement, Diaspora, and Geographies of Identity,* edited by Smadar Lavie and Ted Swedenburg, 1–25. Durham, N.C.: Duke University Press.

Lavoe, Héctor. 1975a. *The Good, The Bad, The Ugly.* Fania 484. Compact disc.

—— 1975b. *La Voz.* Fania XSLP 00461. Compact disc.

—— 1976. *De Ti Depende [It's Up to You].* Fania SLP 00492. Compact disc.

—— 1978. *Comedia.* Fania JM 00522. Compact disc.

—— 1979. *Recordando a Felipe Pirela.* Fania 545. Compact disc.

—— 1980a. *El Sabio.* Fania 58. Compact disc.

—— 1980b. *Héctor's Gold.* Fania 574. Compact disc.

—— 1981. *¡Qué Sentimiento!* Fania 598. Compact disc.

—— 1985. *Revento.* Fania 634. Compact disc.

—— 1987. *Strikes Back.* Fania 647. Compact disc.

—— 1993a. *Héctor Lavoe: The Fania Legends of Salsa, Volume 1.* Fania JM 700. Compact disc.

—— 1993b. *The Master and the Protégé.* Fania 674. Compact disc.

—— 1994. *Héctor Lavoe: The Fania Legends of Salsa, Volume 2.* Fania 701. Compact disc.

Lewis, Oscar. 1966. *La Vida: A Puerto Rican Family in the Culture of Poverty—San Juan and New York.* New York: Random House.

Leymarie, Isabelle. 1994. "Salsa and Migration." In *The Commuter Nation: Perspectives on Puerto Rican Migration,* edited by Carlos Antonio Torre, Hugo Rodríguez Vecchini, and William Burgos, 343–61. Río Piedras, Editorial de al Universidad de Puerto Rico.

Manuel, Peter. 1994. "Puerto Rican Music and Cultural Identity: Creative Appropriation of Cuban Sources from Danza to Salsa." *Ethnomusicology* 38, no. 2 (Spring/Summer): 249–80.

Mato, Daniel. 1997. "On Global and Local Agents and the Social Making of Transnational Identities and Related Agendas." *Identities: Global Studies in Culture and Power* 4(2): 167–212.

McClintock, Anne. 1996. "No Longer in a Future Heaven: Nationalism, Gender, and Race." In *Becoming National: A Reader,* edited by Geoff Eley and Ronald Grigor Suny, 260–84. New York: Oxford University Press.

Negus, Keith. 1999. *Music Genres and Corporate Cultures.* New York: Routledge.

Padilla, Felix. 1989. "Salsa Music as a Cultural Expression of Consciousness and Unity." *Hispanic Journal of Behavioral Sciences* 11(1): 28–45.

Pagan, Adam. 1997. "Indestructible: The Young Lords Party and the Cultural Politics of Music in the Construction of Diaspo-Rican Identity." Paper presented at "The Rhythms of Culture: Dancing to Las Américas, An International Research Conference on Popular Musics in Latin[o] America" at the University of Michigan, Ann Arbor, 21–22 March.

Pérez, Jorge. 1991. "La plena puertorriqueña: de la expresión popular a la comercialización musical." *Centro de Estudios Puertorriqueños Boletin* 3(2): 51–55.

Pérez, Richie. 1996. Interview by the author. Tape recording. New York, 8 July.

Portelli, Alessandro. 1991. *The Death of Luigi Trastulli and Other Stories: Form and Meaning in Oral History.* Albany: State University of New York Press.

Pratt, Mary Louise. 1991. "Arts of the Contact Zone." *Profession* 91: 33–40.

Quintero-Rivera, Angel. 1989. "Music Social Classes, and the National Question in Puerto Rico." Working paper 178, Woodrow Wilson International Center for Scholars, Washington, D.C.

——— 1998. *Salsa, sabor y control: sociología de la música tropical.* México: Siglo Veintiuno Editores.

Quintero-Rivera, Angel and Luis Manuel Alvarez. 1990. "¡Libre combinación de las formas musicales en la salsa!" *David y Goliath* 57 (October): 45–51.

Roach, Joseph. 1996. *Cities of the Dead: Circum-Atlantic Performance.* New York: Columbia University Press.

Rodríguez, Nancy. 1996. *Ritmo y Aché Radio Program Special on Héctor Lavoe.* Pacifica Radio, 8 September.

Rodríguez Juliá, Edgardo. 1991. *El entierro de cortijo.* San Juan: Ediciones Huracán.

Román-Velázquez, Patria. 1999. *The Making of Latin London: Salsa Music, Place and Identity.* Brookfield: Ashgate.

Rondón, Cesar Miguel. 1980. *El libro de la salsa: crónica de la música del caribe urbano.* Caracas, Venezuela: Editorial Arte.

Rúa, Mérida. 2000. "Porto-Mexes and Mexi-Ricans: Inter-Latino Perspectives on Language and Cultural Identity." Paper presented at the Shades of a New Era: Pushing Intellectual Boundaries in Theory and Practice Conference at the University of Michigan, Ann Arbor, February 11–12.

Ruiz, Mario. 1996. Interview by the author. Tape recording. Brooklyn, New York, 27 June.

Samuel, Raphael and Paul Thompson. 1990. *The Myths We Live By.* New York: Routledge.

Scarano, Francisco. 1996. "The Jibaro Masquerade and the Subaltern Politics of Creole Identity Formation in Puerto Rico, 1745–1823." *American Historical Review* 101 (December): 1398–1431.

Shank, Barry. 1994. *Dissonant Identities: The Rock 'n' Roll Scene in Austin, Texas.* Hanover, N.H.: Wesleyan University Press.

Slobin, Mark. 1994. "Music in the Diaspora: The View From Euro-America." *Diaspora* 3(3): 243–51.

Taussig, Michael. 1993. *Mimesis and Alterity: A Particular History of the Senses.* New York: Routledge.

Torres, Jaime Torres. 1993. "Desconsuelo a Héctor Lavoe." *El Nuevo Día.* 2 Julio. p. 25.

Valle, Antonio del and Carlos Méndez. 1993. "Felicitaciones por el Program Sobre Héctor Lavoe." Carta. *El Nuevo Día,* 29 de julio, p. 125.

Vázquez, Luis A. 1999. "Salsa as a Discourse, Salsa as Practice." Unpublished manuscript.

Young, Robert J. C. 1995. *Colonial Desire: Hybridity in Theory, Culture and Race.* New York: Routledge.

CHAPTER EIGHT

Hip-Hop, Puerto Ricans, and Ethnoracial Identities in New York

Raquel Z. Rivera

> *Word Up* magazine did an article where they mentioned me and it was
> called "The Latinos in Hip-Hop." What's wack about that is that they
> have to separate us [Latinos] [from blacks]. And I hated that. I was in
> the same article as Kid Frost, you know, [who did the song] "La Raza."
> And I was like, come on, man, what do I have to do with Kid Frost?
> It's just totally different things and they're trying to funnel us all to-
> gether. You never hear an article called "The Blacks in Hip-Hop."

The above is a fragment of a conversation I had in 1995 with Q-Unique, a
skilled and feisty MC who is a member of the Arsonists (a popular New
York underground rap group that released its debut album, *As the World
Burns,* in August 1999 with Matador Records) and the Rock Steady Crew
(the legendary hip-hop organization better known for its contributions to
the dance form known as breaking). A self-described hip-hop[1] activist committed to nourishing a socially responsible, historically grounded, holistic
hip-hop creativity, Q. deeply resents being segregated, as a Puerto Rican,
from a hip-hop cultural core that is assumed to be African American.

The problem that Q. describes is two-fold. First, hip-hop is ahistorically
taken to be an African American expressive culture. Latinos (Puerto Ricans
included) are thus excised from the hip-hop core on the basis of a racialized
panethnicity. Second, as Latino population numbers and visibility increase
in the United States, a variety of national-origin groups (Puerto Ricans,
Chicanos, Dominicans, and so on) with different experiences of colonization, annexation, and/or immigration to the United States, as well as different histories of structural incorporation and racialization, are lumped
under the Latino panethnic banner (Flores 1996a; Oboler 1995). This wider
social phenomenon manifests itself within the hip-hop realm when Latinos
are grouped together on the hip-hop margins under the presumed commonalties shared by Latino hip-hoppers.

What does a New York Puerto Rican MC like Q. have in common with
a West Coast Chicano artist like Kid Frost? According to Q., the answer is,

not necessarily more than what he shares with an African American MC from New York City. The ethnic funneling that he criticizes relies on pre-scribed experiential and artistic commonalties based on a panethnic label. Facile and questionable panethnic connections are thus drawn—in this case, between Puerto Ricans and Chicanos on opposite coasts—which may actually serve to erase other more concrete, historically-based, transethnic connections—as those between Puerto Ricans and African Americans in New York.

Puerto Ricans in the United States are commonly thought of as being part of the U.S. Hispanic or Latino population. But Puerto Ricans are also considered an exception among Latinos. Their exceptionality is based on a history that diverges from what has been construed as the Latino norm and happens to share much in common with the experience of African Amer-icans (Chávez 1991; Flores 1996a; Massey and Bitterman 1985; Smith 1994).

This essay explores the ways in which New York Puerto Ricans have navigated the murky waters of ethnoracial[2] identification within the hip-hop realm. My main contention here is that those Puerto Ricans who take part in New York's hip-hop culture construct their identities, participate, and create through a process of negotiation with the dominant notions of blackness[3] and latinidad. Puerto Ricans fit in both categories and yet in neither.

What follows is an exploration of several moments in hip-hop's two decades and a half of history. Through it, I aim to discuss how constructions and experiences of class, ethnicity, and race have had bearing on the crea-tive participation of Puerto Ricans in hip-hop culture. I maintain that cer-tain articulations of class and ethnoracial identities have resulted in the construction of Puerto Ricans as virtual Blacks[4], made them seem an ex-ception for dominant definitions of Latino panethnicity, and facilitated their construction as part of a hip-hop Afro-diasporic "ghetto-ethnicity" (McLaren 1995:9).[5] On the other hand, understandings of Puerto Rican identity that privilege a Latinidad constructed in opposition to Blackness have landed Puerto Ricans participating in hip-hop culture in the precarious position of defending their Afro-diasporic ghetto-ethnicity and their history and crea-tive role in hip-hop. The privileging of this kind of Latinidad leaves Puerto Ricans who participate in hip-hop explaining why they take part in a cul-ture (mis)understood to be African American cultural property.

Hip-hop is one of the most vibrant products of late-twentieth-century youth culture. New York Puerto Ricans have been key participants, as pro-ducers and consumers of culture, in hip-hop art forms since hip-hop's very beginnings during the early 1970s in the South Bronx (Cross 1993; Flores 1988; Rose 1994; Toop 1991). This essay is meant as a contribution to the history of Puerto Rican hip-hop heads in New York as well as a necessary angle from which the Latinization of New York must be explored.[6] Useful insights can be obtained through studying how the younger generations of the Latino group with the longest, most visible presence in New York—namely, Boricuas—have grappled with and been affected by said Latinization. So here we go.

THE 1970S: IT'S JUST BEGUN

The South Bronx is widely recognized as the place where the art forms that make up the expressive foundation of hip-hop—MCing, or rhyming; DJing; breaking (b-boying/b-girling); and graffiti writing—first came together under very specific terms during the first half of the 1970s. African Americans, Puerto Ricans, and West Indians were the groups most heavily involved in the development of these expressive forms (Rose 1994; Thompson 1996).

Puerto Ricans made up the majority of the population in the South Bronx at the time (Rodríguez 1991:109). Together with African Americans and other Caribbean people, they accounted for an overwhelming proportion of the population in this impoverished Bronx area in 1970. Consistent with these groups' class standing, hip-hop was created by poor and working-class youth. In the words of Q-Unique and b-boy Ken Swift, among countless others, it began as a ghetto phenomenon (Q-Unique 1995a; Verán 1991).

Hip-hop was an ethnoracially inclusive sphere of cultural production. During hip-hop's formative years, "the strongest move was unity" (as Sekou Sundiata [1998:4] says of the previous decade), but ethnoracial distinctions and tensions still manifested themselves. These distinctions and tensions varied depending on various factors, among them neighborhood and art form.

The participation and perceived entitlement of Puerto Ricans with respect to hip-hop art forms were contingent upon locality. The South Bronx and East Harlem evidenced relatively subtle ethnoracial rifts and more transethnic cultural interaction; these rifts seemed to be greater and transethnic interaction less pronounced in other neighborhoods, particularly those with greater ethnic residential segregation.

The perceived entitlement to hip-hop of Puerto Ricans also depended on the art form. Whereas graffiti and breaking were largely taken to be multi-ethnic inner-city forms, MCing and DJing—though widely practiced by various Afro-diasporic ethnic groups—were identified more with one group, namely, African Americans.

Puerto Ricans were, for the most part, welcome and active participants in hip-hop. But even during these early times, Puerto Ricans had to step lightly on hip-hop's cultural ground—particularly when it came to MCing and DJing. They were largely considered partners in creative production, although at times the bond was reduced to a junior partnership (Flores 1992–1993, 1996b).

The perception of Puerto Rican full entitlement to graffiti and breaking versus their perceived limited entitlement to MCing and DJing could be traced to the overwhelming participation of Puerto Ricans in the first two. However, these different rates of participation may not have been the cause of these notions of entitlement but rather an effect. Most probably, rhyming and DJing were from the beginning more ethnoracially identified with African Americans and closed to perceived outsiders by virtue of their relying on dexterity in the English language, being most easily traceable to a U.S. Black oral tradition, and primarily employing records of music considered to be Black.

Hip-hop's musical side seems to have been premised upon an Afro-diasporic urbanity in which, though the participation of Caribbeans was pivotal (Flores 1988; Hebdige 1987; Rose 1994; Toop 1991), it was often narrowly identified with an ethnoracial Blackness (Flores 1996b; Rivera 1996). A distinction must be made, however, between the experiences within the hip-hop realm of West Indian Caribbeans (primarily Jamaicans and Barbadians) and Latino Caribbeans (primarily Puerto Ricans). West Indians are commonly thought to stand comparatively closer to Blackness than Latino Caribbeans. That is the case even for black Latinos. Though West Indians may be perceived as not ethnically Black (i.e., African American), they are, as a group, thought of as racially black (Foner 1987; Kasinitz 1992; Waters 1996). Given their relative proximity to an ethnoracial Blackness, West Indian entitlement to hip-hop as a Black-identified musical expression has not been as much of an issue as it has been for Puerto Ricans.

The position of Puerto Ricans within hip-hop must be understood within the historical context of Puerto Rican migration to New York City, their placement within the city's racial and socioeconomic hierarchies, and their relationship with African Americans.

Puerto Ricans and African Americans, though having had a presence in the city since the previous century, became thought of as the new wave of immigrants during the 1920s. Both groups were incorporated into the lowest rungs of the labor structure under similar circumstances and since then have lived parallel experiences of racialization, marginalization, and class exclusion (Grosfoguel and Georas 1996; Rodríguez-Morazzani 1996; Torres 1995). Their histories of unemployment and underemployment, subjection to police brutality and racial violence, negative portrayals in academic literature and media (Pérez 1990; Rodríguez 1997), and housing and employment discrimination have been not only similar but also linked. Puerto Ricans have come to be considered a native minority that shares the bottom of the socioeconomic structure with African Americans (Ogbu 1978; Massey and Bitterman 1985; Gans 1992; Smith 1994). The histories of Puerto Ricans and African Americans in New York may not be identical, but they are certainly analogous, related, and at times even overlapping (Flores 1996a; Urciuoli 1996).

Puerto Ricans were initially a confusing lot because being even more visibly multiracial than African Americans, they could not be easily cast as black or white. Eventually, Puerto Ricans became a new racialized subject, different from both but sharing with African Americans a common subordination to whites (Grosfoguel and Georas 1996). Puerto Ricans came to be racialized as dark, dangerous others who, though different from African Americans, share with them a multitude of social spaces, conditions, and dispositions. Points of contention and separation might arise between the two groups, but there is a fundamental shared exclusion from the white, middle-class world.

Hip-hop's ethnoracial inclusiveness must be contextualized not only within this common structural history of African Americans and Puerto Ricans but also within a long-standing history of political alliances (Rodríguez-Morazzani 1996; Torres 1995) as well as joint cultural production (Boggs 1992; Flores 1988; Toop 1991).

Youth culture is one of the sites where cultural interaction and hybridization between African Americans and Puerto Ricans have been most intense. Urciuoli uses Bourdieu's concept of *habitus*[7] to illustrate how the experiences and actions of Puerto Ricans and African Americans are congruent given that their lives are structured by similar conditions and result in similar understandings of themselves and the world. She points out that the degree of congruence varies depending on other mediating factors such as gender, age, family role, and generation. Adolescent boys exhibit the highest levels of congruence (Urciuoli 1996:66). Hip-hop, as a youth cultural manifestation dominated by young males (Guevara 1987; Rose 1994), is the quintessential expression of this structural and cultural congruence.

Congruence, however, does not translate into an absence of rifts, tensions, and exclusions. The marginalizations experienced by Puerto Ricans in the hip-hop realm have not been fortuitous or circumstantial but are related to the historical relations between both groups and the particular position that each occupies in the city's racial and socioeconomic hierarchies. Cultural identity, production, and entitlement have most often been invested with the notion that Puerto Ricans are *like* blacks but *not* black. In Flores's words, "cultural baggage and black-white racial antinomies in the U.S. thus conspire to perpetuate a construction of Puerto Rican identity as non-black" (1992–1993:28). Part of this cultural baggage is a very eurocentric notion of Latinidad (Flores 1996a; Fox 1996; Pabón 1995; Thomas 1967). Puerto Rican Latinidad is constructed in such a way that precludes its coexistence with Puerto Rican Afro-disporicity.

Furthermore, understandings of cultural identity and practice are frequently decidedly un-Afro-diasporic so that the connections between those who populate what Gilroy (1993) has termed "The Black Atlantic" are camouflaged. Hip-hop, as a site of internal movement and contentions, includes challenges as well as abidances to these un-Afro-diasporic understandings of history and culture. If, given these un-Afro-diasporic assumptions, the connections between African Americans and West Indians are disregarded, the ruptures become even more intense in the case of Latino Caribbeans such as Puerto Ricans.

These un-Afro-diasporic visions have had direct bearing on hip-hop. Despite the fact that, in practice, hip-hop has been an Afro-diasporic form, it has still been marred by narrow understandings of blackness.

FROM 1979 TO THE EARLY 1980S: THE DAWN OF THE RAP GAME

During Spring 1979, a funk group called Fatback released what can be considered the first commercial rap record, entitled "King Tim III (Personality Jock)." But that record's popularity was no match for the wide commercial acclaim with which "Rappers' Delight" was greeted a few months later. "Rappers' Delight," released on Sugarhill Records by an unknown group that called itself the Sugarhill Gang, was undoubtedly the record that signaled the commercial rise of rap, reaching number 36 on the U.S. charts and becoming the biggest-selling twelve-inch record ever (Toop 1991:81). MCing and DJing thus began their steep rise in mass-mediated popularity with the release of "Rappers' Delight".

Though most of the artists popular during rap's first five years as a mass-mediated consumer product (1979–1983) were African Americans (some of them West Indian, such as Grandmaster Flash and Kool Herc), Puerto Ricans were far from absent in this scene. DJ Charlie Chase of the Cold Crush Brothers, The Fearless Four's Devastating Tito and DJ Master O.C., The Fantastic Five's Prince Whipper Whip and Rubie Dee, Prince Markie Dee Morales of the Fat Boys, and The Real Roxanne were popular figures in commercial rap's early times.

Given rap's identification as a Black (i.e., African American) musical form, Puerto Ricans participated within a perceived Black matrix. This had been the case since hip-hop's beginnings in the early 1970s. But rap's mass-mediated commodification in the late 1970s led to an even more intense ethnoracialization of rap. Furthermore, if the cultural entitlement of Puerto Ricans to rap was sometimes ambivalent in the New York context, this ambivalence was magnified in other locations, most often landing them on the outsider side of the fence. The Afro-diasporic New York context in which Blacks and Puerto Ricans are neighbors, friends, and allies is a precious exception and hard to conceive of in most other U.S. locations. Hip-hop's initial Afro-diasporic ghetto base was hard to translate into highly segregated contexts with no corresponding histories of transethnic, Afro-diasporic cultural production. Audiences unfamiliar with New York life for the most part did not (and could not) distinguish between Blacks and Puerto Ricans. After its commercialization, rap remained class identified, but its ethnoracial scope shrunk.

THE LATE 1980S: BLACK NOISE

After breaking and graffiti crash-landed in terms of mass-mediated popularity around 1985 following their brief but intense media-propelled flight,[8] hip-hop became synonymous with the one art form that had from its inception been most intensely Black-identified, namely, rap. Subsequent creative developments and mass-marketing strategies (which did not operate independently of each other) further intensified this identification.

The explicit voicing of ethnoracial (African American) concerns by popular rap artists through rhymes, statements, and samples was one of the factors that further contributed to the ethnoracialization of hip-hop as African American (Henderson 1996; Rodríguez-Morazzaun 1996). In other words, the voicing of Black-identified perspectives and concerns led to the increasingly narrow identification of hip-hop with this specific group.

Throughout its history, rap music has manifested different approaches to and articulations of Blackness. Explicit references to Blackness in the early 1980s, though elaborated and displayed, were not omnipresent. The late 1980s and early 1990s, however, saw an explosion of Black nationalist sentiment (Allen 1996).

The ideological and aesthetic reverberations of this period are still being felt, for it set the stage for creations and transformations to follow. The Pro-Black, Afrocentric, or Black Nationalist school of rap had a lasting impact on the hip-hop collective imagination—its faddish qualities notwithstanding. These formulations of an explicit ethnoracial agenda cloaked hip-hop with garb that seemed several sizes too big (or small, depending on how one looks at it) for Puerto Ricans—among plenty of others.

Louis, a Puerto Rican teenage rap fan during rap's Black Nationalist phase, recalls that when he first heard Public Enemy, it was like a revelation. He went straight to the library to look up this Huey Newton they were talking about. That's when it really hit him that they were talking about important Black historical figures and events. His first reaction to the information to which he was being exposed was pride in "us Black people." But then it started dawning on him that he was not exactly Black, given the way Blackness was being formulated. It was a Blackness whose referents were not inclusive of his side of the Caribbean because they did not fully acknowledge the cultural hybridity and fluidity of the Black Atlantic. Louis realized that he and "his people" were not quite part of the history about which Public Enemy was talking and rhyming. This point was driven home by his close friends—many of whom were African Americans—who teased him with the question, "Why can't *your* people make good hip-hop?"

Louis's experience illustrates the ambivalent position that Puerto Ricans (and other New York Caribbean Latinos) held given hip-hop's growing identification with a musical expression increasingly perceived as exclusively Black. Boricuas could be included or excluded, depending on the situation.

I mentioned earlier that both creative developments and marketing decisions worked together in the ethnoracialization of hip-hop as African American. So the issue was not as simple as Run DMC, Public Enemy, X-Clan, and others deciding to write African American–centric lyrics. The identification of hip-hop as Black must be contextualized in hip-hop's growing mass-mediation and popularity and, thus, its expansion outside territory where Puerto Ricans are a familiar presence—whether as neighbors, family, playmates, or artists. As hip-hop's scope of consumption and production grew, new players integrated themselves into the field of participation—players decidedly unfamiliar with Puerto Rican hip-hoppers. The imagined links between what was variably referred to as the hip-hop community or hip-hop nation were increasingly premised upon African Americanness so that hip-hop's Afro-diasporicity became increasingly obscured, even in its New York breeding grounds (which remained a fertile and influential spot of hip-hop creativity).

Hip-hop's Black identification must also be contextualized in the vilification/romanticization of African Americans in U.S. popular culture (Allinson 1994; Ross 1989) and the profitability of its commercial packaging. One of the hottest selling points of hip-hop has been its association with a raw, outlaw, ghetto-based, Black-identified (and particularly male) experience and image (Allinson 1994; Rose 1994; Samuels 1995). Allinson argues the relationship between rap's appeal and "a long-established romanticization of the Black urban male as a temple of authentic cool, at home with risk, with sex, with struggle" (1994:449).

Puerto Ricans, though considered virtual Blacks for some purposes, are considered nonblacks for others. Within the U.S. context, they have always had their ghetto nonwhite credentials up to date; their blackness, however, has been a different issue. So if hip-hop's mass-mediated popularity is closely connected to a romanticization/exoticization of blackness, why risk investing in a tepid/lighter/unstable version of blackness—in the form of a Puerto Rican—when you can have the real thing (Báez 1998)?

Puerto Ricanness in rap was (and still is, but less so) deemed a potential liability. Numerous Puerto Rican MCs recount being explicitly told by artists and repertory executives (A&Rs) and other industry people that they were talented but that their ethnicity worked against them.

Puerto Rican marginalization in rap has also been related to purist and narrow definitions regarding what is Black expressivity and what is Latino expressivity. Rap has been viewed as a new expression among a Black-music continuum and deemed as a breaking away from Latino music.

Rap presented similar problems for the perceived boundaries of Latino musical expression, as those that the Latin soul (which included bugalú) of the 1960s and early 1970s had presented (Flores 2000; Roberts 1979; Salazar, 1992). Though many of the critiques of Latin soul emphasized the musical inexperience of its musicians and its faddish qualities, much of the discomfort with this genre harked back to a deviation from tradition. Unflatteringly described by bandleader Willie Rosario as "American music played with Latin percussion" (Roberts 1979:167), bugalú violated the bounds that kept distinct what was Black and what was Latino/Puerto Rican.

Hip-hop's African Americanization to the exclusion of Puerto Ricans was not a product of circumstance. Neither can it be explained away by invoking only African American creative volition. The increasing Black identification of hip-hop must be understood within the steadfastness of ethnoracial categories in this country. These categories translate into a perceived limited potential for transethnic cultural production, solidarity, and political organizing. Cultural hybrids such as hip-hop threaten those categories and the comforting, simplifying myths built around them.

THE LATE 1980S: WHAT IS THIS "LATIN" IN LATIN HIP-HOP?

A twist in the story of Puerto Ricans in hip-hop came with the commercialization and popularity of two Latino-identified genres: freestyle in the late 1980s and Latin rap in the early 1990s. Terminology here provides a bit of confusion, because both were also often referred to as Latin hip-hop. But this apparent terminological confusion actually proves to be illuminating. The term *Latin hip-hop* points to the fact that both genres were somehow related to, yet distinct from, hip-hop; and key in their difference from hip-hop was a shared Latin element.

Toop describes freestyle as "faithful to the old electro sound of 'Planet Roc' adding Latin percussion elements and an overlay of teenage romance" (1991:174). Others describe it in starkly unflattering terms as the "synth-heavy bubble-salsa of Lisa Lisa and her big-haired descendants" (Morales 1991:91) and "bubble-gum ballads over drum-machine beats" (del Barco 1996:84). Groups such as Cover Girls, Exposé, TKA, and Latin Raskals and artists such as George LaMond, Sapphire, and Brenda K. Starr were among the best-known freestyle artists. The overwhelming majority of these were New York Puerto Ricans. Freestyle's audience was also primarily Puerto Rican.

In terms of vocal style, lyrics, and sound, freestyle was very different from the rap music of the time. Freestyle vocalists sang (not rapped) sticky-sweet (at times bittersweet) lyrics centered on the vagaries of love, whereas hip-hop MCs broached topics more concerned with ghetto life, racial strife, and personal/artistic prowess. Freestyle's sound was electropop, while hip-hop was usually backed by harsh funk with booming bass lines.

Toop talks of a division arising between African American and Hispanic audiences in 1987, which he attributes to "Hispanics stay[ing] faithful to the old electro sound of 'Planet Roc' " in the form of freestyle while African Americans followed the increasingly Black-identified rap music of the time (1991:174). But he offers no possible explanations and leaves one wondering, why did that separation happen?

Popular taste and cultural production can hardly ever be fully or accurately explained in cause-effect fashion. However, influential factors can be identified with relative certainty. One of the factors at play in the late 1980s schism along ethnoracial lines between hip-hop and freestyle audiences had to do with notions of cultural property and entitlement.

The growing African Americanization of hip-hop during the 1980s—largely media-driven, premised upon a reductive notion of blackness, and suffering from severe cultural-historical amnesia—prefaced the increasing alienation of Puerto Ricans (and other New York Caribbean Latinos) from hip-hop. Cultural entitlement to hip-hop was explained as a non-Latino-inclusive "Black thing" (Allinson 1994; Hochman 1990).

Freestyle, as a new genre, was in great part young Latinos' response to media marginalization—which included marginalization in rap (Rodríguez 1995; Panda 1995; Q-Unique 1995a). Discussions of the emergence, popularity, and cultural significance of freestyle must take into account this desire of Puerto Ricans and other Latinos to see "their own" in the limelight, to have a music that was theirs.

George LaMond, a popular freestyle singer during the 1980s, recalls: "I felt like I was representing my hometown and my Puerto Rican people. It made me that much more proud of being a Latino" (Parris 1996:31). Andy Panda, a key song writer, producer, and media personality of what he terms "the freestyle movement," adds: "I think it gave kids a sense of identity because finally we had something that was ours. We didn't have much of a cultural identity in the music industry other than Spanish-language music" (Parris 1996:30).

Such desires must be contextualized within Latino invisibility in mass media (E. Morales 1996; Rodríguez 1997), in general and the prevailing notion that hip-hop was Black cultural property in particular. They must also be understood with respect to the will of second- and third-generation Puerto Rican (and other Latino) youth to expand the bounds of collective expression outside of Spanish-language Latin music.

What was perceived as culturally theirs by these youths exceeded the bounds of Latinidad orthodoxy, which considered Spanish language and Latin American–originated sounds as a necessary component of music worthy of the label *Latin*. Latinos and so-called American music seemed disparate partners in terms of cultural legitimacy. In that sense, the participation of Puerto Ricans and other Latinos in Latin soul (in the 1960s), hip-hop (in the late 1970s and 1980s), and freestyle (in the 1980s) all shared an element of challenge to the dominant notions of Latinidad.

Resistance to this challenge to Latinidad took many forms: Willie Rosario's insistence on identifying bugalú as "American" music (Roberts 1979:167), Puerto Rican parents complaining of their children's fascination with so-called nigger music (i.e., hip-hop), A&Rs refusing to sign Puerto Rican MCs because "Puerto Ricans don't sell," George García being persuaded by his label to launch his freestyle career as George LaMond because his last name was considered a commercial drawback (Parris 1996).

Though grassroots perceptions are often more responsive to innovations and changing conditions than market-oriented ones, both coincided in their difficulty to grapple with the younger generation's will to embrace their New York–based, English-dominant, Afro-diasporic, lived cultural experiences. Freestyle was, in this sense, an artistic liberation from stifling (in terms of creativity and cultural identity) parameters of conformity with the reigning notions of Latinidad.

At the same time, though, that freestyle pushed the envelope with respect to second- and third-generation identity and artistic production, it also reproduced other reductive notions of identity, experience, and solidarity. It reinforced the myth of pan-Latino commonality and the drawing of puertorriqueñidad and latinidad as identity categories in great part defined through nonblackness.

Orsi proposes that the fissures and conflicts between racialized groups have much to do with anxieties regarding group definition. "Strategies of alterity" have served to define "self-constitution through the exclusion of the dark-skinned other" (1992:336). His study of East Harlem reveals how Italians struggled to separate themselves from the "dark" African Americans, Puerto Ricans, and other Caribbean immigrants. "Proximity—actual and imagined—to the dark-skinned other was pivotal to the emergence of the identity 'Italian American' " (1992:318). Similarly, Puerto Ricanness and latinidad have been informed by a desire to distinguish these groups from the darker African Americans.

These anxieties regarding ethnic and racial identity affect understandings of artistic production in peculiar ways. Not only can a certain mode of expression, such as freestyle, be said to be Latino because New York Puerto Ricans are the most distinguished, popular, or numerous participants, but a certain genre can also be said to be Latino because it is informed by specific modes of speech or experiences that are identified with Latinos living in the United States. But also certain myths based on a stereotypical ethnoracial ethos come to define what may or may not be Latino. Panda directed the following comment at George LaMond during an interview: "George, you never sounded black and yet everyone respected your talent as a vocalist because what you did was uniquely Latino. Black artists traditionally sing with soul. We sing with passion. We sing with sex. We sing with emotion" (Parris 1996:31).

Panda's belief in a self-evident soulful black sound distinct from a Latino sex-heavy sound is by no means peculiar to him, freestyle, or those of his generation. Similar essentialized and naturalized identity markings are often thrown around in the media, street corner cyphers, and domestic conversations.[9] These essentializing myths serve to cement difference as further strategies of alterity.

The list of areas in which difference is believed to be patently clear thus grows. Ethos, aesthetics, themes, ideas, language, and musical references and sources can all be pointed to as examples of group difference. What is African American can thus be pretended to be easily discernible from what is Puerto Rican or Latino.

Whereas certain audience segments and critics celebrated the dawn of Latin hip-hop, there was a strong feeling of suspicion and betrayal among those who felt themselves part of an urban Afro-diasporic, Black-matrixed hip-hop culture. Edward Rodríguez (1995), a Puerto Rican hip-hop journalist, bitterly explains the appearance and popularity of freestyle as a denial of Latino Afro-diasporicity.

Freestyle began as an artistic outlet within a context of Latino media marginalization and a prescribed latinidad orthodoxy. Ironically, it also had ghettoizing and stifling consequences in terms of media perception as well as popular cultural identity. Many Puerto Ricans divested themselves from hip-hop to pursue something that was truly their own. The fickleness of mass-mediated taste did away with the basket in which many Puerto Ricans had placed their eggs. The commercial popularity of freestyle ended up taking a nosedive that affected not only its artists but also Puerto Rican MCs. Freestyle, as Latin hip-hop, cemented the idea that Puerto Ricans were marginal to the hip-hop core.

Freestyle was only one side of Latin hip-hop. Latin rap fell under the same rubric. Compared to freestyle, Latin rap stood a lot closer to hip-hop in terms of form and style. Vocal flows were rapped, and topics were ghettocentric. It was basically rap music done by Latinos, often code-switching, with topics and references particular to inner-city Latino communities.

Contrary to freestyle, whose artists were overwhelmingly New York Puerto Ricans, Latin rap was largely coming out of the West Coast and had few Puerto Rican exponents. Kid Frost (nowadays known simply as Frost), a Los Angeles Chicano who released his first album, *Hispanic Causing Panic*, in 1990, was one of the first Latino rappers to receive wide media recognition. Other artists that came out under the Latin rap rubric were Mellow Man Ace (a Cuban, also from Los Angeles), Latin Alliance (headed by Frost), and the infamous Gerardo (an Ecuadorean, aka Rico Suave).

New York Puerto Ricans never ceased being active in the local underground hip-hop scene. But in terms of Latin rap's mass-mediated exposure, they were nearly invisible. Latin Alliance had two New York Puerto Rican members, Rayski and Markski. A Nuyorican duo by the name of Latin Empire had garnered some local exposure earlier in the 1980s and even landed a deal with Atlantic Records; however, they never achieved the popularity of later Latin rap artists.

Though most commonly treated as such, Latin rap is neither a self-explanatory nor unproblematic label. Is it simply rap done by Latinos, regardless of style or content? Is it rap done by Latinos that is also necessarily related to Latino life or a Latino aesthetic? How could that reality or that aesthetic possibly be defined? Whose definition do we use? Can non-Latinos who use Spanish in their rhymes or other elements of that hypothetical Latino aesthetic also make Latin rap?

The Latin rap label has been used to categorize artists such as Kid Frost, Mellow Man Ace, Gerardo, Latin Alliance, and Latin Empire—all U.S.-based Latino artists whose music, rhymes, and themes include elements commonsensically identifiable as Latino. It has also been used to describe Latin America–based artists such as Vico C., Lisa M., and El General (Manuel 1995) whose rhymes are in Spanish (though sometimes incorporating words in English here and there). For my present purposes, the most difficult questions regarding definition and inclusion within the Latin rap category have to be asked when U.S.-based Latino artists create music that doesn't conform to the most commonly accepted bounds of Latino identity, experience, or creativity.

Cypress Hill, for example, was criticized for being too Anglocentric (Morales 1991). This Los Angeles–based trio is made up of Sen Dog (a Cuban—and incidentally, Mellow Man Ace's brother), B-Real (a Chicano), and DJ Muggs (an Italian American who spent his early childhood in Queens, New York). The assumption seems to have been that because two of its three members were Latinos, Cypress Hill had to conform to a certain mold of latinidad. They, however, never claimed to be doing Latin rap. In fact, they scoffed at the thought and explicitly resented being boxed into the category to which others presumed they belonged (Cross 1993).

Sen Dog and B-Real were actually the first Latino artists to be deemed part of the hip-hop core—as opposed to the fringes that Latin rap artists occupied. These discussions of how Latino or Anglocentric their artistic production is or is not completely lose sight of other aspects of their music, which are more directly relevant to the social milieu in which rap is produced and consumed.

Morales has defined Latin hip-hop as "the polyphonic outburst of recent rap-oriented records" such as *Latin Alliance* (Virgin), *Dancehall Reggaespañol* (Columbia), and *Cypress Hill* (Columbia), which is "in step with the world-wide Afrocentric cultural revolution that will carry us into the next century." One of its virtues, according to Morales, is its "development of a nationwide Latino/Americano hip-hop aesthetic" that permits artists from both coasts who were once strangers to "become one nation kicking Latin lingo on top of a scratchin', samplin' substrate." He argues for an inclusive notion of this aesthetic so that Cypress Hill doesn't have to be dismissed as "de-Latinized, stoned-out Beastie Boys." Though their rhymes are mostly English, they still kick some bilingualism and their "relative Anglocentrism" doesn't necessarily "mean they're not reaching *vatos* in the hood" (1991:91).

Instead of questioning the stifling assumptions regarding ethnoracial identity and artistic expression that underpin this charge of Anglo-centrism,[10] Morales explains what he sees as Cypress Hill's redeeming qualities. After all, they do inject some Spanish into their rhymes, plus they are probably reaching a vato audience. Seeking redemption through these means seems less pertinent than asking why Latino artists are, in the first place, expected to adhere to a certain orthodox Latino aesthetic (in terms of language, topics, and/or music) or to cater to a Latino audience.

This issue becomes particularly relevant in the case of Puerto Ricans in New York, whose cultural production and identity have been so tightly linked with that of African Americans that it begs the question, Why assume the naturalness or necessity of a Latino aesthetic and cultural product (myopically defined, to boot) over and against Afro-diasporic ones?

The Hispanocentric bent of the dominant definitions of latinidad (Fox 1996; Pabón 1995) has (at times) led to Puerto Ricans placing themselves and (often) being placed by others outside the bounds of latinidad. A cornerstone aspect of the Latin rap aesthetic was the use of bilingualism or only Spanish. However, many of those Puerto Rican participants who rejected what they perceived as the Latin rap pigeonholing sought to emphasize a U.S.-based Afro-diasporic identity. Edward Rodríguez (1995, personal communication) explains why some MCs refused to go the Latin rap route: "MC's don't wanna come out as exclusively Spanish 'cause they don't wanna exclude people. Black people are their people."

Then there's also the issue of second- and third-generation Puerto Ricans (and other Latinos) expressing themselves more comfortably in English than in Spanish. As the South Bronx's Fat Joe (Joseph Cartagena) says, even though—by virtue of being Puerto Rican—promoters expected him to rhyme in Spanish, "I can't really kick it in Spanish, I couldn't really feel the vibe, so I'm not even gonna try and make myself look stupid." Prince PowerRule (Oscar Alfonso) has the following comment to add: "There's so many Latino people in the United States that don't speak Spanish, so they don't wanna hear that bilingual rap. They're just like us; they're Americans." (del Barco 1996:82)

Similarly to the case of freestyle, the appearance of Latin rap as a Latino-specific realm within rap music on the one hand expanded the bounds of participation and expression of Latinos in hip-hop but on the other hand also ended up making the existing divides between Puerto Ricans and African Americans even deeper. The nonblack latinidad on which Latin rap was based further put into question the Afro-diasporicity of Puerto Ricans and their position within hip-hop as a Black-matrixed culture.

THE 1990S: GHETTOCENTRICITY, BLACKNESS, AND LATINIDAD

The Afrocentric emphasis in rap of the late 1980s started shifting toward a more ghettocentric (Kelley 1996; McLaren 1995) approach in the early 1990s

(Boyd 1997; Smith 1997). Blackness did not cease being a crucial identity marker within rap's discourse; it just became more narrowly identified as a *ghetto* blackness. According to Smith, "in rap's dominant market paradigm, blackness has become contingent, while the ghetto has become necessary" (1997:346).

As rap's discursive and performative focus shifted from a blackness primarily defined through (a narrow, nondiasporic take on) African American history and ancestry to one more based upon contemporary socioeconomic conditions and lived culture (as opposed to traditional, inherited, or ancestral culture), a slight relaxing of blackness's ethnoracial scope occurred. The blackness formerly restricted by the bounds of an ethnoracialized African Americanness began expanding to accommodate certain Latino groups—most notably, Puerto Ricans—as a population whose experiences of class and ethnoracial marginalization are virtually indistinguishable from the ghettocentric African American experience.

Hip-hop, during the late 1980s and early 1990s, used to be frequently described by participants as "a Black thing, you wouldn't understand"; since the mid-1990s it has become increasingly common to hear hip-hop explained in everyday conversation, as well as in mass-mediated and academic forums, as a Black and Latino phenomenon (Dennis 1992; Jiménez 1997; Lascaibar 1997; McLaren 1995; Smith 1997). Today's near-dominant convention of describing hip-hop culture (and within it, rap) as Black and Latino and the increased mass-mediated visibility of Latinos/Latinas within hip-hop would not have come about had it not been for this shifting conception of blackness that emphasizes the ghetto experience.

Rap is a central part of mainstream U.S. pop culture, has multiracial audiences all over the globe, and is immersed in the politics of the transnational music industry. Still, hip-hop authenticity—signified through the tropes of a class-identified blackness/nigganess—is contentious ethnoracial territory, and its borders are zealously policed by its participants. The ethnoracial scope of authenticity has been expanded somewhat but only to incorporate (though not always smoothly) the Latino experience.

Authenticity has been broadened to accommodate a group that is perceived to be quite close to Blackness to begin with. Latino blackness, or virtual Blackness, is thought of as a product of social, political, and economic circumstances that have led to shared lived and historical experiences in the ghetto with African Americans. But Latino authenticity is not only conceived within hip-hop in terms of socioeconomic structures; it is also constructed as related to Afro-diasporic ethnoracial identities, cultural history, and cultural formations.

But hold up! Wait a minute. To talk about a shared Afro-diasporicity between African Americans and Latinos entails that we must be talking about only a sector of Latinos, namely, Afro-diasporic Latinos. To talk about shared experiences in the ghetto means we must distinguish the intense experiential similarities between Blacks and Caribbean Latinos in New

York from the comparatively more distinct experiences of Chicanos and Blacks in Los Angeles or Chicago and from the completely divergent experiences of African Americans and Cubans in Miami. This may seem all too obvious, yet it is another example of the specificities that are smothered under the seductive weight of the pan-Latino discourse.

The acknowledgment of hip-hop in both the academic and journalistic literature as an urban Black *and* Latino cultural expression has suffered from the perils of panethnic abstraction. In the haste to rescue Latinos from the hip-hop historical invisibility in which they were submerged for a period and to acknowledge the present role played by Latinos within core hip-hop, essentialized connections are drawn and crucial differences among groups within the Latino panethnic conglomerate are slighted.[11] The historical and present connections between Afro-diasporic Latinos and African Americans in New York are, at times, muted or even drowned out by the naturalizing call of panlatinidad.

THE LATE 1990S: LATINAS GET HOT

As I explained in the previous section, the rise of rap's ghettocentricity as a selling point in the latter half of the 1990s has played a part in Latinos' relegitimization as core participants of hip-hop. This legitimization is manifested in various ways: the greater media visibility of Latino hip-hop artists; the rise in the use of Spanish words and phrases in songs by the most popular African American rap artists; and widespread references to and images of Latinos and Latinas in rhymes, videos, and articles. A whole slew of artists dedicated lines or even whole songs to the *mamis*. Latina mamis actually became one of the latest faddish hip-hop fetishes. Tropicalized[12] (Aparicio and Chávez-Silverman 1997), exoticized, eroticized, and romanticized, Latinos in hip-hop have, as of late, most often been portrayed as virtual Blacks with the ghetto nigga stamp of approval and, particularly in the case of females, a sexualized flair.

New York's Afro-diasporic multi-ethnic hip-hop culture and the integral role of Caribbean Latinos—particularly Puerto Ricans—within it has set the tone for transregional, mass-mediated Latino hip-hop images. But this is a subtlety that largely remains unspoken. Therefore, oftentimes the pan-Latino aggregate is awarded a blackness really meant for Caribbean Latinos.

Let's take the example of the recent Latin mami fetish. Though most often generically referred to as Latinas, when the mamis populating rappers' wet dreams are referred to by specific national origin, it is almost invariably Boricua (and increasingly, Dominican) females that are invoked. And even when their Puerto Ricanness is not stated explicitly, subtle and not-so-subtle clues reveal these mamis as Puerto Ricans.

Puerto Rican women had had a presence in rap lyrics (almost invariably as objects of desire) before salivating after mamis became a commercial gimmick. "I like 'em yellow, brown, Puerto Rican and Haitian," A Tribe Called Quest's Phife had said of his taste in women in 1993's "Electric Relaxation." A member of the Wu-Tang Clan, using the metaphor of ice cream flavors in 1995's "Ice Cream," lusted after Chocolate Deluxes, French Vanillas, and Butta Pecan Ricans (Raekwon 1995).

The difference between then and now is that a theme that used to be occasionally touched upon—namely, the hot Latin mami—has nowadays become a market cliché. Another difference is that as New York becomes more Dominicanized, the local long-standing interchangeability of Spanish/ Hispanic/Latino for Puerto Rican (Flores 1996a) has come to be expanded to include Dominicans next to Puerto Ricans.[13] Puerto Ricans used to be the prototype of the exotic/erotic New York mami; now Dominicans also inform the prototype.

Latinas are certainly not the only females that get hypersexualized through rap images and rhymes. Far from it. As Irving accurately states, the role of Black women in rap has "more often than not, been limited to those voiceless images projected unto the extended wet dream of music videos" (1998:34)[14] Within rap's heterocentric discourse, where African American male subjectivities reign supreme, Black women are the norm, the ethnoracial self—othered and hypersexualized for gender reasons—but in ethnoracial terms they are the familiar and familial. Puerto Rican women, on the other hand, are familiar yet still exotic. At times they may even be considered part of the family—but always one step removed. Black women are the "sistas"; Puerto Rican women are the othered, tropicalized, and exoticized mamis.[15]

Asian women have also had the questionable honor of occasionally populating rap's wet dreams. Similarly to Latinas, Asian women are viewed as erotic/exotic creatures. Unlike Latinas, however, their exoticism is not stamped by the U.S. ghetto experience and spliced with images of south-of-the-border tropicalism. Mamis are inner-city exotics, tropicalized ghetto creatures. They are brash, loud, hot, hard, street savvy, and bold—in terms of movies, think Rosie Perez's characters in *Do The Right Thing* and *White Men Can't Jump* and Rosario Dawson's Lala Bonilla in *He Got Game;* in terms of rap music, think Puff Daddy's "Spanish girl" in the interlude right before his 1997 song "Señorita" from the CD *No Way Out* or Lissette and Joanne in the late Big Punisher's 1998 interlude "Taster's Choice."[16] This ghetto tropical spitfire exoticism greatly differs from the common exoticization of Asian women based on an imputed silence and subservience.[17]

The commercial hip-hop image of the Latina mami is most often based on a tropicalized virtual Blackness. The mami is typically taken to be an exotic (and lighter) variation on black womanhood. How? Lets see.

An ad[18] for the Cocoa Brovas[19] album *The Rude Awakening* features a cardboard cup full of steaming cocoa. Six chocolate-drenched young women are partially immersed in the liquid. On the right-hand side of the cup appear the erroneously accented words *Chocolaté Calienté*.

The words in Spanish seem to be indicating that these women (or at least some of them) swirling in hot chocolate and sexily awaiting ingestion are Latinas. They are all various shades of caramel—unquestionably black by this country's standards but still light skinned. Their relative lightness and the fact that all but one have straight or slightly wavy hair go with the Butta Pecan Rican Myth, i.e., the popular perception of Puerto Ricans as golden-skinned and "good-haired" [sic!].[20] But butta pecan is somehow still imagined to be a variation on chocolate. Butta Pecans are, after all, a crucial ingredient in the Cocoa Brovas recipe for chocolaté calienté. The bottom line is that these hot cocoa girls' latinidad does not take away from their blackness. What their latinidad does do is add an element of exoticism — signified through the ad's use of Spanish—to their blackness.

The accentuation of words that, according to Spanish orthographic rules, should not be accented serves to further intensify a sense of exoticism. Accents are deemed exotic characteristics of an exotic language. Whether this erroneous accentuation was a mistake or was done on purpose does not change the fact that the accents in *chocolaté* and *calienté* serve as tropicalizing markers of difference.

Let's move on to another example. "Set Trippin'," a review of ten popular rap videos in *Blaze*'s premier issue, includes Big Punisher's "Still Not a Player." The reviews consist of short blurbs under specific headings such as Plot, Ghetto Fabulous, Estimated Budget, and Black Erotica. The following comments under Black Erotica regarding "Still Not a Player" caught my eye: "Dozens of scantily clad, lighter-than-a-paper-bag sistas and mamis end up dancing outside. Sounds like a red-light district" (Carasco 1998:207).

It is significant that the Black Erotica category includes mention of both sistas and mamis. These may be two ethnically distinct female populations, but both are included in the realm of eroticized blackness. The fact that their light-skinnedness makes the set seem like a red-light district is a commentary on gendered color-chaste hierarchies (hooks 1994) that equate lightness with sexual desirability as well as an acknowledgment of the figure of the prostitute as the embodiment of male sexual fantasy. Considering the common coding of Puerto Ricanness as butta pecanness, it is evident that their attributed phenotypic lightness plays a part in the collective erotization of Puerto Rican females.[21]

The text of "Still Not a Player" itself poses Puerto Rican and African American women as two distinct groups. Its sing-song chorus, which consists of multiple repetitions of "boricua, morena / boricua, morena," differentiates these two groups of women through the use of Puerto Rican ethnoracializing terminology. The video adds a visual dimension to the distinction as the camera alternates between a group of lighter-skinned women when the word *boricua* is being uttered and a group of comparatively darker-skinned women when the chorus mentions *morena*. The tiny chihuahua that one of the Boricuas is holding serves as yet another mark of difference. Chihuahuas are a dog breed considered in New York ghetto lore to be popular among Puerto Ricans, but they also invoke the tropicalized panlatinidad of Dinky, the infamous chihuahua of the late-1990s Taco Bell commercial campaign. However, though distinct, these two groups come together by virtue of Big Pun's sexual desire:

> I love 'em butter pecan
> The black, brown molass
> I don't discriminate
> I regulate every shade of that ass
> [spanking sound followed by a woman's moan] . . .
> I want a ghetto brunette
> With unforgettable sex . . .
> Since I found Joe
> Every pretty round brown ho
> Wanna go down low (Big Punisher 1998)

Pun boasts of not discriminating because he sexually engages "every shade of that ass." But the shades that he regulates are specifically three: butter pecan, black molasses, and brown molasses. Using the language of "gastronomic sexuality" (Aparicio 1998:147) that also informs the aforementioned Cocoa Brovas ad, Pun focuses his desire on African American and Puerto Rican "ghetto brunette[s]." Boricuas and morenas may be distinct but, as Pun constructs them, they are both sweet, thick, pretty, round, and various shades of brown. And, evidently, that is how he likes his hos.

The Cocoa Brovas ad as well as Pun's pronouncements are only two examples among many of rap's dominant masculinist ghetto nigga discourse, in which African American and Caribbean Latino men construct a landscape of desire where sistas and mamis take center stage as "their" women.

THE LATE 1990S: PUERTO RICANS' TROPICALIZED AFRO-DIASPORICITY

Rap music's late-1990s commercialized ghettocentricity and fetishization of mamis have helped legitimize and even trendify Puerto Ricans—and by extension, Latinos as a whole. This renewed embracing of Puerto Ricans as entitled hip-hop participants invested with cultural authenticity is also connected to the wider social context of the United States, where the rising population numbers, political clout, and media visibility of Latinos highlight their desirability as consumers and/or objects of mass-mediated exoticization.

Hip-hop's late-1990s "Latino Renaissance" (R. Morales 1996) has signaled an era of greater legitimacy and visibility for Puerto Rican (and other Latino) participants and expanded their opportunities for participation and expression. At the same time, the potential for a wider range of creative expression often fails to be fulfilled given the constraints placed on artists through flavor-of-the-month fetishization and tropicalization.

This redrawing of the realm of creative expression is reminiscent of freestyle music in the late 1980s, which pushed the bounds of New York Puerto Rican creativity through the inclusion of second-generation perspectives but reproduced other essentialist myths regarding Latino cultural production. As I explained earlier, one of its central myths was the construction of a Latino aesthetic that was imagined as excised from the Afrodiasporic history and present context of Caribbean Latino cultural expression in New York.

Despite the similarities—in terms of redrawing essentialist ethnoracialized boundaries—among freestyle in the late 1980s, Latin rap in the late 1980s/early 1990s, and Latino hip-hop participation in the late 1990s, a crucial distinction must be made. Although freestyle and Latin rap were defined as Latino cultural realms, core hip-hop is a Black-matrixed cultural sphere shared by African American and Latino youth. Caribbean Latinos may tropicalize themselves and be tropicalized by others, thus being readily distinguishable from African Americans. However, their participation in hip-hop is grounded in and celebrated as part of an Afro-diasporic cultural realm.

CONCLUSION

The 1980s were dubbed the Decade of the Hispanics in the media and saw an acknowledgment of the diversification and growing numbers of the Latino population—a belated recognition, because this phenomenon had actually begun more than a decade earlier (García 1988). Puerto Ricans made up 80 percent of the Latino population of New York in 1960; by the 1990s, this number had dropped to 50 percent (Flores 1996a:173).

With the growing plurality of Latino groups, numbers, experiences, and voices began the perception of the exceptional character of Puerto Ricans with respect to other Latino groups. It also became apparent that the same factors that made Puerto Ricans a distinct case among Latinos were the same ones that they shared with African Americans.

Certain factors pull Puerto Ricans into the Latino narrative (Spanish language; other historical and cultural factors related to Spanish colonization; and later, U.S. imperialism), but others pull them closer to African Americans and toward a virtual Blackness (English language among the

Victor's Cafe 52: enshrining the past. Wall display featuring prerevolutionary
Cuban currency. Photograph by Lisa Maya Knauer.

Generic (but class- and race-specific) tropicalism. Dining room mural at Victor's
Cafe 52. Photograph by Lisa Maya Knauer.

Spanish-only placards announcing daily specials at La Esquina Habanera (Havana Corner), Union City, N.J. Photograph by Lisa Maya Knauer.

Ethnic eatery as a portable homeland: La Esquina Habanera, Union City, N.J. Photograph by Lisa Maya Knauer.

Patron dancing columbia at the Sunday evening rumba performance. La Esquina Habanera, Union City, N.J. Photograph by Lisa Maya Knauer.

Mixing secular and sacred modes: dancing for Eleggua at the Sunday evening rumba. La Esquina Habanera, Union City, N.J. Photograph by Lisa Maya Knauer.

Ethnicity on display: Gran Parada Cubana, New York
City, May 1998. Photograph by Lisa Maya Knauer.

Marking the clave at the weekly rumba in New York's
Central Park, May 1998. Photograph by Lisa Maya
Knauer.

Note: In summer 2000, the Central Park rumba, an
ongoing informal performance over the last 35-plus
years, was shut down by the NYC police and forced to
relocate outside the park.

Gran Parada Cubana, New York City, May 1998. Photograph by Lisa Maya Knauer.

Rumbeando in Central Park, May 1998. Photograph by Lisa Maya Knauer.

Outdoor exhibitions like this one were a common component of El Taller Boricua's activities in the mid 1970s. Shown here are silkscreen prints from Puerto Rican artists used to announce and commemorate cultural events. Photographer unknown. Photo courtesy of El Museo del Barrio.

Another outdoor exhibition of paintings by members of El Taller Boricua. The painting in the foreground by Manuel Otero features Puerto Rican nationalist leader Pedro Albizu Campos. Photographer unknown. Photo courtesy of El Museo del Barrio.

second and third generations, residential segregation, labor marginality, poverty, and negative symbolic capital and public image).

Young New York Puerto Ricans have often either found themselves excluded or have excluded themselves from the generally accepted bounds of latinidad, given the constitutional urban Afro-diasporicity of their cultural identity. Puerto Ricans who participate in hip-hop culture have, for the most part, sought to acknowledge their Afro-diasporic Caribbean latinidad without wholly submerging themselves under the reigning definition of latinidad or merely passing as virtual Blacks.

Despite the growing appeals to an increasingly abstracted panlatinidad, Puerto Rican hip-hoppers still privilege their New York Afro-diasporic lived experience. As Q-Unique (1995b) says in his song "Rice and Beans":

no, not Latino
drop that "o"
Latin's just a language, yo

NOTES

1. Hip-hop is most commonly described by its participants as an Afro-diasporic urban youth culture with origins in the 1970s South Bronx. Among its primary venues of creative expression are MCing (rapping), DJing, writing (graffiti), and breaking (dancing). See Flores (1988), Norfleet (1997), and Rose (1994).

2. I use the term *ethnoracial* to acknowledge the constitutional racialization of ethnic categories.

3. In my writing, I will be using *black* and *Black* to refer to two distinct concepts: *black* as the racial or sociocultural category that refers to people of the African diaspora and *Black* as the U.S.-based ethnoracial category that refers specifically to the population known as African American. In this manner, I am seeking to distinguish between the perceived blackness but non-Blackness of Puerto Ricans (and others from the Spanish-speaking Caribbean) and the double blackness/Blackness of African Americans.

4. Thanks to Philip Kasinitz for the concept of Puerto Rican virtual Blackness.

5. Peter McLaren places rap ("gangsta rap" [sic]) within an Afro-diasporic context and a history that features economic exploitation. His case for rap's "ghetto-ethnicity" relies on the centrality of the ghetto within the rap discourse and the shared experience of African Americans and Puerto Ricans.

6. Flores (1996a) argues that the history of Puerto Ricans in New York, rather than being posited and dismissed as an exception among Latinos, can serve to illuminate and guide efforts to understand and further the position and prospects of other Latino groups.

7. Bourdieu explains *habitus* as a "system of structured, structuring dispositions" (1993:482). Urciuoli (1996) applies it in the case of African Americans and Puerto Ricans to indicate that their experiences, perceptions, and actions are shaped by common historical circumstances or "conditions of existence," thus

leading to similar understandings of and approaches to the world around them. This is not to say, however, that experience and action are strictly determined by these two groups' shared conditions of existence.

8. See Hazzard-Donald (1996), Tompkins (1996), and Verán (1996).

9. See Menéndez (1988) and Aparicio (1998:147).

10. If Latino rappers use English in their rhymes, it is because rap is an Afro-diasporic oral/musical form of expression that originated in the United States among English-dominant Afro-diasporic youth. The assumption that the use of English by Latino rappers equals Anglocentrism whereas the use of Spanish or bilingualism signals some kind of adherence to latinidad points to severe conceptual problems. Equating the use of English with Anglocentrism negates the appropriation and transformation of the colonizers' language by Afro-diasporic people (which includes certain Latino populations). Furthermore, not only are Latinos following rap's Afro-diasporic English-based orality, but their use of English also derives from their most immediate communicative experience as young people raised in the United States. Another problem with these charges of Anglocentrism is that they assume that a language equals a culture. Flores, Attinasi, and Pedraza (Flores 1993) challenge the notion that the use of English or Spanish indicates how much assimilation has occurred. Puerto Ricans, as well as other Latinos, assert their cultural identity through their particular way of speaking English (Urciuoli 1996; Zentella 1997).

11. For journalistic examples, see Baxter (1999) and Weisberg (1998). For examples in the academic literature, see McLaren (1995) and Smith (1997).

12. Aparicio and Chávez-Silverman forward the notion of a tropicalized latinidad, drawing from Fernando Ortiz's concept of transculturation, Pratt's contact zones, and Said's orientalism: "To tropicalize, as we define it, means to trope, to imbue a particular space, geography, group, or nation with a set of traits, images, and values" (1997:12).

13. On the initial Puerto Ricanization of Dominicans in New York, see Grosfoguel and Georas (1996).

14. See also Morgan (1996) and Rose (1994).

15. Rap's Puerto Rican (as well as other Latino) male subjects also eroticize mamis. The difference is that, in these cases, mamis are eroticized not as a tropical (ethnoracial) Other but as a tropical self.

16. Big Punisher, a Puerto Rican rapper from the Bronx and member of the Terror Squad, was the first Latino solo act to reach platinum sales with his 1998 debut album *Capital Punishment* (Loud Records, 1998).

17. The Latina spitfire stereotype is by no means a recent phenomenon. It has populated mass-mediated images in the United States since this century's early decades (Rodríguez 1997). Lupe Vélez and the "Carmelita" character she played in various highly successful movies of the 1930s represents an early example. Rita Moreno, tellingly nicknamed "Rita the Cheetah" by the press, had a hard time breaking out of the spitfire mold in the 1950s. These early portrayals of the spitfire, as is the case with today's mami, were typically grounded within a gendered lower-class identity.

18. See *The Source* 101 (February 1998):36.

19. The Cocoa Brovas are a rap duo of African American MCs.

20. On the aesthetic and representational marginalization of black Puerto Ricans, see Jorge (1986), Gregory (1995–1996), Thomas (1967), and Tate (1995). On skin tone and Puerto Ricans, see Jenkins and Wilson (1998).

21. Samara, a dark-skinned African American twenty-six-year-old "veteran of live sex shows in New York City," says of her experience looking for work in strip clubs: "Some clubs did not want to hire me because I was black. . . . Some like black girls, but black girls who have either big tits or light skin, who tend to look more like Puerto Ricans" (Samara 1987:37).

REFERENCES

Allen, Ernest, Jr. 1996. "Making the Strong Survive: The Contours and Contradictions of Message Rap." In *Droppin' Science: Critical Essays on Rap Music and Hip Hop Culture*, ed. William Eric Perkins, 159–91. Philadelphia: Temple University Press.

Allinson, E. 1994. "It's a Black Thing: Hearing How Whites Can't." *Cultural Studies* 8(3): 438–56.

Aparicio, Frances. 1998. *Listening to Salsa: Gender, Latin Popular Music, and Puerto Rican Cultures*. Hanover: Wesleyan University Press.

Aparicio, Frances, and Susana Chávez-Silverman. 1997. Introduction to *Tropicalizations: Transcultural Representations of Latinidad*, ed. Frances R. Aparicio and Susana Chávez-Silverman, 1–17. Hanover, N.H.: University Press of New England.

Arsonists. 1999. *As the World Burns*. Matador OLE 343–2. Compact disc.

Báez, Alano, vocalist for Ricanstruction. 1998. Interview by author. East Harlem, Manhattan, New York, June 15.

del Barco, Mandalit. 1996. "Rap's Latino Sabor." In *Droppin' Science: Critical Essays on Rap Music and Hip Hop Culture*, ed. William Eric Perkins, 63–84. Philadelphia: Temple University Press.

Baxter, Kevin. 1999. "Spanish Fly: Latinos Take Over." *The Source* 113 (February): 136–41.

Big Pun. 1998. *Capital Punishment*. Loud/RCA 07863 67512–2. Compact disc.

Boggs, Vernon. 1992. *Salsiology: Afro-Cuban Music and the Evolution of Salsa in New York City*. New York: Greenwood Press.

Bourdieu, Pierre. 1993. "Structures, Habitus, Practices." In *Social Theory: The Multicultural & Classic Readings*, ed. Charles Lemert, 479–84. Boulder, Colo.: Westview Press.

Boyd, Todd. 1997. *Am I Black Enough for You?: Popular Culture from the 'Hood and Beyond*. Bloomington and Indianapolis: Indiana University Press.

Carasco, Rubin Keyser. 1998. "Set Trippin'." *Blaze* (Fall): 206–7.

Chávez, Linda. 1991. *Out of the Barrio: Towards a New Politics of Hispanic Assimilation*. Basic Books.

Cross, Brian. 1993. *It's Not About A Salary: Rap, Race and Resistance in Los Angeles*. New York: Verso Books.

Dennis, Reginald. 1992. Liner notes in *Street Jams: Hip Hop from the Top, Part 2*. Rhino R4 70578. Cassette.

Flores, Juan. 1988. "Rappin', Writin' & Breakin'." *CENTRO* 2, no. 3 (Spring): 34–41.

—— 1992–1993. "Puerto Rican and Proud, Boyee!: Rap, Roots and Amnesia." *CENTRO* 5, no. 1 (Winter): 22–32.

—— 1993. *Divided Borders: Essays on Puerto Rican Identity*. Houston: Arte Público Press.

—— 1996a. "Pan-Latino/Trans-Latino: Puerto Ricans in the 'New Nueva York'." *CENTRO* 8, nos. 1 and 2 (Spring): 171–86.

—— 1996b. "Puerto Rocks: New York Ricans Stake Their Claim." In *Droppin' Science: Critical Essays on Rap Music and Hip Hop Culture*, ed. William Eric Perkins, 85–105. Philadelphia: Temple University Press.

—— 2000. "Cha Cha with a Backbeat: Songs and Stories of Latin Boogaloo." In *From Bomba to Hip Hop: Puerto Rican Culture and Latino Identity*, ed. Juan Flores, 79–112. New York: Columbia University Press.

Foner, Nancy. 1987. "The Jamaicans: Race and Ethnicity Among Migrants in New York City." In *New Immigrants in New York*, ed. Nancy Foner, 195–217. New York: Columbia University Press.

Fox, Geoffrey. 1996. *Hispanic Nation: Culture, Politics, and the Constructing of Identity*. Tucson: University of Arizona Press.

Gans, Herbert. 1992. "Second-Generation Decline: Scenarios for the Economic and Ethnic Futures of the Post-1965 American Immigrants." *Ethnic and Racial Studies* 15(2): 173–92.

Garcia, F. Chris. 1988. Introduction to *Latinos and the Political System*. Notre Dame: University of Notre Dame Press.

Gilroy, Paul. 1993. *The Black Atlantic: Modernity and Double Consciousness*. Cambridge, Mass.: Harvard University Press.

Gregory, Deborah. 1995–1996. "Lauren Vélez." *Vibe* 3, no. 10 (December/January): 129.

Grosfoguel, Ramón and Chloé Georas. 1996. "The Racialization of Latino Caribbean Migrants in the New York Metropolitan Area." *CENTRO* 8, nos. 1 and 2 (Spring): 190–201.

Guevara, Nancy. 1987. "Women Writin', Rappin', Breakin'." In *The Year Left*, ed. Mike Davis, 160–75. London: Verso Books.

Hazzard-Donald, Katrina. 1996. "Dance in Hip Hop Culture." In *Droppin' Science: Critical Essays on Rap Music and Hip Hop Culture*, ed. William Eric Perkins, 220–35. Philadelphia: Temple University Press.

Hebdige, Dick. 1987. *Cut 'N' Mix: Culture, Identity and Caribbean Music*. New York: Methuen.

Henderson, Errol A. 1996. "Black Nationalism and Rap Music." *Journal of Black Studies* 26, no. 3 (January): 308–39.

Hochman, Steven. 1990. "Hispanic Rappers Stake Out New Turf." *Rolling Stone*, November 15, 36–37.

hooks, bell. 1994. "Back to Black: Ending Internalized Racism." In *Outlaw Culture: Resisting Representations*. New York: Routledge.

Irving, Antonette K. 1998. "Pussy Power: The Onerous Road to Sexual Liberation in Hip-Hop." *The Source* 101 (February): 34.

Jenkins, "Satchmo" and "Belafonte" Wilson. 1998. "Shades of Mandingo: Watermelon Men of Different Hues Exchange Views." *Ego Trip* 4(1): 24–26.

Jiménez, Roberto "Cuba" II. 1997. "Vanishing Latino Acts." *The Source* 95 (August): 22.

Jorge, Angela. 1986. "The Black Puerto Rican Woman in Contemporary Society." In *The Puerto Rican Woman: Perspectives on Culture History and Society,* ed. Edna Acosta-Belén, 180–87. New York: Praeger.

Kasinitz, Philip. 1992. *Caribbean New York: Black Immigrants and the Politics of Race.* Ithaca, New York: Cornell University Press.

Kelley, Robin D. G. 1996. "Kickin' Reality, Kickin' Ballistics: Gangsta Rap and Postindustrial Los Angeles." In *Droppin' Science: Critical Essays on Rap Music and Hip Hop Culture,* ed. William Eric Perkins, 117–58. Philadelphia: Temple University Press.

Lascaibar, Juice (TC-5). 1997. "Hip-Hop 101: Respect the Architects of Your History." *The Source* 95 (August): 47–48.

Manuel, Peter. 1995. *Caribbean Currents: Caribbean Music from Rumba to Reggae.* Philadelphia: Temple University Press.

Massey, Douglas S. and Nancy A. Denton. 1991. "Trends in the Residential Segregation of Blacks, Hispanics and Asians 1970–1980." In *Majority and Minority: The Dynamics of Race and Ethnicity in American Life,* ed. Norman R. Yetman, 352–78. Boston: Allyn and Bacon.

McLaren, Peter. 1995. "Gangsta Pedagogy and Ghettoethnicity: The Hip Hop Nation as Counterpublic Sphere." *Socialist Review* 25(2): 9–55.

Menéndez, Marilú. 1988. "How to Spot a Jaguar in the Jungle." *The Village Voice,* August 9, pp. 20–21.

Morales, Ed. 1991. "How Ya Like Nosotros Now?" *The Village Voice,* November 26, p. 91.

——— 1996. "The Last Blackface: The Lamentable Image of Latinos in Film." *Sí* (Summer): 44–47.

Morales, Robert. 1996. "Fat Joe: Heart of Bronxness." *Vibe* 4, no. 2 (March): 84.

Morgan, Joan. 1996. "Fly-Girls, Bitches and Hoes: Notes of a Hip Hop Feminist." *Elementary* 1 (Summer): 16–20.

Norfleet, Dawn Michaelle. 1997. " 'Hip Hop Culture' in New York City: The Role of Verbal Musical Performance in Defining a Community." Ph.D. diss., Columbia University, New York.

Oboler, Suzanne. 1995. *Ethnic Labels, Latino Lives: Identity and the Politics of (Re)Presentation in the United States.* Minneapolis: University of Minnesota Press.

Ogbu, John U. 1978. *Minority Education and Caste: The American System in Cross-Cultural Perspective.* New York: Academic Press.

Orsi, Robert. 1992. "The Religious Boundaries of an Inbetween People: Street *Feste* and the Problem of the Dark-Skinned Other in Italian Harlem, 1920–1990." *American Quarterly* 44(3): 313–47.

Pabón, Carlos. 1995. "De Albizu a Madonna: Para armar y desarmar la nacionalidad." *bordes* no. 2: 22–40.

Panda, Andy. 1995. Talk given at Muévete!: The Boricua Youth Conference, Hunter College, New York City, November 11.

Parris, Jennifer. 1996. "Freestyle Forum." *Urban* 2(1): 30–31.

Pérez, Richie. 1990. "From Assimilation to Annihilation: Puerto Rican Images in U.S. Films." *CENTRO* 2, no. 8 (Spring): 8–27.

Puff Daddy & The Family. 1997. *No Way Out*. Bad Boy 78612–73012–4. Cassette.

Q-Unique (Anthony Quiles), rapper and member of the Arsonists. 1995a. Interview by author. Tape recording. Lower East Side, Manhattan, New York, October 12.

—— 1995b. *Rice and Beans*. Unreleased cassette.

Raekwon. 1995. *Only Built for Cuban Linx*. RCA 66663–4 07863. Cassette.

Rivera, Raquel. 1996. "Boricuas from the Hip Hop Zone: Notes on Race and Ethnic Relations in New York City." *CENTRO* 8, nos. 1 and 2 (Spring): 202–15.

Roberts, John Storm. 1979. *The Latin Tinge: The Impact of Latin American Music on the United States*. Oxford: Oxford University Press.

Rodríguez, Clara E. 1991. *Puerto Ricans: Born in the U.S.A.* Boulder: Westview Press.

—— 1997. "The Silver Screen: Stories and Stereotypes." In *Latin Looks: Images of Latinas and Latinos in the U.S. Media*, ed. Clara E. Rodríguez, 73–79. Boulder, Colo.: Westview Press.

Rodríguez, Edward. 1995. Hip Hop Culture: The Myths and Misconceptions of This Urban Counterculture. Tms. unpublished manuscript.

Rodríguez-Morazzani, Roberto P. 1991–1992. "Puerto Rican Political Generations in New York: Pioneros, Young Turks and Radicals." *CENTRO* 4, no. 1 (Winter): 96–116.

—— 1996. "Beyond the Rainbow: Mapping the Discourse on Puerto Ricans and 'Race'." *CENTRO* 8, nos. 1 and 2 (Spring): 151–69.

Rose, Tricia. 1994. *Black Noise: Rap Music and Black Culture in Contemporary America*. Hanover, N.H.: Wesleyan University Press.

Ross, Andrew. 1989. *No Respect: Intellectuals and Popular Culture*. New York: Routledge.

Salazar, Max. 1992. "Latinized Afro-American Rhythms." In *Salsiology: Afro-Cuban Music and the Evolution of Salsa in New York City*, ed. Vernon Boggs, 237–48. New York: Greenwood Press.

Samara. 1987. In *Sex Work: Writings by Women in the Sex Industry*, ed. Frédérique Delacoste and Priscilla Alexander, 37. Pittsburgh: Cleis Press.

Samuels, David. 1995. "The Rap On Rap: The 'Black Music' That Isn't Either." In *Rap On Rap: Straight-Up Talk On Hip-Hop Culture*, ed. Adam Sexton, 241–52. New York: Dell Publishing.

Smith, Christopher Holmes. 1997. "Method in the Madness: Exploring the Boundaries of Identity in Hip-Hop Performativity." *Social Identities* (3): 345–74.

Smith, Robert. 1994. " 'Doubly Bounded' Solidarity: Race and Social Location in the Incorporation of Mexicans Into New York City." Paper presented at the Conference of Fellows: Program of Research on the Urban Underclass, Social Science Research Council, University of Michigan, June.

Sundiata, Sekou. 1998. "The Latin Connection." Essay in playbill for the Black Rock Coalition's music performance *The Latin Connection*, BAM Majestic Theater, Brooklyn, New York, June 27.

Tate, Greg. 1995. "Bronx Banshee." *Vibe* 3, no. 9 (November): 44.

Thomas, Piri. 1967. *Down These Mean Streets*. New York: Vintage Books.

Thompson, Robert Farris. 1996. "Hip Hop 101." In *Droppin' Science: Critical Essays on Rap Music and Hip Hop Culture*, ed. William Eric Perkins, 211–19. Philadelphia: Temple University Press.

Toop, David. 1991. *Rap Attack 2: African Rap to Global Hip Hop*. London: Serpent's Tail.

Tompkins, Dave. 1996. "Hollywood Shuffle." *Rap Pages* 5, no. 8 (September): 16–17.

Torres, Andrés. 1995. *Between Melting Pot and Mosaic: African Americans and Puerto Ricans in the New York Political Economy*. Philadelphia: Temple University Press.

A Tribe Called Quest. 1993. *Midnight Marauders*. Jive Records 41490. Compact disc.

Urciuoli, Bonnie. 1996. *Exposing Prejudice: Puerto Rican Experiences of Language, Race and Class*. Boulder, Colo.: Westview Press.

Verán, Cristina. 1991. "Many Shades of Our Culture: A History of Latinos in Hip Hop." *Word Up!*, 24–26.

—— 1996. "That's the Breaks." *Rap Pages* 5, no. 8 (September): 6.

Waters, Mary. 1996. "Ethnic and Racial Identities of Second-Generation Black Immigrants in New York City." In *The New Second Generation*, ed. Alejandro Portes, 171–96. New York: Russell Sage Foundation.

Weisberg, Chang. 1998. "Hip Hop's Minority?: The Past, Present, and Future of Latinos in Hip Hop." *Industry Insider* 15: 50–57, 96–97.

Zentella, Ana Celia. 1997. *Growing Up Bilingual: Puerto Rican Children in New York*. Malden, Mass.: Blackwell Publishers.

CHAPTER NINE

Ambiguous Identities!

The Affirmation of Puertorriqueñidad in the Community Murals of New York City*

Elsa B. Cardalda Sánchez

Amílcar Tirado Avilés

> —Hola . . .
> —¡ No, BUENAS!
>
> *—At a casita, conversation between one of the authors*
> *and a Loisaida resident*

This essay explores the social representations of Puerto Rican cultural identity through the study of muralism in El Barrio. For the last three decades a tradition of muralism in New York City has been used by Puerto Ricans to express their socioeconomic and political concerns. Therefore, we ask what muralism in El Barrio says about the community and about puertorriqueñidad as well as why it has arisen with such force recently.

The selection of El Barrio for conducting our study is based on its historical and symbolic importance for Puerto Ricans, who have occupied this neighborhood for over seven decades. The discourse of puertorriqueñidad has been a historical formation maturing since the 1920s and more recently a metonymic base supporting current conceptions of latinidad in New York City. Thus, our essay relates to the general discussion of this book regarding the genealogy of discourses of latinidad and presents the mural as an emblematic montage of identity in the City.

Our essay reports on the El Barrio Murals Research Project, which we developed from the perspectives of social psychology and history. We view

*In memory of Andrés E. Cardalda (Papi).

Special thanks to Mayra Berríos, Nancy Llera, Nitza L. Guadalupe, Dr. José Rodríguez, and Dr. Daniel Martínez from the Caribbean Center for Advanced Studies in San Juan, Puerto Rico; to Blanca Vázquez and Pedro Rivera in New York; and to David Fontánez in Puerto Rico.

Photos by Amílcar Tirado Avilés and Elsa B. Cardalda Sánchez murals as social chronicles of the community and as unofficial historical documents. The popular iconography of murals can be approached from the Social Representations theory of Serge Moscovici.[1] There is little research about the iconic side of social representations. Therefore, we will be contributing in that area. Our analysis of the social representations of puertorriqueñidad/latinidad is limited to the muralism examined in El Barrio. From a historical perspective, this essay represents another contribution because despite the seniority and large number of Puerto Ricans living in this area, still we lack a history of them in El Barrio.[2] Given this need, the essay includes a brief section on the history and socioeconomic profile of Puerto Ricans in this neighborhood that serves as the context for evaluating the current diversification of Latino nationalities in El Barrio.

We contend that murals are visual voices that represent an affirmation of puertorriqueñidad. Community muralism in El Barrio suggests a symbolic cultural resistance in the face of material poverty and spiritual desolation. These visual voices convey a public claim, written in the walls; they express and articulate the imagery of a Puerto Rican cultural identity and project a determination not to be erased from history. El Barrio has been changing, so the effervescence of muralism may be related to recent gentrification and its implications in terms of displacement and deterioration of the institutions of the Puerto Rican community. As displacement, dispersion, and decay undermine the fabric of the Puerto Rican community, and as Puerto Rican centrality in El Barrio is challenged by the language of Latinidad, there is a perceived threat of the symbolic nexus of El Barrio as a key place of Nuyorican identity. Murals serve as a medium to study the social web that El Barrio is becoming and as a cultural barometer to examine relations between Puerto Ricans and recent Latino immigrants.

The third question is, Have murals adopted a panethnic Latino identity following recent changes in the composition of the neighborhood? Contemporary proposals for the study of Latinos in the United States express that the convergence of groups under the notion of pan-Latinism represents a dominant force in their everyday life. Therefore, if the murals speak about identity in a place that is changing economically, culturally, and demographically, then this fluid form of social representation should surface. Another line of thinking postulates that national identifications supersede pan-Latin identifications. This essay contributes to the discussion presented by López and Espíritu[3] and questions the degree to which panethnic labels among Latino groups represent a genuine generalization of ethnic solidarity and identity, as opposed to alliances of convenience. Pan-Latinism appears in the murals studied as emerging social representations that are still in flux, lack a core, and are not widely used. Thus, a potential issue implicit in our examination is whether these peripheral elements will crystallize into a particular social identity, transforming or coexisting among national social identities.

EL BARRIO, MURALS, AND SOCIAL REPRESENTATIONS

El Barrio is one of the most important settlements in New York City for Puerto Ricans owing to its historical and "mythical" force.[4] This is the case because large numbers of Puerto Ricans settled there and formed community organizations and political alliances. As an entry point in the global city, El Barrio has the characteristics of economic informality and social marginality that arise in certain groups in postmodernity.[5] The Latino community of El Barrio is mainly working class, with an annual per capita income of less than $6,000.[6]

The murals of El Barrio represent one of the existing "cultural texts"[7] of greatest vitality that serve as social chronicles of the community. We believe that murals reflect feelings of desolation or despair in the contested terrain of interstitial communities during transitional periods. The mural as social tableau seems to arise in New York City mostly where ghettoization prevails. As public resources, murals are part of the community work of casitas and gardens. Murals, like casitas, operate on a landscape of despair to produce their own architecture of resistance. About the genesis of this desolation, Luis Aponte-Parés makes the following observation:

> Market forces have brought desolation and despair to the inner
> city, rendering the urban fabric into residual and discontinuous
> fragments attended by a loss of memory and identity, producing
> a lumpenography of capital, "reserved" neighborhoods with
> arrested development potential analogous to the industrial
> reserve of workers. [Therefore] families choose to take an active
> role in reshaping landscapes of despair into landscapes of hope.
> Transforming fragmented and discontinuous urban landscapes
> into cultural forms with continuity, rich in values, and bringing
> forth a sense of attachment.[8]

As visual voices, murals sustain a dialogue with the community, and this communication constitutes a form of knowledge production. They are designed to create a reflection and evoke a visual/verbal response in an urban setting where cultural amnesia has been induced by the dominant commercial culture. Murals are public art that fills the community with pride. With respect to the social impact of mural production, barrio based artist James De la Vega claims that the act of creating art in the streets for the people is a way of fostering a sense of place in the neighborhood: "I want my paintings to be seen as the voice of the neighborhood, a record of what was happening here."[9]

Community muralism entails a public claim for place and identity in the configuration of New York City. As such, it takes part in the cultural wars for public space. At issue is why Puerto Ricans and other working class Latinos are being displaced from Manhattan and from the city. Why the condition of economic and social marginality of a substantial percentage of the Puerto Rican community of East Harlem? In light of this, murals are cultural practices that serve to commemorate hope and a determination to survive in the face of an economy of violence and death. Racialized working-class neighborhoods become instead places of self-affirmation and community making. Muralism has been interpreted as an event signaling change in the community. In the words of Puerto Rican muralist María Domínguez:

> Ese movimiento de los murales reflejaba que había un cambio.
> . . . El arte público tiene el gran poder de reflejarle a la
> comunidad que va a haber un cambio, y el [mural *Nuestro
> Barrio*] que yo hice en El Barrio que es en la 104, ese lo hice
> puramente intencional para reflejar la cultura puertorriqueña la
> cual algún día no va a existir en El Barrio. Entonces escogí el
> Taller Boricua que fue una de las primeras organizaciones que se
> afincó, . . . la Marqueta, . . . El Museo del Barrio, the Harbor
> Conservatory for Music. . . . So I chose those four organizations
> who have long established Puerto Rican culture in El Barrio and
> not just to say "This is ours" but just to say "No one is
> documenting this." . . . Los que en realidad deben heredar El
> Barrio se van a quedar sin nada.[10]

In this sense, muralism seems a communal vehicle during a period of crisis that speaks about a threat, which may be the massive displacement gentrification and marginalization of Puerto Ricans from El Barrio and from Manhattan.

To interpret this situation, we turn to social representation theory as expressed by Serge Moscovici, who states that "when studying a representation, we should always try to answer the unfamiliar feature which motivated it and which it has absorbed. . . . All representations arise from the need to turn the strange into something familiar."[11] These processes stabilize the social world.

Moscovici defines *social representations* as "a network of interacting concepts and images whose contents evolve continuously over time and space."[12] Social representations "always have two facets, which are as interdependent as the two faces of a sheet of paper: the iconic, and the symbolic facets. We know that: Representation = image/meaning; in other words, that it equates every image to an idea, and every idea to an image."[13]

The space between icon and symbol is the locus of social representations. Social representations recreate identities by means of communication channels and generate a map to make sense of the vicissitudes of life.

Social representations are structured in a figurative nucleus and periphery. Moscovici proposes that all representations have a nucleus, a core strongly anchored in collective memory and shared by all people that is the most stable part of its grouping. They also have a periphery, images or meanings associated with a different context. However, some social representations don't have a nucleus and are still in a state of flux.[14]

Community murals in El Barrio suggest polemical social representations because the affirmation of identity is rooted in denial of resources and social conflict. As argued by Moscovici, polemical social representations

> are representations generated in the course of social conflict,
> social controversy, and society as a whole does not share them.
> They are determined by the antagonistic relations between its
> members and intended to be mutually exclusive. These polemical
> representations must be viewed in the context of an opposition
> or struggle between groups and are often expressed in terms of a
> dialogue with an imaginary interlocutor.[15]

On the one hand, there is the conflict with the dominant culture, which generates an affirmation of the cultural identity of a subaltern group. And on the other hand, there is the situation in which long-term residents of El Barrio may feel threatened by recent migrants, fueling a process of affirmation of puertorriqueñidad over latinidad. This frames intralatino conflicts thus rendering polemical social representations on both sides of this dynamic. Here, competition among primarily working class Latino nationalities often takes the form of differences between long-term residents (or older immigrants), in this case Puerto Ricans, and new immigrants, in this case mostly Mexicans and Dominicans.

PUERTO RICAN ROOTS AND SOCIOECONOMIC PROFILE OF EL BARRIO

Historically, the Puerto Rican community established in East Harlem has maintained a remarkable position as center and symbol of the Puerto Rican presence in the United States. The 1990 census data indicate that of the 92,241 persons residing in East Harlem, Puerto Ricans (41,902) and African Americans (41,156) constitute the two largest ethnic groups. Puerto Ricans represent the group with the largest population among Latinos settled in this sector of the city, followed by Dominicans (2,691) and Mexicans (2,418), groups that may be seriously undercounted because of their uncertain immigration status.[16]

The development of the Puerto Rican community in East Harlem has been a process spanning the twentieth century. By 1920, the Harlem settlement represented one of the three enclaves constituting the Puerto Rican community in the city (the Navy Yard in Brooklyn and Chelsea in Manhattan were the other two). According to the 1930 census, Manhattan had the largest number of Puerto Ricans living in the city (34,715 of 44,908), with most of them concentrated in the Harlem area (26,118 persons).[17]

The number of Puerto Rican migrants to the city increased from the mid-1940s until the 1960s; most were still living in Manhattan, particularly in East Harlem. The 1970 census established a Puerto Rican population in the United States of over a million (1,379,100), with 811,800 living in New York City. Although East Harlem remained a focal point of the Puerto Rican population in the city, it should be noted that the census registered a decrease of the concentration of Puerto Rican population in Manhattan and an apparent movement toward the Bronx and Brooklyn.[18] During the 1980s, the tendency among Puerto Ricans living in the city (now numbering 860,552) was to move out of the traditional areas of settlement, particularly New York. The most recent census indicated that the Puerto Rican population in New York City had a modest increase, reaching 896,763.[19]

From its beginnings, the Puerto Rican community established in El Barrio was essentially of working-class background and limited economic resources. The area has been labeled as one of few job opportunities and suffers from discrimination and inadequate municipal and state services. During the course of the twentieth century, the neighborhood has been extremely poor, characterized by displacement and population substitution. As Nuyorican writer Ed Vega expressed: "The departure of the Italians ceded the land East Harlem with all its joys and sorrows, to the Puerto Ricans."[20]

Gentrification, deindustrialization, and economic restructuring foster competition between racialized working classes who are displaced from the labor and housing markets, and new immigrant workers who replaced them in the lower echelons of labor (now the new service economy). Hence, the rise of latinidad and the new affirmations of puertorriqueñidad ought to be framed in terms of this global context of neo-liberal economic restructuring and the tremendous increase in global labor migrations. Intralatino contests are beginning to be noticed in the cultural arena, in new small businesses, and in religious festivities. El Museo del Barrio, founded during the 1970s as a Puerto Rican institution, is today projecting itself as a Latino institution. In another case, a new cultural institution has been named the Julia de Burgos Latino Cultural Center (linking the name of a Puerto Rican poet who died in East Harlem in 1953 with the most recent approach of Latinos). Bodegas and small businesses are no longer Puerto Rican–owned, and a large number of participants of the informal economy, such as flower vendors, are from other Latino groups. In the religious arena, the new cultural influences and displacing forces were felt when Mexicans raised concerns about which aspect of the Virgin Mary should be the object of their devotion at a local church: The Virgin of La Providencia or the Virgin of Guadalupe.[21]

The main job sources for El Barrio residents have historically been the needle industry, the service sector, and those jobs defined as semiskilled or unskilled. As a result of the city's economic restructuring during the 1940s, many Puerto Ricans moving to East Harlem were able to find jobs in the city. Puerto Rican migrants represented the kind of workers needed to occupy semiskilled and unskilled jobs. Nevertheless, the transformation of the city's economy during the past thirty years to a banking and technology center, and the relocation of main industries to other areas of the country or abroad are contributing factors in explaining the high unemployment and accompanying poverty among Puerto Ricans.

It can be concluded that El Barrio has not been historically the main employment center for Puerto Ricans. Its main contribution has been to serve as housing space and as a community that projects itself as a symbol of puertorriqueñidad. The community has been identified as the place where people made "primary life spaces," i.e., "the areas people occupied in which their dreams were made, and their lives unfolded" and where historical events could be recorded and then remembered.[22]

THE PUERTO RICAN COMMUNITY IN NEW YORK AND MURALISM: A HISTORICAL NOTE

The history and documentation of muralism at the local level has yet to be written.[23] Puerto Rican muralism in New York City is a case in point; information is scarce and scattered in a few publications. Nevertheless, a series of factors and precedents that influenced the development of contemporary U.S. muralism can be cited as factors that also marked the development of Puerto Rican muralism in the city.[24]

The first precedent entails the works in the United States during the 1920s and 1930s of Mexican artists Diego Rivera, David Alfaro Siqueiros, and José Clemente Orozco. These artists contributed to murals taking on a role as vehicles for communicating social messages with themes that often had controversial political and social content.[25] The legacy of these painters informs us that a connection exists between muralism and workers' struggles, the first serving as a means to express a message of the second (particularly those in the urban sector). These Mexican muralists have influenced the works of Puerto Rican painters such as James de la Vega, a protagonist of the current muralista movement in El Barrio.[26]

The second precedent is from the New Deal period, when the Works Project Administration (Federal Arts Project) sponsored the creation of murals in public buildings in the United States. Some of these murals were also controversial because of their social and political messages. Regarding Puerto Ricans, there is the case of Rockwell Kent, who sparked a controversy in 1937 owing to the political and anticolonial message he portrayed. The objection centered on the mural including an inscription of a letter that Eskimos had sent to Puerto Ricans ("To the people of Puerto Rico, our Friends! Go ahead. Let us change chiefs. That alone can make us equal and free").[27]

A third precedent was the muralism developed during the social movements of the 1960s and 1970s. The civil rights and student movements of that era, as well as the struggle for the recognition of ethnic/racial identities of groups such as Chicanos and Puerto Ricans, influenced this period of muralism. Chicanos in the Southwest developed a muralist movement that gave visual voice to images of identity and history and reflected pride in their origins. At the same time, they wanted to expose in their murals a series of social problems afflicting them as a group, such as discrimination, exploitation, unequal and inadequate government services, and the drug problem in their communities. Puerto Rican communities in the United States were confronting similar issues, and the muralism developed by them was analogous to that of Chicanos.

Other local factors contributed to the development of Puerto Rican muralism in New York. The founding of Cityarts in 1968, under the auspices of the New York City Department of Cultural Affairs, provided guidance and support to mural projects related to the various ethnic/racial groups in New York. Cityarts initially concentrated its work in the Lower East Side (Manhattan), particularly in the African American community. Afterwards, Cityarts expanded its projects to other spaces and ethnic/racial groups throughout the City. Some of the murals sponsored by Cityarts relating to Puerto Ricans were *Ghetto Ecstasy,* which included the figure of Puerto Rican patriot Ramón Emeterio Betances (1973, directed by James Jannauzzi, Lower East Side) and *Puerto Rican Heritage Mural* (1975, directed by Alfredo Hernández, Lower East Side).[28]

Other mural projects developed independently from Cityarts, a great number of them with political and social protest iconography. One of the most common images in these murals was the Puerto Rican flag;[29] others incorporated images of Pedro Albizu Campos and Che Guevara, and some of them were dedicated to the freedom of the Puerto Rican Nationalist political prisoners. In East Harlem, murals adorned the entrance of the original site of El Museo del Barrio (Third Avenue and 107th Street). From 1974 to 1978, Hank Prussing and Manuel Vega developed a mural, *The Spirit of East Harlem,* showing an idyllic representation of the community in daily activities, i.e., men playing dominoes, friendly policemen shaking hands with tenants, etc. However, one should recall that during this period the neighborhood was at the height of confrontation between community and government agencies. Deliberate municipal neglect was the target of a political offensive by the Young Lords Party. Manuel Vega recently renovated this mural in 1998. Hope Community, Inc., a housing renewal organization that holds a business interest in changing the façade of the neighborhood, sponsored both the original work and the restoration.

Current muralism in East Harlem is dominated by the work performed by James De la Vega and by projects sponsored by El Museo del Barrio under the direction of artist María Domínguez. In addition, other groups and individuals such as the Comité de Afirmación Puertorriqueña and the Puerto Rico Collective, a young generation of activists, have practiced muralism in the community, and their work continues to express ideas of social identity and political issues concerning Puerto Ricans. Several objectives may be identified when studying murals. Murals are vehicles for the representations of cultural identity, particularly through images representing history and cultural and social traditions. They serve to express messages of social protest, unearthing discontent with some situation that is happening. Murals constitute a space that serves as a forum for the discussion or dialogue on topics of particular interest for the community (e.g., Fuerzas Armadas de Liberación Nacional, political prisoners, memorials to fallen youth). They also represent a kind of art accessible to a large number of people. Nitza Tufiño, an artist affiliated with El Taller Boricua, developed colorful mosaics filled with symbols associated with the Taíno, which were sponsored by the Metropolitan Transit Authority (MTA) for the 103rd Street subway station so it can "allow anyone who uses the subway to see some art every day." The community artist Manuel Vega has also sponsored mosaics that he dedicated to Afro-Caribbean symbols because "we have to remember who we were to know who we are."[30]

There is no guarantee regarding the longevity of murals. They can suffer destruction because of demolition and/or reconstruction of the spaces where they are located, or they may be painted over so that new murals can be put up in their place (a practice used by De la Vega). Another characteristic of murals is the dialogue they sustain with the public. Both instances of destruction and dialogue are represented in our sample.

Murals, although not exclusive works of particular communities, tend to be employed more frequently in densely populated urban areas of limited economic resources. They do not represent exogenous elements to the community but constitute an integral part of and reflect pride in the social space in which they happen, enjoying the approval of the residents. Murals serve to express the concerns of people in a visual language they can understand.[31] However, on some occasions murals may be interpreted as portraying antagonistic messages toward the community or its members. In such circumstances, murals can suffer alterations, mutilation, or destruction by those who feel offended by the message.[32]

The murals constitute a historical response of affirmation and resistance both to North American colonialism and, more specifically, to the socioeconomic limitations in which the community is currently immersed. Murals in El Barrio have become a way of expressing, performing, and imaging Puerto Rican identity. Migration, as Jorge Duany states, has not automatically made

Puerto Ricans into just another ethnoracial group in the United States. Puerto Rican affirmation of cultural identity continues to be expressed in several forms.[33] Such responses are not exclusively centered in a political discourse but also respond to the myriad of problems that the community confronts (drugs as well as cooperation and competition among the ethnic/racial groups). Murals are also aesthetic practices, and as such they are expressive of desires, pleasures, and of the collective and individual imagination.

EL BARRIO MURALS RESEARCH PROJECT

Initially, we in El Barrio Murals Research Project defined murals as wall art framed in a rectangle, treating a single theme, and signed by an author. However, this definition was expanded to include painting on the sidewalk and unsigned work (e.g., flags). Also, it was important to distinguish murals from graffiti work; we defined *graffiti* as a form of writing, but if there was an iconic side to a representation, then we counted it as a mural. Using this definition, we ended up with a group of murals inspired by graffiti but with iconic representations. Another element of the definition was counting each discrete unit because some murals are painted in a montage style. Murals designed with a montage technique offer a density of elements, where one piece can be erased from a wall and another produced in its place, forming a new gestalt. As murals have a relationship with their context, adjoining murals form a background for a piece. There is another arrangement of murals in which the montage is developed sequentially in different places of the neighborhood.

The fieldwork of the project was conducted during 1998–99, photographing 228 murals from El Barrio in Manhattan, covering from 96th to 125th streets.[34] We walked the neighborhood in a grid pattern, covering most of it except for some streets that we are planning to do. El Barrio muralism is constantly evolving, and this required us to go back to streets already covered. We went to places of high human concentration such as strips of shops, subway stations, and important streets. At other times, artists directly indicated where their work was. For De la Vega's work, we enjoyed a tour by him.

Murals were photographed and their addresses noted. We took several pictures of each mural and catalogued it as an item. In addition to taking photos of the murals, the field research included observations, analysis of a documentary video, community contacts, perusal of daily newspapers, and interviews with muralists. Also, we researched books looking for murals from El Barrio ($n = 19$). This type of archival data served to interpret contemporary murals against earlier work. For additional thematic comparisons, we sampled murals from the community of the Lower East Side (Loisaida).

For the analyses of murals, we identified categorical themes. Then we identified redundant Puerto Rican and Latino topics across the themes. While looking at the murals, we considered the icons and verbal texts and analyzed these conjointly and separately. Therefore, we moved from a descriptive plane of ordering themes and examining their topics to interpreting the structured meaning of the iconic matrix. Finally, from the network of social representations, we distilled thematas, or fundamental notions.

Themes and Topics

Thematic categories were defined based on the plots exhibited in the murals. Murals were categorized as showing a theme according to their dominant elements. Themes were assigned on an exclusive basis to a mural. Social scientists (two psychologists and a sociologist) and a historian attributed the thematic categories to murals.

With respect to themes, murals in El Barrio were categorized as Political, People, Religious, Memorial, Commercial, Artistic, Customs/Folk, Homage/Allegory, Graffiti, Education, and Sports. Of the murals studied, the most frequent category was Political, with 23 percent of the total (52 of 228). Next, in descending order of frequency, is the broad category labeled People (40 of 228), followed by Religious (33 of 228), and so on. Of significance is the scarcity of murals in the category of Education, with only 1 percent.

To validate these themes, categorizations were compared with statements about De la Vega's work by others as well as by the artist himself. Results indicated that there is a clear correspondence among these categorizations, with themes concerning political, cultural, and religious aspects of the community. Themes in El Barrio muralism are also consistent with a sample of 202 murals from the Lower East Side. A similar network of themes is sustained; the political theme remained one of the most frequent as well. The consistency in the iconic matrix led us to inquire whether social representations in murals were featuring aspects of Puerto Rican cultural identity. Thus, we examined each theme in terms of topics that might pertain to Puerto Rican cultural identity. Another question was if murals had changed historically in El Barrio. An archival search of murals in El Barrio referenced works as early as 1974 but were less covered in print than those of the Lower East Side. This search was less informative than anticipated. On the one hand, muralist María Domínguez has argued that murals in New York City were more politicized before than nowadays.[35] On the other hand, political themes were most frequently identified in our contemporary sample. We are still locating sources of earlier material to examine this further. Nevertheless, as can be judged from current newspaper coverage, murals have become very popular phenomena.

Across all themes we uncovered topics concerning Puerto Rican cultural identity. Topic analysis included the iconic and verbal elements in each mural. We are aware that there are discussions on the authenticity of cultural symbols; nevertheless, given a constructivist standpoint, we selected the most conventionally known, which, of course, are open to debate.[36]

The Puerto Rican flag was the most prominent topic in murals with fifty-six instances, counting the Lares flag (symbol of the 1868 insurrection) and the official *monoestrellada* flag. How are we to interpret the ubiquitous presence of flags? We suggest two ways to examine this question. First, with what are flags associated in the compositions? Second, in what performative contexts do flags appear?

Puerto Rican flags are anchored to political heroes, with the towering presence of Pedro Albizu Campos prevailing in seven instances.[37] A pantheon of national heroes in the mural *Celebrating Puerto Rican History* included Ramón Emeterio Betances, Arturo Schomburg, Luis Muñoz Marín, and Lolita Lebrón. Two murals seemed to commemorate the historical moment in 1977 when the National Congress for Puerto Rican Rights wrapped the Puerto Rican flag around the Statue of Liberty. These two instances relate the flag with a narrative of Puerto Rican history as a juxtaposition of protagonic figures, and with an anticolonial action reflecting a symbol that defines and represents Puerto Ricans.

Flags frame other topics as exemplified in murals about the Puerto Rican parade in New York (the first annual Puerto Rican Parade was held entirely in El Barrio), the Young Lords Party (established in El Barrio), and a song by Rafael Hernández relating to the migration experience ("The motherland is calling. Puerto Rico is pure flame and here I am freezing to death"). Furthermore, verbal texts inscribed in flags held quotes by Lolita Lebrón "Si los hombres no pelean por la libertad de Puerto Rico, nosotras las mujeres lo haremos," "Yo no vine a matar, yo vine a morir;" Lebrón is a fervent nationalist involved in the 1954 attack on the U.S. House of Representatives in Washington, D.C.

Polyvalent symbols are interwoven in the narrative anchored to flags: the coquí (a species of small amphibian exclusive to Puerto Rico), garitas/ morro (sentinel box in Spanish military installations), and a pava (a Puerto Rican peasant hat, the symbol of a political party on the island). Other polysemic historical protagonists are a machetero (a sugar cane cutter), a fisherman, and a jíbaro (a Puerto Rican peasant participating in the Great Migration). A painting by Ramón Frade called *El pan nuestro* representing a Puerto Rican jíbaro has been incorporated in various murals. Iconic representations accompanied by verbal texts also mentioned Taínos[38] (e.g., "Strictly Taíno. Siempre pa'lante"), Boricuas (e.g., "Absolut Boricua"), and "our people" ("Justice is especially blind when it comes to our people".)

The uses of Puerto Rican flags transcend the political theme and cross over the categories of Artistic, Memorial, Customs/Folk, and Commercial murals. Flags proudly identify those known to have died as victims of the drug trade, memorialized as dignified Puerto Rican people, renewing family and social ties to the deceased. Some sources have interpreted the display of flags in memorials as a sign of collective loss, an affirmation that these people were loved members of a community.[39]

Puerto Rican flags adorn an artistic mural entitled *Celebrating Puerto Rican Musicians. Celebrando nuestra cultura* that depicts a magnificent Hall of Salsa whose members include Ismael Rivera, Héctor Lavoe, La India, Marc Anthony, Tito Puente, Tito Rojas, and Gilberto Santa Rosa. Remember that many salsa musicians are related to El Barrio. Salsa is one of the main domains of cultural creation through which puertorriqueñidad composes latinidad. Artistic themes exalt the preeminent place of music in Puerto Rican culture through the representations of musical instruments and rhythms (bolero, salsa, rap, and bomba). We also see the presence of Puerto Rican poets (e.g., Julia de Burgos) and sports figures (e.g., Cheguí Torres) as an avenue of cultural identity. A mural entitled *Nuestro Barrio* argues for a place to preserve Puerto Rican heritage through institutions such as El Museo del Barrio, El Taller Boricua, and La Marqueta.

To evaluate the possible meanings of displaying Puerto Rican flags, we visited other performative contexts in the community. We observed flags in the following contexts:

- Rallies for freedom of political prisoners displayed the flags of Puerto Rico, the Dominican Republic, and Mexico in an act of solidarity.
- An ecumenical demonstration in support of removing U.S. military presence from Vieques displayed the flags of Puerto Rico and Lares.
- A Puerto Rican parade displayed the flags of Puerto Rico and Lares.
- Casitas in public gardens displayed the Puerto Rican flag.

So what is the equation here? We conclude that murals, like other performative contexts, are using the flag as a national symbol to affirm the cultural identity of Puerto Ricans as a people in conflict with a dominant culture. This manifestation of ethnic pride seems to provide a sense of belonging. But as it reflects a particular national identity submerged under the imperial gaze, it is a polemical social representation rooted in social conflict.[40]

Conflict crisscrosses the terrain of muralism. Based on reports and observations, we present some anecdotal evidence that suggests social conflicts:

- When asked why he included Malcolm X in a mural ("¿Por qué estás poniendo ese prieto ahí?" [Why are you painting that dark-skinned man over there?]), De la Vega responded by explaining the importance of this historical figure and expressing that everyone could learn from his teachings. The muralist interpreted this incident as an expression of racism in Harlem, which manifests as conflict between Puerto Ricans and African Americans.
- Somebody defaced the figure of Luis Muñoz Marín in a mural, *Celebrating Puerto Rican Heritage,* writing in graffiti the word *colonialism* over it.[41] In this mural also appears Pedro Albizu Campos, thus suggesting a debate between the contiguous representations of commonwealth versus independence options for Puerto Rico. De la Vega informed us that the graffiti drawn over his mural initially "bothered" him, but that now he sees it as a form of "dialogue" between muralist and community.
- In a mural, Pedro Albizu Campos had a gun but later this part was erased (it's unclear who did it).
- De la Vega did a mural of Mexican singer Alejandro Fernández in a building where the majority of the tenants were Puerto Ricans. To add insult to the injury, the mural of Mexican revolutionary leader Emiliano Zapata located on 110th Street was also erased.
- When De la Vega painted his adaptation of Picasso's *Guernica* at 111th Street and Lexington Avenue, he represented a needle going into an arm. The community objected, and he painted over it. This seems to be a denial of the subculture of drugs in the community or an indication that a negative portrayal of the community is not acceptable.
- A mural dedicated to Vieques by the Puerto Rico Collective included a Lares flag. While they were working on it, a man reacted, "What is that flag doing beside the Puerto Rican flag? Several attempts were made to explain to him that the flag depicted was from El Grito de Lares and not Dominican. Ironically, the Lares flag was inspired in the flag of the Dominican Republic that was an independent nation when the Cry of Lares.
- Other erasures were found on murals representing people of the community. It is known that turf rivalry motivates the defacement of some memorials.

Semiotic Lines and Thematas

What are the narrative linkages among topics and themes? What are the dimensions sustaining the meanings of the iconic matrix? The community muralism of El Barrio represents a fin de siècle struggle that reflects in its iconography a dimension of resistance-repression regarding Puerto Rican cultural identity (see Figure 9.1), This axis is evident in the preponderance of political themes depicted in the murals. Another dimension of the iconography is the semiotic axis related to hope-desolation in the midst of a situation of poverty and oppression. This dimension registers the suffering of Puerto Rican people and is evident most poignantly in the mural representation of religious themes and memorials to those, often the young, who have died. To understand this sphere of oppression, which is an expression of "internal colonialism,"[42] we would have to mention how pockets of extreme poverty have been created in the urban environment and how members of this community have developed a social identity that narrates a chronicle of desolation.

It is our interpretation that the axis of resistance-repression pertains more directly to Puerto Rico's colonial relationship to the United States, whereas the axis of hope-desolation relates to the condition of internal colonialism for those residing on the mainland. However, these are not independent vectors but rather interlocking forces that create a dynamic tension. The intertwined dimensions of resistance-repression and hope-desolation act as visual voices. For example, in Figure 9.2 a graffiti comment transforms an icon signifying sacrifice into a message of freedom.

Social representations embedded in El Barrio's muralism seem structured along dimensions leading to psychological processes of affirmation or suffering. On the one hand, the positive interaction of the dimensions of hope and resistance leads to a process of affirmation that seems to follow the primary objectives of contemporary mural making, those of cultural identity and social protest.[43] On the other hand, the interaction of desolation and repression leads to a process of suffering.

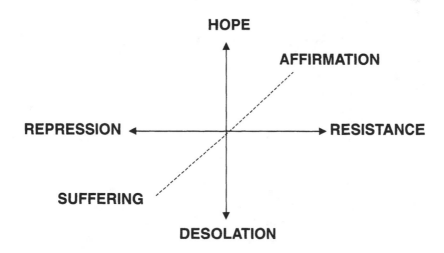

Given these dimensions, what are the thematas that potentiate pro-cesses? Thematas function as nuclear contents to the social representations. On the positive side, concerning the condition of affirmation, we recognized thematas such as the need to forge ahead and the struggle for independence.

On the negative side, regarding the condition of suffering, we recognized themata such as social/political subjugation and the protection of higher powers while facing dangers.

A belief system and an affective component sustain the themata potentiating processes. For instance, flags strongly pull for a *sentir patriótico* and grief is worked through in memorials. Religious imagery powerfully presents *Nuestro Via Crucis* as people targeted by social epidemics. Only the strongest determination can face the extent of our marginality. In an age of skepticism about nationalist discourses, it is impressive how muralism constructs a cultural defense anchored in narratives and icons establishing a sense of "invented tradition."[44]

Pan-Latinism

An inspection of the cultural confluences portrayed in murals suggests emerging social representations. However, these are not yet widely used and lack a nucleus because they are in flux. According to Moscovici, social representations should show a patterned "figurative nucleus, a complex of images that visibly reproduces a complex of ideas."[45] Hence, the question is, Do these emerging social representations constitute a crystallized social identity? To answer this, we attend to the issue of structuralization of social representations.

Icons were defined as pan-Latin depending on the association of contiguous Latin American cultural confluences. This definition of pan-Latinism was based on the thinking of López and Espíritu. Cultural confluences can be associated into levels of social influences forming attitudes and beliefs. Three levels of cultural confluences emerged in the murals: identification, exchange, and proximity.

Identification was clearly displayed with joined flags (e.g., Puerto Rico's and Cuba's) or the concurrence of political heroes (e.g., Albizu Campos and Che Guevara). Most often, the classical amalgamation of national symbols conveyed a sense of latinidad. A remarkable example is a mural of the flags of Puerto Rico, Mexico, and the Dominican Republic united under the title *El Barrio* (see Figure 9.3) Although not entirely explicit, this may suggest that nationalistic imagery is not abandoned in favor of latinidad; instead, the images are juxtaposed, forming a periphery to the core identity in recognition that these groups are living in the same neighborhood but that each one remains attached to its own nationality. Some murals exhibit a duality in terms of affirming Puerto Rican/Latino topics. For instance, there is a salsa mural that connects Puerto Rican musicians to the Cuban Celia Cruz and Panamanian Rubén Blades. Although this mural provides an iconic Latino message, it bears the message "Celebrating Puerto Rican Musicians" and is adorned only with Puerto Rican flags. In the arena of music there is another mural dedicated to a Latino rap artist, but underneath appears "Puerto Rico." The Latino nomenclature is also used in a mural advertising a music store called Casa Latina. If the definition of pan-Latinism is enlarged to include not only Latinos, then other examples emerge. Such is the case with a mural dedicated to Comandante Marcos, José Martí, the Young Lords, and Malcolm X. All of these figures represent an ethnic/racial group that has been an integral part of the community. Hence, at the highest level, cultural confluences are structured by identification.

In an intermediate level, cultural confluences are structured by exchange. An example of this type of exchange is a Santería mural by Cuban artist Salvador González with the dedication "Al Barrio Latino." Thus, another common denominator among Latinos is popular religion. Religious and memorial murals are richly immersed in a version of popular Catholic iconography. Therefore, in broad terms, cultural confluences coincide in three areas: politics (flags and heroes), music (salsa, bolero, rap) and religion (Santería and Catholicism).

If the notion of pan-Latinism is extended to consider proximity, then we find the prints of other groups. For instance, in two murals dedicated to Mexican popular figures, one for the singer Selena, and the other for revolutionary hero Emiliano Zapata, James de la Vega explicitly authored a welcoming to Mexican immigrants from Puerto Ricans of El Barrio.[46] In this zone of cultural contact and transculturation,[47] we see several murals representing new Others in El Barrio: non-Hispanic Caribbeans, Africans, Mexicans, and Dominicans. References are also made to the established African American group sharing East Harlem.

Location

Another analysis performed concerned the location of murals. We observed that murals are designed to be seen, that they are meant to resignify the environment in which they act as visual voices. Murals are intended to reach particular publics and places in the neighborhood, people whose lives transverse and interact on those specific streets. The location of a painting invites a dialogue between mural and community. To this effect De la Vega said, "The placement of the painting is very important. It is an art in itself". For example, neighboring 104th Street we found many murals (e.g., *The Spirit of East Harlem, Nuestro Barrio, Celebrando Nuestra Cultura*, and *El Framboyán*). This street has witnessed a long historical trajectory of the Puerto Rican community.[48]

Murals are close to commercial areas such as Lexington and Third Avenues. Merchants of El Barrio, for example, seem to use Puerto Rican symbols to protect themselves from potential vandalism and stimulate local commerce.[49] Murals are also on the way to subway stations located at 103rd and 110th streets. A large number of community people walk by these streets every day, making these walls into a public gallery. Therefore, although community history may be unrecorded and officially ignored, murals serve as a tool of popular education to anchor memory and collective action. In general, murals in the community are respected when placing propaganda, i.e., usually people do not plaster flyers over the murals but neatly incorporate them with the rest of the wall.

People sometimes superimpose graffiti comments on murals. For instance, on a mural by De la Vega about *The Last Supper,* people responded in graffiti writing "Cristo sana y salva." De la Vega commented that "graffiti and murals live on each other, both express." Graffiti response is one of the ways in which the dialogue between muralist and community occurs. In fact, graffiti is part of the vernacular of Puerto Rican youth. Puerto Rican artists who have dominated the graffiti medium developed the memorial mural genre.

Other ways by which dialogue is stimulated is by indenting chunky verbal texts and by community celebrations (inaugurating murals or performing wakes in memorials). In itself, the creation of a mural is a group activity. Muralist Annabelli Rivera told us that when she and her friends were painting a mural of Vieques, people would often stop and talk about their relationship to Puerto Rico.[50] James De la Vega and María Domínguez also had incorporated young students in their mural works.

Authorship

A methodological problem with the analysis of murals is that De la Vega has authored many murals in El Barrio, limiting a generalization from the material. In fact, it has been argued that he might be overrepresenting himself, seeking celebrity on the basis of his privileged education or sponsorship from a community agency. De la Vega has authored 113 murals; 115 were produced by other artists/makers. Of interest is that De la Vega's main themes are People and Religion. The fact that the majority of murals with a political theme are not by De la Vega is important given that, in the total sample, that is the most popular theme. Other themes not dominated by De la Vega are the Memorial and Commercial categories. Nevertheless, De la Vega's muralism shows a wide range of categories.

There are issues about who is representing what agenda. Table 9.1 provides a survey of authors, agents, and sponsors. As can be seen in this table, there is a wide array of authors on the scene coinciding with political groups that favor *independentismo* for the island. Some artists, such as De la Vega, seem to be moving toward commercialization, but others, such as María Domínguez, hold steadfastly to artistic and political meanings. Hope Community, Inc., is relatively vested in sponsoring local murals that make the neighborhood attractive, given its crusade for affordable housing. A ques-

Table 9.1

Authors, Groups, and Sponsors of Murals Representing Puerto Rican
Cultural Identity and Confluences

Authors	
De la Vega	Oliver Rios
Puerto Rican Collective	No signature
Comité Afirmación Puertorriqueña	Unclear signature
The Death Squad	Wippler
Maria Domínguez et. al.	Vagabond
Zena	Daisy Pagán
TATS cru	Shark Unit Gear Inc.
Manny Vega et. al.	Brother Lee
Oyola	Vivian Linares et al.
Raimund	Nitza Tufiño
Salvador	Colion
Augie	Mig & Mari

Political Groups
Puerto Rican Collective
Comité Afirmación Puertorriqueña
ARM

Sponsors
HOPE Community
Cityarts Workshop
El Museo del Barrio
Metropolitan Transit Authority

tion for the future is how sponsors will play into this field, potentially changing the shape of social representations in performative scenarios.

CONCLUSION

In sum, the current mural movement of East Harlem is not simply the result of the authorship of James de la Vega and the mural project of El Museo del Barrio. The murals that embellish walls, mailboxes, storefronts, empty lots, gardens, and casitas in East Harlem should be read as aesthetic strategies of survival, resistance, and self-affirmation in the context of savage capitalism (i.e., economic restructuring), urban gentrification, and abject racialization that characterize the current neo-liberal period of world capitalist modernity and its local manifestation in the global city.

The murals of El Barrio embody images that are expressive of cultural strategies for affirming Puerto Rican identity and dignity in opposition to the colonial conditions of Puerto Rico and Puerto Ricans. The community murals under consideration are also expressive of the negotiations of nationality and pan-ethnicity that are so central to the very definition of latinidad. In our study the main focus was in the relationship between puertorriqueñidad and latinidad. El Barrio, as its familiar name connotes, has historically been a bastion of both puertorriqeunization and latinization. As latinization increasingly means dominicanization and mexicanization, the murals of El Barrio signify both the affirmation of puertorriqueñidad and the increasing significance of latinidad for Puerto Rican identities as well as for the shifting meanings of El Barrio and its Latino/a identities and cultures.

Murals serve as frameworks for the retrieval of memory and as spaces to perform rituals of community making. The community murals of El Barrio express and serve as a platform for the negotiations of space, culture, and identity between the long-term Puerto Rican community of East Harlem and the new Latino immigrants who are transforming the visual economy of the neighborhood. As visual voices they speak loudly about the complex and contradictory processes through which Puerto Rican and other Latino/a identities are conceived and enacted. In this respect murals act as public signatures to transgress the colonial violence that provokes invisibility. As long as El Barrio is able to survive the corrosive forces of gentrification and racial vilification, in so far as its Latino residents can effectively fight against the attempts from the anglocore establishment to colonize public space in the city and particularly to relegate Puerto Rican and Latino popular cultures to invisibility; as an art form through which subaltern sectors appropriate and redefine public space to claim collective memory, identity, and dignity; community murals indicate the pulse of the culture wars and social struggles of El Barrio.

NOTES

1. French psychologist and originator of the widely known theory of social representations, whose work has been disseminated in a number of articles and books in Europe and North America.
2. One of the limitations to the study of the Puerto Rican community in East Harlem arises from the lack of publications about the social, cultural, and political history of Puerto Ricans in this neighborhood. The occasional articles in newspapers, magazines, and journals and the mentions in books don't fill the need for a history of El Barrio. In addition, taking into consideration that the Puerto Rican presence in East Harlem did not happen in a vacuum, there is a need for comparative research linking Puerto Ricans with other ethnic and racial groups who have shared the neighborhood, African Americans, Italians, Dominicans, and Mexicans among others. Robert Orsi's essay, "The

Religious Boundaries of an Inbetween People: Street Feste and the Problem of the Dark-Skinned Other in Italian Harlem, 1920–1990," *American Quarterly* 44, no. 3 (1992): 313–47, represents a work comparable to the one to which we are referring.

3. David López and Yan Espíritu, "Panethnicity in the United States: A Theoretical Framework," *Ethnic and Racial Studies* 13, no. 2 (1990): 198–224. The authors define panethnicity as "the development of bridging organizations and solidarities among subgroups of ethnic collectivities" (98). Also see the definition by Juan Flores in "Pan-Latino/Trans-Latino: Puerto Ricans in the New Nueva York" *Centro* 8, nos. 1 and 2 (1996): 176: "Latinos as a 'pan-ethnicity,' a group formation that emerges out of the interaction or close historical congruence of two or more culturally related ethnicities."

4. Ed Vega, "The Mythic Village of El Barrio," in *Spanish Harlem,* ed. Joseph Rodriguez (Washington, D.C.: National Museum of American Art, 1994), 7–16.

5. Edwin Meléndez, "The Economic Development of El Barrio," in *Borderless Borders: US Latinos, Latin Americans and the Paradox of Interdependence,* ed. Frank Bonilla, Edwin Meléndez, Rebecca Morales, and María de los Angeles Torres (Philadelphia: Temple University Press, 1998), 105–27.

6. Christopher Hanson-Sánchez, *New York City Latino Neighborhoods Data Book* (New York: Institute for Puerto Rican Policy, 1996).

7. R. G. Mendoza and C. Torres, "Hispanic Community Murals and Social Technology," in *Handbook of Hispanic Cultures in the United States: Anthropology,* ed. Nicolás Kanellos and Claudio Esteva-Fabregat (Houston: Arte Público Press, 1994), 77–84.

8. Luis Aponte-Parés, "What's Yellow and White and Has a Land Around It?: Appropriating Place in Puerto Rican Barrios," *CENTRO* 7, no.1 (Winter 1994/ Spring 1995): 11–13. The author states that "casitas built around the City belong to a family of balloon-frame wooden structures-shacks, bungalows or cottages—generally identified with Third World vernacular architecture" (10).

9. Jeffrey Cornwell, "James De la Vega," *Folk Art Messenger* (Summer 1998): 13.

10. María Domínguez, interview in New York by the author, February 12, 1999. [That mural movement reflected a change. . . . Public art has the power to reflect to the community an upcoming change, and the mural that I did in El Barrio, *Nuestro Barrio,* which is on 104th Street, I did with the pure intention of reflecting Puerto Rican culture, which one day won't exist in El Barrio. Then I selected El Taller Boricua, one of the early established organizations, the Marqueta, El Museo del Barrio, the Harbor Conservatory for Music. . . . Who should inherit El Barrio will have nothing.]

11. Serge Moscovici, "The Phenomenon of Social Representations," in *Social Representations.* ed. R. M. Farr and Serge Moscovici (Cambridge, England: Cambridge University Press, 1984), 28.

12. Serge Moscovici, "Notes Towards a Description of Social Representations," *European Journal of Social Psychology* 18: 220.

13. Moscovici, "The Phenomenon of Social Representations," 17.

14. Serge Moscovici, "Cognition and Culture," class offered in 1992, The New School for Social Research, New York.

15. Moscovici, "Notes Towards a Description of Social Representations," 221. Likewise, Daniel Mato, "On the Making of Transnational Identities in the Age

of Globalization: The US Latina/o 'Latin American' case," *Cultural Studies* 12, no. 4 (1998): 598–620, argues that "identities are not legacies passively received but representations socially produced, and—in this sense—matters of social dispute" (598).

16. Hanson-Sánchez, *New York City Latino Neighborhoods Data Book,* 325–35.

17. Lawrence R. Chenault, *The Puerto Rican Migrant in New York City* (New York: Russell and Russell, 1970), 63.

18. U.S. Department of Labor, Bureau of Labor Statistics, *A Socioeconomic Profile of Puerto Rican New Yorkers.* New York: U.S. Department of Labor, Middle Atlantic Regional Office, Regional Report 46 (July 1975), 8–32.

19. Francisco Rivera-Batiz and Carlos Santiago, *Puerto Ricans in the United States: A Changing Reality* (Washington, D.C.: Puerto Rican National Coalition, 1994), 20–24.

20. Vega, "The Mythic Village of El Barrio," 7.

21. Juan González, "Cultures Clash at Church in El Barrio," *Daily News,* January 10, 1997, pp. 6, 30.

22. Aponte-Parés, "What's Yellow and White," 12.

23. Allan W. Barnett, *Community Murals: People's Art* (New York: Art Alliances Press, 1984).

24. The mural art tradition in Puerto Rico is not discussed in this essay. *La Gran Enciclopedia de Puerto Rico* (San Juan, Puerto Rico, 1976) contains information about this topic.

25. The historical interpretation of Orozco was controversial in the work performed at the Baker Library of Dartmouth College. The mural commissioned to Rivera by John D. Rockefeller was censored for having included the image of Lenin. Part of the censorship to which these artists were submitted was based on anticommunist sentiments toward the artists' socialist positions, which were reflected in themes such as agrarian reform, revolution, and anti-imperialism in their murals.

26. James De la Vega, interview in New York by the author, February 11, 1999.

27. Karal Ann Marling, *Wall to Wall: A Cultural History of Post-Office Murals in the Great Depression* (Minneapolis: University of Minnesota Press, 1982), 88. Also see Carlos Rodríguez-Fraticelli, "U.S. Solidarity with Puerto Rico: Rockwell Kent, 1937," in *Colonial Dilemma: Critical Perspectives on Contemporary Puerto Rico,* ed. Edwin Meléndez and Edgardo Meléndez, (Boston: South End Press, 1993), 189–98.

28. Allan W. Barnett, *Community Murals: Peoples Art* (New York: Art Alliances Press, 1984), 217–19.

29. Ibid., 215.

30. *The New York Times,* March 16, 1998, p. E3.

31. In the words of Alfredo (Freddy) Hernández, a Lower East Side muralist, the reason to use walls in the murals is that "people enjoy seeing them, seeing a painting in the streets." Quoted in Philip Pocock, *The Obvious Illusion: Murals from the Lower East Side* (New York: George Braziller in association with the Cooper Union for the Advancement of Science and Art, 1980), 16.

32. Barnett, *Community Murals: People's Art,* 17; Pocock, *The Obvious Illusion,* 7.

33. Jorge Duany, "Imagining the Puerto Rican Nation: Recent Works on Cultural Identity," *Latin American Research Review* 31, no. 3 (1996): 252.

34. El Barrio is located within the physical boundaries of East Harlem. Both

terms *(El Barrio/East Harlem)* are used interchangeably, although the boundaries of El Barrio have changed historically.

35. María Domínguez, interview.
36. See Arlene Dávila, *Sponsored Identities: Cultural Politics in Puerto Rico* (Philadelphia: Temple University Press, 1997).
37. Pedro Albizu Campos was an anticolonial patriot and president of the Nationalist Party in Puerto Rico who advocated for the independence of Puerto Rico.
38. Taino is the name Spaniards gave to the native peoples of the island of Puerto Rico (that indeed was called Borikén by the Amerindians).
39. Martha Copper and Joseph Sciorra, *R.I.P. Memorial Wall Art* (New York: Henry Holt, 1994).
40. Other routes of expression of cultural identity are popular religious icons such as saints, virgins, Christ, and *Los Tres Reyes Magos*. In fact, El Museo del Barrio organizes the traditional parade of the Three Kings. Cultural topics such as the flamboyán tree, tropical palms, *amapolas* (poppy flower), and *mangles* (mangrove) seem to nostalgically evoke the island's natural beauty. Customs/Folk themes represent traditional domino games, the fable of the chupacabra and *refranes populares* (proverbs, such as "la muerte en bicicleta" and the characteristic expression of "Ay Bendito!").
41. Luis Muñoz Marín was a politician, poet, and leader of the Popular Democratic Party, advocating for an autonomous relationship with the United States. He was the first Puerto Rican elected as governor of the island in 1948. For the concept of internal colonialism, see Mario Barrera, *Race and Class in the Southwest: A Theory of Racial Inequality.* (Notre Dame: University of Notre Dame Press, 1979), and Robert Blauner, *Racial Oppression in America* New York: Harper & Row, 1972).
42. For the concept of internal colonialism, see Mario Barrera, *Race and Class in the Southwest: A Theory of Racial Inequality.* (Notre Dame: University of Notre Dame Press, 1979), and Robert Blauner, *Racial Opression in America,* (New York: Harper & Row, 1972). Ramón Grosfoguel, "The Divorce of Nationalists Discourses from the Puerto Rican People: A Sociohistorical Perspective," in *Puerto Rico Jam: Rethinking Colonialism and Nationalism,* ed. Frances Negrón-Montaner and Ramón Grosfoguel (Minneapolis: University of Minnesota Press, 1997), 57–76.
43. Barnett, *Community Murals: People's Art.*
44. Jorge Duany, "Después de la modernidad: debates contemporáneos sobre cultura y política en Puerto Rico," *Revista de Ciencias Sociales,* Nueva Epoca 5 (1998): 218–41.
45. Moscovici, "The Phenomenon of Social Representations," 38.
46. De la Vega, interview.
47. According to Pratt, *contact zones* are "social spaces where disparate cultures meet, clash, and grapple with each other, often in highly asymmetrical relations of domination and subordination." Mary Louise Pratt, *Imperial Eyes: Towards Writing and Acculturation* (New York: Routledge, 1992), 4.
48. See Piri Thomas, *Down These Mean Streets* (New York: Knopf, 1967).
49. Meléndez, "The Economic Development of El Barrio."
50. Annabelli Rivera, interview in San Juan, Puerto Rico, by the author, July 20, 1999.

FIGURE 4. Los Pleneros de la 21 in the "Festival de las Cruces" in El Barrio, mid 1980s. Photo by Máximo Colón

FIGURE 5. Break dancing in West 92nd Street. Photo by Máximo Colón 1984

FIGURE 6. A rendition of the Mexican, Dominican Republic, and Puerto Rican flags by an unknown artist in El Barrio, the Latino community in East Harlem. Photo by Elsa B. Cardalda Sánchez and Amílcar Tirado Avilés

FIGURE 7. The Spirit of East Harlem, mural by Hank Prussing and Manuel Vega. Photo by Arlene Dávila

PART III

Latino/a Identities and the Politics of Space and Place

CHAPTER TEN

Making Loisaida

Placing Puertorriqueñidad in Lower Manhattan

Liz Ševčenko

> He had been born in Loisaida: his mother had told him that in Puerto Rico there was a village of blacks in which the slave prison of a sugar cane refinery had been, that the village was named Loíza and the Rio Grande flowed nearby, its crystal waters becoming like mulch each time Ochún bathed in the waters of his love. His mother had told him what at first seemed to be an African fairy tale, that the first Puerto Rican emigrant who arrived in Loisaida had been born in Loíza Aldea and that he, only he, had baptized this impoverished neighborhood with the sacred name of Loisaida. . . . He knew that his mother's insanity had made it possible for him to feel at home in this world and to know his real name.
>
> —*Manuel Ramos Otero, "The Point-Blank Page."*[1]

In 1976, real estate developers described the area just north of Houston Street as a "vast wasteland." One out of every five lots was either empty or contained the remains of crumbling, abandoned buildings.[2] From this rubble a handful of Puerto Rican community organizers built Loisaida: a territory, a movement, and an identity constructed to claim resources for the working-class residents of the area. The making of Loisaida—officially the area between Houston and 14th streets and between Avenue A and the East River—stamped a new Puerto Rican territory on the map of Manhattan and marked a significant step in the latinization of New York City. But from its birth in the mind of a poet in 1974 to its officialization in a street sign in 1987, Loisaida was about more than claiming space as Puerto Rican. The Loisaida movement, as it came to be called, constructed a neighborhood-specific discourse of puertorriqueñidad born from its political relationship to urban space. The movement organizers' goals were to mobilize the neighborhood's majority Spanish-speaking but multi-ethnic residents to claim their rights to city land and resources. They therefore needed to develop a discourse of puertorriqueñidad that could build a multicultural coalition—among Puerto Ricans, Argentineans, Cubans, Eastern European Jews, and others—and establish a historical claim to land. The Loisaida movement did more than claim streets and services; it suggested a new physical and discursive place for Puerto Ricans and puertorriqueñidad in the postindustrial city.

Discourses of latinidad had an ambiguous relationship to place in New York City in the half-century before Loisaida. Although by the 1920s East Harlem already housed the majority of Puerto Ricans and other Latinos living in New York, the name El Barrio was not yet commonly applied to it. Instead, those working to build unity among Spanish-speaking New Yorkers used the concept of *la colonia hispana,* which denoted a group of people who shared a common regional, class, or political background but was not defined on any geographical area in the city. Puerto Rican socialist and communist organizations, for instance, who were very active in organizing tobacco workers and other Latino laborers in New York in the 1920s and 1930s, called their membership "the Hispanic workers' colony."[3] The workers' colonia, as these labor organizations defined it, was a community of people who knew each other or of each other individually and were connected by a common cause, though they might not live in the same area. On the other hand, "Notas de la Colonia," the society section of *La Prensa,* the primary Spanish-language newspaper in the city, established the boundaries of the bourgeois Latino community.[4] By 1950, the more geographically restricted term *El Barrio* began to circulate more widely. It often described "the most typical" and "most picturesque . . . of all the Hispanic sectors in the city" but did not assert a political claim to the space.[5] The celebration of El Barrio was soon mitigated by Puerto Rican advisors to the War on Poverty, who believed that the best way to lift the Latino out of the ghetto was to disassociate latinidad from particular neighborhoods and promote instead a citywide, assimilated community.[6] The Loisaida movement's struggle to make a political claim to local territory and the discourses of puertorriqueñidad it used to make them—born from the specific circumstances of deindustrializing New York—disrupted previous conceptions of la colonia hispana and the Puerto Rican community.

THE CREATION OF THE LOISAIDA LANDSCAPE

In the 1960s and 1970s, the landscape of the Lower East Side and other working-class neighborhoods of the city changed dramatically. As part of a nationwide deindustrialization of urban economies, the manufacturing industries that had employed a large number of the neighborhood's Puerto Rican residents relocated to areas outside New York City. Between 1960 and 1975, 55 percent of the city's manufacturing jobs disappeared.[7] These trends combined with deliberate strategies by the city and private investors to place a growing number of Puerto Ricans below the poverty level. Landlords, for instance, saw little hope of recovering any profits from their tenants, the majority of whom had little money to spend on rent. All over the Lower East Side, landlords stopped investing in the upkeep of their buildings but continued to collect rent until tenants abandoned their apartments. Their ultimate goal was to make the buildings disappear: some stopped paying real estate taxes and waited for the city to seize the building and take the responsibility off their hands; others torched the buildings, hoping to salvage some lost earnings in insurance money. This disinvestment was compounded by banks and insurance companies, who "redlined" certain areas from which they withheld investment money.[8] Finally, city government hammered the final nail in the coffin of New York's poor neighborhoods. Desperately seeking a way out of the fiscal crisis of the early 1970s, New York's Housing and Development Administrator initiated a policy of "planned shrinkage," in which the city would cut all spending on services such as fire stations and public schools in poor neighborhoods, making these sections of the city uninhabitable and forcing people to leave so that the city could bulldoze these areas.[9]

The result was a landscape of deteriorating buildings that were either abandoned or without services such as heat or hot water and of rubble-strewn empty lots from buildings that had been demolished. By 1976, there were 100 vacant lots and 150 vacant buildings in the thirty-six-block area between Avenue A and the East River and between Houston and 14th streets.[10]

In response to these conditions, a large number of residents began to move out of the neighborhood. In just five years, between 1974 and 1979, the Lower East Side as a whole lost two-thirds of its population.[11] The drop was even more severe in the northeastern section, which housed the greatest number of Puerto Ricans. Between 1970 and 1980, the number of people living in the blocks from avenues B and C and from 3rd and 12th streets dropped from 14,908 to 4,597.[12] This exodus was not part of the nationwide, so-called white flight, in which middle-class white residents abandoned deteriorating inner cities to poorer people of color. García remembers that "a lot of the working-class people left the neighborhood" and that many of them were Puerto Rican.[13]

But although the barrio of the Lower East Side, like El Barrio and the South Bronx, was abandoned by investors, city government, and its own residents, it faced additional territorial pressures unknown to other Latino enclaves because of its position in the city. Sandwiched between Greenwich Village and Soho, two recently gentrified neighborhoods, and minutes from Wall Street, the new economic center of the city, the northern Lower East Side was, despite appearances to the contrary, ripe for reinvestment. The biggest threat to Puerto Rican working-class survival in the Lower East Side came from the rash of speculative development that began in the late 1970s. More than anything else, it was the threat of gentrification—the threat of the disappearance of affordable housing and displacement of working-class residents—that inspired activists to make a concerted claim to the neighborhood. In 1977, local housing organizers Ruth and Roberto Nazario implored, "Will the reinvestments occur as rehabilitation of the existing housing stock, or will the neighborhood first be reduced to uninhabited piles of rubble, the community scattered to the winds, so the new construction becomes the only remaining alternative? Who will have the opportunity to live in the new and improved Lower East Side?"[14]

The mid-1970s was a crucial moment for the abandoned northern Lower East Side. The neighborhood was destroyed but was on the brink of a momentous transformation whose future benefits were as of yet unclaimed. To save the neighborhood for the Puerto Rican and other working-class people who lived there, activists realized they needed to claim the barren terrain before someone else did. They needed to define it publicly for themselves and the city at large before it was defined in the interests of outside investors. Their task was not only to claim a geographical territory but to endow this urban space with an identity and an ideology that would support its residents' needs.

THE NAMING OF LOISAIDA

The most powerful way to claim an urban territory and define its identity is to give it a name. In the early 1970s, the northeastern section of the Lower East Side did not have one. Abandonment, the rise of poverty, and the rise of drugs and drug-related crime had erased the neighborhood from the map of palatable New York. As part of their preparation for reinvestment, developers began to look for new ways to name the area, to give the wasteland a marketable identity. Community organizer Chino García remembers:

> One of the biggest problems we were having then was gentrification. So therefore, what gives flame to this gentrification? Names of neighborhoods. They begin to rename areas like Soho, Noho, so we knew . . . that's the mechanism that some people use for this type of thing. Usually, it's in order to chase out the poor.[15]

Neighborhood activists began to mobilize to make their own claim to the territory in the interests of its poor and working-class residents. The first step was to define its boundaries and develop a concept of it as a separate, locally organized entity. Community organizations and concerned residents began to formalize their discussions about the nature and the future of the neighborhood in regularly scheduled, public *reuniones del pueblo,* which was translated into English as "town meetings," evoking a bucolic community shielded from the industrial anonymity of the city at large.

Initially, organizers at these town meetings sought to reclaim the heritage of the Lower East Side, to put the "town" on the map by associating it with an important space in the city's—and the nation's—history. García explained:

> In the early 70s we was trying to look for a name to call the
> neighborhood because the developers was already calling it
> Alphabet City, the East Village, and they started using names
> like that in order to make it attractive, to start selling property,
> to the outsiders, to the gentrifiers. They won't use names like the
> Lower East Side. They used names like the East Village, because
> that makes it more attractive. . . So in a conscious manner,
> organizations like Charas, Adopt-A-Building, and other
> community organizations, we had a few Town Meetings in the
> early 70s, and that was one of the discussions that we was
> concerned was the fact that we should plug the name, the 'Lower
> East Side,' more. The Lower East Side itself is a historical
> neighborhood, one of the neighborhoods in this country that got
> the most history, I think.[16]

For García and his colleagues, the power of the name *Lower East Side* lay in its ability to give its residents a strong history and heritage. But the historical identity of the Lower East Side, and therefore the identity it would bestow on its current residents, was a fiercely contested one in the 1960s and 1970s. Writing about the decision a few years later, a group of activists remembered that claiming the history of the Lower East Side had at first seemed a powerful way to legitimize a working-class, immigrant claim to the neighborhood. It had a "rich cultural and political history . . . as the home of poor immigrants for two centuries ." But what was the meaning, or memory, of the poor immigrant? On the one hand, it evoked a noble struggle, the rags part of the rags-to-riches story. If Lower East Side residents identified themselves with this story, their current poverty would seem a temporary condition, nothing more than a brief chapter in an inevitable narrative of upward mobility. On the other hand, the poor immigrant and poverty could be associated with destitution and social decay: "The name Lower East Side connotes poverty and crime," the activists worried, and as such was a 'stigmatic name.' "[17] In a moment when unemployment among Puerto Ricans and other Latinos was rising rapidly, accompanied by an explosion of writing by social scientists and political commentators condemning the failure of the new immigrants to assimilate and advance in comparison to their European predecessors, the legend of upward mobility that the Lower East Side contained threatened to reinforce racist discourses of urban pathology and the punitive policies they produced.

Ultimately, the most important consideration was that the name be a simple, effective organizing tool. Rather than adopt the name *the Lower East Side,* organizers Latinized it for the area's Spanish-speaking residents. During the time the name *Lower East Side* was being revived, Chino García and Bimbo Rivas, a local poet and activist, were collaborating on a play entitled *Don Quixote of the Lower East Side.* García remembers:

> We felt that that name, *The Lower East Side,* was too long. So we wanted to come out with a more simple name. So Bimbo then used the technique of Spanglish, which is a mixture of English and Spanish, and said, "Let's call it *El Don Quixote de Loisaida."* Some people asked, "Why you call it Loisaida? What's that?" And we explained that Puerto Ricans have a hard time saying *Lower East Side,* so we figured we'd give a Spanish rhythm to it, and it's easier for them to pronounce.[18]

The name *Loisaida* was born in the Adirondack mountains in 1974 when Bimbo Rivas, on a writing retreat with Chino García, composed the poem "Loisaida." Part of it reads:

> Lower East Side
> I love you
> You're my lady fair
> No Matter where I am
> I think of you!
>
> The mountains and the
> valleys cannot compare
> my love, to you.
> Loisaida, I love you!
>
> I dig the way you talk
> I dig the way you look ...
> En mi mente, mi amada,
> yo te llamo Loisaida.

Employing the style of a patriotic ode, the poem worked to communicate a pride in and identification with the neighborhood, crucial for the stabilization of a transient population that was rapidly abandoning the area. The anthem's play between English and Spanish, a hallmark of the emerging Nuyorican literary movement, endowed Loisaida with a specifically Puerto Rican migrant identity.

García argued that the success of the name lay in its ability to be marketed to the community as a cultural product with an accessible slogan:

LS : Why do you think it caught on so fast?

CG: It's easy to pronounce. I think that's a very important
matter. It's like people call Exxon. Exxon, I forgot they used to
have a long name at one time, and then they just changed it to
Exxon. Situations like that, you create names like that. So
Loisaida was perfect, especially for people that didn't know
English, or had a hard time pronouncing *Lower East Side* by
giving them that opportunity of saying *Loisaida.* It was easy.[19]

Loisaida was not to remain a private concept "en mi mente" for long.
Although the name was accessible and immediately popular, it did not naturally attach itself to the neighborhood. García and his colleagues launched
a concerted campaign to promote the name to local residents. In 1974, Pupa
Santiago, a musician working on the Lower East Side, created A Band
Called Loisaida, a music group founded to publicize the name and the ideology it communicated: "This whole attitude of community, and being involved, and going out there and making changes." Santiago "started doing
shows with Bimbo, with the whole entourage, and the word, the concept
started catching on. . . . So out of that whole concept of energy, of going out
there and doing this whole thing, the name started—we started promoting
the name through the band. No one had really heard of the name before we
started promoting it and promoting it."[20]
For their part, García and Rivas promoted Loisaida to local residents
as a place and an identity by performing skits from their play *El Don Quixote
de Loisaida* on the streets of the neighborhood. García recalls:

In the story that we was writing, we did it for that purpose also,
to create a place, a neighborhood, a community, or a village,
called Loisaida. . . . So Bimbo and I used to do a lot of skits. So
then it caught on. People would say, "Where are you from?"
"From Loisaida."[21]

As a result of these marketing efforts, the name was soon made official
and visible in the neighborhood. In the 1975 town meeting at which Bimbo
Rivas first recited his poem "Loisaida," Ruth García Nazario, a resident
involved in community organizing for housing, proposed that the community formally adopt Loisaida as the name of the neighborhood. Soon afterwards, community organizations rehabilitated a building in which to hold
regular meetings and hung a large sign over the door that read "Loisaida
Town House." García remembers: "And it took off, from that town meeting,
people opened up Loisaida restaurant, Loisaida pharmacy, Loisaida incorporated, people started using it."[22] Santiago, too, remembered that "stores
started opening up on the corner, Loisaida Restaurant, over here these peo-

ple started naming another thing Loisaida, and before we knew it, every-body started using the name Loisaida. So it became like a community."[23] By 1978, Freddy's Luncheonette on Avenue C and 4th Street was advertising *comidas loisaideñas* (Loisaidan dishes).[24]

"The Ideology of Loisaida"

Loisaida communicated far more than a place. It was an identity, a belief system, and a social movement. In 1979, Carlos Quiñones, a neighborhood resident, published an article in the local newspaper *Quality of Life in Loisaida/La Calidad de Vida en Loisaida* entitled "The Ideology of Lo-isaida." "To those who are walking around the local streets still not know-ing what is meant by Loisaida, read on," he wrote. For him, the idea went far "beyond the drawing of boundary lines at 14th Street, Houston Street, and Avenue A."[25] For the most part, the many projects to develop the neigh-borhood were self-help efforts that depended not only on the support but also on the active participation of the community. To inspire large numbers of people to unite to change their immediate environment, organizers had to do far more than mark territory as the property of a particular ethnic group. They had to endow this territory with a meaning and identity that would support their efforts. They did so by defining the identity of the neighborhood and its people as an Afro–Puerto Rican struggle to defend the values of working-class autonomy and self-help. The neighborhood and the people who lived there both came to be referred to as the Loisaida movement, in which the fight to save urban space was equated with a fight to save a people and an ideology. The language of puertorriqueñidad that the movement produced thus articulated both a physical and a discursive space for Puerto Ricans in the postindustrial city.

Loisaidan activists worked to define a cultural identity for the neigh-borhood and its residents that reflected the new experiences of Puerto Ri-cans in New York. Perhaps more than any other efforts, what put Loisaida on the map was the intense activity of artists, musicians, and poets who gave shape to the idea of what came to be known as Nuyorican culture and language starting in the mid-1970s. The work of the Nuyorican poets and musicians, like that of other Loisaida organizers, was related to the neigh-borhood and the efforts to improve its physical conditions. The most widely acclaimed institution was the Nuyorican Poet's Café, founded in 1976 as a place where artists and other Loisaidans gathered to listen to readings of local poets. Miguel Algarín, founder of the café, believed that poets could play a crucial role in the transformation of urban neighborhoods. "The poet juggles with every street corner east of First Avenue and south of Four-teenth Street ending at the Brooklyn Bridge," he wrote, alluding to the boundaries of Loisaida. "Poetry is the full act of naming. Naming states of mind . . . . To stay free is not theoretical. It is to take over your immediate environment."[26]

In their play *El Don Quixote de Loisaida,* Chino García and Bimbo Rivas named Loisaida to encourage idealism and community action, spreading this idea through the skits they performed in the streets of the neighborhood. García remembers that the play "is about a neighborhood more than anything else, and how two Puerto Rican guys . . . solve the problems of the neighborhood." Rivas writes:

> Loisaida, like Dulcenea [sic] , the heroine of Don Miguel de Cervantes's *Don Quixote*, is an entity that dwells in the minds of its creators and its lovers. . . . With the purest motivation in his own conviction [Quixote] embarks upon a series of adventures all leading toward the rescue and liberation of his princess.[27]

Though the struggle to resume a neighborhood devastated by abandonment, drugs, and crime might seem quixotic, Rivas and García argued that if the community could retain a blind faith and idealism, they just might succeed.

Pupa Santiago also used the name to communicate ideology as well as territory. He remembers:

> We started promoting it, not only like a word, or a community, but as a state of mind, as a type of fight back. Because at that time, we were telling people, "Listen. The Lower East Side's getting gentrified. Pretty soon they're gonna burn down this whole neighborhood and then a whole bunch of people are gonna come in and claim it, and then all these people are gonna have to move out and a lot of high rises, and a lot of people with expensive rents, and stuff like that are going to come in."[28]

Loisaida, then, communicated action as well as urban space. Only those people who took action were considered residents of the space. Rivas described organizers and those residents working to improve the neighborhood as "the self-selected citizens of Loisaida." Apathetic neighbors, though they might live on its streets, are nonetheless not "citizens" of this ideological community.

FORGING PUERTORRIQUEÑIDAD LOISAIDEÑA

Integral to the work to improve the physical conditions of the neighborhood, and integral to the ideology of community action in Loisaida, was the development of a *puertorriqueñidad loisaideña* that would effectively mobilize the community and serve the movement's goals. In 1979, Miriam Rivas, director of the dance group Loisaida Folklórica, claimed that

> the purpose of Loisaida is to conserve the Puerto Rican culture.
> By doing so they reaffirm their unity as one people whether from
> the island of Puerto Rico or from the United States. Loisaida
> Folklórica see themselves as part of the Loisaida movement by
> being able to reconstruct their culture while reconstructing their
> buildings.[29]

But what was the Puerto Rican culture to Loisaida activists, and how would it help to mobilize neighborhood residents to take over territory? Puertorriqueñidad loisaideña had four characteristics that activists instrumentalized in their organizing efforts: it stressed Afro-Indian over Spanish heritage, it argued for the inherent multiculturalism of puertorriqueñidad as an ethnicity of many races (African, Indian, and European), it promoted Puerto Ricanness as the umbrella identity of all New York Latinos, and it argued for colonized people's inherent rights to U.S. land. The Loisaida movement, then, involved the self-conscious construction of an ethnic identity that was inextricably linked to urban space.

In constructing this ethnicity, organizers had to negotiate with other discourses of puertorriqueñidad circulating in the city. During the 1950s and 1960s, many Puerto Rican leaders in New York sought to create avenues for middle-class advancement by working to integrate Puerto Rican identity and people into the cultural fabric of the city at large. War on Poverty organizations such as the Puerto Rican Forum combated the image of the unassimilable, isolated ghetto-dweller by promoting a citywide, mainstream middle-class Puerto Rican community through such performances as the Puerto Rican Day Parade. The parade was not attached to a particular neighborhood but marched the same central path down 5th Avenue as many other ethnic parades.

By the late 1960s, the ideal of unified, upwardly mobile de-ethnicized minority groups as symbolized in the Puerto Rican Day Parade suffered attacks from African American, Mexican American, Native American, and other radical ethnic pride movements across the country. Inspired by many of these grassroots efforts, neighborhood-based organizations of working-class Puerto Ricans organized in New York to combat the conditions in which they lived. In so doing, they posed serious challenges to elite definitions of Puerto Rican ethnicity and community. The Young Lords Party and other Puerto Rican national organizations like the Movement for Puerto Rican Independence and the Puerto Rican Socialist Party became impatient with the poverty programs proposed by middle-class leaders, feeling that their assimilationism perpetuated the colonial status of the island

and the subjugation of working-class Puerto Ricans on the mainland. They articulated a new puertorriqueñidad that supported their efforts to organize working-class people of color to protest the deteriorated conditions of their neighborhoods. They spread this message on the Lower East Side through the many community education classes, breakfast programs, and street rallies they held there as well as by distributing newspapers like the Young Lords' *Pàlante* at local newsstands.[30]

The puertorriqueñidad of the Young Lords and other radical Puerto Rican organizations contained three characteristics that would inform the Loisaida movement. First, the Puerto Rican ethnicity and heritage they constructed was a specifically working-class one (embodied in *el jíbaro*, or peasant, who symbolized an ideal of anticolonial self-sufficiency) and was rooted in African and Indian, more than Spanish, race and culture. The Lords' mission was to "unite the two most oppressed classes, the lumpens and the workers, and also the two social groups in which our people are divided, the most oppressed Afro-Puerto Ricans and the jíbaros."[31] They offered classes in Afro–Puerto Rican history on the Lower East Side and around the city, believing that it had important implications for present-day Puerto Ricans:

> All of this information about our African origin is not just good
> to know. For centuries under Spanish colonialism, Puerto Ricans
> suffered from slavery and racism. Today the United States
> continues to try and divide black from lighter-skinned from
> brown Puerto Ricans by trying to indoctrinate us with their
> racism. . . . But we must not allow the oppressor to divide us. . . .
> We are a beautiful, strong, and hard-working people.[32]

The Young Lords' puertorriqueñidad, then, celebrated through both heritage and contemporary culture, was a crucial organizing tool in their struggle to claim rights for oppressed Puerto Ricans.

Second, the Lords' Puerto Rican community was rooted in specific urban neighborhoods. They contested middle-class leaders' vision of an upwardly mobile Puerto Rican community assimilated into the city at large as performed in the Puerto Rican Day Parade. In 1971, the Lords launched a public protest against the parade, arguing that

> the Puerto Rican Day Parade should reflect the reality of life for
> Puerto Ricans. Puerto Ricans are poor and Puerto Rico is a
> colony. . . . We will not allow the parade to become a one-day
> trip to fantasy land, where we march on fifth ave—as if that will
> make us forget what our own barrios are like. The Puerto Rican
> Day Parade will begin in the Puerto Rican community.[33]

The Lords rooted their puertorriqueñidad in local barrios and argued that activism should start there.

Third, and perhaps most important for the Loisaida movement, the Lords argued that as a colonized people, Afro-Indian Puerto Ricans had a historical claim to U.S.—and New York City's—land. Following their legendary occupation of an East Harlem church, the party encouraged poor Puerto Ricans all over the city to seize urban spaces in the name of their identity as a colonized people struggling for control of their own land and institutions. Celebrating the occupation of an abandoned building by several Puerto Rican families in the Bronx, *Pàlante* rejoiced, "The Land is Ours! We're Taking it Back!"

> The white man ripped this land off from our Indian brothers and sisters. Then he drew up pieces of paper, said they represented ownership of the Indians' land, and traded and bought and sold them. Well chump, you ripped it off by force from our brothers and sisters; and now we're ripping it off from you in the name of the Indians, the Puerto Ricans and all Third World People![34]

The Lords' puertorriqueñidad—with its emphasis on Afro-Indian, working-class heritage, neighborhood identity, and historical rights to land—offered Lower East Side activists a language with which to claim Loisaida.

NARRATING ORIGINS, LOCATING ROOTS

Organizers of the Loisaida movement adopted much of their radical predecessors' conceptions of puertorriqueñidad. They created an oppositional, Afro–Puerto Rican heritage for the neighborhood, and by extension its people, by claiming that Loisaida's spiritual origins lay in the like-sounding Puerto Rican village of Loíza Aldea. In claiming this legacy, Loisaida activists had to contend with middle-class interpretations of the village's significance. The contrasting interpretations of the Fiesta de Loíza Aldea, a parade that had been celebrated for many years in Puerto Rico and began to be celebrated in the United States in the 1970s, revealed a contest over how the racial and cultural identity of Loíza—and of the New York neighborhood that claimed it as its legacy—were to be defined. Although the fiesta was held in East Harlem, it was created by a resident of Loisaida, and Loisaidans participated in it. The meaning of the fiesta was interpreted very differently by *El Diario/La Prensa*, a paper that still primarily represented assimilationist, middle-class interests, and by *Palante* and Loisaida cultural organizers. The Fiesta de Loíza Aldea, *El Diario* explained, is "a tradition that Puerto Ricans inherited from the Spanish colonizers of celebrating the festival in honor of Santiago the Apostle, patron saint of Spain."[35] The Young Lords, by contrast, had celebrated Loíza Aldea as a historic site of slave resistance against the Spanish, as the African root of Puerto Rican culture. Because the Africans of Loíza Aldea resisted Spanish occupation, the Lords explained, "Loíza Aldea stayed pure Black and the result is that today in Loíza we have an Afro-Boricua culture which we relate directly back to the original African culture which our forefathers brought with them."[36] Loisaida organizers claimed the African story for Loíza Aldea and, by extension, Loisaida. Bimbo Rivas, the original inventor of Loisaida, described the fiesta as a key celebration in the Loisaida calendar, "a pageantry of dance and chorus reflecting the ancestral heritage the Loisaida citizens received from the African slaves that were brought to Puerto Rico by the Spanish."[37] To publicize this heritage, several music and dance groups organized classes of bomba and plena, two Puerto Rican traditions with strong Afro–Puerto Rican roots, and performed in community spaces and on the streets of Loisaida. The dancers felt that the traditions they communicated would give Loisaidans the strength and understanding they needed to cope with the present-day conditions they faced:

> "La bomba" is a lively rhythmic Puerto Rican folk dance, with echoes from our African ancestors who were brought to the island of Puerto Rico. . . . The Puerto Rican people in the United States are under the same feeling of oppression, although it no longer comes in the same form of slavery. It comes in other disguises such as poor education, unemployment, substandard housing, etc. In spite of all these negative forces, somehow Loisaida Folklórica finds time to love, caress, express, and purify their souls with the beauty transmitted through the centuries in the rhythms, sounds, vibrations and songs of their ancestors.[38]

Rivas and other participants in the Fiesta, then, constructed a history and heritage specific to Loisaida that celebrated the resistance of people of color to European colonial authority, a story that reflected the position of many Loisaida residents.

But Loisaida activists moved beyond the legacy of Afro-Taino pride they inherited from the Young Lords and other radical movements, constructing a puertorriqueñidad that served their specific needs and circumstances. Where the Young Lords worked all over the Northeast to address specifically Puerto Rican concerns on the island and the mainland, the Loisaida movement was concerned with mobilizing the ethnically diverse residents of a single neighborhood. In the 1970s, Puerto Ricans and other Latinos made up less than 70 percent of the total population in Loisaida.[39] Activists would therefore need to create an identity for the neighborhood that simultaneously celebrated ethnic pride and built coalitions across ethnic groups.

The answer lay in constructing a puertorriqueñidad that was inherently multicultural. Many believed in a larger Latino race and culture, itself a mix of three different ethnicities, that was inherently inclusive. One Argentinean organizer explained, "In general, by birth, we [Latinos] have to be more inclusive than other cultures, because when you say *Latin,* even the census is confused here, we have black, we have blond, we have black with blue eyes, we have absolutely everything."[40] In 1978, a group of Loisaida women performed resident Edgar Rivera's song, "Soy Puertorriqueño," for a large audience in the Plaza Cultural, an outdoor gathering place in the neighborhood that community workers had constructed. They sang, "I'm not white, I'm not yellow, neither olive or black, I'm the rainbow of colors, the spectrum of light. I'm the salt and the spice. . . . Soy Puertorriqueño de corazón, soy Puertorriqueño con todo mi amor."[41] Puertorriqueñidad loisadeña, then, celebrated Latinos as inherently inclusive people, genetically predisposed to coalition building across ethnic lines and therefore ideally suited to leading the Loisaida movement, "a melting pot of poor workers coming together to rebuild and reorganize our neighborhood."[42]

Puertorriqueñidad loisaideña attempted to built coalition not only among Europeans, Asians, African Americans, and Puerto Ricans but also among the many different Latin American and Caribbean peoples living in the neighborhood. Here, as in other places in the city, Puerto Rican heritage and culture stood for latinidad, serving as an umbrella identity for all Latinos living in Loisaida. Bernardo Palombo, an Argentinean Loisaidan, remembers:

> In Loisaida . . . out of historical karma or whatever, the first ones who came here, the ones who really paid *derecho de piso,* were the Puerto Ricans. So most of the stuff that happens is under that symbol, if you want. The whole Latin community finds an identification with their own culture through a symbol that by birth is Puerto Rican, and *Caribe. . . .* [The name Loisaida] ha[s] not just the power of Puerto Rican. It's the power of Latin, or not just Latin, a lot of people here are beginning to identify with anything that is inclusive and open.[43]

As an ethnic neighborhood, then, Loisaida celebrated an identity of multiculturalism contained in the symbol of Puerto Rican ethnicity. It created a puertorriqueñidad that promoted racial tolerance and could be used to mobilize a diverse group of Latin American, European, and other residents.

PUERTORRIQUEÑIDAD LOISAIDEÑA AND THE URBAN LANDSCAPE

The ideology of Loisaida—a spirit of working-class activism and ethnic pride expressed in a defined geographic area—did not represent a simple symbolic appropriation of a neighborhood. It was designed as a tool to mobilize residents to roll up their sleeves and physically take over their environment. The name *Loisaida* was created to defend a working-class neighborhood from developers. The majority of the organizers working in Loisaida were primarily concerned with developing and maintaining decent, affordable housing for the area's residents. In the years after the naming of Loisaida, organizations working to improve housing and other conditions in the neighborhood proliferated. Over the course of the 1970s, Interfaith Adopt-A-Building and other housing organizations, in conjunction with independent tenants' associations, rehabilitated over thirty buildings in the thirty-six-block area. By 1981, eighty buildings were represented by tenants' associations that either owned their buildings or managed them independently.[44]

Community activists sought to root the ethnic identity and heritage of Loisaida in the neighborhood itself. They struggled to define success and upward mobility as staying in the neighborhood and working to improve it. The motto of one neighborhood cleanup campaign was "Mejore, No Se Mude" ("Improve, Don't Move").[45] Rivas praised Loisaida children for not following in the footsteps of their Lower East Side ancestors. Loisaida's children worked to improve empty lots "where proud edifices once stood built by immigrants whose children used the very same stones to climb away from the Lower East Side and into the voids of the American Dream." Rejecting this neighborhood heritage of abandonment and upward mobility, Loisaida children are instead "proud of their immediate heritage"[46] in the neighborhood, that is, of their many elders who struggled to improve conditions in the area. Adopt-A-Building praised the commitment of dancer Angie Hernández, who "as the mother of four . . . has a stake in the future, and it is firmly planted here in Loisaida where she lives. She is sure that even if she had 'a lot of money' she wouldn't move away."[47]

These urban homesteaders claimed their buildings in the name of Loisaida in the ways they named them and decorated their facades. Several tenants' associations adorned their buildings with signs bearing their names. Using cloth banners and painted wood, these associations worked to build a landscape that expressed the values of a working-class Puerto Rican identity and visibly claimed each block in the name of Loisaida. A pedestrian walking the streets of Loisaida in the late 1970s would pass the three-foot high announcement of the Loisaida Town House on Avenue C and 4th Street.[48] Nearby, a banner reading "La Fortaleza" claimed its building in the name of El Morro Castle in San Juan, known for its role in defending the island from British invaders in the eighteenth century. Three blocks over, a mural depicting the Second Street and Avenue B Block Association's official emblems floating over a garden of brightly colored flowers decorated one of its rehabilitated buildings.[49] Around the corner, the Coquí Tenants' Association illustrated the building it owned with its namesake, the popular folk motif.[50] On a twenty-three-unit building two blocks up, a twelve-foot-high, thirty-foot-long mural displayed the words "Neighborhood Housing Movement" surrounding an image of the Puerto Rican flag.[51] Residents rendered the landscape even more Puerto Rican through the design of community gardens. On a wall overlooking one such garden, a mural was painted that contained excerpts from the poetry of leaders of the movement for Puerto Rican independence. In some of these gardens, loisaideños erected casitas, small wooden houses modeled after rural homes in Puerto Rico, literally building a jíbaro heritage for Loisaida.

In addition to developing private homes and empty lots in the name of Loisaida, organizers sought to create a public space where people could gather together and define themselves as a community and from where the message of Loisaida could be broadcast. In May 1976, Charas received a lease agreement from the city to develop an empty lot on 9th Street into La Plaza Cultural, designed to "exhibit the multi-cultural arts and talents of the people of Loisaida and to encourage the community's development, with the objective of reversing the trend of physical deterioration and social disintegration."[52] Flanked by murals that read "La Lucha Continúa," the plaza contained an amphitheater for performances and a playground for children. From the 1970s on, countless neighborhood activities were held there, from music and dance performances to religious festivals, such as the Fiesta de la Cruz. In 1979, Loisaidans held a celebration of the birthday of Puerto Rican nationalist Don Pedro Albizu Campos. Rivas remembers that at the celebration, "one of the poets reciting remarked to the hundreds of spectators at La Plaza Cultural, 'If anyone should ask you where the spiritual guidance comes from to the people of Loisaida, you can answer immediately: Don Pedro Albizu Campos!' "[53] In these performances, the ethnic, class, and ideological identity of Loisaida was defined and promoted.

Organizers also developed a Loisaida calendar of public parades and street festivals in the neighborhood. In the summer of 1979, the first Loisaida Festival was held on 11th Street between avenues B and C. Beginning in 1978, Adopt-A-Building organized a Three King's Day parade in the neighborhood. Long celebrated by Puerto Ricans in El Barrio, this parade was specific to Loisaida and again celebrated both Puerto Rican ethnic heritage and community activism. The parade began at the Loisaida Town House, the site of the official naming of Loisaida, and ended at the Nuyorican Poet's Café. In addition to claiming the neighborhood for the day, the parade made a more lasting visual claim to the streets it walked. Before the beginning of each year's parade, Adopt-A-Building announced the "Miracles of Loisaida" for the previous year. These were most often buildings, empty lots, or other urban spaces that had been successfully rehabilitated. The parade would process these miracle sites and hang a banner on each that read, "I am a miracle of Loisaida." According to Rivas, "the banners stay up until they are destroyed by the wind, snow, heat, or rain"[54] as visual reminders of the identity of the territory and the ideology of self-help and improvement it represented.

RECOGNITION: LOISAIDA, NEW YORK

Many developers and other New Yorkers continued to identify the area as a barren frontier. But Loisaida did not go unrecognized by the rest of the city for long. Loisaida sent representatives to public events around New York. In 1979, the Loisaida dance group, Loisaida Folklórica, performed in the Fiesta de Loíza Aldea held uptown and was awarded first prize.[55] By the end of the decade, Loisaida had its own float in the Puerto Rican Day Parade and sent dancers and musicians to Central Park to represent the neighborhood in the annual Fiesta Folklórica. Loisaida announced itself to other cities in the country, as well: in the summer of 1980, the Loisaida Baseball League, composed of 150 children between eight and twelve years old, traveled to Boston to play the Boston Baseball League.[56]

City officials soon realized the neighborhood contained an extremely politically active constituency that should be courted on its own turf. By the late 1970s, it behooved anyone campaigning in Lower Manhattan to recognize the territory of Loisaida and the interests it represented. In early 1978, just over three years after Bimbo Rivas wrote his legendary poem, Manhattan Borough President Andrew Stein attended a day-long workshop at the Loisaida Town House to develop a strategy for neighborhood improvement, campaigning for a newly recognized pocket of Latin voters.[57] Beginning in the early 1980s, Councilwoman Miriam Friedlander acknowledged and publicized the territory of Loisaida by politicking in its landscape, making official speeches from the Plaza Cultural and other public spaces constructed by Loisaida activists. In the spring of 1986, in celebration of local housing organizations' rehabilitation of several buildings along Avenue C, Mayor Koch proclaimed May 31 to be Loisaida Day.[58] Finally, that June, Koch came down to the neighborhood himself to officiate the Viva Loisaida Awards Presentation, a ceremony honoring the efforts of individuals and local organizations to improve the neighborhood. "I commend your hard work, dedication and tireless efforts," he proclaimed, "to make Loisaida a place that we can all be proud of."[59] With Loisaida now on the mayor's lips, local activists began to lobby city government to make Loisaida an officially recognized section of New York City. In May, a collection of local organizations brought a proposal to the Community Board to rename Avenue C from Houston to 14th streets "Loisaida Avenue."

How would the complex ideology of Loisaida be translated in this official representation? What identity would ultimately be communicated to the city at large? And how did residents not involved in the movement understand the new territory in which they found themselves? In the course of the negotiations over the name of Avenue C, what had been conceived as a multi-ethnic, working-class, activist self-help movement under Puerto Rican leadership came to represent a homogeneous ethnic territory and voting bloc. Before the proposal was even brought to the Community Board, a group of concerned residents who had caught wind of the idea of the name change banded together in protest to form the Avenue C Preservation Committee. After collecting 700 signatures of support, topping the 400 collected in favor of the name change, the committee and other protesters defended their position in several letters to the Mayor. For these residents, Loisaida Avenue represented an officialization of the neighborhood as a homogeneous Hispanic community that excluded residents of other backgrounds. "This is a very ethnically diverse community," objected Susan Vaughn of the 7th Street Block Association in her letter to Mayor Koch, "and the name [Loisaida Avenue] is inappropriate."[60] "Using the name Loisaida connotates [sic] the neighborhood as Hispanic—which is an untruth," echoed Mary Tolman, cochairperson of the Avenue C Preservation Committee. "No one group should be permitted to claim it as their turf."[61] The committee proposed that the name be attached to something more isolated, such as a square or a post office. Puertorriqueñidad loisaideña was evidently not as effective a coalition-building tool as organizers hoped. Although organizers tried to promote it as an ethnicity that was inherently multicultural and inclusive, for many residents it represented a specific, alien group invading their territory.

The bill that was ultimately proposed to the Committee of Parks, Recreation and Cultural Affairs did attempt to use the concept of puertorriqueñidad loisaideña to strike a balance between a Hispanic and multicultural identity. "Loisaida is the Spanish translation for lower east side [sic]," it explained. "Approximately 60 percent of the present population of this area is Hispanic." This statistic, portraying the neighborhood as majority Hispanic, justified the use of the Spanish name to the Avenue C Preservation Committee, which had quoted a figure of 37 percent. But lest the bill imply that the city was intending to acknowledge the area as a homogeneous ethnic community, it added, "The use of the designation Loisaida will serve as a recognition of the community's diversity."[62]

The Mayor's Office sat on the bill for the remainder of the year, waiting for the controversy to die down. In January 1987, it sought advice from John Cinque-Sacarello, advisor to the mayor for Hispanic affairs, and from Bruce Feld, director of the Community Assistance Unit. "I am aware of the considerable debate that has raged in the community over this proposal," the mayor's representative wrote, "and I would appreciate your views on whether we should take a position either way."[63] The Community Assistance Unit, responding in the name of a multi-ethnic, local geographic community, wrote, "Given the strongly divided community opinion, we advise that the Mayor not take a position on the bill."[64] The Office of Hispanic Affairs, responding in the name of a citywide ethnic community, recommended that the mayor endorse the street renaming, arguing that "the community is already known informally as 'Loisaida' " and reminding the mayor that he was beholden to the "many community based organizations as well as local residents" to whom he had already acknowledged the term on previous occasions.[65] The mayor took the advice of the Office of Hispanic Affairs and moved to sign the bill into law the following month.

To turn to the Office of Hispanic Affairs was to ask whether Loisaida should be acknowledged as part of the mayor's Hispanic constituency and whether it should be catered to as such. Throughout the 1970s and early 1980s, Loisaida had received little recognition from larger citywide Hispanic institutions. *El Diario/La Prensa*, for instance, consistently referred to the area as "Bajo [Lower] Manhattan" when it mentioned it at all. With its recommendation, the Office of Hispanic Affairs not only made Loisaida an official part of New York but an official part of Hispanic New York as well. At the public hearing on the signing of the bill, the mayor acknowledged the multi-ethnic heritage of the neighborhood, describing the Lower East Side as "long a first home to the many ethnic groups that have created the great diversity that is our city." But he made it clear that Loisaida Avenue meant to represent Loisaida as a definitely Hispanic neighborhood. "The name change," he explained, "is designed to reflect the contributions of the increasing Hispanic influence in that community."[66]

Loisaida was made an official part of the city in the name of a different concept of community than it originally represented. In the 1970s, local organizers sought to mobilize neighborhood residents by promoting the concept of Loisaida as a multi-ethnic, neighborhood-based movement for working-class self-help under Puerto Rican leadership. In the 1980s, the city government recognized Loisaida as a homogeneous ethnic territory that was part of a citywide ethnic constituency. By 1992, *El Diario/La Prensa* referred to Loisaida as a Hispanic voting district.

THE IMPACT OF LOISAIDA

How effective was the Loisaida movement in creating community identity? Although artists and community organizers energetically worked to promote the concept of Loisaida as an ideology of working-class activism and pride in a multi-ethnic Puerto Rican identity, they were not always successful in mobilizing the community to their cause. In an article titled "Loisaida Spirit," *The Quality of Life in Loisaida* announced in bewilderment,

"It has come to our attention from several sources that, while a certain number of people here are aware that this is a neighborhood engaged in a unique struggle to improve itself in every way, there are many who go on from day to day as if nothing were happening."[67] Rivas lamented, "The colonial dependency state of mind is one of Loisaida's greatest enemies. . . . The dependency syndrome infuriates the organizers who are trying to motivate these people to do something for themselves, to be self-starters."[68] But for many poor and working-class Puerto Rican migrants and Latino immigrants who had been forced from place to place by urban renewal programs and rising rents, the ideology of Loisaida, its rootedness and commitment to the neighborhood, was a powerful concept. Bernardo Palombo, an Argentinean musician in Loisaida in the 1970s, remembers that the development of an identity for Loisaida was empowering for him and his neighbors:

> Here, in the land of immigrants, where you don't have political representation, when half of the people are running away from immigration when the other half don't have green card. . . . you feel kind of in a limbo situation. Suddenly, somebody says well, this is Loisaida. Because it's a place where for many years Latins have been living, and are still living, culture happens here. It is important.
>
> We were the invisible men, over there. Well, yeah, we were the crack dealer, or the Latin *pendejo* who is selling the café, some of the stereotypes. Suddenly, when you have a name, no matter how much scum you have around, you are in the map. You have the special to be put in the map. In Spanish, to be killed is to disappear of the map, lo desapareció del mapa. So to appear in the map is almost like to be alive suddenly.[69]

Loisaida, therefore, could provide a territory to the deterritorialized, whether to Puerto Rican American citizens or to illegal Latin American immigrants.

But how effective was the Loisaida identity in the fight to improve its residents' material conditions? In the 1980s, developers continued their attack on the neighborhood. Landlords often harassed low-income tenants and used other illegal tactics to chase residents out of rent-controlled buildings. After the successful gentrification of the adjacent areas of Soho and Greenwich Village, financial institutions viewed Loisaida as a less risky prospect and lent money to developers for further investment. In 1982, a real estate broker advertising a tenement on Avenue A and 11th Street billed the neighborhood as a "Soho-like area."[70] Another real estate agency echoed this image by calling itself "LoHo Associates," implying that the area would be, like Soho, completely transformed by gentrification. In some cases, the image of the neighborhood that García and his colleagues had so carefully constructed could contribute to its own demise. In 1982, one reporter noted that "more progressive people" were "delighted by the flavor of the Hispanic neighborhood north of Little Italy" and were paying astronomical prices for the privilege of living there.[71] As a result, between 1980 and 1990, the number of blocks whose residents were over 50 percent Latino was reduced by half.[72]

Much of the work of the Loisaida movement, however, prevented a complete takeover of the neighborhood during the 1980s. The Loisaida ideology's encouragement of attachment to and identity in place—the anti-upward mobility, "Mejore, No Se Mude" campaign—paid off for many residents. As one study of the area demonstrates, the many city-owned buildings that were appropriated and rehabilitated by Loisaidan tenant associations formed a barrier that thwarted the complete gentrification of the area.[73] García believes that the name and ideology of Loisaida helped to defend affordable housing in the neighborhood:

> [The name] helps you a lot. It gives you a sense of identity as a people. . . . It gives you a sense of identity as a community, to challenge people. . . . Basically [the name] worked in our favor. A lot of the private property still got gentrified, but a lot of the public property, we managed to develop it, and now a lot of working-class and poor people are living in them. So we succeeded to a great extent.[74]

Organizers such as García claimed the territory of Loisaida in the name of a multi-ethnic coalition of working-class people who collectively identified with the anticolonial struggles of Afro-Indian Puerto Ricans. This territory would not only represent this identity and its values to the residents of the community but, by appearing on the map, would also make Loisaidan people and their struggle an official part of the larger city. It was an attempt to reify ideals and identity in urban space, to define a new place for puertorriqueñidad in Nueva York. For at least fifteen years, the Loisaida movement proved an effective strategy against the displacement of working-class people.

EPILOGUE: LOISAIDA IN THE 1990S

Loisaida continued to be an important organizing tool in the revanchist New York City of the 1990s. As the real estate market skyrocketed to an all-time high, the Office of Mayor Rudolph Giuliani joined private developers in the battle for Loisaida land. Whereas during the fiscal crisis of the 1970s the city had struggled to rid itself of costly abandoned properties, by the mid 1990s it fought to reclaim the now extremely valuable buildings community groups had restored. Although those properties that Loisaidans had managed to legally purchase from the city were protected, others had been rented under a long-term agreement. As part of its "quality of life" campaign, the Mayor's Office now worked to evict its less profitable tenants and sell properties to developers.

One target was Charas/El Bohio Cultural and Community Center, one of the original organizing bases of Loisaida and the institutional home of its founder, Bimbo Rivas. Charas spent over twenty years restoring an abandoned school building into classrooms, theaters, and dance and studio space and providing cultural and educational programs to neighborhood youth and adults. It also served as a center for community organizing, providing space to dozens of other groups active in issues such as housing, drug use, police brutality, and the environment. During the mid- and late-1990s, the city placed Charas on the auction block several times. Each time, Charas mobilized the community and its supporters under the name of Loisaida to protest the auction. Carrying banners that read "Viva Loisaida," protesters successfully blocked the sale, either by pressuring the city to take it off the auction block or by intimidating potential developers into not bidding on the property.

The entrance of the city into the fight for land complicated the battle considerably because it brought political as well as economic pressure on organizers and on the ideology of Loisaida itself. Whereas developers denied Loisaida and its claims to land by denigrating its geographic territory as a wasteland, the city attacked Loisaida's politics and activities. During the public relations battle raging around the auctions, some of Giuliani's officials described Charas as a false organization that ran no programs at all or as a dangerous community center that harbored criminals. Although the ideology and organizing base of Loisaida managed to fend off the sale of Charas for more than five years, it could not compete with the power of the Mayor's Office. In 1999, the building—one of the largest and last remaining centers of the Loisaida movement—was sold to a private developer. As of this writing, community protest and legal pressure have prevented the occupation of the building, but Charas and Loisaida are facing their greatest threat since their founding in the 1970s. The map of New York City is being radically redrawn. The geographical and political place of puertorriqueñidad in Lower Manhattan is uncertain.

NOTES

1. Manuel Ramos Otero, "The Point Blank Page," in *Low Rent: A Decade of Prose and Photographs from the Portable Lower East Side* (New York: Grove Press, 1994), 16–17.

2. Joan Turner, "Building Boundaries: The Politics of Urban Renewal in Manhattan's Lower East Side" (Ph.D. diss., City University of New York, 1984), 307, 312.

3. All translations are mine. Alianza Obrera Puertorriqueña, meeting announcement, 1924.

4. "Notas de la Colonia," *La Prensa*, December 17, 1936.

5. Felipe Arana, "Los hispanos de Harlem," *Ecos de Nueva York*, February 26, 1950, 10.

6. Judith Herbstein, "Rituals and Politics of the Puerto Rican 'Community' in New York City" (Ph.D. diss., City University of New York, 1978), 117, 131, 137, 142.

7. Turner, "Building Boundaries," 107.

8. Ibid., 108.

9. Malve von Hassell, *Homesteading in New York City, 1978–1993: The Divided Heart of Loisaida* (Westport, Conn.: Bergin & Garvey, 1996), 53–54.

10. Edward Kirschner, Eve Bach, and Thomas Brom, *Memorandum on Loisaida* (Oakland: 1977), 2.

11. Linda Cohen and Brent Sherman, "Rebuilding a Community," *WIN*, December 20, 1979, 10.

12. Martin Gottlieb, "Space Invaders: Land Grab on the Lower East Side," *The Village Voice*, December 14, 1982, p. 10.

13. Chino García, interview by the author, New York, December 4, 1996.

14. Kirschner, Bach, and Brom, *Memorandum on Loisaida*, 3.

15. García, interview.

16. Ibid.

17. WIN Collective, "Loisaida," *WIN*, December 20, 1979, 2.

18. García, interview.

19. Ibid.

20. Pupa Santiago, interview by the author, New York, November 27, 1996.

21. García, interview.

22. Ibid.

23. Santiago, interview.

24. Advertisement for Freddy's Luncheonette, *The Quality of Life in Loisaida*, November–December 1978, p. 16.

25. Carmelo Quiñones, "The Ideology of Loisaida," *The Quality of Life in Loisaida*, March–April 1979, p. 15.

26. Miguel Algarín and Miguel Piñero, eds., *Nuyorican Poetry: An Anthology of Puerto Rican Words and Feelings* (New York: William Morrow and Company, 1975), 11–12.

27. Bimbo Rivas, "Loisaida: The Reality Stage," *WIN*, December 20, 1979, 6.

28. Santiago, interview.

29. Miriam Rivas, "Dancing from the Heart and Soul," *WIN*, December 20, 1979, 22.

30. "Palante on New York Newstands [sic] Starting August 31," *Palante*, August 16, 1972, p. 9.

31. "Ideology of the Young Lords Party" pamphlet, vertical files, Centro de Estudios Puertorriqueños.

32. "Loiza Aldea," *Palante*, August 15, 1970, p. 6.

33. "Puerto Rican Day Parade," *Palante,* June 7, 1971, p. 11.

34. "The Land is Ours! We're Taking it Back!" *Palante,* August 15, 1970, p. 3.

35. "Fiestas de Loíza Aldea—herencia hispánica . . . y afro en Puerto Rico y las otras Antillas," *El Diario,* June 1, 1978, p. 36.

36. "Loiza Aldea," p. 6.

37. Rivas, "Loisaida: The Reality Stage,"8.

38. Ibid.

39. Christopher Mele, "Neighborhood 'Burn Out': Puerto Ricans at the End of the Queue," in *From Urban Village to East Village: The Battle for New York's Lower East Side,* ed. Janet Abu-Lughod (Cambridge, MA: Blackwell, 1994), 130, 137.

40. Bernardo Palombo, interview by the author, New York, November 1996.

41. Gary Greenstein, "The Salt and the Spice," *WIN,* December 20, 1979, 25.

42. Quiñones, "The Ideology of Loisaida," 15.

43. Palombo, interview.

44. Brent Sharman, "Don't Be Forced Out! Join the Loisaida Neighborhood Tenant's Council," *The Quality of Life in Loisaida,* December–January 1981, p. 10.

45. *El Diario,* July 1, 1979, p. 15.

46. Rivas, "Loisaida: The Reality Stage," 6.

47. "Dancing Feet," *The Quality of Life in Loisaida,* March–April 1979, p. 3.

48. Marci Reaven and Matias Bienvenida, *El Corazón de Loisaida* (New York: Unifilm, 1979).

49. Walter Robinson and Carlo McCormick, "Slouching Toward Avenue D," *Art in America* 72, no. 6 (1984): 134.

50. Quiñones, "The Ideology of Loisaida," 15.

51. *City Limits,* September 1978, 10.

52. Josie Rolon, "Doing More With Less," *WIN,* December 20, 1979, 12.

53. Rivas, "Loisaida: The Reality Stage," 7.

54. Ibid.

55. Rivas, "Dancing from the Heart and Soul," 21.

56. Alfredo Irizarry, "Loisaida's Baseball Team," *The Quality of Life in Loisaida,* June–July 1980, p. 9.

57. "'Town Meeting' Termed Success," *City Limits,* March 1978, 14.

58. Proclamation of the Office of the Mayor of the City of New York, Folder for Local Law 3, 1987, New York City Municipal Archives.

59. Letter from Mayor Edward Koch to Loisaida, Inc., June 9, 1986, Folder for Local Law 3, 1987, New York City Municipal Archives.

60. Letter from Susan Vaughn to Mayor Edward Koch, May 26, 1986, Folder for Local Law 3, 1987, New York City Municipal Archives.

61. Letter from Mary Tolman to Mayor Edward Koch, June 3, 1986, Folder for Local Law 3, 1987, New York City Municipal Archives.

62. Introductory Number 717, November 6, 1986.

63. Memo from Liz Berger to John Cinque-Sacarello, January 8, 1986, Folder for Local Law 3, 1987, New York City Municipal Archives.

64. Memo from Bruce Feld to Liz Berger, January 20, 1987, Folder for Local Law 3, 1987, New York City Municipal Archives.

65. Memo to Liz Berger from John Cinque-Sacarello, January 20, 1987, Folder for Local Law 3, 1987, New York City Municipal Archives.

66. Transcript of the Stenographic Record of the Public Hearing on Local Laws Held Before the Honorable Edward I. Koch, Mayor at City Hall, City of New York, February 19, 1987, Folder for Local Law 3, 1987, New York City Municipal Archives.

67. "Loisaida Spirit," *The Quality of Life in Loisaida,* December 1979, p. 2.

68. Rivas, "Loisaida: The Reality Stage," 8.

69. Palombo, interview.

70. Gottlieb, "Space Invaders," p. 10.

71. Ibid., p. 11.

72. Mele, "Neighborhood 'Burn Out,' " 128.

73. Ibid., 183.

74. García, interview.

CHAPTER ELEVEN

The Manifold Character of Panethnicity

Latino Identities and Practices Among Dominicans in New York City

José Itzigsohn

Carlos Dore-Cabral

This paper addresses the question of the formation of a Latino identity among Dominican immigrants. We attempt to answer three questions: Do Dominicans define themselves as Latinos? If so, what does that definition mean? And finally, how do they act based on a Latino identification? Answers to these questions will provide a better understanding of the process of incorporation of Dominicans to U.S. society and the processes of formation of individual and collective identities.

When immigrants cross borders, they confront systems of symbolic classification, systems of organization of social reality that are strange to them and force them to look for new individual and group identities. The rise of new individual and collective identities, however, is not a given but the result of processes of out-group labeling and internal self-definition; a result of the interplay of the symbolic classifications of the new society and the cultural categories that immigrants bring with them. In the eyes of mainstream U.S. society, the Latino or Hispanic label designates a new ethnic group composed of immigrants from different Latin American countries and their offspring. For the people who are labeled in this way, the meaning of this identity is complicated by two elements. The first one is the diversity of people to whom it applies. The national histories and experiences of different Latino groups are very different from one another. The second element is that this new ethnic group is also a racialized other. Latinos not only enter an ethnic system of classification but also, and perhaps more important, a racial system of classification that operates with binary categories and classifies Latinos as nonwhite. Moreover, this panethnic group is multiracial, encompassing people all along the color spectrum. So the Latino label defines, in fact, a group that is at the same time multiethnic and multiracial. The rise of a common group identity would appear, in these circumstances, rather difficult (Oboler 1995; Grosfoguel and Georas 1996; Duany 1998).

The labeling of all the people with origins in a Spanish-speaking country as Hispanic or Latinos has been strongly criticized because it combines people from different nationalities and races, mixing people with a history of oppression in the United States with new immigrants who arrived in search of a better economic future. The different Latino groups vary greatly not only in their national origin but also in their time of entry to U.S. society and their mode of incorporation into it. Different immigrant groups encounter different state policies toward them and different mainstream attitudes and may also find a preexisting ethnic community with its own characteristics (Giménez 1992; Massey 1993).

These critiques are appropriate, as the Latin American population is indeed extremely heterogeneous. They do not take into account, however, the fact that the constant use by different social actors of these inappropriate names can sometimes "give rise in reality, by the specific effectiveness of evocation, to the very thing they represent" (Bourdieu 1991:224). Every day we encounter people who define themselves as Latinos and act upon this identification, and we witness the production of Latino culture and politics. We could ask, however, whether the Latino label means the same thing for all the people who identify as Latino and whether different expressions of Latino culture and politics share elements in common. This paper attempts to provide answers to these questions by looking at the case of Dominican immigrants in New York City. We will do so by looking at three areas of social action in which identities are formed: the racial classification system, the political arena, and the social services field.[1]

LATINO IDENTITY: ETHNICITY AND RACE

Group identities provide individuals with a sense of belonging and a reference group for accepted values and behaviors. Ethnic and racial identities and their social valuation help to determine the status of individuals in the material and symbolic stratification systems of their society. Looking at the ways in which immigrants identify themselves helps us understand their experience of incorporation into U.S. society. Waters (1994) argues that immigrants choose between different identities according to their perceptions of the opportunities open to them in the United States and their understanding of the dynamics of race and ethnic relations in this country. Immigrants can choose among different identities to gain access to certain material benefits, to achieve what they perceive as higher social recognition, or to recreate an imagined community that will provide them with a sense of understanding and control of their social reality. For immigrants of color, however, the ethnic choices are severely restricted by the imposition of racial and ethnic labels by mainstream society. For immigrants of color in United States, ethnicity is racialized.

The study of the process of identity formation among Latinos focuses on two issues: the formation of a panethnic Latino identity and the positioning of Latinos within the U.S. binary racial classification system. Latino immigrants have to find a position within the parameters of the dominant racial symbolic system—a symbolic system that is alien to them and assigns them negative characteristics (Grosfoguel and Georas 1996; Moore 1990; Oboler 1995; Padilla 1985; Rodríguez and Cordero-Guzmán 1992).

The formation of a Latino ethnic identity is neither a simple nor an unambiguous process. A key step in the study of the rise of Latino panethnicity is the work of Felix Padilla (1984, 1985). Padilla argues that a Latino ethnic consciousness, which he calls "Latinismo," arises out of the interaction of two or more Latino groups in a situation in which those groups share common interests. The Latino consciousness is not a spontaneous one but arises out of the action of Latino organizations in the political field. This identity is situational; that is, it arises out of a specific political situation and does not necessarily continue after that situation is resolved. This Latino consciousness does not replace a national consciousness, but it coincides with it throughout the time that the circumstances that gave rise to it continue. Moreover, Padilla reminds us of possible contradictory interests among those Latino groups that have been historically oppressed minorities in the United States, concretely Mexican Americans and Puerto Ricans, on the one hand, and other newer immigrants who enjoy a better situation in this country, such as Cubans or South Americans, on the other.

On a similar vein, López and Espíritu (1990) argue that the rise of panethnic organizations is ultimately the result of the mobilization of middle-class activists. They compare the effects of cultural and structural variables in the emergence of panethnic organizations among Asian Americans, Native Americans, Indo-Americans, and Latinos. They find that structural commonalties, among which they include race, class, generation, and geography, are a better field for the rise of panethnicity than a shared culture. They conclude that because Latinos diverge more along structural lines than the other three groups, they are less likely to develop panethnic organizations. The work of Padilla and López and Espíritu offers important insights into the constitution of a field of ethnic political competition. However, their focus on the action and discourse of political organizations and elites precludes them from looking at the self-definition of the constituencies of these organizations.

Oboler (1992) affirms that it is necessary to go beyond Padilla's view of Latinismo as a situational identity, arguing that a generation of U.S.-born or U.S-raised descendants of Spanish-speaking immigrants has grown up between two cultures, belonging to both and to neither of them and experiencing discrimination as Latinos. These conditions may lead some of these people to identify as a unified ethnic group in the United States, erasing, or at least attenuating, the national and historical differences that separate them. Joan Moore (1990) argues along similar lines, asserting that among the different Hispanic groups there is a growing need for a collective common identification. This need arises out of the changing situations of Hispanics at the regional and national levels, but it transcends the simple need for political alliances. She suggests that the second generation of Hispanics may grow up identifying with a pan-Hispanic identity. This identity, she argues, will be a form of secondary identity that is looser and shallower than the national origin identity that will still be the primary basis of identification. Oboler (1995) also shows how gender, class, and race mediate the construction of a Latino identity.

The question of the racial identity of Latinos is addressed in the work of Clara Rodriguez (Rodríguez 1992; Rodríguez and Cordero-Guzmán 1992). Looking at racial formation among Puerto Ricans in the United States is very important for us, because the social constructions of race among different Caribbean peoples have a lot in common. Rodríguez argues that Puerto Ricans in the United States do not accept its dichotomous construction of race. They do not identify themselves racially simply as black or white. They are aware of how they are seen by Americans, but they see themselves in a different way. When Puerto Ricans answer "other" to the census racial question, they are not choosing an intermediate racial category but are choosing culture and ethnicity over phenotype as a basis for racial identification (Rodríguez and Cordero-Guzmán 1992).

We suggest that to understand the processes of emergence of Latino (or other) panethnic identities, we ought to look at the position of the different national groups in the fields of symbolic and material competition in U.S. society. This will allow us to understand what the adoption of one or other ethnic identity may mean to the people involved in those fields of competition. We adopt the notion of field from Pierre Bourdieu (1991). A *field* is a place of struggle between individuals who try to affect the distribution of the forms of capital particular to that field (e.g., symbolic, political, or economic capital). We attempt to take an initial step by looking at the presence of panethnic self-identification among one particular group, Dominican immigrants, in one particular location, Washington Heights, New York City. We argue that identities and practices based on that identity are constituted in different social fields and that we ought to look at the logic of those fields to understand the identities and practices that emerge. We will look at three social fields: the symbolic system of racial classifications, the political arena, and the social services fields. Latino identities and practices are produced in each of these fields in ways that do not necessarily coincide with one another. Looking at these three fields will provide a sense of the different forms and meanings of a Latino identity among Dominicans.

RACE AND NATION IN THE DOMINICAN REPUBLIC

A central element of the experience of Dominican immigrants in the United States stems from the different social construction of racial differences in the two countries. The U.S. system of racial classifications is based on two binary distinctions: a general one between white and nonwhite, and a more specific one between white and black. These dichotomous classifications are based on a combination of phenotype and national and family origin. The Dominican system of racial classification, instead, is based on the recognition of intermediate racial categories, based mainly on skin color—and other physical elements such as facial features, type of hair, and cultural elements such as language, education, and religion—and on the ideal of whitening.

The Dominican elites who guided the process of nation building since the middle of the nineteenth century adopted a racial ideology of whitening and negrophobia. As a result, the official discourse associated Dominicanness with things Hispanic (referring to Spain), Catholicism, and whiteness. The goal of public policy, from education through immigration, was to "whiten" the population (Duany 1998; Torres-Saillant 1998). Dominicans "range phenotipically across the entire color spectrum from black to brown to white" (Duany 1998:162) and could not be considered white, but they were defined as categorically nonblack, the black category being reserved for Haitians. This political-discursive strategy reached its peak during the Trujillo regime—and found its most horrifying expression in the expulsion and massacre of Haitians in 1937—but it did not end with the death of Trujillo in 1961. It continued during the years of Balaguer's hegemony and is still present today.

The result of the superposition of blackness and Haitians is the deemphasizing of the racial differences among Dominicans. Dominicans use different terms to refer to different shades of skin color, such as *mulato, jabao, trigueño,* and others, all of which are intermediate categories between black and white. All these terms, however, are included within the category *indio,* a term that encompasses all the intermediate categories. Dominicans distinguish between shades of color referring to people as *indio claro* (light Indian) or *indio oscuro* ("dark Indian") but reject being categorized as black (Dore-Cabral 1995).

As said before, in the Dominican Republic, the category *black* is reserved for Haitians. Haitians fulfill the most menial jobs in the Dominican

Republic and are discriminated against on both national and racial bases. The Haitian population is less racially mixed than the Dominican population, but Haitians are physically indistinguishable from dark-skinned Dominicans. Nevertheless, only the former are referred to as black, whereas the latter are referred to as *indio oscuro*. In the absence of visible physical markers, the boundaries between Dominicans and Haitians are expressed in language and in certain central cultural elements such as music or religion.

DOMINICANS IN NEW YORK CITY

Dominicans began to migrate in large numbers to the United States after 1965, following the invasion of the island by U.S. troops. The United States accepted the Dominican migration as a way to lower the social tensions on the island. The early migration was mostly urban, lower-middle-class people. With the deterioration of the economic conditions on the island in the early 1980s, migration to the U.S. became an option for almost every sector of Dominican society, from unskilled laborers to middle-class professionals (Grasmuck and Pessar 1995; Hernández, Rivera-Batíz, and Agodini 1995).

Dominican immigrants entered the U.S. labor market mostly as low-wage manual workers. They are concentrated mainly in clerical, operatives/labor, and personal service occupations. The Dominican community is also affected by a high percentage of unemployment (Hernández, Rivera-Batíz, and Agodini 1995). This mode of incorporation was, in part, the result of the process of racialization of Dominicans within the New York economy, which led Dominicans to fulfill similar socioeconomic and symbolic positions as Puerto Ricans (Duany 1998; Grosfoguel and Georas 1996). A growing number of Dominicans, however, are opening their own businesses and seeking upward mobility through self-employment (Guarnizo 1994).

Dominican immigrants in the United States maintain a vibrant Dominican cultural life. Guarnizo characterizes the Dominican community in New York City as "a non-assimilationist, persistently ethnic group" (1994:80). Duany (1994) analyzes the process of formation of a transnational identity that encompasses elements from the home country and U.S. cultures. The main orientation of this identity, in terms of significant symbolic elements and in terms of long-term expectations, is toward the Dominican Republic. Dominican migrants reproduce their life on the island in the streets of New York City. Through recreating their culture, Dominicans affirm their distinct national identity and differentiate themselves from Puerto Ricans or African Americans (Duany 1994). Dominicans in the United States also maintain close ties with the island and have become an important factor in the economy of the Dominican Republic: migrant remittances are second only to tourism as a source of national revenue (Itzigsohn 1995).

In New York's social and political life, Dominicans constitute one of the many racialized immigrant groups in the city. Grosfoguel and Georas (1996) show how the political and ideological needs of the U.S. state led to divergent processes of racialization for different Caribbean groups. Puerto Rican immigrants were incorporated into the U.S. economy as manual laborers and racialized as nonwhite. Dominicans occupied the same socioeconomic position of Puerto Ricans and were identified with them in the symbolic racial stratification system. Cubans, and to a certain degree West Indians, were identified as model minorities. As a result, these groups could transform this symbolic capital into economic success. This success was then counterposed to the presumed failure of Puerto Ricans, Dominicans, and African Americans.

Thus, when Dominican migrants enter U.S. society, they move from a society where race is a pervasive element of social classification but is covered by a language of nationality and where it is Haitians that are most discriminated against on a racial basis to a society in which race is a central feature of daily life and where they themselves suffer discrimination due to their skin color and ethnicity. Although in the Dominican Republic the main logic of racial/national classification system is the positioning of Dominicans as nonblack, in the United States the main logic of the racial classification system—the one-drop rule—classifies Dominicans as nonwhite. The question that prompted our research was how Dominicans would identify racially when confronted with a society that defines them as black. In the Dominican Republic, Dominicans tend not to see themselves as black. Has the U.S. experience changed that self-perception? We hypothesized that exposure to a society that sees most of them as black will lead Dominicans to abandon their rejection of blackness and identify as black. Our results do not support this hypothesis.

HISPANO AS A RACIAL AND PANETHNIC CATEGORY

The findings of this study are based on two sources of data: a small survey ($n = 60$) conducted in Washington Heights, upper Manhattan, in Spring 1991 and a series of semistructured interviews with key informants conducted in Fall 1996. The purpose of the survey was to capture the immigrants' racial and ethnic self-identification as well as their perception of other ethnic groups in New York City. The sample was built using the snowball technique with multiple points of entry (to avoid getting locked into only one network). The interviews were conducted in person with a structured questionnaire. The interviewers were Dominicans, and the interviews were conducted in Spanish.

The interviews with key informants were part of a large project studying transnationalism in which the authors are involved. We interviewed thirty-two people: twenty-two men and ten women. The interviewees were chosen because of their central position in different fields of Dominican communal activities. The interviews included an open-ended question about racial and ethnic self-identification that often resulted in long conversations about the issue, showing its importance in the personal life of the interviewees. These findings provide qualitative depth to the results of the survey. In addition to the interviews, we draw on our observation of different organizations, institutions, and practices. The strength of these two studies is that they allow a close look at the question of identity formation. Their weakness is their small size and the nonrandomness of the selection. The evidence we have gathered so far is exploratory, and we continue our research on this issue. Nevertheless, we believe that our findings provide some important indications into the processes of Latino identity formation and suggest avenues for further research.

Table 11.1 presents the main characteristics of the first study's sample. The mean age of the respondents is relatively high, and a very small number of respondents are citizens of the United States (this was very common until the recent changes in immigration law drove large numbers of permanent residents to naturalize). The mean years of education of our sample is higher than that of the population in general. Three-quarters of the sample socialize mainly with other Dominicans; moreover, three-quarters

Table 11.1 Characteristics of the Sample ($n = 60$)

Variables		Numbers, Percentages, Means[1]
Women		29 (48.3%)
Age (mean)		34.8
Years of Education (mean)		12.0
Years in the United States (mean)		10.8
U.S. citizens		10 (16.7%)
Most friends are Dominicans		45 (75.0%)
Would like to return to the Dominican Republic		45 (75.0%)
Racial self-identification	Hispano/a	28 (46.7%)
	Latino/a	10 (16.7%)
	Black	14 (23.3%)
	Indio/a	5 (8.3%)
	White	2 (3.3%)

[1]Some numbers do not round up due to missing values.

would like to return to the Dominican Republic. This profile suggests a community whose referents for self-identification are both here and on the island.[2]

The question that prompted the research was how Dominicans would identify themselves racially when confronted with a society that defines them as black. The survey attempted to capture racial self-identification by asking an open-ended question: we asked the respondents to "which race they belong in the United States." We did not give the respondents any particular set of choices. Although the question was posed in racial terms, the answers to our question regarding racial self-identification were expressed in panethnic terms: Hispanos or Latinos. Table 11.1 shows that 46.7 percent of the sample identifies as Hispano, and another 16.7 percent identify as Latino.[3] Only 23.3 percent identify as black and 3.3 as white. As a mode of comparison, in the 1990 census 24.3 percent of New York Dominicans identified themselves as white; 25.2 percent, as black; and 50.1 percent, as other (Grasmuck and Pessar 1995).

The fact that so many people gave a panethnic answer to a question on racial identity presents a very interesting puzzle. We need to understand this pattern of answers. It could be argued that this is an artifact of language use. In the everyday Spanish of Dominicans and other Latino groups, the word *raza* has a different connotation than the English word *race*. It is very common to hear Dominicans use *raza* to refer to the Dominican people, to other Latino nationalities, or to Latinos in general, hence the ethnic answer. Nevertheless, we asked a similar question on racial self-identification in the Dominican Republic, and the answers given to this question used the Dominican racial categories, suggesting that the respondents understood the question in racial terms. Table 11.2 shows the cross-tabulation of the answers to the questions on racial self-identification in the United States and the Dominican Republic. Although most of the respondents choose Hispano

Table 11.2 Racial Self-Identification in the Dominican Republic and the United States (parentheses indicate column percentages)

	Race in the U.S.				
	Hispano/a or Latino/a	Black	Indio/a	White	Total
Race in the Dominican Republic					
Black	12 (37.5)	11 (91.7)			23 (46.0)
Indio/a	16 (50.0)	1 (8.3)	5 (100.0)	1 (100.0)	23 (46.0)
White	4 (12.5)				4 (8.0)
Total	32	12	5	1	50 (100.0)

or Latino as their racial identification in the United States, close to half of the sample choose black as their racial identification in the Dominican Republic, and the same number choose to identify as indio.[4] It is important to note that the percentage of respondents who self-identify as black is larger for the Dominican Republic than for the United States. Out of the twenty-three people who self-identify as black in the Dominican Republic, only eleven identified as black in the United States. The other twelve choose the Hispano or Latino label. These responses contradict the initial hypothesis that motivated this research.[5]

The results of the 1991 survey suggest that the labels Hispano or Latino operate as racial categories. The Hispano or Latino identity allows many Dominicans to find a position within the U.S. racial symbolic field, which is hierarchically organized in a binary distinction between whites and non-whites and, more specifically, between whites and blacks. These binary classifications are strange to Dominican people and do not address their former experiences. For some Dominicans, embracing the Hispano or Latino label is a way of rejecting being labeled as black and choosing what is perceived as an intermediate label. In the field of symbolic racial classifications, the Hispano/a label parallels the indio/a label in Santo Domingo. This appeared clearly in a conversation with a recent Dominican immigrant. He defined himself as "indio Hispano." Asked about the meaning of that classification, he explained that in the United States people are classified as either white or black, whereas in the Dominican Republic people distinguished between shades of color, and because he was Hispano, he was indio. Asked what would he be if he was not Hispano, he answered that in that case he would be black.

Torres-Saillant (1998) points to another important aspect of this racial/ethnic dynamic, arguing that in many cases Dominicans are not recognized as black by African Americans owing to the cultural/ethnic differences between both groups. Embracing Hispano/a or Latino/a as a self-definition may also be related to the recognition of certain national/ethnic common experiences. This is best expressed in the answer of a Dominican woman whom we interviewed in New York, an immigrant who arrived to the United States in the mid-1980s and is actively involved in the New York branch of one of the large Dominican political parties. She affirms "I am Hispanic, Dominican, I am not black nor white." In her answer, panethnicity is equated with nationality, and both are opposed to the racial white/black binary.

These findings seem to coincide with the Puerto Rican case described by Rodríguez and Cordero-Guzmán (1992). Like Puerto Ricans, Dominicans reject the white/black dichotomy. Nevertheless, their choices are limited by the classification system of mainstream society. Contrary to Rodríguez's interpretation, we argue that Dominicans cannot transcend the system of classification established by mainstream U.S. culture. This appears clearly in the words of a recent immigrant living in New York. When asked about his racial self-identification, he answered, "I am Hispanic; that is how we are called here." The self-definition as Hispanic is linked in this case to the way mainstream society defines Dominicans.

To what extent does the adoption of the Hispano/a or Latino/a label indicate the emergence of a Latino imagined community? Table 11.3 shows two interesting results. The first one is that in spite of the large percentage of people who identify themselves as Hispanos or Latinos, a large segment of the 1991 sample claims that Dominicans are discriminated against by other Latinos. The second one is that the perception or experience of conflicts with other Latinos does not seem to affect identification as Hispanos. Those who self-identify as Hispanos or Latinos tended to think that other Latinos discriminate against Dominicans or to report the actual experience of discrimination by other Latinos. We do not suggest that there is a direct connection between experiences of discrimination by other Latinos and self-identification as Hispanos. We argue that self-identification as Hispano or Latino is related to the process of incorporation into U.S. society (Itzigsohn and Dore 2000). Dominicans who are more incorporated into this society are exposed to and compete with people from other Latino national groups, and as a result, they are more likely to experience discrimination from these groups.

So far we have argued that self-identification as Hispano or Latino allows Dominicans to find a place within the U.S. racial classification system and that self-identification as Latino or Hispano does not erase tensions between the different Latino groups. These findings do not preclude the possibility of the emergence of Latino panethnic identities and practices in certain social fields. In the last part of this section, we look at ways in which self-identification as Hispano/a or Latino/a operates as a form of emergent panethnic identity in the political and social services field. The political field

Table 11.3 Perceptions and Experiences of Discrimination by Other Latinos by Racial Self-Identification as Hispano or Latino

	Hispano/a or Latino/a	Other	Total
Believe that other Latinos discriminate against Dominicans			
Yes	29 (76.3)	14 (66.7)	43 (72.9)
No	9 (23.7)	7 (33.3)	16 (27.1)
Experience discrimination by other Latinos[1]			
Yes	12 (35.3)	3 (14.3)	15 (27.3)
No	22 (64.7)	18 (85.7)	40 (72.7)

[1]The results for the experience of discrimination are statistically significant at the .08 level.

is the locus of Padilla's (1985) argument, and it is the area that justifies many of the existing panethnic projects. The social services field is interesting because it is an area in which numerous Latino institutions and organizations are created. These institutions, in turn, produce Latino practices and identities.

Dominicans constitute the majority of the population in Washington Heights, and they have built powerful Dominican-based political and social organizations. Graham (1997) documented the struggle of Dominican residents in Washington Heights for the recognition of dual citizenship by the Dominican state and the formation of a Dominican district in the city council. Both goals were achieved, and as a result Dominicans do not lose their Dominican citizenship when they naturalize, and the District 10 (Washington Heights) councilman is a Dominican, Guillermo Linares. The state representative for the sector is also a Dominican, Adriano Espaillat, and Dominicans in New York are arguing for the right to be represented in the Dominican congress. Dominican political parties are active and have offices in the area, and numerous town committees link people in the neighborhood with their hometowns in the Dominican Republic. Such a cursory look at this field of action suggests that the main forms of identity and collective organization and action are Dominican based.

The local Latino political field in New York is certainly not devoid of interethnic competition. As different groups attempt to attain political and economic power, they compete with each other, generating ethnic tension. Nevertheless, the relationships among the different Latino ethnicities are complex. A Dominican leader whom we interviewed asserted that Puerto Ricans have been fighting for political access for a long time and see Dominicans as recently arrived competitors. The same respondent, who is a prominent local activist and has been working for years to create a Dominican power base in the sector, stated that "at the grassroots level, the relationships with Puerto Ricans are very good, but at the level of leaders it is different" and added that marriages between Dominicans and Puerto Ricans are on the increase.

The commentaries of another Dominican leader further show the complexity of the Latino political identities. He argued that "the Dominican identity is very important for me, but my political identity is Hispanic." This response associates the rise of a Hispanic identity to politics. What is interesting is that the political activities of this respondent are focused almost exclusively on the Dominican Republic. This respondent lived in New York for more than thirty years, and during all those years he had been continuously involved in Dominican politics as an important member of one of the large Dominican parties. He argues that "Dominicans here are as Dominican as those who live there." Nevertheless, he defines himself politically as Hispanic.

These two responses point to existing tensions in the organization of the political field. Although there is a strong support and a large base for

Dominican-based organization and identity, the large presence of other Latinos in the city—mainly but not only Puerto Ricans—creates not only
ethnic tensions but also the recognition for some form of a wider base of
organization and identity. Another activist explained this tension, arguing
that Dominican politicians have to respond to their constituencies, which
are mainly Dominican, and at the same time convince other Latino groups
that they also represent them.

Admittedly, it is necessary to expand this inquiry to concrete forms of
political organization rather than interviews with actors. Nevertheless, it
appears from our interviews that the dynamic of the political field leads to
the creation of dual forms of identification: an anchoring Dominican identification and a secondary Latino identification. This situation is somehow
similar to that described by Padilla (1985). In both cases the national identity is the basic and anchoring one. Nevertheless, although in the case described by Padilla the Latino identity seemed to be punctual and conjunc-
tural, in this case these two forms of identification coexist with one another.
There are often tensions between these two forms of identification, and in
those cases, the Dominican identification almost always prevails, but nevertheless, to a certain extent, it has to accommodate the Latino identification
as well.

This situation is different, for example, from the Miami Cuban case as
described by Cortina (1990). Miami Cubans tend to identify and organize
as Cuban, rejecting alliances and identification with other Latinos. Cortina
points out that this case is special in the sense that Cubans in Miami have
acquired an unprecedented amount of political and economic power that
they don't intend to share with other Hispanic groups, leading them to focus
on their national identity. We can then pose the following hypothesis: In
those places in which one national group is hegemonic in terms of numbers,
political, or economic power, that hegemonic group will tend to reject the
panethnic identity. On the other hand, situations in which there is no hegemonic group are more propitious for the rise of secondary panethnic identities and practices.

The field of social services is also an interesting site to look at the rise
of Latino identities and practices Many organizations serve the Latino
population in areas such as health, housing, education, English-language
instruction, and immigration law, among others. The biggest social services
organization in Upper Manhattan is probably Alianza Dominicana, a
Dominican-based organization, and there are several other smaller Dominican organizations. Nevertheless, there are several organizations that are
Latino or immigrant based in the area. Those organizations provide assistance to the whole Latino immigrant population, and although to a large
extent the people working for those organizations and using their services
are Dominicans, they are not recognized as Dominican organizations. The
organization of the field of social services as expressed in the access to
services and access to funds for community services organizations presup-

poses the recognition of some form of panethnic identification—at least by funding agencies and users.

People working for these organizations may or may not identify as Latino/a or Hispano/a. For example, one of the workers in these organizations argued that he is "Dominican by nationality, Latino because I speak Spanish, and Black due to the African Heritage," differentiating between the national, ethnic, and racial components of his identity. Another worker of a different social service organization, a successful second-generation Dominican professional who has difficulty speaking Spanish, after thinking for a while chose to identify as Dominican American, rejecting the Latino label. In spite of these differences, both attended the October 1996 Latino March on Washington. A third person involved in a social services organization told us about his involvement in the creation of District 10, the Dominican district for the New York City council, and emphasized how Dominicans were interested in a Dominican rather than a Latino district. Yet, in his everyday life this person works in an organization structured on the premise of serving the whole Latino community. People who work or receive the services of these organizations, through their everyday actions, are defining a field of panethnic practices regardless of how they choose to identify themselves.[6]

CONCLUSION: THE MANIFOLD CHARACTER OF LATINO/A IDENTITY AND PRACTICES

In this paper we analyzed three different social fields in which panethnic identities and practices are produced. We found that the encounter between the U.S. racial classification system and the Dominican racial categories leads some Dominicans to choose the Hispano/a label as an intermediate racial category. We saw that the logic of alliances and competition in the political field leads to the emergence of an often tenuous secondary Latino/a identification among people involved in this field, and we argued that the structure of the social service field leads to the constitution of organizations that presuppose a Latino community and as such create practices based on that identity. Our results suggest the need to abandon the search for consistent and fixed forms of individual and group identities, for either/or forms of categorization. Identities are multiple, variable, and not necessarily consistent, responding to the demands of the different social fields in which they are constituted.

It is important to remark that although identities are decentered and vary, they are not arbitrary; they are constituted in social fields that constrain the options and pressure in certain directions. That is perhaps the most important theoretical-methodological aspect of our work. To analyze the manifold character of Latino identities and practices, we have to look at the structure of the different fields in which they are constituted. The fields in which identities are constituted are themselves not fixed and changing, but at every particular time and place we can identify certain structural pressures for the raising of certain identities and practices.

The identities that emerge in different fields do not necessarily mean the same even if they use the same label. Similarly, practices that construct panethnic social identities need not be based on individual panethnic identification. For example, a person can choose to identify ethnically as Dominican, racially as indio/a—that is, using Dominican racial categories—and work for an organization structured around the Latino/a identity. Another can spend most of his or her time working for Dominican political organizations but at the same time identify as Latino/a. These different identities sometimes coexist without tension and sometimes conflict with one another, forcing people to choose one or another aspect. In cases of conflict between individual and group national and panethnic identities, it is most often the national one that prevails. Nevertheless, all the time that there are field pressures for the constitution of panethnic identities, the latter resurface. In the three social fields we looked at, there are definite structural pressures for the rise of some form of secondary Latino/a identity and/or practices in addition to the anchoring national Dominican identity.

NOTES

1. Of course, these are not the only areas of social actions in which identities are formed, but an analysis of these three particular areas provides us with a range of the different meanings of the panethnic labels.
2. Parts of tables 11.1 and 11.3 appeared originally in Itzigsohn and Dore (2000).
3. There is considerable debate over the appropriateness of the Hispano/a or Latino/a labels, and it would have been interesting to explore the differences between those who choose one or the other. Unfortunately, the small size of the sample does not allow such analysis. Nevertheless, it is our impression that this debate is stronger among academics and activists and that most people use both words interchangeably.
4. Not all of the twenty-three cases used the indio/a identification. We put together all those who used intermediate racial categories under this label.
5. Some recent articles present evidence in favor of the hypothesis that the U.S experience increases Dominicans' identification as blacks (Duany 1998; Torres-Saillant 1998). These findings call for further research in this area.
6. Although we don't analyze the issue in this paper, we argue that a similar process is occurring in Latino churches.

REFERENCES

Bourdieu, Pierre. *Language and Symbolic Power.* Cambridge, Mass.: Harvard University Press, 1991.

Cortina, Rodolfo J. 1990. "Cubans in Miami: Ethnic Identification and Behaviour." *Latino Studies Journal* 1 (1990): 60–73.

Dore-Cabral, Carlos. "Encuesta *Rumbo*-Gallup: La población dominicana es mas antihaitiana que racista." *Rumbo,* May 29, 1995, pp. 8–12.

Duany, Jorge. *Quisqueya on the Hudson: The Transnational Identity of Dominicans in Washington Heights.* New York: The City University of New York Dominican Studies Institute, 1994.

——— "Reconstructing Racial Identity: Ethnicity, Color, and Class Among Dominicans in the United States and Puerto Rico." *Latin American Perspectives* 25, no. 3 (May 1998): 147–72.

Giménez, Martha E. 1992. "U.S. Ethnic Politics: Implications for Latin Americans." *Latin American Perspectives* 19(4): 7–17.

Graham, Pamela. 1997. "Reimagining the Nation and Defining the District: Dominican Migration and International Politics." In *Caribbean Circuits: New Directions in the Study of Caribbean Migration,* ed. Patricia Pessar, 91–126. Staten Island, N.Y.: Center for Migration Studies.

Grasmuck, Sherri and Patricia Pessar. *Between Two Islands: Dominican International Migration.* Berkeley: University of California Press, 1991.

——— "First and Second Generation Settlement of Dominicans in the United States: 1960–1990." In *Origins and Destinies: Immigration, Race and Ethnicity in America,* ed. Silvia Pedraza and Ruben Rubmaut. Belmont, Calif.: Watsworth Press, 1995.

Grosfoguel, Ramon and Chloé S. Georas. "The Racialization of Latino Caribbean Migrants in the New York Metropolitan Area." *Journal of the Center for Puerto Rican Studies* 8, nos. 1 and 2 (1996): 191–201.

Guarnizo, Luis E. "Los Dominicanyorks: The Making of a Binational Society." *Annals of the American Academy of Political and Social Sciences* 533 (May 1994): 70–86.

Hernández, Ramona, Francisco Rivera-Batíz, and Roberto Agodini. *Dominican New Yorkers: A Socioeconomic Profile.* New York: The City University of New York Dominican Studies Institute, 1995.

Itzigsohn, José. 1995. "Migrant Remittances, Labor Markets, and Household Strategies: A Comparative Analysis of Low-Income Household Strategies in the Caribbean Basin," *Social Forces* 74, no. 2 (December 1995): 633–57.

Itzigsohn, José and Carlos Dore-Cabral. 2000. "Competing Identities? Race, Ethnicity and Panethnicity among Dominicans in the United States." *Sociological Forum* 15, no. 2.

López, David and Yen Espíritu. "Panethnicity in the United States: A Theoretical Framework." *Ethnic and Racial Studies* 13, no. 2 (April 1990): 198–224.

Massey Douglas S. "Latinos, Poverty, and the Underclass: A New Agenda for Research." *Hispanic Journal of Behavioral Sciences* 15, no. 4 (November 1993): 449–75.

Moore, Joan. "Hispanic/Latino: Imposed Label or Real Identity?" *Latino Studies Journal* 1 (1990): 33–47.

Oboler, Suzanne. "The Politics of Labeling: Latino/a Cultural Identities of Self and Other." *Latin American Perspectives* 19 (Fall 1992): 18–36.

——— *Ethnic Labels, Latino Lives.* Minneapolis: University of Minnesota Press, 1995.

Padilla, Felix. "On the Nature of Latino Ethnicity." *Social Science Quarterly* 65 (1984): 651–64.

——— *Latino Ethnic Consciousness.* Notre Dame, Ind.: University of Notre Dame Press, 1985.

Rodríguez, Clara E. "Race, Culture, and Latino 'Otherness' in the 1980 Census." *Social Science Quarterly* 73 (1992): 931–37.

Rodríguez, Clara E. and Hector Cordero-Guzmán. "Placing Race in Context." *Ethnic and Racial Studies* 15, no. 4 (October 1992): 523–41.

Torres-Saillant, Silvio. "The Tribulations of Blackness: Stages in Dominican Racial Identity." *Latin American Perspectives* 25, no. 3 (May 1998): 126–46.

Waters, Mary. "Ethnic and Racial Identities of Second-Generation Black Immigrants in New York City." *International Migration Review* 28, no. 4 (1994): 795–820.

CHAPTER TWELVE

Immigration Status and Identity

Undocumented Mexicans in New York

*Jocelyn Solís**

DISCOURSES AND COUNTERDISCOURSES OF ILLEGALITY

Some could argue that the adoption of discourses that label and identify are a necessary aspect of social life. One cannot have an identity unless one is named. As I approach the issue of illegal Mexican immigration, especially as it is taking place in New York City, it is important to keep in mind the problems that being classified as "illegal" can cause for an individual who must learn to navigate within and outside of the many sources of meaning that such an identity carries.

This essay will discuss the close link between discourse and identity and the complex conditions that produce an illegal or undocumented identity. As others have argued, identity is a locus of convergence of both societal and individual conditions (Deaux 1991). Although traditional studies of psychology define *identity* as a composite of traits inherent to an individual, social constructionist accounts of self and identity instead argue that social, political, and interactive conditions make certain identities possible (Gergen 1991). Sociocultural theory would further argue that the emergence of a psychological form rests on the transformation of the individual's manipulation of external conditions or resources into a bidirectional function-

*I am greatly indebted to the editors and anonymous reviewers of this volume as well as to my faculty and colleagues for their constructive comments and suggestions to earlier drafts of this manuscript, which continue to be instrumental in the shaping of this work.

ing between the individual's external *and* mental conditions (Van der Veer and Valsiner 1994).

In this frame, identity is derived as a psychological form from the individual's manipulation of preexisting social conditions. I will discuss how one possible identity that preexists for would-be immigrants in the United States is illegality, an identity that emerges from existing social conditions and structures. Mexicans who immigrate to New York enter into particularly new social positions as they cross invented geographical borders, political systems, and institutions that produce certain discourses about who they are. The notion of a border to be crossed and laws that determine who may and may not cross it as well as how the border ought to be crossed presuppose the existence of both legal and illegal immigrants. They involve discourses that reproduce relations of power stemming from a particular ideology (Parker 1992). That is, the border, its militarization, and immigration laws in their respective functions produce a discourse about a U.S. population composed of those who are insiders and those who are outsiders, those who have certain rights and those who do not; moreover, they are structures that afford a discourse based on value judgments about why some belong in the country and why others are not authorized to enter. Mainstream media often maintain and reproduce such discourses of power in their depiction of Mexican immigrants as unwanted invaders and dangers to U.S. society (Edstrom 1993). Undocumented immigrants are positioned by the discourses of such social structures as undesirable foreigners and as threats to the welfare of the United States. In this manner, some social structures afford immigrants the identity of illegality, laden with negative meanings without even needing to take the individual into account.

An individual exists nonetheless. Undocumented immigrants must either adopt or reappropriate this social position to express their identity and exist within a preestablished social order. To reiterate, identity is the adoption of a social position couched in relations of power and discourse (Harré and Gillett 1994). Nevertheless, although discourse can be normative, it is also a tool that is culturally created and therefore malleable. Consequently, a counterdiscourse can emerge that contests the discourse produced by those in power. A counterdiscourse emerging from those in a weaker position of power can serve to readjust the meanings underlying who undocumented immigrants are and thus function to reclaim identity if it is recognized by those with the authority to legitimate it. The challenge for undocumented immigrants, therefore, is how to reclaim their identity as undocumented immigrants without invoking its meanings already established by structures of power and without provoking action to be taken against them. Undocumented immigrants have rights in the United States of which they are often unaware and that are often abused (Mirandé 1985). To be able to seek their rights and report an abuse of those rights, undocumented immigrants would have to disclose their identities as such. In doing so, they would also be forced to risk deportation. I argue in this paper that one resource undocumented immigrants use to enable their identities as undocumented immigrants to emerge publicly is community organization.

As a Mexican American woman from New York who has witnessed the changes taking place within the Mexican population in the city, I maintain not only an intellectual interest in this topic but a deeply personal one as well. My awareness of the hardships and barriers that undocumented immigrants face as they move to this country, and of the persistence, bravery, and dignity that characterize many of these people, is part of a history that informs my perspective. In fact, I consider knowledge of these everyday stories to be an important part of the oral history of the Mexican community in the United States. As a partisan of an ethnic community of which I am a member, I find it important to explore the manner in which research and theory can address issues that on a sociopolitical level impinge on the lives of individual people. However, I do not intend by any means to be a spokesperson for an entire population.

To understand the perspectives of other informal participants and advocates who work with this population, this essay is further informed by interviews I conducted in the past year with an attorney and with community leaders in a few nonprofit organizations. Another objective of conducting these interviews was to reveal how undocumented Mexican immigrants are identified by some public institutions in the city. In addition, the ideas presented in this essay are based on my participation as a volunteer in one of the nongovernment, community organizations I originally interviewed. The purpose is to discuss the complex problem of identity formation as it is further complicated by the overtly politicized situation of illegal Mexican immigration by providing a critical perspective on the mutual role that U.S. society and undocumented Mexican immigrants have on this formation.

Although the organization of this paper moves between general, historical, and more local accounts of Mexican immigration, these levels of description are always located within national conditions (in the form of various institutions) that intersect with personal, everyday conditions to produce certain identities. In a sociocultural and historical framework (Scribner 1985), I argue that identity is a form that develops, that comes into existence under some circumstances and is reinvented under others for a purpose. In a general sense, an identity functions to group people artificially, overlooking differences found within the group. That is, identities can function to essentialize or homogenize groups in ways that do not necessarily speak to the everyday experience of individuals. In a particular sense, the manipulation of social structures and the positions they afford serves as a means of reappropriating identity. Nevertheless, the sociopolitical milieu provides the conditions for certain kinds of groupings (e.g., based on legal status) to emerge during certain historical periods. Once the historical and actual conditions in which identities emerge are recognized, one cannot speak of identity as a stable or unitary category. Identity is always contextual, couched in the everyday, and variable.

To distinguish between identity as it is produced by those in a predominant power position in society (e.g., lawmakers) and identity as it is counterproduced by those in a weaker position of power (e.g., undocumented immigrants), I will refer to the former as an *illegal identity* and the latter as an *undocumented identity*. This essay attempts to open possibilities for further theory and research that investigate how *indocumentados,* undocumented Mexican immigrants, come to terms with one position (illegal immigrant) and its meanings made available to them by U.S. structures upon entry and consequent participation in this country. I will explore the historical conditions in which an illegal identity has emerged and the different means through which this has occurred. Then I will discuss how an undocumented identity can emerge, particularly through the involvement of allies of immigrants in some city institutions as well as through immigrants' own involvement in organizations. First, however, I will review the situation of undocumented Mexican immigrants in New York.

THE EMERGENCE OF MEXICAN MIGRATION TO NEW YORK

In spite of the fact that New York City has historically been a site for the settlement of new Latin immigrants, Mexican immigration to New York City only escalated relatively recently for economic as well as legal reasons. Flores (1996) reports that changes in immigration law in 1965 that ended the quota system based on national origin opened the country to Latin American immigrants who had been previously disfavored in comparison to those from western and northern Europe. Mexicans, however, were not among the Latin-origin groups entering New York in fairly large numbers until the 1980s.

The Mexican population in New York City has grown so considerably and quickly in recent years that it is counted among the five largest Latino groups in the city (Flores 1996). According to Mollenkopf (personal communication, October 1999), there are an estimated 300,000 Mexicans living in New York. Because many of these new immigrants are undocumented, estimates of the size of the population are difficult to come by; Smith estimates that of the most recent immigrants, at least half are undocumented (personal communication, October 1999). As far as visibility is concerned, the population has made itself known in a variety of public arenas such as diverse workplaces, social and religious domains, and both English- and Spanish-language media in ways that affect both the economic and cultural capital of the city. Whether they are seen in the workplace, selling flowers, working in delis or restaurants, making deliveries, laboring as domestics, or participating in public protests or marches, Mexican men, women, and children are now a significant, noticeable part of New York City.

Smith (1996) has found that immigration to New York City began in the early 1940s in the Mixteca Baja region of Mexico, an area comprising the southern part of the state of Puebla, the northern part of Oaxaca, and the eastern part of Guerrero. This migration pattern continued until the late 1960s, when the percentage of Mexicans moving to the city began to increase, and then spiraled in the mid-1980s when an economic crisis in Mexico fell especially harshly on the Mixteca Baja region. Immigration to New York seems to have increased steadily from then and escalated considerably again following a second economic crisis in 1994.

Smith (1996) states that Mexicans seem to be settling in Manhattan temporarily while they find larger, cheaper housing in other boroughs. In this respect, the Mexican population has not settled in one neighborhood but in several neighborhoods around the city that have been historically occupied by Latin-origin groups. According to the Institute for Puerto Rican Policy's *New York City Latino Neighborhoods Data Book* (Hanson-Sánchez 1996), each of the city's five boroughs now houses Mexican immigrants; according to this source, the largest Mexican neighborhoods are in Sunset Park, Brooklyn; Mott Haven, the Bronx; and El Barrio/East Harlem in Manhattan. As one *New York Times* article puts it:

> In past decades, the city attracted a small group of Mexican professionals, businessmen and artists. But the most recent migration, which gathered steam about five years ago, is bringing many poorer, mostly illegal Mexican immigrants. Many of them have settled in small pockets in the city's established Hispanic neighborhoods, like East Harlem in Manhattan, the Williamsburg section of Brooklyn and the Tremont section of the Bronx. (González 1991:A1)

Thus, one can see a growing Mexican population in traditionally immigrant neighborhoods such as Jackson Heights, Queens, where a stroll along Roosevelt Avenue will reveal all kinds of small Mexican businesses ranging from restaurants, *panaderías* (bakeries), and groceries to *taquerías* and music stores.

STRUCTURES OF SOCIAL ORGANIZATION AND IDENTITY

Unlike other parts of the United States, New York City affords a particularly unique situation for Mexican immigrants as they enter new racial and pan-ethnic classifications and social memberships in which they are identified as Latinos. The emergence of these "new New Yorkers" (Flores 1996:172) has greatly diversified the Latino presence in the city. As Flores notes, being Latino in New York had at one point been synonymous with being Puerto Rican; now the classification includes these new immigrants who do not share the same experience or history as other older, Latin-origin immigrants. This panethnic identity, however, is obviously a nationally recognized identity; that is, it is not particular to New York City although its functions may be reproduced locally. Nationally, the term *Latino* was designed to describe all persons of Latin American descent, regardless of race, social class, gender, or religion as a response to the government-imposed term *Hispanic,* a term that privileges Spanish or European heritage over indigenous and African origins (Oboler 1995). Thus the reappropriation of identity through the construction of a new label, Latino, was a political move meant to redefine oneself and one's social memberships according to geographic origin, in spite of within-group differences of race, nationality, gender, class, language, or dialect.

Nonetheless, in a society organized according to race, the terms *Latino* and *Hispanic* often become confounded as racial identities whose meanings must constantly be negotiated in social practice. Such racial or panethnic identities cannot be immediately adopted by newcomers to the United States; recent immigrants, such as Mexicans in New York, must be socialized into understanding a new system of identity politics and manifestation. Their new social position as Latinos or Hispanics is based on an abstracted classification that cannot do justice to within-group variations yet whose adoption is necessary for political activity and presence. Labels and categories used to represent some unitary whole often ignore geographic, language, gender, and class distinctions as well as the social categories and meanings that new immigrants carry with them into the United States.

Among the sources of diversity, some within-group variations to which I would like to call particular attention as they currently impinge on Mexican identity in New York City are time of entry into the United States and immigration status. I maintain that ethnic and panethnic labels on several scales (global, national, and local) come to be intertwined at times with labels of status, including legal/illegal immigration status, as they are each based on distinctions between a predominant "us" and a marginalized "other." Seen within a historical context, Oboler argues that "people of Latin American descent in the United States have long been perceived homogeneously as 'foreign' to the image of 'being American' since the nineteenth century regardless of the time and mode of their incorporation into the United States or their subsequent status as citizens of this nation" (1995:18).

She explains how the discourse of superiority of U.S. mainstream society over the rest of the Americas, as a homogeneous block, was manifested in the early nineteenth century:

> As early as 1823, the Monroe Doctrine determined that the entire hemisphere was to come under the sphere of influence of the United States. Initially an economic rather than political declaration ... the Monroe Doctrine had in effect early on begun to establish a homogeneous approach to relations between the United States and Latin American nations and was to have far-reaching implications in forging a public American identity in relation to the other emerging nations in the hemisphere. (1995:33)

The view of a homogenous United States is counterposed to that of an other, a homogeneous Latin America. In a similar fashion, this view persists today vis-à-vis illegal immigration. The currently fierce campaign to curtail entry by undocumented immigrants along the U.S.-Mexico border through increases in border patrols and new policies that restrict basic human rights to undocumented Mexicans, as supported by the passing of Proposition 187 in California (Quiroga 1995; Smith and Tarallo 1995), can be understood as a continued, national crusade to maintain this image of a homogeneous United States that should not be corrupted by the perceived other. Similarly, within the country, processes of categorization that distinguish between an "us" and a "them" reify relations of power. For example, distinctions between the white mainstream and racial minorities ignore within-group differences in the process of identification, such as that between U.S.-born and immigrant minorities (Gibson and Ogbu 1991), yet these distinctions identify all minorities in relation to an unvarying, white cohort.

Thus, the organization of society according to race/ethnicity follows from a long history of nationalist ideologies that attempt to distinguish between the mainstream and everyone else. At the same time, however, other social structures permit within-group variation. Latinos are others, one minority group that can be further differentiated according to legal status. Entry into the United States itself is an initial locus of labeling. Particularly if one is Mexican, one can enter either illegally or not; one can be either a legal or illegal alien. The identity category legal/illegal alien is already available to immigrants before they even cross into the country. Although anyone who falls outside of the mainstream may be considered a foreign other, a subcategory further dichotomizes the other by predominant national immigration standards that distinguish between those others who live in the country legally or illegally.

A process of categorization, as is made evident in the emergence of the social position legal/illegal immigrant, serves to stabilize identity by classifying activity (that of entering and residing in the country under some conditions at a particular moment), turning an unfolding process into a constant feature of individuals. Thus, the activity of living illegally in the United States is made static by grouping individuals into a dichotomous category. *Illegal alien* is an imposed term generated by government standards on immigration that fail to address the complex conditions that lead to such a state of being. Furthermore, the language of this social position functions to uphold a negative image of undocumented immigrants by portraying them as something like "outlaws from another planet" (Conover 1987:xiv). Undocumented Mexicans are indeed foreigners to U.S. society, yet the term *illegal* blurs the line between what counts as an illegal action, such as crossing the border without the necessary documents, and what counts as a criminal act that warrants punishment. Thus, discourses of illegality further criminalize undocumented immigrants without consideration of the social forces that foment illegal immigration or of the individual immigrant's interpretation of her or his own situation within this preexisting social order.

However, contradictions also arise in the ways that nonmainstream groups are identified on a societal scale. For example, Oboler illustrates how Latinos are increasingly stigmatized when they are associated with such social problems as high drop-out rates, teenage pregnancy, AIDS, drugs, and crime, yet "from the perspective of business entrepreneurs ... the term 'Hispanic ethnicity' identifies a lucrative market segment and good box-office" (1995:14).

Undocumented immigrants may be identified as criminals, as the term *illegal* would imply, but are simultaneously seen as consumers and serve as cheap labor, both necessary for the country's economic prosperity. The manner in which these contradictions unfold among undocumented Mexicans in New York City can only be understood by paying close attention to their individual experiences embedded within the conditions afforded by the societies in which they live. In this sense, contradictions found within the process of defining identities appear on societal scales yet must somehow be negotiated on local, individual levels. Illegality produces a contradictory social position that historically preexists immigrants, yet serves as a psychological tool for the individual to have an identity that is recognized by the larger society. Thus, identity must be understood as a product of its historical and personal specificity.

THE HISTORICAL EMERGENCE OF AN ILLEGAL IDENTITY

The history of undocumented Mexicans migrating to and living in New York differs radically from the history of Mexicans settling in the Southwest (Meier and Ribera 1993; Sánchez 1993). Although Mexican immigration history itself is different from that of other Latin American groups, methods of incorporation into the United States are also different for subgroups of Mexicans settling in geographically different areas of the country. In other words, Mexican immigrants to the United States can be subdivided into those who have migrated to traditionally Mexican parts of the country (such as the Southwest), and those who are migrating to newer settlement areas (such as New York City).

Mexicans living in the Southwest have a long history of settlement in the United States that spreads over generations and encompasses people who may never have immigrated to the United States at all. After the Mexican War ended in 1848, land that was once considered Mexican territory became part of the United States, and Mexicans were given the opportunity to stay and retain their land as U.S. citizens according to the Treaty of Guadalupe-Hidalgo. Oboler cites Richard Griswold del Castillo on this matter: "While many won their cases, hundreds were ultimately displaced from their lands—whether as a result of unscrupulous lawyers and unfair judicial practices, of pressure to give up the land, or of confusion about their titles and the new land laws and language" (1995:23). Often referred to as outsiders in their own land, generations of Mexicans of the present-day U.S. Southwest never actually crossed the border. As a result of their incorporation into a new society largely organized according to race, some Mexicans of the Southwest could identify themselves as Hispanic or Spanish American as a means of deemphasizing their mestizo roots and tracing their ancestry back to racially "pure" Spaniards. This identity has also functioned to distinguish them from working-class, newly arrived, undocumented Mexicans.

Labor shortages during World War II resulted in the *bracero* program, bringing 4.8 million Mexicans into the southwestern United States from 1943 to 1964. Midwestern urban centers, such as Chicago, then drew Mexican agricultural workers from the Southwest into the railroad industry there (Guerra 1998). Although the bracero program was continuous, these same Mexicans were considered illegal after the war ended and their services were no longer needed; at this time, the government began efforts to deport them. The point is that Mexican braceros were brought to the country by the U.S. government and became illegal as a result of their overstay rather than as a result of physically crossing the border in an unauthorized manner.

The appearance of student and working-class organized campaigns such as the Chicano/a Power movements and the founding of both the United Farm Workers under the direction of César Chávez and La Raza Unida in the 1960s were motions designed to reorganize and reappropriate Mexican identity in the United States for political ends, mitigating internal divisions stemming from differences in class, generation, and immigration status. Each of these movements attempted to unite urban and rural Mexicans as well as newly arrived Mexican immigrants with older generations of Mexican Americans. Their efforts sought to curtail the antagonisms rising between older and newer Mexicans or between those who had been born here and those who had just crossed the border, legally or illegally. In this way, Mexicans of different generations were able to reorganize existing social positions according to their own needs and interests.

BEYOND A HOMOGENEOUS MEXICAN IDENTITY

Mexicans in New York have not experienced this same history. At most, New York can see a first and second generation of Mexicans who are generally from the working class participating in a new process of identification that is situated historically in a unique way. Due to the recency of their migration and new destinations, their identity has origins different from that of Mexicans in other parts of the country. For instance, in a three-year ethnographic study of Mexican families living along the Texas-Chihuahua border, Valdés (1997) found that although most of the families she studied had crossed the border illegally, the act itself was not considered a major turning point in their lives. All of them had lived along the Mexican border, and living on either side did not make much difference to them. They were used to crossing the border with or without *papeles* (legal documents).

New York Mexicans, on the other hand, generally do not share the same border lifestyle and history. Mexicans in New York are mostly migrating from south-central parts of Mexico. The geographic distance alone is greater for them to traverse than it is for Mexicans of the borderlands. New York Mexicans are not coming into a city with a preestablished Mexican community or with forceful political movements under way, although some organization is already taking place, especially by nongovernment organizations. Moreover, contact with people of other races as well as contact with other Latinos is prevalent in New York City and unique to those Mexicans migrating into this city. Mexicans are entering an unparalleled situation in New York City as they find a vast array of Latino immigrant groups facing some of the same challenges they are. According to Flores (1996), as of 1990, the five largest Latino groups in New York were Puerto Ricans, Dominicans, Colombians, Ecuadoreans, and Mexicans; although none of these groups share the same history of migration, what does unify these various ethnic groups is New York City itself as the common locus of identity formation and reformulation.

As a result of their entry into both a racialized society and a particularly cosmopolitan city, Mexicans in New York are identified in ways that are singular to this historical period and geographic locale. They are Latinos who come into contact with other Latinos in their neighborhoods and workplaces, yet in spite of their common racial identity and social class, many differ along one fundamental aspect: legal status. Particularly, contact between Mexicans and Puerto Ricans, who are both the largest Latino ethnic group in New York *and* U.S. citizens, has led to hostilities and conflicts that often surface in public forums. For example, consider the following comment about new Latino immigrants in New York City, especially Mexicans and Dominicans, by Herman Badillo, a Puerto Rican excongressman:

If you go to El Barrio in East Harlem, 115th Street, you see a sign that says "Mexican Meat Market." Then you turn around the corner, then you see "Mexican Grocery Store." Why should there be? . . . This is supposed to be a Puerto Rican area, it's all Mexicans. (September 22, 1999, transcript prepared by the Office of University Relations of the City University of New York)

Such interethnic conflict is encountered in schools and neighborhoods and is fostered by competing power structures that organize people according to race/ethnicity, social class, and legal status. Close contact between Puerto Ricans and Mexicans in New York, and tensions resulting from their differences in citizenship and immigration status are experiences that have historically not been shared by Mexicans of the Southwest.

NATIONAL ACTIONS AND LOCAL CONDITIONS IN THE FORMATION OF ILLEGALITY

Although larger economic trends affecting the labor market both in Mexico and the United States impact immigration into the United States, policy changes on the part of the U.S. government coupled with community formation and local Mexican settlement patterns also contribute to the emergence of illegality. For example, the introduction of Proposition 187 in California as well as other bills designed to deny basic human rights and birthright citizenship to children of undocumented immigrants (Alarcón 1994; U.S. House 1995) can be understood as political moves intended to curtail illegal immigration. In a similar vein, it is not surprising that a federal analysis of a New York immigration law adopted in 1996 posited that the implications of the law would make it difficult for poor immigrants, especially Mexicans who are among the poorest, to legally bring family members into the United States. Because the law requires sponsors of potential new immigrants to earn at least a $19,500 yearly salary, it is designed to restrict immigration by the poor and thus reduce dependence on public aid. Although the use of public assistance programs by immigrants is a subject of debate, others add that the law may in fact *encourage* illegal immigration (Dugger 1997). Economic need, the strength of family ties, and dependence on family networks in light of a lack of public services for undocumented immigrants in the United States may overpower legal measures to deter illegal immigration.

In many ways, the rejection of poorer classes of immigrants becomes synonymous with the rejection of undocumented immigrants and Latinos in general who may occupy the same spaces. Moreover, lower-income neighborhoods and their inhabitants are often identified as cultivators of crime. Poor neighborhoods of New York City, in particular, are often associated with high crime rates, further entangling the categories of illegality and criminality. For example, when describing the Roosevelt Avenue area of

Queens as a new locus of settlement for poor, undocumented Mexicans, one *New York Times* article described it as a place "where the elevated No. 7 train has long served as a cover for nighttime drug sales and other criminal activities" (Onishi 1996:4). In this way, stigmas against Latinos, the poor, criminals, and undocumented immigrants become confounded as the physical spaces they each occupy are shared.

According to an interview I conducted with a criminal attorney working with the Legal Aid Society, the oldest nonprofit legal organization in the country, once arrested a person is immediately identified according to immigration status for the reason that a criminal conviction affects an immigrant's likelihood of obtaining legal residency. Moreover, a conviction places undocumented immigrants within the justice system, facilitating their deportation. For minor cases, a fine would have to be paid or community service fulfilled. As for undocumented immigrants, a minor case would not place them at special risk for deportation, although this is a potential risk they always face.

Because undocumented immigrants are ordinarily also poor, they would be likely to seek Legal Aid's services. This attorney estimates that 99 percent of her Mexican clients are undocumented. She also stressed that most of them are generally first-time offenders charged with misdemeanors, such as consuming alcohol in public, driving under the influence of alcohol, or driving without a license. The undocumented Mexicans with whom she has been in contact generally do not get rearrested or serve time in prison because they are not usually charged with major crimes.

Although undocumented Mexican immigrants are equated with criminals in the public eye, in order to make such an assumption, one would need to also examine publicly and thoroughly the rates with which they are arrested, the kinds of crimes they commit, as well as the reasons for which Mexicans cross the border illegally. Generalizations about undocumented Mexican immigrants are thus based on incomplete social analyses that publicly ignore the activities and practices that would define more accurately who undocumented immigrants are.

HIDDEN DISCOURSES OF ILLEGALITY

The United States assumes the right to control its own territory and exclude certain entrants, such as undocumented immigrants. At the same time, however, one finds that minimum-wage laws are supposed to protect all workers in the United States regardless of legal status. In spite of a demand in the United States for undocumented workers, the consequences of such contradictions result in many kinds of abuse as in the form of extremely low or unpaid wages, dangerous working environments, and even physical maltreatment. Mirandé (1985) corroborates that undocumented Mexicans generally assume jobs that domestic workers do not want because of their physical difficulty, long hours, low pay, and working conditions that often fall below minimum standards. He also postulates that if displacement of domestic employees by undocumented workers were a true concern, it could be easily abolished if minimum wage legislation were honored and equal pay given to all employees, regardless of their legal status. He goes as far as to encourage an open border, unconditional amnesty for all foreigners, and cessation of border patrol and immigration surveillance, a series of goals common to immigrant organizations in New York City. To understand how undocumented workers are simultaneously benefiting the country and being accused of abusing it, one has to consider conditions that do not often enter public, mainstream discussions of this problem.

Nowhere have the abuses toward undocumented Mexicans in New York City been made more evident in both Spanish- and English-language media than in the case of a group of deaf-mute Mexicans who were severely exploited, and sometimes physically and sexually abused, as they worked for fellow Mexicans in New York. Known as a national smuggling ring with connections in Chicago and other cities in California and North Carolina, undocumented Mexicans' stories of poverty, abuse, and exploitation emerged in the media as tales of

> deaf people being promised opportunity in the United States that
> they were denied in Mexico, only to work as slaves for a deaf
> Mexican family named Paoletti. The peddlers told authorities
> that they sold trinkets on the subway 16 hours a day, and that
> every dollar they collected was turned over to a superior. But the
> abuse extended beyond servitude. . . . The peddlers have told of
> being beaten and sexually abused, of being denied contact with
> their families in Mexico. (Barry 1997:26)

Although the exploited deaf Mexicans were granted temporary, and eventually permanent, legal residence in the United States (Ojito 1997), their stories generated strong emotions in the media, conjuring images of slavery, peonage, and servitude; the case, in some instances, was also used to uphold the image of a United States of liberty and equal opportunity tainted by newer, undocumented immigrants:

> Those who have always had their doubts about immigration will
> surely find in the news from Queens confirmation of their fears
> that immigrants undermine the American way of life. . . . That
> immigration has brought to our shores the kind of peonage
> abolished in this country long ago would seem to confirm the
> belief that allowing indiscriminate entry into the United States
> would corrupt our most fundamental values. . . . Moved by the
> plight of people barely capable of communicating their distress,

we might decide that the nation has a humanitarian duty to help the vulnerable, especially those attracted to this country by the opportunities it offers. That would be a wrong conclusion. This was not, after all, a tale of wealthy Americans exploiting helpless immigrants, but of one group of immigrants exploiting another in a country to which neither belonged. (Wolfe 1997:A21)

Such opinions maintain the vision of a country that, without the interference of undocumented immigrants, protects the liberty and human rights of its people. A more realistic account of the news would not place the blame on foreign others who do not even belong in the country but instead represent the deaf victims as an extreme example of the kind of exploitation inherent to living illegally, which conditions in both the United States and Mexico foster.

According to my interview with the criminal attorney, during investigations of the case of the deaf-mute Mexican immigrants, some Legal Aid attorneys were present throughout questioning sessions to make sure that this particular group of undocumented immigrants did not criminally implicate itself and that they were not being threatened by the Immigration and Naturalization Service (INS) to give information unrelated to their questioning as witnesses. As undocumented immigrants with special needs who were both witnesses and victims of a crime, they were granted special visas to stay in the country and testify during the trial. Throughout this process, however, their status caused them to remain in the custody of the INS, which meant that they were not free to come and go as the pleased; actually, they were housed in a motel whose entrance was watched by security guards. Several of the women being detained were pregnant or mothers of very young children. Everyone was housed as a prisoner in the building, with armed officers stationed in the hallways that served as playgrounds. Such an understanding of the real practices surrounding undocumented immigrants reveals how undocumented Mexicans are simultaneously identified as victims of other outsiders, as corruptors of the liberal values of U.S. society, and as a result of their immigration status alone, as criminals.

ECONOMIC AND SOCIAL NETWORKS PRODUCE ILLEGALITY

An examination of the manner in which socioeconomic conditions in both countries have historically and continuously provided undocumented Mexicans as human currency is absolutely lacking in public discourses on immigration. Complex economic transactions between both the United States and Mexico set up conditions that foment illegal immigration. Changes in the Mexican economy from traditional to liberal policies, as exemplified in the North American Free Trade Agreement, have fostered migration from rural to urban centers. Because periods of fast industrialization are inherently difficult, Mexico has been undergoing extreme economic hardships (Baker et al. 1998). As a consequence, instead of moving from a rural to an urban center within the country, many migrants leave rural areas in Mexico and move directly to urban centers in the United States. Nevertheless, economic circumstances alone are important but not sufficient for understanding why Mexican migration to New York has increased so quickly or the manner in which this occurs. They do not explain why some people do migrate or how they make such a decision and find the means to realize it.

Smith (1996) reports that a major factor precipitating Mexican immigration to New York specifically was that traditionally Mexican parts of the United States were saturated with newer Mexicans, rendering employment scarce. Once information about the availability of cheap labor and willingness to hire Mexicans in New York spread, the flow of immigration began to increase dramatically. Generally, the use of such information networks has enabled the Mexican population in the city to find housing and employment. For instance, Smith (1996) finds that networks are formed by small groups of people who find work through each other, spreading the word about potential employers, generally involving some sort of service work, including jobs in grocery stores, dishwashing, or domestic work. Although employers are generally of a different ethnic/racial group, Smith (1996) has found that Greeks and Koreans, for example, tend to hire large groups of Mexicans for various reasons. Primarily, employers' demand for cheap labor is met by Mexicans due to their recency in the country and undocumented status. For example, Kim (1999) finds that Mexicans request employment in Korean businesses once word spreads that Koreans are hiring Mexicans or other Latinos. This situation is particularly interesting given the fact that ethnic ties have historically been important in promoting cooperation for economic mobility within particular ethnic groups. However, Kim documents how co-ethnic solidarity for Korean business owners has been changing along with immigration trends in recent years. Business competition by fellow Koreans and increasing availability of cheap labor by Mexicans have transformed dependence on co-ethnics into dependence on non-co-ethnics for the promotion of their businesses.

Mexicans who are in dire economic need are willing to take difficult jobs with little pay to meet basic needs for themselves here as well as for their families back home. Flower vendors, for instance, have worked about twelve hours a day and earned between $175 and $200 over a seven-day work week (James 1991). In spite of very low wages, the U.S. dollar is still highly valued by Mexican immigrants in comparison to the economic power of salaries they would earn at home. Due to their status as undocumented immigrants, Mexicans occupy a weak bargaining position; they cannot obtain the higher-skilled, higher-paid positions because they lack legal documents even though they may possess the required skills. Their legal status also makes it difficult for them to demand back wages or to make other claims. Language differences only add to the difficulty. For the undocumented immigrants whom Kim interviewed, many seemed to desire legalizing their status so that they could travel back and forth between their home countries and the United States to visit family. This mind-set of return, regardless of actual practice, originates in migrants' planning activities before leaving Mexico. It may be sustained in the United States as a result of living in a place where legal and human rights to which undocumented immigrants are entitled are not enforced if you are not a citizen. As I mentioned earlier in this essay, the challenge for undocumented immigrants is finding the means through which they can make a reasonable living in the United States, demand that their rights be enforced, *and* have their social existence recognized.

COUNTERDISCOURSES OF ILLEGALITY

Luis Moll (1997) has documented the cultural practice of networking intellectual and material resources between Mexican families in the Southwest as "funds of knowledge." In this sense, knowledge about how to be undocumented, that is, knowing how to cross the border illegally, find work, and reside in the United States without placing oneself in jeopardy, is circulated internally, among individuals who belong to this particular community. These activities set the stage for understanding the hidden discourses of illegality and how certain kinds of identities are communicated. Networking facilitates access to resources and information that is otherwise undisclosed and is also an activity that may function to identify one as undocumented. However, this form of networking is itself a hidden discourse of identity as it remains internal to the community. As long as their identity remains suppressed, undocumented immigrants cannot make public demands. A counterdiscourse, on the other hand, publicly resists predominant discourses of illegality. I argue that for an undocumented identity to become public, the institutionalization of networking practices is necessary. The public, institutional form of undocumented identity is found in community organizing and may be the kind of activity that leads to permanent settlement among undocumented Mexican families in New York. This a possibility that has not been investigated among Mexicans in this city.

For example, Hondagneu-Sotelo (1995) has found that in California, women contribute significantly to permanent settlement among undocumented Mexican immigrant families; Mexican women are found to be central to the settlement process as fundamental facilitators for families to establish stable employment, build community, and supply the resources necessary for sustenance and reproduction, especially as this is brought about through their involvement in public institutions. As increasing numbers of women and children make their way into New York City (González 1991), particular attention to them as participants in the formation of the

Mexican setting here is especially due. Smith (1996) finds that amnesty granted to undocumented Mexicans in New York by the 1986 Immigration Reform and Control Act practically disintegrated intentions of permanent return to Mexico. This does not explain, however, the settlement of those families that remain undocumented. In addition, legal status has implications for the way parents socialize their children, whose resulting permanent settlement and participation in society would involve negotiating the official discourse of their illegitimacy along with their own awareness of hidden or counter discourses that produce an undocumented identity. Therefore, an understanding of the ways in which Mexican families participate in public institutions and organizations is still needed to specify how and where an undocumented identity may emerge.

IDENTIFYING HEALTH CONCERNS AND THEIR RELATION TO IMMIGRATION STATUS

One nonprofit organization I contacted and interviewed was established as a result of identifying the Latino population in New York as one in need of information in Spanish and of services related to health, particularly HIV/AIDS awareness, prevention, and treatment. This organization centers around these concerns, and the representative whom I interviewed stressed that the organization provides no direct treatment but rather initiates outreach programs to the general Latino population in New York to educate and raise consciousness, defend the rights of Latinos with HIV, and make referrals. In addition, the organization communicates with other community organizations and service providers to sensitize them to the health needs of Latinos living in New York and to encourage them to make HIV/AIDS education a part of their agenda.

My informant, a Mexican activist whose ethnic background allows him access to other Mexicans in the city, affirmed that although the organization does not center around issues of legality, immigration status is an important way of framing health issues among Mexican immigrants as there is a close relationship between the two. Legal immigration status and citizenship is now unavailable to people with HIV except under extraordinary circumstances. Persons applying for a change in immigration status are required to be tested for HIV. However, if a person is HIV positive and does not receive counseling the virus can spread here; if the person is deported or returns home, the virus spreads in Mexico as well. In fact, this organization finds that most Mexican immigrants, especially those from rural parts, first become infected while they are living in the United States. As a result of their traveling back and forth with the virus, along with poor education on the subject, the incidence of HIV/AIDS in Mexico has risen. These are health concerns that require immediate attention as they can seriously affect the population in both countries as well as the infected person's chances of survival both in the United States, where access to health care is already limited to emergency situations, and in Mexico, where certain medication and treatments may be unavailable or very costly.

Again, government decisions in the United States exclude certain people from a legitimate place in society and identify poor, undocumented people with HIV and AIDS as especially unwanted social dangers. Policies and public discussion, however, ignore the process by which health matters enter the picture to begin with and how people may live in the United States with HIV, without documents, and without medical treatment. As a consequence of poor information and education in both countries, immigrants place themselves and others in risky situations not only for cases of HIV/AIDS but also for any case of undiagnosed or untreated disease. In a more general sense, my informant also stressed that a sensitivity to cultural differences and legal status is lacking on the part of service providers, who need to understand that they cannot assume immigrants know certain information or will provide details as seemingly meaningless as a Social Security number. Thus, this organization focuses on health concerns as a way of mediating between the general Latino population and social or health service providers; in the process of doing so, undocumented Mexican immigrants are identified according to further-specified needs within the Latino population. In the next section, I will discuss how else the undocumented Mexican population redefines itself through institutions in New York City.

SOCIOCULTURAL AND SPIRITUAL DISPLAYS OF COMMUNITY

Smith (1996) finds that the incorporation of Mexican immigrants in New York City is taking place through social and political forms of organization. For example, he argues that a newly formed "Mexican consciousness" is emerging due to the formation of social, civic, and sports clubs under the direction of the Mexican consulate in affiliation with the Mexican government. By keeping connections between Mexico and New York, Smith (1996, 1998) posits that many new Mexican immigrants are involved in the establishment of a transnational community through government means. However, it is important to keep in mind that Mexicans are often suspicious of government involvement with good reason; the Mexican government was dominated by a single party for over seventy years, and its continued practices of corruption, many immigrants would argue, depleted the country of its resources and fostered extreme poverty and emigration.

Nonetheless, ties between both countries are sustained by travel back and forth (even without documents) as well as by the exchange of "new communication technologies" through television, audio/video tapes (Gendreau and Giménez 1998), and of course monetary remittances

(Cederström 1998). When considering this kind of exchange, then, one has to consider both receiving ends. In other words, transnational ties are based not only on whether immigrants send things home as a way of staying connected to Mexico but also on the ways immigrants transform their surroundings in the United States and Mexico by bringing and integrating certain cultural practices into existing structures. In the case of undocumented Mexican immigrants in the United States, the activities of nongovernment organizations are essential because they further strengthen these practices (Gutiérrez, 1998). They also serve as a psychological tool to then re-present the *public* front of this particular population, a goal that would be difficult to achieve individually.

For example, ties between life in Mexico and in New York are displayed on spiritual levels. The church of Our Lady of Guadalupe on Manhattan's Lower West Side has historically been a center of Mexican immigrants' demonstrations of faith. Year after year on December 12, Mexicans unite at this church at dawn with offerings of flowers and mariachi music to celebrate this feast day as is done in Guadalupe's basilica just outside Mexico City. Now, with the involvement of one Mexican grassroots organization, the feast of Our Lady of Guadalupe is celebrated in churches all over New York City, accompanied by the running of a torch, *la Antorcha Guadalupana*. The strength of those who are *guadalupanos* is seen in their organization of this day in honor of Guadalupe, one of the most important holidays in Mexico. Moreover, this nongovernment organization has sought the city's recognition of this date as a holy day of rest. In this way, all Mexicans in the city, mostly undocumented workers who have no days off or paid vacation, would be able to use their rights as workers to claim one day of rest as their religious observance requires. By working together within the U.S. legal structure, immigrants are seeking to enforce their rights regardless of their legal status and incorporate new practices into the city.

It is not surprising that Guadalupe would act as an emblem of those Mexicans who are struggling and undocumented, as in the case of those living in New York. As a powerful icon of faith, nationality, womanhood, and historic ties between indigenous and colonized people of Mexico (Castillo 1996), *la virgen de Guadalupe* has also come to represent the lives of the oppressed, marginalized, and poor Mexicans of the United States. Anzaldúa writes:

> Our faith is rooted in indigenous attributes, images, symbols,
> magic, and myth. Because *Guadalupe* took upon herself the
> psychological and physical devastation of the conquered and
> oppressed *indio,* she is our spiritual, political, and psychological
> symbol. As a symbol of hope and faith, she sustains and insures
> our survival. . . . To Mexicans on both sides of the border,

> *Guadalupe* is the symbol of our rebellion against the rich, upper
> and middle class; against their subjugation of the poor and the
> *indio.* . . . *La Virgen de Guadalupe* is the symbol of ethnic identity
> and of the tolerance for ambiguity that Chicanos-*mexicanos,*
> people of mixed race, people who have Indian blood, people who
> cross cultures, by necessity possess. (1987:30)

Even though Anzaldúa primarily speaks of Mexicans of the U.S. borderlands when describing how political and psychological identities are im-
pressed on their faith, the largely undocumented, Catholic Mexican population in New York City is no exception.

Their organization at the grassroots level has demonstrated how intricately their ethnic, legal, and spiritual identities are interwoven. I recall one
occasion when a group of teenagers visited the organization to make picket
signs that members would carry later that afternoon in front of the offices
of the INS. Not accidentally, this event was taking place on Good Friday.
In remembrance of Christ's sacrifice, some of the signs read "STOP THE
CRUCIFIXION OF IMMIGRANTS." Although this is only one organization's method of portraying undocumented immigrants (as victims of government actions), it serves to illustrate the idea that individuals use the
resources they have at their disposal to construct their identities in such a
way that is never easily separated into clear pieces. Rather, identity takes
on form through the integration of social means; in this case, those are legal,
political, religious, and ethnic affiliations that operate together for people
to be able to make demands en masse by repositioning themselves in the
face of certain structures of power.

Rather than silently accepting the discourses of illegality that position
them as criminals and outsiders, some undocumented immigrants are attempting to reclaim their identity through communal, public actions. Although their status may not change, one way immigrants transform their
social position is to publicly advocate for an undocumented identity that is
couched in the notion that they are people entitled to basic human rights
and whose hard labor and economic, cultural, and historical contributions
to the United States make them deserving of legal rights as well. Their
activism functions as a public rejection of illegality as a dehumanizing, unfair, and hypocritical form of identification. This kind of counterdiscourse,
or reaction to predominant views of undocumented immigrants, is captured
clearly in a message delivered during protests and marches: NO HUMAN
BEING IS ILLEGAL.

Positions of identity in the United States carry with them a multiplicity of
meanings that are generated through processes of interaction between individuals acting in groups embedded in societies that quite often cross national borders. Although an understanding of the origins of certain social

positions such as Latino reveals part of the meanings that identities carry with them, other meanings are also created according to the position of power from which they are produced. Changing panethnic labels from Hispanic to Latino may have been an originally empowering move, yet as has been discussed, Latinos have also become associated with social evils such as poverty, school failure, illegal immigration, etc. A mere replacement of labels is insufficient in restructuring the ongoing social processes that give them their meanings. Therefore, a mere replacement of terms from *illegal* to *undocumented* is insufficient in transforming relations of power that afford immigrants a particular place in the preexisting social order. However, the activities and discourses through which immigrants participate, including but not limited to a change in identity terminology, are the places where psychological transformations of identity are situated. Illegality is a preexisting condition that functions as a psychological tool when immigrants deliberately reposition themselves in society.

All identities I have discussed (Hispanic, Latino, Mexican, illegal, or undocumented) are constructed in relation to homogeneous U.S. national and societal standards. For any individual who falls under any or all of these categories, the meanings that each social position carries may vary a great deal at different moments. An undocumented immigrant who identifies with other *ilegales* may not consider him- or herself to be a criminal but rather a member of a type of community through which information addressing particular needs (such as finding employment without proper documents) may be found. This is an internal process of identification in the sense that it is private to the culture of undocumented immigrants. An external process of identification, however, operates as a public reaction entailing the personal adoption of an undocumented identity to resist widespread misunderstanding and injustice.

This is indeed a controversial yet provocative time and place for understanding the process of identity formation in the making. Recent Mexican immigrants in New York are involved in fundamental changes to assimilationist views of immigrant incorporation and challenge individualist, U.S. values of self-gain and independence as they maintain family and community ties both in Mexico and the United States. An interesting question arises as to how recognition of transnational communities, such as the Mexican one in New York, will affect the assimilation process. For example, if recognition of transnational and global interchange begins to dismantle national borders, perhaps the discourses of assimilation into an allegedly homogeneous nation will also crumble.

Many undocumented Mexican immigrants in New York are making use of institutions and community organizations as a means of making their identities public, making demands, and enforcing the observance of their rights. This is one way immigrants are able to transform a public resource into a psychological tool that allows them to act on their worlds in a deliberate way. As a result, they are able to make use of this public front to uncover unjust practices, challenge existing relations of power that identify undocumented immigrants in derogatory ways, and reposition themselves in a dignified manner. The interviews I conducted along with my observation and participation in the community reveal some of the ways in which large-scale misunderstanding of undocumented immigrants may be experienced by individuals and how those experiences, in turn, are transformed and re-presented publicly through communal institutional activity. This kind of reappropriation of identity illustrates how a psychological form emerges from the individual's manipulation of preexisting social conditions.

A question remains as to how far undocumented immigrants can provoke change from the marginal spaces from which they speak and act. Although a reappropriation of identity as undocumented immigrants is necessary for individuals to achieve some purpose (such as protection of their rights within a preexisting social/legal order), radical movements call for an eradication of any identity that originates from legal status. This is a proactive rather than a reactive stance that requires a complete reorganization of existing power structures. Acknowledgment of the uncertainty about undocumented immigrants' transformative power is reflected in recent campaigns for general amnesty for all immigrants and in public encouragement of participation in census counts. Without voting power and representation, the strength of undocumented immigrants' political motions remains present yet limited.

However, certain world views that Mexican immigrants bring with them can also challenge predominant ideologies in U.S. society. Valdés (1997) has found that for Mexican families in Texas, personal fulfillment was not contingent upon monetary rewards and rights. These families expected to live economically stable lives in which they could provide an education for their children who would, in turn, mature into socially responsible adults and maintain connections to their families. Such differences in world views need to be understood better in their relation to immigration status. For instance, U.S. standards define citizenship according to legal status embodied in certain documents (i.e., a passport, Social Security card, or driver's license). Yet for undocumented Mexican immigrants, who are organizing themselves, citizenship is an earned outcome of everyday economic, social, and cultural contributions; political involvement; and community memberships in the United States.

The implications of legal status on identity development for undocumented Mexicans in New York may be significant to other undocumented immigrants in the city. However, a further analysis of how undocumented Mexicans' experience of identity formation in New York is unique compared with that of other undocumented immigrants or other Latinos or other Mexicans in the United States remains to be completed. For example, Suárez-Orozco (1991) conducted a study with children of Latin American immigrants to elicit personal narratives. Generally, the same recurring themes emerged, such as the need to repay their families, share success with their families, and be educated as well as feelings of guilt about being educated at the expense of the families' or communities' sacrifices. In a similar vein, Smith (1998) finds that one of the functions of establishing a transnational community between New York and Mexico has been for immigrants to be able to contribute something back to the homeland. Furthermore, these immigrants' social status is increased in their hometown as a function of their children's success in the United States. Therefore, transformations of identity need to be understood both here and in Mexico in their historically, geographically, socially, and individually specified emergence. The actual, day-to-day transactions and discourses through which certain identities are formed, along with the specific psychological functions they serve, must continue to be revealed.

REFERENCES

Alarcón, R. 1994. *Proposition 187: An Effective Measure to Deter Undocumented Migration to California?* San Francisco, Calif.: Multicultural Education, Training and Advocacy.

Anzaldúa, G. 1987. *Borderlands/La Frontera: The New Mestiza.* San Francisco: Aunt Lute Books.

Baker, S. G., F. D. Bean, A. Escobar Latapi, and S. Weintraub. 1998. "U.S. Immigration Policies and Trends: The Growing Importance of Migration from Mexico." In *Crossings: Mexican Immigration in Interdisciplinary Perspective,* ed. M. M. Suárez-Orozco, 79–105. Cambridge, Mass.: Harvard University Press.

Barry, D. 1997. "Pair Arrested in Chicago in Smuggling-Ring Inquiry." *New York Times,* July 27, pp. 1, 26.

Castillo, A., ed. 1996. *Goddess of the Americas. Writings on the Virgin of Guadalupe.* New York: Riverhead Books.

Cederström, T. 1998. "La vida ya no está como antes: The Multidimensional Impacts of Migrant Remittances in the Mixteca Baja of Puebla and Oaxaca." Paper presented at the conference on Mexican Migrants in New York and Mexico: New Analytical and Practical Perspectives on Transnationalization and Incorporation, New York, October.

Conover, T. 1987. *Coyotes: A Journey Through the Secret World of America's Illegal Aliens.* New York: Vintage Books.

Deaux, K. 1991. "Social Identities: Thoughts on Structure and Change." In *The Relational Self: Theoretical Convergences in Psychoanalysis and Social Psychology,* ed. R. C. Curtiss, 77–93. New York: Guilford Press.

Dugger, C. W. 1997. "Immigrant Study Finds Many Below New Income Limit." *New York Times,* March 16, p. A1.

Edstrom, M. 1993. "La imagen de México en Estados Unidos: La inmigración mexicana en los medios impresos estadounidenses, 1980–1988." *Revista Mexicana de Sociología* 54(4): 21–65.

Flores, J. 1996. "Pan-Latino/Trans-Latino: Puerto Ricans in the 'New Nueva York.' " *Journal of El Centro de Estudios Puertorriqueños* 8(1,2): 170–86.

Gendreau, M. and G. Giménez. 1998. "Between Popocatepetl and Brooklyn: Migration and Mass Media Effects on Regional Identity in Atlixco, Puebla." Paper presented at the conference on Mexican Migrants in New York and Mexico: New Analytical and Practical Perspectives on Transnationalization and Incorporation, New York, October.

Gergen, K. J. 1991. *The Saturated Self: Dilemmas of Identity in Contemporary Life.* New York: Basic Books.

Gibson, M. A. and J. U. Ogbu, eds. 1991. *Minority Status and Schooling: A Comparative Study of Immigrant and Involuntary Minorities.* New York: Garland Publishing.

González, D. 1991. "Poor and Illegal, Mexicans Lose Hope in New York." *New York Times,* May 19, p. A1.

Guerra, J. C. 1998. *Close to Home: Oral and Literate Practices in a Transnational Mexicano Community.* New York: Teachers' College Press.

Gutiérrez, D. G. 1998. "Ethnic Mexicans and the Transformation of "American" Social Space: Reflections on Recent History." In *Crossings: Mexican Immigration in Interdisciplinary Perspective,* ed. M. M. Suárez-Orozco, 307–35. Cambridge: Harvard University Press.

Hanson-Sánchez, C. 1996. *New York City Latino Neighborhoods Data Book.* New York: Institute for Puerto Rican Policy.

Harré, R. and G. Gillett. 1994. *The Discursive Mind.* Thousand Oaks, Calif.: Sage.

Hondagneu-Sotelo, P. 1995. "Beyond 'The Longer They Stay' (and Say They Will Stay): Women and Mexican Immigrant Settlement." *Qualitative Sociology* 18(1): 21–43.

James, G. 1991. "A Flower Vendor Dies After Youths Beat Him." *New York Times,* June 17, p. B3.

Kim, D. Y. 1999. "Beyond Coethnic Solidarity: Mexican and Ecuadorean Employment in Korean-Owned Businesses in New York City." *Ethnic and Racial Studies* 22(3): 581–605.

Meier, M. S. and F. Ribera. 1993. *Mexican Americans/American Mexicans: From Conquistadors to Chicanos.* Rev. ed. New York: Hill and Wang.

Mirandé, A. 1985. *The Chicano Experience: An Alternative Perspective.* Notre Dame, Ind.: University of Notre Dame Press.

Moll, L. C. 1997. "The Creation of Mediating Settings." *Mind, Culture, and Activity* 4(3): 191–99.

Oboler, S. 1995. *Ethnic Labels, Latino Lives: Identity and the Politics of (Re)Presentation in the United States.* Minneapolis: University of Minnesota Press.

Ojito, M. 1997. "Deaf Mexicans Are to Remain as Witnesses." *New York Times,* August 3, pp. 1, 29.

Onishi, N. 1996. "Motive Sought in Killing at a Church." *New York Times,* June 4, p. B4.

Parker, I. 1992. *Discourse Dynamics: Critical Analysis for Social and Individual Psychology.* New York: Routledge.

Quiroga, A. 1995. "Copycat Fever: California's Proposition 187 Epidemic Spreads to Other States." *Hispanic* 8(3): 18–24.

Sánchez, G. J. 1993. *Becoming Mexican American: Ethnicity, Culture and Identity in Chicano Los Angeles, 1900–1945.* New York: Oxford University Press.

Scribner, S. 1985. "Vygotsky's Uses of History." In *Culture, Communication and Cognition,* ed. J. Wertsch, 119–45. New York: Cambridge University Press.

Smith, M. P. and B. Tarallo. 1995. "Proposition 187: Global Trend or Local Narrative? Explaining Anti-Immigrant Politics in California, Arizona, and Texas." *International Journal of Urban and Regional Research* 19(4): 664–76.

Smith, R. C. 1996. "Mexicans in New York: Membership and Incorporation in a New Immigrant Community." In *Latinos in New York: Communities in Transition,* ed. S. Baver and G. Haslip-Viera, 57–103. Notre Dame, Ind.: University of Notre Dame Press.

——— 1998. "Transnational Localities: Community, Technology and the politics of Membership within the Context of Mexico and U.S. Migration." In *Transnationalism from Below,* eds. M. P. Smith and L. E. Guarnizo, 196–238. New Brunswick, NJ: Transaction Publishers.

Suárez-Orozco, M. M. 1991. "Immigrant Adaptation to Schooling: A Hispanic Case." In *Minority Status and Schooling: A Comparative Study of Immigrant and Involuntary Minorities,* ed. M. A. Gibson and J. U. Ogbu, 37–61. New York: Garland Publishing.

——— ed. 1998. *Crossings: Mexican Immigration in Interdisciplinary Perspectives.* Cambridge, Mass.: Harvard University Press.

U.S. Congress. House. Subcommittee on Immigration Claims and Subcommittee on the Constitution of the Committee on the Judiciary. 1995. *Societal and Legal Issues Surrounding Children Born in the United States to Illegal Parents.* 104th Cong., 1st sess., December 13.

Valdés, G. 1997 *Con Respeto: Bridging the Distances Between Culturally Diverse Families and Schools: An Ethnographic Portrait.* New York: Teachers' College Press.

Van der Veer, R. and J. Valsiner. 1994. *The Vygotsky Reader.* Oxford: Blackwell.

Wolfe, A. 1997. "Immigration Angst." *New York Times,* July 23, p. A21.

CHAPTER THIRTEEN

Outside/In

Crossing Queer[1] and Latino Boundaries

Luis Aponte-Parés

> Beware of saying to them that sometimes different cities follow one another on the same site and under the same name, born and dying without knowing one another, without communication among themselves.[2]

During an early evening "round" of Parque Zamora in Veracruz during December 1997, two Mexican men signaled me. As I approached them, they asked, "¿Qué busca?" And I answered, "Maricones." Like so many other places throughout Latin America and elsewhere, Zamora Park in Veracruz is one of the many "furtive night landscapes"[3] or "queerscapes"[4] that gay men have invested with meaning and historically used to contest urban narratives. It has been a project of mine to decipher the way in which Latinos and Latino queers have invested with meaning the spaces of everyday life because "space has no natural character, no inherent meaning, no intrinsic status as public or private."[5] We do not live in a void but "inside a set of relations that delineates sites which are irreducible to one another and absolutely not superimposable on one another."[6] Furthermore, the "class, gender, cultural, religious, and political differentiation in conceptions of time and space frequently become arenas of social conflict."[7] My interest has been to examine how these transgressions, "arenas of social conflict," have developed in *el Norte*, the northern cities, where so many of us have come to reside; perhaps producing what Foucault has called *heterotopias*, "counter-sites" that "are simultaneously represented, contested, and inverted."[8] How do Latino queers construct their spaces outside and inside the spaces of the perceived other twice over, locales perceived by some in both the Latino and white communities to threaten the heteronormative status quo? To be sure, these new locales still remain "largely unstable, vulnerable, 'nomadic.' "[9]

In this essay, I posit that to fully grasp the degree to which Latinos have latinized New York City's landscapes, the role Latino queers play in this process merits examination.[10] Latino queers have begun to challenge queer institutions. They also aim to be coproducers of a queer imaginary and appropriate places of queer culture, thus Latinizing queer culture. They also claim a role in the coproduction of a Latino imaginary. By adding sexual orientation to this identity, queers indeed "queer," mariconear, decenter heteronormative Latino culture, perhaps producing a new "conception of 'identity,' which lives with and through, not despite, difference," but "by hybridity."[11] In a city where queers play a significant role in politics, economics, culture, and the construction of its "imagined environment," Latino queers increasingly have a role to play, a role emerging primarily from the dynamics of their dual Latino and gay identities, increased numbers, and an activism that challenges marginalization by virtue of their being outsiders to both communities. If one wants to be outside/in, move from periphery to center, one cannot latinize the queer community without queering the Latino community, la comunidad, and vise versa.

Population increases and expanded political activism of Latino queers have intersected cultural changes transforming the landscapes of certain districts in U.S. cities into what Gómez-Peña calls a "huge border zone," a "borderless society."[12] When cultural changes brought about by queers in the United States are considered, new possibilities become apparent, creating opportunities for Latino queers to transgress and transform the boundaries of the Latino and gay communities. By building their own organizations and networks, Latino queers have created spaces in which to build community, resulting in greater visibility and political activism.[13] As these organizations have matured, Latino queer activists have challenged their dual oppression in both communities with a discourse aimed at debunking and subverting the stereotypical views that queers hold of Latinos and that Latinos hold of queers, a "demand for respeto" being central to their full "cultural citizenship" within both communities.[14] This new discourse enables Latino queers to work on the deconstruction of the diasporic/immigrant imaginary of Latino/Latin American queers by offering a new one in which queer and Latino are not exclusive categories.

As Latinos disperse throughout the New York metro area, many neighborhoods in the city have been appropriated culturally by both Puerto Ricans and other immigrant Latino communities, transforming them into diasporic/immigrant enclaves, where they build places that "look like them," those "discrete if 'elastic' areas in which settings for the constitution of social relations are located and with which people can identify."[15] Latino gay men and women have also claimed spaces in both communities by challenging and collaborating with traditional organizations in the Latino community by breaching the boundaries and "queering" traditional Latino social and cultural organizations and events while appropriating and reterritorializing white queer spaces and institutions as well as countless gay bars in Manhattan and Queens. This bodes well for the latinization of New York City: the representation of Latino sensibilities and imaginary on the city's imagined environment, which includes Latino queers. How and where Latinos are appropriating spaces is the focus of this work.

APPROPRIATING SPACES AND PLACES

In *The Practice of Everyday Life,* Michel de Certau provides clues on where and how to identify the actions of people as they go about producing their everyday lives. He differentiates between strategies and tactics. A *strategy,* he argues, is "the calculation (or manipulation) of power relationships that becomes possible as soon as a subject with will and power . . . can be isolated. It postulates a *place* that can be determined as its *own* and serves as the base from which relations with an *exteriority* composed of targets or threats . . . can be managed."[16] On the other hand, *tactics* are calculated actions "determined by the absence of a proper locus. . . . The space of a tactic is the space of the other."[17] For example, opening a gay bar and establishing a Latino gay organization are strategies, whereas marching as queers in the Puerto Rican Day Parade is a tactic, a site-specific intervention. In the first instance, Latino queers have the power to delimit their own place; in the second, Latino queers take advantage of opportunities. It depends on them how to build up their own position and plan raids.[18]

I set about a research agenda to examine the way Latino queers devised their strategies and tactics in queering the Latino community and latinizing the queer community. As a Puerto Rican/Latino queer activist and founding member of two groups, I was unable to disassociate my activism from my research. Owing to my relationship with these groups, I have gathered materials produced by them as well as maintained friendships with many of their members. Thus, the work presented here is not detached, and the boundaries between researcher and activist will always remain ambiguous. I am also cognizant that my choice to recover the recent history of Latino queers and how we have chosen to represent ourselves is a political act. Moreover, I aim to minimize the dichotomy present in the larger queer community, where there is a marked difference between the discourse of activists and academics. This dichotomy separating theory from praxis is a luxury that Puerto Ricans/Latinos may not be able to afford. Our ranks are too thin, our resources are too limited, and our needs are too great not to join our efforts in a common discourse and coalesce around common agendas for action.

I conducted over thirty in-depth and open-ended interviews with activists and nonactivists in New York City.[19] All informants articulated the difficulties they have had with both their communities, queer and Latino, on an individual, family, and institutional basis. A majority come from middle- and working-class families, and they represent a full range of occupations, with a large number working in human services, the arts, and other professional jobs. They are not a representative group of Latino gay men in New York City. A good number of them have worked or volunteered for AIDS organizations. They ranged in age from the early twenties through the late forties. Of those who visited queer bars regularly, most went to both mixed and Latino bars. Many others opted to visit other queer sites, including gyms, theaters, the Lesbian and Gay Center, and other places of queer culture. However, most preferred to socialize at private parties.

CHANGING URBAN LANDSCAPES AND REPRESENTATIONS OF IDENTITY

We live in times "where space and time cross to produce complex figures of difference and identity, past and present, inside and outside, inclusion and exclusion."[20] Suppressed voices have come forward to claim spaces and a place in U.S. urban narratives. However, Latino urban history, particularly the history of Puerto Ricans in New York City, has been poorly documented. As a result, Puerto Ricans and Latinos are absent from most accounts of the history of the city and remain generally invisible. The spaces and places created by the settlement of Puerto Ricans for the past century have been all but destroyed with an attendant loss of memory: a community deterritorialized.[21] This loss compounds the view that Latinos are all immigrants, that they have not contributed to the development of New York City, and that somehow Latinos do not have a place in the city's history.[22] However, the demographic explosion of Latinos in New York City and their increased political activism have made it all but impossible to keep them invisible anymore. Increased Latino presence intersects profound changes to the landscapes of U.S. cities.

The descriptive terms *theme park, global city, fortress city, informational city, analogous city, virtual city, edge city, exopolis,* and *megalopolis,* to name a few, attempt to describe the way changing economic, political, and cultural forces of the global economy are being articulated in U.S. cities. These changes stem from the restructuring of international capital and labor markets; a global economy that increasingly relies on the growth of international financial markets; an expansive service sector, along with a global network of factories; and the concentration of financial centers in a select number of global cities.[23] Edward Soja and others add that the process also entails deindustrialization and reindustrialization resulting in the loss of jobs, the lowering of wages and the quality of life in certain centers.[24] These forces have brought about profound transformations of urban landscapes during the second half of the twentieth century, namely, suburbanization and class- and ethnic-specific segregation of residential districts, with the poor and people of color isolated in distressed neighborhoods while the wealthy converge in well-appointed and protected enclaves. The privatization and subsequent loss of public space, with the concomitant exclusion of the poor and people of color from it and the increased employment of "stage set" concocted environments or "theme park" architecture and urban design solutions are utilized to revitalize cities.[25]

Peter Marcuse has specified these changes by using a wall metaphor, suggesting deep social divisions that characterize the postmodern city.[26] He argues that the apparent chaos of postmodern cities may indeed "cloak" the "visible (and visual) anarchy" in "an increasingly pervasive and obtrusive order" that covers an "increasingly pervasive pattern of hierarchical relationships among people."[27] He also identifies five distinctive types of residential quarters: the controlling city, the city of advanced services, the city of direct production, the city of unskilled work and the informal economy, and the residual city.[28] People of color, Latinos in particular, are residents in the last two and visitors to the first three quarters.

Latino barrios are scattered throughout the city, and certain neighborhoods have become closely identified with them. Latino barrios, however, differ greatly. Some, such as East Harlem and the Lower East Side, have been devastated by disinvestment (in the former) and gentrification (in the latter), resulting in the displacement of Puerto Ricans and other Latinos from their historical homelands for most of the century. For over two decades now, Mexicans and Dominicans, however, have begun to repopulate East Harlem and to appropriate West Harlem and Washington Heights, juxtaposing borderlands with the traditional ghetto. In Queens, Jackson Heights, Elmhurst, Woodside, and Corona, there are other borderlands where new immigrants congregate. The neighborhoods have become important places for unskilled work and the informal economy. Images emerging from these enclaves are dissonant from those produced by the culture industries, so essential to the image of the city, the "imagined environment," which increasingly relies on the symbolic economy, i.e., the utilization of culture as a means of redeveloping the image of the city. For sure, those at the top, the elites, including wealthy gay men, continue to establish "their identity as a patrician class, [to] build the majestic art museums, parks, and architectural complexes" to represent New York as a world-class city.[29] Latinos in general, and Puerto Ricans in particular, remain at the bottom of the social and economic ladder in New York City, residing in neighborhoods labeled by some the "lumpengeography of capital."[30] This has not deterred them from mapping their identities in the cultural geography of the city. Indeed, their ability to imprint their identity in space remains a primary area of contention, as "power struggles over mapping (. . .no matter if these are maps of so-called 'real' or metaphorical spaces) are therefore fundamental moments in the production of discourses."[31]

Generally, Latino queers reside in Marcuse's cities of unskilled work and the informal economy and the residual city and are visitors to queer neighborhoods, which are usually located in the city of advanced services. Like other people of color and immigrants, Latino queers are not part of queer-centered neighborhoods such as Chelsea and Greenwich Village in Manhattan, where street life has clear signs and representations of queer culture, spaces "where production and consumption of gay identity and gay community is visualized and made possible on many levels."[32] However, "there are many 'invisible' bodies on Christopher Street. The lesbian body and bodies of color only nominally appear in the storefront aesthetics and the heart of the street life."[33] Yet while walking Christopher Street on any night, the presence of people of color is felt on many corners, particularly the waterfront landscapes, where Latino queers have carved their own spaces.[34] Visiting the city of advanced services, however, can be dangerous. Excluded from many bars, watched as criminals by store owners, or harassed by policemen, Latino queers know that every visit to Chelsea or the Village is an act of courage. Visiting these neighborhoods, although usually framed in terms of "going to the land of queers" by many informants, can also be construed as a political act. To some, for example, visiting these neighborhoods means that they have to divest themselves from their ethnicity by "acting white." To others it is the only place in the city they can be themselves, that is, they can be as queer as they want, a "free fag" like one of the characters in Jaime Manrique's novel.[35]

Feeling unwelcome in the white queerscapes of the Village and Chelsea, many Latino queers have produced their own places in the locales of the other, such as the South Bronx, Washington Heights, Woodside, and Jackson Heights. Although historically communities of color have been gay unfriendly, Latino queers have also begun appropriating places in their own neighborhoods. By "acting gay" in their own communities, Latino queers challenge the community's conception of itself. Latino and Latin American queers from Colombia, Venezuela, the Dominican Republic, Central America, and elsewhere have greatly increased their visibility in Woodside and Jackson Heights. Lining Roosevelt Avenue, for example, and almost undistinguishable from other storefronts, are a number of gay bars such as Friends, Luchos, and Zodiac, which intermix with storefront churches; Colombian, Peruvian, and Korean restaurants; and other immigrant sites. Located along main streets, these bars are more visible than previous ones, such as the old La Escuelita, which was sited in the garment district in Manhattan, with no outside signage, and which required patrons to go "down into the darkness of basements without windows outside the view of the outside view."[36] The streets are clear sites of the informal economy, of cultural displacement, and the reterritorialization of urban narratives. Latino queers are adding a new element to this process of reterritorialization by producing Latino queerscapes.

LATINO QUEER ORGANIZATIONS AND LATINO QUEERSCAPES

Latino queer institution building has been a struggle.[37] Individual acts of courage occur every day and are fundamental in the development of personal identity and survival. Queer organizations have played a major role in the development of this identity, particularly in queering the Latino community and latinizing the queer community at the institutional level. Organizing has provided Latino queers a foundation, a place of their own, and a base from which relations with their other two communities can be managed. To understand this role, the way these groups developed their agendas through time, and the spaces they have created, one needs to review the story of Latino queer organizations in New York City.

I propose four stages in the post-Stonewall period.[38] The Pioneering stage spans between the late 1960s and the mid-1970s, when activists such as Sylvia Rivera and others attempted to be part of the movement and were turned away by racism. In the Puerto Rican/Latino community, those who attempted to come out within political organizations were shunned or expelled by the radicals of the period. Those who remained active were sent back to the closet. The Foundation stage spans between the early 1970s and the mid-1980s, when groups began the difficult enterprise of bringing together those activists concerned with the way the gay movement had ignored Latino issues as well as the way the Latino community had dismissed gay issues.[39] During this period many who remained closeted became militants in radical groups in the Latino community and had to "prioritize their struggles," as Juanita Ramos has suggested.[40] The Developmental stage began in the mid-1980s and lasted through the early 1990s.[41] This stage brought to the forefront new queer leaders who had been activists in housing, the arts, health, and so forth who came out of the closet and expanded the working agenda to deal with both the Latino and gay communities. How to envision their two identities, Latino and gay, was central to all groups leading to a "construction project": "inventing themselves" with the formulation of a Latino queer imaginary "fashioned creatively on the basis of shared memory and desire, congruent histories, and meshing utopias."[42]

With the founding of Latinos Latinas de Ambiente New York (LLANY), Puerto Rican Initiative to Develop Empowerment (PRIDE), the Colombian Lesbian and Gay Organization (COLEGA), and Mano a Mano, for example, a new stage characterized by collective work, coalition building, and greater militancy as well as a new and younger generation of activists has begun. Some groups have become not-for-profit corporations, giving them the added stability that previous organizations lacked. This added formality has provided members with a predictability missing in earlier organizing as well as a long-term commitment to institutionalize.[43] Missing, however, is an intense discussion of the complex issues that surround Latino gay identity: class, national cultures, sexualities, and race.[44]

Gay men with different histories, cultures, time of arrival, and conceptions of homosexualities find themselves grouped and identified as Latinos by the receiving society. Furthermore, differences between Puerto Ricans and other Latinos, and particularly between those Puerto Ricans born on the island and those born in New York City, intersect social class and racial/ethnic issues revealed when better-off Latinos resent the minority status of Puerto Ricans. This has led to a dual strategy of organizing around the broader concept of Latino queers as well as nation-specific groups like COLEGA, Latitud Cero (Gay and Lesbian Ecuadorean Movement), Colectivo Mexicano, the Gay and Lesbian Association of Cuban Exiles, the Venezuelan Gay and Lesbian Association, and many others. This suggests that a fixed identity as a Latino gay man remains elusive. How each member of that larger imagined community identifies with it differs and remains a work in progress. I should note that both Latino[45] and queer remain contested identities.[46]

When I speak in this essay of a *Latino community*, both in the general and queer sense, I am referring to a group using a "negotiated identity," in which the "Latino 'experience,' the group's demonstrable reality and existence, includes but is not coterminous with its self-consciousness" and "the way it thinks, conceives of, imagines itself."[47] Similarly, identifiers such as *queer community* and *gay and lesbian community* also require specification because there is no agreement on what they constitute and who they purport to represent. Although identity politics has been severely criticized as divisive, by playing on their Latino queer identity, Latino queers perhaps see its use as "strategic provisionality," an identity that can "become a site of contest and revision"[48] in both communities. It is also important to note that although the Latino gay movement has never ceased to be political, always linking its struggle with other struggles, the mainstream gay movement has always had difficulties linking with other struggles and has most recently moved, like the rest of society, to more conservative positions. In the mainstream gay and lesbian community, the recent debate between Sex Panic! and major queer activists such as Michelangelo Signorile and Gabriel Rotello around issues of liberation versus assimilation is exemplified by a recent essay by Frank Browning in which he summarizes the debate as one where liberation and "the pursuit of sexual pleasure as a legitimate social concern has disappeared from the movement's public agenda. In its place has come the right to participate in war, the right to marry, the right to adopt children, and so on."[49]

QUEERING LA COMUNIDAD / LATINIZING LOS BLANCOS

Difficulties encountered by Latino gays and lesbians working with white queer organizations have remained central to Latino queer organizing.

Furthermore, Latino queers individually suffer on a daily basis from the exclusion from commercial, social, institutional, and other places under the control of whites. Similarly, there have been countless difficulties in working with the Latino community. Owing to the complexity of issues confronting them, Latino queers have vacillated in their priorities as to what to do first: to confront and transform homophobia in the Latino community or to challenge racism in the white queer community and gain a space in the movement. At times, Latino queers create alliances with white queers to challenge the Latino community. The opposite, however, has been more difficult. In this essay I examine a few examples that illustrate the strategies and tactics utilized by Latino queer organizations to address both communities. I have chosen examples in two areas: co-producing an imaginary, and transgressing boundaries.[50]

Coproducing an Imaginary

How do white queers view Latino queers? How does the Latino community view its queers? How do Latino queers want to be viewed and represented in both communities? How does one engage in the production of a new imaginary that is inclusive? Stuart Hall reminds us that cultural identity is a "production" always "constituted within, not outside, representation."[51] The production of Latino identity in general and Latino queers in particular can be found in the social sciences and the arts, particularly in literature.[52] Furthermore, there are two important sites in the production of imaginaries: mass cultural forms such as the media and social/cultural and political institutions. To queers, the media is part of an array of mass cultural forms that highlight "certain questions about the circulation of representations and, specifically, the positions occupied by lesbians and gay men within public discourse."[53] The debate a few years back about the cancellation of the TV show *Ellen* suggests that at the national level the portrayal of gays and lesbians remains problematic.

Generally, Latino queers are absent from gay media. Viewing the pages of *The Advocate* or *Out,* two nationally distributed gay magazines, reveals that gay men are still portrayed as white and middle class. Institutional inclusion or exclusion also provide the bases by which representations of a particular group are portrayed. The ongoing debate in the school systems of the nation, where conservatives do not want to include any positive representations of gays or lesbians for fear that young minds could fall into sin, is a case in point. Thus, how society portrays queers in the public eye remains critical in understanding them. For example, two recent references to Latino queers appeared in New York City:

> *La especie no necesita de homosexuales para su mantenimiento.* He aquí la desgracia de ser homosexual: el amor erótico por el

propio sexo no puede reproducirse; es híbrido; no puede engendrar naturalmente ni criar a un hijo dándole todas las opciones de identificación.[54]

The Male Room Presents. *Sucking off Puerto Rican Drug Dealers in the bathroom contest.* Hosted by Your "connection" Mark Allen. Contest at 12 Unless we get busted. Wednesday, January 11, 1995 at Webster Hall, 125 E. 11th St. NYC.[55]

The above quotes summon the stereotypes used by Latinos and white gays when referring to Latino gays, i.e., *una desgracia,* a disgrace, and drug addicts, "street people."

"Una desgracia." The first quote comes from a guest essay in *El Diario* and is symptomatic of the uneasiness that the principal Spanish daily for Latino New Yorkers had in dealing with gay and lesbian issues and specifically of its homophobic leanings during the early nineties. It also conjured painful images, using the negative language with which Latino gays had been portrayed in their countries of origin. Many of my informants characterized themselves as "sexiles," as Manolo Guzmán calls them, that is, men and women who felt that they could not develop their identities in full within the cultural constraints of their country of origin. In June 1991, a protest letter was sent by community leaders to Fernando Moreno, then editor of the daily.[56] A few months later, *El Diario* answered the letter with an editorial entitled "Homophobic Violence," castigating homophobia by referring to the Julio Rivera assassination and quoting statistics from the Gay and Lesbian Anti-Violence Project (AVP), information that had been included in the referred letter. However, the editors failed to endorse an antibias bill pending for many years in Albany. The editorial, nevertheless, signaled that the daily was willing to entertain changing its view of Latino homosexuals. Changing *El Diario's* editorial orientation was the goal, and the editorial was a clear tactical success, particularly given the daily's historical role in producing a Puerto Rican and Latino imaginary for all New Yorkers. Most importantly, although challenging *El Diario* was a major endeavor, the organizations had grown secure enough to plan their strategies in response. As one member of the group that met with the daily states:

Ya estabamos cansados. Cuando vimos el artículo inmediátamente llamamos a una reunión. We decided to approach *El Diario* with a range of political and health organizations. We planned our agenda, sent them a letter, and finally they called for a meeting. They called us back for a meeting. I believe that they were not expecting people from so many different organizations. From that day on I believe *El Diario* changed their view of us.[57]

Such was the impact that for the past five years *El Diario* has both increased and produced positive images of gays and lesbians. This has taken place through the publication of articles and op-ed essays friendly to queers. During the recent past, the daily has published gay-friendly essays examining an aspect of Latino queer life the day before the Gay and Lesbian Pride March every June. Although positive portrayals have a ways to go, the editors' willingness to hire openly gay queer activists such as Juan Méndez as part of their editorial staff (he serves as opinion editor) and publish the work of Gonzalo Aburto, a queer Mexican journalist who writes a weekly Latin Rock column, bodes well for the future.

"Puerto Rican drug dealers and street people." The second quote purported to represent an erotic image of Latino men, specifically Puerto Ricans. Like African American men, Puerto Rican men have been portrayed as dangerous. As colonial people, Puerto Ricans, particularly Puerto Rican men, have been construed as "degenerate types on the basis of racial origin."[58] Like African Americans, Puerto Ricans are pictured by many white gays as sexually uninhibited and passionate: "they want to be dominated by this dark man with this humongous dick."[59] Soon after the despicable ad appeared, the Latino queer community came together to challenge the promoters and the magazine that printed the ad. Under the leadership of Frank Guzmán, a young queer activist and founding member of LLANY and PRIDE, a major campaign was organized with three purposes: to get the event canceled, to get both the promoters of the event and *HX* magazine to print an apology in its next edition, and to alert the Latino queer community to the threat to their dignity that was being perpetuated on them. As Frank Guzmán, the protest organizer puts it:

> We started faxing Latino organizations, both gay and straight. I called a meeting and almost all organizations contacted came. We set out a plan of action and chose to picket on the night of the "party." That night 75 to 100 Latino and non Latino queers (mostly people of color) picketed the entrance for several hours demanding an apology in writing. We demanded *HX* to print an apology and to guarantee us that they would never again print or accept commercial ads for events like that one.[60]

The overall strategy went beyond producing positive images or contesting stereotypes. It went on to "constitute and sustain discursive and institutional networks" by gaining access to the same media channels that whites had.[61] Organizing the protest also provided Latino gays the tools to examine their own understanding, demystify the historical depiction of Latinos, and join forces with other nongay Latinos and others in a common project: deconstructing the images of Latinos in general as well as of Latino gays in particular. What brought about this examination was that one of the promoters was a Latino. As Guzmán also states:

> He had no excuse. In fact, it came to my mind that he must really be a self-hating Latino in order to be part of such despicable action. The other promoter was a white guy who thought of the idea. The Latino promoter had the courtesy to send me an apology. The white promoter restated that he was from Iowa and he had heard that a lot of Puerto Ricans were drug dealers. Can you believe that?[62]

Self-hating Latino queers has been a deep concern and was an issue that had been debated earlier by other groups. However, to the new generation of activists it was difficult to fathom. After all, it was 1995, and possibly one in four queers in New York City was a Latino; many had hoped that old stereotypes had faded away.

The protest was a success. By utilizing Latino gay and nongay organizations and networks, organizers felt they had the strength and were in control of the event. When the interviewer from Gay Network filming the protest asked the organizers, "Why have there not been more demonstrations?" a protester replied, "Perhaps with the AIDS crisis our community was involved in self-healing. But we never lost sight that like the rest of society, many gays and lesbians are racists. This is a warning to those who think that they can get away with business as usual. No more." Another protester stated, "All clubs are exploitative. If I did not participate in anything racist or anything derogatory towards the Spanish, I would not participate in anything."[63] In other words, racism is expected by most Latinos as they go about in their everyday living, and many just get used to it. Another protester commented that Mark Allen, the event promoter, had said that "he was not aware that Puerto Ricans were activists." The question would resonate in some of the protesters' heads. It summoned a sense of powerlessness for Latinos to control their own images and the abysmal lack of knowledge the white queer movement had about Latino queers and their organizations.

One significant result of the event was that Gay Network TV aired the protest and invited a number of speakers to comment on the need of the white gay community to examine its racism and the stereotypes it uses to represent Latino men. It was a recognition that Latinos were increasingly more vocal and would challenge the white community in its own places, its bars, and on its own terms. Refusing to remain invisible and to accept the stereotyping without a fight signaled that Latino queers were ready to transgress white spaces collectively. Organizers thought the days of referring to Puerto Ricans/Latinos as *street people,* a common term utilized historically to refer to working-class people of color, were over. However, recent publication of negative stereotypes of Puerto Rican/Latino gay men suggests that many other media outlets are still portraying them as dangerous. In a 1998 issue of *Next,* a gay weekly, Latinos were listed among "five types of men that cannot be trusted" and portrayed as "romantic, but most of them are alcoholics—not to mention those explosive hot tempers." Banjee boys (usually Latino or African American) were portrayed by the same author as "fierce" and having "ended up stealing all [his] designer gowns."[64]

Crossing Boundaries

Boundaries are either visible or imaginary, physical or symbolic. Some boundaries are delineated by walls, "tangible or intangible, physically effective or physically symbolic of social and economic barriers."[65] Frequently, boundaries emerge to provide protection and perhaps cohesion and solidarity, such as those erected symbolically or territorially by immigrants as they go about building their enclaves. Other boundaries become walls, such as those defining ghettos and places of confinement.[66] Others delineate private from public space. Socially, boundaries can be erected by class distinctions, cultural differences, or areas of interest. For gays and lesbians, "environmental activism has been constrained by a host of unresolved issues concerning the entitlement of sexual minorities to public space in patriarchal and heteronormative contexts."[67] Latino queers, like other queers everywhere, have been walled in by social mores that establish "compulsory heterosexuality" as the "original, the true, the authentic"[68] sexual expression in all societies. In Latin America and the Caribbean, these mores remain powerful reminders of supremacy of the macho imaginary. To break the compulsory boundaries imposed by society such as those of the closet, Latino queers must cross over to the site of the other and make it their own. For the past decade Latino queers in New York City have been transgressing boundaries. Many times these transgressions stem from deliberate strategies chosen by groups as ways to expand their influence.

El Desfile. Perhaps an event that has addressed and crossed the boundaries most in both the Latino and gay communities has been the participation of Latino queers in the Puerto Rican Day Parade, El Desfile.[69] El Desfile is perhaps the most important event of the Puerto Rican community, the day when Puerto Rican identity, its imaginary, la comunidad puertorriqueña, is manifested in its most conspicuous way in New York City. El Desfile itself is an act of transgression of New York City's landscapes by all Puerto Ricans. Once a year, Puerto Ricans appropriate, map, and decenter privileged sites such as Fifth Avenue if only for six hours: reterritorializing Manhattan, the symbolic center of the city, home to the controlling city and the city of advanced services, where the privileged other lives. Some observers estimate that close to one million people either participate in or observe El Desfile. These numbers suggest that the event may be one of those rare occasions in New York City where many social classes come together to share a common experience. The open participation of Latino queers in El Desfile becomes a double transgression: Latino queers overrun the traditional boundaries of the Puerto Rican/Latino community, which, by appropriating Fifth Avenue that day, is transgressing the boundaries of the privileged other.

In 1989, Boricua Gay and Lesbian Forum (BGLF) brought together a large contingent of queers from several organizations to transgress the Puerto Rican Day Parade. The goal was to open up the march and expand the definition of what is Puerto Rican. As one activist remembers:

> Once we decided to go to El Desfile, we called a coalition that
> included both men and women, Latino and non-Latino
> organizations. We then applied for a permit and it was denied.
> We challenged the denial, and after the intervention of Dinkins's
> Gay and Lesbian Liaison, we got the go-ahead.[70]

Every year since then, organizers have permitted Latino queers to be a regular contingent in the march. Although it has not been easy, opening this major space has provided countless queers with the energy to deal with their own sexualities. After all, performing one's queerness in front of one million people can be intimidating as well as exhilarating.

> I don't particularly like to expose my sexuality in front of others.
> You know, it is a very personal thing. However, I believe that I
> am as Puerto Rican as everyone else in the parade. Why can't
> they just understand that we are familia. What I don't like is the
> looks I get from some of the people watching the parade. But at
> the same time, it feels good when so many also give us a thumbs-
> up. It just feels good and is worth the aggravation.[71]

Of all ethnic parades or marches in the city, El Desfile is the only one where queers have gained the right to establish a beachhead of sorts. By invading the space of the heterosexual other, Latino queers have effectively built a countersite where their sexual identity is in the open. By joining other Puerto Ricans in reterritorializing Fifth Avenue, Latino queers begin to reimagine Puerto Rican identity in New York City.

Puerto Rican Association for Community Affairs. Collaborating with gay-friendly Latino organizations has provided many Latino queers with the grounds to expand their influence. In 1993 the executive director of the Puerto Rican Association for Community Affairs (PRACA) asked Richard Irizarry and me to help her in an endeavor.[72] As an agency dealing with foster parents, its staff was aware of problems arising from the adoption of gay children by straight Puerto Rican/Latino parents. These parents needed guidance in dealing with gay and lesbian youth. The result of the meeting was that PRACA agreed to bring George Ayala, then director of Hettrick Martin Institute, to provide their board, staff, and parents with training on how to deal with queer issues. The request was emblematic of the changing landscapes of Puerto Rican/Latino agencies making attempts at adding sexual identity to their service paradigm. This technical assistance provided by Hettrick Martin was a sign that a progressive gay organization was willing to recognize the importance of working with the Latino community.

Between 1995 and 1999, a number of Latino queer organizations were able to utilize the offices of PRACA. Due to their relative newness, most of the groups are unable to stand on their own, i.e., they lack office space, telephones, computers, and so forth. Latino Gay Men of New York (LGMNY), LLANY, PRIDE, and other groups share offices in PRACA's headquarters. As the agency's executive director stated recently in an informal exchange with me, "After a while, by having gays and lesbians share the same offices with our regular staff, even the most homophobic has been sensitized, and I believe that a climate of mutual respect has been achieved." A good number of my informants have visited PRACA for meetings, mailings, etc., or know about the agency's support for Latino queers. Some of these new organizations could not have survived without the support they have received from the agency. The most common comment I heard my informants make was "gracias a PRACA mi organización existe" (thanks to PRACA, my organization exists). In fact, one organization member went as far as to state that when they started their organization, which centers on providing drugs for people with AIDS and HIV in Latin America, they first went to Gay Men's Health Crisis and were denied space. But PRACA provided them with desks and computer access and permitted them to put together a program that is now serving countless men and women in Mexico, Venezuela, and Colombia who would have never had access to these drugs.

The amount of support that PRACA has offered queer and AIDS organizations raised a question in my mind: how come these groups had such an easy entry into one of the oldest and most important Puerto Rican/Latino social service organizations? Why couldn't they have had the same support from their queer brothers and sisters? One Latino gay activist, Louis Ortíz, has suggested that in "dealing with the Latino community, there is only one major issue, gayness. We share all other issues, problems, cultural bonding, etc. However, in the gay community there are differences in culture, economic status, language, religion, education, etc." He further stated:

The Latino community is willing to accept issues of the lesbian and gay community, but they must be brought to their attention by proven Latino activists. In other words, they feel more comfortable with long-term activists who have a proven record in other community issues. The fact that I worked in ASPIRA and PRACA helped a lot to bring about changes.

When I asked him where he saw the boundaries between each community, he also added:

The only boundaries I see are in people's minds. I think that the Latino community is already dealing with the broader picture. As long as we, those who still have internalized our homophobia, don't confront it, it will remain preventing us from having a greater impact in the community. The example of what I am saying is the response of the Puerto Rican community to us in the Puerto Rican Day Parade. That experience is overwhelmingly positive. Those boundaries are internalized. They are more internalized within the Latino gay community than with the straight community.[73]

State senate race in East Harlem. Perhaps one case could illustrate the way Latino queers have both latinized the queer community and queered the Latino community, transgressing one (Latino) while collaborating with the other (queer). In 1992, playwright Richard Irizarry ran for state senator for East Harlem and Washington Heights against Olga Méndez.[74] The campaign was emblematic of the schism between the Puerto Rican and gay communities: both communities had been invisible to the other. Gay elected officials such as Tom Duane and Deborah Glick, for example, represented districts in the controlling city and the city of advanced services. All Latino elected officials represented people from the residual city and the city of unskilled work and the informal economy. The political constituents of Puerto Rican/Latino and gay elected officials differed in their needs, their politics, and the kinds of agendas that represented their views. Although all Latino and gay elected officials were members of the Democratic Party, their political prisms differed greatly. One group did not see the other unless party affiliation was called upon for political expediency. And an openly gay Latino man running in a Latino district was a new species.

As the campaign developed, a number of issues began to emerge. Irizarry ran on a progressive platform and allied his campaign across racial, ethnic, and class boundaries. Furthermore, many of the traditional allies of Ms. Méndez provided the campaign with resources and support. Some Latino elected officials privately commented on the need for leadership change and welcomed Irizarry. Most, however, could not openly support Irizarry but were willing to remain neutral. (In politics, *remaining neutral* usually means "not supporting the incumbent.") Ms. Méndez ran on her record. The problem was that her record was challenged by many, including *El Diario* and the *New York Times,* both of which endorsed Irizarry. Feeling threatened by the loss of endorsement by those newspapers and by the neutrality of some of her previous political allies, Méndez's campaign shifted gears and focused on two issues: that Irizarry was gay and HIV positive and that he was possibly not Puerto Rican but Cuban, a certain kiss of death in a Puerto Rican community.

Late in the campaign, a candidates' night was sponsored by many community organizations from East Harlem. During the evening, an exchange took place between Irizarry and Méndez: "The gay agenda is harmful to the Puerto Rican agenda," sputtered Senator Méndez, while Irizarry answered, "Olga, there are gays in the Puerto Rican community. I am Puerto Rican and gay. My agenda is a Puerto Rican and gay agenda." What struck the audience most about the exchange between candidates was Irizarry's fearlessness as he queered the event in opposition to the homophobic comments of his opponent. Community leaders admired Irizarry's campaign as a model of the politics of inclusion; his campaign brought together Puerto Ricans, Dominicans, blacks, whites, gays and lesbians, and straights from uptown and downtown, from among the poor and the well-to-do. The campaign headquarters, a dingy storefront, was located on 112th Street, and its immediate neighbors, working-class and poor Puerto Ricans and Dominicans, adopted the campaign. Some commented that in all the years they had lived on the street, nobody of importance, particularly a political candidate, had ever visited them and listened to their issues. A second campaign office was located in Washington Heights and fully supported by Dominicans. This Upper Manhattan office provided an ample example that the community was willing to accept a queer son who addressed their needs.

The whole leadership of LGMNY became involved in the campaign, and scores of the group's members worked on a daily basis from doing errands to fund raising. The support that Irizarry received from gay political clubs, Pride Agenda, and Tom Duane, the first openly gay elected official in New York City, pointed towards a recognition by the downtown gay political machinery that there *were* Latino gays and that Latinos were going to increase their visibility in both communities. Irizarry lost the campaign because he could neither raise the money nor put together the political machinery that the Méndez dynasty could. Irizarry's campaign, nevertheless, opened a space never before opened in the Puerto Rican and gay communities: an openly gay and HIV-positive candidate who claimed both identities.[75] Perhaps the recent victory of Margarita López in the Lower East Side of Manhattan could in some ways be attributed to the space created by Irizarry's campaign.

CONCLUSION

Although Latino queers remain marginalized from mainstream queer and Latino organizations in New York City and although the agenda for Latino queer organizations remains long and complex, the advances made in the last decade have been significant. Latino queers are increasingly present in boards of queer organizations, and their presence in major events such as the Pride March during the month of June has increased their visibility. In the Latino community, Latino queers are also increasingly able to come out of the closet and be part of organizations, perhaps the best example being the work of a number of Latino queers in *El Diario*. Issues of race, class, and nationality among Latino queers remain unresolved. The dual strategy of organizing as Latinos and as nation-specific groups represents a challenge in the development of a political agenda. Problems faced by a Colombian queer differ from those of a Dominican or a Puerto Rican queer, and visions of homosexuality may also differ because there is no one Latin American homosexuality. Nation-specific organizing, on the other hand, is perhaps a form of resistance to homogenization.

Last Fall, as I went for an evening "round" on Roosevelt Avenue in Jackson Heights, Corona, and Elmhurst, I recalled my travels in Mexico and the furtive night landscapes of Parque Zamora in Veracruz. Walking to Friends or perhaps Zodiac, I feel that the streets of New York are increasingly being invested with meaning by Latino queers and that the streets of many neighborhoods in Queens will never be the same.

NOTES

1. Although the term *queer* is not commonly utilized by Latino gays and lesbians, I am using it as shorthand to refer to gay, lesbian, transsexual, and other homosexualities. I am aware that the term connotes a number of problematic issues. For a very thorough discussion of the term *queer* and queer theory, please see Michael Warner, *Fear of Queer Planet. Queer Politics and Social Theory* (Minneapolis: University of Minnesota Press, 1993).
2. Italo Calvino, *Invisible Cities,* trans. William Weaver (New York: Harcourt Brace Jovanovich, 1974), 30–31.
3. Gordon Brent Ingram, "Marginality and the Landscapes of Erotic Alien(n)ations," in *Queers in Space: Communities/Public Places/Sites of Resistance,* ed. Gordon Brent Ingram, Anne-Marie Bouthillette, and Yolanda Retter (Seattle: Bay Press, 1997), 43.
4. Ibid., 29.
5. George Chauncey, "Privacy Could Only Be Had in Public," in *Stud. Architectures of Masculinity,* ed. Joel Sanders (New York: Princeton Architectural Press, 1996), 224.
6. Michel Foucault, "Of Other Spaces," in *Diacritics* (Spring 1986): 23.
7. David Harvey, *Justice, Nature and the Geography of Difference* (Cambridge: Blackwell Publishers, 1996), 225.

8. Foucault, "Of Other Spaces," 24.

9. Ingram, "Marginality," 50.

10. Owing to self-imposed limits, I have focused my research primarily on Latino gay men. Latina lesbians have been pioneers in the queering of Latino institutions as well as in challenging traditional gay and lesbian institutions. Indeed, most significant transgressions into mainstream Latino institutions were spearheaded by women. For example, the decision of Boricua Gay and Lesbian Forum (BGLF) to breach the Somos Unos conference in Albany was the work of both men and women in the organization, particularly Brunilda Vega, a BGLF founder. Furthermore, it was also BGLF that organized the first consistent presence of queers in the Desfile Puertorriqueño in 1989, with Las Buenas Amigas being the largest and most visible contingent. However, due to my involvement with Latino gay men's organizations that provided me full access to their meetings, data, and other documents, I found that at this stage of my research, documenting Latino men would be most appropriate. This in no way means that the work and struggles of Latina lesbians are less important. It is my expectation that Latina women will find their own voices and meet Latino men in documenting the important role they have had in the development of queer organizations and their leadership in transgressing/transforming, queering, and tropicalizing/latinizing mainstream institutions.

11. Stuart Hall, "Cultural Identity and Diaspora," in *Contemporary Postcolonial Theory,* ed. Padmini Mongia (London: Arnold, 1996), 120.

12. Guillermo Gómez-Peña, "Beyond the Tortilla Curtain. Welcome to the Borderless Society," *Utne Reader,* January-February 1995, 38.

13. For a more detailed analysis of the early Latino queer movement in New York City, see Luis Aponte-Parés and Jorge Merced, "Páginas Omitidas. The Gay and Lesbian Presence," in *The Puerto Rican Movement: Voices from the Diaspora,* ed. Andrés Torres and José Velázquez (Philadelphia: Temple University Press, 1998).

14. Renato Rosaldo, "Cultural Citizenship, Inequality, and Multiculturalism," in *Latino Cultural Citizenship. Claiming Identity, Space, and Rights,* ed. William V. Flores and Rina Benmayor (Boston: Beacon Press, 1997), 38.

15. John Agnew, *Representing Space* (New York: Routledge, 1993), 263.

16. Michel de Certau, *The Practice of Every Day Life,* trans. Steven Rendall (Berkeley: University of California Press, 1984) 35–36.

17. Ibid., 36–37.

18. Ibid.

19. My sample is not a scientific sample. There were two kinds of informants: activists and nonactivists. I interviewed around fifty activists during a period of two years, between 1996 and 1998. Nonactivists were also interviewed during the same period. Activists were members, founders, and/or leaders in the development of a Latino gay organization. They were out to their peers and willing to be spokespersons for their causes. They were selected among key members of these organizations. Nonactivists were selected more at random. Many were self-selected in various social and cultural meetings in places such as the Lesbian and Gay Community Center. Others were casual encounters at bars and other places queers congregate. Material developed through these interviews has been utilized in several other articles on the

subject. Over 50 percent of them were Puerto Rican, and the rest were Dominican, Cuban, Colombian, Mexican American, Venezuelan, and other nationalities. About half were born in New York City, whereas others were born in the Caribbean, Latin America, or elsewhere in the United States. Many date only Latino men, whereas others did not have a particular choice. Two-thirds were Latino activists and were members or had some relationship with an organization. About half had been activists in nongay organizations, such as community agencies or political parties, whereas others were new to social activism.

20. Homi Bhabha, "Introduction. Locations of Culture," in *The Location of Culture* (New York: Routledge, 1994) 1.

21. See Luis Aponte-Parés, "What's Yellow and White and Has Land All Around It: Appropriating Place in Puerto Rican Barrios," in *The Latino Studies Reader. Culture, Economy and Society,* ed. Antonia Darder and Rodolfo D. Torres (New York: Blackwell, 1997).

22. See, for example, the special section "Then and Now, 100 Years of New York City," in the *Sunday New York Times,* January 25, 1998. If one were to understand the presence of Puerto Ricans and other Latinos in the history of New York from this document, their history seems to begin in the 1980s rather than the 1890s.

23. Saskia Sassen, *The Global City: New York, London, Tokyo* (Princeton, N.J.: Princeton University Press, 1991).

24. Edward Soja, *Postmodern Geographies: The Reassertion of Space in Critical Social Theory* (New York: Verso, 1989).

25. Michael Sorkin, ed., *Variations on a Theme Park: The New American City and the End of Public Space* (New York: Noonday, 1992).

26. Peter Marcuse, "Not Chaos, but Walls: Postmodernism and the Partitioned City," in *Post Modern Cities and Spaces,* ed. Sophie Watson, and Katherine Gibson (Cambridge, Mass.: Blackwell, 1995).

27. Ibid., 243.

28. Ibid., 247.

29. Sharon Zukin, *The Culture of Cities* (New York: Blackwell Publishers, 1995), 7–8.

30. Richard Walker, "Two Sources of Uneven Development Under Advanced Capitalism: Spatial Differentiation and Capital Mobility." *Review of Radical Political Economy* 10, no. 3 (1978): XX.

31. Harvey, *Justice, Nature, and the Geography of Difference,* 112.

32. James Polchin, "Having Something to Wear: The Landscape of Identity on Christopher Street," in *Queers in Space: Communities/Public Spaces/Sites of Resistance,* ed. Gordon Brent Ingram, Anne-Marie Bouthillette, and Yolanda Retter (Seattle: Bay Press, 1997), 383.

33. Ibid., 387.

34. During the past decade the increased presence of young queers of color on the streets of Greenwich Village has threatened many white queers, particularly store owners. In early 1992 many of our members in Latino Gay Men of New York (LGMNY) complained of police harassment when they visited Christopher St.

35. Jaime Manrique, *Latin Moon in Manhattan* (New York: St. Martin's Press, 1992), 45.

36. Manolo Guzmán, " 'Pa'La Escuelita con Mucho Cuida'o y por la Orillita': A Journey Through the Contested Terrains of the Nation and Sexual Orientation," in *Puerto Rican Jam. Rethinking Colonialism and Nationalism,* ed. Frances Negrón-Muntaner and Ramón Grosfoguel (Minneapolis: University of Minnesota Press, 1997). Since publication of his article, a new bar, La Nueva Escuelita, has opened at the same site. The new one differs greatly from the old one in the use of the space as well as the quality of the environment. No longer is La Escuelita dirty or smelly, and neither does going there feel like slumming. The most striking difference, however, is that the entrance has been changed to 39th Street, and it now has an awning announcing it. No longer is La Escuelita hidden from view.

37. Elsewhere I have examined the barriers encountered by Latino queers as they conceive and build their own institutions (Aponte-Parés and Merced, "Páginas Omitidas").

38. Research on the pre-Stonewall period has been lacking. My proposal is tentative and needs further development.

39. Groups such as the Comité Homosexual Latino Americano (COHLA), Hispanos Unidos Gay Liberados (HUGL), and others were founded during this period. For a historical sketch of these groups see Aponte-Parés and Merced, "Páginas Omitidas."

40. Juanita Ramos, ed. *Compañeras: antología lesbiana Latina* (New York: Latin Lesbian History Project, 1984), 96.

41. Some of the groups founded during this period were a new HUGL (Hispanic United Gays and Lesbians); BGLF; Las Buenas Amigas; ACT UP Latino; and in 1991, Latino Gay Men of New York.

42. Juan Flores, "The Latino Imaginary: Dimensions of Community and Identity," in *Tropicalizations. Transcultural Representations of Latinidad,* ed. Frances R. Aparicio and Susana Chávez-Silverman (Hanover, N.H.: University Press of New England, 1997), 188.

43. It is too early to know if institutionalization will bring long-term benefits. One of the best characteristics of previous organizing efforts was that the voluntary nature of their commitment was very genuine. However, in this day and age, with most Latino queers holding jobs that do not give them flexibility and not being bearers of great personal wealth, this strategy may be the most logical and beneficial.

44. This issue was raised in a Christmas 1999 letter by Andrés Duque, the cyber connector of Mano a Mano, a coalition of several Latino lesbian and gay groups.

45. Latino community is a complex label, a bridge identity for a number of people sharing common heritage but who differ by class, ethnic composition, race, nationality, and time of arrival in theUnited States. In 1990 the distribution of Latinos was the following: 49.5 percent Puerto Rican, 19.1 percent Dominican, 4.9 percent Colombian, 4.5 percent Ecuadorean, 3.3 percent Cuban, 3.2 percent Mexican, 1.4 percent El Salvadorian, 1.3 percent Peruvian, 1.3 percent Honduran, and 0.5 percent Nicaraguan. Among Latinos, furthermore, social and economic indicators differ greatly.

46. It is beyond the scope of this work to enter into the debate around identities. The literature on Latino, queer, gay, and lesbian identity is extensive. We have argued elsewhere (Aponte-Parés and Merced, "Páginas Omitidas") that Latino gay identity remains an elusive identity, and is also a bridge identity. Nevertheless, all informants in this study identified themselves as Latino gays while maintaining the national identity as well.

47. Flores, "The Latino Imaginary," 185.

48. Judith Butler, "Imitation and Gender Insubordination," in *inside/out. Lesbian Theories, Gay Theories,* ed. Diana Fuss (New York: Routledge, 1991), 19.

49. Frank Browning, "Sex, Pride, and Desire," *The Harvard Gay and Lesbian Review* 5, no. 2 (Spring 1998): 33.

50. In a longer version of this essay, I examine the development of Latino gay bars in Queens and the Bronx. Bars remain a major site of cultural representation in the Latino queer community.

51. Hall, "Cultural Identity and Diaspora," 110.

52. There is a vast literature on the cultural identity of Latino queers, and commenting on it lies beyond the scope of this paper. For two recent compilations, see David W. Foster, *Gay and Lesbian Themes in Latin American Writing* (Austin: University of Texas Press, 1991); and Emille L. Bergmann and Paul J. Smith, eds., *¿Entiendes? Queer Readings, Hispanic Writings* (Durham, N.C.: Duke University Press, 1995). For the past decade the production by Latino gay artists in the United States has increased significantly. At the national level there is Luis Alfaro, and in New York City there are many artists such as Jorge Merced, Arthur Aviles, Janet Astor, and so on who have chosen to integrate their artistic production with their gayness.

53. Martha Gever, "The Names We Give Ourselves," in *Out There. Marginalization and Contemporary Culture,* ed. Richard Ferguson, Marta Gever, Trinh T. Minh-ha, and Cornel West (Cambridge, Mass.: MIT Press, 1990), 192.

54. Orlando García, "Homosexuales en marcha," *El Diario/La Prensa,* 21 de marzo de 1991, p. 37. Bold added by author.

55. Words of an ad that appeared in the January 1995 edition of *HX* magazine. I do not have copies of the original but rather a reproduction that was utilized by Latino queers in their flyer calling for a demonstration on that same night.

56. The letter was signed by the executive director of the Hispanic AIDS Forum, Las Buenas Amigas, Latino Gay Men of New York, the NYC Lesbian and Gay Anti-Violence Project (AVP), the editor of SIDAhora, and the Spanish Communications Committee of ACT UP. It was a major milestone. Those who signed were not always in agreement over many issues in both Latino and gay communities. However, the blatant homophobic leanings of *El Diario* led to a rare coalition of forces from the Latino gay, lesbian, and AIDS community leadership.

57. Subject 1 (name withheld), interview by the author, San Juan, Puerto Rico, January 8, 1998.

58. Bhabha, *The Location of Culture,* 70.

59. Joe DeMarco, "Gay Racism," in *Black Men White Men,* ed. Michael J. Smith (San Francisco: Gay Sunshine Press, 1983), 113.

60. Frank Gúzman, interview by the author, New York City, July 8 and 9, 1998.
61. Cornel West, "The New Cultural Politics of Difference," in *Out There. Marginalization and Contemporary Culture,* ed. Richard Ferguson, Marta Gever, Trinh T. Minh-ha, and Cornel West (Cambridge, Mass.: MIT Press, 1990), 29.
62. Gúzman, interview.
63. Videotape of Gay Network program, n.d.
64. Miss Guy, "Five Types of Men That Cannot Be Trusted," *Next,* February 13, 1998. The reaction to this latest publication of stereotypes has been well managed. Mano a Mano, a coalition of queer groups, has engaged in a concerted effort to eradicate the use of Latino stereotypes. After initial attempts to get the editors of the publication to publish an apology, Mano a Mano was able to get *LGNY,* a gay weekly, to publish their letter and pressure their white brothers to react. If *Next* continues to ignore the Latino queer community, Mano a Mano is ready to begin a boycott of commercial establishments that advertise in the weekly.
65. Marcuse, "Not Chaos, but Walls," 249.
66. Ibid., 248.
67. Gordon Brent Ingram, Anne-Marie Bouthillette, and Yolanda Retter, "Lost in Space: Queer Theory and Community Activism at the Fin-de-Millénaire," in *Queers in Space: Communities/Public Places/Sites of Resistance,* ed. Gordon Brent Ingram, Anne-Marie Bouthillette, and Yolanda Retter (Seattle: Bay Press, 1997), 14.
68. Butler, "Imitation and Gender Insubordination," 20.
69. In 1972 COHLA attempted to march in the Puerto Rican Day Parade. Although unsuccessful, this attempt positioned the early *movimiento* into strategies and tactics to challenge for years to come the imagined community that Puerto Ricans and other Latinos held of themselves, as well as challenging the gay movement to link their struggle with the issues of people of color.
70. Louis Ortíz, interview by the author, New York City, August 12–14, 1998.
71. Arnaldo Meléndez, telephone interview by the author, September 11, 1998.
72. The Puerto Rican Association for Community Affairs is one of the oldest social service organizations of the Puerto Rican community. It is a multiservice agency serving all Latinos throughout New York City.
73. Ortíz, interview.
74. I am completing research on an essay to record this campaign for an essay, "Challenging Puerto Rican Politics: Richard Irizarry's 1992 Campaign for State Senate."
75. During that same summer there were three other gay Latino candidates running for office: Pedro Velázquez (a policeman and chairman of Gay Officers Action League), Antonio Pagán (who was outed by the *Village Voice*), and Joe Franco (a former Hispanic AIDS Forum employee). Except for Irizarry and Franco, none of the other candidates chose to link both identities in their public postures.

CHAPTER FOURTEEN

Engendering and Coloring Labor Unions*

Transcultural Readings of Latin American Women's Ways

Mary Garcia Castro

This article is based on an old affair of alliances: my research on activism among Puerto Rican women in labor unions in New York City during two different historical periods and on union women in Brazil in the city of Salvador, Bahia.[1] Latin American working-class women in New York reconstruct an engendered and enraced class, deterritorializing "nuestra America, la America mestiza" (Martí 1983:20) or multiplying its northern territories through continuities and ruptures with Latin American identities (or their stereotypes) in the process. These trends are present in the narratives of *pioneras* —Puerto Rican women who arrived in New York in the early part of the twentieth century and worked in the garment industry (Benmayor 1992) and are still present today in the voices of their heirs, Puerto Rican women in leadership positions in labor unions, whom I began to study in 1993 and whom I shall refer to as the 1970s generation.

A focus on union women had been part of my work in Brazil since 1989, and after returning from New York, in transcultural readings of my Bahian work, I discovered new issues, some commonalities with Latinas[2] in New York but also many differences in practices and visions on gender, class, and race. In both places, the ways that women labor activists understood and combined gender, race, and class were an exercise in transcul-

*This article was made possible by support from the PRONEX-Brazilian Government/UNICAMP-CEMI Project. Thanks also to Lisa Earl Castillo for her input and for editing the final drafts of this paper.

turation:[3] women labor leaders in both places translate race, gender, and class according to their specific goals as well as to political, economic, and cultural constraints that are part of the history of workers, of women, and of ethnically subaltern groups in both places.

THE IMPORTANCE OF PUERTO RICAN EXPERIENCE ON GLOBALIZATION, MIGRATION, AND GENDER AND LABOR UNIONS: A BRAZILIAN READING

Economic globalization, its links to a new international division of labor, and its effects on women's participation in the labor market constitute a very recent focus in the academy, but among Puerto Rican intellectuals such a perspective was already de rigueur by the 1970s (Lauria-Perriceli 1989; Bonilla and Campos 1986; Rios 1983; Morales and Bonilla 1993; among others). A laboratory in the 1950s by virtue of Operation Bootstrap, Puerto Rico would by no means exemplify a Latin American leftist utopia during the decade to come. With the Economic Commission of Latin America/ United Nations emphasizing an import-substitution model and the construction of a national bourgeoisie, Puerto Rico was led down the path of an industrialization oriented by U.S. interests, creating a neocolonial state/ status. In a certain way the neoliberal models so often used today, with renewed imperialist ties and the subordination of local economies to multinational interests, were inaugurated in Puerto Rico decades ago.

Indeed, Puerto Rico was an unsettling reality in the Latin American nationalist imaginary of the 1960s, especially considering the other utopian dream-come-true of the period, the Cuban revolution. Puerto Rico became something not to deal with. The silence on Puerto Rico in Brazilian and other Latin American academic production in social sciences and literature of the period is not just an indifference toward an uncomfortable, unframed other (see Franco in Flores and Yúdice 1993) but also an avoidance of the pain of discovering the commonalities of destiny.

My focus on Puerto Rican women in labor unions also stems from another process that has recently been attracting more and more attention from Brazilian scholars concerned with the articulation of gender, race, and class. In the literature on Latinas in the United States, it is quite common to call attention to the resistance of Puerto Rican women in terms of multiple processes of subalternities and the way they historically have dealt with transits and negotiation of identities in spaces such as labor unions. Puerto Rican women have participated in the New York garment industry since the early part of the twentieth century (Ortíz 1994), illustrating that economic globalization (as well as its lackey, labor migration) is an ongoing transformative process that in addition to imposing patterns of work control and exploitation in Third World countries also affects Third World migrants in the United States and the economies into which they are packed.

The history of Puerto Rican women in the U.S. labor force also calls attention to the pitfalls of a labor movement whose origins were compromised by a probusiness model that reproduced systems of gender and racial discrimination. Authors such as Ortíz (1994) and Laurentz (1980) document how the International Ladies' Garment Workers' Union (ILGWU) maintained a political hierarchy in which positions of high leadership were reserved for males of European descent, excluding Latinas from decision-making processes at the same time that its organizing emphasized their recruitment (NACLA 1988). Some authors argue that the union's rigid internal hierarchy and its practice of negotiation with the bosses were linked to the general anticommunist hysteria that prevailed in the United States as well as to collaboration by the labor movement with those politics in the 1950s and more recently (Laurentz 1980). They also argue that the unions' fears about the garment industry's lack of competitiveness, especially in New York, resulted in an emphasis on job protection at the expense of working conditions and wages.

In a certain way, similar concerns are found in contemporary Brazilian debates on labor unions such as the persecution of labor unions and activists related to what are considered far-left currents by the government and the so-called modernization of the labor union model through social pacts between the government and employers in an effort to guarantee jobs, given the shortage of positions available in certain sectors of the economy due to automation and other transformations in the workplace. The limits of compromises with the government and employers and their effects on specific worker constituencies such as women form an ongoing debate in the Brazilian labor movement.

INTERROGATING PAST PRACTICES FOR ENGENDERING AND COLORING LABOR UNIONS—THE TESTIMONIES OF PIONERAS

The historical context for pioneras' testimonies is the New York Puerto Rican community during the 1940s and 1950s and the dynamics of the garment industry of the period, especially ILGWU shops. A complete analysis is beyond the scope of this paper; however, a basic framework for understanding is the crisis that hit the industry at that time. In an early manifestation of a symptom that would later become recurrent in the era of the globalization of capital, the garment industry was hit by long-term international and regional competition, with the cheap labor of migrant women emerging as the solution.

Pionera Gloria Maldonado presents insightful analyses of globalization's effects on workers as early as the 1950s, including imports, runaway shops, the exploitation of undocumented migrants, and the use of cheaper labor abroad. Maldonado suggests that the decline of the national garment industry as an employment source for migrants and the U.S.-born alike is not a new phenomenon, but her discourse also reveals an ambiguous border between conflicting identities. Despite some solidarity with Third World workers, she favors a closed market for U.S. workers:

> Unfortunately we were sleeping when it started [referring to the interviewer's comment on the debate that "nowadays there are not so many jobs because they are sending the work to Taiwan"]. . . . *These are . . . underdeveloped countries that need a boost and they don't have the qualification that a lot of us have.* So . . . making garments is one of them, you know, you don't need so much experience to do garments. And it started little by little tripping out, then the big . . . multinationals, the big corporations . . . I don't wanna say another word because then they'll think I'm too much to the left. [laughs] But *capital people,* they saw the advantage of making good money at the expense of other people's misery and at the expense of our people working here. . . . And we're not the only industry, we have the auto, the steel workers, the electronics. A lot of the things you buy now, radios, television, whatever, you know, they come from outside, especially from Japan. . . . So if all the work, or most of the work is sent out there then we are suffering. . . . When we call it a run-away shop is when it's a union shop and it closes. . . . The run-away shops, if they go to another part of the country at least somebody's working, whether they're union or nonunion. But if it comes from outside, if it goes outside of the United States *it's not our people making the profit, or having jobs, it's somebody else. . . . Why take the food from our table to give to somebody else? We know there's poverty, you know, you always try to help but should we help with our people, you know, being the ones that are losing out?* (Gloria Maldonado, interviewed by Rina Benmayor; italic emphasis mine.)

Pioneras paint vivid pictures of poverty and the daily struggle to survive both on the island and on the mainland during the Depression as well as of the forms of labor exploitation used by the garment industry in New York. Decades later, women of the 1970s generation witnessed many of these forms as well: there were still runaway shops, nonpayment of wages, lack of benefits, low wages, and control techniques based on the manipulation of fear in an era when jobs were scarce and unemployment high, using the workers' lack of English proficiency as an intimidation tactic. These stories of exploitation are mixed with other tales illustrating the "political ethics of everyday life" (Heller 1994:35) among workers. But in the case of the pioneras, I see an accent of collective organizing, as in pionera

Eva Monje's story of how she threatened to call the union if the boss did not pay Dominican workers who could not speak English their wages. Other women spoke of employers limiting the time they spent in the bathroom. In a similar vein, a contemporary Brazilian labor unionist commented: "Every time I went to the bathroom, the bosses were sending someone after me to see if I was trying to organize the people in there" (Castro 1995:39).

Pioneras also bore witness to racism on the shop floor during the 1930s. This history is an open-ended one with which women of the 1970s generation also grappled: in 1993, Rosa García, a labor lawyer with ILGWU, often spoke of issues of race and class, even when not describing it in so many words. She sees ethnic discrimination as an ongoing strategy for garment-industry employers, feeding on rivalries among workers of different nationalities. Pioneras recall conflicts between Italians and Puerto Ricans in their neighborhoods and on the shop floor and how management used language as a tool in controlling workers.

The pioneras' present-day heirs make similar observations. Indeed, Puerto Rican women of the 1970s generation also speak of conflicts among the oppressed and of the insidiousness and pervasiveness of the racial/ethnic system of power in the United States today. Their interviews speak of racism in the workplace and in labor unions in New York in the 1950s and 1970s but also show how the victims themselves are trapped in categories that exclude the perceived other—another migrant or another person of color—and how labor unions contributed to reproducing antagonisms among migrants:

Habían [en la directiva del sindicato] *morenas,* habían varias puertorriqueñas y, esto, *all nationalities.* Habían sirianas, judías, italianas. . . . Yo la conocía porque yo conozco todos los business agents, yo como pertenecía a la directiva los conocía a todos. Entonces voy y le digo, *ella era una judía but very nice. (*Eva Monje, interviewed by Ana Juarbe)

Another pionera, Lucilla Padrón, speaking of her first job in a unionized shop, also indicated conflicts with coworkers of other ethnicities:

Bueno, ahí [primer empleo] había unión pero era así. No me unioné na' porque, fíjate, ¿cómo me iba a unionar si no. . .? ¿Sabes lo que pasa? Que eran todas italianas, ¿tú ves? Y cuando allí todas son italianas, no te quieren, no te quieren. Antes era así. Todo el mundo era italiano y tú caes mal. Latino, ¿no?
    Entonces después la unión esa la cambiaron pa' el 23. . . . Nos separamos. Separaron los italianos del resto de la gente. Dejaron la 22 sólo para los italianos, para las mujeres italianas. Entonces

en la 23 habíamos latinas de Puerto Rico, West Indians, jamaiquinas, de todas las otras razas. Esa era la 23—para todas las otras razas. Pero la 22 era separada, nada más que para los italianos. (Lucilla Padron, interviewed by Ana Juarbe)

In looking for evidence of the production of subjectivity, a striking feature of these narratives is how in the women's memories of their work as chairladies, as residents of El Barrio or members of Puerto Rican clubs and associations, metonymic uses of language emerge through expressions such as *like a family, my Puerto Rican people,* and *take care of my own— cuidar de los míos, ayudar los míos.*

Nationality appears as a political identity in opposition to the colonial situation, a mixture of working-class solidarity and ethnicity. This is still a hypothetical reading—the narratives collected from the pioneras contain little information on political imagery other than their activism as chairladies. Still, it would be reductive to describe their narratives using exclusively social imagery, even if the direct reference suggests, among other cultural ethos: 1) an ethic of "everyday life" (Heller 1994:35); 2) a female tradition for caring and nurturing others, because they are homemakers par excellence; 3) a humanitarian liberal trend; 4) a socialist ethics of solidarity among equals; and 5) a Latino practice of community-building based on a common cultural background (Sánchez-Korrol 1983). Such ethos need not be mutually exclusive. I see a working-class notion of nationality as the privileged site of a singular subjectivity, underlining narration on resistance. I draw evidence for this reading from the women's stories of their practice as rank-and-file labor unionists, which indicate more loyalty to a social practice of labor unionism that they themselves constructed in everyday life—a union by and for the workers with whom they worked on a day-to-day basis and with whom they shared neighborhoods—than to the formal, more abstract structure of the international union.

Of course, focusing on the past, colored discourse on an anticolonial working-class identity might be disputed as imposed translation, because there is not an explicit political project of reference as part of pioneras' repertoire of motifs as there is in the writings of Jesus Colón (1982), a Puerto Rican socialist writer of the same period. Indeed, the international socialist accent, as well as the independentist option, is more explicit in Jesus Colón's sketches and also in discussions I had with some of the women of the 1970s generation, discussed in the next section.

Still, the point is to question simplistic liberal interpretations of expressions such as *cuidar de los míos* and the like as essentialist illustrations of a woman's voice. I argue that these expressions take on special meaning when utilized by working-class activist women in a colonial context. Most pioneras were asked to join ILGWU by union business agents because of demonstrated commitment and creativity in defending worker rights on the shop floor. They were elected as chairladies by the rank and file, and that was the level at which most stayed. The pioneras engendered unions by their direct practice, protecting women workers on the shop floor, sometimes even from the abuses or omissions of higher-level union organizers. They also colored the unions by defending the rights of Latino workers.

INTERROGATING THE PRESENT: WOMEN OF THE 1970S GENERATION[4]

Puerto Rican women of the 1970s generation witnessed an era of dramatic changes and setbacks in the labor movement brought about by economic globalization.[5] It was a time when both union and nonunion garment jobs in the United States were being lost to lower-wage, mostly nonunion shops in Latin America and Asia. Many saw the United States as the site of struggle but from the vantage point of their condition of otherness, framed by multiple references including gender, class, race, ethnicity, and nationality as well as by inequalities between Anglos and Latinos and tainted by Puerto Rico's position as an *estado asociado*. The importance of this may even diminish that of other borders among Latinos, such as gender. Rather than being a natural or atavic condition, this is an otherness imposed by the Anglos, as I read in the following piece:

> No es ni intencional, ellos [los norteamericanos blancos] siempre me recuerdan que soy una puertorriqueña y muchas veces por la forma de ignorarme o al ignorar mi país. Estoy hablando de líderes sindicalistas norteamericanos. (Puerto Rican woman employed at Local 1199 [National Union of Hospital and Health Care Employees] who asked not to be identified, 1993)

The women often emphasized the common finding in research on organized labor in the United States that despite the backdrop of backlash against unions[6] in the 1980s, there were also the seeds of a backlash against the backlash, which in a certain way grew to maturity with the AFL-CIO's 1995 election. Rachleff considered that a labor resurgence would take place, especially given some labor unions' concern for organizing the unorganized "to give greater voice to workers," "to face the resistance of its old bureaucratic leadership" (1994:21), and to reach out to the community and to organized workers in other countries. In sum, organized labor in the United States, in Rachleff's words, does not need a "revival" of the 1920s CIO model but must "shift from a culture of business unionism to what activists are calling an 'organizing model' and 'social unionism'" (1994:22).

Creative concepts of labor unions' revival such as the accent on workers' internationalism were addressed in the narratives of the women of the 1970s generation. To my question, "What do you think about the thesis that 'labor unionism is dead', especially in the United States?" Rosa García replied:

> Indeed the situation is making it hard for labor unions. But *I* believe that the idea of labor unionism, that the need of labor unions are not dead. Today even more than in the past workers need labor unions. *I* argue that labor unions, especially in this country have to find a new way to arrive to this sector [the workers]. They need more *creativity.* Some practices of the past perhaps are not working anymore . . . but labor unions are as important as they were 30, 40, or even 50 years ago. We are facing a situation when there is less and less jobs, and people are fighting to secure jobs. In the same way that capital *gets to be international,* that all industries come to an agreement, the union has to follow this path. *We, the workers,* have to be organized in Brazil, in Mexico, in Dominican Republic, in Haiti and in the U.S. If *we* do not do it, *we* are going to get in trouble, because *we* are competing against each other for the same jobs. (Rosa García, 1993; italic emphasis mine)

She also stressed the need for closer contact between labor unions and community-based organizations and for unions to support autonomous movements in the community. But her narratives also suggest that part of her effectiveness as an activist may stem from her very separation of spheres, with her work at the union on the one hand and in community movements, such as the creation of a bilingual education school in Brooklyn, on the other. In answer to my question, "Why do so few women participate in labor union activities?" Rosa García's response was:

> I think that educational opportunities at the labor unions are quite restrictive. Unions should offer more educational activities at the level of the shop floor. People have to learn more about *community* sense. Power has to be given to people in a way that workers can participate of those activities. There is a combination of causes, and many women are afraid to face the idea they have to fight, and many of us accept the role imposed on us by society. (Rosa García, interviewed by Mary Garcia Castro, italic emphasis added)

Like other women I interviewed, Rosa García spontaneously brought up the subject of labor unions on the island. On her father's side, she comes from a family of labor union activists, and she lived on the island until she was twenty-five, when she came to New York to pursue a master's degree. Now thirty-nine, she maintains close contacts with organized labor in

Puerto Rico. Rosa García suggests ways of engendering unions on the island, focusing on the role of women activists in the debate on the double day, on sexual harassment, and on domestic violence, noting that this last issue is not dealt with by women's groups in the United States focusing on labor unions. Nevertheless, she spoke of ILGWU as having a broad anti-discrimination policy in relation to race, sex, and sexual preference.

ILGWU and Local 1199 have different histories and practices, and most interviewees talked about those operative in the period during which the interviews were conducted. They considered that there was more room for Latinos, Latinas, and African American men and women at Local 1199, that it was a more democratic, more progressive union, representing social labor unionism. Reaching out to the community, a common thread in the narratives of several Latinas with whom I spoke at ILGWU and at Local 1199, was seen as an issue particularly affecting people of color in New York:

> In this country the struggle has to be given at different levels. We
> have to fight for the housing question; we have to fight for better
> schools for our children, demanding the right for a better
> education. At last, all these struggles we are related to in other
> levels are those that really will allow us to move ahead. . . . To
> *the Latina community,* school is a very important issue. In almost
> 45 percent of the schools where the children are, they are not
> learning anything. . . . Teachers are underpaid. . . . We have to
> create mechanisms *in our own communities in order to help each*
> *other,* so we can get involved in so many things. (Rosa García,
> interviewed by Mary Garcia Castro; italic emphasis mine)

When asked about the links between labor unions and community activities, Rosa replied:

> I think that still in the majority of the labor unions, they [labor
> unions and community] are separated worlds, with some few
> exceptions. I think that this is a mistake, it is very important to
> unions that they make linkages with the communities. We have
> been working in organizational campaigns like those in Brooklyn
> in order to have contacts with the Church, and other communal
> groups, to build up a supportive net. (Rosa García, interviewed
> by Mary Garcia Castro)

Community also emerges as a key concept in the narratives of Sonia Larracuente, who was in charge of educational programs at ILGWU when I interviewed her. In the texts of many of the Puerto Rican women I interviewed, community is understood as barrios, Latino neighborhoods—and sometimes it is understood by the same person as also meaning Puerto Rican nationality and the struggle to preserve Puerto Rican pride, dignity, and culture. In a certain way community is understood as citizenship, but not just as a right: it is an abstract means of political resistance that goes beyond the local, beyond immediate experience. As a Puerto Rican female labor organizer from ILGWU, who asked not to be identified, put it: "Acuérdate que entre Puerto Rico y Estados Unidos hay una relación colonial que lo pinta todo." My reading suggests that despite the truism that class, gender, race, and ethnicity must be joined, at the level of discourse one site of oppression tends to assume a privileged role, without necessarily nullifying the others. The broader power structure tends to orient which will be chosen as sites of rebellion.

Like her contemporary Rosa García and some other pioneras, Sonia Larracuente came from a family of political activists: she is the daughter of pionera Gloria Maldonado. Life histories such as hers and her mother's suggest the building of a unique national community. Sonia speaks with enthusiasm about her mother's importance as a role model for her own activism:

> My mother was the only Latin woman who in 1940 worked in a *taller* where all other workers were men, Italians, Jews, and older. She was sixteen years old, they were forty or fifty years old. She worked for twenty-five years in this type of job *(en esto)*. Then she became an activist, and after a while she began to participate in programs of the Department of Education here in New York, in technical education and formation. I always had a fascination for her work.
>
> After she left the factory, for twenty-three years she was active, working in the union. She retired when she was sixty-two years old. She did everything in the taller: contracts, organization, etc. . . . But she did not reach the high leadership. She was never a manager or a vice president. Anyhow she was in all branches of the daily work. (Sonia Larracuente, 1993 interview)

In the early 1990s, Sonia Larracuente was quite active in the Latin American Committee for Advancement (LACRA), in which many labor unions participate as institutional members. She not only engenders the labor union through her educational programs for delegates, business, agents, and organizers but also by advancing the cultural and formal empowerment of Latinas as privileged arenas. With LACRA, she was involved in setting up classes for women on chairing meetings and in competing for formal positions in the union as well as cultural activities related to Puerto

Rican cultural expressions, such as courses in bomba and plena, traditional dances from the island.

In some of the narratives of Puerto Rican women in leadership positions in labor unions, I see back-and-forth transitions between nationality, class solidarity, family, dignity, pride in being Puerto Rican *(orgullo de ser puertorriqueño)* that are direct, or a part of the same narrative. In other cases, more than the place of speech, it was the woman's tone of voice that suggested the importance of nationalism and the identity of Puerto Rico as a nation. I read these topics as related to a project: "the defense of my people," "the importance of being Puerto Rican and presenting oneself as such in the United States" (common expressions in different interviews), or as Aida García, vice president of Local 1199, put it, "la puertorriqueñidad." Other topics I brought to the interviews, such as feminism, relations between Latinos and African Americans, the life of the union, or even types of discrimination, did not engage these women as much as the debate on *ser latino* and *ser puertorriqueño*.

LATIN AMERICAN WOMAN WARRIORS: TRANSCULTURAL READINGS BETWEEN NEW YORK AND BRAZIL

When power and gender are taken together, commonalities among Latina labor activists in Brazil and in the New York emerge. In different countries, an unequal gender culture occurs in the world of organized labor. Labor unions are spaces where women are not quite at home, despite exceptions and changes over time, especially when taking into account high-level decision-making positions (Castro 1998, among others). In New York, Puerto Rican women of the 1970s generation spoke of the need to bridge gaps between communities and labor unions, a strategy that might assist unions in recovering from the general crisis provoked by the contemporary transformation of labor and economic globalization. These women utilized innovative strategies for serving workers: through education programs that target unorganized migrants as well or participating in school boards in their barrios. Their strategies demonstrate an understanding of the working class as being produced and politically represented much more through social movements other than labor unions. Despite their emphasis on terrains beyond the union hall, these women also indirectly engendered the unions. By reaching out to the community, they brought reproductive, citizenship, and family rights to the political agenda of traditional labor agencies. They struggled against the sexual division of labor and power, being outstanding leaders in the male-oriented world of the workplace, and in caring for their families, their communities, and their nation. They supported institutional legal action as a strategy for defending women's rights but were suspicious of an essentialist women's movement, combining concerns with different types of identities. Yet their feminist agendas might suggest a more conservative or realistic perspective when compared to the broader women's movement. They tended toward supporting affirmative action, equality in the workplace, campaigns against sexual harassment, and the like. The flexibility of their concept of class is also worth noting, although class was not a concept commonly referred to in their discourse.

The Brazilian union leaders whom I interviewed in Bahia (Castro 1995, 1998) were quite young—their average age was twenty-seven—and commonly were the first generation of activists in their families; the Puerto Rican women whom I interviewed, however, were in their forties or fifties and were more likely to come from families of political activists, thus combining the private and the public and suggesting that the formation of class identity is part of their life histories. In Brazil, trade unionists seldom refer to themselves without stressing class and a socialist utopia as a collective social project or stressing class as a social relation that designates antagonic positions in the economic structure. Yet in Brazil labor unions still employ a narrow, traditional concept of class that does not concern itself with workers not employed in the formal economy or with the unemployed and retired, despite worldwide labor turmoil and despite the fact that blacks, especially black women, are more visible in the informal sector and among the unemployed. Also, because race/ethnicity is narrowly addressed as a cultural issue in itself, social movements are considered the appropriate arena for the struggle against racism, and labor unions do not include the struggle against racism in the workplace or discriminatory recruitment practices as basic parts of their agenda. However, over the past five years the discourse of upper-level leaders has included those topics as well as discrimination against women and some specific organized activities.

In comparing Puerto Rican union women in New York to their sisters in Bahia, I suggest the following hypotheses.

First, different forms of complementarity between visions come to light. *Community* is an important reference in the narratives of Puerto Rican union women in New York, whereas *society* is a more common term among Brazilians. *Community* assumes a politico-cultural connotation with different meanings. I read *resistance* but one not necessarily associated with long-term projects that question the establishment. But society as a project also allows multiple references when gender and race are the issue. For Brazilian union men (Castro 1998), discussions of issues such as "the socialism we want," "the struggle against the bankers and the conservative, authoritarian state government," "our union's strength against the employers," or "our perspective on politics and that of the workers from other political parties" are dear to their hearts. With the union women I interviewed in Brazil, these issues also came up, but they focused more on the need for an internal gendered democracy in the union, in which different types of languages can be heard and respected—a point stressed by their sisters in New York as well.

I claim that it is neither by chance nor individual choice that Brazilian labor women privilege gender and class as sites to be combined in the production of subjectivity. Their narratives are located in a rigid authoritarian society still caring for the wounds of fourteen years of repression and a military coup. They consider the union to be *theirs,* and union men are *companheiros* first in a common struggle against employers and a certain type of society (capitalist society, neoliberal society, and the like).[7]

Second, gender undergoes a peculiar transculturation in both cases. Brazilian union women criticize male-female relations within unions, but at the same time, union men are their *companheiros.* Still, the women invest in "a long-term project to change their macho mentality" (Castro 1995). They keep their distance from gender perspectives they associate with middle-class feminism and from class visions reduced to equality or reducing workers to a homogeneous mass. They also stress a concern with the combination of equality and differences. In their view, differences among women should also be highlighted, taking into account not just race and class positions but also political perspectives and alliances.

In contrast, the issues dear to the hearts of the women in New York were their community, the colonial status of Puerto Rico, and Puerto Rican identity in the United States. For ILGWU women, not all male colleagues were described as *compañeros,* and in some cases the union was not really "their" union. In the narrative of one, "The union is a job; the struggle is out there, in the community." The word *ours* was, however, commonly employed by female union leaders at Local 1199 when speaking of the union, as it was in Brazilian women's testimonies. Some Puerto Rican women, such as Rosa García and Aida García, stressed their belief in unions' importance in fighting for workers' rights and for women's rights as workers. But they were not so optimistic about changes in gender relations, given the rigid hierarchies within the union (especially ILGWU) that go beyond gender lines.

The Brazilian activists, however, had faith in unions, like political parties, as basic vehicles for social change. They stress that general cultural patterns on gender, as well as those more often found in labor unions, might be challenged when bridges are made with social movements that are also concerned with class projects, such as working-class feminism (Castro 1998). Latinas in New York and their Brazilian *companheiras* in Bahia both defined themselves as feminists, yet both groups added a "but" afterwards. All of the Puerto Ricans I interviewed were critical of white North American feminist currents for not incorporating the issue of colonial status and, some said, for employing rigid separations between men and women. From their position as colonized, working-class women of color in the United

States, gender is a site of rebellion within organized labor; for Latinas, gender is referred to as a specific constituency.

Third, the concept of race also gave rise to transcultural readings and translations. For many Brazilian labor activists, race-related issues are described as being out of their territory. Despite a long history of blacks at decision-making levels in unions, not until 1995 would racism be defined as a class issue in Brazilian labor unions.[8] Male and female union leaders often see themselves as antiracist, but race is not privileged as an explicit site for stimulating rebellions against work relations. Since the foundation in 1933 of the Bank Workers Union of Bahia, there have been blacks on its board of directors. In 1998, out of the board of directors' seventy members, by Brazilian standards about 70 percent would be characterized as *negros* because of their hair and skin, whereas by U.S. standards, 85 percent would be considered black. Nonetheless, racism in the workplace is less of an issue in union struggles than sexism, a struggle spearheaded, in this case, by women union leaders. In Brazil, a recent debate on race/ethnicity in the workplace has been limited to the relationship between discrimination and underrepresentation of blacks in formal sectors of the economy and inequalities between black and white employed workers. There is a controversy over a government proposal for implementing an affirmative action program in schools and workplaces. Less attention is given to the political and cultural reproduction of racism, especially when combined with sex/gender discrimination. Racial inequalities among workers, for instance, are more focused in debates related to government proposals than institutionalized racism and the role of neoliberal politics in its reproduction. Few black women's organizations or workers' movements address questions related to the complex combination between politics, culture, and economy, including women's self esteem; male/female relations among blacks; the role of conventional parameters of beauty in discriminating against black women for jobs in the service sector; the relation between class and race; the link between high levels of poverty in the black population and black marginalization; the politico-cultural ethos of Brazilian society against domestic work, an occupation that survived slavery; and the Western consumerist model of development and its codes of beauty, or how this model, on the one hand, marginalizes the nonwhite other and, on the other hand, transforms mixed-race women *(mulatas)* into commodities in the sex-tourism industry.

In labor unions, the fact is that race/ethnicity is not regarded as an arena to be conquered, which questions the emphasis on quotas for blacks in decision-making positions. As previously mentioned, many Brazilians of African descent hold leadership positions in labor unions. Although lately the issues of race as a system of privilege as well as of racism in the workplace and in society are gaining ground in speeches by labor union leaders, they are less prominent among rank-and-file workers, male and female. The damage done during the era of slavery to the collective imagery of blacks and whites at work—a racial and sexual division of labor—is addressed more via discourse on/against discrimination. Less space is left for race/ethnicity as a language of rebellion not restricted to a space, a position, or a social movement (Gilroy 1991).

Race is also an ambiguous reference in the narratives of pioneras and women of the 1970s generation—but it takes peculiar forms, made more complex owing to national/political boundaries. The narratives of some pioneras reveal discriminatory remarks against other groups, such as Jews and Italians. References to race mingle with allusions to ethnicity and national roots, being used as emblematic signs of resistance identity to differentiate themselves from the Anglos. Puerto Ricans commonly referred to cases of racial discrimination in the workplace and other spheres of U.S. society as a strong division among workers. Racism is ambiguously understood as discrimination against Latinas, and black women were more vocal about discrimination that they suffered as Latinas than as black women.

In contrast, Gloria Maldonado shows a unique alchemy (Castro 1993:10) of the circulation between multiple systems of privileges as a subaltern/subversive other:

> I'm the only woman here, the only woman officer and the only Hispanic business agent. The boss is Hispanic but . . . you know, the manager, he's Puerto Rican. But I'm the only woman. And I have three points: I'm dark, so some people say, "She's black." [laugh] 'Cause, you know, some people consider us in between, you know, but for some people if you got a little black blood, you're black. So I don't care, I'm proud of my black heritage too anyway. *So I'm Puerto Rican, I'm a woman and I'm black. I got three Affirmative Action points.* [laughs] (italic emphasis mine)

I noted a strikingly similar collapsing of categories with some union women in Bahia. When I asked Creuza Maria Oliveira, president of the Domestic Workers' Union, "What color are you?" she replied, "I am a black woman domestic worker." (Castro 1993:16). These ambiguous uses of race and class, collapsing or separating them, recall Gilroy's thesis on the complex identity of each system: "The problems are particularly acute when writers have resisted the idea that 'race' and class [and, I would add, gender in its homo and hetero forms] belong to separate spheres of experience with different epistemological and ontological valences" (1991:4).

The problem becomes acute when different equals have to face the limits of their equality, the fragility of fragmented identities, and their differences not in written texts but in their daily experiences of life. It is the complexity and pain of these experiences that make narratives such as those of Gloria Maldonado and Creuza Maria Oliveira pioneering voices for projects of collective subjectivity that go beyond essentialist perspectives.

CONCLUSION

The women whom I interviewed in U.S. labor unions, from their borders as Latinas and as women from the working class, deal with the borderlands Anzaldúa 1987) imposed on them, switching codes and figures of language in their narratives where *the workers, the community, our people, our Puerto Rico,* and *we Latinas* are fundamental references. These are the sites from which they envisage the engendering and coloring not of labor unions but of Latino resistance, which is thought of as lying elsewhere. They also recognize that in the United States the emphasis on institutional measures is a necessary one in the fight against discrimination. All interviewees considered laws against racism and sexism to be important, and many believed that affirmative action programs in the workplace and labor unions had allowed them some social mobility.

A slightly different strategy is employed by women in the northeastern Brazilian labor union. A subtle investment in a de-recoding of cultural politics takes place in the union through women's agency. Indeed, through references to a gendered class perspective, the Brazilian working-class feminists in labor unions use other codes. They still invest in reaching the *companheiros* and transforming not one space but the whole structure, the labor union and the Brazilian society, all together. They search for "a new language" but do not invest in the "language of the borderlands" (Anzaldúa 1987:5). In producing their subjectivity as political subjects, they strive toward a transborder language in alchemical combinations (Castro 1993) of private and public, general and specific, equality and difference, gender and class. Some, even quite a few, even go beyond, "race-ing" it all. They are not limited by recognizing limits or borders but are still engaged in the master narrative perspective of transformation of the whole, which sometimes appears as the labor union and other times as "this society."

NOTES

1. I first addressed the narratives of Brazilian union women during research at the bank employees union in Bahia—Sindicato dos Bancários da Bahia (1989–1993)—see Castro (1995) and Castro (1998). The Brazilian women to whom I briefly refer here are today members of that labor union. It is a relatively powerful union in the state and in the country. Before 1995 it used to organize massive strikes. Even today it is active in street demonstrations, but those are less frequent today, when more attention goes to the increasing layoffs of bank employees due to automation in the financing system and to the neoliberal

politics of the current government, by which workers' historic gains are undermined. In 1993 there were 25,000 bank employees in the state of Bahia; by early 1995 that figure had been reduced to about 17,000, and by mid-1998 the number had dropped to less than 9,000.

The New York project was carried out in 1993 and 1994 when, as a Rockefeller fellow in humanities at the Centro de Estudios Puertorriqueños of Hunter College, I explored interviews filed in the *Pioneras*—Oral History Archive and was able to discuss my findings with staff members there, including Rina Benmayor, Antonio Lauria, and William Flores as well as with Ana Juarbe and Alicia Díaz Colón.

A third source of information were twenty structured interviews I conducted in New York with women who had emigrated from different Latin American countries, thirteen of whom were Puerto Rican. Most occupied intermediate leadership positions or were responsible for programs in the New York office of the former ILGWU and Local 1199 (National Union of Hospital and Health Care Employees). In this article I refer only to interviews conducted with Puerto Rican women. See the appendix to this article for names and biographical summaries.

2. I should emphasize that the term *Latina* was quite often used by the Puerto Rican women I interviewed as well as by those interviewed by other researchers. Still, I am aware of its limits (see Flores and Yúdice 1993, among others) and its potential for contributing to a counterhegemonic bloc formation. According to Flores and Yúdice, immigrants from Latin America are "conquered minorities" in the United States, but they "do not comprise even a relatively homogeneous 'ethnicity' " (1993:199).

3. The concept of transculturation, first developed by Cuban anthropologist Fernando Ortíz (in 1940–1955) and revived by Angels Rama (cited in Pratt 1992) and by Pratt (1992), involves an intellectual reasoning construction that is appropriated here with some simplification. I did not perform in-depth historical-anthropological studies like those conducted by Ortíz (1995) and Pratt on social and imaginary formations.

4. In this section I refer to the testimonies of some Puerto Rican interviewees who were on the staff of ILGWU and Local 1199 in 1993 and 1994 (see the appendix).

5. Recent changes in U.S. labor unions include the merging of ILGWU with the Amalgamated Textile Workers' Union; the recent visibility and legitimacy of gender and race in the AFL-CIO and its 1995 elections; and the empowerment of Latinos, male and female, in terms of formal representation. Linda Chávez Thompson, a Chicana, was nominated for vice president of the AFL-CIO, and the current president, John Sweeney, has stressed the importance of orienting programs toward migrant workers and of being more attentive to Latino issues in the workplace and the community.

6. The backlash against labor unions in the United States in 1993 and 1994 is well summarized by Rachleff: "From 19.4 percent of the work force ten years earlier, unionized labor plummeted to 10.2 percent. The strike had virtually disappeared as a weapon of labor. Where 4 million workers had hit the bricks a decade before, now only 300,000 dared to do so. As the labor movement withered, wages stagnated and the work week lengthened despite a doubling of

manufacturing output. Inequality grew, as the top one-tenth of 1 percent of the social pyramid took in as much income as the bottom 42 percent" (1994: 226).

7. The class-based unionism from which Brazilian women union leaders speak is far from the "bread-and-butter" unionism of Samuel Gompers, who maintained that "labor should stick to bread-and-butter demands and steer clear of politics" (NACLA 1988:25). Brazilian unionism rose up against the military dictatorship in the 1970s and along with other social movements pushed for the impeachment of then president Collor in 1992. But it is facing a backlash against neoliberalism not only due to increased unemployment but also to ideological divisions—with a growing center-right tendency—and internal power disputes (see Antunes 1991).

8. In September 1995 the first international conference on racism in the workplace to be held in Brazil occurred in the city of Salvador with financial support from the AFL-CIO. The Brazilian worker confederation CUT—Central Unica dos Trabalhadores—has denounced the Brazilian government in international court in Geneva for failing to comply with Convention 111 of the International Labour Office against racism in work relations. Seminars and programs on racism in the workplace have been taking place, but racial/ethnic awareness is still a banner of CUT and quite a few other labor unions.

REFERENCES

Antunes, Ricardo. 1991. *O Novo Sindicalismo.* São Paulo: Editora Brasil Urgente.

Anzaldúa, Gloria. 1987. *Borderlands—La Frontera: The New Mestiza.* San Francisco: Aunt Lute Books.

Benmayor, Rina. 1992. "Gender and Concepts of Community in Life History Narratives." Paper prepared for Recovering the U.S. Hispanic Literary Heritage Project, November..

Bonilla, Frank and Ricardo Campos. 1986. *Industry and Idleness.* New York: Centro de Estudios Puertorriqueños.

Castro, Mary García. 1993. "The Alchemy of Social Categories in the Production of Political Subjects. Class, Gender, Race and Generation in the Case of Domestic Workers' Union Leaders in Salvador-Bahia, Brazil." *The European Journal of Development Research* 5, no. 2 (December): 1–22.

——. 1995. "Gênero e poder no espaço sindical." *Revista Estudos Feministas* (Rio de Janeiro), 3(1): 29–51

——. 1998. "The Gendered (Di)-vision of the Rebellion. The Public and the Private in Life Histories of Female and Male Union Leaders, Salvador-Bahia-Brazil." *Identities—Global Studies in Culture and Power* 5, no. 1 (April): 65–96.

Colón, Jesus. 1982. *A Puerto Rican in New York and Other Sketches.* New York: International Publishers.

Flores, Juan and George Yúdice. 1993. *Divided Borders. Essays on Puerto Rican Identity.* Houston: Arte Público Press.

Gilroy, Paul. 1991. *There Ain't No Black in the Union Jack.* Chicago: University of Chicago Press.

Heller, Agnes. 1994. "The Elementary Ethics of Everyday Life." In *Rethinking Imagination Culture and Creativity,* edited by Gillian Robison and John Rundell. New York: Routledge.

Laurentz, Robert. 1980. "Racial/Ethnic Conflict in the New York City Garment Industry, 1933–1980." Ph.D. diss., State University of New York at Binghamton.

Lauria-Perricelli, Antonio. 1989. "A Study in Historical and Critical Anthropology: The Making of the People of Puerto Rico." Ph.D. diss., New School for Social Research, New York.

Martí, José. 1983. *Nossa América, Antologia*. São Paulo: Ed Hucitec.

Morales, Rebecca and Frank Bonilla, eds. 1993. *Latinos in a Changing U.S. Economy*. London: Sage.

North American Conference on Latin America (NACLA). 1988. "Neither Pure nor Simple. The AFL-CIO and Latin America—The NACLA Report." *NACLA—Report on the Americas* 22, no. 3 (May-June): 10–30.

Ortiz, Altagracia. 1994. " 'En la aguja y el pedal eché la hiel': A History of Puerto Rican Women in the Garment Industry of New York City, 1920–1980." N.b.r.

Ortiz, Fernando. 1995. *Cuban Counterpoint. Tobacco and Sugar.* Durham, N.C.: Duke University.

Pratt, Mary Louise. 1992. *Imperial Eyes. Travel Writing and Transculturation.* New York: Routledge.

Rachleff, Peter. 1994. "Seeds of a Labour Resurgency." *The Nation,* January 21, 21–27.

Rios, Palmira. 1983. "Women Under Colonialism. The Case of Puerto Rico." Reproduced from *Transafrica Forum* by WIRE. New York.

Sánchez-Korrol, Virginia E. 1983. "On the Other Side of the Ocean." In *From Colonia to Community. The History of Puerto Ricans in New York City. 1917–1948.* London: Greenwood Press.

APPENDIX: BACKGROUND ON PUERTO RICAN INFORMANTS

Pioneras

Source: Puerto Rican Pioneras Oral History Archives, Centro de Estudios Puertorriqueños, Hunter College/City University of New York.

Gloria Maldonado. A chairlady in garment factories and educational program officer of ILGWU, she was a union activist for almost thirty years up to 1950. Gloria Maldonado is a black Puerto Rican, born in the United States in 1928. Interviewed by Rina Benmayor, Blanca Vásquez, and Celia Alvarez on September 28, 1984, and February 17, March 17, and July 26, 1985; interviews transcribed by Alicia Días Concepción.

Eva Monje. A chairlady in garment factories for ILGWU in the 1940s, she was elected chairlady in 1956. She was born in Puerto Rico and came to the mainland when she was a child in the 1920s. Interviewed by Rina Benmayor and Ana Juarbe on August 7, 1984, and July 22, 1985; interview transcribed by Alicia Días Concepción.

Louise Delgado. A chairlady and business agent in garment factories for ILGWU and a board member of the union, she was an activist in the 1930s, 1940s, and 1950s. She was born in Puerto Rico and arrived in the United States as a child in 1923. Interviewed by Rina Benmayor, Celia Alvarez, and Blanca Vásquez

on August 15, 1984, and February 17 and 22, 1985; interview transcribed by
Alicia Días Concepción.

Emilia Giboyeaux. A chairlady in garment factories for ILGWU in the 1930s, she
retired in 1962. She was born in Puerto Rico in 1926 and arrived in the United
States as a child. Interviewed by Rina Benmayor and Ana Juarbe on August 1,
1984; interview transcribed by Alicia Días Concepción.

Lucilla Padrón. A chairlady in garment factories for ILGWU, she worked in the
garment industry from the 1940s until 1973. She was born in Puerto Rico and
arrived in the United States at the age of seventeen. Interviewed at the age of
seventy by Ana Juarbe and Rina Benmayor on April 5 and July 6, 1984;
interview transcribed by Lisa Davis.

1970s generation

Source: Interviews by the author conducted in 1993. All tapes are part of the Oral
History Archives, Centro de Estudios Puertorriqueños, Hunter College/City
University of New York.

Rosa García. Born in Puerto Rico and an activist in student movements there, she
came to the United States to pursue a master's degree in Central American
and Caribbean studies and later received a degree in law. Thirty-nine years
old at the time of the interviews, she has worked at ILGWU since the 1970s.
In 1993 she was assistant general counsel at ILGWU headquarters in New
York.

Sonia Larracuente. Daughter of Gloria Maldonado, in 1993 she was vice president
of the Women's Caucus of LACRA-Latin American Committee for
Advancement, affiliated with the AFL-CIO. She began to work in ILGWU in
the late 1970s and now works in the education department of ILGWU
headquarters. Born in the United States, Sonia studied sociology and political
science and has been involved in union's activities since the age of fourteen.
She was forty-eight years old at the time of the interviews.

Aida García. In 1993 she was vice president of the Local 1199, National Union of
Hospital and Health Care Employees. Thirty-seven years old at the time of the
interviews, she has been quite active in all spheres of the union. Born in
Puerto Rico to a family active in union movements, her parents returned to
the island about fifteen years ago, and she maintains contacts not only with
her family but also with Puerto Rican organized labor.

FIGURE 8. Lucky Cienfuegos, poet and representative of the Nuyorican Poets Movement in the 1970s. Photo taken in Charas Cultural Center in Loisaida. Photo by Máximo Colón

FIGURE 9. The Quisqueya on the Hudson Dominican Festival in Washington Heights. Photo by Arlene Dávila, 1999

PART IV

Latinizing Cityscapes

CHAPTER FIFTEEN

The Latin Side of Madison Avenue

Marketing and the Language that Makes Us "Hispanics"

Arlene Dávila

Latinos currently make up a coveted U.S. marketing segment. No other ethnic group in the United States is targeted by such a vast network of advertising agencies and an entire marketing industry selling them consumer products by addressing them as a common people and a market. In this context, Hispanic marketing has become one of the primary institutional forces fueling a common Latino/a identity, prompting analyses of this industry in relation to contemporary Latino cultural politics.[1] Today, Hispanic marketing agencies can be found in every city with sizable Latino populations, over fifteen of which operate in the U.S. advertising capital, New York City, the birthplace of the Hispanic advertising industry and the second largest Latino market.

This essay explores the origins and current scope of New York's Hispanic marketing industry as well as its impact on the creation of panethnic categories and images of and for Latinos.[2] I consider this industry as an arena of Latino self-representation that, dominated by corporate intellectuals of Latin American backgrounds in the United States and tied directly to the dominant structures of the U.S. economy, serves as a fruitful entry point into the complex interests involved in the public representation of latinidad. In particular, I argue that this industry is directly involved in the maintenance of latinidad's Hispanic core through its economically driven need to emphasize the permanence of the Spanish language as the basis for Latino/Hispanic identity to ensure and perpetuate its own existence and profitability. The industry's common name, Hispanic marketing, is indicative of its nature and scope: its premise is not only that there are basic differences between Latinos and other consumers that need to be addressed through culture- and language-specific marketing but also that there is a continuous influx of Spanish-speaking populations who would be left out of corporate America were it not for this type of marketing. The implications of such Spanish-centered definitions of latinidad come to the forefront in New York City, where there is indeed a growing number of Spanish-speaking Latino populations but also many older-generation Latinos for whom a common identity may not be based on a Spanish-centered notion of hispanidad or on the notions of authenticity that sustain this industry's existence and continued profitability.

This essay is also motivated by my interest in going beyond the current emphasis on the images and discourses of latinidad to probe the negotiations and compromises involved in the homogenization of a heterogeneous population into a culturally specific market. Oftentimes, following the still-dominant tendency of media studies, research on the Hispanic media and advertising industry has focused on the finished images and the texts generated to represent this market, leaving largely unexplored the interests that shape and constrain their development. Accordingly, culture-specific marketing is either praised or censured according to its perceived representation of the Latino community. Thus, some have argued that this type of advertising provides positive images for this population and that it helps counter its omission in mainstream media, whereas others point to advertising's commodification of Latino culture and its continued reproduction of dominant stereotypes, such as the association of Latino culture with the subjects of hypermasculinity, authenticity, and nationalism (Alaniz and Wilkes 1995; Nuiry 1996; Peñaloza 1997). Less discussed, however, are the interests and processes that shape these types of representations and how they may be related to dominant notions of hispanidad, the greater politics of representation in U.S. society, or the interests of the global market. To address these gaps, I draw from a year-long ethnographic study of the city's ad agencies and the making of their ads and, in particular, will place less emphasis on the finished images and texts generated to represent Hispanics relative to the political-economic interests involved in their production, particularly in the promotion of Spanish as the primary trait of latinidad.

I will start by briefly reviewing this industry's origins and transnational foundations as evinced in New York City and then move to analyze some of the dominant definitions of this market. I conclude with a consideration of what commercial representation of U.S. Latinos disseminated by the Hispanic media and marketing industry may be communicating to and about U.S. Latinos concerning the scope and nature of their identity as well as the centrality of the Spanish language to these constructions. Through this focus, my aim to is to highlight the New York origins of this industry while simultaneously examining what these ad agencies may reveal about the processes by which nationwide generic conceptions of hispanidad are currently being shaped.

ORIGINS AND DISCOVERY OF NEW YORK'S HISPANIC AD INDUSTRY

Advertising for U.S. Latino populations spans the very origins of Spanish-language media at the turn of the century, but the development of Hispanic marketing and advertising as a specialized industry, however, was a primarily New York City development and one fueled by a conjuncture of factors ensuing in the 1960s.[3] Among them were the rapid growth of the city's Latino population and the particularities of the Cuban and Puerto Rican migrations to the city. Specifically, by the 1960s, a steady influx of the mostly working-class Puerto Rican migrants to New York City had contributed a sizable Spanish-speaking presence in the city, providing a strong incentive for the development of media programming and marketing efforts to this population. Cuban immigration after the Cuban revolution, for its part, brought key figures of the well-developed Cuban publicity and marketing industry ready to tap into the marketing opportunities ensuing from the changing demographics in the city. In fact, it was Cuban executives who were behind the development of the first and largest advertising agencies targeting populations of Latin American background not only in New York City but in the United States. This was the case of Spanish Advertising and Marketing Services (SAMS), founded in 1962, whose chairman, Luis Diaz Albertini, had owned a successful agency in Cuba prior to leaving the island. Other early agencies also owned and led by Cubans throughout the late 1960s and early 1970s included Conill Advertising, headed by a husband-and-wife team that had also worked in advertising in Cuba, as well as Castor Advertising and later Font and Vaamonte, founded in 1977, and Siboney, which was first established in Cuba in 1954, later moved to Puerto Rico, and finally opened in the U.S. market in 1983.

Many of these Cuban advertising executives already had significant knowledge of U.S. corporate culture and products and most importantly enjoyed contacts with U.S. corporate clients, which facilitated their entry into corporate America. In fact, because some of them were already involved in U.S. transnational ventures in Cuba, from which they represented U.S. products throughout Latin America, the work of this first wave of Cuban advertising entrepreneurs to create and reinforce the idea of a nationwide Hispanic market is better seen as the extension and transposition of an already existing vision to the U.S. context—the idea of Latin America as a common market to the United States, though Latin America was now transposed within the very confines of the United States.[4]

Also aiding the consolidation of the Hispanic market as a Spanish-speaking market was the advent of network television,[5] which provided continuous programming for Spanish-speaking populations and hence a dependable and steady base for advertising. Directly linked to two of the most influential media empires in Latin America, Azcarraga's Televisa International of Mexico and Cisnero's Venevision Media Group of Venezuela, and historically organized as a "transnational," not "ethnic," media that drew heavily on Latin America as source of talent and programming, the Spanish TV networks would become one of the greatest defenders of Spanish as the base of Hispanic marketing as a specialized industry.[6] Finally, the promotion of the category of Hispanic by the U.S. Census Bureau was also pivotal to the growth of this industry. Although complex and contradictory, this category fitted accurately the needs of the advertising industry, which, following the trend of the commercial networks, saw in Spanish the core of a common identity for the diversity of populations of Latin American background in the United States. Now advertisers could legitimately draw major name brands with the existence of an untapped market as well as lure clients into developing profitable nationwide campaigns for the totality of the Hispanic market. This category also strengthened their case for unique advertising—not advertising that is dubbed and adapted but rather reconceptualized in altogether new campaigns specifically geared and targeted to the supposedly distinct Hispanic consumer.

By staking exclusive claim over what was being rapidly recognized as a profitable and growing target, Hispanic advertising soon emerged as a thriving industry, albeit one that remained peripheral to mainstream agencies. By the early 1980s, some of the largest Hispanic agencies, such as New York City's Conill Advertising, handled close to $15 million in advertising monies and counted with national clients like Pepsi, Greyhound, and McDonald's ("¡Piense en Español!" 1982). And not surprisingly, this rapid success would also mark the end of the Cuban-owned agencies' exclusive domain over the Hispanic market. Throughout the 1980s, as part of global trends in advertising toward segmented and targeted marketing (Turow 1997), knowledge of the potential profitability of Hispanic marketing led to a surge of mergers and buyouts of the Hispanic-owned agencies by major transnational agencies: SAMS was bought by the no-longer-existing De-Garbo, Conill Advertising was bought by Saatchi and Saatchi, Siboney U.S.A. was integrated with True North Communications, and Font and Vaamonte became part of Grey Advertising. The result is that today this industry is mostly dominated by global advertising networks, adding to the variety of interests profiting from the existence of some definite ideas about the identity of Hispanics and how best to sell products to them, and it is to these ideas that I now turn.

"DON'T PANIC, I'M HISPANIC!"—THE PEOPLE AND THE MARKET

Primary among the ideas feeding this industry's existence and profitability are the putative expertise, authenticity, and Latinness of Hispanic marketers. Though owned by global advertising chains, their artistic, creative staff has historically sold themselves on the claim that they, too, are Hispanic, thus reassuring clients that they are experts on this market. Indeed, "Don't Panic, I'm Hispanic" could well have been the slogan behind the rapid growth of the Hispanic advertising industry after the 1960s. Not only were the founders of these agencies Cuban-born, "authentic" Spanish-speaking Hispanics, but their staff has since also been dominated by Latin American marketers, whose knowledge of Latinos has also been argued on the basis of similar claims. Most are either Latin American born or have lived and worked in Latin America and, most importantly, are what the industry calls "Spanish-dominant" Latinos, people who have relocated to the United States as adults, often to pursue advanced studies, and are oftentimes even recruited from advertising agencies in the major U.S. markets in Latin America such as Mexico, Venezuela, and Puerto Rico. Similarly, it is the recently arrived Latin American, not yet "tainted" with U.S. culture, who constitutes the model Hispanic consumer. An ad executive explained this preference as follows: "We know that there are three kinds of Latinos: the Latino who has just arrived, who is 100 percent Latino; the Latino who arrived as an adult, lives here for over twenty years, and continues being Latino; and the one who is born here and becomes an American, even if they seek to identify themselves as a Latino." As he later stated, it was not to "gringos" but to "Hispanics," Spanish-speaking Hispanics, that he directed his productions.

The result is that it is mostly educated, Latin American corporate intellectuals from middle-class and upper-class backgrounds, rather than U.S.-born Latinos, who are behind the creation and dissemination of U.S. Hispanic images. English-dominant Latinos, in contrast, are more likely to be found in client services requiring their so-called more Americanized skills or are else altogether ignored as consumers or producers of these representations, a situation that is, of course, not unique to Hispanic marketing. The Spanish TV networks have long been implicated in relegating U.S. Latinos to the status of second-class producers and audiences by closing opportunities for English-dominant Latino producers and productions, which are thereby excluded from both the mainstream media and the one that is supposed to represent them (Gutiérrez, quoted in Avila 1997).[7] Feeding this trend is the already mentioned Latin American/transnational nature of all Hispanic programming that has been historically at the heart of the Spanish TV networks programming. This revolves around the importation of cheaper Latin American shows and talent to the U.S. market and developing U.S. productions with both the U.S. Hispanic and Latin American market in mind.[8] Such a trend has helped increase the marketability of U.S. Hispanic products throughout Latin America and aided the construction of a trans–Latin American notion of latinidad, but not without relegating U.S. Hispanics as producers and consumers in the media.

Disjunctions such as these, however, are constantly veiled in this industry, which projects itself as the authentic "spokesman" for the entire U.S. Latino population and its staff as rightful advocates for Hispanics vis-à-vis corporate America. Not only has this presentation allowed the industry to lessen its disregard of class, race, or language differences among Latinos, but, most importantly, it has also vested it with the legitimacy to profit from Latinos' marginality in greater society by presenting itself as a public voice for all Latinos. During my interviews, for instance, marketers repeatedly credited themselves with playing a key role in challenging stereotypes and promoting a more sophisticated view of Hispanics and with contributing to the increased representativity to which, as a substantial percentage of the population, Hispanics are "entitled." Indeed, the industry's peripheral position in relation to mainstream agencies and the fact that advertising in the Hispanic market lags well behind advertising in other markets—according to the Association of Hispanic Advertising Agencies, it actually constitutes only 1 percent of all advertising spending in the United States, even though Latinos are believed to constitute about 11 percent of U.S. population (Riley 2000)—corroborate this common industry claim. Accordingly, the argument goes, attracting advertising monies from corporations relative to the percentage of Latinos entails increasing the power and representativity of the Latino population.

Evidence of these dynamics was not hard to find during my research. Within weeks of my having settled in the city, a memo by Katz Radio Group containing derogatory remarks against African Americans and Latinos and implying that advertising for these audiences was appealing to "suspects, not prospects" came to light and became the subject of great controversy in the industry and public at large (*Hispanic Market Weekly*, 1998). This memo, followed shortly by one of the last *Seinfeld* episodes, in which Kramer stomps over a flaming Puerto Rican flag during the Puerto Rican day parade, triggered demonstrations in front of Young and Rubicam's headquarters over the issue of equity in advertising budgets for African Americans and Latinos during the summer of 1998 and turned the disparity in advertising budget into a contentious political issue throughout the year. New Yorkers saw Senator Efrain González, president of the National Hispanic Caucus of State Legislators, team up with African American activist Al Sharpton to demand that corporations advertise more in the Hispanic market and to organize the Invitational Summit on Multicultural Markets and Media in New York City in 1999. Aimed at exposing inequalities in corporate advertising spending in general and ethnic markets, the summit was symbolically scheduled on Martin Luther King's birthday to emphasize the political basis of their claim for equal advertising as a right and for the need for increased corporate spending in these markets. These are the kinds of appeals and strategies through which investing in culturally specific advertising for Hispanics becomes politicized as an issue of representativity for the totality of the Hispanic population.

Moreover, far from being a purely strategic move, the industry's self-representation as the rightful advocate for U.S. Hispanics is foremost sustained by the dominant view that some essential and intrinsic characteristics are indeed shared by all Hispanics. Despite their class background or knowledge or lack thereof of U.S. Latinos, for their Anglo clients, Hispanic marketers are as Hispanic as anyone in El Barrio, the Bronx, or Los Angeles and are therefore able to speak for and represent the totality of the Hispanic population. In this context, marketers' role has been mostly that of strengthening and contributing to the already widespread view that essential and unique commonalities do exist among Hispanics. That is, advertisers have become key "tropicalizers," to follow Aparicio and Chávez-Silverman, circulating and profiting from dominant representations of latinidad that draw on the exotic and the putative essential characteristics of Latinos (1997). Primary among these conventions is the common marketing conception that Hispanics constitute a nation in and of itself, with its own idiosyncrasies and particularities. The founder of Font and Vaamonte, Cuban-born Pedro Font recalled during an interview that from early on, Latinos had to be seen "as a country that is separate and apart from the U.S." if they were to become a profitable market, one with its own unique language and a totally different culture. In this nation, differences among Latinos are rendered as irrelevant and immaterial, as are differences across the U.S. market, an analogy that some marketers have used to persuade clients into paying them to find an acceptable image that would lure the Puerto Rican in New York as much as the Mexican in California. A creative staff member at Siboney Advertising explained, "I always tell my clients that just as they don't do a different ad for Arkansas and Massachusetts, we don't need to do something different for New York or California. We find something that is acceptable for all. It is like a good stew; you need to know how to cook." In fact, it is to a Hispanic nation to which most of these ads transport viewers, a nation in which there is little reference to the greater U.S. society in which they now live. As another put it: "This is like an ideal world, where there aren't gringos, no one to think you are ugly, where you don't have to struggle to be heard, where you are not a minority, and where if you go into a bar, everyone there is Hispanic, and everyone is your friend."

Even though erased as a visual reference in most advertising, the United States has nevertheless been a key symbolic reference in the advertisers' conceptualization of the Hispanic consumer, one that has also allowed them to project commonalities and override differences of race, class, or ethnicity among Hispanics. Moreover, it is in opposition to the "American" that Hispanics are most often defined in the advertising world, following the same dichotomous frameworks in which Latin American intellectuals have defined Latin American cultures as more moral, spiritual and "whole" than the materialistic U.S. culture (Flores 1979; Fernández Retamar 1973). One need only talk to marketing staff to perceive the preponderance of these ideas. On and on, Latinos are described as people who are "conservative, who care about their culture, who are respectful of their elders and traditions, and who love to eat rice and beans," among a plethora of overculturalist characterizations of the market that recycle a view of a "traditional" Hispanic in opposition to the "American."

These generalizations are also reflected in the variety of publications on how to market to Latinos that are staple reading among Hispanic marketers. Consider, for instance, Isabel Valdés and Marta Seoane's (1995) book on Hispanic marketing, which tags itself as the "bible of Hispanic marketing" and was prominently displayed by all the agencies I visited. In it, one will find numerous charts in which Latinos are described as more communally and family oriented, emotional, spontaneous, affectionate, and spiritual as opposed to Anglos, who are planners, materialistic, individualistic, self-oriented, and efficient. Thus, we see campaigns like that for Avon, which, as its creative staff explained, was based on the view that unlike Anglo women, Hispanic women beautify themselves not for "selfish, me-oriented purposes" but rather to please others and obtain their approval and praise.[9] This also explains the preponderance of family images and references in Hispanic ads, which could well be considered the ultimate advertising "referent system" in this market; more than any other theme or image, the family has been associated with Latinos' intrinsic Latin spirit and morality and their collective rather than individualist orientation.[10] Through this and other strategies, Latinos are consistently portrayed as loving and socially caring individuals but not without simultaneously reproducing the same Anglo-versus-Hispanic behavioral dichotomies that have long patterned Hispanic stereotypes and hierarchies along the lines of values and disposition among Anglos and Latinos. Are there no motivated and self-reliant Latinos? Could it be something other than their culture that turns them on? As if reminding Latinos to keep their culture but to keep it packaged, the commodification of Latinos ends up involving their reauthentication into the right way of being an "ethnic," requiring them to be exotic, that is, culturally different, but only within normative patterns that are always associated with an aspirational Anglo (not Latino) world, the specter of Latinos' putative culture of poverty always constant and lingering in the background.

Of course, it is not solely through an emphasis on its putative commonalities that advertisers construct the Hispanic market as a unique and contained entity and thus as one suitable to be sold and projected in the media. Reminiscent of Foucaldian technologies and strategies of power, the containment and managing of the heterogeneity among Hispanics is also a way of constituting the market as a unique entity. Hispanic marketers have long had to learn the regional specificities of the Hispanic market in San Antonio, Los Angeles, and Miami as well as generational differences and differences in the levels of acculturation among the conglomerate regarded as "the Hispanic consumer." Thus, it is common practice to use salsa musical backgrounds for advertising for East Coast audiences and to provide a more Caribbean feel to advertising for New York audiences, whereas Mexico is the main reference of any production geared to audiences in the West and thus *conjuntos,* rather than salsa, are employed in ads directed at that market area. Similarly, advertisers have adopted a few strategies to appeal to the so-called acculturated, English-dominant Latino who may watch Spanish television periodically but may not understand Spanish-driven media. One such strategy involves emphasizing images over language as in one ad for milk by the New York– based firm Vidal, Reynardus and Moya (now renamed the Vidal Partnership), which portrays what the creative staff described as a "Puerto Rican from the Bronx"—a middle-aged male individual playing the congas—in which the only spoken message is a sophisticated voice-over (which stands over and apart from the conga man) stating "Leche, ¿por qué no?" [Milk, why not?].

As a general rule, however, awareness of the actual diversity among Latinos—be it along the lines of language use, class, or race—has not led to the development of campaigns that represent this diversity or particularly to showing or evoking the complex experiences of acculturation or the bicultural experiences of this population. At the center of this is the fear of losing the market's perceived value, particularly in light of the ongoing fragmentation of the general market. This trend has diminished the size of other U.S. demographic and marketing segments, contributing to the importance of the Hispanic market, which—as opposed to women or teenagers, who are simultaneously divided into lifestyles, age, tastes, or race—remain a protected segment by their mere definition as a homogeneously bounded, culturally defined niche. At the same time, however, this trend is a constant threat to marketers, pressing them to police rather than show such differences, to manage and contain these differences, to screen out supposedly inauthentic Latinos from definitions of Hispanics, and thus to maintain bases of commonalities in ways that stress the perpetuation of "authentic" Hispanics as a unified marketing segment. And nowhere are these dynamics more evident than in New York City, which features one of the most heterogeneous and oldest, and hence most likely to be bilingual and English-dominant, Latino populations. Thus, it is not at all uncommon for the New York marketers with whom I worked to screen out Spanglish speakers from participating in focus groups' marketing discussions, to film ads in Mexico to secure the casting of "authentic Spanish-speaking Hispanics," or to hire creative staff from Argentina or Venezuela to ensure the "right language and marketing skills." These are some of the strategies through which the industry continues to sustain and refurbish itself, summoning Latin American talent via global cities such as New York.

The construction of the Hispanic market is thus predicated on an unchanging and static vision of Hispanics that are not "contaminated" with U.S. culture. In fact, upon my queries about whether Nuyoricans and second- and third-generation, or what they call "acculturated," Latinos would ever find themselves in these images, I was unrelentingly told that "those populations had already been lost" and that it was now up to the English networks to target this type of consumer. An L.A.-born and raised creative staff member now working in New York put it this way: "We know that this is not a language issue, it is a culture issue, my attitude towards my family and towards my parents, and neighborhood, are all Latino, but then the issue is: how far can you fragment the market before it loses its value?" These are the types of predicaments that led the same marketer, who earlier stated that it is only the recently arrived Latino who could claim to be 100 percent Latino, to rationalize that differences among Latinos were ultimately irrelevant because

> the Hispanic is a very particular race. It has 50 percent of
> similarities, in that we are all the same, you and I are attached to
> our families, we love our families, we respect our ancestors and
> are proud of them; unlike the American, we are proud of our
> roots and keep eating rice and beans, but we are 50 percent
> different in that the Cuban is different from the Argentinean and
> he in turn from the Colombian. What we seek is to tap into that
> 50 percent that makes us all the same.

The result of this search for the 50 percent that reconciles all differences and makes all of us the same and thus able to be sold, projected, and promoted over the Spanish TV airwaves is easily evident: a preponderance of family scenes, whiter and lighter Latinos, and most of all, the overemphasis on Spanish as the source of Latinos' commonality and cultural heritage. In this way, although Hispanic media and marketing should certainly be recognized for refurbishing Latinos' pride and interest in the Spanish language as well as raising Latinos' visibility in public life, their contradictory aftermaths should also be subject to critical examination.[10]

In keeping with this work's main focus on the Hispanic-centered definitions of latinidad promoted by this industry, I will not delve into these images in any depth here but rather conclude by considering some of their potential implications for contemporary U.S. Latino cultural politics. Briefly, we need to account for the fact that such emphasis undoubtedly provides a repository of language and culture but not without fostering the invisibility and exclusions of some Latinos, namely the non-Spanish-speaking Latinos. In fact, during my research I repeatedly found that U.S.-born and English-dominant Latinos have indeed internalized dominant definitions of latinidad promoted by these representations and that they are fully aware that they may be perceived by others to lack the supposedly appropriate cultural capital of latinidad. While I was recruiting people to participate in focus group discussions of the Latino-oriented media, for instance, more than one English-dominant youth declined to participate on the grounds that they spoke no Spanish until I explained that my study included all Latinos, be they code-switchers or Spanish or English dominant. Another recruit (who failed to appear in the focus group) had identified herself as a second-generation Puerto Rican and a Latina but was ready to add that she may not be the right person for this study because she neither spoke Spanish nor watched the Spanish-language channels, as if qualifying her own authenticity as a Latina on the grounds that she lacked the right language and media skills.

Additionally, we need to contend with the fact that such Hispanic-centered definitions of latinidad have important implications for who is more or less likely to participate and find employment, if not profit—after all, it is ultimately Sony, Televisa, and Young and Rubicam Worldwide who are securing the real profits—from Hispanic marketing. In particular, we are summoned to acknowledge that as long as Spanish remains the base for Hispanic marketing, this industry will likely function along transnational, not ethnic, lines, hindering the involvement of U.S.-born/English-dominant Latinos in the making and imaging of U.S. Latinos as well as the showcasing of U.S.-specific topics and issues that are particular to U.S. Latinos as a U.S. racial/ethnic minority. New York Latinos have responded to this by fleeing to community-access cable channels to develop local interest shows largely absent in the Spanish networks, but this still means that when U.S. Latinos do become producers, it is mainly through local or regional media, which never enjoy the type of nationwide dissemination that the networks do. As a result, there is little space for probing U.S. latinidad by acknowledging or showcasing differences among U.S.-based Latinos and Latin Americans in ways that could potentially facilitate critical dialogue about the status, place, and position of U.S. Latinos within the U.S. context. Lastly, I am not suggesting that bilingual media and marketing initiatives alone could address these issues. At the national level there is now a growth of bilingual print and electronic media targeted to intergenerational and linguistic subsets among Hispanics. Locally New York's La Mega Estación, 97.5 FM, has increasingly adopted a more a bilingual format and remains the number one station among New York Latinos. These developments are challenging prevailing trends in the commercial representation of latinidad but are not necessarily enlarging the public spheres of discussion and debate. For one, they are still predicated on the idea that there is an untainted ethnic base that can be sold and projected in the media and that it is language that provides the greatest variable for defining Latinos' cultural identity. After all, bilingual media are still commodifying Latinos around one single and marketable variable: language, be it English, Spanish, or Spanglish, is constructed as the single and most important variable around which any other differences among this population can be subsumed and contained if it is to be kept authentic and marketable within corporate America. Moreover, these media initiatives are unlikely to pose too many challenges to the fact that within the framework that prioritizes language, only Spanish can effectively attest to the uniqueness of the U.S. Hispanic market. For if it is not language per se that makes Latinos Latinos, what is then the need for ethnic-specific media and programming to begin with? Could Latinos not just be targeted by appealing to culture and lifestyle, as is done to target African Americans, or perhaps simply ignored as a culturally specific niche altogether? These are just some of the concerns that may explain such little innovation in the media airwaves and that are likely to continue to impair attempts at broadening the media's definition of Latinos beyond the current dominant image of the Spanish-speaking and thus authentic Hispanic. Most importantly, these trends do not challenge the fact that over and above how Latinos conceptualize themselves, their language, and their reality, it is corporate and commercial considerations that are likely to guide their commercial representations. And insofar as it is these types of considerations that guide the representation of Latinos, we are likely to see similar discourses of Latino authenticity become tantamount to latinidad in ways that respond more to the demands of particular culture industries for manageable and predictable consumers rather than to Latinos' self-conception of themselves or their realities.

NOTES:

1. In this paper I will use *Hispanic* and *Latino* interchangeably as is common in the advertising/marketing industry, although it is by the name of Hispanic marketing that this industry is most commonly known. This emphasis, as will be seen, is directly related to the role given in the industry to Spanish as the most important marker of Hispanic/Latino identity.

2. This work is part of a larger ethnographic research I conducted from 1998 through 1999 among Hispanic advertising agencies geared at analyzing the production of Hispanic advertisements and their consumption by the people to whom they are geared. Readers interested in learning more about this industry in a more nuanced and detailed analysis of its impact on Latino cultural politics may consult Dávila (2001).

3. See Subervi-Vélez et al.'s discussion (1994) of the origins of commercial advertising for U.S. Latino populations. As noted by Robert Park in *The Immigrant Press and Its Control*, the Spanish press of New Mexico, Texas, and New England had little national advertising. Mostly it advertised for local department stores, businesses, and romantic and religious groups. In New

York City, he also makes mention of a phonograph and phonograph records store on Sixth Avenue that advertised records in twenty-three different languages (1922:133–34). Looking through early issues of *La Prensa,* founded in the early 1900s, one sees advertising for services, such as for shopping assistance and translation, as well as ads for subscription to magazines such as the *Revista Universal,* which claimed to be the official organ of the Hispanic population.

4. A longer discussion of the industry's origins and operations and of the participation of Cubans in its development is included in Dávila (2001). Readers may also consult Pérez (1999) for an analysis of the involvement and employment of Cubans in U.S. advertising firms and how it contributed to their training and knowledge of U.S. advertising.

5. In New York City, channel 47 and channel 41, now with Telemundo and Univision, respectively, began to air in 1965 and 1968 (also respectively). Channel 47 initially operated as a local TV channel for the New York City, not the national, market. Channel 41 was founded by the SIN network, which later became Univision.

6. For a discussion of these distinctions between ethnic and transnational media, see Naficy (1993). For a discussion of ownership patterns for Univision, the largest and most profitable U.S. Spanish network, see Rodríguez (1999) and Wilkinson (1995).

7. These concerns are relevant when considering that the growth of the Hispanic-oriented market has simultaneously fostered the segregation of Latinos from the mainstream media, with companies increasingly targeting Latinos solely through culturally specific marketing (Penaloza 1997).

8. See Wilkinson (1995) and McAnany and Wilkinson (1996).

9. For a discussion of Avon's marketing strategy for Latinos, see Roslow and Decker (1998).

10. For a discussion of the media's role in consolidating a common Latino identity and in promoting the Spanish language, see Flores and Yúdice (1993), Rodríguez (1997), and Fox (1996).

REFERENCES

Alaniz, Maria and Chris Wilkes. 1995. "Reinterpreting Latino Culture in the Commodity Form: The Case of Alcohol Advertising in the Mexican American Community." *Hispanic Journal of Behavioral Sciences* 17(4): 430–45.

Aparicio, Frances and Susana Chávez-Silverman.1997. *Tropicalizations: Transcultural Representations of Latinidad.* Hanover, N.H.: University Press of New England.

Avila, Alex. 1997. "Trading Punches: Spanish Language Television Pounds the Competition in the Fight for Hispanic Advertising Dollars." *Hispanic* January-February, 39–44.

Dávila, Arlene. 2001. *Latinos, Inc.: Marketing and the Making of a People.* In press. Berkeley: University of California Press.

Fernández Retamar, Roberto. 1973. *Caliban, apuntes sobre la cultura de nuestra América.* Buenos Aires: La Pleyade

Flores, Juan. 1979. *Insularismo e ideología burguesa*. La Habana: Casa de las Americas.

Flores, Juan, and George Yúdice. 1993. "Living Borders/Buscando América: Languages of Latino Self-Formation." In *Divided Borders*, edited by Juan Flores, 199–224. Houston: Arte Público Press.

Fox, Geoffrey. 1996. *Hispanic Nation: Culture, Politics, and the Constructing of Identity*. Birch Lane Press.

Hispanic Market Weekly, May 18, 1998.

McAnany, Emile and Kenton T. Wilkinson. 1996. *Mass Media and Free Trade: NAFTA and the Cultural Industries*. Austin: University of Texas Press.

Naficy, Hamid. 1993. *The Making of Exile Culture: Iranian Television in Los Angeles*. Minneapolis: University of Minnesota Press.

Nuiry, Octavio. 1996. "Magazine Mania, Whose Media is This, Anyway?" *Hispanic* December, 53–58.

Park, Robert. 1922. *The Immigrant Press and Its Control*.New York, London:Harper & Brothers.

Peñaloza, Lisa. 1997 "Ya Viene Aztlán." In *The Media in Black and White*, edited by Everette E. Dennis and Edward C. Pease, 113–20. London: Transaction Publishers.

Pérez, Louis. 1999. *On Becoming Cuban: Identity, Nationality and Culture*. Chapel Hill: University of North Carolina Press.

"¡Piense en Español! (Think Spanish)." 1982. *Marketing and Media Decisions*, October, 66–160.

Riley, Jennifer. 2000. "AHAA: Creating a Bridge Between Corporate America and the Hispanic Media." *Hispanic,* June, 40–45.

Rodríguez, America. 1999. *Making Latino News*. Thousand Oaks, Calif.: Sage Publications.

Rodríguez, Clara, ed. 1997. *Latin Looks: Images of Latinas and Latinos in the U.S. Media*. Boulder, Colo.: Westview.

Roslow, Peter and Janet Therrien Decker. 1998. *A Guide to Building Market Dominance, Hispanic Marketing Casebook*. Prepared for the Association of Hispanic Advertising Agencies and Univision Communications, Inc.

Strategy Research Corporation. 1996. *U.S. Hispanic Market*. Miami: Strategy Research Corporation.

Subervi-Vélez, Federico, et al. 1994. "Mass Communication and Hispanics." In *Hispanic Media Handbook of Hispanic Cultures in the United States: Sociology,* edited by Felix Padilla, 304–50.Houston: Arte Público Press.

Turow, Joseph. 1997. *Breaking Up America: Advertisers and the New Media World*. Chicago: University of Chicago Press.

Valdés, Isabel and Marta Seoane. 1995. *Hispanic Market Handbook*. New York: Gale Research.

Wilkinson, Kenton Todd. 1995. *Where Culture, Language and Communication Converge: The Latin American Cultural-Linguistic Television Market*. Ann Arbor: University of Michigan Dissertation Services.

CHAPTER SIXTEEN

Eating in Cuban

Lisa Maya Knauer

Cubanía (Cubanness) is in vogue now throughout the United States, perhaps no place more so than in New York.[1] The "boom Cubano" is perhaps most visible—or audible—in the musical landscape. Jazz at Lincoln Center recently featured a miniseries on Afro-Cuban sounds. According to *New York Times* music critic Peter Watrous, in 1998 almost every week a different musical group from Cuba played at New York clubs.[2] And in the rapidly shifting microclimate of New York's restaurant scene, what we might call with apologies to Appadurai (1997) its "gastroscape," there has been a recent flurry of new Cuban and Cuban-inflected restaurants, ranging from the ultrachic Asia de Cuba, a sleek, slightly gimmicky place that combines Asian-Latin "fusion" cuisine, mandarin-jacketed wait staff, and Cuban music, to Little Havana, which serves up more easily recognizable Cuban fare in humbler surroundings (Asimov 1998; Brooks 1998).

However, alongside this new-found interest in cubanía lies another, partially invisible landscape. When I moved to New York over twenty years ago, the Cuban-Chinese diners seemed a uniquely New York institution. And Cuban restaurants have been a constant presence in New York for decades. Scattered throughout the city are numerous well-established neighborhood establishments—La Rosita and Caridad on the Upper West Side, the National in the East Village, Sam's Chinita in Chelsea. But the ubiquitousness of Cuban eateries is more than just a curiosity. If we analyze when and where these restaurants were established, whom they have served over the years, and how they position themselves in the broader ethnoscape of

New York, we find another set of stories. Some are primarily historic markers of areas that were once Cuban settlements (the Lower East Side, the Upper West Side), whereas others serve as signposts to the remaining scattered nodes of Cuban population: Washington Heights and the adjacent Queens neighborhoods of Corona, Elmhurst, and Jackson Heights (see Ojita 1997).

But this other geography, these other narratives, are largely unacknowledged and are nearly absent from popular discourse. Cubans have lived in New York for over 170 years, yet they remain vastly understudied. Prior to the 1959 revolution, the New York area was home to the most populous Cuban community in the United States, and Cubans were the second-largest Latino group in the city. Although New York was rapidly eclipsed by Miami as ground zero of Cuban America, the metropolitan area still boasts the second-largest concentration of Cubans nationwide. But they are underrepresented in both scholarship about Latinos in New York (which tends to focus on the largest groups—Puerto Ricans and Dominicans) and the growing body of literature about Cubans in the United States—what some are starting to call Cuban-American studies. [3] This lacuna is beginning to be addressed by a handful of scholars such as Nancy Raquel Mirabal (this volume).

This juxtaposition of hot, newfangled Cubanesque restaurants and old-fashioned neighborhood eateries in the urban ethnoscape raises some questions: Why Cuba (again), and why now? What, if anything, do the new-wave establishments have to do with the traditional ones? But this also provides a useful entry point into this complex and multilayered community—or actually, communities. And if we also read, as I do, ethnic restaurants as both real and imagined landscapes of desire and staging grounds for the construction, performance, and negotiation of identities, we can engage broader discussions of diaspora and the role of the imaginary in ethnic and national identities. I have chosen three very different restaurants, each of which frames and engages Cubanness in a unique manner, to begin to explore why cubanía is such an important reference point in the cultural landscape of New York. I also examine what is the Cuba (or perhaps, more accurately, what are the Cubas) that these restaurants invoke or perform and for whom these performances or invocations are intended. Is this a Cuba of the imagination, one rooted in historic or contemporary reality, or somewhere in between? And to whose history, whose imagination, do these restaurants appeal?

For Cuba—as both icon and geopolitical entity—is deeply ingrained in U.S. popular and political culture. Since at least the mid-nineteenth century, Cuba has occupied a place in our national imaginary (see Perez 1999 for an exploration of the role of U.S. culture, and particularly consumer, commercial culture, in the formation of Cuban identity). Prior to the revolution, the island was viewed by many middle-class and wealthy Americans as a playground of sun, sensuality, and sin. Although U.S. policy following the revolution cast Cuba as an outlaw state and U.S. citizens were virtually forbidden to travel there, an even more domesticated version of Cubanness became part of popular cultural understanding via *I Love Lucy*.[4] Fidel Castro is a familiar, iconic (if malevolent) figure on the global political landscape. Cuba has played a disproportionately important role in the formulation of U.S. foreign policy, being one of the focal points of anticommunism. [5]

Cuba still carries a mystique, an aura of the unknown. However, Cuba has resurfaced in the news. The most recent immigrant wave, the *balseros* (rafters), whose numbers increased dramatically during the economic/political crisis of the early-to-mid-1990s,[6] have occupied the national spotlight. The politically powerful anti-Castro Cuban establishment actively works to keep national politicians' attention focused on Cuba and U.S.-Cuba policy.[7] The much-publicized visit of Pope John Paul II in 1998 put Cuba squarely on the (global TV) map. And as I revised this article for publication, the national news in both Cuba and the United States has been occupied with the bizarre, almost surreal custody/immigration case of Elián Gonzalez, a six-year-old rafter whose mother died at sea and who has been claimed by both his Cuban father and his Miami relatives.

Each of my three sites chosen functions within a different cultural economy and social geography. Victor's Cafe 52, which styles itself as a traditional Cuban restaurant, has been in business for thirty-five years. It is listed in many tourist guides to New York as one of the places to go for "authentic" Cuban cuisine and is also featured in Zagat's and other gastronomic bibles. La Esquina Habanera (Havana Corner) is a modest neighborhood corner restaurant in the enclave community of West New York/Union City, New Jersey, still one of the most significant concentrations of Cubans in the United States. Patria is a relatively new, upscale, fusion restaurant imported to New York from Miami.

The purpose of this comparison is not to create a hierarchy of authenticity (during the course of my investigation, friends and colleagues continually asked me who served the best black beans) but to explore how these sites mark, invoke, or enact Cubanness. I also use this study to explore intersections between theories of diaspora, cultural transformation, and tourism. Ethnic restaurants occupy multiple, sometimes conflicting registers. They serve as gathering places for immigrant or diasporic communities; they mark geographic and social boundaries, provide a refuge from the dominant culture, and can serve as memory palaces for exilic nostalgia. They thus form part of a diasporic or subaltern public sphere. But they are simultaneously a specialized kind of tourist production—one that draws upon strategies of place making and multiple touristic discourses. Ethnic restaurants wrap themselves in the language of both heritage and the exotic. For perceived others, they invite travel without leaving home. For visitors, they are part of the attraction of the metropolis. For both homegrown and foreign cosmopolitans (Urry 1995), the city is where you can get the world on a plate (Cook and Crang 1996). They thus become destinations for very different journeys—a voyage to the unknown, an encounter with a neighboring other, or a pilgrimage to a portable homeland (Appadurai 1997).

Restaurants—eating out—have characterized urban life for several centuries. But they play a particular role in distinguishing contemporary cities; "urban promotion is increasingly seeking to capitalize on a city's culinary associations in the race for prominence on the world-city stage" (Bell and Valentine 1997:121). Tourism thus interfaces with what Zukin (1995) calls a cultural strategy of redevelopment. Cultural consumption (museums, gourmet restaurants, boutiques) helps valorize real estate and aids in the process of gentrification. Zones of consumption are created, but consumption—the accumulation of cultural or symbolic capital (Bourdieu 1984)—also becomes what defines (middle-class) values and lifestyle. Food becomes a marker of social position and differentiation, and authenticity becomes incorporated into the matrix of consumption: "A taste for 'the real thing' becomes a strategy of social differentiation. Yet the real thing refers to two quite different sorts of goods. It refers to goods that offer the *authenticity* of the past, and those that suggest the *uniqueness of new design*" (Zukin 1991:202–3; emphasis added).

Middle- or upper-middle-class urbanites, whether they travel the globe or travel across town, are encouraged to learn about other cultures to acquire cosmopolitanism, which "involves the cultivating of 'globalized cultural capital' as a form of lifestyle shopping which, crucially, involves possessing considerable knowledge about 'the exotic,' 'the authentic,' and so on" (Bell and Valentine 1997: 136).[8]

"Kitchen table tourism" is reinforced through the media—food is an increasingly important lifestyle feature in "serious" newspapers such as *The New York Times*, chefs are accorded the celebrity status reserved for rock stars and actors, and food-related TV shows are increasing in number and popularity.

Ethnic restaurants and the ubiquity of ethnic dining experiences in a multi-ethnic global metropolis such as New York, which is both a center for many types of tourism and home to multiple diasporic and ethnic communities, complicate, in an interesting way, descriptive or analytic categories used in tourist analysis and discourse. Who are the tourists at a neighborhood ethnic eatery—everyone from outside the immediate area or everyone who doesn't belong to that ethnic group? Is a native New Yorker a tourist when she treks off in search of the best Turkish, Thai, or Indonesian restaurant?

On the other hand, if ethnic restaurants also represent exilic or diasporic nostalgia, it is too simplistic to assume that everyone from a particular ethnic or national group shares the same social imaginary. Some immigrant groups, such as Cubans, are characterized by distinct migratory waves, which may involve different reasons for leaving the home country and different sets of social and economic conditions in the host country. Later immigrants may find increased hostility, not only from the host culture but also from their own ethnic cohort. Ethnic institutions may become a space for intracultural (as well as intercultural) negotiation and contestation: whose diaspora is this, anyway?

Restaurants are a particular kind of social institution. They are intimately entangled with our personal needs and desires but simultaneously provide an inherently social experience. But they are also businesses, geared not only toward taste making but profit making (the hospitality industry is one of the most rapidly growing sectors of the economy, although the failure rate is extremely high); they "represent the apotheosis of free-market capitalism . . . a consumption economy" (Fine 1996:1).

But viewed from another angle—that of diasporic or immigrant peoples—ethnic restaurants embody multiple movements and dislocations of people.[9] Restaurants occupy and mark particular geographies, both real and imagined. They are part of the production of locality (Appadurai 1997), and their interiors incorporate forms of sociospatial structuring (Crang 1997:147). But they are also temporal. They exist in the lived time of their owners, patrons, and communities but also embody or recall other times and places.

Small businesses such as neighborhood ethnic restaurants or newsstands have often served as an economic stepping-stone for immigrants. They require only modest initial capitalization. Ethnic entrepreneurs who cater primarily to members of their own group do not need fluency in English,[10] and labor costs can be kept low by relying on family members or other recent immigrants who may be willing to work for low wages.[11] These institutions then become a locus for the preservation and transmission of a cultural heritage. Eating a particular "home country" food acquires a symbolic importance in New York that it never had at home (Kasinitz 1992); it serves to distinguish one's community from both the dominant culture and other immigrant groups. And for the U.S.-born second generation, the restaurant or bakery is the home country.

Ethnic businesses also serve as symbolic markers, announcing that the community has reached critical mass and making it visible both to itself and others (Kasinitz 1992:39). In Cristina Garcia's novel, Dreaming in Cuban, when one of the characters is about to open a small business, her father advises her: "Put your name on the sign, too, hija, so they know what we Cubans are up to, that we're not all Puerto Ricans" (Quoted in Grosfoguel and Georas 1996:192). These sites also serve as gathering places for community members; for informal events like birthday and holiday dinners; and more organized activities like club meetings, cultural performances, and beauty pageants (Kasinitz 1992).

Community can be thought of as a locality or territory—that is, as a spatial fact or practice—but also as a series of interrelationships or shared values—in other words, in ideological terms. Food becomes a way of maintaining cohesion, distinguishing oneself from the dominant or host culture and from other ethnic communities: it can even mark resistance. Historically, ethnic foods are initially produced for the community itself, but they can also create a bridge to the host culture. Through hybridization or what Philip Crang (1996) prefers to call displacement, traditional cuisines are adapted and transformed; rather than simply being a static representation of identity, food becomes a terrain in which identify is negotiated (Bell and Valentine 1997). Or, to draw upon a different spatial metaphor, food becomes a theater in and through which cultures are remolded.

Ethnic restaurants can be seen as ethnographic sites that have multiple (and sometimes contradictory) functions because they invite both cultural insiders and outsiders. They can be sites for intercultural encounters. Simultaneously, they can be places to preserve and transmit traditions and fantasy worlds that serve as a surrogate or simulation of real travel.

Restaurants are also sites where social boundaries and structures are experienced and reinforced through a series of codes, which include the architecture, design, "appropriate" behavior, and the food (Shelton 1990:524). I look at restaurants, then, as spaces of performance and spectacle (both museological and theatrical). As Philip Crang suggests, "Tourist places are not just imagined places, they are also performed places." (1997:146).

Victor's Cafe 52 is a sleek, "white tablecloth" restaurant at the northern end of Manhattan's midtown theater district, an area whose side streets are dotted with a variety of restaurants, ranging from matchbox-sized luncheonettes to mid-priced ethnic restaurants such as Cabana Carioca, grand old institutions such as Gallagher's Steakhouse, and upscale establishments. A large awning, visible from halfway down the block, proclaims "Cuban cuisine since 1963." On the sidewalk outside the restaurant are a lone set of hand prints belonging to former boxing champion Roberto Duran, one of the many celebrity friends of the owner, whose pictures line the wall behind the hostess's station/reservation desk inside.

Victor's history typifies a version of the immigrant success story. A self-described *campesino* (peasant) from the countryside surrounding Havana, Victor del Corral worked as a butcher and then ran two restaurants prior to emigrating to the United States. At the time of his arrival, New York was home to the largest concentration of Cubans in the continental United States, including descendants of families who had emigrated in the nineteenth and early twentieth century as well as more recent arrivals who left Cuba in increasing numbers during the 1940s and 1950s for a combination of political and economic factors—recession, unemployment, and political unrest (Boswell and Curtis 1984; Poyo 1984, 1989; Poyo and Diaz-Miranda 1994).

Their visibility was perhaps out of proportion to the community's size; after World War I, New York became the center of the international recording industry and thus an important site for the production and dissemination of Cuban and other so-called Latin music (Glasser 1995). Cuban musicians and other performers such as Desi Arnaz and Chano Pozo flocked to New York from the 1920s through the 1950s, playing in Broadway and Harlem theaters, jazz bands, and Cuban and Latin dance bands.

In the 1940s and 1950s there were numerous Cuban restaurants, butchers, grocers, and other small businesses throughout the city. Most were small, unpretentious, family-run and family-style enterprises and not well known outside of the Latino community. After working at a succession of jobs, Victor opened his first restaurant at what was then a fairly seedy, dangerous intersection at 71st Street and Columbus Avenue.

The restaurant was initially a corner storefront, with a small counter and less than a dozen tables. According to restaurant folklore, the kitchen was so small that Victor's wife baked the desserts in an upstairs apartment and sent them down to the restaurant (Presilla 1987). Although popular with local residents (friends who grew up on the Upper West Side recall it as a hangout or a local place to experiment with an ethnic cuisine other than Chinese or Italian), it attracted people from all over the city, including a carefully cultivated celebrity clientele. For many non-Latino New Yorkers, it became a prototypical or emblematic Cuban (or Latin) dining experience. Victor's Cafe was a place for a special meal or to take out-of-town guests—a destination on a tourist itinerary, a way of demonstrating aesthetic cosmopolitanism (Urry 1995).

Cubans and other Latinos also patronized Victor's. It was one of the Cuban restaurants that offered traditional food in more elegant surroundings, and its popularity among non-Latinos may in fact have served as a sign of legitimacy, of having "made it" for the early exile generation. Especially in the early years, Cubans from the metropolitan area, including from the colonia in New Jersey, came to Victor's for weekend dinners or to celebrate family-oriented holidays such as Mother's Day, Easter, and *Noche Buena* (Christmas Eve). The fact that the restaurant did have a coherent Cuban clientele also served to authenticate it for non-Latinos. Part of Victor's appeal to non-Latinos is as an ethnographic reconstruction. It markets itself as a place where you can go to get real Cuban food; the food thus becomes an ethnographic object, which must then prove its authority and legitimacy.

Motivated as much by entrepreneurial instincts as by a cultural mission, Victor decided to invest in a property in the theater district. Victor's Cafe 52 was opened in April 1980 (ironically, the month that the Mariel boatlift began, bringing over 125,000 Cuban refugees, a much poorer and darker section of the population than those who had emigrated during the 1960s and early 1970s; see Pedraza 1995; Poyo and Diaz-Miranda 1994; Masud-Piloto 1988). The Upper West Side in the late 1970s was already undergoing a process of gentrification; as the neighborhood was transformed into what many people saw as the prototypical yuppie stronghold, Columbus Avenue quickly became a showcase of consumption. By the time Victor opened his midtown location, Columbus Avenue was already being forcibly upgraded. Laundromats, bodegas, and mom-and-pop delis were squeezed aside or replaced by pricey boutiques, middlebrow chains like The Gap, and gourmet cafes and restaurants—what Sharon Zukin calls, in another context, "domestication by cappuccino" (Zukin 1995:xiv).

Victor's Cafe maintained a dual existence for several years. Victor leased the uptown location and the name to his former managers, who ran it as Victor's Cafe until 1993 and as Havana (also serving Cuban food) after a lawsuit over the rights to the name. Havana folded in 1994 or 1995, and the corner is now occupied by a branch of the successful Malaysian restaurant Penang.

Victor's decision to open up shop in the theater district can be read in part as a response to the delatinization of the area around West 71st Street during the 1960s and 1970s; it had to remake itself as a tourist attraction, promoting its own exoticism, othering itself—what Frances Aparicio and Susan Chávez-Silverman (1997) refer to as self-tropicalization. And what better place to do that than the theater district, which has been an important tourist destination and a site of spectacle and theatricality for over a century, where the forces of gentrification were beginning to work their magic, starting the cycle of "creative destruction"[12] that continued through the 1980s and 1990s, tearing down single-room occupancy hotels and renovating and building theaters and hotels.

But Victor's Cafe was always, in some sense, a tourist production. According to Victor and his manager, a longtime family friend, even in its earliest days, the restaurant did not position itself—either geographically or conceptually—to cater to the city's Cuban and Latino communities; its target clientele were residents of the ethnically mixed (but largely white) surrounding area. In other words, from its inception, Victor's was not designed to be primarily a Cuban restaurant for Cubans but a site in which Cuban culture (in the form of its cuisine) would be translated and made accessible to non-Cubans.

According to restaurant personnel, the current clientele of Victor's Cafe 52 is approximately 90 percent non-Latino; that, however, is not a recent development but has been characteristic since the restaurant's opening. The proportion of out-of-towners has increased since the move to the theater district, to about 60 percent. But there is a temporal segmentation of this clientele. Especially in the early years, Cubans from the surrounding area, including the colonia in New Jersey, have used the restaurant as a site for family gatherings, holidays, and other special occasions. It is still a special-event restaurant for Cubans and other Latinos. On weekdays, at lunch, and for pretheater dinners, the customers are overwhelmingly non-Latino and out-of-towners. On weekend evenings and on holidays, the crowd is largely Latino. On a recent Saturday at lunch, the front room was filled with well-dressed, mostly middle-aged whites, while in the back room a large, extended Latino family held a lavish baby shower. The restaurant can thus be seen, in some ways, as a form of cultural brokering—it serves to mediate and negotiate representations of one cultural group to another cultural group or the society at large.

Victor's Cafe 52 does not fully disclose itself to the street; its windows offer only a partial view inside. It is a large, high-ceilinged space, decorated in a subdued fashion. Most of the chairs and tables are wooden, solid, and heavy. They have the patina of family heirlooms. Plates and silverware are also large, heavy, and distinctly premodern. One wall of the back room is covered with a large mural painted in bright colors depicting a variety of scenes of people enjoying themselves in tropical locations. It draws upon widely circulated and non-site-specific images of the Caribbean as a vacationer's paradise. The people depicted are happy, having fun, and mostly white or light skinned.[13] The images may not be site specific, but they are class specific: this is a vacation paradise for the elite. There is little (to my eye) that marks these images as specifically Cuban. The visual iconography is thus of a generic tropicalism, designed to be consumed by those who can afford it. The mural invites and implies, in fact almost demands, a touristic gaze (Urry 1990).

However, there are artifactual displays and museological flourishes that invoke memories (or fantasies) of a more specifically Cuban setting. On the walls of the front room, there are three glass picture frames containing distinctly prerevolutionary Cuban icons. One displays several engraved cigar-box designs; another, prerevolutionary Cuban currency; and the last, a neat arrangement of swizzle sticks from swank Havana nightclubs and restaurants of the 1940s and 1950s. Cubanía is also coded and invoked through the music played in the dining room.

The restaurant thus deploys a series of codes and images that are open to multiple interpretations by cultural insiders and outsiders. Both the generic and specific references would be recognizable as tropical by non-Latinos. For most Latinos, these would read as Cuban. For Cuban exiles of Victor's generation, the references would be even more specific: these images work as a nostalgic invocation of a (vanished) world they left behind. But these icons are even more narrowly referential. Both aural and visual icons are relics of pre-1959 Cuba; in other words, they are temporally, spatially, racially, and class specific. There is an almost religious quality to the way these artifacts are framed and presented: the word *reliquary* came to mind. This dovetails with MacCannell's description (1989) of the process of sight sacralization, which involves framing, elevation, and enshrinement. For the exiles of the 1960s, who still "dream in Cuban," Victor's recalls the comfortable lifestyle they were forced to abandon. It is what French historian Pierre Nora (1989) calls a *lieu de mémoire,* a memory site.

Victor's Cafe prides itself on serving traditional Cuban cuisine. The menu features well-known standards such as *lechón asado* (roast suckling pig), *frijoles negros* (black beans), and *ropa vieja* (literally, "old clothes," a dish of shredded beef). But to differentiate itself from "ordinary" Cuban and Latin restaurants like Caridad or La Esquina Habanera and to continue to attract upscale customers whose expectations have been honed by recent trends toward fusion or pan-Latino cuisine, the menu has been expanded to include innovative dishes, and all of the dishes are plated with an eye to visual presentation.

Ropa vieja, a Cuban standard, is still cooked according to the restaurant's time-honored recipe but is served in a basket of plantain strips (a presentational strategy developed by Patria's Douglas Rodriguez), and the plate is sprinkled with chives. In addition to *yuca con mojo* (boiled cassava with garlic sauce, a standard side dish), yuca is also served in the form of fingers with a cilantro salsa. Portions are reasonable, but the emphasis is on presentation and not quantity.[14]

One of Victor's Cafe 52's challenges is to educate non-Cubans about Cuban food. As noted previously, the restaurant estimates that 90 percent of its customers are non-Latino and that perhaps 60 percent are from out of town (this 60 percent, of course, includes Latinos from out of town). According to then-manager Clara Chaumont, a lot of people don't know what Cuban food is: "They come in, they say, 'Cuban, is it like Mexican food?' " (personal communication). Like a museum, then, the restaurant has a pedagogic mission: most simply put, to demonstrate that it is not Mexican. In other words, it has to differentiate Cubanness as a specific other within a world of others.

To look at it another way, the restaurant has a multifaceted ethnographic project: cultural preservation, transmission, and translation. The culture is preserved as both a lieu de mémoire for older-generation Cubans, a place of vicarious memory for younger Cubans who were born or grew up in the diaspora, and a way of encountering difference for non-Cubans.

The written menu thus functions as a guidebook for the uninitiated or as a set of explanatory labels. The text is vivid, enticing, but more descriptive than evocative. The names of the dishes are given in Spanish; the accompanying text is sometimes simply a translation of that name but more often includes details on seasonings and preparation. Even something as simple and standard as black beans is presumed to need explanation:

Frijoles negros: Quintessentially Cuban, a velvety-rich black bean potage scented with the aroma of bay leaf, cumin, and oregano. Victor's specialty.

For most Latinos, the bulk of the menu reads as familiar cooking but served in elegant surroundings—in other words, edible heritage. For non-Latinos, these same dishes are a trip into the unknown—that is, the exotic, a different "world on a plate" (Cook and Crang 1996)—and the written menu and verbal assistance from the wait staff are designed to provide information and reassurance.

In many ways, Victor's Cafe 52 can be interpreted as a heritage site. Both Victor and Clara emphasized the restaurant's "traditional" nature. Callers who get put on hold are reminded that Victor's has been "serving *authentic* Cuban food for over thirty years."[15] One of its heritage narratives is the restaurant's own history. The restaurant's longevity is emphasized through multiple media—in all the restaurant's print advertising, on the outdoor awning, and in the outgoing phone message. The numerous photos of Victor surrounded by well-known entertainers underscore the importance of this narrative of crossover success. The restaurant published a small booklet[16] for its twenty-fifth anniversary, which situates the history of Victor's Cafe within a broader historical/ethnographic narrative about the evolution of Cuban cooking from pre-Conquest times to the present (Presilla 1987). The management designed a new menu for the thirty-fifth anniversary, which features a collage of images including the Cuban flag, an American car from the 1950s,[17] and photos of Victor and his family upon their arrival in the United States. The restaurant then becomes, in part, a museum of itself.

La Esquina Habanera—Havana Corner, a name that directly evokes the homeland—is imbricated within a very different cultural and economic geography or ethnoscape, across the Hudson River in the enclave community that straddles the towns of West New York, Union City, and Weehawken, New Jersey (I will refer to the area as Union City). During the 1970s and 1980s, the Union City area became the second-largest Cuban settlement in the United States after Miami. A large number of the Cubans who arrived in the Mariel boatlift settled in the Union City area (Boswell and Curtis 1984; Poyo 1994). According to 1990 census figures, approximately 80 percent of the area's population is Hispanic, and of that number, a majority are of Cuban origin.[18] Bergenline Avenue, the main commercial street in Union City, is lined with photo studios, florists, bakeries, restaurants, music stores, and other businesses catering to Cuban émigrés. Although there are pockets of Cubans, and Cuban-owned businesses, scattered throughout the metropolitan area, these establishments are more geographically concentrated in Union City, and in some ways this community functions as a symbolic center, or at least a point of reference, for other Cubans in the area.[19] Many Cubans who live in other parts of the metropolitan area have friends and family in Union City, or they travel there from time to time to shop, eat at Cuban restaurants, and soak up atmosphere.

La Esquina Habanera is one of dozens of small, informal Cuban restaurants that line the main avenues of Union City. There are also some fancier, although still very traditional, white-tablecloth restaurants on Bergenline Avenue. The nearby suburbs also boast at least one or two trendier establishments, whose menus, style of food presentation, and promotional strategies are clearly influenced by New York's fusion or pan-Latino eateries such as Patria.[20] La Esquina Habanera (also the name of a restaurant in Miami's Little Havana district) was established by Tony Zequeiros, a balsero who arrived in 1991—prior to the large wave of balseros, which peaked in 1993–1994.

However, the surrounding community has changed. There has been an modest influx of new Cuban émigrés—the balseros and those who have emigrated legally through the lottery established in 1994. As the earlier generations of Cuban émigrés have matured, there has been a modest exodus from the Union City area in two directions. Some have moved to more affluent and suburban parts of New Jersey. In addition, many Cubans did not entirely choose Union City. Between the mid-1960s and the early 1980s, new Cuban arrivals were strongly encouraged to settle outside of Miami, and the U.S. Cuban refugee program offered economic incentives to prevent an "overconcentration" of Cubans in Miami and Florida (see Croucher 1998; Masud-Piloto 1988; Grenier 1998; Grosfoguel and Georas 1996). Many Cubans, after living in New Jersey for a decade or more, have moved to the Miami area to rejoin family and friends, to get away from the colder climate of the Northeast, or to take advantage of real or imagined business opportunities offered by Miami's recent—and volubly hyped—economic ascent.[21] There is a popular perception among many local Cubans that "everyone's moved to Miami ... almost every week someone else leaves for Miami" (Armando Guiller, personal communication).

But Union City's demographics have also shifted in response to new immigration from other parts of Latin America and the Caribbean. As Cubans have moved out, other Latinos have moved in. The changing composition of the community can be seen along Bergenline Avenue, where decades-old Cuban-owned businesses have been joined or replaced by El Salvadoran, Ecuadorean, and Colombian restaurants, bakeries, and travel agencies.[22] A recent feature article in *The New York Times* dubbed this "A Pan-American Highway of Food on Avenida Bergenline" (Louie 1997).

La Esquina Habanera, then, is one of the remaining bastions of cubanía in a community where Cubans may still constitute a majority of the Latino population but are seen—and see themselves —as losing ground. The restaurant looks like a typical neighborhood ethnic eatery. The furnishings are modest—formica tables and lunch counter, red leatherette cushions on the stools and chairs. For most of the week, it primarily serves the nearby community. It's not a place to which one would travel just because of the food, which typifies Finkelstein's description of an ethnic cafe: "These restaurants are inexpensive enough to allow individuals to dine there regularly and the foodstuffs are consistent enough to give patrons confidence in what to expect" (1989:97). This familiarity extends beyond the food: most of the patrons seem to know each other, the owner, and the wait staff.

The written menu is not automatically proffered, although visibly non-Latino patrons are sometimes asked if they want to see a menu. The restaurant presumes that customers and staff form a gastronomic or culinary knowledge community and that there is no need to interpret, translate, or even, in some cases, inform customers about the food. Posters on the outside window announce the $3.49 lunch special and some of the restaurant's specialities. At the inside counter, other signs announce daily specials and fast-food offerings such as batidos and croquetas de papas. None of this signage is translated into English. The written menu is bilingual, but the menu simply lists the titles of the dishes and translates them. The menu is straightforward and basic, featuring standard offerings of black beans, roast pork, steak, Cuban sandwiches, and yuca con mojo. There are no surprises and no gestures toward or acknowledgement of other gastronomic cultures. Portions are generous, but the food is simply heaped onto a plain white porcelain plate; there are no flourishes, garnishes, or architectural renderings here. La Esquina Habanera does not try to translate Cubanness for non-Cubans.

Although the decor, at first glance, seems nondescript and unimportant, it provides an extremely useful gloss on the site's exilic performativity. The glass-walled front room is fully visible from the street. Examining the restaurant as theater, during daylight hours, the street is an omnipresent backdrop for indoor performances. In a series of photomontages shot in Miami's Little Havana, photographer Arturo Cuenca uses the ironic title "This is not Havana" to interrogate and disturb exilic nostalgia. Union City may not be Havana, but the restaurant's street corner setting and the way it creates a dialogue between exterior and interior echo the intensely social and interactive street life of many Havana neighborhoods. The windows are about both looking out and looking in, and they allow for an ongoing interplay between the street and the restaurant.[23] The window also frames the restaurant's interior as a diorama to be viewed from the street.

There are decorative elements that utilize stereotypical tropical motifs, such as palm leaves. But its place-making iconography is largely site specific: murals painted on the walls offer Havana streetscapes recognizable to most patrons. One, called La Memoria (The Memory), depicts the Paseo del

Prado, a well-known avenue in Old Havana. Patrons are thus invited to imagine themselves somewhere else—transported back home (for Cubans) or to a strange new place.

But La Esquina Habanera enacts and stages Cubanness more evocatively and dramatically through the live musical performances it hosts on weekend evenings and some special occasions like New Year's Eve. On Friday and Saturday, to attract or be responsive to an increasingly diverse Latin population, dance bands play a variety of Latin music. Cubanía is certainly present but downplayed. The crowd varies, but the core of regulars seems to be a heterogeneous mix of Latinos. On Sunday nights, however, cubanía—in an overtly performative and somewhat folkloricized (Hagedorn 1995) or touristic mode—comes to the fore when La Esquina Habanera hosts a weekly rumba. *Rumba* refers to both a complex of music and dance forms combining African and Spanish musical elements and an event featuring rumba music and dance. Rumba is performed with percussion and voice and involves call-and-response singing; stylized, often erotic dance gestures; and usually improvisation.

Rumba has been part of New York's musical landscape for at least forty years. As in Cuba, rumba occupies multiple performative registers: there are spontaneous and informal performances in people's homes or in public spaces (such as Central Park or a street corner in Washington Heights) and theatrical, folkloric performances. The Sunday-evening rumba at La Esquina Habanera was started in 1996 by Cubans who felt that the informal rumbas were too sloppy and did not do justice to the tradition. It is a staged spectacle, with a house band, professional dancers, and clearly defined sets. Although audience participation is permitted, it is somewhat contained (although on occasion, it threatens to break into disorder).

The crowd is intensely if not exclusively Cuban, largely black and *mulato,* and primarily made up of those who arrived in 1980 or later. There is a loyal crowd of regulars who come from throughout the New York/New Jersey area. The rumba generates a feeling of community, and for many Cuban patrons, it invokes memories of home. It becomes a living, active lieu de mémoire. Rumba itself is also a result and a medium of traveling culture, rooted in the forced migration/ displacement of Africans to Cuba. The site can be understood as series of overlapping spatial axes—the double diaspora from Africa to Cuba to the United States—and time frames—precolonial Africa to colonial Cuba to the premigratory moment (which could be 1959, 1980, 1994, or last week) to the present day. The rumba thus functions as a heterotopia but one that encompasses multiple chronotopes (Bakhtin 1981; for a fuller discussion of rumba and diaspora, see Knauer 1997).

La Esquina Habanera also points to ways in which culture refuses to respect neatly ordered categories or locations. Before shows and during the breaks, video projection screens show music videos and programs from Cuban TV. Many of the restaurant's Cuban patrons, as well as the owner, maintain regular communication with their families on the island, thus confounding commonsense understandings of the relationship between the island and the diaspora. Through these informal means, La Esquina Habanera has come to occupy a place in Havana's social imaginary. Many rumba performers in Havana know about it and make a point of visiting and sitting in if they come to New York. Tony wants to promote the restaurant as a performance venue, and with the help of his sister Mercedes, who lives in Havana, he schedules special shows featuring musicians from the island that draw over-capacity crowds. There is intense audience interest and participation at these shows, which also provide a unique opportunity for musical interchange and dialogue between the Cuban guests and the locally based performers, momentarily eliding or blurring territorial, ethnic, and generational boundaries. (See Duany 1997 for a fuller discussion of the renegotiation of Cuban identity between the island and the diaspora.)

La Esquina Habanera also points to ways in which boundaries are blurred between the secular and the sacred, the commercial and the folkloric. There are visual and performative references to the Afro-Cuban religion of La Regla de Ocha, or Santería. There is an altar to the goddess Ochún on the side of the stage, and the rumba always begins with an invocation to Elegguá, the orisha who guards the crossroads. The restaurant has increasingly sponsored *bembes,* or drum feasts, to celebrate popular orishas such as Changó, Ochún, and Babalú-Aiyé. It is a restaurant and not a religious community, but these are hybrid events, somewhere in between a folkloric performance and a ceremony. They have become a kind of invented tradition (Hobsbawm and Ranger 1983).

Patria is a sleek, ultrachic restaurant on Park Avenue near Gramercy Park, an area that in recent years has become one of a series of new gourmet meccas, a highly visible zone of consumption. It does not style itself as a Cuban restaurant but rather as a pioneer in what former chef/co-owner Douglas Rodriguez labels *nuevo latino* cuisine. Rodriguez was born and raised in New York City; his parents left Cuba in the 1950s. Patria is the most high-profile of my three sites; it has become a benchmark of the kind of cross-cultural innovation currently in vogue. Rodriguez has become a celebrity chef; his cookbook, *Nuevo Latino,* has generally received good reviews. Rodriguez is often mentioned and quoted in newspaper stories about food trends, and recipes from Patria frequently appear in *The New York Times.*[24]

Its outgoing phone message encapsulates the restaurant's mission, message, and strategy:

> Welcome to Patria, the *home* of nuevo Latino. New York Times
> *three-star chef* Douglas Rodriguez has reinterpreted *classical
> Latin American dishes* with an emphasis on flavor, freshness and

exotic ingredients. Patria combines an extremely unique dining *experience* that is fun and exciting with an atmosphere that is lively and elegant. (emphasis added)

This restaurant is thus a place not merely to seek nourishment but to have an experience. We are invited into a thematized environment that draws upon both heritage discourse ("classical Latin American dishes") and tourisms of the exotic (exotic ingredients, unique experience); the language, in fact, suggests the restaurant as theme park (fun, exciting, and lively). Rodriguez's cookbook also plays upon this mixture of heritage and exoticism:

Many Latins will recognize the foods *from their homeland,* but will notice that they are served in nontraditional ways. For many non-Latins, this book will be an *adventure into the unknown* and an introduction to dishes that instantly become new favorites. For me, cooking is all-consuming, and a creative connection with my *heritage.* All of my dishes are founded on *tradition* and home cooking—the type of food I was raised on and still love. I invite you to *enter my world* of cooking. . .Nuevo-Latino style. (1995:2; emphasis added)

Patria's interior is sleek, ultramodern, and somewhat subdued. The bar occupies a central and elevated location, and a long curved counter in the back is a visible staging area where finishing touches are placed on plates before they are carried to tables. The decor is tropical postmodern—an unobtrusive elegance replete with tropical references (paintings of tropical fruit, brightly colored mosaics, and an extravagant floral arrangement at the entrance). The wall art is paintings and not murals, framed and hung gallery-style, which heightens the museumlike character. Patria courts both Latino and non-Latino customers; according to Rodriguez, non-Hispanics come looking for something different, whereas Latinos come to experience familiar ingredients in nonfamiliar interpretations. There is also an appeal to ethnic pride: "They [Latinos] also like the fact that it's a white tablecloth restaurant with a good wine list and stylish food that places an emphasis on presentation. . . . It's a restaurant they can be proud of." (Quoted in *The New York Times,* January 17, 1996, p. C1).

The restaurant's clientele is fairly heterogeneous, at least in terms of race and ethnicity, and homogeneous in terms of class. On the nights I have been there, the majority of customers were not Latino, but the restaurant does attract affluent Latinos. The restaurant's management estimates that 80 percent of the clientele is from the New York area.

The food is complicated, and the presentations are meticulous, whimsical, and almost extravagant. Some dishes are so elaborately constructed that they look like a miniature stage set. A whole fish is balanced vertically on a brilliant transparent blue plate so that it appears to swim. The restaurant's signature dessert is called a "chocolate cigar." A plate appears with a perfect cigar-shaped cylinder molded from dense chocolate cream, with a foil label reading "Douglas Rodriguez." An edible matchbook is placed to one side, with the "matches" sticking upward. These are meals that have to be consumed visually. The food is literally staged and becomes a performing object. Or one can look at the food presentation as a form of framing and display. We might, then, look at Patria as object theater, museum theater, or a hybrid of both.

The written menu is surprisingly restrained. The language is descriptive rather than romantic/evocative; the text is nearly adjective free. But reading the menu is like taking a quick journey through the Americas: Honduran ceviche, Colombian *arepas* (corn cakes), Cuban sandwich, Chilean salmon. On one level, this can be read as an overdone pastiche, food that belongs to everywhere and thus nowhere. This is heritage in a blender, Latin America under glass. But it can also be read as an attempt at interculinary/cultural dialogue. Patria's heterotopia also encompasses multiple chronotopes or at least chronotopic elements.

Although not a Cuban restaurant per se, it does invoke Cuba and Cubanness through multiple strategies. *Patria* means "homeland" or "fatherland"; nationalist discourse in most Latin American countries is replete with references to *la patria*. But *Patria* was also the title of a newspaper published in New York by Cuban exiles fighting for independence from Spain. Cuban patriot José Martí served as its editor for many years. So even though Patria's fusion cuisine connotes layers of displacement, multiple diasporas, and hybridizations and bespeaks a kind of placelessness, it is possible to read the restaurant's name as a (coded) marker of Cubanness.

Patria also references Cuba through its use of background (and occasionally performed) music. Discerning listeners will recognize that Patria moves to a distinctly Cuban beat—the restaurant's soundtrack is comprised primarily of Cuban music from the 1950s and Cuban-inflected, classic salsa from the 1960s and 1970s.

Patria thus situates Cuba securely within an (imagined) pan-Latino cultural-culinary community. In this regard, it stands as a salutary rebuttal to continued efforts to isolate or exclude Cuba from the hemispheric community. It also can be viewed as an attempt to transcend a rigid nationalism that has unfortunately characterized much political and cultural discourse in Latin America over the last century. We might read Patria as an embodiment of Cuban patriot José Martí's sweeping, hemispheric vision of *nuestra América*—our America (Martí 1891).

It is tempting to read the three restaurants as embodying the worldview or structure of feeling of distinct generations of Cuban migration to the United States. Victor's, as I have noted, is in many respects a chronotope, a memory palace of pre-1959 Cuba. Its glitz and showbiz associations correspond to an ethos of successful entrepreneurship, of Cubans as a successful immigrant community, a so-called model minority. The more modest accomplishments of La Esquina Habanera can be read as a parable about the less-than-meteoric success of the post-1980 Cuban immigrants, who did not receive the same economic and social benefits as pre-1980 Cuban immigrants and have not assimilated or acculturated as much. Patria, on the other hand, reflects the aspirations of a hip, younger cohort of Cubans, who were either born in the United States (and thus called second-generation in migration studies) or at least raised here (dubbed the "1.5 generation").

Clearly, a full demographic/sociological study of the restaurants, their staffs, and their clientele are beyond the scope of this study. A more complete analysis would also have to look more closely at the social, economic, and population dynamics of the surrounding areas, which I have only been able to sketch in a very summary fashion. Another useful frame would be to look at the multiple and perhaps colliding cartographies of Cuban life in the New York area. How do these and other Cuban restaurants, together with other physical gathering places (cafés, nightclubs) and cultural/social institutions that are not place bounded (clubs, social or political organizations, concerts and informal musical performances) combine to map the Cuban community(-ies) and interact in the production of an exilic or diasporic imaginary?[25] And perhaps most interestingly, how have those maps and imaginaries shifted and changed over time? However, I was surprised to find that these restaurants exhibited more similarities than I had expected. They initially appeared worlds apart from each other, occupying completely different market niches and performative registers. If I had to encapsulate each site, I would say that Victor's is about translating Cuba for non-Cubans, as producing itself as a site of differentiated otherness, through ultranarrow and generic strategies. La Esquina Habanera's goal is to maintain itself as an outpost of Havana, playing upon nostalgic and site-specific memories. Patria embodies a grand cosmic vision of postnational, panethnic latinidad. But as I have stressed, all of these sites involve multiple frames and cartographies. Each restaurant draws upon heritage and tradition but also appeals to the exotic. I also argued that each of these sites incorporates both chronotopic and heterotopic elements. I choose to look at them as three different instances of how Cubanness is framed, utilized, and consumed. None of these instances is complete, seamless, or universal, but taken together, they provide interesting insights into the production and performance of multiple diasporic identities and the various ways these spaces invite all of us to eat (in) Cuban.

NOTES

1. This essay was originally written for Barbara Kirshenblatt-Gimblett's Spring 1998 seminar on Tourist Productions at New York University (NYU). I am

indebted to her for proposing this topic, which allowed me to combine an interest in Cuba and Cubanness with the constraints of conducting fieldwork in New York City, and to the editors of this volume for their support and patience. A shortened version of this essay was presented at the Cuban Research Institute's (CRI) Second Conference on Cuban and Cuban-American Studies at Florida International University in March 1999. Many useful comments and suggestions came from participants in the NYU seminar; the CRI conference; two anonymous readers; and several colleagues, including Jorge Duany, Roman de la Campa, and George Yudice. I also want to thank the staffs of La Esquina Habanera, Patria, and Victor's Cafe 52 for their graciousness and generosity.

2. In an important, almost seismic, shift, contemporary music from Cuba (as opposed to pre-1959 classics or music produced by in the United States by émigré musicians) has begun to penetrate the cultural landscape of Miami.

3. For example, the CRI at Florida International University, which has played an important role in bringing together Cuban and U.S.-based scholars, now advertises its biennial gathering as a conference on Cuban and Cuban-American studies.

4. Though Ricky Ricardo may have been a parody or burlesque, he was indelibly and specifically Cuban. For a discussion of Desi Arnaz and cubanía, see Perez-Firmat (1994) and Fusco (1995).

5. U.S. foreign policy initiatives in Nicaragua and elsewhere in Central America, for example, were often couched in terms of the Cuban threat; we had to prevent Nicaragua or El Salvador from becoming "another Cuba."

6. The crisis is arguably still in effect. Although the severe economic depression probably hit bottom in 1993, the economy has not fully recovered from the cutoff of Soviet aid. The decision in the early 1990s to focus on expanding tourism, promoting biotechnology, and encouraging foreign investment has helped but has also created a new set of social, cultural, and political problems.

7. Recently, this establishment has shown its fissures, as several conservative Cubans have lobbied to ease travel restrictions for Cuban Americans and permit family remittances and humanitarian aid.

8. Clifford (1997) and other writers have suggested rethinking cosmopolitanism in a less ethnocentric, class-bound framework to include types of other travel and knowledge.

9. Relevant here is Paul Gilroy's work on the emergence of a specifically "black British" diasporic culture, which draws upon Caribbean traditions but is firmly rooted in everyday life in contemporary England. See Gilroy (1987, 1993).

10. Victor, who has lived in the United States for over forty years, has limited proficiency in English; our conversations were conducted entirely in Spanish. Tony, the owner of La Esquina Habanera, who arrived in the Mariel boatlift of 1980, also does not speak fluent English.

11. Family members, especially spouses and dependent children, may often work for little or no formal wages. Although wages are notoriously low, often far below the legal minimum, restaurants are seen as an attractive workplace for new immigrants because they frequently provide employees with most or all of their meals.

12. A term that Sharon Zukin has borrowed from economist Joseph Schumpeter (Zukin 1991).

13. This image reminded me of several friends' description of paper placemats they used to encounter at Cuban luncheonettes that featured a map of the island and statements or statistics that underplayed or erased the black and mulatto presence on the island (one friend, who grew up in Union City in the 1970s, recounted a placemat that read "There are no blacks living in Cuba") (Various sources, personal communication).

14. By contrast, "everyday" Cuban and Latino restaurants are widely known for serving gargantuan portions.

15. Transcribed from outgoing phone message at Victor's Cafe 52, April 10, 1998.

16. Sponsored by Bacardi and written by an eminent food historian, Maricel Presilla, who happens to be Cuban.

17. U.S. cars from the 1950s are an icon associated in many people's minds with middle-class life in prerevolutionary Havana. Many cars of this vintage are still seen on the streets of Havana, as few people can afford to buy new cars.

18. *The New Jersey Municipal Data Book* (Palo Alto, Calif.: Information Publications, 1994), 502; conversation with Union City town clerk.

19. For example, there are numerous references to Union City in Cuban author Miguel Barnet's ethnographically based fiction, *La Vida Real,* whose protagonist is a Cuban émigré who has lived in New York since the 1940s.

20. WCBS radio's food reporter, Anthony Dias Blue, reviewed Azucar, a new Cuban restaurant in Edgewater, New Jersey, as "charging *New York prices* for *mod* Cuban eats. . . . Azucar food is appealing, often *plated* on a banana leaf " (emphasis added). From http://newsradio88.com/style/foodwine/archive/august_1995/august_4.html.

21. Some wealthier metropolitan-area Cubans maintain vacation residences in Florida.

22. These developments in many ways parallel the increasing diversification of the Latino community/-ies throughout the metropolitan area.

23. Every time I have eaten there, several people have dropped in to visit (but *not* dine) with other patrons, chat with the owner, inquire about mutual friends, or exchange gossip with the wait staff.

24. The public announcement that Douglas Rodriguez was leaving Patria's staff came while I was completing final revisions on the manuscript (Winter 2000). It is too soon to tell what the impact of his departure will be on the specific themes I have addressed in terms of the restaurant's invocation or performance of Cubanness.

25. I have taken this concept from a presentation by Bertha Jottar Palanzuela at the Spectacles of Religiosity conference sponsored by the Performance Studies Program, New York University, April 20, 1998.

BIBLIOGRAPHY

Aparicio, Frances R. and Susan Chávez-Silverman. 1997. *Tropicalizations: Transcultural Representations of Latinidad.* Hanover, N.H., and London: University Press of New England.

Appadurai, Arjun. 1997. *Modernity at Large: Cultural Dimensions of Globalization.* Minneapolis and London: University of Minnesota Press.

Asimov, Eric. 1998. "Ceviche and Filet Mignon, Courtesy of Cuba." *The New York Times,* February 18, p. F10.

Bakhtin, Mikhail. 1981. "Forms of Time and The Chronotope in the Novel." In *The Dialogic Imagination,* edited by Michael Holquist. Austin: University of Texas Press.

Bell, David and Gill Valentine. 1997. *Consuming Geographies: We are Where We Eat.* New York: Routledge.

Boswell, Thomas and J. Curtis. 1984. *The Cuban American Experience: Culture, Images and Perspectives.* Totowa, N.J.: Rowman and Allanheld.

Bourdieu, Pierre. 1984. *Distinction.* London: Routledge.

Brooks, Patricia. 1998. "Where Rum and Seafood May Top the List." *The New York Times,* February 15, p. 14CN19.

Clifford, James. 1997. *Routes: Travel and Translation in the Late 20th Century.* Cambridge, Mass.: Harvard University Press.

Cook, Ian and Philip Crang. 1996. "The World on a Plate: Culinary Culture, Displacement and Geographical Knowledges." *Journal of Material Culture* 1, no. 2 (1996): 131–53.

Crang, Philip. 1996. "Displacement, Consumption, and Identity." *Environment and Planning A*(28): 47–67.

——. 1997. "Performing the Tourist Product." In *Touring Cultures: Transformations of Travel and Theory,* edited by Chris Rojek and John Urry, 137–54. Routledge: London and New York.

Croucher, Sheila L. 1998. "Ethnic Inventions: Constructing and Deconstructing Miami's Culture Clash." Paper prepared for the conference "Orange Empires: Miami and Los Angeles," Huntington Library, Los Angeles, California, February 27–28.

Duany, Jorge. 2000. "Reconstructing Cubanness: Changing Discourses of National Identity on the Island and in the Diaspora." In *Cuba, The Elusive Nation: Interpretations of National Identity,* edited by Damien J. Fernández and Madeline Cámara Betancourt. Gainesville: University Press of Florida: 17–42.

Fine, Gary Alan. 1996. *Kitchens: The Culture of Restaurant Work.* Berkeley and Los Angeles: University of California Press.

Finkelstein, Joanne. 1989. *Dining Out: A Sociology of Modern Manners.* New York: New York University Press.

Fusco, Coco. 1995. *English Is Broken Here: Notes on Cultural Fusion in the Americas.* New York: New Press.

Gilroy, Paul. 1987. *There Ain't No Black in the Union Jack: The Cultural Politics of Race and Nation.* London: Hutchinson.

——. 1993. *The Black Atlantic: Double Consciousness and Modernity.* Cambridge, Mass.: Harvard University Press.

Glasser, Ruth. 1995. *My Music Is My Flag: Puerto Rican Musicians and Their New York Communities, 1917–1941.* Berkeley: University of California Press.

Grenier, Guillermo. 1998. "Exiles in Power: Miami, Immigration, and Social Change." Paper prepared for the conference "Orange Empires: Miami and Los Angeles," Huntington Library, Los Angeles, California, February 27–28.

Grosfoguel, Ramon and Chloé S. Georas. 1996. "The Racialization of Latino Caribbean Migrants in the New York Metropolitan Area." *CENTRO* 8 (1,2): 191–201.

Grunwald, Michael. 1998. "Cuban Music Eases Exiles' Pain in Little Havana." *The Boston Globe,* February 27; www.latinolink.com/art/art98/0227amia.htm.

Hobsbawm, Eric and Terence Ranger, eds. 1983. *The Invention of Tradition.* Cambridge, U.K.: Cambridge University Press.

Kasinitz, Philip. 1992. *Caribbean New York: Black Immigrants and the Politics of Race.* Ithaca, N.Y.: Cornell University Press.

Knauer, Lisa Maya. 1997. "Rumba, comunidad e identidad en New York." *Temas* 10 (Fall): 13–21.

Louie, Elaine. 1997. "A Pan American Highway of Foods on Avenida Bergenline." *The New York Times,* April 30, p. C3.

Martí, José. 1891. "Our America." In *The America of José Martí: Selected Writings of José Martí,* translated by Juan de Onis, 138–51. New York: Funk & Wagnalls.

Maśud-Piloto, Felix Roberto. 1988. *With Open Arms: Cuban Migration to the United States.* Totowa, N.J.: Rowman & Littlefield.

MacCannell, Dean. 1989. *The Tourist.* 2d ed. New York: Macmillan.

Mirabal, Nancy Raquel. 2000. "No Country but the One We Must Fight For."

Nora, Pierre. 1989. "Between Memory and History: Les Lieux de Mémoire." *Representations* 26 (Spring): 7–25.

Ojita, Mirta. 1997. "As Cubans Replaced by Other Hispanics, Community Shifts Accent." *The New York Times,* January 28; www.latinolink.com/life/life97/0128LCNY.HTM.

Pedraza, Silvia. 1995. "Cuba's Refugees: Manifold Migrations." Paper presented at the Nineteenth International Congress of the Latin American Studies Association, Washington, D.C., October 1995.

Perez, Louis Jr. 1999. *On Becoming Cuban: Identity, Nationalism, and Culture.* Chapel Hill and London: University of North Carolina Press.

Perez-Firmat, Gustavo. 1994. *Life on the Hyphen: The Cuban-American Way.* Austin: University of Texas Press.

Poyo, Gerald E. 1984. "Cuban Communities in the United States: Toward an Overview of the 19th Century Experience." In *Cubans in the United States,* edited by Miren Uriarte-Gaston and Jorge Canas Martinez, 43–67. Boston: Center for the Study of the Cuban Community.

——. 1989. *"With All and for the Good of All": The Emergence of Popular Nationalism in the Cuban Communities of the United States, 1848–1898.* Durham, N.C.: Duke University Press.

Poyo, Gerald E. and Mariano Diaz-Miranda. 1994. "Cubans in the United States." In *Handbook of Hispanic Cultures in the U.S.: History,* edited by Alfredo Jimenez. Houston: Arte Público Press.

Presilla, Maricel E. 1987. *Celebrating Cuban Cuisine: In Commemoration of Victor's Cafe 52 25th Anniversary.* Privately published.

Rodriguez, Douglas (with John Morrisson). 1995. *Nuevo Latino: Recipes that Celebrate a New Latin American Cuisine.* Berkeley: Ten Speed Press.

Shelton, Alan. 1990. "A Theater for Eating, Looking and Thinking: The Restaurant as Symbolic Stage." *Sociological Spectrum* 10 :507–26.

Urry, John. 1990. *The Tourist Gaze: Leisure and Travel in Contemporary Societies.* London: Sage Publications.

———. 1995. *Consuming Places.* New York: Routledge.

Zukin, Sharon. 1991. *Landscape of Power: From Detroit to Disney World.* Berkeley: University of California Press.

———. 1995. *The Cultures of Cities.* Cambridge, Mass., and Oxford: Blackwell Publishers.

CHAPTER SEVENTEEN

Taking "Class" Into Account

Dance, the Studio, and Latino Culture

*Karen Backstein**

I walked into Clark Center for the first time, and at the sign-in desk I immediately ran into a friend I hadn't seen in awhile.

"What class are you taking?" she asked.

"Loremil Machado's."

"*Loremil's?*" The note of surprise in her voice was unmistakable. "Have you ever done an African-based dance class before?"

"No," I said, suddenly feeling a bit nervous, wondering what I was in for.

She chuckled. "Well, you'd better warm up!"

Em busca	In search of. . .
Em busca de um novo El Dourado	In search of a new El Dorado
Viajei	I traveled
P'ro melhor lugar do mundo	To the best place in the world
Fui tentar a minha sorte na 46	To try my luck on 46th [Street in New York City].

—*"Uma Rua Chamada Brasil," samba enredo in honor of New York's "Little Brazil" by Império Serrano, Carnaval 1999*

I found myself irresistibly drawn to Clark Center after seeing Brazilian dancer/choreographer Loremil Machado perform in a free outdoor concert at Lincoln Center. Inside the white buildings, entered only with high-priced tickets, was the ballet I'd loved since childhood, with mostly adult spectators sitting silently until the proper moment came to applaud. Outside, in the sunshine, samba, the orixas, and capoeira; lots of children; gleeful shouting; and movement rippling through an audience thoroughly enraptured by Loremil's puckishness, energy, and acrobatics. Then I overheard someone behind me make a comment about Loremil teaching a class, and when I spotted him later on the plaza, I ran over to get a schedule.

---

*Em memória do meus caros amigos brasileiros: Loremil, que me ensinou a sambar, e querido Arlindo, meu parceiro favorito. I will forever miss your fleeting steps, thrilling and invigorating music, and glorious presences.

And to Robert Stam—without your abiding and infectious love for Brazil, none of this would have happened.

Of course, this indoor/outdoor dichotomy is far too simple and neat. Ballet and its high-art sister, modern dance, have long since folded popular forms into their refined techniques, while Brazilian companies such as Balé Folclórico da Bahia put on a bravura display of fiendishly difficult samba steps in major New York City theaters. But the comparison does suggest the rich variety of dance styles and spaces that New York offers, the way in which different practices commingle or simply jut up against each other, producing new meanings—some of which concern not just performance but ways of and reasons for transmitting culture.

When I first began studying Brazilian dance, in the midst of writing a dissertation on cinema and choreography, I saw class as a place to gain firsthand knowledge of all the form's intricacies, both academically and physically. As both Barbara Browning (1995) and Yvonne Daniel (1995) have pointed out, to truly understand a dance, you must partake of it yourself. I didn't know at the start exactly how much information Loremil would impart along with the steps, but I knew he would at the very least teach me to recognize the movement patterns of samba and Candomblé dances and that he would possibly serve as a source as I went about my research.

Now, after nearly fifteen years of Brazilian and Afro-Caribbean classes, I want to talk about the experience of learning movement itself, to focus directly on the dance studio and the classroom. What does it mean to teach Latino dance in a formalized setting? How does the culture of New York City affect these classes—and how do they in turn affect the city? What kind of teaching style predominates, and how does it differ from classical and modern forms?

Before proceeding, two methodological questions require attention. The first concerns the definition of *Latino* used here and whether it should rightly include Brazilian culture, as I am doing. The second issue involves the type of dance classes included in this study.

In the introduction to *Negotiating Performance: Gender, Sexuality & Theatricality in Latin/o America*, Diana Taylor focuses on the term *Latino*, pointing out that it usually refers to "peoples of 'Hispanic' descent who were born or live permanently in the United States." Then she elaborates on the definition: "Latinos . . . tend to identify ideologically with the so-called 'third world,' with 'people of color' or economically and politically disenfranchised minorities. They take pride in their indigenous and African origins" (Taylor and Villegas 1994:5).

Clearly, as regards the first point, far fewer Brazilians than Cubans, Puerto Ricans, Dominicans, and Mexicans have become a regular part of the fabric of U.S. life. They do not walk the borderline between cultures so often. And neither have Brazilians amassed the political force or social influence of the larger Hispanic population, which has struggled to affect everything from school policy to trade agreements with their home nations. Brazilians have not even traditionally had a separate category in the U.S.

Census, as Maxine L. Margolis has pointed out (1994:254). Rather than count themselves as Spanish/Hispanic and writing in their nationality, as they were expected to do, many instead identified themselves according to race, ensuring their invisibility as a group. Also, as Margolis notes, most initially come here for transitory stays (1994:vii), meaning they haven't the same investment in making long-term change as do Latinos who have planted permanent roots, such as the Nuyoricans or the Cubans who fled Castro's regime.

The absence of a shared language is also of paramount importance, as Spanish remains a highly privileged signifier of Latino identity and resistance as well as a prime isolator of Brazilians both within and without the United States. Reminiscing about his first visit to Cuba in 1978, where he met and interacted with Latin American intellectuals and artists from many nations, Brazilian composer/singer Chico Buarque noted that

O brasileiro, na verdade, nunca teve essa raiz latino-ameriana, nenhuma ligação com o resto do continente. . . . O que me impactou em Cuba, ao ver aquelas pessoas todas, é que entre elas estavia uma certa identidade, un trânsito livre, e que um brasileiro sentia-se isolado. [The Brazilian, to tell the truth, never had these Latin American roots, or any connection with the rest of the continent . . . What had an impact on me in Cuba, seeing all these people, is that they shared a certain identity, a free transit, and that the Brazilian felt himself isolated.] (Buarque 1989)

Taylor doesn't even address the issue of Portuguese and how it might fit in. However, one can also argue that despite the linguistic schism, the social differences between, say, Argentina and Cuba are far greater than the differences between Cuba (or Puerto Rico) and Brazil—especially in relation to dance and music. Here, the Third World cohesion to which Taylor alludes builds a crossroads where Brazilian and Latino cultures meet both literally—in terms of a shared African influence—and structurally, given the similar processes of syncretism. The orishas of Santería and the orixas of Candomblé frequently overlap, whereas on the secular front, the Cuban rumba, the Puerto Rican bomba and plena, and the Brazilian samba have all succeeded in surviving official, sometimes vicious, attempts to stamp them out. Most of the dances I will discuss in this paper had the full weight of legal restrictions brought to bear on them during the colonial period and faced critical vitriol for their "unseemliness" and "immorality."[1] In the everyday life of many Latin countries, these dances of African origin embody national pride, pleasure, and festivity.

Within the New York dance class scene, these classes also are grouped together as they would not be in their native context, owing to their similar movement styles; their mutual foreignness within the framework of U.S. culture; and their shared history as expressions of the African diaspora. Here, in the city, Latin and Brazilian dance and music are subject to layers upon layers of interpretation. Depending on the viewer's perspective, styles such as samba and salsa can either be a source of pride in one's own native culture (for Latinos), evidence of the retention of African structures (for African Americans), or a reflection of the so-called melting pot that is New York City (for white non-Latinos).

Historically, one must consider the ever-fluctuating ideas of what constitutes latinidad as well as the ways in which South American and Caribbean countries have been linked in both the U.S. and Latin American popular imagination. Going back to the "Good Neighbor" policy during World War II, the U.S. government forged a strategic political and ideological connection between Brazil, Argentina, Cuba, and Puerto Rico. The State Department heavily targeted Brazil and Argentina, considering them almost as a single problem: entities that required recruiting to the Allies, a situation that deeply entangled Puerto Rico as well.

The idea of a generalized "Latin American neighborhood" seeped into the culture at large, particularly the media and arts. Taking their cue from Washington, films as radically different as Disney's blinkered *Tres Caballeros* and Orson Welles's more nuanced, unfinished *It's All True* tackled several South American nations (plus Mexico) at once. Hollywood musicals went *Down Argentine Way* with "Brazilian bombshell" Carmen Miranda and not a tango step visible anywhere. In dance studios and ballrooms, the Latin Dancing category included the samba, maxixe (a Brazilian waltz), tango, rumba, and others, making little or no distinction between country of origin. As Chico Buarque noted in his sly song "Las Muchachas de Copacabana" from his political musical *Ópera do Malandro*:

Se o cliente quer rumbeira, tem	*If the client wants a rumba dancer, we have one*
Com tempero da baiana . . .	*With the flavor of a baiana . . .*
Nos somos las muchachas de	*We are the girls of Copacabana*
Copacabana	(Buarque 1985)

Today, a new crop of ballroom films still continues to present a generalized Latin potpourri. *Dance with Me,* about the relationship forged on and off the dance floor between a Cuban émigré to the United States and a (very light-skinned) African American woman, primarily features several variations of rumba and salsa, ranging from the most traditional (within Cuba) to the social (in clubs) to the stylized and professional (in dance studios and competitions). One snippet of choreography in the final, gala showdown, however, is performed to Sergio Mendes's version of Carlinhos

Brown's "Magalenha," a fine example of Bahian samba-reggae—and a highly contemporary and Africanized shift from the usual ballroom samba.

And neither is the interchange and linking of diverse national forms limited only to U.S. popular culture. Within Latin American productions, too, a mélange of styles appear, suggesting a free interplay between cultures. *Carnaval Atlântida,* a prime example of the Brazilian musical-comedy genre known as *chanchada,* prominently showcases Mexican actress Maria Antonieta Pons as a Cuban dancer throughout. Pons interestingly takes over the stereotype of the "hot Latina" that in Hollywood frequently fell to Carmen Miranda. In the Mexican cabaretera *Aventurera,* Ninon Sevilla performs several Brazilian numbers whose spirited rhythms and happy lyrics contrast with the more melodramatic Spanish-language songs recounting tales of aching heartbreak and loss.

Within the recording world, too, cultural exchange and borrowing take place throughout the Americas, clearly evidencing mutual interests, both politically and musically. Brazilian singer/songwriters such as Chico Buarque and Milton Nascimento participated in the socially conscious pan-Latino Nueva Canción movement—not surprising, as Brazil shared with both Chile and Argentina the unhappy distinction of living under a repressive and murderous military government. Salsa powerhouse Willie Colón incorporated Brazilian songs into his repertoire,[2] and he convinced Célia Cruz to do the same; on her *Duets* CD, she harmonizes with Caetano Veloso on Gilberto Gil's and Capinam's bilingual "Soy Loco Por Ti, América." David Byrne, inspired by the "stuff I have been listening to in New York for eight or nine years," (Hilburn 1989:5) recorded *Rei Momo,* his own quirky take on salsas and sambas, assisted by renowned musicians such as Cruz, Johnny Pacheco, and Cyro Baptista. And on a lighter note, during the lambada's brief spurt of popularity, song versions came out in both Portuguese and Spanish, while in New York clubs Dominicans danced to its swift rhythms using the movements of their own merengue. Established dance techniques, such as Katherine Dunham's, also freely mix Latin, Brazilian, and above all Haitian styles, based on their shared African origins.[3] This focus has also contributed to the formation of many Africanist dance companies, including some groups, such as Marie Brooks's in Harlem and the Batoto Yetu dance company, dedicated to teaching African American children their history.[4]

DANCE CLASS: MOVEMENT, TECHNIQUE, ETHNICITY, AND THE EXOTIC

As host city to all these cultures, and one that tends to celebrate (at least on the surface) multiculturalism, New York offers dance classes of many types and in many venues. These days, salsa, rumba, and samba have become an integral part of many gym programs as a fun type of exercise and an alternative to mindless aerobicism;[5] in ballroom dance studios that teach stylized versions for social occasions; and even in clubs like SOBs and outdoors at Lincoln Center's Midsummer's Night Swing, where a quick lesson precedes each performance so that a mixed group of spectators can have the wherewithal to enter into the experience.

The focus here will be instead on what are known as ethnic dance classes—usually understood as African, Caribbean, Brazilian, and Haitian as well as Oriental, or "belly," dance and flamenco. They're taught side by side with ballet, modern, and jazz in dance schools and sometimes absorb aspects of those techniques. Such classes obviously exist elsewhere, both in the United States and out. But given its huge Puerto Rican population, plus its reasonably sized Brazilian one (not to mention the Latinos and Brazilians who pour in from the nearby New Jersey area), the Big Apple clearly is a privileged metropolis for looking at the widespread dispersion of dance/musical forms. Additionally, since the late 1940s and the heyday of the famed Palladium, New York has had a long-standing history of Latin dance culture in which non-Latins participate, a general popularity made visible in city-set television shows of that time, such as *I Love Lucy* and *The Honeymooners*. Undoubtedly, the inroads made by African American dance, which at least since the Roaring Twenties has been the primary influence on popular choreography, eased the way for broad acceptance of the mambo, cha-cha, salsa, and merengue.

The very term *ethnic dance* is, in itself, an interesting and loaded phrase, erroneously suggesting that although some forms of choreography have cultural roots, others (such as ballet) have somehow succeeded in loosening these connections and eluding their social origins. Yet, as Joanne Kealiinohomoku (1983) so rightly pointed out, no dance can escape ethnicity. A culture's ideas about body, gender, and movement are built into the use of weight, posture, and partnering as well as the organization of patterns. Ballet's upright lightness, along with its often-linear hierarchical arrangements, says as much about Western European society's view of god and heaven existing above, in the skies, as the bent-over, grounded posture assumed in many African dances does about their veneration of the earth. However, once a dance goes into circulation, it becomes reformed, transformed, and even deformed according to the purposes of the dominant culture. The romantic ideology of high art is well served by conveniently ignoring ballet's aristocratic history and locating it solely in an artificial, theatrical sphere. Consigning such forms as mambo, samba, and tango to the ghetto of ethnicity both deemphasizes the technical demands of the dance and also places it in the realm of life as opposed to art.

Context is all-important, however: *ethnic dance* can also resonate positively, referring to a movement form that actively acknowledges and embraces, rather than effaces, cultural background. Given the mixed student composition in ethnic dance classes, this historical perspective has practical connotations. It forces us to take into consideration what the class offers people from outside the culture, how the dance might be read, and how teachers construct those readings. The phrase *ethnic dance*, in this instance, signifies an oppositional practice dedicated to restoring history and valorizing cultural creativity, rather than a judgment on the quality of the dance itself.

Traditionally, ethnic dances had folk roots, with a permeable and always shifting divide between audience and performers and teaching that took place in the body of the community, usually from childhood on. One Brazilian friend recalled that as a small child her mother made her hold on to a chair and practice the sliding, slippery foot movements of samba until she had mastered them. Frances Aparicio, in her study of salsa, similarly emphasizes the importance of a lifetime's worth of exposure to that form of music in the household, which she contrasts with the "exoticism" of the Anglos who have become interested in the style as adults. Anglos, Aparicio feels, use salsa as mere distraction and entertainment, ignoring issues of politics and identity in favor of fetishizing the dance's "intoxicating" effects:

> Most of my Latina/o students in courses on popular music have reaffirmed the serious political value and cultural urgency underlying their identification with salsa music. The process of signifying, of producing meaning and reaffirming cultural identity and boundaries through the music, stands in sharp contrast to the controversial and much discussed 'intoxicating' effects that some Anglo students have described to me in their intercultural experience of dancing to salsa music. (1998:99)

Aparicio's formulation manages at once both thoroughly to reverse and play into the usual reduction of dance to mindless physical pleasure. Here salsa becomes, both musically and physically, a purely intellectual and political concept—one that seems to ignore other statements by her Latino subjects, the physiology of dance, and the functional history of movements created to bring gods (who themselves deeply enjoy the bawdy satisfactions of the body) down to earth. Interestingly, many of the European dance and cultural critics who have studied the phenomenon known as raves specifically focus on the politics behind ecstasy (both the drug and the emotion) and the group cohesion forged by hundreds of bodies bound in the mutual rapture of high-energy, nonstop motion.[6] Aparicio falls into the trap of logocentrism, privileging lyrics as a special site of meaning and downplaying specifically musical issues, including the appeal of tempo, harmony, arrangement, and vocal quality.[7]

Indeed, as I will discuss in more detail further on, there is a joy in exploring movement that contests the rigid notions of Anglo motion, whether it be the tightly ruled steps of ballet or the so-called freer, more natural movements of modern dance. If Anglos look for alternative kinetic possibilities in oppositional and demonized forms, are they engaging in exoticization? How would one reconcile the desire by Latinas for this same freedom, so visible in Aparicio's own account of salsa and analysis of patriarchal critiques, as well as in Yvonne Daniel's history of the danzón, which repeatedly refers back to issues of sexuality and upper-class fear?

Aparicio's discomfort with the broadened audience for Latin music and dance is mirrored by Paul Gilroy, who goes even further in his denunciation of the appropriation of black culture. He sees an opposition between dance as a living, breathing form, developed by practitioners engaged in displaying their powers of creativity and cultural affirmation, and the present state of dance in our society, where black culture and black bodies have become a thing of exotica. Comparing the modern phenomenon of hip-hop to past modes of African American dance, he notes:

> The "traditional" counter-values forged on the slave plantations, and reactivated in condensed form in those circles that endorsed the mutant offspring of Capoiera (sic) and the Caribbean dancehall, have been dissipated. They have been painted over in the sparkling logos of an indifferent corporate appropriation of blackness that would harness the insurgent vitality of the abject and make it into nothing more than an exciting means to dwell in the body. Carefully simulated black subcultures supply an ecstatic but unsyncopated soundtrack for the joyous discipline of Working Out. (1997:23)

Certainly Gilroy has a point: the dominant culture has always seized upon what it perceives as aberrant cultural forms, surreptitiously working to incorporate them into the mainstream, turning them into pure aesthetics, draining them of revolutionary power, and rendering them acceptable. A recent *New York* magazine article on capoeirista Edna Lima would seem to confirm his worst fears: Lima, the first woman in Brazil to become a capoeira mestra, has developed a capoeira-based workout that has now penetrated such New York gyms as Chelsea Piers, Equinox, Duomo, and New York Sports Club. As the article put it, "Now capoeira . . . a 400 year old Brazilian martial art, has bankers and supermodels learning the same moves that supposedly once helped set African slaves free. . . . Critical mass is critical for any trend, but a strategic marketing plan is what has saved capoeira from being consigned to the closet like so many striped leg warmers" ("Kick Starting a Trend":12).

Here, the movement is clearly deracinated and even physically altered to effect the switch from fighting form to workout style. But the type of dance class to which I am referring doesn't fit quite so comfortably in the negative world of corporate logos, pure style-as-meaning, and ahistoricism: the acquisition of muscle has never eclipsed the spiritual, and as we will see later in the paper, cultural contextualization is present at nearly every moment.

In fact, as Randy Martin has pointed out in his writing on hip-hop aerobics classes in Los Angeles, even those programs that focus primarily on the workout leave their traces on the body:

> One could ask whether in the appropriation of otherness that
> has been profitable in myriad forms over centuries of capital, you
> ever really get it for free. Here, dance insinuates a difference
> from what the body had been to now enlarge its capacity for
> being. It inserts into that model of sameness . . . an other truth of
> body's ideality, one that never quite fits and helps to break up
> the authority of that ideal. (1998:147)

The complexity of the process Martin outlines—which, importantly, he in no way idealizes—concerns *potential* and the possibility of employing culture for the purposes of political mobilization.

Marta E. Savigliano, in her lively, poetic, and theoretical study of tango, also tries to unravel a knotted tapestry of fascination, appropriation, and exoticization. She looks back to the turn of the century, when a craze for that hot-blooded dance first flourished, and demonstrates how an entire colonialist "economy of passion" developed around its scandalous choreography. In what was probably one of the first instances of widespread ethnic dance classes in Europe, Parisians rushed to learn the steps, wear the costumes, and patronize the tango clubs and teas. Savigliano fully demonstrates how this enthusiasm ultimately served to turn Argentines into exotic others, but she, like Martin, sees a price paid and a struggle set into motion. What she refers to as a "disciplining process" emerged, in which dance masters and others attempted to tame the movement: "Through these dances [waltz, polka, can-can, apache, and tango] for over a century bodies in movement successively (and successfully) broke rules. . . . It was said that dancing bodies could hardly lie. For this very reason, dancing was also dangerous" (1995:98–99).

Savigliano's analysis of what at first might seem like a cultural victory for the Argentines—the popularity and embracing of their native art form— unpacks what is, ultimately, a negative progression but one filled with contradiction and almost unresolvable difficulty.

In "Goulash Americano: Are We Dancing Like the Natives?" an article published in the ballroom dance magazine *Dancing USA,* Esther Kando Odescalchi discusses "the real thing" versus ballroom stylization, relating a story about what happened when she took the "true" Dominican merengue onto the dance floor where couples tended to dance a modified, "toned-down" version: "I proudly demonstrated [the merengue] at a ballroom dance in New York. As I walked off . . . instead of the expected acclaim for my 'authenticity,' the reaction of my dancing friends was anything but flattering. . . . 'You looked like a street girl wiggling like that' " (1999:16).

After admitting that the experience of performing the Dominican merengue in a club felt very different than "dancing it under the stars of Santo Domingo," Kando Odescalchi argues for the U.S. variation in the U.S. context. She affirms, "This is, after all, the land of freedom and entrepreneurship—to fit our purposes, we customize what we like and adapt them to our environment" (1999:16).

In this postmodern age, the lines between popular, mass, and theatrical cultures have become blurred for a multitude of reasons, ranging from consumer marketing that has given birth to the category of world music to political changes that led to the widespread relocation of populations and popularized cultural products that formerly had a limited audience. Authenticity has become an important commodity, and this cannot be entirely separated from ideas of race, ethnicity, and resistance. As George Lipsitz has pointed out, the commercial product of transnational companies "goes far beyond their role as commodities . . . [providing] a powerful illustration of the potential . . . to carry images, ideas, and icons of enormous political importance between cultures" (1994:27).

In the realm of dance, things become yet more complicated because it is not an art form easily packaged as a mass commodity, like a CD or video. And at this point in time, dance education is an even less commercial proposition, especially in New York City where rents are high and schools are continually forced to switch locations.[8] However, alterations in musical taste, purchasing decisions by customers, and newspaper coverage of such trends do have an impact on people's awareness of the styles that surround them: at the end of 1998, the *New York Times* ran article after article noting significant world music CDs as well as small clubs where Brazilian and Latin music could be heard . . . and where a dance floor was available to enjoy. So although many writers, including Aparicio, relate a history of continued and systematic "whitening" of culture, dance classes have moved in the other direction, searching for the most African-based versions rather than the ballroom adaptations of Latin dances that became so prevalent in the 1950s.

A predilection for more traditional styles has occurred not only in the United States but also in the countries of origin for these dances. Yvonne Daniel pinpoints changing sites of training in Cuba, due to the "codifying" and crowning of rumba in that nation's postrevolutionary culture. Elite academies not only use professional ballet masters to teach but also bring into the classroom "experts" who had not formerly worked as professionals, thus ensuring the perpetuation of the culture with the details intact. (This has not, of course, eliminated what Daniels calls the "rumba event," a looser, more freewheeling, rum-filled, fight-filled, family-filled occasion in which rumba is transmitted through less formal means—although even this is now often "sanctified" by the government, which sponsors many such occasions.)

The establishment of training centers for a dance—its professionalization, in short—leads to increased respect. As Frances Aparicio has pointed out regarding salsa musicians in Puerto Rico, education implies that the material requires specialized talent and work in order to be properly grasped (1998:73). Writer/performers covering Haitian (Katharine Dunham), Cuban (Daniel), and Brazilian dance (Browning) have repeatedly attempted to redress misperceptions about the reputed lack of technique in these styles and to emphasize how highly the culture regards extraordinary ability.

The teaching of rumba, samba, and other ethnic styles has now fallen in line with ballet class, which in the past has served not only as a place to master a set of complex steps but also as a lesson in the accumulation of cultural capital. There teachers instilled in groups of (mostly) little girls ideas of grace and comportment developed a few centuries ago in the French courts. In "Programme for a Sociology of Sport," Pierre Bourdieu speaks about how "the progressive constitution of a relatively autonomous field reserved for professionals is accompanied by a dispossession of the profane, who are little by little reduced to the role of spectators; in opposition to village dancing, often associated with ritual functions, courtly dance . . . presupposes specific forms of knowledge" (1990:165).

Ironically, in the present day, a certain form of exchange has taken place: even as the ritual functions behind the dance gradually fade from the ballet class, they turn up freshly in the ethnic arena, which is finally enjoying that same "presupposition of knowledge" by people both in and out of the diaspora. In discussing the role of the capoeira academy in Brazil, Browning notes that it has become "the controlled space [for playing capoeira]. . . . And yet ostensibly the academy serves the function of an educational space. Politicized black parents today send their children to capoeira academies to learn about their cultural heritage. . . . The *way* we read, teach, and write about culture is as important as the particular manifestations we're considering" (1995:98–99).

Contrast this with ballet class as described by Leslie-Anne Sayers, in "Madame Smudge, Some Fossils, and Other Missing Links: Unearthing the Ballet Class:" "In the steps and rituals we might expect to find encoded memory, evidence of mutations, mergers, influences absorbed and transformed, changing ideals; an evolution of form. But how many children lining up at their weekly ballet class know the significance of a ronde de jambe beyond what it is as a step and perhaps what it can do for your legwork?" (1997:131).

In place of past meaning is pure movement. Within the United States, this shift has occurred thanks in part to ballet's formalization and also to the schism between the dance's aristocratic roots and the democratically oriented U.S. population. American dancers long for facility in the courtly forms despite never having had the advantage of belonging to the originating culture.

Even if the ballet's ideology somewhat obscured its history, at least the form wasn't widely and negatively distorted. Popular accounts of Latin dance, as least as they have been disseminated in the United States, have desperately needed revision. Jesus Colón, in his pungent article "The Origin of Latin American Dances according to the Madison Avenue Boys," sarcastically slashed to bits a television program on the subject hosted by Edward R. Murrow; Xavier Cugat; and Cugat's wife, singer Abbey Lane:

> For example, this is what the Cugats had to say on the origin of the merengue, the dance from Santo Domingo so popular today in every dance hall in New York.
>
> It seems that an Irish captain with a peg leg arrived in Santo Domingo. As he could not dance like everybody else, having to drag his wooden leg with him over the dance floor, the Irish sea captain started to dance one-sided giving a lame effect to his dancing. From then on all the dancers of Santo Domingo followed the way the Irish captain with the peg leg danced the merengue! (1988:79)

Colón then goes on to detail an equally sorry narrative of tango's origins, in which Argentineans, unable to count the simple one-two-three of the waltz rhythm, "hit on the 'less difficult' dance we now call the tango" (1988:80). To anyone who has ever seen, much less tried to master, that fiendishly difficult style, with its intertwining of legs, sudden weight shifts, and small, sharp little kicks, this story is nothing short of ridiculous. A renewed interest in roots in New York City, both within the dance classroom and out, has in some small measure redressed years of misinformation. But the question remains: What form of cultural capital do students who take ethnic classes gain for our multicultural times/multiethnic city? Do classes offer an entrance into a world increasingly defined by Latin rhythms, food, and icons . . . or a road to the exotic, as Aparicio sees it? Do these dances refresh a curriculum filled with forms, such as ballet, that may seem out of sync with modern life, or are they a way back to the past, to a time when culture emanated from community, not a corporation? Do they offer, for Anglos, the pleasure of links forged with another culture or, for African Americans and Latinos, a knowledge of roots? Of course, there is the dance itself, with its appealing formal qualities, the draw of the live music, and the energy fostered by the class's nonstop movement. Yet these qualities alone cannot explain why so many of the students do not limit themselves to the acquisition of mere technique but become wide-scale consumers of the culture in much the same way as Savigliano's Parisian tango-philes, although perhaps with a more politicized perspective fostered by the culture at large and the classes themselves.

These questions have never ceased to circulate in my mind from the moment I started studying, although the answers barely come into clear focus but instead appear more a series of competing discourses, positives and negatives, pleasures and concerns about where and why those pleasures arise. As a white, Ashkenazi Jewish woman—one of a number there, I might add[9]—and an academic keenly trained to self-interrogation, I am also well aware of my forerunners in the more anthropological and cultural aspects of my work (including Maya Deren, Mura Dehn, and Ruth Landes[10]) and have wondered not only what brought so many "outsiders" such as myself into class but what has led us to delve very deeply into the culture beyond dance, from the language to the music. Clearly, I have a very particular point of view, one that is very different from that of Latinas or, for that matter, African Americans connecting with manifestations of their own traditions. My choice, along with others in the class, has been to delve deeply into another group's culture rather than my own. When faced with critiques like those of Aparicio or Gilroy, there is always the nagging fear of having impure motives, of misunderstanding and essentializing this world that I have come to love.

THE "STUDENT BODY": DEFINING THE DANCER

A few New York downtown dance studios may fill up with earnest (if a little ridiculous) women like myself yearning correctly to imitate an African god's motion.

—*Browning 1995:37*

Buried in Barbara Browning's description is a fact worth pondering: the majority of students are women. Rarely do more than five or six men attend class, and they are sometimes encouraged to dance in a group—even provided with gender-specific steps. To some extent, this is a natural outgrowth of the female-centered nature of dance in the United States, but when one takes into account the fact that rumba and samba are equally welcoming to men and women in Latin cultures, the imbalance cannot be shrugged off so easily. (The issue of religious dances is somewhat more complex in this regard; although Santería, especially the Cuban version, may be slightly more male dominated, within Brazil, Candomblé is very often the province of women and gay men, who are considered more open to the spiritual.)

What pleasures might these dances offer women in particular? First, when performing the orishas/orixas, women have the opportunity to represent both male and female saints, a fact discussed in different ways by Maya Deren in relation to Vodun[11] and Browning in relation to Brazilian dance. There is a constant play with identities and movement strategies, although the female orixas are by no means solely the quiet ones. For every deeply feminine Iemanjá caressing her braceleted arms or Oxum stroking her hair and gazing into a mirror, there exists a fiercely dancing Iansã stirring up the winds or a Pomba Gira who guzzles from a bottle. And every Xangô/Changó, full of fire and thunder, is matched by a quieter male orixa, like the aged, stooped Omulú, god of sickness.

There is also the issue of movement and sexuality, a vexed question demanding a delicate negotiation between a series of essentialist tropes—namely, the primitive at the negative pole and the too easy "liberated body" at the other, utopian end.

Without a doubt, motions that have traditionally been forbidden or discouraged in Anglo, upper-class, and patriarchal systems—of the lower body, of discrete parts moving separately rather than in "graceful" harmony—form an integral part of the Africanist lexicon, giving it strength and complexity. And if, to use Martha Graham's famous axiom, "bodies don't lie," then there is an important connection between stretching the bounds of the physical and expanding one's emotional realm: "For all the anxiety which samba's eroticism causes many from the United States, whether for reasons of morality or politics, I have found its *auto*erotic potential to be extraordinarily liberating. In a culture in which racism and sexism are articulated in each other's terms, I was beginning to get some kind of bodily comprehension of the race politics of Brazil" (Browning 1995:33).

Class indeed encouraged this "autoeroticism": in Loremil Machado's studio, samba often demanded the breaking of certain taboos, occasionally to the evident discomfort of some. The samba's roots may lie in African fertility dances, and the Bahian *samba de roda* (the circle that dancers enter to perform) has retained the ancient *umbigada,* a move in which someone exiting the dance space bumps bellies to nudge the next person into the circle. The sexual connotations of the dance persist, visible in many of the steps; in the standard teasing interplay between dancing couples; and, on the stage or float, in the barely there costumes of the mulatas in the samba schools. At Loremil's request and by his demonstration, we became part of this tradition, pointing to or directly touching our own bodies while dancing, highlighting with our arms areas of erotic interest. Hands flowed over the breasts, moving to hips, and brushing past the pelvis.

It is also true that a sense of freedom can sometimes be more easily experienced in the restricted arena of the dance class. Kando Odescalchi's report of bringing authentic forms into contemporary clubs suggests that, at the very least, in the wrong space one can become an unhappy spectacle. Barbara O'Connor, in her article "Safe Sets: Women, Dance and 'Communitas,' " suggests that within a classroom a community can grow, one that contrasts with the larger, and perhaps colder, space of the big city, in which people of different backgrounds come together, sharing the pleasure of achievement in the dance. But unlike clubs, a dance class operates under a strict set of rules, and the comfort level is higher than it might be within a public space where a woman may be perceived as prey." In the studio, hips fearlessly swivel, pelvises thrust, and torsos shimmy.

For Aparicio, one result of fear and control in the outside world is the limitation of women's dance technique and motion more generally. Referring to the lyrics in female-centered salsa that refer to walking and "free movement," she avers: "This emphasis on free movement . . . contests . . . not only the boundaries of the domestic sphere imposed on women but also the rigid disciplines and limitations of bodily movements, gestures, and comportment imposed on a feminine body by society's standards. Acceptable feminine movements, in contrast to men's, are systematically more centripetal and rigid, unwittingly expressing a sense of closure" (1998: 131–32).

Motivations for performing undoubtedly vary, from those more spiritually inclined to those who crave the destruction of physical limitations to those who merely think the movement looks like fun.

MUEVE LA COLITA AND EXPLORE YOUR SOUL

If you find yourself in an exercise rut, mueve la colita and explore something new. Go to an Afro-Cuban dance class, where you will get a workout (worthy of the spirits, or orishas) that pairs muscle and aerobic training with live musicians singing and playing congas and bongos.

A typical Afro-Cuban dance class will reflect the rich diversity of our heritage with people of all shapes, sizes, ages, and colors moving a Latin rhythm."

—*"Conga Workout" 1998:38–39*

This quote, from the bilingual magazine *Latina* (its dual language and dual focus on the "border" and the mainstream already a prime example of the tightrope walk that is latinidad in theUnited States), was followed by a photo essay of exercises to strengthen and tighten the tummy, arms, and legs. It illustrated moves from dances dedicated to Yemayá ("Represent casting evil out to sea") and Aganyú ("Represent a deity's journey"), although the writer couldn't successfully find an orisha to label the crunches, considered to "center the mind and body." In addition, the article included a listing of studios in New York, Los Angeles, and Miami Beach where prospective students could start simultaneously training their physical, spiritual, and cultural selves. The New York *Daily News* considered this article worthy enough to mention in a list of items to look for in upcoming magazines of that month. The collapsing of different forms of consciousness, from the narcissistic cult of beauty to the religious cult of Santería, speaks to the increasing social desire to infuse even the seemingly simple act of exercise with a soul-filling pleasure.

Significantly, the article emphasizes the variety of body types, age groups, and races found in these classes: ethnic dances are perceived as being more open and welcoming to the outsider, without the same rigid preexisting standards for success as ballet, which presently requires a long-limbed, bone-thin physique as well as early childhood training to build complete flexibility and turnout (the rotation outward from the hips). My own experience backs this up. A large percentage of the students are not Latina. Those who are frequently stand out and perhaps even teach as well as take class. Often, heavier women perform exquisitely, their talent visibly appreciated and acknowledged by both the teachers and the musicians. Many pupils are older and have been in the studios for the more-than-a-decade in which I've attended classes. But this should in no way be confused with easiness: the moves are often highly energetic and tricky to do well, demanding a fully polyrhythmic body with arms, shoulders, and legs working in different counts. The torso vibrates and undulates, and arms cut a sharp swath through the air like a slicing knife or machete. Dances of the orishas/orixas depend for their effect on the evocation of a recognized and worshiped being; an Ochún/Oxum that doesn't flow with liquidity and suggest the breathtaking beauty possessed by this river goddess is not Ochún/Oxum at all.

Bringing religion into the classroom is a vexed issue: sacred space touches the secular, with a "congregation" consisting of people with varying degrees of knowledge, with their own belief systems, and with their assorted reasons for being in the class. One Jewish woman, for instance, clashed with a dance teacher over the required bowing to the musicians because it defies her own religion's rules. Further exacerbating the problem are this society's frequently negative representations of both Santería and Candomblé, representations deeply encrusted (at least in the Unites States) with layers of fearfulness, dark mystery, and black magic and images of strange sacrifices.

The dance class does differ from the "conga workout," however, in that the emphasis lies on doing the choreography with respect for the gods and on capturing the essence of the orishas/orixas rather than on "shaping up." In this uncertain space, part school and part temple, dancers have actually fallen into trance, deeply affected by both the dance and the music. Teacher Richard Gonzáles is well aware that some of these religious and cultural requirements may at first not have meaning to some of the students, and he has spoken about his own beginnings as a dancer and how what first was done as a matter of course, simply following instructions, became more and more significant to him emotionally and intellectually. What one is exposed to regularly may, indeed, lose its strangeness and become ordinary, everyday—and then compelling.

Rarely does the choreography consist of extremely extended dances, though it does include combinations of seven or eight different movements, usually performed across the floor from one end of the studio to another. To learn the gestures and the emotional shadings, movements may hew somewhat to the dramatic; Barbara Browning talks about dancing her Ogum for a mãe de santo (literally, "mother of the saints [orixas]") in Bahia and the woman's reaction to the demonstration: "Who taught you Ogum's arms like that. . . . *Que merda,* those who don't know go like that, but we who understand these things do *this"* (1995:46).

The scolding focused on the "excessive mimesis," which Browning traces back to her more theatrical training and the need for the gestures to tell a story: thus connotation became denotation, a situation definitely true for the classroom, where students from different origins must learn concrete meanings. It is the difference between the religious and the dramatic, of dance for possession versus dance for presentation. Both styles, however, despite their varying approaches, do have similar goals: to convey accurately the spirit of a god.

Many of the students study (or have studied) a variety of styles, and their performances reveal a range of variations and shadings. Those who primarily take pure African classes will do the Cuban or Brazilian movements (modified by the variety of influences upon them) with greater force and use of space. The indefinable issue of feel and authenticity—what makes the movement seem native owing to the correct stress, accenting, tension, and the additional little filigrees that have developed through time—is a point difficult to discuss, hard to pin down, and purely dependent upon one's perspective. From a personal point of view, I can generally see the difference when Latinas born to the culture move in class. As with ballet, childhood training develops body memory that allows a person to fall easily into a given posture and energy of motion. It is as hard for late learners to replicate their precise motions as it would be to imitate perfectly the inflections of a vocal accent.

FROM PLIÉ TO RODA: STEPS, COMBINATIONS, CHOREOGRAPHY

AFRO BRAZILIAN:
ORIXAS
Mainha D'Oxum
Special Guest from Bahia, Brazil

Come learn the dances of the orixas
with Mainha who has over
50 years of experience
This is an opportunity!!!

Muevete means
Come
Ignite your spirit!
Express your self thru
African-based movement
that
combine the Spiritual,
the Sensuous,
the Strengthening,
the Passionate!

[and written around a picture of hands drumming]
Brazil Cuba Haiti Puerto Rico
afro-caribbean dance with rosamaria

This last flyer, printed on orange paper, has a delicate border and small drawings of bodies lined up holding hands, as well as of a pair of hands on a drum. The entire image sends out a joyfully carnivalesque message and suggests the warmth of community that these classes carefully cultivate. It also, notably, includes Brazilian in "afro-caribbean," suggesting once again the fashion in which similar philosophical and physical stances overcome the small matter of geography.

How exactly are these classes organized? The warm-up generally is balletic or modern dance–based in nature, often the already more ethnically inflected Dunham technique that has absorbed movements from various areas of the Caribbean and South America. This consists of a mixture of pliés, stretches, and other strengthening exercises; jazz isolations; and motions specific to the dance style, such as hip swivels; undulations to loosen the back; short, quick tremors and vibrations in the torso; and arm movements that appear later in lengthier dance combinations.

The dancers then begin to move across the floor, performing a series of combinations that grow increasingly complex. Usually broken up into a mixture of orisha and secular dances, the process of learning movements starts with mastering individual steps and then fragments of choreography that build on each other until they become full dances. The class may end with a *roda,* or circle, which students enter to perform and show off. Depending upon the teacher, the shyer or newer dancers may be urged or even playfully pushed inside. This is the moment for joyful improvisation, and it allows everyone to experience the unfettered delight of dancing whichever steps feel most comfortable—even if the movements are drawn from slightly different techniques. Above all, the roda provides a small but delicious taste of what goes on in real social situations in Brazil, Cuba, or Puerto Rico, where dancers cheerfully—but definitely competitively—try to one-up each other.

A tendency to recreate the world in which the dances were born permeates the class, even in the face of great difficulty. For example, in line with the inseparability of music and movement in most African-based cultures, singing and chanting make up an integral part of the lesson. Because many of the students haven't fluency in either Spanish or Portuguese—much less Nago or Lukumí, the Yoruba dialects in which several of the Candomblé and Santería songs, respectively, are still sung—the words must be phonetically taught and their meaning translated, a sacrifice of time willingly made. Even the salute to the drummers to give thanks for the music, which consists of bowing down and touching the floor (symbolic of the sacred earth) in front of them, brings an extra touch of the culture into the classroom. (By contrast, in ballet the class must curtsy and bow to the teacher but never to the musician; here it works quite the other way round.)

Throughout, the teachers usually provide, to a greater or lesser extent, historical or religious information on the dance. Not only does this transmit the necessary knowledge of the dance's background, but it also guides the student to the correct quality of movement. The instructions convey the fact that gripping the thumb and finger in a certain way signifies an arrow for the hunter god Ochosi/Oxossi or that an arm curving up and "pouring" evokes Yemayá/Iemanjá scooping up rivulets of ocean water and spilling it over her bejeweled body but also the realization that Changó/Xangô, who rules over thunder and lightning, must move with force, strength, and swiftness because those qualities form the bedrock of his personality. Secular dances, too, such as the samba, also received more than just the mere technical details of movement; even facial expressions merited comment. When the students' faces occasionally contorted or frowned in concentration, teacher Edson Ferreira would admonish, "A samba done without a smile just isn't samba!"

RETRATO DE UMA AULA E ALÉM/PORTRAIT OF A CLASS AND BEYOND: LOREMIL MACHADO

Eu nao sou daqui	I'm not from here
Eu nao tenho amor	I don't have love
Eu sou da Bahia	I am from Bahia
De Sao Salvador	From Sao Salvador

—*"Marinheiro Só," traditional capoeira chant*

Each class provides a tour through the teacher's territory and to some extent a tour through the teacher's own life, politics, and perspective. To understand the dynamic and the widespread influence of these classes, I am going to focus on Loremil Machado, who in many ways remains the exemplar of an ethnic dance teacher. A Baiano born of a poor family, he had come to New York City after touring with local dance companies, and as such his very presence in the city attested to its magnetism for artists who often made a go of it at home only with difficulty. Once here, at just the point when Brazilian culture became somewhat trendy, he helped change the city almost as much as it changed him.

Trained thoroughly in capoeira but "street-practiced" in his samba, this *mestre* was one of the first pied pipers of Brazilian dance to a passel of eager students whom he taught four days a week at Clark Center, a studio with an illustrious history, particularly in relation to African American dance. In exchange, Clark Center gave him a valuable site from which to view a variety of techniques he had not studied while growing up—especially ballet and jazz—all of which took root in his fertile choreographic mind and insinuated their way into his warm-up and long combinations.

For a considerable amount of time, his musical ensemble, the Sarava Bahia Band, played regularly at the then-hot club SOBs (Sounds of Brazil), which became a hangout for a large percentage of the class—not only when he played but also when other musicians from Brazil appeared. And after leaving the group he had coformed with fellow Baiano Jelom Vieira, Capoeiras da Bahia (captured for posterity by filmmaker Warrington Hudlin in 1980), Loremil established his own dance company. In general, neither Loremil nor his students were unusual in forging a relationship that went beyond the classroom. In the studios hang fliers advertising arts-and-culture-oriented trips to Cuba, Brazil, and Africa, sometimes run by the teachers there and sometimes (especially in the case of Cuba) run by local companies. My own first trip to Brazil was run by Ligia Barreto, who at the impromptu request of several students arranged a tour group along with dance classes at local studios in Salvador, Bahia. Most of the teachers perform either in their own small dance companies or with larger ones or play in a band. (In some respects the Cuban and Puerto Rican teachers and musicians have less opportunity, given their larger population and greater competition posed by professional groups who play and visit, such as Las Muñequitos de Matanzas or Los Pleneros de 21. Brazilian stars visit more rarely, leaving a regular space for those who have settled here.)

Incorporating a tremendous number of styles in his class, Loremil succeeded in painting quite a full portrait of Brazilian choreography, one thus far unequalled in the many lessons I have taken. He typically presented reasonably sized chunks of orixa dances (those of Xangô, Ogum, Iemanjá, Iansã, Oxumare, Omulú, Oxum, Ossâe, and his own saint, Oxossi, among them); multiple versions of samba, from Rio's upright style to Bahia's bent-low and shuffling samba de roda; the bounding, athletic *frevo* from Recife in the northeast; *caboclo,* with its tripping, almost drunken-looking motion; the *puxada de rede,* a fisherman's dance that mimics pulling in the net with the catch; *maculêlê,* a dance fight using sticks; and even, occasionally capoeira—never enough to make anyone an expert, but its presence provided the opportunity to discuss the form's history during slavery.

Lacking the codified nature of ballet as well as its highly organized and refined syllabus, much of this class depended upon one's ability to follow steps and patterns quickly shown. Loremil himself rarely had the inclination to break down what he had learned as naturally as breathing. Unlike others—such as Ligia Baretto, who taught beginners the abc's of samba with a simple toe/toe/heel/heel shift that sped up until the motion became fluid—Loremil demonstrated the movement as a whole and dared the class to follow, a method that often left hapless newcomers somewhat lost . . . myself included. I needed at least six months to begin to feel any confidence and was hardly alone in approaching the members of his company, who regularly attended his lessons, to ask for additional help. What he substituted for the mechanics of the steps was the energy and joy of a piece of choreography performed full out. Once mastered, his irresistible combinations could make you feel as if you were flying. Indeed, Loremil's teaching style, and that of most other ethnic dance teachers, is distinguished by their own classroom performance. In Randy Martin's explication of university dance teaching he notes that "since the teacher will tend to indicate the movement rather than dance it fully, it requires someone in the midst of the room to emerge as one who corporealizes it. This person . . . gets featured . . . as a model. This too may have an influence on what the phrase ultimately becomes, hence shifting the authority of movement from teacher to dancer" (1998:164).

Although the "first line" that dances the combination across the room in my Brazilian and Cuban classes may exert a powerful influence on those who follow, if too much of a breakdown in the original combination occurs toward the back of the group, it is far more typical of the teacher to step in, dance alongside the students, and provide another view of the steps done correctly. (Loremil's situation was a bit more complex, because for many years the first group consisted of members of his company whom he trusted as role models while he went to join the musicians.)

The issue of pedagogy becomes quite interesting in relation to ethnic classes, with their new professionalization and increased popularity with dancers initially unfamiliar with the culture. Though in every respect as old (or even older than) ballet or modern dance, only recently have teachers truly developed a logical, methodological approach to passing on so-called folk dances, although there is no standardization. For example, Richard Gonzáles, a master teacher of Afro-Caribbean dance who not only works in New York but travels throughout the country, has developed a beautifully and carefully leveled warm-up that grows and develops from week to week, building on technique, speed, and clarity. As a devoted proselytizer in behalf of his culture as well as a dancer, he constantly focuses on the relationship of motion to meaning in every gesture, extensively breaking down each aspect of the movement, pointing out each detail, from the smallest absence of a required undulation or continuous vibration to the weakness in a gesture that should bristle with energy.

If, for Aparicio, a " 'state of disembodiment,' this radical fissure between body and mind ... informs Anglo constructs of salsa music," (1998:104), dance class attempts to stitch up that split. And as I began with a story that illustrated confusion and uncertainly when first confronted with "performing culture," I wish to end it with another tale of a different form of confusion. During my first trip to Brazil, on a Bahian bus filled with merrymakers looking forward to carnaval just a few days away, some men began singing samba de roda tunes. I happily listened to the rhythms drummed on the seat and the voices joyfully raised when I suddenly recognized several of the songs ... from my class in New York.

At that moment, the two spaces converged in my mind, as the music from Bahia and the classes in New York where I had first heard it became inseparable.

NOTES

1. See Browning (1995), Aparicio (1998), and Backstein's unpublished dissertation, "Dancing Images: Cinema, Choreography and Culture" (New York University, 1996), for more on this subject.
2. See Sue Steward, "Dancing with the Saints: The International Sound of Salsa," in *World Music: The Rough Guide,* ed. Simon Broughton, Mark Ellingham, David Muddyman, and Richard Trillo; contrib. ed. Kim Burton (London: Rough Guide, 1994), 485.
3. It is also interesting to consider that Dunham worked in the entertainment industry, often choreographing pieces for exotic scenes in plays and film, as well as running a theatrical dance company. Because of her widespread renown, she did contribute to popular ideas about these dances. However, it would be unfair to her many courageous cultural and political acts—including a hunger strike in support of Haitian causes—to limit her in this way.
4. See *New York Times,* "From Dance Fledglings, An Ideal of Africa and Family," August 17, 1999, p. E1.
5. See the following articles in the *New York Times:* Janny Scott, "Flirting with the Tango," June 11, 1999, pp. E1, 8; Amanda Hesserl, "How to Build Abs of Undulating Steel," *New York Times* July 20, 1999, p. F8; Alex Witchell, "With a Huff and a Puff," November 14, 1999; as well as "Fit Buzz: The Thrill from Brazil," *Fitness,* July 1999, 21 ; and Ruth Bashinsky, "Shake It!: The Ricky Martin–Inspired Workout for a Fabulous Butt," *New York Daily News,* October 21, 1999, p. 61.

6. See Helen Thomas, ed., *Dance in the City* (New York: St. Martin's Press, 1997), for several articles on different aspects of rave.

7. This problem—the talking around dance and music rather than about it—recurs all too often. See Celeste Fraser Delgado and José Esteban Muñoz, eds., *Everynight Life: Culture and Dance in Latin/o America* (Dunham and London: Duke University Press, 1997), allegedly about dance and yet so often about only its history and its representation in language and literature. Only three contributors, Jane Desmond, Barbara Browning, and Ana Lopez, become more specific—and the first two are dancers as well as academics.

8. See Janet Allan, "Lights Dim for Dance Studios," *New York Times,* June 20, 1999, section 14, p. 6.

9. The heavy participation of Jewish students in ethnically tinged dances is true not only in New York but also in Los Angeles; Eve Babitz, in *Two by Two: Tango, Two-Step, and the L.A. Night,* notes that "the two-step [is] the only dance not overrun with Jews (like tango, salsa, ballroom, or even swing)" (1999:63).

10. Maya Deren spent over ten years researching and filming Vodun dances and rituals in Haiti; Mura Dehn directed a jazz dance company and for decades extensively filmed black dance, from plantation forms to break dancing; and Ruth Landes's groundbreaking work on Candomblé, *City of Women* (1994), challenged many assumptions about that religion during the 1940s.

11. See Maya Deren's *Divine Horsemen: The Living Gods of Haiti* (London and New York: Thames and Hudson, 1953; reprint, Kingston, N.Y.: McPherson and Company, 1991).

REFERENCES

Aparicio, Frances R. *Listening to Salsa: Gender, Latin Popular Music, and Puerto Rican Cultures.* Hanover N.H.: Wesleyan/New England, 1998.

Babitz, Eve. *Two by Two: Tango, Two-Step, and the L.A. Night.* New York: Simon & Schuster, 1999.

Browning, Barbara. *Samba: Resistance in Motion.* Bloomington: Indiana University Press, 1995.

Bourdieu, Pierre. "Programme for a Sociology of Sport." In *In Other Words: Essays Towards a Reflexive Sociology.* Stanford: Stanford University Press, 1990.

Buarque, Chico. "Los Muchachas de Copacabana." Marola Edicões Musicais Ltda., 1985.

——. "Nossa América." www.chicobuarques.com.br/texto/entrevistas/entre_1989 .htm, 1989.

Colón, Jesús. "The Origin of Latin American Dances (According to the Madison Avenue Boys)." In *A Puerto Rican in New York and Other Sketches.* Masses and Mainstream, 1961; reprint, New York, International Publishers, 1988.

"Conga Workout," *Latina,* June 1998, 38–39.

Daniel, Yvonne. *Rumba: Dance and Social Change in Contemporary Cuba.* Bloomington: Indiana University Press, 1995.

Dunham, Katharine. *Dances of Haiti.* Los Angeles: Center for Afro-American Studies/University of California, 1983.

Gilroy, Paul. "Black Bodies in the Black Public Sphere." In *Dance in the City*, edited by Helen Thomas. New York: St. Martin's Press, 1997.

Hilburn, Robert. "Byrning Up the Music World." *Los Angeles Times*, Calendar section, October 8, 1989.

Kando Odescalchi, Esther. "Goulash Americano: Are We Dancing Like the Natives?" *Dancing USA*, October-November 1999, 16–17.

Kealiinohomoku, Joanne. "Ballet as a Form of Ethnic Dance." In *What Is Dance : Readings in Theory and Criticism*, edited by Roger Copeland and Marshall Cohen. Oxford: Oxford University Press, 1983.

"Kick Starting a Trend." *New York*, January 31, 2000, 12.

Landes, Ruth. *City of Women*. Albuquerque: University of New Mexico Press, 1994.

Margolis, Maxine L. *Little Brazil: An Ethnography of Brazilian Immigrants in New York City*. Princeton, N.J.: Princeton University Press, 1994.

Martin, Randy. *Critical Moves: Dance Studies in Theory and Politics*. Durham, N.C., and London: Duke University Press, 1998.

O'Connor, Barbara. "Safe Sets: Women, Dance and 'Communitas.' " In *Dance and the City*, edited by Helen Thomas. New York: St. Martin's Press, 1997.

Savigliano, Marta E. *Tango and the Political Economy of Passion*. Boulder/San Francisco/Oxford: Westview Press, 1995.

Sayers, Leslie-Anne. "Madame Smudge, Some Fossils, and Other Missing Links: Unearthing the Ballet Class." In *Dance and the City*, edited by Helen Thomas. New York: St. Martin's Press, 1997.

Taylor, Diana and Juan Villegas, eds. *Negotiating Performance: Gender, Sexuality & Theatricality in Latin/o America*. Duke University. Press, Durham, N.C., and London, 1994.

CHAPTER EIGHTEEN

Deceptive Solidity

Public Signs, Civic Inclusion, and Language Rights in New York City (and Beyond)

Vilma Santiago-Irizarry

Some years ago, when I was teaching courses on Latino identity and culture at the City University of New York's John Jay College of Criminal Justice, my Latino students would argue that the course material I was assigning was too dark.[1] Drawing upon my training in anthropological modes of cultural critique as well as my own knowledge and experiences in and of the United States, I wanted my students to challenge essentializing definitions of cultural identity as well as received historical accounts that reduce the complex processes shaping ethnoracial histories in the United States to dominant narratives of eventual assimilation, incorporation, and success derived from typified (and somewhat dubious) "white ethnic" experiences (di Leonardo 1998; Urciuoli 1996).

This, I believe, is crucial in these times when dominant neoconservative discourses capitalize upon widely held beliefs that inequality and exclusion in the United States have been vanquished through institutional, legal, and sociocultural advancement. In these discourses, current advocacy is often represented as the product of self-interested ethnic political activism.[2] Contemporary demands for equality, entitlement, and inclusion are deemed unnecessary, even spurious.[3] Yet, even admitting to some degree of change, the multiple Latino histories in the United States are still embedded in a sociocultural context permeated by inequality of conditions. Latinos are also affected by monocultural and monoglottic[4] ideologies and practices that prevail in spite of current mainstream claims to multiculturalism and plurality (Darder and Torres 1998). The trend for acknowledging the Latino presence as the latest prominent minority group in the nation—in tones implying that others must deal with it as one does with any intractable problem—has not necessarily translated into full enfranchisement. Yet this discourse sustains and contributes to the validation of the nation's congratulatory self-perceptions as an egalitarian—minimally, inclusionistic—society of immigrants.

Language understandably occupies a major problematic space in these developments. Language difference, after all, is still a prime marker of identity for Latino communities and is equivocally addressed within the English-monoglot terrain of the United States. This is especially salient within New York City's public and institutional spaces. My own experience of these paradoxes has led me, years later, to reconsider the notion of language rights in New York City within the context of the city's (arguable) latinization. In considering the effect that language rights developments have upon actual linguistic practices and ideologies, I have become increasingly concerned about the wholesale application of legal discourses to struggles over language parity. Drawing upon the law as the foremost corrective for solving current language wars imbues any achievement or concession with a deceptive aura of closure and permanence, an aura of solidity that may not necessarily be warranted.

This piece represents my initial attempt to broach these issues. First, I examine how the presence of Spanish in New York City's public and institutional spaces acquires significance among Latino "natives" for engaging in empowering processes of cultural maintenance and reproduction; secondly, I discuss the fragmentation that characterizes the field of language rights in the United States because the nation's legal and cultural history undermines, rather than warrants, the maintenance of any other language but English. Zentella's excellent documentation (1997b) of Spanish in New York City shows that Spanish has a highly visible (audible?) place in it. Some may argue that language issues among the city's Latino communities are relatively unproblematic, perhaps even nonexistent, considering developments in other latinized sectors of the United States such as California's infamous Proposition 227, which basically dismantles state-supported bilingual education and garnered so much media exposure.[5] One only has to ride the New York City subway in the middle of the afternoon, when schoolchildren are on their way home, to witness clusters of young Latinos skillfully and expressively codeswitching among their multilingual and multidialectal speech repertoire without dropping a beat. This linguistic vibrancy evinces how the city's Latino youth have become accomplished linguistic practitioners.

If one agrees that education is the bellwether of attitudes and policies toward linguistic difference in the United States (Conklin and Lourie 1983:229), New York City holds pride of place. In 1974, it subscribed a relatively bloodless consent decree in a class action suit filed by Aspira, the

Puerto Rican advocacy group, demanding the institutionalization of bilingual education. Contemporary to the U.S. Supreme Court's decision in *Lau v Nichols* (414 US 563), the precedent-setting case on bilingual education originating in San Francisco that was filed on behalf of children of Chinese descent, the New York City decree, still in effect, guaranteed bilingual education for the city's Spanish-speaking children (Crawford 1989:35). It eventually provided the jural and institutional bases for other public school students when it was extended to speakers of other languages. Aspira's contribution was thus writ large as a significant landmark of Latino activism that contributed to the maintenance, through public means, of the city's historic multilingualism and cultural diversity (García 1997).

Yet in spite of its expressive vitality, cultural significance, formal propriety (as documented by scholarly research), local ubiquity, and official validation, Latino bilingual and multidialectal ways of speaking remain stigmatized and stigmatizing language codes in New York City (Urciuoli 1996; Zentella 1997a). Ironically, considering how many perceive Spanish as perilously encroaching upon the city's (and the nation's) public spaces,[6] long-term data show that it is rapidly being lost, particularly among younger Latinos. Complex ideological and institutional factors, Hispanophobia prominent among them, have converged to militate against the survival of Spanish among Latino speakers (Zentella 1997a, 1997b).

I suggest that how Latino language issues and practices in New York City remain ambiguous, bitterly contested, and challenged, with the very public and institutional presence of local Latino Spanish fragmented and underappreciated, underscores the dubiousness of relying on the law as the prime guarantor of linguistic parity. I here draw upon work in legal anthropology that is critical of cultural notions about law as an autonomous, supposedly objective, and just social leveler for remedying complex sociocultural situations. My past experience practicing law confirms these scholarly interpretations. I do not expect to exhaust the complexities of these issues in a single article, though. My purpose is more modest: I wish to add to the ongoing dialogue about the meaning and viability of linguistic parity in the United States today, particularly as it relates to Latino modes of speaking that have been particularly stigmatized while being officially recognized in a variety of domains.

STATING THE SUBJECT, LOCATING THE ISSUES

To amend my dark vision, my students would urge me to acknowledge the assortment of perceptible public signs inscribed in New York City's urban spaces. They saw in them an increasing prevalence of Spanish in assorted domains—in public notices and forms, subway and traffic signs, advertisements, television, magazines, and so on. Place names, official or otherwise, were often invoked to the same effects: El Barrio, Luis Muñoz Marín Boulevard, Quisqueya Heights, even the *Village Voice*'s trendy appropriation of Loisaida ("Lower East Side," presumably as pronounced by its Spanish-speaking Latino residents).[7]

Those of my students who held relatively prestigious positions—paralegals, administrators, computer programmers, and analysts—would likewise point out that their bilingual competence, as their employers had assured them, had been crucial to their hiring. Bilingualism has become a desired asset in New York City's workplaces in these globalizing times. What is valued, though, is so-called standard Spanish, a monolithic and idealized norm (practically unused in speech), not Latino modes of speaking that are perceived as ungrammatical and accented (Urciuoli 1996). Within this context, some of my students challenged the propriety of validating the bilingual and multidialectal array that characterizes Latino speech repertoires and its cultural value as a significant identity marker. Spanglish, the equivocal label applied to the use of Spanish and English dialects especially in the form of intrasentential codeswitching,[8] stands particularly damned. Others maintained that ways of speaking were important for processes of Latino identity construction:[9] strategically, though, they argued that one should strive to accommodate dominant ideas about proper speech.

As New York City Latinos, these students were hyperconscious of the paradoxes that attach to disparaged linguistic codes that the dominant culture correlates with similarly disparaged and stigmatized identities (Zentella 1997a:13). Imbued with the ethos of upward mobility that marks one's experience in and of the city, they wanted to reconstruct themselves and claim sociolinguistic profiles that revalued their culture and language while enhancing their own desire and potential for upward mobility.

In sum, contra the darkness of scholarly critiques, the public presence of Spanish in New York City constitutes mundane signs of inclusion that carry, in native minds, great symbolic capital and material possibilities. Visibility can be interpreted as empowering. These signs appear to embody and communicate a mainstream acknowledgment that the city's Latino presence is important, that Latinos are essential players in the city's pluralistic sociocultural life—in its politics and economy, in the arts, in its public service institutions, in the corporate sector, in media, and in other such key domains from which, as members of a racialized, stigmatized, and ghettoized culture, they are generally presumed to be either absent or merely menial and passive participants.

Resignifying strategies may thus be based on perceptions about the local deployment and use of linguistic signs. In everyday life, language in public spaces represents the potential to override other indices of low socioeconomic performance—the statistics, census reports, demographics, and other instruments generated and used by social scientists and public officials for locating communities within dominant structures but that have also filtered into the popular imagination. As urban natives, my students were cognizant of the dominant linguistic semiotics as well as of the material and symbolic capital that attaches to local hierarchies of language codes and pragmatic communicational choices (Bourdieu 1991; Urciuoli 1996; Zentella 1997a). Through their life experiences and desire for mobility and change, they were conscious of the facts of local linguistic domination by which English, as the prestige language, renders Spanish in an ambiguous position as language of identity and of solidarity but not necessarily of power (Woolard 1985, 1989; Urciuoli 1996; Zentella 1997a).[10] It was precisely this consciousness that led these students to articulate strategies that challenged the hierarchy.

Their strategies, I would suggest, pursued two basic goals. One was to revalue Spanish, precisely because its ubiquity in the city's public and institutional spaces signaled acknowledgment and inclusion and even enhanced occupational mobility. The other was to critique the local Latino dialectal formations and uses, the very ones that stigmatized them: Spanglish was to be avoided, and correct (standard) Spanish became a desired norm. I was not surprised at these strategies: I was teaching in an institution of higher education that, whatever its profile in the national educational hierarchies, still partakes of its institutional function to socialize individuals into the dominant material and symbolic orders (Bourdieu and Passeron 1977; Zentella 1997a:78). Conveniently, the very ordinariness of the linguistic signs that proliferate around New York City heightened their impact; they matter-of-factly signaled mundane inclusion. These signals of inclusion were thus different from those implicated in institutional practices, which operate by assigning nonstandard status to certain communities and stigmatize them by prescribing for them specialized treatment. The therapeutic ethos so prevalent in U.S. sociocultural life,[11] these students wisely realized, was not necessarily empowering.

MASTER NARRATIVES AND SOCIAL MOBILITY

I wish to underscore two aspects in these critiques that are relevant in considering issues of language parity. Both, I suggest, are crucial for examining our own widespread reliance on the law in attempting to revalue subordinate language codes and practices given the monoglottic dominance of English (Silverstein 1987). First, social actors locate signs of inclusion in a variety of domains *that may or may not* coincide with core institutional ones usually targeted and addressed by political activists and language rights movements through the legal order: education, voting, criminal procedures, public services, and others. Second, one must note the ambiguities, ambivalence, and contestation surrounding the coexistence of unequal language codes and their value. Reactions to linguistic ideologies and practices are not monolithic but critically permeated with contradiction.

Thus, in spite of their critique, my students at John Jay *did* identify with the experiences of racism and discrimination addressed in the material I assigned. They certainly were not advocating or supporting neoconservative assimilationist views; neither were they arguing for cultural divestment. On the contrary, their very presence in my courses documented their investment in asserting their own Latino identity as well as those of their local communities.

But while recognizing inequality and racism, they would advance a variety of commonplaces that, however unintentionally, mitigated and defused our mutual experiences of racialization:[12] that times had changed, that New York City was altogether different from the rest of the nation where so-called middle Americans hold xenophobic sway, that Latinos had advanced in multiple ways and repositioned themselves in the nation's structures, and so on. Perhaps, they would acknowledge, Latinos had not achieved incorporation to the degree that other groups in the city or in the nation had, but they had definitely advanced relative to their previous histories and in many regions of the United States. New York City, of course, was the prime urban space where pan-Latino enclaves had best (re)constituted themselves as powerful sociocultural actors.

Dominant migration myths of inclusion, mobility, and success were thus being rearticulated. These Latino college students were engaged in drawing from dominant notions of civic inclusion to differing degrees of consciousness. Yet they also recognized how their experiences of racism and nativism intersected with other ideological proposals, such as manifest destiny and U.S. exceptionalism, to locate and relocate them as threatening presences and indices of national decline.

This ambivalence likewise indexed the experiential, generational, and ideological gaps that foregrounded our own mutual differences. These reactions underscored the contestation intrinsic to processes of identity construction in the United States and the ideational and institutional slippages that characterize the process. We were all engaged in complex strategies for positioning ourselves and constructing a sense of agency. Given my student's socialization in New York City's schools, status as mostly second-generation or older Latinos, and historic experience growing up in an increasingly conservative sociopolitical environment, their reactions were not unexpected; my own contradictions and ambivalence, after all, were rooted in my biography as an island-born and -raised Puerto Rican from a transitional generation that experienced the pervasive poverty of a pre-industrial colony along with the short-lived opportunities of Operation Bootstrap, which had positive effects upon my own occupational trajectory yet are to me ideologically repugnant.[13]

Other concerns further evinced the contestation intrinsic to the cultural processes that my students and I were both experiencing and enacting. On their surface, these concerns appeared to contradict some of their critiques—their dismissal of Latino ways of speaking, their espousal of proper speech as defined by the dominant culture, and their panglossian arguments about the value that attaches to Spanish and such other Latino signs in New York City's public spaces. Salient among them were childhood horror stories about their experiences of the kind of bilingual education inflicted upon them within the city's public school system.

I was already familiar with these local narratives because I have done fieldwork in the city's public schools. I documented similarly scathing accounts about the actual administration of bilingual programs, especially from Latino parents and educators. Parents in particular would invoke the general lack of resources, bureaucratic confusion, and ideological premises that permeate the system as a whole. They maintained that the low quality of bilingual education programs in New York City was the product of racist assumptions about non-English speakers, especially the Spanish-speaking Latino children who constitute their bulk. Latino parents would often tell me that, however much they wanted their children to become or remain competent bilinguals, they would fight their child's placement in a bilingual education program because most bilingual education programs were little better than special education and unequal tracking that hampered their children's' educational advancement. These experience-based assessments are further complicated by the fact that the city's bilingual education programs are unevenly implemented: *some* programs, in *some* neighborhoods, bear out their potential, making language acquisition and maintenance contingent rather than systematic. Whatever its potential, though, bilingual education remains a contested measure, and bilingual education programs are strained of resources, a situation that hinders their adequate implementation; most are strongly informed by an assimilationist ethos that defines bilingualism as a transitional condition toward the achievement of the culturally favored English monolingual competence.

Nearer home, the Puerto Rican student organization at John Jay was then engaged in a struggle with the college's administration over the language requirements that the institution was applying to Latino students. Identified as Spanish-speaking bilinguals as a matter of course, they were routinely exempted and actively discouraged from taking basic Spanish courses even when many of them *wanted* or felt they needed basic Spanish courses for a variety of reasons: some were conscious of their largely emblematic use of the language, others thought they were only partially competent in Spanish, and yet others desired to achieve full literacy. The college's language policies, ironically, were advantageously positioning non-Spanish speakers for achieving bilingual competence while fostering the erosion of Spanish competence that Latino students felt had begun with faulty precollege schooling and continued unabated into their college years. The irony was compounded by the state of the city's job market, increasingly favorable to bilingual competence but as defined in terms of standard Spanish rather than of the stigmatized codes and accents characteristic among these Latino students. Yet the college was limiting their ability to acquire standard Spanish and tap into the symbolic capital it represents.

Yet one other ambivalent dimension articulated the two aspects I here stress: To what degree do these public signs of inclusion, whether inscribed in urban spaces or embodied in institutional practices, truly index a mainstream acknowledgment of cultural and linguistic authority, acceptance, and parity? Although I do not deny that the public presence of Spanish could have such effects, I believe that its underlying motivations were more ambiguous and fulfilled other purposes. Some of these signs responded to the rationalistic, instrumental need for public institutions, agencies, and officials to establish order in the city's urban spaces and control them by circumscribing people's actions. Subways signs in Spanish, for example, are devised to forestall riders' injuries, perhaps indirectly investing public officials with an illusionary mantle of altruism, but they are principally designed to prevent personal injury suits, in that conflation of communal care and state self-interest that so much characterizes contemporary urban life.

Many of the prominent public signs in Spanish are thus not necessarily intended as expressions of inclusion but as ordering devices for the instrumental organization of everyday life. A number of them are mandated by legislation or case law. For example, the bilingual political brochures on voting procedures and candidates that we all, as New York City voters, received during election periods are under the purview of federal legislation on bilingual voting ballots and informational material. Signs per se do not represent gracious acquiescence toward the Latino presence in the city; neither are they primarily based on an ideologically committed recognition of cultural parity. Many are the outcome of a complex history and often trenchant politico-legal processes of demanding, contesting, and negotiating claims in a variety of domains. Other signs—most obviously advertisements and media—are devised to beguile Latinos to consume the services, commodities, and products of corporate capitalism. Thus, as Flores and Yúdice (1990) argue, the processes at work in the production of these signs operate to define and position Latinos either as populations in need of public state services or as targets for the consumerism that characterizes advanced capitalism in the United States.[14]

I am keenly aware that signs can be polysemic and context dependent. In this sense, within the context of New York City, something as seemingly trivial or instrumental as subways signs may be interpreted as indexing inclusion when they are written in a minority language, especially when it involves a cultural group that has for decades engaged in a struggle for recognition. They may be even regarded—though, obviously, of a radically different order—as paralleling the elimination of segregation signs identifying facilities as "Negro" or "white": they can be read as attempts to metonymically reconstitute local histories of interracial relations and symbolically restructure each group's mutually determinative social location. I believe, though, that it is still important to foreground the ambivalences that surround public uses of language and the meaning of such uses in New York City. Even while acknowledging the polysemic potential in the signs, it is more relevant for my arguments that, after all, the elimination of racist segregation signs did not entail the obliteration of the racism, civic exclusion, and inequality that have affected African Americans or even the deracialization of U.S. society.

FRAGMENTED LEGAL HISTORIES, INFIRM RESOLUTIONS

Conklin and Lourie anticipated the current struggles over minority language rights and policies in the United States when they point out that

> throughout its first century, the United States was an openly
> multilingual nation. . . . Subsequently, in the latter half of the
> nineteenth and first half of the twentieth centuries, the rights of
> non-English speakers were eroded by anti-foreigner and racist
> sentiment and action. In recent years, however, federal court
> rulings and legislation have reinstated many minority language
> rights. In the 1980s we are witnessing large-scale legal and illegal
> immigration from Mexico, resettlement of Southeast Asian
> refugees, and an influx from various Caribbean and Central
> American countries. The U.S. government may react by
> restricting minority civil and language rights, just as it did after
> the earlier periods of massive population shift.
>
> In the past quarter century of struggle for their civil rights,
> non-English and nonstandard-speaking groups throughout the
> country have strongly demanded redress of grievances against
> federal, state, and municipal policies. Federal policy has shifted
> to reflect these renewed demands but not without opposition.
> Language issues such as bilingual education, non-English ballots,
> and the status of nonstandard varieties of English have become
> the focus of heated public debate that will determine not just the
> linguistic future of this country but our commitment to
> maintaining a multicultural society. (1983:226)

Similarly addressing a fragmented legal situation, Norgren and Nanda portray the historic context of legal struggles over language rights as one in which there has never been an official national language policy. Language policies are contingent to "territorial expansion, shifts in ... immigration history, and perceived threats to ... national security" (1996:225–26). It is precisely to emphasize how this context has generated contestation rather than stability in language domains that I characterize the legalization of language rights as deceptively solid.

Dominant cultural ideologies in the United States imbue the law with an aura of objectivity, fairness, infallibility, and resolution that renders those events, relationships, and situations articulated through a legal discourse as decultured domains of action (Moore 1978; Bourdieu 1991:169). But these are reductionistic ideations because law cannot exhaust the complexities of language difference and the public debates generated in situations of linguistic stratification (Bourdieu 1991). Actual political relations of domination and subordination contribute to the reproduction of the existing inequalities embodied in dominant language hierarchies. Yet the prevalent legalism of the United States surrounds policy pronouncements, decisions, and practices with a deceptive aura of authority and permanence because their operationalization is actually vitiated by racialization and the diminishment of subordinate language codes. Legal determinations do not, by themselves, automatically eradicate the assignation of a subordinate position to Spanish dialects vis-à-vis the supremacy that English enjoys in the United States across all cultural domains. Much less do they, ipso facto, assuage their stigmatization because this emerges from a complex matrix where history, culture, and ideology converge.

This is all particularly paradoxical in the United States, where a dominant ideology constitutes the law as the prime means for leveling inequality and redressing injustice. Ideas of law and order as facilitating equality are deeply ingrained in cultural modes of self-definition and inform common practices. Actually, "legal orders *create* asymmetrical power relations, [and] ... the legal system does not provide an impartial arena in which contestants from all strata of society may meet to resolve differences" (Starr and Collier 1989:7; my emphasis).

Given the centrality of legality in U.S. society, it is strategically valuable to mobilize its instrumentality in advancing minority interests and challenging the status quo. But one can neither overestimate the effects of legal processes nor expect that they will achieve closure to sociocultural tensions that are thick with contradictions. Indeed, the law itself is not immune to incoherence and paradox. As Merry (1990) argues, the great paradox at the core of the law is precisely that although it creates and embodies asymmetrical power relations, it also provides the means to mobilize it against the very inequalities it sustains; the law is thus manifold and contradictory, at one and the same time accommodating, even inviting, dissent while constituting the very conditions that foster it—thereon the contested nature of legality, the law, and the legal system. Insofar as one uses and mobilizes the law to delegitimize the status quo, one contributes to validating the legal system as the utmost means for regulating relations and assigning meaning to sociocultural relations (Merry 1990).

Norgren and Nanda establish the strongly Anglocentric character of the nation:

> The controversies over acceptance and public recognition of second languages—in courts, voting, government, business, and education—were generally heavily weighted toward the dominant assimilationist view of the early settlers and those that shortly followed them from English-speaking countries. From the first, English was established as the lingua franca of the colonies. In 1814, De Witt Clinton, soon to become governor of New York, commented with undisguised pleasure: "The triumph and adoption of the English language have been the principal means of melting us down into one people, and of extinguishing those stubborn prejudices and violent animosities which formed a wall of partition between the inhabitants of the same land." This view is still widely shared today. Former Secretary of Education, William Bennett, said, "American citizens must share a common language in which to discuss our common affairs." The *New York Times* [in 1985] agrees, echoing Governor Clinton in 1814: "English is the pot in which the melting takes place." (1996:226)

The linguistic hegemony of English has thus been naturalized as an essential historic condition for national unity. This premise fragments a legal field torn between homogenizing nationalism and actual conditions of cultural plurality that need to be institutionally validated through invocations of equality. Such is the ideological context for language rights litigation, legislation, and case law; English dominance and linguistic homogeneity establish the parameters within which only certain kinds of linguistic behavior will be authorized and tolerated. The historic and the legal records indicate a continuing tension between assimilationist and multiculturalist/multilingualist forces; this tension is not necessarily amenable to facile resolution. The fragmentation of the legal field keeps entitlement vague and contestable.

Norgren and Nanda summarize the state of the field thus:

> *The legal ambiguity regarding language rights in education is paralleled by the lack of a clear judicial pattern on language rights in general. Language rights have been manufactured piecemeal by judges and are inconsistent and even contradictory; the major effect of the courts has been to ensure constitutional rights otherwise guaranteed to non-English speakers, and to prohibit discrimination*

on the basis of national origin, and by extension, language.

In the 1980s and 1990s, perhaps as a result of the perceived legislative and judicial support for minority language rights in voting, schools, and employment, combined with changes in immigrant patterns, pressures to assure the predominance of English in the United States became more organized and more vocal, leading to the growth of the English-Only and Official English movements. Among other things, the ultimate aim of these groups is ratification of a constitutional amendment making English the official language of the United States. This would outlaw the mandating of bilingual programs and services provided by all levels of government, effect congressional repeal of the bilingual ballot requirements under the 1965 Voting Rights Act, and sharply reduce federal programs for bilingual education. Some prominent Latinos support the movement because they feel that bilingual education programs particularly impede Latino assimilation by delaying or impeding the acquisition of English fluency. Their support, therefore, is predicated more on the harm that multilingualism does to the Latino community than on the harm it does to the nation. (1996:230; my emphasis)

This evinces the embeddedness of the field of language rights within highly contested sociocultural relations as well as its fragmentation. Articulating the recognition of vested rights in terms of national origin reinforces the quality of otherness that has been the Latino fate in the United States in spite of our lengthy hemispheric presence; it both signals and reconstitutes the boundaries of exclusion that have been persistently drawn around Latino communities across the nation.

CONCLUSION

In problematizing the issue of language rights, I have tried to advance our dialogue, debates, and struggles over the place of Latino communities in the United States. I argue that the law is not the leveling, restitutive, and equalizing force that it is usually represented to be. The fragmentation within the field of language rights attests to this. But I have also tried to argue and document how many of us locate cultural and linguistic authority in extralegal public signs, including the most mundane ones that we encounter in our everyday experiences and practices; this, however, can represent its own set of problematic ironies.

New York City, with its stable Latino communities, represents a prime sociocultural space for these embodiments, one in which we may read how Latinos are attempting to reconstitute and revalue themselves, their communities, their ways of speaking, and their cultures to become considerable presences in the city's and in the nation's life. Yet this process of revaluing continues to be contested, open ended, and contingent. The city's alleged latinization thus represents the outcome of uneven processes and propositions that, much as happens with the apparent solidity of legal achievements, cannot necessarily become a condition to be taken for granted.[15]

NOTES

I wish to thank Ana Celia Zentella for her contributions to this essay. I inherited it from her but she directed me to relevant works and sources. I draw greatly on her own analyses and arguments, trying to produce work informed by the notion, of her devising, of an anthropolitics of language that indexes a committed scholarly practice addressing actual sociocultural conditions. She encouraged me when I discussed with her my concerns about our own dubious reliance upon legality and legal discourses for advancing language parity for Latinos in the United States. I do not develop this theme here as fully as I would have wished, but the piece represents my initial attempt to tease out the complexities of the situation. I am, of course, fully responsible for the arguments, and all the conceptual flaws in the piece are purely mine.

1. Among other texts, I used Steinberg's (1989:5–43) work on "the ignominious origins" of cultural diversity in the United States, which argues that the way in which different peoples have been incorporated into the nation's social structure shapes their current sociocultural location. Racialized groups incorporated through conquest and colonization, such as Latinos, were differentially incorporated into the nation's capitalist class structure, precluding their upward mobility. Steinberg demystifies the "migration myth" and contemporary processes of ethnicity construction based on a dominant narrative of democratic inclusion, structural equality, and full civic participation. His arguments were particularly appropriate for my purposes teaching courses on ethnicity and race in a city much beguiled by the mystique of Ellis Island and the Statue of Liberty. Neither of these icons seems particularly relevant to the history of Latinos in New York City, whose relationship to it is somewhat more complex and mutually ambivalent. Sánchez-Korrol (1984) documents how the Puerto Rican presence in the city since the early nineteenth century responded to a variety of political, economic, and colonial purposes that are generally overlooked, as is the lengthy Latino presence in the city.

   I also used Arnoldo de León's (1983:14–23) depiction of the nineteenth-century encounter in Texan territory between Anglo Americans and mejicanos. A paradigmatic historic moment of intercultural contact for Latino populations, it generated racialized stereotypes that are still with us. Anglo Americans perceived mejicanos as racially liminal, as a category of people that could not be slotted into the dominant racial hierarchies of identity produced in the European contact with indigenous and imported African peoples. Mejicanos were constituted as a mixed-blood category that could not be understood in its own right but rather marked an identity that had to be signified through the essentialistic racial labels—niggers, redskins—generated and applied to the other "others" who were perceived as nonwhite within the period's dominant Anglo culture. These racial semiotics eventually produced "greasers" as an identity label for mejicanos, underscoring how negatively they were being perceived and categorized. The label was predicated upon alleged similarities between skin color and the contaminating qualities of grease (de León 1983:16). Blu (1978) points out that the biologization and naturalization of cultural difference entailed in the production of phenotypical racial categories has moral overtones. Ethnic categories, perceived as categories in culture, presuppose the existence of a community that provides individual members with a sustaining collective moral order; racial categories, understood as categories in nature, are viewed as devoid of any such communal morality. This was another reading I assigned in my courses.

2. Minority political mobilization and activism are themselves represented as proof of equality and inclusion, as an indication that the system works.

3. Micaela di Leonardo (1998:79ff) aptly summarizes the recent history of these ideological developments within the context of contemporary anthropological practices that continue to efface issues of unequal power relations within the United States, particularly as regards women and ethnic communities. I share her concern about this blind spot in U.S. anthropology that continues to self-define as the field of inquiry that focuses on exotic and primitive others while casting itself and U.S. society in the role of unmarked category and deculturated normative center—this, in spite of a long-standing Americanist tradition as well as the articulation of the anthropological enterprise, à la Margaret Mead, as a venue for the nation's self-understanding. As di Leonardo points out, anthropologists have contributed to the production and reproduction of entwined noble and nasty savages in the scholarly and in the popular imagination by exoticizing both foreign and local others.

   I am equally concerned about the erasure of the *longue durée* regarding Latinos and their history of relations with and in the United States, especially their political activism and resistance. Di Leonardo herself does not totally escape the predominant trend that constitutes Latino political mobilization solely as issuing from the example of African American activism and the 1960s civil rights era, thus effacing a history of resistance that goes back, at the very least, to the nineteenth century. Oboler's excellent critique (1995) of labeling and identity construction among Latinos in the United States also tends to simplify this history, though, to her credit, she is historicizing Hispanic/Latino as an identity category in the United States, which *is* a post–civil rights era development and one devised to diffuse Latino activism. Limón (1994) contributes to "thickening" the history, though in a work that is strongly localized. He underscores the continuing nature of the war of internal colonialism that shapes Latino-Anglo American relations in the United States, beginning in the nineteenth century, as it pertains among Mexican American communities in south Texas.

4. I here wish to evoke Silverstein (1987) but also Bakhtin's notion of monologism (1980) with its metaphoric implications of attempted unicity and

imposed singularity that systematically function to constrain other voices within particular sociocultural contexts and relations.

5. Proposition 227, approved in a state-wide referendum celebrated in the summer of 1998, is currently under legal, institutional, and grassroots challenge. California has a history of previous anti-immigrant and antibilingualism measures that strongly index an anti-Latino agenda. Woolard (1989) describes how advocates of these measures engage in certain rhetorical strategies to mobilize high numbers of voters in minority communities whose sphere of action would be equally curtailed, symbolically or in practice, by the approval of propositions affecting vested minority rights. She describes a case—a San Francisco proposition against bilingual ballots—that is particularly instructive. It involves the approval of a city ordinance challenging legislation in a field preempted by the federal government. Neither the referendum nor the city measure whose approval it pursues could have any legal or practical effect on the federal legislation and regulations or their implementation. The referendum was thus purely symbolic, animated by xenophobia and racism.

6. Allegations of Latino language loyalty are exploited in ethnocentric, xenophobic, and linguocentric movements such as English Only and Official English for self-legitimation, eliding the fact that Spanish is dying in the United States.

7. This particular appropriation is akin to the use of mock Spanish by Anglo Americans in the Southwest (Hill 1993). Within the unequal structure of relations in which Spanish-language features are appropriated and the pragmatic purposes for which they are used, they constitute indices of racism and racist language ideologies. I relate the popularization of *Loisaida* to the convenient exoticization of the Lower East Side as it was being gentrified and commodified in the 1980s and 1990s, marginalizing local communities, predominantly Latinos, who found themselves losing their space to the brand of yuppie chic that has been increasingly colonizing New York City's neighborhoods.

   As to Latino place names, generally, my experience is that the public is not necessarily cognizant of them. As with many other eponymous spaces, their history, relevance, cultural meaning, and importance are usually unknown and/or soon forgotten by most of the city's inhabitants.

8. Switching languages *within* the sentence rather than between sentences. Intrasentential codeswitching is perhaps the most controversial feature of Latino linguistic practices because it appears to violate the norms of a strongly sentence-based linguistic ideology.

9. The importance of this is documented in the scholarly literature, which includes Fishman et al. (1971); Durán (1981); Poplack (1981, 1982); Amastae and Elías-Olivares (1982); Sánchez (1983); Ramírez (1988); Zentella (1980, 1990a, 1990b, 1997a, 1997b); Urciuoli (1991, 1996); Silva-Corvalán (1994); Torres (1997). These are some of the scholars who have focused specifically on Latino linguistic repertoires, competence, and practices (as opposed to codeswitching in other speech communities). They are not uncritical about the linguistic relativism that appears to underpin their analyses. Zentella (1997a), in particular, has developed the notion of an anthropolitics of

language to bridge the gap between pure research and public policies to effect ideological and practical change.

10. Of course, these hierarchies are not intrinsic to the codes in question but commensurate with their speakers' structural positions. Neither are power and solidarity fixed polarities but rather relational and contextual attributions that may be located in either dominant or subordinate language.

11. See Lears (1981) and Trachtenberg (1982) on the therapeutic mindframe and progressivism.

12. I use *racializing* and *ethnicizing* after Urciuoli (1996), who rearticulates race and ethnicity as semiotic elements, de-essentializing these constructs and bringing them into the realm of dynamic discursive practices.

13. Lassalle and Pérez (1997:65ff) examine the intricate tensions that emerge when Puerto Rican anthropologists attempt to teach Puerto Rican students about their culture within the context of institutionalized ethnic studies programs in the United States. Their felicitous coining of the "virtuality" of Puerto Rican culture and identity and their discussion of their own experiences as scholars entangled in the array of contested claims to that identity are instructive for understanding the situation I here describe with its intersecting hierarchies and loci of power, experience, and difference.

14. Flores and Yúdice also argue, interestingly, that the meaning, transgressive nature, and expressive potential of Latino bilingualism has been well recognized and incorporated in advertising. Advertising agencies are careful in their translation of commercial names and slogans but also exploit the bilingual imagination for coining puns and word games that profitably sell their products. The same cannot necessarily be said of official government translations, which, in my experience, either use culturally specific dialectal forms assumed to be standard—Castilian Spanish, for example—or disregard dialectal variations. Berk-Seligson(1990) notes similar problems among court interpreters engaged in simultaneous trial translation.

15. As I was working on this paper, the *New York Times* published a piece on bilingual education in New York City in its Sunday magazine (Traub 1999). Attempting to be critical about bilingual education, the author argues that bilingual education is particularly ineffective for Latino students who are, according to him, the ones who "place more stock" in it. He documents his arguments on the basis of visits to three different bilingual education classes in a junior high school in Brooklyn for Russian, Chinese, and Latino students. The author tries to give some depth to his piece by addressing "cultural" differences—i.e., the Russians and the Chinese students are middle or upper class and have educated parents, whereas the Latino students come from more diverse rural and urban backgrounds and class positions. However, these are structural positions rather than actual culture. Traub fails to contextualize his analysis in broader ideological and historic conditions. He characterizes bilingual education as a purely political phenomenon and dismisses claims to its place in a child's development. He does not discuss research on the cognitive advantages of bilingualism or its benefits in these globalizing times. The desirability of English and monolingualism is the piece's animating principle, a sort of ground zero for any consideration of language ideologies

and policies. The piece is typical of the media treatment of bilingualism, with its not-so-subtle implications of Hispanophobia.

REFERENCES

Amastae, Jon and Lucía Elías-Olivares, eds. 1982. *Spanish in the United States: Sociolinguistic Aspects.* Cambridge, Mass.: Cambridge University Press.

Bakhtin, Mikhail. 1980. *The Dialogic Imagination.* Austin: University of Texas Press.

Berk-Seligson, Susan. 1990. *The Bilingual Courtroom: Court Interpreters in the Judicial Process.* Chicago: University of Chicago Press.

Blu, Karen. 1978. "Race and Ethnicity: Changing Symbols of Dominance and Hierarchy in the United States." *Anthropological Quarterly* 52(2): 77–85.

Bourdieu, Pierre. 1991. *Language and Symbolic Power.* Cambridge, Mass.: Harvard University Press.

Bourdieu, Pierre and Jean-Claude Passeron. 1977. *Reproduction in Education, Society, and Culture.* London: Sage Publications.

Comaroff, John. 1992. "Of Totemism and Ethnicity." In *Ethnography and the Historical Imagination,* edited by J. and J. Comaroff, 49–67. Boulder, Colo.: Westview Press.

Conklin, Nancy Faires and Margaret A. Lourie. 1983. *A Host of Tongues: Language Communities in the United States.* New York: The Free Press.

Crawford, James. 1989. *Bilingual Education: History, Politics, Theory, and Practice.* Trenton, N.J.: Crane Publishing Company, Inc.

——. 1992. *Hold Your Tongue: Bilingualism and the Politics of "English-Only."* Reading, Penn.: Addison-Wesley Publishing.

Darder, Antonia and Rodolfo D. Torres, eds. 1998. "Latinos and Society: Culture, Politics, and Class." In *The Latino Studies Reader: Culture, Economy, and Society.* Oxford: Blackwell.

de León, Arnoldo. 1983. *They Called Them Greasers: Anglo Attitudes Toward Mexicans in Texas, 1821–1900.* Austin: University of Texas Press.

di Leonardo, Micaela. 1998 *Exotics at Home: Anthropologies, Others, American Modernity.* Chicago: University of Chicago Press.

Durán, Richard (ed.) 1981. *Latino Language and Communicative Behavior.* Norwood, N.J.: Ablex Publishing.

Fishman, Joshua, Robert Cooper, Roxana Ma, et al. 1971. *Bilingualism in the Barrio.* Bloomington: Indiana University Press.

Flores, Juan and George Yúdice. 1990. "Living Borders/Buscando America: Languages of Latino Self–formation." *Social Text* 29(2): 57–85.

García, Ofelia. 1997. "New York Multilingualism: World Languages and their Role in a US City." In *The Multilingual Apple: Languages in New York City,* edited by O. García and J. Fishman, 3–50. Berlin: Mouton de Gruyter.

Hill, Jane. 1993. " 'Hasta la vista, baby!' Anglo Spanish in the American Southwest." *Critique of Anthropology* 13(2): 145–76.

Lasalle, Ivonne and Marvette Pérez. 1997. " 'Virtually' Puerto Rican: 'Dis'locating Puerto Rican-ness and its Privileged Sites of Production." *Radical History Review* 68(Spring): 54–78.

Lears, T. J. Jackson. 1981. *No Place of Grace: Antimodernism and the Transformation of American Culture 1880–1920.* New York: Pantheon Books.

Limón, José. 1994. *Dancing with the Devil: Society and Cultural Poetics in Mexican American South Texas.* Madison: University of Wisconsin Press.

Merry, Sally Engle. 1990. *Getting Justice and Getting Even: Legal Consciousness Among Working Class Americans.* Chicago: University of Chicago Press.

Moore, Sally Falk. 1978. *Law As Process.* London: Routledge and Kegan Paul.

Norgren, Jill and Serena Nanda. 1996. *American Cultural Pluralism and Law.* 2d ed. Westport, Conn.: Prager.

Oboler, Suzanne. 1995. *Ethnic Labels, Latino Lives: Identity and the Politics of (Re)Presentation in the United States.* Minneapolis: University of Minneapolis Press.

Poplack, Shana.1981. "Syntactic Structure and Social Function of Codeswitching." In *Latino Language and Communicative Behavior,* edited by R. Durán, 169–84. Norwood, N.J.: ABLEX Publishing.

——. 1982. "Sometimes I'll Start a Sentence in Spanish and *termino en español:* Toward a Typology of Codeswitching." In *Spanish in the United States: Sociolinguistic Aspects,* edited by J. Amastae and L. Elías-Olivares, 230–63. Cambridge, MA: Cambridge University Press.

Ramírez, Arnulfo G. 1988. "Spanish in the United States." In *The Hispanic Experience in the United States,* edited by E. Belén-Acosta and B. Sjostrom, 187–206. New York: Praeger.

Sánchez, Rosaura. 1983. *Chicano Discourse: Socio-Historic Perspectives.* Houston: Arte Público Press.

Sánchez-Korrol, Virginia. 1984. *From Colonia to Community: The History of Puerto Ricans in New York City.* Berkeley: University of California Press.

Silva-Corvalán, Carmen. 1994. *Language Contact and Change: Spanish in LA.* Oxford: Clarendon Press.

Starr, June and Jane Collier. 1989. Introduction to *History and Power in the Study of the Law.* Ithaca, N.Y.: Cornell University Press.

Silverstein, Michael. 1987. "Monoglot 'Standard' in America: Standardization and Metaphors of Linguistic Hegemony." Working papers and proceedings of the Center for Psychosocial Studies no. 13. Chicago: Center for Psychosocial Studies.

Steinberg, Stephen. 1989. *The Ethnic Myth: Race, Ethnicity, and Class in America.* Boston: Beacon Press.

Torres, Lourdes. 1997. *Puerto Rican Discourse: A Sociolinguistic Study of a New York City Suburb.* Mahwah, N.J.: Lawrence Erlbaum Associates.

Trachtenberg, Alan. 1982. *The Incorporation of America: Culture and Society in the Gilded Age.* New York: Hill and Wang.

Traub, James. 1999. "The Bilingual Barrier." *The New York Times Magazine,* January 31, pp. 32–35.

Urciuoli, Bonnie. 1985. "Bilingualism as Code, Bilingualism as Practice." *Anthropological Linguistics* 27(4): 363–86.

——. 1991. "The Political Topography of Spanish and English: The View from a New York Puerto Rican Neighborhood." *American Ethnologist* 18(2): 295–310.

——. 1996. *Exposing Prejudice: Puerto Rican Experiences of Language, Race, and Class.* Boulder, Colo.: Westview Press.

Woolard, Kathryn. 1985. "Language Variation and Cultural Hegemony: Toward an Integration of Sociolinguistic and Social Theory." *American Ethnologist* 12(4): 738–48.

———. 1989. "Sentences in the Language Prison: The Rhetorical Structuring of an American Language Policy Debate." *American Ethnologist* 16(2): 268–78.

Zentella, Ana Celia. 1980. "Language Variety Among Puerto Ricans." In *Language in the USA,* edited by C. Ferguson and S. B. Heath, 218–39. New York: Cambridge University Press.

———. 1990a. "Lexical Leveling in New York Spanish Dialects: Linguistic and Social Issues." *Hispania* 73(4):1094–1105.

———. 1990b. "Return Migration, Language and Identity: Puerto Rican Bilinguals in *dos* Worlds/Two *mundos.*" *International Journal of the Sociology of Language* 84:81–100.

———. 1997ab. *Growing Up Bilingual: Puerto Rican Children in New York City.* Oxford: Blackwell.

———. 1997b. "Spanish in New York." In *The Multilingual Apple: Languages in New York City,* edited by O. García and J. Fishman, 167–201. Berlin: Mouton de Gruyter.

FIGURE 10. A promotional float for Knorr products during the Puerto Rican parade on Fifth Avenue. Photo by Arlene Dávila, 1999

FIGURE 11. Ad boards strategically placed over a fruit stand in the Bronx. Photo by Arlene Dávila

FIGURE 12. Loremil Machado, Capoeira teacher from Grupo Musical Loremil Machado and Saraba Bahia Band at a festival in Central Park. Photo by Máximo Colón, mid-1980s

FIGURE 13. Advertisements in Spanish at El Barrio. Photo by Arlene Dávila